S0-BBV-434

The Glannon Guide to Civil Procedure

EDITORIAL ADVISORS

Vicki Been
Elihu Root Professor of Law
New York University School of Law

Erwin Chemerinsky
Dean and Distinguished Professor of Law
University of California, Irvine, School of Law

Richard A. Epstein
Laurence A. Tisch Professor of Law
New York University School of Law
Peter and Kirsten Bedford Senior Fellow
The Hoover Institution
Senior Lecturer in Law
The University of Chicago

Ronald J. Gilson
Charles J. Meyers Professor of Law and Business
Stanford University
Marc and Eva Stern Professor of Law and Business
Columbia Law School

James E. Krier
Earl Warren DeLano Professor of Law
The University of Michigan Law School

Richard K. Neumann, Jr.
Professor of Law
Maurice A. Deane School of Law at Hofstra University

Robert H. Sitkoff
John L. Gray Professor of Law
Harvard Law School

David Alan Sklansky
Yosef Osheawich Professor of Law
University of California at Berkeley School of Law

Kent D. Syverud
Dean and Ethan A. H. Shepley University Professor
Washington University School of Law

The Glannon Guide to Civil Procedure

Learning Civil Procedure Through Multiple-Choice Questions and Analysis

Third Edition

Joseph W. Glannon
Professor of Law
Suffolk University Law School

Wolters Kluwer
Law & Business

Copyright © 2013 CCH Incorporated.

Published by Wolters Kluwer Law & Business in New York.

Wolters Kluwer Law & Business serves customers worldwide with CCH, Aspen Publishers, and Kluwer Law International products. (www.wolterskluwerlb.com)

No part of this publication may be reproduced or transmitted in any form or by any means, electronic or mechanical, including photocopy, recording, or utilized by any information storage or retrieval system, without written permission from the publisher. For information about permissions or to request permissions online, visit us at www.wolterskluwerlb.com, or a written request may be faxed to our permissions department at 212-771-0803.

To contact Customer Service, e-mail customer.service@wolterskluwer.com, call 1-800-234-1660, fax 1-800-901-9075, or mail correspondence to:

> Wolters Kluwer Law & Business
> Attn: Order Department
> PO Box 990
> Frederick, MD 21705

Printed in the United States of America.

3 4 5 6 7 8 9 0

ISBN 978-1-4548-2746-7

Library of Congress Cataloging-in-Publication Data

Glannon, Joseph W.
    The Glannon guide to civil procedure : learning civil procedure through multiple-choice questions and analysis / Joseph W. Glannon, Professor of Law Suffolk University Law School.—Third edition.
        pages cm
    Includes index.
        ISBN 978-1-4548-2746-7
    1. Civil procedure—United States—Problems, exercises, etc. I. Title. II. Title: Guide to civil procedure.

    KF8841.G59 2013
    347.73′5076—dc23

                                                                    2013021395

About Wolters Kluwer Law & Business

Wolters Kluwer Law & Business is a leading global provider of intelligent information and digital solutions for legal and business professionals in key specialty areas, and respected educational resources for professors and law students. Wolters Kluwer Law & Business connects legal and business professionals as well as those in the education market with timely, specialized authoritative content and information-enabled solutions to support success through productivity, accuracy and mobility.

Serving customers worldwide, Wolters Kluwer Law & Business products include those under the Aspen Publishers, CCH, Kluwer Law International, Loislaw, ftwilliam.com and MediRegs family of products.

CCH products have been a trusted resource since 1913, and are highly regarded resources for legal, securities, antitrust and trade regulation, government contracting, banking, pension, payroll, employment and labor, and healthcare reimbursement and compliance professionals.

Aspen Publishers products provide essential information to attorneys, business professionals and law students. Written by preeminent authorities, the product line offers analytical and practical information in a range of specialty practice areas from securities law and intellectual property to mergers and acquisitions and pension/benefits. Aspen's trusted legal education resources provide professors and students with high-quality, up-to-date and effective resources for successful instruction and study in all areas of the law.

Kluwer Law International products provide the global business community with reliable international legal information in English. Legal practitioners, corporate counsel and business executives around the world rely on Kluwer Law journals, looseleafs, books, and electronic products for comprehensive information in many areas of international legal practice.

Loislaw is a comprehensive online legal research product providing legal content to law firm practitioners of various specializations. Loislaw provides attorneys with the ability to quickly and efficiently find the necessary legal information they need, when and where they need it, by facilitating access to primary law as well as state-specific law, records, forms and treatises.

ftwilliam.com offers employee benefits professionals the highest quality plan documents (retirement, welfare and non-qualified) and government forms (5500/PBGC, 1099 and IRS) software at highly competitive prices.

MediRegs products provide integrated health care compliance content and software solutions for professionals in healthcare, higher education and life sciences, including professionals in accounting, law and consulting.

Wolters Kluwer Law & Business, a division of Wolters Kluwer, is headquartered in New York. Wolters Kluwer is a market-leading global information services company focused on professionals.

I dedicate this book to my children, Sam and Hallie

Contents

Acknowledgments

In addition to those who assisted me with the first edition of this book, I appreciate the very capable assistance of Dana Wilson from Wolters Kluwer in editing and producing this new edition.

Thanks, too, to those benumbed students from law schools across the country who took a much needed break from studying Civil Procedure to compose limericks for my amusement and yours.

The Glannon Guide
to Civil Procedure

1

A Very Short Introduction

~

While studying the Glannon guide,
It's best to keep it at your side.
The procedure is civil,
Over details they quibble,
Professor—you've saved my hide.

S.K. Suffolk University Law School

~

This book provides a short, clear, efficient review of basic topics in Civil Procedure, organized around the theme of multiple-choice questions. In each chapter, the individual sections explain fundamental principles of a topic—such as stream-of-commerce jurisdiction, joinder under Rule 14, or the requirements for res judicata—and illustrate them with one or two multiple-choice questions. After each question, I explain which answer is right, and why the wrong answers are wrong. These short explanations allow me to discuss the black letter rules in the context of the questions. Hopefully, this format will engage you in the study process, so you'll develop a stronger understanding of the basics of procedure. That will pay dividends at the end of the course, whether your exam includes multiple-choice questions or not.

So, the book provides a topically organized review of basic Civil Procedure issues, and clear explanations tying that review to the questions in between. It will be useful either in conjunction with your class study of each topic, or for review toward the end of the course. Even if you just read it to get ready for the final, even if you don't *want* to learn the first year's most mysterious course, working through this short book is going to make some lights go on about some complicated concepts.

Don't expect any magic formulas for Mastering the Multiple-Choice Question in the pages that follow. I don't have any. I don't think there are any. That's why multiple-choice questions are a legitimate testing format: You can't "psych out" a good multiple-choice question, you have to *analyze* it. My students routinely implore me to tell them the secret to improving their performance on multiple-choice exams. All I can tell them is that they need to understand the underlying legal rules, and articulate in their heads the problem with each answer until they find one that's unassailable. That may be good advice, but it never makes them feel much better. But *practice* on good questions, with clear accompanying explanations of the law, will help. I think you will find that this book provides an intelligent, slightly seductive vehicle for learning a complex subject.

Drafting multiple-choice questions for practice can be dicey. There is a risk that the questions will be too complex, or too ambiguous. Fairness demands that a multiple-choice question have one clearly preferable answer. The questions in this book are fair—if you think any are not, please let me know for the next edition—and the explanations explain why. I've also included brief explanations of the law relevant to the questions right along with them, to assist in learning the doctrine and answering the questions. Glannon's Picks at the end of each chapter, recaps the answers to all questions for quick reference.

There are several ways to use this book. The first is to read each introduction, then work through the question, make a considered choice of the right answer, and then read my analysis. This is the best approach, because reading the introductions will provide you with the substantive background to address the question, and reinforce your understanding of it.

Another way to use the book is to read the question, choose the best answer, and then look at Glannon's Picks at the end of the chapter. If you got it wrong, go back and read my analysis of the various choices. This has the advantage that, if you really know the point, you don't have to read about it. But a quick recap of the law will usually be worth the extra time to read the introductions. The advantage over the first approach is meager.

The third way to use the book is to read the question, guess the answer, compare my answer at the end, and shrug your shoulders if you missed it. Not much value here; you might be better advised to save yourself the cost of the book.

Oh, one more thing. Just to lighten things up a little, I've started off each chapter with a limerick. Admittedly, some of them are pretty bad. If you can write a better one, e-mail it to me at jglannon@suffolk.edu and I'll consider it for the next edition. For some other students' offerings, see Closing Openers, the last chapter in the book.

2

Diversity Jurisdiction:
The Basic Rules

It may seem like a lot of falarfel
To claim the state court stands impartial,
But though it's perverse,
Opponents must be diverse
'Cause that's the holding . . . from Chief Justice Marshall.

CHAPTER OVERVIEW
A. State citizenship in diversity cases: The domicile test
B. The difference between intent and evidence: Proof of domicile
C. Chief Justice Marshall's *Strawbridge* rule: The requirement of complete diversity
D. Determining a corporation's principal place of business
E. Diversity in cases involving foreign citizens
F. The relation between statutory diversity jurisdiction and the constitutional grant
G. The amount-in-controversy requirement
H. Aggregation of damages in diversity cases
I. The Closer: Another shot at the domicile test
◈ Glannon's Picks

We have to start somewhere, so let's start with federal court jurisdiction over diversity cases, a fairly straightforward topic to get us going. As I promised in the first chapter, for each topic my introductions will explain the basic doctrine, followed by a multiple-choice question and my analysis of the choices. Perhaps you already know the doctrine. If so, the introductions will provide a quick run-up to the questions. If you don't, it will supply an efficient infusion of black letter law.

A.   State citizenship in diversity cases: The domicile test

Under federal diversity jurisdiction a citizen of one state may sue a citizen of another in federal court, even though her claim arises under state law, if she has a colorable claim for more than $75,000. The state citizenship of a person — as opposed to that of a corporation — is determined by her domicile, that is, the most recent state where she has (1) resided with (2) the intent to remain indefinitely. The "residence" requirement is easily satisfied. Staying overnight in a hotel or a tent will establish "residence" in a state. It is the intent-to-remain-indefinitely prong that gives students problems.

A person intends to remain indefinitely in a state if she is residing in the state on an open-ended basis, without the intent to leave at a definite time or on the occurrence of a definite event. You don't have to swear allegiance forever to a state to acquire domicile there; you only need to reside there "indefinitely," that is, on an open-ended basis. If a party is living in a state without definite plans to leave, the domicile test regards that state as her "home." She is there, not as a visitor, but as a citizen. She is, psychologically speaking, at home there, rather than passing through. She may choose to move on, as we all may, but at the moment she has no plans to do so.

Remember that, until the two prongs coincide in a new state, your old domicile continues, whether you plan to return to that state or not. If Acari, from Hawaii, leaves for a one-year job acting in a play in California, planning to go to New York afterwards, he remains domiciled in Hawaii, even if he swears that he will never return to Hawaii. He hasn't acquired a domicile in California, because he doesn't plan to stay there indefinitely. He hasn't acquired one in New York either, since he doesn't reside there yet. Domicile doctrine abhors a vacuum, so it holds that Acari keeps his Hawaii domicile until the two prerequisites come together in another state.

In analyzing the question below, assume that the court applies the reside-with-intent-to-remain-indefinitely test, and consider where Marla has established a residence with the requisite "indefinite" intent.

QUESTION 1. Moving Marla. Marla, who grew up in Montana, moved to Colorado after high school to enter a two-year program for hair stylists at the Denver Beauty School. She wasn't sure if she really wanted to be a stylist, but she was anxious to get away from home, and her parents agreed to foot the bill, so off she went. She figured she'd stay if she liked it, and get a job as a stylist afterwards, in Denver or elsewhere in the West (including Montana). Or she would leave the program if she didn't like it and look for work, hopefully in Denver. She took an apartment on a six-month lease. After moving to Denver, Marla

A. remains domiciled in Montana, because the program is only for two years.
B. remains domiciled in Montana, because she may return there to work as a stylist.
C. remains domiciled in Montana, because she was domiciled there before she left for Denver.
D. is domiciled in Colorado, because she resides there with the intent to remain indefinitely.

ANALYSIS.   Don't be fooled by **A**. Although Marla's program is for two years, that doesn't mean that Marla will be there *only* for two years. The question indicates that she might stay in Denver after finishing the program, or she might leave for a job in some other Western state. Or, she might leave the program if she doesn't like it and stay in Denver. Thus, she may leave Colorado, or she may not. Since she is not definitely planning to leave Colorado at the end of the program, her stay is not clearly limited to the two years of her academic program.

How about **B**? It sounds seductively reasonable. But the test for domicile isn't whether you might someday go back to the state from which you came. The test is your attitude toward the state where you are. If you live in a state indefinitely, you acquire domicile there, even if you think you might go somewhere else, or back where you came from, at some point in the future. Here, Marla's state of mind is that, whether she finishes the program or not, she may stay in Colorado, or she may leave. That certainly does not show an intent to leave at a definite time. She is in the state with no definite plans to leave. The possibility that Marla might move on at some time in the future does not make her current stay a "definite" one. She might leave Colorado, or she might not. That's "indefinite" intent.

C would only be right if Marla has not established a new domicile in Colorado. If she went to Denver for a fixed period, she would retain her Montana domicile. However, if she's in Denver without definite plans to leave, she establishes a new domicile there. The facts suggest that her stay is open-ended, so she has established a Colorado domicile. **D** takes the prize.

B.   The difference between intent and evidence: Proof of domicile

Cases analyzing domicile for purposes of diversity frequently cite evidence about the person's practical affairs, in order to establish a party's intent. The court may rely on facts such as where the party votes, has health insurance, has a driver's license, rents an apartment, has a bank account, registers her car, and so forth. Certainly, such facts are relevant evidence of a person's intent to remain in a state, or not to. But keep in mind that the *test itself* is the person's intent. Evidence about her practical affairs may help to demonstrate her subjective intent, but a person is not automatically domiciled where she has an apartment, or votes, or maintains her health insurance. If she were, *that would be the test,* rather than her subjective intent.

Parties introduce such practical evidence about a person's conduct to prove the ultimately relevant fact: her intent. But a person could be domiciled in Wisconsin, even though most of these practical factors point to Illinois. It's all a matter of trying to ascertain a subjective fact based on all the evidence. A court will certainly look at the party's testimony in assessing intent, but will also consider whether her practical conduct corroborates or refutes that testimony.

Consider this example.

QUESTION 2. **Wedding plans.**   Rossi grew up in Erie, Pennsylvania. In August 2012, she departed for college in Idaho. After starting school in Idaho, she registered her car there and established a bank account there. She gets health coverage through the college. She has an apartment there, which she has taken on a one-year lease. She has a part-time job in Idaho, and has Idaho state taxes taken out of her check. On her application for the job she listed her Idaho address and telephone number. Her plan is to complete a two-year computer technician degree, and then return to Pennsylvania, where her fiancee has just taken over his family's construction business in Erie. (They have reserved a hall for their wedding in June 2014.) However, she may need a bit more than two years to finish the degree, if tuition goes up too much.

Three months after arriving in Idaho, Rossi brings suit against a Pennsylvania surgeon, for an injury suffered in an operation performed in Pennsylvania a year before. She sues in federal court on the basis of diversity. The court will probably conclude that Rossi is domiciled in

A. Pennsylvania, since she is only in Idaho as a student.
B. Pennsylvania, since she intends to return to Pennsylvania when she finishes her degree.

C. Idaho, since she has an apartment there, goes to school there, has a job there, has health coverage there and pays Idaho state taxes on her income.
D. Idaho, since she doesn't know when she will finish the college program.
E. Idaho, if she testifies in her deposition that she plans to remain there indefinitely.

ANALYSIS. Let's start with **C**, which suggests that the court will find Rossi domiciled in Idaho because she has an apartment there, an Idaho job, health insurance there, and so on. The example illustrates a situation in which most of these practical facts suggest that one state is the domicile, but it probably isn't. Here, there are good reasons for Rossi to arrange her practical affairs as she has, even if she plans to leave Idaho. If you went to school in a state, wouldn't you need a place to live? Wouldn't you get a job if you needed money? Wouldn't you give your local address so the employer could get in touch with you? Wouldn't you join the college health plan? Very likely, you would do all of these things, whether you intended to leave the state when you finished the degree or not. In this case, there's a perfectly good explanation for all these practical choices, even if Rossi has definite plans to leave the state. So, these facts do not themselves establish that Rossi has an open-ended commitment to living in Idaho. So **C** is wrong.

D suggests that Rossi is domiciled in Idaho, because she doesn't know exactly when she will finish her degree. However, while Rossi doesn't know when she will finish, she does have definite plans to leave Idaho when she does. Since she plans to leave upon the occurrence of a particular event, her stay is not open-ended. She's a Idaho visitor, not a domiciliary, under domicile analysis.

But **A** isn't right either. It implies that you can never establish a domicile by going to a state as a student. That isn't so. If you go to a state to attend school, without definite plans beyond your studies, you can establish a domicile there. Many students do satisfy the reside-with-intent-to-remain-indefinitely test by going to school. A case in point, on which this example is very loosely based, is *Gordon v. Steele*, 376 F. Supp. 575 (W.D. Pa. 1974).

How about **E**, which takes the position that the court will find Rossi domiciled in Idaho if she testifies that she plans to remain there indefinitely? Would this be dispositive? Surely not. People do sometimes lie. More often, some motive, such as access to federal court, may color their view of a subjective fact. In determining Rossi's domicile, the court would look at all the evidence, not just her testimony. Here, the facts pointing to Idaho are easily explained on another basis. And the fact that her fiancee has taken over the family business and they plan to marry at the time she will likely complete her studies very strongly suggests that she intends to return. Her testimony is important evidence about her intent, but not solely dispositive.

So **B** is the best answer. Rossi has not established a domicile in Idaho, because she went there with clear plans to leave when she finished her degree. The question *tells you* that she plans to leave, and her engagement clearly corroborates her intent to go back to Erie.

So the point is that the practical factors may be useful in evaluating a person's subjective intent. But the ultimate fact to be proved, under the domicile test, is the intent itself.

C.   Chief Justice Marshall's *Strawbridge* Rule: The requirement of complete diversity

Very early on, the Supreme Court held that diversity jurisdiction is only proper if all plaintiffs are citizens of different states from all defendants. *Strawbridge v. Curtiss*, 7 U.S. 267 (1806). You can have multiple defendants from the same state, and multiple plaintiffs from the same state, but no plaintiff can be from the same state as any defendant or her presence will "destroy diversity." (In the real world, of course, a plaintiff can cure the defect by dropping the nondiverse plaintiff, or a defendant from the plaintiff's state, to "perfect diversity.")

A twist in applying the *Strawbridge* rule arises in cases involving corporations. The Supreme Court has held that corporations are state "citizens," but courts cannot determine their citizenship by the domicile test, since a corporation can't have "intent" the way a person can. Consequently, Congress has defined the "state citizenship" of a corporation in the diversity statute itself. 28 U.S.C. §1332(c)(1) provides that a corporation is a citizen of the state in which it is incorporated, and also the state in which it has its principal place of business.

I find that my students resist looking at statutes and rules to the death. They will go to almost any lengths to avoid consulting the governing provisions of law! That's a shame, because the statutes and rules that establish procedural lore answer a lot of questions. I always let my students bring the federal rules pamphlet into the exam, since I want them to focus on applying the rules and statutes, rather than memorizing them. My questions in this book *assume that you have the relevant rule or statute in front of you* to help in analyzing the question. However, it's essential to find out your professor's policy on bringing the rules book into the exam. If she doesn't allow you to, you will obviously need to spend more time absorbing the details of the rules likely to be tested.

Here's a straightforward question — more straightforward than my usual fare — that probes the complete diversity requirement.

> **QUESTION 3. Foundering fathers.**   In which of the following cases
> would the federal court *lack* diversity jurisdiction? (Assume in each case that
> the suit is for more than $75,000.)
>
> A. Madison, from Virginia, Jefferson, from Virginia, and Gerry, from
>   Massachusetts, sue Hamilton, from New York and Franklin, from
>   Pennsylvania.
> B. Madison, from Virginia, sues Lafayette, from Maryland, and Washington
>   Corporation, incorporated in Delaware with its principal place of
>   business in Maryland, and a large office in Virginia.
> C. Madison, from Virginia, sues Adams Corporation, incorporated in
>   Delaware with its principal place of business in Virginia.
> D. The court lacks jurisdiction in choices **B** and **C**.

ANALYSIS.   Questions with double choices, like **D** here, can be excruciating. You review the answers and find one that is "right." You think you're all
set, and then realize that you aren't, since two may be right. Back to the
drawing board. One lesson, of course, is to read all the choices very carefully.

A is a proper diversity case (and therefore not the right answer) since no
defendant is from the same state as any plaintiff. **C** is not a proper diversity
case, since Adams Corporation is from the same state as Madison: Its
principal place of business is in Virginia. Adams can't argue that there's
diversity because it is from Delaware, where it is incorporated. The point of
28 U.S.C. §1332(c)(1) is that the corporation is considered a citizen of *both*
states, and is not diverse from a citizen of either. So we have one right
answer. The tougher question is whether there is diversity jurisdiction in **B**,
in which Washington Corporation is not incorporated in Madison's state,
and does not have its principal place of business there, but does have a
substantial place of business there.

The statute provides that a corporation is a citizen of the state of "the"
principal place of business, suggesting that only one will be chosen, even if the
corporation has large establishments in several. That has been the holding of
the courts. A corporation — say, McDonalds, of hamburger fame — may
have many restaurants and a great deal of business in lots of states, but under
§1332(c)(1) the court must choose one as its "principal" place of business. The
question tells you that Washington Corporation's principal place of business
is Maryland. It can't be diverse from a Marylander, but is diverse from
Virginians. So **B** is a good diversity case; the right answer is **C**.

By the way, this question suggests two useful hints about taking
multiple-choice questions.

- First, read the question with excruciating care. Here, it would be easy
  to read the question as "In which cases would the court *have*

jurisdiction?" If you do, of course, you will get it wrong. In a lecture by an expert on the multistate bar exam (which consists solely of multiple-choice questions) the speaker described the multistate exam as "an exercise in reading comprehension." I would be willing to wager that most students get more questions wrong by failing to read carefully than they do from lack of substantive knowledge.

- Second, when a question tells you something is true, take it on faith. Here, for example, don't go questioning whether Washington Corporation's large office in Virginia might be its principal place of business. Your professor is the boss in the artificial world of the exam. If she says its principal place of business is Maryland, answer the question based on that premise, whether you believe it or not.

Here's a question that applies the *Strawbridge* rule to a case involving both corporations and individuals. To answer it, remember that 28 U.S.C. §1332(c)(1) provides that a corporation is a citizen, for diversity purposes, of its state of incorporation and its principal place of business. The domicile test discussed above applies to the citizenship of human beings.

QUESTION 4. **Onofrio's revenge.** Onofrio lives in Oregon, with no plans to leave. He works in Idaho. He brings an action in federal court in California against Corcoran, an Idaho citizen, and Brainard Corporation, which is incorporated in California, with its principal place of business in Idaho. He seeks $200,000 in damages against each defendant. Brainard has a large sales office employing 125 people in Oregon. Rivera, the president of Brainard Corporation, lives in Oregon.

A. The court lacks jurisdiction over the action, because Brainard's president is domiciled in the same state as Onofrio.

B. The court lacks jurisdiction, because a substantial part of Brainard's daily activities take place in Oregon, where Onofrio is domiciled.

C. The court lacks jurisdiction, because Onofrio's place of business is in Idaho, and Corcoran is a citizen of Idaho.

D. Jurisdiction is proper.

ANALYSIS. Let's go through the answers in order. **A** is wrong, because the domicile of Brainard's president or other officers is irrelevant. Onofrio hasn't sued Rivera, he's sued the corporation. So we look at the corporation's state citizenship under 28 U.S.C. §1332(c)(1), not at Rivera's. **B** is also wrong. Under §1332(c)(1), a corporation is a citizen of the state in which it is incorporated and the state of its principal place of business. It is not a citizen of other states in which it does business, even a lot of business. Brainard can have huge amounts of daily activity in many states, but we still only look at the state of incorporation and the state of its principal place of business in measuring diversity, because Congress has told us to in §1332(c)(1). So it is irrelevant that Brainard has a large facility in Oregon. The hypo *tells you* that Brainard's principal place of business is Idaho, not Oregon. Once again, when the question tells you something is true, answer the question on that basis.

C is wrong, because the place where Onofrio works is irrelevant in determining the citizenship of the parties. He's a person, and a person's citizenship is measured by his domicile, not his place of business. A court would choose the state in which he lives, the center of his domestic life, as his domicile, even if he works across the border. So he isn't a citizen of Idaho.

D, then, is the right answer. This is a case between Onofrio, a citizen of Oregon, and Corcoran, a citizen of Idaho, and Brainard Corporation, a citizen of California and Idaho. Since there are no Oregonians on the right side of the "v," it's a good diversity case, and federal jurisdiction is proper. The fact that the defendants are both from Idaho does not "destroy diversity."

D. Determining a corporation's principal place of business

Congress has provided that a corporation is a citizen of the state in which it is incorporated and the state of its principal place of business. 28 U.S.C. §1332(c)(1). So, to apply the *Strawbridge* complete diversity rule to corporate parties to a diversity case, courts have to determine where a corporation's principal place of business is. Corporations conduct their business in many different ways. Most corporations are small, and are incorporated in one state and do all their business in that state. These corporations are citizens of only one state. But large corporations might have extensive activities in many states — think Home Depot, or McDonalds. And some corporations will incorporate in one state, concentrate their manufacturing activities in another, and maintain their headquarters, where the corporation's high-level decisions are made, in a third.

Until 2010, federal courts took several approaches to determining a corporation's principal place of business under 28 U.S.C. §1332(c)(1). Some held that the state of a corporation's headquarters is the state of its principal place of business, even if the corporation's manufacturing or service activities took place elsewhere. Other courts, however, applied a "daily activities" test if a corporation's productive activities were primarily concentrated in a single state, reasoning that the corporation will be perceived as "local" in that state, since it will have the most contact with the public there. If the productive activities were widely spread among states, these courts would look to the state where the corporation has its headquarters or "nerve center," since the diffused activities would all be coordinated from that state.

All of this is now interesting history, because in 2010 the Supreme Court held, in *Hertz Corp. v. Friend*, 559 U.S. 77 (2010), that the corporation's principal place of business for diversity purposes is the state of its headquarters in all cases. After *Hertz*, a corporation is citizen of the state in which its headquarters are located, even if all of its actual manufacturing or service activities take place elsewhere. The Court emphasized the importance of having a relatively clear rule that will avoid uncertainty and litigation about whether diversity jurisdiction is met in cases involving corporate parties.

QUESTION 5. Business principals. Angus and Phillips, from Texas, bring a breach of contract action against Apex Corporation in the federal district court for the Western District of Texas. Apex is a corporation that manufactures lawnmowers. It is incorporated in Delaware. It assembles the mowers at its plant in El Paso, Texas, which employs five hundred employees. It has another factory in Tennessee, which manufactures handles for the mowers and employs twenty-five employees. Its corporate headquarters occupy a small suite of offices on the twelfth floor of an office building in Tulsa, Oklahoma. Fifteen officers and employees work out of the headquarters office.

The court will find that there

A. is complete diversity and proceed with the case.
B. is not complete diversity because the case is brought in a Texas court, and the plaintiffs are both Texas citizens.
C. is not complete diversity because both plaintiffs are from Texas.
D. is not complete diversity between the plaintiffs and Apex. Under 28 U.S.C. §1332(c)(1) Texas is Apex's principal place of business, because Texas citizens in El Paso will think of Apex as "local," while hardly anyone in Oklahoma will know anything about Apex Corporation, which has very low visibility in Oklahoma.
E. is diversity between the plaintiffs and Apex, because Apex is a citizen of Delaware based on its incorporation there.

ANALYSIS. The wrong answers in a multiple choice question are called "distractors." Beguiling choices like **B** suggest the reason. There is something so *plausible* about it, isn't there? The suit is brought in the state where the plaintiffs live, so no diversity? Of course this doesn't make sense, but it threatens to distract you from the business at hand. To determine diversity, we compare the state citizenship of the plaintiffs and the defendants, not the plaintiffs' citizenship and the place where the suit is brought. If the parties are from different states, it does not matter that one of the parties is a citizen of the state in which the suit is brought. The case is a proper diversity case, *no matter what state the suit is brought in.*

C should not fool any but the truly unprepared. Under *Strawbridge v. Curtiss*, you can have a hundred plaintiffs from the same state, as long as no defendant is from that state. So the fact that both plaintiffs are from Texas does not defeat diversity jurisdiction. And you should have rejected **E** quickly as well. A corporation is a citizen of *both* its state of incorporation and the state of its principal place of business, so we need to determine that here in order to apply the *Strawbridge* complete diversity rule.

D is beguiling, because it would make a lot of sense for a court to treat Apex as local in the state where its daily productive activity is centered. Many courts did apply this approach before the Supreme Court decided *Hertz Corp. v. Friend.* But that case is a Supreme Court case; its decisions are the supreme law of the land, and in *Hertz* the Court held that a corporation's principal place of business for diversity purposes is in the state where it has its central offices—its headquarters from which it directs corporate operations. Here, that state is Oklahoma, so Apex is a citizen of Oklahoma and of Delaware, and there is complete diversity between it and the Texas plaintiffs. **A** takes the prize.

E. Diversity in cases involving foreign citizens

Article III, §2 provides that federal courts may hear not only claims between citizens of different states, but also claims between citizens of a state and "foreign . . . Citizens or Subjects" (usually called "aliens"). So, a case between a citizen of Oregon and a citizen of Spain is within the constitutional grant of federal subject matter jurisdiction in Article III, §2. And, 28 U.S.C. §1332(a)(2) provides statutory authority for the federal district courts to hear such cases. By extrapolation, courts have held that a case between citizens of different states, with an alien added as an additional plaintiff or defendant, is also proper. See 28 U.S.C. §1332(a)(3). However, interpretive questions arise when an alien is domiciled in one of the American states. Suppose, for example, that Frankel, a New Yorker, sues Leduc, a citizen of France living in New York. The courts have held that there is federal jurisdiction over this case, since Leduc, though living in the plaintiff's state, is a foreign national (an alien). For diversity purposes, a person can't be a "citizen" of a state unless she is also a citizen of the United States. Since Leduc is a French citizen, he cannot be a citizen of New

York, even if he is domiciled there. To be a New York citizen, a person must both be domiciled in New York and a citizen of the *United States.*

The diversity statute has a special provision, however, that changes the result in Leduc's case if he has been "admitted for permanent residence in the United States." Section 1332(a)(2) now provides that an alien admitted for permanent residence and domiciled in a state cannot bring a diversity action against a citizen of the state in which she is domiciled. Leduc is thus treated as "local" in his state of domicile if he is here as a permanent resident. However, if Leduc has not been admitted for permanent residence (which apparently equates under immigration law to having a "green card"), Frankel could sue him in federal court under §1332(a)(2).

Conversely, a person may be a citizen of the United States without being a citizen of any state. If Frankel moves to Gambia and establishes a domicile there, he is still a United States citizen, but he is not a citizen of any American state, since he isn't domiciled in one. However, he isn't an alien either, as long as he remains an American citizen. So the diversity jurisdiction doesn't apply. This problem arose in *Twentieth Century-Fox Film Corp. v. Taylor*, 239 F. Supp. 913 (D.C.N.Y. 1965). Twentieth Century Fox sued Elizabeth Taylor for her shenanigans during filming of the movie "Cleopatra." Although Taylor was an American citizen, she was living — indefinitely — in England. Consequently, she was not domiciled in any state and could not be sued in federal court based on diversity. She wasn't an alien, since she had not renounced her American citizenship. Nor was she a citizen of any American state, since she was domiciled in Great Britain.

QUESTION 6. At home and abroad. Crandall, a citizen of Missouri, and Rizzouti, a citizen of Iowa, sue Janssen, a citizen of Vermont; Gompers, an American citizen who lived all his life in Florida but recently moved to Great Britain and plans to remain indefinitely; and Toussaint, a French-woman who has moved to Iowa to take a one-year visiting professorship at the University of Iowa, hoping to get tenure there and stay. The suit is brought in federal court based on diversity jurisdiction. (Assume that Toussaint has not been admitted to the United States for "permanent residence.")

A. There is no jurisdiction over the action because Toussaint is a citizen of Iowa.

B. There is no jurisdiction if Gompers remains in the case, but the action could proceed between the plaintiffs Crandall and Rizzouti and defendants Toussaint and Janssen.

C. There is no jurisdiction over the claims against Toussaint, because she is an alien domiciled in Iowa.

D. There is jurisdiction over the entire action.

ANALYSIS. This question should help to sort out the complexities of applying diversity to cases involving American citizens and aliens. The crux of the problem is the point made above: To be a "citizen" for diversity purposes, you must be *both* a citizen of the United States and domiciled in a state. Here, Toussaint, while domiciled in Iowa, is not a citizen of Iowa, because she isn't an American citizen. She's a French national, and therefore, under Article III, §2, she is an alien ("a citizen or subject of a foreign country"). (The exception in §1331(a)(2) does not apply, because Toussaint has not been admitted for permanent residence.) So **A** is wrong.

C is wrong, too. Article III authorizes suits between citizens of a state (or, as here, of several states) and aliens. It is irrelevant that Toussaint is domiciled in Iowa; she remains a Frenchwoman until she becomes an American citizen (or is admitted for permanent residence, under §1332(a)(2)).

And **D** is wrong, because Gompers is not a citizen of any state. Remember that, to be a citizen of a state you must be both an American citizen and domiciled in a state. Gompers is an American citizen, but he isn't domiciled in any state, since he is living in Great Britain with the intent to remain there indefinitely. The claim against him would have to be dropped for lack of subject matter jurisdiction. Consequently, go with **B**.

F.   The relation between statutory diversity jurisdiction and the constitutional grant

Article III, §2 of the Constitution creates diversity jurisdiction in very general terms. It does not expressly state whether there must be "complete diversity," or whether diversity might be satisfied if *some* plaintiffs are diverse from *some* defendants. *Strawbridge v. Curtiss,* of course, held that all defendants must be diverse from all plaintiffs, but for many years it was unclear whether *Strawbridge* interpreted Article III or interpreted the statute by which Congress conveys diversity jurisdiction to the lower federal courts. If *Strawbridge* interpreted the language "citizens of different states" in Article III, the complete diversity rule would be constitutionally required, and could not be changed . . . unless the Court overruled *Strawbridge.*

In *State Farm Fire & Casualty Co. v. Tashire,* 386 U.S. 523 (1967), the Supreme Court held that *Strawbridge* interpreted the diversity statute, not Article III. It further held that, for Article III purposes, a case is "between citizens of different states" so long as at least one plaintiff is diverse from one defendant. Consequently, it is now clear that diversity jurisdiction exists under Article III as long as there is "minimal diversity," that is, as long as some plaintiff is diverse from some defendant. However, *Strawbridge,* which interprets the diversity statute, 28 U.S.C. §1332(a), to require complete diversity, has never been overruled.[1] Nor has Congress amended §1332(a) to allow diversity jurisdiction based on minimal diversity. But it *could be* changed by Congress. Recall that the jurisdiction allowed under the Constitution is not self-executing. The lower federal courts derive their jurisdiction from Congress. Congress may authorize jurisdiction over all cases described in Article III, or it may authorize the federal district courts to hear only some subset of those cases.

The following example illustrates the relationship between the scope of diversity jurisdiction permissible under Article III and the Congressional grant of diversity jurisdiction to the federal district courts.

QUESTION 7. Smith's amendment.   Congressperson Smith introduces a bill that would provide for diversity jurisdiction "so long as at least one plaintiff in the case is a citizen of a different state from one defendant."

A. Smith's bill would be constitutional, since Congress may expand or restrict the jurisdiction of the federal district courts as it sees fit.

B. Smith's bill would be unconstitutional, since it allows jurisdiction over cases that do not satisfy the complete diversity rule of *Strawbridge v. Curtiss*.

C. Smith's bill would be constitutional, because the scope of diversity jurisdiction in Article III includes minimal diversity cases.

D. Smith's bill would be unconstitutional, since Article III, §2 alone determines which cases the federal district courts may hear.

ANALYSIS.   It's crucial to understand why **D** is wrong. Article III of the Constitution doesn't create federal district courts, and doesn't directly bestow any jurisdiction on them. Section 1 of Article III authorizes *Congress* to create lower federal courts if it chooses to. This power to create lower federal courts (or not to) carries with it the implied authority to create them, but to authorize them to hear only some of the cases listed in Article III, §2. See *Kline v. Burke Constr. Inc.*, 260 U.S. 226, 233-234(1922). In other words, Article III, §2 defines the universe of cases that federal courts may potentially hear, but Congress creates the lower federal courts and can give them as much or as little of the Article III jurisdiction as it chooses to. It need not — and never has — bestowed all of the constitutionally permissible jurisdiction on the lower federal courts.

So **D** is wrong because Article III does not directly grant jurisdiction to the federal district courts; Congress does. **A** is wrong too, because Congress

---

1. Congress has, however, enacted various statutes authorizing jurisdiction in some categories of cases based on minimal diversity. See, e.g., 28 U.S.C. §1332(d)(2) (certain class actions cases); §1369(a) (certain mass accident cases).

cannot give the lower federal courts any jurisdiction it wants. It may only grant jurisdiction over cases within the categories listed in Article III, §2, which defines the outer limits of the federal judicial power. And **B** is also wrong, because *Strawbridge*, we now know (from the *Tashire* decision), interpreted the federal diversity statute, not Article III, §2. Since it is the statute, §1332(a) (as interpreted by *Strawbridge*), that requires complete diversity, Congress could change it. Ironically, of course, it was really Chief Justice Marshall who established it, in *Strawbridge*. But he interpreted the diversity statute to require complete diversity, not the Constitution, and the statute may be changed by Congress. So don't blame Marshall alone for the rule; Congress hasn't changed it in two hundred years. Thus, **C** is right. Smith's bill would authorize jurisdiction based on "minimal diversity." *Tashire* holds that "minimal diversity" cases are proper diversity cases, within the meaning of Article III, §2, so Congress could authorize federal district courts to hear them.

G. The amount-in-controversy requirement

As the previous section explains, the scope of diversity jurisdiction in Article III and that conveyed to the federal district courts by Congress aren't the same. The *Strawbridge* rule illustrates one situation in which the statutory grant is narrower than the constitutional authority. Another example is the amount-in-controversy requirement. Article III, §2 contains no monetary restriction on diversity jurisdiction; it broadly authorizes jurisdiction over all cases between citizens of different states. Congress's grant of diversity jurisdiction to the federal district courts, however, includes an amount-in-controversy requirement, in order to keep small diversity cases out of federal court. See 28 U.S.C. §1332(a) (granting jurisdiction over diversity cases in which "the amount in controversy exceeds the sum or value of $75,000, exclusive of interest or costs").

Here's a mediocre question, included to make a point.

> **QUESTION 8. By the numbers.** A diversity case cannot be heard in federal court unless the amount in controversy is at least
>
> **A.** $75,000, counting interest and costs as well as the plaintiff's damages.
> **B.** $75,000, not counting interest and costs.
> **C.** $75,000.01, counting interest and costs.
> **D.** $75,000.01, exclusive of interest and costs.

ANALYSIS.   This is what I would call a "pure knowledge" multiple-choice question. It simply asks a factual question and gives you four choices, one of them right (**D**). To answer it, you simply need to remember a fact, not analyze a problem. This is easier, and less imaginative, than questions that require you to apply a concept to a subtle set of facts. Analytical questions call for a higher order of reasoning than this amount-in-controversy hypo.

Most professors will test your analytical skills, since they are trying to teach you to think, not memorize. So I think you will find the more analytical examples in this book more representative of law school exams — either multiple-choice or essay exams. Similarly, the multi-state bar exam also focuses on proper application of legal rules to facts, not memorization of black letter law.

One problem with requiring a minimum amount in controversy is that you have to know how much is "in controversy" in order to determine whether the court has jurisdiction. Courts generally determine their jurisdiction at the outset of a case, but how can they determine the amount in dispute between the parties without gathering evidence or trying the case?

The Supreme Court addressed this conundrum in *St. Paul Mercury Indemnity Co. v. Red Cab Co.*, 303 U.S. 283 (1938). Under the "*St. Paul Mercury* rule," the court will find the amount requirement met as long as it is possible that the plaintiff's claim would support a recovery of more than $75,000. If the judge, evaluating the plaintiff's injuries or damages, concludes that a jury would likely award more than $75,000, she will find the amount requirement met. If she concludes that a jury probably would award less than $75,000, but *might* rationally award more, she would still find the amount requirement met. If, on the other hand, she concludes that a verdict over $75,000 would be irrational, that the claim is "to a legal certainty" worth less than the amount required, she would dismiss for failure to meet the amount-in-controversy requirement.

This approach gives the plaintiff the benefit of the doubt. Where her damages might exceed the required number, the amount requirement is deemed satisfied, and the case may go forward in federal court. It is only where her injuries or losses could not rationally support a verdict for the jurisdictional amount that her claim will be dismissed.

Here's a question that probes the application of the *St. Paul Mercury* rule.

QUESTION 9. *St. Paul* misery.   Wanda brings a diversity action against Peroski in federal court for injuries suffered in a construction accident. As a result of the accident, Wanda suffered a badly sprained ankle. She alleges that Peroski's negligence caused the accident. However, Peroski denies that her conduct was negligent. Wanda demands $100,000 in damages for her injuries.

A. To determine whether the amount-in-controversy requirement is met, the court will consider whether Wanda is likely to be able to prove that Peroski was negligent.
B. To determine whether the amount-in-controversy requirement is met, the court will have to determine whether a reasonable jury could award more than $75,000 for the injuries Wanda alleges.
C. The amount-in-controversy requirement is met if it is clear, to a legal certainty, that Wanda's damages exceed $75,000.
D. The amount-in-controversy requirement is met, because Wanda seeks $100,000 in damages.

ANALYSIS. If **D** were the right answer to this question, the amount-in-controversy requirement would be a dead letter. Plaintiffs would simply demand large damages in their complaints, and the federal court would have to hear their cases. Surely, federal judges are too savvy to leave it at that. The court won't simply accept the number Wanda's lawyer asks for in damages; it will look at *the actual injury Wanda has suffered,* and consider whether those injuries could rationally support a verdict over the required amount.

The rule suggested by **C** also misperceives the meaning of the *St. Paul Mercury* test. It suggests that the amount requirement is only satisfied where the plaintiff will definitely recover more than $75,000. Under this test, if the plaintiff might recover more, but also might recover less, there would be no diversity jurisdiction. Under *St. Paul Mercury,* the presumption is the opposite: if the damages are in the debatable range, where a reasonable jury might award more, or might award less, the amount requirement is met. Only where it is clear, as a matter of law, that the award will be *less* is the amount requirement not met.

A can't be right either: the amount-in-controversy question is not whether the plaintiff is likely to win her case on the merits, but whether, if *she does,* she might recover more than $75,000. After all, §1332(a) requires that more than $75,000 must be "in controversy," not actually recovered. If the court had to consider the strength of the plaintiff's proof of her claim in order to decide whether the amount-in-controversy requirement was met, it would not be able to decide this preliminary issue without developing the facts through discovery and litigating the merits of the case. That would be a poor rule indeed for a question of jurisdiction, which should be settled at the outset of the case.

So **B** is the best answer. The court will look at Wanda's damages, a sprained ankle, and consider whether a reasonable jury could award more than $75,000 for that injury. Seems like a good case for dismissal to me, but you don't have to decide that to answer the question.

H.   Aggregation of damages in diversity cases

If a plaintiff brings more than one claim, can she add her damages on the claims together to meet the amount-in-controversy requirement? Suppose, for example, that Harris brings a federal diversity action against Tanfredi for $60,000 in damages suffered in an auto accident, and also, in the same suit, seeks $40,000 from him in damages for breach of a contract. This "aggregation" problem bedevils law students, and makes good fodder for testing. The basic rule is that a plaintiff can add up the amounts for all her claims against a single defendant, whether they are related or not. However, she cannot "aggregate" claims against *different* defendants, except in the unusual situation where they are sued on a "common, undivided interest." (Please disregard this exception for the moment.) Harris meets the amount requirement in the example just given. However, if she sued Tanfredi for $60,000, and Vincent, in the same action for $40,000, she would not meet the amount requirement against either, since she cannot add together the amounts sought against different defendants to meet the requirement.

The situation is less clear where two plaintiffs join together to sue a defendant, and one sues for more than $75,000 but the other for less. Prior to enactment of 28 U.S.C. §1367, the supplemental jurisdiction statute, the answer was clear: each plaintiff had to meet the amount requirement on her own. If Couples and Jenks sued Barone, and Couples sought $50,000 in damages, and Jenks sought $60,000, neither met the amount requirement. If Couples sought $90,000 and Jenks joined with him, seeking $20,000, Couples met the requirement, but Jenks did not. Now, however, 28 U.S.C. §1367 has changed this result in the multiple-plaintiff situation. This problem is discussed in more detail at Chapter 14, p. 279.

You can analyze this question without worrying about the supplemental jurisdiction statute, since it involves claims against multiple defendants, not by multiple plaintiffs. As to multiple defendants, the traditional rule, that the plaintiff must meet the amount requirement separately against each, still applies.

QUESTION 10. Aggravation of damages.   Maurice sues O'Connell in federal court based on diversity jurisdiction, seeking recovery on a libel claim for $25,000 and an unrelated negligence claim, for $65,000. He also joins Parker as a codefendant on the negligence claim, seeking his $65,000 in negligence damages from Parker. Assume that Maurice's claims do not involve a "common undivided interest."

A. Maurice does not meet the amount-in-controversy requirement against Parker, but does against O'Connell.

B. Maurice meets the amount-in-controversy requirement against both defendants, since he seeks $90,000 in total recovery.

> **C.** Maurice meets the amount-in-controversy requirement against both defendants, as long as the claim against Parker arises from the same events as that against O'Connell.
>
> **D.** Maurice does not meet the amount-in-controversy requirement against either defendant.

ANALYSIS. Let's review the choices in reverse order. **D** is wrong, because Maurice does meet the amount requirement against O'Connell. One plaintiff can add up whatever claims he asserts against a particular defendant to meet the amount requirement, so Maurice can add his $25,000 and $65,000 claims against O'Connell to meet the requirement.

C doesn't cut the mustard either. The courts have generally taken the position that Maurice must seek more than $75,000 against Parker to meet the amount requirement.[2] He can't bootstrap a claim against Parker for less than the required amount onto his claim against O'Connell for more. And **B** is wrong, because the aggregation rules don't allow aggregation of amounts sought against different defendants.

A is correct. Maurice meets the amount requirement against O'Connell, by adding his two unrelated claims against him. But he cannot add Parker as a codefendant, since he seeks less than $75,000.01 in damages from him.

Frequently, a plaintiff sues two or more defendants on a tort claim for injuries arguably worth more than $75,000. Suppose, for example, that Epstein suffers nerve damage during surgery, and that the damages are $90,000. He sues Dr. Smith and Dr. Doe for his injury, claiming that the negligence of each during the operation contributed to the injury. Does he satisfy the amount-in-controversy requirement against the doctors?

Under the law of damages in tort cases, he does, because either of the doctors might be held liable for the entire injury. Suppose that the jury finds that the injury was Smith's fault alone. It would return a verdict against Smith for $90,000. So, Smith might be liable for more than the jurisdictional amount. Alternatively, if the jury found that the injury was Doe's fault alone, it would return a $90,000 verdict against Doe. So he also might be liable for the jurisdictional amount. Thus, the court cannot say to a legal certainty that Epstein could not recover the required amount from Smith, or from Doe. The amount requirement is met against either.

Suppose the jury found that they were both negligent and contributed to the harm? On this assumption, the result turns on the tort law of the state. In

---

2. The analysis here is more complex since the enactment of 28 U.S.C. §1367(a), the supplemental jurisdiction statute. See Chapter 14, p. 279. However, this case would not be authorized under §1367 either, since §1367(b) bars supplemental jurisdiction over claims by plaintiffs against parties joined under Rule 20, if they are inconsistent with the requirements of §1332.

some states, they would find Smith and Doe "jointly and severally liable" for $90,000, which means that each would be held liable for the full amount, and Epstein could collect $90,000 from either.[3] In other states, they would each be held liable for parts of the loss, based on their percentages of negligence. But the amount requirement would be met in either type of jurisdiction. As long as either defendant might be held liable for the full $90,000, that amount is "in controversy" between her and the plaintiff. Since either Smith or Doe might be found solely at fault, either might be held liable for the full $90,000.

To illustrate:

QUESTION 11. Stooges do the math. In which of the following cases can all the claims properly be brought in federal court (assume that the traditional aggregation rules apply)?

A. Larry and Moe (both from New York) sue Curly (from Iowa) for negligence. Larry seeks $60,000 for his injuries in the accident and Moe seeks $25,000 for his.

B. Larry (from New York) sues Curly (from Iowa) for his injuries in an accident, seeking $60,000. Curly counterclaims for $100,000 for his injuries.

C. Larry (from New York) sues Curly and Moe, two Iowa citizens, for injuries he suffered when Curly and Moe's cars collided. He claims that one or the other, or both, were negligent, and seeks $100,000 in damages for his injuries.

D. Larry (from New York) sues Curly (from Iowa), and Dr. Moe, also from Iowa. He claims that Curly caused the accident, and that he suffered $60,000 in damages from a broken leg suffered in the accident. He further claims that Dr. Moe negligently set the leg after the accident, causing an additional $30,000 in damages.

ANALYSIS. Let's dispose of Larry, Moe, and Curly, and then we'll move on to other matters. The last choice, **D**, is the most interesting here, but it isn't the right answer. Under the law of causation in tort law, Curly would probably be liable for the $60,000 in initial injuries to Larry and the additional $30,000 due to Dr. Moe's malpractice. Larry would not have suffered the malpractice if he had not been injured in the accident, so most jurisdictions would hold Curly liable for this additional loss as well as the broken leg. So, the amount requirement is met as to him. But Dr. Moe is only liable for the $30,000 in damages that he caused, so the amount requirement is not met as to him. And Larry cannot aggregate his claim against Dr. Moe with his claim against Curly.

---

3. No, he couldn't get $90,000 from each, for a total of $180,000. Once the damage amount has been paid, his claim is "satisfied," and he cannot seek more from a second tortfeasor, even one who has been adjudged liable for it.

Under the traditional aggregation rules, the plaintiff must seek more than $75,000 from each defendant. And that rule has not been changed by 28 U.S.C. §1367, the supplemental jurisdiction statute. See 28 U.S.C. §1367(b) (barring supplemental jurisdiction over claims by plaintiffs against persons made parties under Fed. R. Civ. P. 20).

A isn't right because the amount requirement is not met by either plaintiff, and they can't be added together. **B** is no good either. The amount requirement must be assessed based only on the plaintiff's claim, without regard to the value of any counterclaim. If Curly had brought the initial suit (and the claim for $100,000 were colorable), the court would have had jurisdiction. But Larry brought it, and sues for less, so his claim does not support original jurisdiction. The claims in **C** do satisfy the amount requirement, however. Here, either defendant might be found to have negligently caused Larry's injuries, so either might be liable for his full $100,000 in damages. Go with **C**.

I.   The Closer: Another shot at the domicile test

In each chapter I'll include a "Closer," a fairly challenging example to push the analysis and test your understanding. Because the concept of domicile is always confusing to students, especially that elusive "intent-to-remain-indefinitely" principle, let's try one more example on the domicile requirement. In analyzing it, assume that the court applies the reside-with-the-intent-to-remain-indefinitely test, and focus on the main point: Where is the last state in which the two prongs of the test — residence and intent to remain indefinitely — coincided at the same time?

QUESTION 12. **Flaky Filbert.**   Filbert is flaky. He moved to Nebraska from Chicago, Illinois, to go to law school, planning to return to Chicago after law school to practice law. After his first year, he did a summer clerkship at a Denver, Colorado, law firm. They liked his work and indicated that they would hire him after graduation. Filbert decided he would go back to the firm after graduation. During his second year, he received a letter from the firm indicating that they would probably not have an opening for him after graduation. Consequently, he clerked in an Omaha, Nebraska, firm after his second year, and accepted an offer to join the firm after graduation.

In the middle of his third year, the Denver firm called him up and made him an offer. The offer was too good to resist, so he decided to renege on the Omaha job and go to Denver when he finished school. Immediately after the events described,

A. Filbert is domiciled in Nebraska, because it is the last state in which he has met the two prerequisites for domicile.
B. Filbert is domiciled in Illinois, because when he moved to Nebraska he did not intend to remain there indefinitely.
C. Filbert is domiciled in Colorado, because while he was there he decided he would take the job with the Denver law firm after graduation and now intends to do so.
D. Filbert is domiciled in Nebraska, because he lives there now and has no plans to return to Illinois.

ANALYSIS. C seems like a reasonable answer to this question: Filbert did decide at one point to move to Colorado. He even decided that he would do so while he was in Colorado, But at the time he made that decision, he planned to leave to finish school in Nebraska. A court would likely hold that this intent was to *become domiciled* in Colorado two years later, so that Filbert did not establish a residence in Colorado at the same time that he had the intent to remain there indefinitely.

B is also wrong, although many of my students routinely choose it. Although Filbert did not plan to stay in Nebraska when he went there to go to school, he later decided to stay while he was residing there — when he accepted the job at the Omaha firm. At that moment, the two prerequisites coincided, and his domicile changed to Nebraska — remember, they don't have to coincide on the day you enter the state. Although Filbert moved to Nebraska planning to leave, he later formed the intent to remain indefinitely. When his intent changed, he acquired domicile in Nebraska. Even though he now plans to leave for Colorado, he hasn't acquired a residence there yet, so he keeps his Nebraska domicile until he physically relocates to the new state.

So the answer is **A. D** is right, in a sense, but the reason offered is insufficient. In evaluating the distractors, you should focus not only on the "bottom line," but also on the reasoning offered to support it. Here, **D** says "Nebraska," which is right, but the reason it gives is not. One does not necessarily acquire a domicile by living in a state with no plans to go back to a former state, as the Hawaii example at the beginning of this chapter (see p. 4) illustrates. One acquires a domicile by residing in that state with intent to remain *in that state* indefinitely.

Glannon's Picks

1. Moving Marla	D
2. Wedding plans	B
3. Foundering fathers	C
4. Onofrio's revenge	D
5. Business principals	A
6. At home and abroad	B
7. Smith's amendment	C
8. By the numbers	D
9. *St. Paul* misery	B
10. Aggravation of damages	A
11. Stooges do the math	C
12. Flaky Filbert	A

3

Federal Claims and Federal Cases

When an accident left the Mottleys in pain,
They settled for passes on the train.
The railroad wouldn't renew
So they decided to sue,
Which gave rise to a rule most arcane.

CHAPTER OVERVIEW
A. The toughest nut: The *Mottley* rule
B. What is a "well pleaded complaint?"
C. The *Grable* problem: State law claims that require proof of federal law
D. The relation between constitutional and statutory limits on "arising under" jurisdiction
E. Federal law in state courts
F. Law and facts
G. Mongrel jurisdiction: Supplemental claims
H. Challenges to subject matter jurisdiction
I. The Closer: Arising-under jurisdiction in the Supreme Court
◈ Glannon's Picks

Always keep in mind that federal courts are courts of limited subject matter jurisdiction. Actually, I suppose that is true of *all* courts, short of the Pearly Gates. I can't think of any court, state or federal, that can hear every type of case.

But the federal courts are courts of *really* limited subject matter jurisdiction. They only have authority, under the federal constitution, to hear about ten categories of cases, all listed in Article III, §2 of the Constitution. Some of those categories are pretty arcane, such as cases involving ambassadors and consuls, or cases involving land grants, and consequently of little concern to first-year law students. Two categories of Article III cases — diversity cases and cases arising under federal law — account for the lion's share of federal court litigation, and therefore get a lot of attention in Civil Procedure. This chapter addresses the second of these, federal jurisdiction over cases "arising under" the Constitution and laws of the United States.

A.   The toughest nut: The *Mottley* rule

The most fundamental point about arising-under jurisdiction is that many cases that involve federal issues do not "arise under" federal law. This is the essential message of that civil procedure chestnut, *Louisville & Nashville R.R. v. Mottley*, 211 U.S. 149 (1908). In *Mottley*, the plaintiffs sued the railroad for breach of contract, and alleged in their complaint that the railroad had breached the contract because it believed that a federal statute prohibited it from renewing their passes for free travel. In fact, when it answered the complaint, the railroad did rely on the federal statute as their justification for denying the passes. The parties then litigated that federal question and the federal trial court held that the federal statute did not bar renewing the passes.

The United States Supreme Court reversed and ordered the case dismissed for lack of subject matter jurisdiction. The Court held that a case only "arises under" federal law, within the meaning of the federal statute granting arising-under jurisdiction, if the *plaintiff relies* on federal law as the source of her right to relief. That wasn't true in *Mottley*: the plaintiffs had sued for breach of contract, a state law claim. Although a federal issue was litigated, because the railroad raised a defense based on federal law, the plaintiffs did not base their claim on federal law.

The fundamental premise of the *Mottley* rule is that we must assess the federal court's subject matter jurisdiction based on the plaintiff's complaint. There is no inherent reason why this must be so. Presumably, the court could wait to see whether the defendant's answer raises defenses based in federal law, or asserts a counterclaim under federal law, and allow the court to hear the case if she does. Such later pleadings may inject important federal issues into the case, as they did in *Mottley*. There's a good argument that this would be a sensible interpretation of the arising-under statute. Indeed, the American Law Institute recommended some years ago that removal be authorized where the plaintiff sues in state court and the defendant asserts a federal law defense. See American Law Institute, Study of the Division of Jurisdiction Between State and Federal Courts, §1312(a)(2) (1969). But *Mottley* is still good law in the federal courts.

Here's a fairly straightforward question that illustrates the point.

QUESTION 1. Making a federal case. Consolidated Corporation sues Garces, a former employee, for business libel, a tort claim. The suit is brought in federal court, and alleges that Garces falsely reported to a federal agency that Consolidated was using watered-down concrete on a federal construction project. Garces answers, admitting that he had made a report to the agency, but alleging that his report was protected by the First Amendment to the United States Constitution, which guarantees the right of free speech. He also files a counterclaim against Consolidated, based on the Federal Whistleblower Act, which authorizes damages for anyone who is dismissed or disciplined for reporting fraud on the federal government. After answering the complaint, Garces moves to dismiss for lack of subject matter jurisdiction. (Assume that there is no jurisdiction based on diversity.) The motion should be

A. granted, because the court lacks subject matter jurisdiction over the case.
B. denied, because the complaint alleges that Garces reported the violations to a federal agency.
C. denied, because the case involves a question arising under the Constitution of the United States.
D. denied, because Garces's counterclaim arises under federal law.
E. denied, because Garces waived his objection to jurisdiction by answering the complaint and asserting a counterclaim against Consolidated.

ANALYSIS. While it might make sense to allow federal jurisdiction whenever an issue of federal law is raised in a suit, this has not been the Supreme Court's interpretation of the arising-under statute. Under *Mottley*, we don't consider federal questions injected into the case by the defendant. Consequently, **C** is wrong; the fact that the case *involves* a federal question isn't enough to satisfy *Mottley*. We need to look at the plaintiff's claim only. Here, the law that creates Consolidated's right to sue is libel law, which is state tort law; the federal law issue only enters the case as a defense.

D is wrong for the same reason. Just as we don't consider federal defenses raised in the answer, we don't consider counterclaims (that is, claims for relief asserted by the defendant against the plaintiff) in assessing arising-under jurisdiction. One irony here is that Garces could just as well have been the plaintiff in this dispute. Both parties had claims against the other. If Garces had filed suit first, his claim under the Federal Whistleblower Act would have supported federal arising-under jurisdiction. But he didn't file first, and under *Mottley* the court will only consider Consolidated's claim in assessing its jurisdiction. Consequently, Garces will end up litigating his federal law defense and counterclaim in state court. **A** is the correct answer.

When I test this issue, I always like to have one choice in which there's a vague federal presence that is not directly the source of the claims in the action. Here, **B** is wrong because the fact that the report was made to a federal agency doesn't mean that Consolidated's claim arises under federal law. There's a vague federal flavor here, but if we ask what Consolidated is suing Garces for, the answer is, for libel, a claim arising under state law. Under *Mottley*, such peripheral involvement of federal law will not suffice to support jurisdiction. See, however, Section C below, which illustrates a situation in which a federal issue embedded in a state claim may support jurisdiction.

E is emphatically wrong, because an objection to subject matter jurisdiction may be raised at any time during the case. If the court lacks subject matter jurisdiction over a case, it must dismiss, even if the defendant wants the court to hear it, asserts her defenses and counterclaims, and proceeds to litigate there. *Mottley*, in which the parties litigated to judgment in the trial court and appealed, illustrates the point. Although the parties wanted the Court to reach the merits, it dismissed because the federal trial court lacked subject matter jurisdiction over the case.

B.   What is a "well pleaded complaint?"

Remember that *Mottley* is frequently referred to as the "well-pleaded complaint" rule, because it requires the court to consider not what the plaintiff has pleaded, but what she *needed to plead* to state her cause of action. Just because the plaintiff makes allegations involving federal law in her complaint (as the Mottleys did to rebut the railroad's anticipated defense) doesn't mean that her case arises under federal law. The court will ask what she would plead if she were just stating her own claim and not gilding the lily to get into federal court.

This is puzzling for first year law students. You are just learning the elements of different legal claims, so it's hard to know what allegations are essential to a claim and which are not. But it's fairly clear on the facts of *Mottley* that the plaintiffs did not have to breathe a word about the federal statute in order to assert a valid complaint against the railroad. They certainly didn't claim that they could get relief *because* of the federal statute, but rather in spite of it. The basic syllogism that supports their claim is "We made a contract with the railroad, it didn't perform its obligations, we want an order to it to do so." That is the substance of the Mottleys' position, and it states a basic claim for breach of contract without any reference to a federal issue.

Of course, the Mottleys *did* refer to federal law in their complaint: they alleged that the federal statute was the railroad's reason for refusing to perform the contract. But they didn't *have to* allege that to state their contract claim, so the Supreme Court held that this superfluous allegation should be ignored in determining whether the case arises under federal law.

The Court didn't make this distinction just to wallow in technicalities. It did so to prevent manipulation by plaintiffs. If plaintiffs could "make a federal case" out of a state law claim by including unnecessary references to federal law in their complaints, arising-under jurisdiction could be created by simply including peripheral or even irrelevant references to federal issues in the complaint. By asking not what is in the complaint, but what has to be, the court can limit the opportunity to manipulate the federal courts' jurisdiction.

Let's try another problem that illustrates the well-pleaded complaint limit under *Mottley*.

QUESTION 2. Olefsky's plea for relief. Olefsky, from Florida, is diagnosed with leukemia. Testing of his well determines that it is polluted with toxic chemicals, which may have caused his disease. Officials investigate and determine that the chemicals had migrated through the ground-water from a nearby landfill run by Acme Disposal Corporation, a New York corporation with its principal place of business in Florida. The landfill is completely lined, to prevent leaching into the groundwater, but several years ago one of Acme's drivers had dumped a load outside the lined area. The investigation also revealed other problems with Acme's waste management practices. For example, Acme had violated the Federal Toxics Transportation Act, by failing to file manifests with the Environmental Protection Agency detailing the contents of shipments of hazardous wastes, as required by the Act.

Olefsky sues Acme in federal court, claiming that the dumping created a nuisance (a state law tort) that led to his injuries. The complaint also alleges that Acme violated the Federal Toxics Transportation Act, by failing to file manifests (though it does not allege damages arising from those violations). Acme moves to dismiss for lack of subject matter jurisdiction.

A. The motion will be denied if Acme violated the Federal Toxics Transportation Act.
B. The motion will be denied, because Olefsky has alleged a violation of federal law in his complaint.

C. The motion will be granted, even if the case arises under federal law, because Acme's principal place of business is in Florida, so that the parties are not diverse.

D. The motion will be granted, since Olefsky's case does not "arise under" federal law, as that phrase is interpreted in 28 U.S.C. §1331.

ANALYSIS.   Sometimes the most basic points about a subject are the most confusing. It's very important to recognize what is wrong with the third choice here. **C** suggests that there must be both diversity *and* a federal question in order to sue in federal court. Not so; a plaintiff may sue in federal court as long as her case satisfies *one category* of federal jurisdiction . . . it doesn't have to fit into two, or ten! Thus, if this case arises under federal law, it can be brought in federal court, even though the parties are both from Florida. Conversely, if they were diverse, the case could be brought in federal court even if it arose under state law.

Does Olefsky's case arise under federal law? **A** suggests that it does if Acme violated the Federal Toxics Transportation Act. However, even if Acme violated the Act, that doesn't mean that Olefsky's case arises under it. His claim for damages does not arise from the failure to file EPA reports; it arises from dumping by Acme's driver in an unlined area. So what if they violated the federal reporting statute? How does that strengthen Olefsky's case? He's suing for nuisance, a state tort theory based on different acts by the defendant. It's irrelevant to Olefsky's case that they violated other federal pollution requirements.

Suppose Acme had violated a federal accounting statute, and Olefsky found that out. Could he sue for his pollution claim and argue that it arises under federal law because they violated a federal law irrelevant to his claim? Certainly not. Olefsky may have alleged a federal violation in his complaint, but it doesn't *have to be in there* to state his claim against Acme. His "well pleaded complaint" — one that contains the allegations that entitle him to sue Acme for damages, but *only* those allegations — would contain nuisance allegations, but nothing about the Federal Toxics Transportation Act. Indeed, Olefsky's right to recover would be exactly the same if there were no Federal Toxics Transportation Act. If that is true, the statute is obviously irrelevant to his claim, and throwing promiscuous references to it into the complaint will not make the case "arise under" federal law.

Thus, **A** is wrong, and that means that **B** is too. If it's irrelevant that Acme violated the statute, it's also irrelevant that Olefsky alleged that they did. **D** takes the prize. This case asserts a state tort claim and therefore does not arise under federal law within the meaning of 28 U.S.C. §1331.

C.   The *Grable* problem: State law claims that require proof of federal law

Under *Mottley*, the court must look to see whether the plaintiff asserts a right to relief under federal law. If she does, the case "arises under" federal law, so the court has jurisdiction under 28 U.S.C. §1331. In *American Well Works v. Layne*, 241 U.S. 257, 260 (1916), Justice Holmes suggested a commonly cited test for arising-under jurisdiction, that a suit arises "under the law that creates the cause of action." The Mottleys' claim flunked the Holmes test, since state contract law created their right to sue for their passes.

It would be nice if the Holmes test decided all cases, but the law in this area just isn't that tidy. The Supreme Court has occasionally held that a case in which state law creates the plaintiff's cause of action still "arises under" federal law, where the plaintiff, in order to establish her state law claim, must prove a substantial issue of federal law. See, in particular, *Smith v. Kansas City Title and Trust Co.*, 255 U.S. 180 (1920). In *Smith*, the plaintiffs sued to enjoin a corporation from investing in certain bonds, claiming that doing so would exceed the corporation's powers under state corporation law. The claim the plaintiffs asserted was a state law claim, but to establish that it was illegal for the corporation to invest in the bonds, they had to establish that the federal statute authorizing issuance of the bonds was invalid. Thus, they did not have to *plead* federal law to allege a valid cause of action, but they had to *prove* a proposition of federal law to establish their state law claim. The Supreme Court held that this claim arose under federal law, even though the case clearly would not satisfy the Holmes test.

In *Grable & Sons Metal Products Inc. v. Darue Engineering and Manufacturing Co.*, 545 U.S. 308 (2005), the Supreme Court reaffirmed the principle relied on in *Smith* to support arising-under jurisdiction. In *Grable*, the plaintiff brought an action to quiet title—a state law property claim—to recover property sold by the Internal Revenue Service to Darue after it took the property from Grable for non-payment of taxes. Although Grable sued under state law, it claimed that the tax taking was invalid because the IRS had not complied with the notice required by the federal internal revenue code. Thus, it would have to establish a proposition of federal law—the type of notice required by the federal statute—in order to prove its state law quiet title action. The Supreme Court held that the federal district court had subject matter jurisdiction over the claim under 28 U.S.C. §1331.

However, *Grable* did not hold that arising-under jurisdiction would attach every time the plaintiff had to prove some federal issue to establish a state law claim. The federal issue must be "substantial," 545 U.S. at 312, and the court would have to consider various other policies—such as avoiding interference with state court jurisdiction, the need for uniform interpretation of a federal issue and the risk of bringing too many claims into federal court.

After *Grable*, federal courts must make sensitive judgments about the importance of the embedded federal issue, and such issues will sometimes, but not always, support arising-under jurisdiction. If this standard appears murky, it is, but perhaps has to be to accommodate the various interests at stake in such cases.

Here are two questions to test your understanding of this problematic exception to the well pleaded complaint rule.

QUESTION 3. A *Mottley* matter.   In 2012, the Mottleys are denied renewal of their free passes on the Louisville and Nashville Railroad. They sue the Railroad for breach of contract, claiming that it had agreed to renew their passes for life, in return for a release of liability for injuries in an accident on the Railroad. They allege that the Railroad refused to renew their passes because of a new federal statute barring free passes, but also allege that the statute only applies to passes granted after its enactment. Both parties are from Kentucky. The Railroad moves to dismiss the case for lack of subject matter jurisdiction.

After the Supreme Court's decision in *Grable & Sons Metal Products Inc. v. Darue Engineering and Manufacturing Co.*, the court will

A. grant the motion, applying the well pleaded complaint rule.
B. deny the motion if it determines that there is a substantial question as to whether the federal statute applies to the Mottleys' passes, issued prior to its passage.
C. deny the motion, because the Mottleys, in order to prove their state law claim, must establish a proposition of federal law.
D. grant the motion only if it concludes that the federal statute does not bar renewal of the Mottleys' passes.

ANALYSIS.   The correct answer is **A**; the case should be dismissed for lack of subject matter jurisdiction. This case is not like *Grable*, because the Mottleys do not have to prove any proposition of federal law to establish their claim. All they need to prove is that they had a contract and that the railroad has failed to perform it. (So **C** is wrong.) There is no federal issue embedded in their claim. The federal statute will be raised as a defense by the railroad. After *Grable*, as before, courts still look only to the plaintiff's case to determine whether the case arises under federal law. The plaintiffs' case here does not require any allegation or proof of a proposition of federal law.

B is also wrong, because even if the applicability of the new federal statute is a substantial question of federal law, it is not one that the Mottleys must establish to prove their claim — the railroad must prove it to establish a defense. **D** is wrong too. The federal court need not decide whether the statute bars renewal . . . in fact, it can't decide that, because it doesn't have subject matter jurisdiction over the case. After *Grable*, as before, this case does not qualify for arising under jurisdiction.

Here's another question on this embedded-federal-issue problem.

QUESTION 4. Making a federal case, part 2. Marston, a lawyer, represented Green in a suit for patent infringement. (Patent cases arise under federal law and must be brought in federal court under 28 U.S.C. §1338(a).) The court held that Green's patent was invalid because he had not filed for patent protection within one year of commencing sale of the product for which he sought a patent.

After he lost his infringement suit, Green sued Marston for legal malpractice, a state tort claim, in state court. Green asserted that Marston had failed to raise an obvious argument in the earlier case that, if presented, would have led the court to find his patent valid. Marston moved to dismiss the state law malpractice action, arguing that it had to be brought in federal court because it arose under the federal patent statute.

A. It is unclear, under *Grable*, whether this case would arise under the patent statute or not.
B. The case arises under federal law because Green seeks relief under the federal patent laws.
C. The case arises under federal law, under *Grable*, because there is a federal patent issue embedded in the plaintiff's state law malpractice claim.
D. The case belongs in state court because it does not involve any federal issue.

ANALYSIS. This example is take from *Gunn v. Minton*, 133 S. Ct. 1059 (2013). *Gunn* presents a nice set of facts for assessing the meaning of *Grable*'s approach to embedded federal issues. First, **D** is wrong, because there is a federal issue "involved" in Green's case. Green argues that Minton was negligent for failing to assert an argument for patent validity under the federal patent laws. Surely that is an issue of federal law, and one that Green will have to establish to win his legal malpractice case. Yet **B** is not right either. Green does not seek relief under the federal patent statutes; he seeks relief on a cause of action for legal malpractice, which is a state law negligence claim. Under the frequently cited "Holmes test," this claim does not arise under federal law, because it is state negligence law that "creates the cause of action."

While Green is not suing under the federal patent statute, there is a patent issue embedded in his legal malpractice claim. In order to prove that negligence claim, he must prove that Minton failed to make an argument about federal patent law that would have led to grant of a patent to Green. So this is the same configuration as cases like *Grable* and *Kansas City Title & Trust*. But **C** is still not right. It says that Green's case arises under federal law because there is a federal patent issue embedded in the plaintiff's state law malpractice claim. Yet *Grable* did not say that every case in which the plaintiff must establish a federal issue in order to prove a state law claim arises under federal law. It said such cases will *sometimes* "arise under," depending on whether the federal issue is substantial, possible interference with state court jurisdiction, the need for uniform interpretation of a federal issue, and the risk of bringing too many claims into federal court.

So sometimes when a plaintiff must prove a federal issue in order to establish her state law cause of action, the case will "arise under," but in other cases it will not, depending on some fairly broad standards. That makes **A** the best answer here. In fact, in *Gunn* the Supreme Court applied those factors and concluded that the legal malpractice case did not arise under the patent laws, even though Gunn would have to prove a proposition of federal patent law to recover for legal malpractice. The court relied primarily on the fact that this would bring many legal malpractice cases, which are typically handled in state courts, into federal court, and would turn on issues that (even if they were federal issues) were of importance merely to the parties to the case, not "substantial" federal issues of broader application.

D.   The relation between constitutional and statutory limits on "arising under" jurisdiction

Article III, §2 of the Constitution provides that federal courts may hear cases "arising under" federal law. And 28 U.S.C. §1331, the statute conveying arising-under jurisdiction to the federal district courts, uses the same language. A student, or a lawyer, might reasonably conclude that this language means the same thing in the statute and in the Constitution. Since the Supreme Court has interpreted the phrase "arising under federal law" in the statute to focus solely on the plaintiff's complaint, shouldn't that phrase mean the same thing in Article III, §2?

Article III defines the constitutional limits of the jurisdiction of all federal courts, including the Supreme Court. If the *Mottley* rule were an interpretation of Article III, it would drastically restrict the power of all federal courts, including the Supreme Court, to consider cases that involve federal defenses and counterclaims. For example, the Court would have no power to hear an appeal in a case like Consolidated's in Question 1, which raises a federal issue, but does not satisfy the *Mottley* test. The state courts would then have the final authority to decide the federal law questions raised by the case.

Not surprisingly, the Supreme Court has interpreted the scope of the Article III arising-under jurisdiction much more broadly than *Mottley's* construction of the arising-under statute. In *Osborn v. Bank of the United States*, 22 U.S. 738 (1824), Chief Justice Marshall concluded that the Article III grant of jurisdiction over cases arising under federal law applies as long as a question of federal statutory or constitutional law "forms an ingredient" of the case. Certainly, federal law "forms an ingredient" of a case if a federal issue is raised as a defense or as a counterclaim. Thus, because the Article III grant extends to such cases, Congress could do away with the *Mottley* rule (what law student would miss it?) by amending 28 U.S.C. §1331. Although this has been clear since *Osborn*, Congress has never repudiated *Mottley*, because it provides a clear rule that allows federal courts to determine their jurisdiction at the outset of the case, and limits the potential for parties to manipulate federal jurisdiction.

To illustrate the distinction between the reach of arising-under jurisdiction in Article III and under §1331, consider the following question.

QUESTION 5. Mix and match. Eleanor sues Franklin for breach of contract, claiming that he agreed to sell her certain high-risk securities on January 1, 2011, but failed to deliver them on the appointed date. Franklin defends on the ground that after he agreed to the sale, but before the delivery date, a federal statute was passed making such sales illegal.

A. This case "arises under" federal law as that phrase is construed in 28 U.S.C. §1331, but not as it is construed in Article III, §2 of the United States Constitution.

B. This case "arises under" federal law as that phrase is construed in both 28 U.S.C. §1331 and in Article III, §2 of the United States Constitution.

C. This case "arises under" federal law as that phrase is construed in Article III, §2 of the United States Constitution, but not as construed in 28 U.S.C. §1331.

D. This case "arises under" federal law as that phrase is construed in both 28 U.S.C. §1331 and in Article III, §2 of the United States Constitution, if the case is removed to federal court after the defendant has answered the complaint in state court, asserting his federal defense.

ANALYSIS. The point of this example is to illustrate the distinction between *Mottley's* narrow interpretation of arising-under jurisdiction in 28 U.S.C. §1331 and *Osborn's* much more expansive interpretation of the same language in Article III, §2. The facts here are essentially a clone of *Mottley*. The plaintiff sues under state contract law, and the defendant asserts a federal defense to the claim. This is clearly not an arising-under case under the

Mottley interpretation of §1331, because the plaintiff's well-pleaded complaint asserts only a state law claim. So **A** and **B** are both wrong: in order to satisfy the arising-under statute, §1331, the plaintiff herself must assert a right to relief under federal law, and Eleanor's claim is based on state contract law.[1] And since, under *Mottley,* the court will only look at the plaintiff's complaint, not at the answer, in determining whether it has jurisdiction under §1331, **D** is wrong as well. The defendant's federal defense in his answer will be disregarded in evaluating the court's jurisdiction, even if the answer is already before the court when it determines the jurisdiction question.

So **C** is the right answer. The case is within the constitutional grant of arising-under jurisdiction in Article III: Franklin's federal law defense makes federal law an "ingredient" of the case, even though that ingredient is injected by the defendant, not the plaintiff. But the case is not proper under §1331, because *Mottley's* well-pleaded complaint rule (still the governing interpretation of §1332(a)) requires that the plaintiff rely on federal law to make her claim.

Thus, with arising-under cases as with diversity cases, it is always necessary to analyze the constitutional scope of jurisdiction and Congress's grant of that jurisdiction separately. In arising-under cases, as in diversity cases, Congress has never chosen to authorize the federal district courts to exercise all of the Article III jurisdiction. Here's another example to drive home the point.

QUESTION 6. Limiting the limits. Congressperson Smith introduces a bill to add a $75,000.01 amount-in-controversy requirement to 28 U.S.C. §1331.

A. Smith's bill would be constitutional, since Congress may expand or restrict the jurisdiction of the federal district courts as it sees fit.

B. Smith's bill would be unconstitutional, since it would restrict the right of plaintiffs to take some cases that arise under federal law to federal court.

C. Smith's bill would be constitutional, because Congress may grant less than the full Article III jurisdiction to the federal courts.

D. Smith's bill would be unconstitutional, since Article III, §2 authorizes the federal district courts to hear all cases arising under federal law.

ANALYSIS. Smith's bill would impose an additional limit on the jurisdiction of the federal district courts in arising-under cases. Not only

---

1. This case assumes there is no argument for jurisdiction under the *Grable case,* of course.

would the *Mottley* rule apply, but even cases that satisfy *Mottley* could not be heard if less than $75,000.01 was in controversy. Clearly, this would prevent the district courts from hearing cases that are within the constitutional grant of arising-under jurisdiction. If Isaacs sued Eagleton under the federal Age Discrimination in Employment Act (ADEA) but only sought $25,000 in damages, his case certainly involves a "federal ingredient," his claim under a federal statute. His case even satisfies the *Mottley* rule, since he seeks relief under the federal statute. But Smith's bill, if enacted, would prevent him from bringing this federal law claim in federal court.

Not a problem. Article III establishes the outer limits on federal court jurisdiction, but the cases make it clear that, within those limits, Congress decides which cases they want the federal district courts to hear. Congress could grant arising-under jurisdiction very broadly, by authorizing the federal district courts to hear any case that "involves" federal law. This would convey virtually all of the jurisdiction permissible under *Osborn's* "federal ingredient" test. Or it could grant arising-under jurisdiction very selectively. For example, Congress could authorize jurisdiction over cases arising under the federal tax laws, but no others. Or it could grant none of the arising-under jurisdiction, if it chose to do so.

Under this principle, **D** is incorrect. It implies that the federal district courts automatically have all the arising-under jurisdiction in Article III, so that Congress could not limit it. That is not the accepted interpretation. Article III describes the outer limits of the federal judicial power, but within those limits Congress regulates the federal district courts' jurisdiction. It must authorize them to hear cases by statute. It can, and always has conveyed jurisdiction selectively. It isn't enough that a case is within the outer bounds of Article III; it must also be authorized in a jurisdictional statute. **B** is off the mark for the same reason; there is nothing unconstitutional about Congress's limiting the arising-under jurisdiction of the federal district courts.

Perhaps the most plausible "distractor" is **A**, which takes the position that the bill is constitutional because Congress may "expand or restrict the jurisdiction of the federal district courts as it sees fit." This isn't quite true. It may *restrict* their jurisdiction as it sees fit, but it may not *expand* their jurisdiction as it sees fit. Article III sets the outer limit. If Congress passed a statute authorizing federal district court jurisdiction over divorces, that statute would be unconstitutional, because nothing in Article III (leaving diversity aside, anyway) authorizes federal courts to hear divorce cases.

That leaves **C**, which is the right answer. If Congress wants to limit the district courts to "big" federal question cases through an amount-in-controversy requirement, it may do so. While this would indeed "restrict the right of plaintiffs to take some cases arising under federal law to federal court" (**B**), Congress may do that. It always has in diversity cases, and at one time, did in arising-under cases as well. See Pub. L. No. 96-486 (1981) (repealing $10,000.01 amount-in-controversy requirement formerly required under §1331).

E.   Federal law in state courts

Our analysis of arising-under jurisdiction demonstrates that a great many cases that raise federal issues cannot be brought in federal court. Cases like *Mottley*, in which federal law is raised as a defense, or cases in which a federal law counterclaim is asserted, are not within federal court arising-under jurisdiction. So what becomes of them? They are brought in state court, of course. State courts are competent to decide issues of federal law, and in cases like these they must do so.

Suppose, however, that the plaintiff has a case that is within federal arising-under jurisdiction, even as narrowly construed under 28 U.S.C. §1331, but wants to bring it in state court. Can she do that? Put another way, *must* a case be brought in federal court if it satisfies the *Mottley* standard for arising-under jurisdiction?

Generally, the answer is "no." Most cases that arise under federal law may be brought in state court if the plaintiff prefers to do so. For example, if Isaacs has a claim under the federal Age Discrimination in Employment Act, it clearly arises under federal law and may be filed in federal court. But Isaacs would have the right to sue in state court instead, if she prefers. If she sues under 42 U.S.C. §1983, for violation of her federal civil rights, she could certainly do so in federal court under *Mottley*, but again, she doesn't have to. The jurisdiction of the federal and state courts over most types of federal law cases is said to be "concurrent," that is, the courts of both systems can entertain these cases.

Like so many legal principles, this one has an exception. It has long been held that Congress may, if it chooses, provide by statute that the federal courts' jurisdiction over a particular type of federal claim is exclusive, that is, that those federal claims *must* be brought in federal court. See, e.g., *Bowles v. Willingham*, 321 U.S. 503, 511-512 (1944). Congress has mandated suit in federal court in some categories of cases. For example, 28 U.S.C. §1338(a) provides in part that "[n]o State court shall have jurisdiction over any claim for relief arising under any Act of Congress relating to patents. . . ." Occasionally, too, the Supreme Court has concluded that Congress intended federal court jurisdiction to be exclusive, even though the statute isn't clear on the point. But this is quite rare. In most cases, jurisdiction is concurrent with the courts of the states, unless the federal statute conferring jurisdiction confines jurisdiction to the federal courts. See generally C. Wright, *The Law of Federal Courts* 43-44 (5th ed. 1994).

With this background, the following problem should be pretty easy.

QUESTION 7. Concurrents. Plaintiff wishes to sue Defendant under the Lanburn Act, a federal statute. Which of the following is true?

A. Plaintiff must file in federal court if the Lanburn Act itself restricts suits under the Act to federal court.
B. Plaintiff must file suit in federal court, because the case arises under federal law.
C. Plaintiff must file suit in federal court, unless Congress has expressly authorized filing of Lanburn Act suits in state court as well.
D. Plaintiff must file in federal court if there is complete diversity between the parties.

ANALYSIS. **D** is a truly distracting distractor. It suggests that a federal question case must be brought in federal court if the parties are diverse. That isn't so. The plaintiff here has sued under a federal statute, so the case is an arising-under case. As discussed above, state courts have concurrent jurisdiction over most arising-under cases. The state citizenship of the parties is utterly irrelevant to an arising-under case. The plaintiff may bring it in state court if she likes, whether she is diverse from the defendant or not. Or she could bring it in federal court, again, whether she is diverse from the defendant or not.

The state courts have concurrent jurisdiction over diversity cases too, by the way. A plaintiff is free to file a case against a citizen of another state in state court if she prefers (unless, of course, she sues the diverse defendant on one of those rare federal claims for which Congress has made federal court jurisdiction exclusive). Indeed, one of the main reasons for removal jurisdiction is to address the situation where a local plaintiff has sued an out-of-state defendant in state court.

B is wrong because it suggests that a plaintiff who sues under federal law must use federal court. That isn't so; federal claims may be brought in state court unless Congress has provided that they must be filed in federal court. And **C** is wrong because it reverses the general presumption. It is based on the premise that Congress must expressly authorize suit on a particular type of federal claim in state court in order for the state court to have jurisdiction. The presumption is the opposite: the state and federal courts have concurrent jurisdiction unless Congress restricts a particular type of federal claim to the federal courts. Only if the Lanburn Act provides for exclusive federal court jurisdiction must the case be brought in federal court. **A** takes the cake.

F.   Law and facts

In litigation, there is many a slip between cup and lip. Sometimes, a plaintiff may allege facts that would support a federal claim, but it is far from clear that she will be able to establish those facts. Here's a question that considers the relationship of such factual disputes to the court's subject matter jurisdiction. In addressing it, ignore the possibility of supplemental jurisdiction under 28 U.S.C. §1367.

QUESTION 8. Polymolysorbate.   Antril, a Florida citizen, sues Manello, from Kentucky, in federal court. She claims that Manello, a driver for Acme Disposal Corporation, negligently drove a hazardous waste truck off the road, leading to a spill that polluted Antril's property with polymolysorbate. She also asserts a claim, in the same action, against Acme, a Florida corporation, for violation of the Federal Toxics Transportation Act (FTTA). That statute bars transporting polymolysorbate in a truck that lacks a secondary containment system, and allows recovery for resulting pollution damages. Antril's damages are, quite probably, several hundred thousand dollars.

Manello answers the complaint denying that he drove negligently. In its answer, Acme admits that the Federal Toxics Transportation Act requires secondary containment for polymolysorbate, but denies that the polymolysorbate spilled from its truck. It alleges that its truck was not carrying polymolysorbate, so it must have come from an earlier spill by a different hauler.

A. The federal district has jurisdiction over the entire action.
B. The federal district court has jurisdiction over the action only if Antril establishes that Acme's truck was transporting polymolysorbate.
C. The federal district court has jurisdiction over the action against Manello, since Antril and Manello are diverse, but does not have jurisdiction over the claim against Acme, because Antril's claim against Acme raises no disputed issue of federal law, only a factual question concerning who spilled polymolysorbate on Antril's property.
D. The federal district court lacks jurisdiction over the suit, since Antril and Acme are both citizens of Florida and thus, under *Strawbridge*, there is no complete diversity.

ANALYSIS.   In this case, Antril has brought a claim arising under a federal statute against one of the defendants, Acme, but Acme claims that it did not violate the statute upon which Antril bases her claim. Suppose it turns out that its defense is right, that they didn't violate the statute because another hauler spilled the chemical? How will that affect the court's subject matter jurisdiction?

First, let's deal with **D**. It is true that there is not complete diversity among the parties, since Antril and Acme are both from Florida. But diversity is irrelevant to Antril's claim against Acme. Antril sued Acme on a claim arising under federal law, so the citizenship of these parties is irrelevant. Leaving aside supplemental jurisdiction (as I asked you to do), Antril's claim against Manello is a state law negligence claim, so it may only be brought in federal court based on diversity. But Antril and Manello are diverse and we can ignore the citizenship of Acme, since Antril sued it on a different jurisdictional basis, a federal question claim.

Just to make this point clear, imagine that Antril had sued Manello and Acme in two separate actions. If so, the federal court would have jurisdiction over the case against Manello based on diversity, and jurisdiction over the case against Acme based on arising-under jurisdiction. If she can do this (and she could) there is no reason why she can't sue them together, and base jurisdiction over the two claims on two separate grounds. Since the only parties to the claim based on diversity are Antril and Manello, diversity jurisdiction is proper over that claim. The fact that Acme is from Florida is irrelevant, since the claim against it is based on arising-under jurisdiction. Its citizenship thus does not defeat diversity jurisdiction over Antril's claim against Manello.

B is clearly a loser. Imagine if the federal court's jurisdiction turned on whether or not the plaintiff's allegations turned out to be true: the court would not be able to determine its jurisdiction until the factual issues were tried. Generally, courts must know whether they have the power to hear a case from the outset, not based on events down the road (so to speak). So the court will not base its jurisdiction on whether Acme has actually violated the FTTA, but whether Antril asserts a colorable claim that it did.

C argues that the claim does not arise under federal law, because no issue of federal law is actually disputed between Antril and Acme. Acme doesn't deny that the Act requires special precautions for transporting poly-molysorbate, or that it would be liable if it violated the Act. Instead, it simply denies that it violated the federal statute. It doesn't deny that the statute would be violated if they did what Antril alleges, it simply argues, "we didn't do it." So the parties will not have to litigate the meaning or the applicability of the FTTA, they will only litigate a factual question: was it Acme that spilled polymolysorbate on Antril's land?

Although this is true, the claim still "arises under" the federal act. Under *Mottley*, arising-under jurisdiction exists if the plaintiff seeks relief under the federal statute. Certainly she does: she claims damages under the FTTA, a federal statute. Although the parties don't contest the meaning or applicability of the federal statute, Antril does seek relief under it. That is all that *Mottley* requires. And it makes sense that parties seeking relief under federal law should have access to federal court, even if the dispute involves a factual application of federal law rather than a legal interpretation. Federal courts play an important role by applying undisputed legal rules even-handedly, as well as by construing the meaning of legal rules. Federal policies can be just as surely undermined by unsympathetic application to facts as by hostile interpretation.

A, after all, is right. The federal district court has jurisdiction over the entire case. It has jurisdiction over Antril's claim against Manello based on diversity, and her claim against Acme because it seeks relief under federal law.[2]

G. Mongrel jurisdiction: Supplemental claims

This is not the place to go into supplemental jurisdiction in detail — we'll do that in Chapter 14. But it is useful to introduce the problem of cases that include some claims that satisfy federal subject matter jurisdiction, but also others that do not. Very commonly, cases involve not one claim, but several — perhaps two, or perhaps ten. Civil procedure has a nasty doctrine called res judicata, which provides that once you have sued a defendant for claims arising out of a set of events, you can't do it again. Consequently, lawyers know that whatever claims they have against a defendant arising from a particular dispute must be asserted when they bring suit the first time.

Suppose, for example, that Greenstein, a New Yorker, sues Panil, another New Yorker, for infringing her patent, claiming that she had licensed Panil to use the patented device for limited purposes, but Panil had exceeded those limits. This claim arises under the federal patent statutes, so the federal court has arising-under jurisdiction to hear it. However, Greenstein might also allege a claim for breach of contract as well, based on the same acts by Panil. This is a state claim between two parties from the same state. It doesn't arise under federal law, and there's no diversity. If it were brought alone, the federal court would not have jurisdiction to hear it.

But it wasn't brought alone; it was brought along with a proper federal claim and arises from the same events. It makes sense that it should be litigated along with the federal claim. But how can it be? Subject matter jurisdiction is fundamental, and what gives the federal court subject matter jurisdiction over Greenstein's contract claim?

The Supreme Court has held that where the plaintiff asserts a claim that properly supports federal court jurisdiction, it is constitutionally permissible

---

2. It would have supplemental jurisdiction over Artril's claim against Manello as well. 28 U.S.C. §1367(a). But the question asks you to ignore that possibility.

for the federal court to hear the entire dispute between the parties, including other claims that arise from the same "nucleus of operative facts" but could not be brought in federal court alone. *United Mine Workers v. Gibbs*, 383 U.S. 715 (1966). And Congress has conveyed such "supplemental" jurisdiction to the federal district courts in 28 U.S.C. §1367(a), which authorizes the federal court, if it has jurisdiction over one claim, to hear other claims that are part of the same "case or controversy." Basically, a claim is part of the same case or controversy as the main claim (the one that gives the federal court jurisdiction) if it arises from the same set of underlying facts, the "common nucleus of operative facts" test of *Gibbs*. So the bottom line is (a little oversimplified, but close enough until we get to Chapter 14) that a plaintiff who has asserted one substantial claim that properly invokes federal jurisdiction may have her entire dispute heard in federal court, including state law claims that couldn't otherwise be brought in federal court.

Here's a basic illustration.

QUESTION 9. Tagging along. Isaacs, a Montana citizen, sues United Tool and Die Corporation, incorporated in Delaware with its principal place of business in Montana, under the Federal Age Discrimination in Employment Act (ADEA). He sues in federal court. Isaacs claims that United fired him because of his age, replacing him with a younger employee. Isaacs also asserts a second claim in his complaint, alleging that firing him constituted a breach of his contract of employment. He asserts a third claim in the complaint, alleging that, a year before he was fired, United had misappropriated a design he created for a new grinding wheel. Isaacs claimed he had invented the wheel on his own, not in the course of his employment, so that United had no right to exploit the idea without his consent.

The federal court has subject matter jurisdiction

A. over all of Isaacs' claims.
B. over none of these claims, because the parties are both from Montana.
C. over the ADEA claim only.
D. over the first two claims, but not the third.

ANALYSIS. B takes the position that the federal court cannot hear cases between citizens of the same state. But they can, so long as the plaintiff relies on some basis of federal jurisdiction other than diversity. If Smith sues Doe, another Nevadan, for a federal civil rights violation under 42 U.S.C. §1983, he may of course do so in federal court, even though both parties are from the same state.

C is also wrong, because, even though there is no independent basis for jurisdiction over Isaacs's state law claims, there will be supplemental jurisdiction over at least one. The supplemental jurisdiction statute authorizes federal courts that have jurisdiction over a case, because a proper federal claim is asserted, to hear the entire "case," that is, the parties' entire dispute arising out of the same underlying facts. That includes claims arising from those events that don't independently qualify for federal court jurisdiction. Here, Isaacs' breach of contract claim arises from his discharge, as his federal ADEA claim does. Since the ADEA claim arises under federal law, it provides a basis for federal court jurisdiction, and supplemental jurisdiction sweeps in other claims arising from the same facts. See 28 U.S.C. §1367(a) (allowing supplemental claims that arise out of the "same case or controversy" as the federally sufficient claim).

The closer choice here is between **A** and **D**. The crucial question is whether the misappropriation claim arises from the same "nucleus of operative facts" as the discharge claims. I would think not. This claim arises from United's use of his design. He would have this claim whether he had been discharged or not, and the claim accrued well before the discharge. The answer might be different, or at least closer, if the question suggested that Isaacs was fired for making a claim to the design, but it doesn't. So **D** is the best answer. The court has supplemental jurisdiction over the breach of contract claim, because it arises from the same underlying dispute as the ADEA claim. But the misappropriation claim arises from other, only tangentially related events, and would not qualify under §1367 (or under *U.M.W. v. Gibbs*) for supplemental jurisdiction.

H.   Challenges to subject matter jurisdiction

Because the outer limits of federal subject matter jurisdiction are established in the Constitution, the federal courts are careful not to exceed those limits. Thus, they will almost always entertain objections to their jurisdiction, even if they were not raised at the outset of the case. See Fed. R. Civ. P. 12(h)(3) (whenever it appears that the court lacks subject matter jurisdiction, court shall dismiss the action). Thus, for example, the parties cannot consent to the federal court hearing a case over which it lacks jurisdiction. Even if none of the parties asserts an objection to the court's power to hear the case, the court will dismiss on its own motion if it appears that there is no jurisdiction over the case.

Consider the following question.

QUESTION 10. Second thoughts. Taney, from Wisconsin, sues Ivanov, his Wisconsin landlord, for damages suffered when the house he rented from Ivanov collapsed. He alleges that Ivanov was negligent in failing to comply with federal structural standards applicable to buildings offered for rent to tenants subsidized under the Federal Housing Act. Ivanov answers the complaint denying liability, and the parties proceed to engage in discovery.

Ten months later, Taney becomes disenchanted with the federal judge assigned to hear the case. Since he has some doubt as to whether his claim meets arising-under standards, he moves to dismiss the suit for lack of subject matter jurisdiction, claiming that the case does not arise under federal law. The motion should be

A. denied, if the case "arises under" federal law within the meaning of Article III, §2, and is thus constitutionally permissible, even if it does not "arise under" federal law within the meaning of 28 U.S.C. §1331.
B. granted, if the court concludes that the case does not satisfy the standard for a case "arising under" federal law.
C. denied, because Taney, by filing suit in federal court, waived any objection to the court's lack of jurisdiction.
D. denied, because Taney waived any objection to subject matter jurisdiction by litigating the case for ten months without raising the jurisdictional issue.

ANALYSIS. **C** seems like a pretty reasonable answer here. Why should Taney, who invoked the federal court's jurisdiction, be allowed to challenge it when the case looks as though it may be going sour? Isn't he manipulating the system, and shouldn't he be estopped from denying jurisdiction, in order to discourage such manipulation?

There's a fair argument for that view, but other considerations outweigh the risk of manipulation. Federal subject matter jurisdiction involves more than the interests of the parties. It implicates the constitutional balance between the federal and state governments. In order to assure that federal courts don't exceed their constitutional authority, they will always entertain a challenge to their subject matter jurisdiction. After all, if the federal court exercises jurisdiction over a case it lacks the power to hear, the resulting judgment will be subject to reversal on appeal, since a judgment rendered without the power to enter it is invalid. To avoid such wasteful and unconstitutional exercises, the trial court will always consider challenges to its jurisdiction. "If the court determines at any time that it lacks subject-matter jurisdiction, the court must dismiss the action." Fed. R. Civ. P. 12(h)(3).

This reasoning disposes of **D** as well. The objection of lack of subject matter jurisdiction is never waived — at least, it remains subject to direct attack on appeal, even if no objection was raised in the trial court. In *Mottley*, for example, the issue was raised by the Supreme Court itself.

Federal Rule 12(h)(3) confirms that this is true throughout the litigation in the trial court, even if it is the plaintiff who raises the problem.

Consider what would happen if the rule were otherwise: Suppose that the parties wanted to litigate a case in federal court that did not satisfy federal subject matter jurisdiction. The plaintiff could file suit in federal court, and the defendant could simply fail to object. If such a failure to raise jurisdictional defects authorized the federal court to hear the case, the parties could evade the constitutional limits on federal judicial power. Of course, the federal judge might note the lack of jurisdiction on her own motion, and dismiss, but the limits on federal judicial power should not be left to discretion or to chance.[3] So Taney has not waived the right to make the motion by failing to raise the jurisdiction issue earlier.

A suggests that the court can retain the case if it "arises under" federal law as that phrase is used in Article III, §2, even if §1331 doesn't authorize federal jurisdiction over it. I suppose the logic here is that, as long as it would not offend *constitutional* limits for the federal court to hear the case, it has the power to do so, even if the case does not satisfy Congress's *statutory* limits on arising-under jurisdiction. However, a federal court exceeds its authority when it exercises jurisdiction that Congress has not granted, just as it would if it exercised jurisdiction not within the constitutional grant. So, the court will dismiss a case that is not authorized by statute, as well as one that goes beyond the Article III constitutional grant.

So **B**, then, is the best answer. To avoid exceeding the limits on its jurisdictional competence, the federal court will dismiss if it determines that it lacks jurisdiction, despite Taney's failure to raise the objection earlier.

I. The Closer: Arising under jurisdiction in the Supreme Court

The preceding sections make clear that state courts are going to decide many questions of federal law. First, they will decide such questions when plaintiffs file cases arising under federal law in state court, if the defendant doesn't remove to federal court. Second, they will decide federal questions when the plaintiff sues in state court on state law claims, and the defendant relies on federal law as a defense, as the defendant did in *Mottley*. And third, they will

---

3. There are limits to this, however. Courts have usually held that a litigant who litigated on the merits in the original suit cannot resist enforcement of a judgment in another state based on the ground that the court that rendered the judgment lacked subject matter jurisdiction over the case. See, e.g., *Chicot County Drainage Dist. v. Baxter State Bank*, 308 U.S. 371 (1940); see generally W. Richman & W. Reynolds, *Understanding Conflict of Laws* 382-384 (3d ed. 2002).

decide federal issues when the plaintiff sues in state court and the defendant asserts a counterclaim arising under federal law.

In all these situations, the courts of the fifty states will be deciding issues of federal law. Naturally, different courts in different states may decide the same issue differently. One state may decide that a claimant must show intent to discriminate under the ADEA, while another may interpret it to bar practices that have a disparate impact on older employees, even if no intent is shown. Suppose one state court holds that the federal statute in *Mottley* bars renewal of passes, but the courts of another state hold that it doesn't? There has to be some court at the top of the system to reconcile such conflicting holdings, to rule definitively on the meaning of federal law.

And that court ought to be a federal court: otherwise the states could undermine federal authority by unsympathetic interpretation or application of federal law. Under our constitutional system, the obvious candidate for this role is the United States Supreme Court. And, under *Osborn*, the Court itself has held that it has the authority to fulfill that role, even in cases involving federal defenses or counterclaims, since federal law is "an ingredient" in such cases.

But, of course, it would be severely hampered in fulfilling that role if its power to exercise judicial review were limited by the *Mottley* rule, if it could only review cases in which the plaintiff asserts a claim arising under federal law. However, 28 U.S.C. §1331, to which the *Mottley* rule applies, *does not address the appellate jurisdiction of the United States Supreme Court*. It addresses the original jurisdiction of the federal district courts, the trial courts of the federal system. The statute that governs the Supreme Court's appellate jurisdiction, 28 U.S.C. §1257, is a great deal broader than §1331.

28 U.S.C. §1257. State courts; certiorari

(a) Final judgments or decrees rendered by the highest court of a State in which a decision could be had, may be reviewed by the Supreme Court by writ of certiorari where the validity of a treaty or statute of the United States is drawn in question or where the validity of a statute of any State is drawn in question on the ground of its being repugnant to the Constitution, treaties, or laws of the United States, or where any title, right, privilege, or immunity is specially set up or claimed under the Constitution or the treaties or statutes of, or any commission held or authority exercised under, the United States.

This statute authorizes the Supreme Court to review cases that come up to it through the court systems of the states. It allows review of cases in which federal issues are raised — by defendants as well as plaintiffs. Suppose, for example, that a town sued a defendant for violating a state adult bookstore zoning statute, and the store owner claimed the statute was unconstitutional under the First Amendment to the United States Constitution. This case could not be brought in federal court under 28 U.S.C. §1331, as interpreted in *Mottley*, since it arises under a state zoning statute. But the state court's decision upholding or invalidating the statute could be reviewed by the Supreme Court under §1257, since it involves a claim (by the defendant) that the state statute is "repugnant to the Constitution."

Consider this example, which analyzes the scope of review in the United States Supreme Court of state court cases posing federal issues.

QUESTION 11. A *Mottley* reprise. Erasmus L. and Annie E. Mottley sue the Louisville and Nashville R.R. Co. for refusing to renew the free passes it had contracted to provide the Mottleys for life. They sue in state court. The railroad claims that a federal statute making free passes illegal bars renewal of the passes, even though they were contracted for before the statute was enacted. The Mottleys claim that the statute should not be interpreted to apply to passes previously granted, and that, if it does apply to such passes, it deprives them of property (their right to the passes) without due process of law under the Fifth Amendment to the United States Constitution.

The court holds (1) that the statute bars renewal of the Mottleys' passes, and (2) that the statute creates an unconstitutional taking of the Mottleys' property. Consequently, the court holds the statute unconstitutional as applied to them, and orders the passes renewed. The state supreme court affirms. The railroad seeks review in the United States Supreme Court. The Court

A. does not have the authority under 28 U.S.C. §1257 to review either holding by the state court, because the Mottleys' case arises under state contract law.

B. has the authority under 28 U.S.C. §1257 to review the state court's holding that the statute is unconstitutional, but not the holding construing the statute itself.

C. has the authority under 28 U.S.C. §1257 to review both of the state court holdings, but §1257 is unconstitutional, since it allows review of the Mottleys' case, which arose under state contract law.

D. has the authority under 28 U.S.C. §1257 to review both of the state court's holdings.

E. The Mottleys' names can't possibly be Erasmus and Annie.

ANALYSIS. **E** is wrong; the Mottleys' names really were Erasmus and Annie.

More importantly, **A** is wrong. Profoundly wrong. It is based on the assumption that the *Mottley* rule applies to the Supreme Court's jurisdiction. It doesn't. As iterated and reiterated, *Mottley* interprets 28 U.S.C. §1331, which conveys part of the constitutionally permissible arising-under jurisdiction to the federal trial courts, the federal district courts. It does not control the jurisdiction of the Supreme Court. For cases coming up for review from the state courts, §1257 does.

B is flawed as well. Section §1257 authorizes Supreme Court review of the state court's holding that the federal statute violates the Constitution ("where the validity of a treaty or statute of the United States is drawn in question"). And it authorizes review of the state court's interpretation of the statute. The railroad, in its defense, had claimed an "immunity" from its obligation to renew the passes under a federal statute ("any title, right, privilege, or immunity . . . specially set up or claimed under the . . . statutes of . . . the United States"). Section 1257 broadly authorizes review where federal issues are decided by state courts, even though they are not the basis of the plaintiff's original complaint.

It is most important to understand why **C** is wrong. It recognizes that Congress has broadly authorized the Supreme Court to review federal issues decided by state courts, but suggests that this authority is unconstitutional because it violates the *Mottley* well-pleaded complaint rule. But (sorry to repeat myself) *Mottley* does not interpret the Constitution, it is an interpretation of §1331, governing the jurisdiction of the federal district courts. *Osborn* held that the *constitutional* grant of arising-under jurisdiction includes any case in which federal law forms an "ingredient" of the case. So the appeal in this example clearly is a proper arising-under case under the Constitution. The Supreme Court has the authority, under §1257 and under the *Osborn's* reading of Article III, to review both rulings. **D** is the right answer. And §1257 expressly authorizes review of both federal issues, even though they were not asserted by the Mottleys in their well-pleaded complaint.

All of this explains how the Mottleys ultimately got their case heard in the U.S. Supreme Court. After their federal suit was dismissed for lack of subject matter jurisdiction, they sued in state court. They won, and the railroad, invoking an earlier version of §1257, appealed to the Supreme Court. Under that statute, the Court had the authority to review the substantive federal issues raised in the state court suit. Unfortunately for the Mottleys, it reversed, holding that the federal statute applied to the Mottleys and could constitutionally be applied to them, even though they had obtained their passes before its passage. *Louisville & Nashville R.R. Co. v. Mottley*, 219 U.S. 467 (1911).

 ## Glannon's Picks

1. Making a federal case	A
2. Olefsky's plea for relief	D
3. A *Mottley* matter	A

4. Making a federal case, Part 2   A
5. Mix and match   C
6. Limiting the limits   C
7. Concurrents   A
8. Polymolysorbate   A
9. Tagging along   D
10. Second thoughts   B
11. A *Mottley* reprise   D

4

Removal Jurisdiction: The Defendant Chooses the Forum

D doesn't like the state judge he must face;
He wants federal court to decide the case.
If federal jurisdiction was there from the first,
Then there's a happy end to this verse:
28 U.S.C. §1441(a) saves him a place.

—*A.M. Thomas Jefferson Law School*

CHAPTER OVERVIEW
A. The basic standard for removal jurisdiction
B. A logical limit on removal of diversity cases
C. Removal later in the litigation
D. Making something out of nothing: Removal of exclusive federal jurisdiction cases
E. Reverse removal
F. Which federal court?
G. The effect of removal on objections to personal jurisdiction
H. Procedural requirements and motions to remand
I. The Closer: Permutations
✦ Glannon's Picks

A s the last chapter illustrates, cases that may be filed in federal court usually don't have to be. The state courts have "concurrent jurisdiction" to hear diversity cases and most cases arising under federal law as well. Where there is concurrent jurisdiction, the plaintiff makes the initial choice between state and federal court, by filing suit in the forum she prefers. In many cases, however, the defendant may prefer to litigate in the other court system.

If the plaintiff chooses state court, federal procedural statutes give the defendant the power to displace the plaintiff's choice by "removing" some cases to federal court. This chapter explores the provisions and the procedure for removing cases from state to federal court.

A.   The basic standard for removal jurisdiction

The basic standard for removal jurisdiction is simple and sensible: a defendant sued in state court may remove a case to federal court if it could have been filed originally in federal court. The rationale for removal is to give both parties access to federal court for cases within the federal court's jurisdiction. So it makes sense that the standard for *removing* a case to federal court should mirror the standard for *filing* one in federal court to begin with. So, 28 U.S.C. §1441(a) provides that "any civil action brought in a State court of which the district courts of the United States have original jurisdiction" may be removed to federal court.

Consequently, the first question to ask in analyzing a removal problem is whether the claim asserted by the plaintiff fits into some category of federal jurisdiction. Is it a diversity case, or an arising-under case? A case between a citizen and alien, or some other case provided for in Article III, §2? If not, it can't be removed. If it is, then, with a few minor exceptions, it can be.

Here's a first example to illustrate this relation between original and removal jurisdiction.

QUESTION 1. Patent medicine.   Castor Chemical Company, a California company, sues Pollux, from California, in state court for breach of contract, claiming that Pollux agreed to manufacture a drug for Castor and then reneged. Pollux answers the complaint, admitting that he refused to deliver the drug, and offering as an affirmative defense that he learned, after making the contract, that the drug was covered by a patent, so that, under federal patent law, he could not manufacture it without a license to do so. After answering, Pollux removes the action to federal court.

A. The action is properly removed, because at the time he removed, Pollux had raised a federal law issue in his answer.

> **B.** The action is properly removed, because the case "arises under" federal law within the meaning of that phrase in Article III, §2.
> **C.** The action is not properly removed, because it is a federal question case, not a diversity case.
> **D.** The action is not properly removed, because the case does not "arise under" federal law within the meaning of 28 U.S.C. §1331.

ANALYSIS.   The third choice, **C**, is particularly illogical. Under 28 U.S.C. §1441(a), cases may be removed to federal court if they are within the original jurisdiction of the federal courts. Cases arising under federal law are within the federal courts' jurisdiction, so they, like diversity cases, may be removed under §1441(a).

The other three options are closer. **A** appears to rest on the premise that a case may be removed whenever it is clear that a federal issue will be litigated in the action. But that isn't the standard under §1441(a); under that section, the case can only be removed if it could have been filed originally in federal court. As we belabored in the previous chapter, many cases that *involve* federal law cannot be filed in federal court. Witness poor Erasmus and Annie Mottley's case. The test for removal is whether the plaintiff could have filed the case initially in federal court, not whether some federal issue is likely to arise or has arisen in the action. This case could not have been filed in federal court, for the same reason that the Mottleys' action was thrown out by the Supreme Court: it arises under state contract law.

There's a difference between this example and *Mottley*, however. Here, at the time of removal, the defendant had *actually asserted* the federal defense in his answer. Thus, the federal issue is already in the case; there is no need to speculate as to whether a federal issue will be litigated in the action. However, this does not change the result. The removal statute provides that only cases that could have been filed originally in federal court may be removed. Castor could not have filed this action in federal court, because it arises under state law and the parties are not diverse. So, the terms of the removal statute itself bar removal here. **A** is wrong.

This point is the key to **B** as well. It is true that this case arises under federal law within the meaning of Article III, §2, as expounded by Chief Justice Marshall in *Osborn*. Pollux has injected a "federal ingredient" into the case by raising a federal defense. But under §1441(a) the case may only be removed if it could have filed in federal court. And we know that to file a case in federal court, it must not only fall within the scope of the Article III grant, but must also be conveyed to the federal district court by statute. Castor's case is within the Article III grant, but it is not within the statutory grant of arising-under jurisdiction in 28 U.S.C. §1331. Under *Mottley*, the plaintiff's complaint must rely on federal law as the source of his right to relief, to "arise under" federal law within the meaning of §1331. The court will not look at the defendant's answer in determining whether the claim arises under federal law. So the case could not have been brought in federal court initially, and therefore cannot be removed. **D** is the winner.

B.   A logical limit on removal of diversity cases

While it is generally true that a case that could have been filed in federal court can be removed there, it is not always true. The removal statute provides that a diversity case cannot be removed if there is an in-state defendant:

> **§1441(b)(2).** A civil action removable solely on the basis of the jurisdiction under section 1332(a) of this title may not be removed if any of the parties in interest properly joined and served as defendants is a citizen of the state in which such action is brought.

This is a sensible limit on removal, given the rationale for federal diversity jurisdiction. The logic for allowing diversity cases to be brought in federal court is the risk of prejudice in the state court; but if a defendant is sued in her home state, she is not at risk of prejudice. If Coretta, from Wisconsin, sues Parkins, from Iowa, in an Iowa state court, there is little reason to allow Parkins to remove. Any prejudice in the state court would be in *favor* of Parkins, so why allow her to bump the case into federal court? Section 1441(b)(2) therefore bars her from doing so.

Consider this illustration.

QUESTION 2. My state, or yours?   Ortiz, a police officer and Georgia citizen, sues Swensson, from North Carolina, and Dracut, from Virginia, in state court in Virginia. He claims that the defendants battered him while he was trying to arrest them. (Battery is a state tort claim.) He credibly alleges $150,000 in damages. Swensson answers the complaint, denying that he battered Ortiz, and asserts in the answer a counterclaim demanding damages under 42 U.S.C. §1983, for violation of his federal civil rights in the course of the arrest. Within the thirty-day period for removal, Swensson files a notice of removal in the federal district court for the Eastern District of Virginia. Assume that Dracut agrees to the removal.

A. The federal court has jurisdiction over the case, because it could have been filed in federal court initially.
B. The federal court lacks jurisdiction over the case, under §1441(b)(2).
C. The federal district court has jurisdiction over the case, based on the federal counterclaim.
D. The federal district court has jurisdiction, because Swensson is an out-of-state defendant.

ANALYSIS. A is tempting, because we know that, usually, if the plaintiff could have filed a case in federal court to begin with, the defendant can remove it. And it is true that this case could have been filed in federal court: It's a case between a Georgian, a North Carolinian and a Virginian, so there's complete diversity, and the amount in controversy is over $75,000.

But we also know that §1441(b)(2) is an exception to the general rule that a case that could have been filed in federal court initially can be removed. That section provides that a diversity case — even one that could have been filed in federal court — can't be removed if there's an in-state defendant. So A is not an accurate statement in this context.

D is also tempting. Swensson, the removing defendant here, is from out of state, so he may fear prejudice in the Virginia court. In fact, he may fear that the court or the jury will favor Dracut, the in-state defendant, over him. Swensson might legitimately prefer to reduce that risk by removing. Unfortunately, under §1441(b)(2), he cannot. A diversity case can't be removed if there is an in-state defendant . . . even if there's *also* an out-of-state defendant.

C is also a loser. It suggests that, if the plaintiff files a nonremovable case in state court, the defendant can make it removable by filing a counterclaim under federal law. This is not generally true. Removal must be based on the plaintiff's case, not on the defendant's defenses or counterclaims. This follows from §1441(a), which makes removal turn (except for the in-state defendant exception just discussed) on whether the case could have been filed initially in federal court. So B is right; under §1441(b)(2) this case is excluded from removal.

C.   Removal later in the litigation

The removal statute sets a strict limit on the time for removing a case to federal court. Under 28 U.S.C. §1446(b)(1), the notice of removal must be filed within thirty days "after receipt by the defendant, through service or otherwise, of a copy of the initial pleading setting forth the claim for relief. . . ." There's a reason for this short window to remove a case. The state court needs to know whether it is going to hear the case or not. Under §1446(b)(1), the case will either be bumped into federal court within thirty days, or the state court will know that the case won't be removed, that it has jurisdiction, and can get down to business.

But there is an exception. Sometimes a case filed in state court is not removable, but *becomes removable* later. For example, McCoy, a Mississippi plaintiff, might sue Caswell, a Mississippi defendant, on a state law claim. The case can't be removed, since there is neither diversity nor a claim under federal law. But later McCoy might amend the complaint to assert a federal claim. Amendments are generally freely allowed, at least in the early stages of the litigation, so this is a realistic possibility. Once the amendment is allowed, the case contains a claim arising under federal law. If it had been filed in this form initially, it would have been removable. Can the defendant remove after the amendment?

Another example: McCoy, a Mississippi plaintiff, sues Gupta, a Texas defendant, on a state law claim, for $200,000, and sues Caswell, a Mississippi defendant, as a co-defendant in the action. This case is not removable, since there is no complete diversity. But suppose that later McCoy dismisses her claim against Caswell? Now the case has become a diversity case. Can the defendant remove?

In such cases, the statute allows removal once the case becomes removable. Section 1446(b)(3) provides that, if the action wasn't removable as originally filed, it can be removed within thirty days after the defendant receives notice of an amended pleading or order that makes the action removable. This is an important provision, which reduces the incentive for the plaintiff to play games with the jurisdictional rules. Without this provision in §1446(b), the plaintiff could file the case in a nonremovable form, let the thirty-day period for removal run, and then amend her complaint to assert a claim under federal law. The defendant would be stuck in state court in a case in which the plaintiff intended all along to seek recovery under federal law. But under §1446(b)(3), this ploy won't work; once the amendment is allowed, adding a claim arising under federal law, and the defendant receives notice of that amendment, she will have thirty days to remove the now-removable action to federal court.

Here's an interesting question on the application of §1446(b)(3).

QUESTION 3. **Professor's delight.** Diversified Investments, Inc., an investment corporation, sues Eagleton for breach of contract, to collect $300,000 due on a margin account she had with Diversified. Diversified is incorporated in Delaware with its principal place of business in Colorado. It has a large office in Salt Lake City, Utah. Diversified brings the action in Colorado. Eagleton, a Utah citizen, answers the complaint, denying that she owes anything on the account.

Four months later, Diversified moves to amend its complaint to add a claim against Eagleton under a federal fraud statute, based on misrepresentations Eagleton allegedly made in establishing her margin account. The motion is granted. Two weeks later, Eagleton removes the action to federal court. Diversified moves to remand the case to state court. The motion to remand should be

A. granted, because the federal court lacks jurisdiction, since both parties are citizens of Utah.

B. granted, because Eagleton did not remove the action within thirty days after the action was filed.

C. denied, because Eagleton had the right, under 28 U.S.C. §1446(b)(2), to remove within thirty days after the amendment was granted.

D. denied, because Eagleton had the right, under 28 U.S.C. §1446(b)(2), to remove within thirty days after receiving notice that the amendment had been granted.

ANALYSIS.   Here, the plaintiff filed suit in state court. The parties started to litigate in state court, and then the plaintiff added a federal claim. After the amendment, Eagleton removes the case, based on the newly added claim arising under federal law. However, §1446(b)(3), read carefully, bars removal. It authorizes removal later in the case if it was not removable as originally filed, but *becomes removable* due to an amendment or for other reasons.

That isn't this case: Eagleton's case was a proper diversity case and was therefore removable when filed. She chose not to remove within thirty days of receiving notice of the original complaint. Now she wants a second bite at the apple, since Diversified has asserted a federal claim and she would rather litigate the federal claim in federal court. Unfortunately for Eagleton, §1446(b)(3) doesn't authorize removal. Both **C** and **D** are wrong, because, if the case was removable originally, and the defendant failed to remove it within thirty days, she has lost the option of federal court. Doubtless, Congress could authorize removal in these circumstances. It could rewrite §1446(b)(3) to allow a second shot when a new basis of federal jurisdiction is asserted. This might even make good policy: a defendant might be perfectly willing to litigate a contract case in the state court, but prefer federal court to litigate the federal claim that is added later. However, the language of §1446(b) just doesn't reach her case.

A should not have thrown you off. First of all, Diversified is not a citizen of Utah just because it has an office there. For diversity purposes, a corporation is a citizen of the state of its principal place of business and state of incorporation. Neither of these is in Utah. So Diversified is diverse from Eagleton. Second, once Diversified adds the claim under federal law, the federal court would have jurisdiction over the case even if the parties are from the same state. So the federal court would have jurisdiction over the case, as amended, if removal was proper. However, under §1446(b)(3), it is not, since the case did not "become removable" by the addition of the federal claim. It already was removable.

So, the answer is **B**. The action should be remanded because it was not removed within thirty days of the original filing.

This question is a "professor's delight," because, while it is fair, it is tricky. The question focuses the student on the amendment adding the federal claim, and invites her to overlook the crucial fact that Eagleton could have removed earlier and did not. Remember the comment that the multistate bar exam (which is all multiple choice) is "an exercise in reading comprehension." Here's a good example of that. You might know the law, or be capable of solving this problem by careful reading of §1446(b)(3) (remember, I'm assuming that you have the statutes in front of you in answering these questions), but miss the point by a mile if you don't analyze the question carefully. Probably students get more questions wrong from such analytical slips than they do from a lack of substantive knowledge.

D.   Making something out of nothing: Removal of exclusive federal jurisdiction cases

It used to be said that a federal court's jurisdiction in a removed case was "derivative," that is, that it acquired its jurisdiction based on a properly filed state law case. A logical corollary of this conceptual thinking was that, if the state court did not have jurisdiction over a case, it could not be removed to federal court. Suppose, for example, that Wyzanski files suit against Koukios for patent infringement in a state court, and that Koukios removes it to federal court. Wyzanski's case arises under federal law, so it is within the federal court's jurisdiction. The twist here, however, is that Congress has provided in 28 U.S.C. §1338(a) that federal jurisdiction in patent cases is exclusive of the courts of the states. Thus, the state court in which the case was filed had no jurisdiction to entertain Wyzanski's claim in the first place.

Under the "derivative jurisdiction" reasoning of an earlier day, Koukios could not remove Wyzanski's suit to federal court. The federal court's jurisdiction was thought to "derive from" that of the state court. If the state court lacked jurisdiction, the federal court could not acquire jurisdiction on removal. You couldn't, under this theory, make something out of nothing. So the court had to dismiss the claim. It couldn't even remand it to state court, since that court had no jurisdiction. The result was that, because the case had to be in federal court, the federal court would dismiss it!

There was a certain formal logic to this rule, but not a lot of common sense. After the federal court dismissed the action, the plaintiff would have to refile . . . in the federal court. So Congress wisely enacted 28 U.S.C. §1441(f): "The court to which such civil action is removed under this section is not precluded from hearing and determining any claim in such civil action because the State court from which such civil action is removed did not have jurisdiction over that claim." Under §1441(f), the federal court acquires jurisdiction over a removed case, even if the state court from which it was removed had none.

This question requires application of §1441(f) and the basics of supplemental jurisdiction. If you haven't studied supplemental jurisdiction, you may want to come back to it.

> **QUESTION 4. Return to sender?**   Toricelli, from New Mexico, sues
> Olsen, also a New Mexican, in state court for copyright infringement and
> for breach of contract. Both claims are based on Olsen's publication of
> Toricelli's book, allegedly in violation of the terms of their contract for
> publication. 28 U.S.C. §1338(a) provides that the federal courts have
> exclusive jurisdiction over copyright claims. Olsen removes the action to
> federal court.
>
> The federal court should
>
> A. dismiss the action, since the state court lacked jurisdiction over the
>   copyright claim.
> B. remand the case to the state court, since it cannot acquire jurisdiction
>   from a court that lacked jurisdiction over the copyright claim.
> C. take jurisdiction over the copyright claim, since it has jurisdiction over
>   it under §1441(f), but dismiss the contract claim, since the parties
>   are not diverse.
> D. take jurisdiction over the entire case.

ANALYSIS.   The options here get stronger as they go along. A reflects the
older rule, that the federal court could not acquire jurisdiction on removal if
the state court lacked it. But that's the old rule, displaced by §1441(f), which
says that it can. So A is wrong. So is B. Even under the older rule the court
couldn't remand: Just as the plaintiff couldn't properly file in state court, the
federal court couldn't properly send a case back to the state court if the state
court had no jurisdiction to hear it.

C is edging closer. It recognizes that §1441(f) allows the federal court to
hear the case, even though it was removed from a state court that lacked
jurisdiction. But it isn't right. Since the court has jurisdiction over the claim
arising under federal law, it will also have supplemental jurisdiction over the
state law contract claim, since it arises from the same underlying dispute as
the copyright claim. See 28 U.S.C. §1367(a). So it has jurisdiction over the
entire case, making D the right answer.

E.   Reverse removal

What do you make of this question?

> **QUESTION 5. Jurisdictional asymmetry.**   Nancy, a Californian, sues
> Jack, from Oregon, on a negligence claim for $300,000. She sues in federal

district court in Oregon. Jack, who would prefer to litigate the case in state court, files a notice of remand in the Oregon state court, removing the action to the state court. The state court should

A. refuse to entertain the action, because Jack, the in-state defendant, is trying to take advantage of local prejudice.
B. refuse to entertain the action, because the state court would lack original jurisdiction over the case, if the claim is for more than $75,000.
C. refuse to entertain the action, since it was filed in federal court and there is no right to remove from federal to state court.
D. take jurisdiction over the case, since state courts have concurrent jurisdiction over diversity cases.

ANALYSIS. The question makes one point only: Removal is a one-way street. The federal procedural statutes make no provision for removal from federal to state court. If the plaintiff files a case in federal court, and the federal court has jurisdiction over it, the defendant is pretty much stuck there. There are some fancy cases dealing with "abstention," the power of the federal court, though it has jurisdiction, to decline to exercise it for various discretionary reasons. But these are exceptional situations. The general rule, which will govern the vast majority of cases, is that the federal court must hear a case within its jurisdiction. In this situation, the plaintiff really is "master of her claim." If she brings a case in federal court over which it has jurisdiction, there is no general procedure that allows the defendant to avoid litigating there.

Note that **B** is just plain wrong. It suggests that a proper diversity case must be heard in federal court. But that isn't so; state courts have concurrent jurisdiction over cases that satisfy the requirements of federal diversity jurisdiction. **D** makes that point, but still isn't right, because if the plaintiff chooses federal court, there is no procedure for reverse-removing it to state court. **A** is wrong, because Jack's motive is really beside the point. Even if Jack's motive were as pure as the driven snow, there is no statutory authority for bumping the case out of federal court. **C** prevails.

F.   Which federal court?

Once the defendant has determined that the case against her is removable, she must consider which federal court to remove the case to. This shouldn't detain her long, because the statute makes it clear that there is only one host federal court for a removed action: "the district court of the United States for the district and division embracing the place where such action is pending." 28

U.S.C. §1441(a). (Divisions are administrative subdistricts within a district.) A defendant sued in Hawaii who prefers to be in California can't get there by removal, because §1441(a) dictates that, if she removes, the case will go to the federal district court for the District of Hawaii.[1] In a state with more than one district, the case must be removed to the federal district that includes the county where the state action was filed. If Smith files an action in Suffolk County, New York, which is within the Eastern District of New York, the suit can only be removed to the federal district court for the Eastern District.

You may have already studied the rules for venue in cases filed *initially* in federal court. Generally, 28 U.S.C. §1391 provides that federal cases must be filed in a district where the defendant resides, or where events giving rise to the claim took place. I can't tell you how many students I have bewildered, however, with multiple-choice questions like this:

QUESTION 6. Your court or mine?   Appleseed, from Connecticut, sues Bunyan, from Vermont, on an unfair competition claim that arose in Vermont. (Vermont and Connecticut each have only one district, consisting of the entire state.) The suit is for $1,000,000. Appleseed files the suit in Greenwich County, Connecticut. Bunyan removes the case to the District of Vermont.

A. Removal is proper because the defendant resides in Vermont and, under U.S.C. §1391(b)(1), the district where the defendant resides is a proper venue.
B. Removal is improper because 28 U.S.C. §1441(a) only allows removal to a Connecticut federal court. However, venue is not proper in Connecticut because the defendant does not reside there and no events giving rise to the claim took place there.
C. Removal is proper, because the case could have been filed initially in the federal district court in Vermont.
D. Removal is improper, because it has been removed to the wrong district.

ANALYSIS. My introductory warning probably prevented you from missing this one. The problem with **A** and **B** is that they both presuppose that §1391, the federal venue statute, *applies to removed cases.* It doesn't. See

---

1. There is always the possibility, however, that the federal court, after removal, would *transfer* the action to another federal district in a different state if, for practical reasons, it should be litigated there. See 28 U.S.C. §1404(a); Chapter 10. A state court can't do that, so this might be one tactical advantage of removal.

28 U.S.C. §1390(c). Just memorize that, and you won't be fooled by questions like this. As the text indicates, the only proper district on removal is the district that physically includes the place where the suit was filed in state court. This one was filed in Connecticut, so it can only be removed to the District of Connecticut. **D** is right. **C** is wrong because, while the action could have been filed in Vermont, a case can't be removed to any district where it might have been filed. Congress could have authorized that, no doubt, but in §1441(a) they did not. Under that statute, the action may be removed to "the district court of the United States for the district and division embracing the place where such action is pending." There, I've said it three times.

G. The effect of removal on objections to personal jurisdiction

My students always get confused about the relationship between removal to federal court and personal jurisdiction. Suppose that a defendant is sued in Arizona and believes that she is not subject to personal jurisdiction there. Naturally, she should object to personal jurisdiction. But suppose further that she isn't sure that her objection will carry the day; it's a close issue, as so many personal jurisdiction issues are under minimum contacts analysis. And suppose that her tactical judgment is that, if she must litigate in Arizona, she would rather litigate in federal court in Arizona. What should she do?

One thing she could do is to move to dismiss in the Arizona state court. But that motion is not likely to be ruled on within thirty days, and if she's going to remove, she's got to do it within thirty days. So she could do one of two things: She could move to dismiss for lack of personal jurisdiction in the state court (assuming that the state rules allow her to do that) and *then remove to federal court* within the thirty-day period. Her motion would then be pending in federal court instead of state court, and the federal court would rule on it. Or she could remove the case before a response was due in state court, and then, after removal, raise her objection to personal jurisdiction by a Rule 12(b)(2) motion to dismiss or in her answer to the complaint in federal court.

Either way, the point is that removal *does not waive* the defendant's right to object to personal jurisdiction. It simply changes the court in which the objection will be litigated. It is true that, after removal, the question will be whether the *federal* court has personal jurisdiction. But generally the scope of personal jurisdiction in the federal court will be the same as that of the state court, because the Federal Rules require the federal court in most cases to conform to state limits on personal jurisdiction. Fed. R. Civ. P. 4(k)(1)(A).

I've stumped a multitude of students on this point. Consider the following two cases to clarify the point.

QUESTION 7. A switch in time. Yasuda, from Oregon, sues Boyle, from Idaho, on a state law unfair competition claim, seeking $250,000 in damages. He sues in state court in Oregon. Ten days later (before an answer is due in state court), Boyle files a notice of removal in federal court. Five days after removing, Boyle answers the complaint, including in her answer an objection to personal jurisdiction. Boyle's objection to personal jurisdiction is

A. invalid, since she waived it by removing the case to federal court.
B. invalid, since she waived it by failing to assert it before removal.
C. not waived by removal, but will be denied because the federal courts have power to exercise broader personal jurisdiction than the state courts.
D. not waived by removal. The court should dismiss if there is no personal jurisdiction over Boyle in Oregon, even though the case was properly removed.
E. waived, because this is a diversity case over which the federal court has original jurisdiction.

ANALYSIS. There are so many ways to go astray on this issue that I had to include five choices . . . and I could have made it seven! Surely the farthest astray is **E.** The fact that the court has subject matter jurisdiction over this diversity case does *not* mean that it has personal jurisdiction over Boyle. Though easily confused, the subject matter and personal jurisdiction analyses are separate; the court must have both subject matter jurisdiction over the case and personal jurisdiction over the defendant in order to proceed with the case.

   A reflects the faulty assumption that removal waives objections to personal jurisdiction. It doesn't; it simply changes the forum in which the personal jurisdiction question will be litigated. Boyle may remove the case, and then respond to it, raising his defenses and jurisdictional objections in federal court. And **B** is wrong, because Boyle removed the case before the answer was due in state court. It is true, under some states' procedural rules, that answering a complaint without including an objection to personal jurisdiction would waive it. But where a defendant removes before a response is due in state court, she does not waive any defenses by removal. She simply changes the forum in which such defenses will be raised. See Fed. R. Civ. P. 81(c)(1) (Federal Rules govern procedure after removal).

   C is also wrong, because it suggests that, after removal, personal jurisdiction over Boyle will be tested by a different standard from that used in state court. In a diversity case, the reach of the federal court's personal jurisdiction is governed by Fed. R. Civ. P. 4(k)(1)(A), which provides that the defendant is subject to personal jurisdiction in the federal court if she "is subject to the jurisdiction of a court of general jurisdiction in the state where the district court is located." In other words, if the state courts of Oregon could exercise jurisdiction over Boyle, the Oregon federal court can; otherwise not.

    D is the correct answer. Boyle has not waived his objection to personal jurisdiction. If the federal court lacks jurisdiction over Boyle, it should dismiss the case, even though it was properly removed.

    Now, another.

QUESTION 8. Another switch. Yasuda, from Oregon, sues Boyle, from Idaho, on a state law unfair competition claim, seeking $250,000 in damages. He sues in state court in Oregon. Assume that Oregon follows the special appearance rule, under which the defendant may appear to challenge jurisdiction, but waives the objection if she raises any other issues. Boyle answers the complaint in state court, raising her defenses on the merits and including an objection to personal jurisdiction. Three days later Boyle files a notice of removal in federal court. Five days after removing, Boyle renews her motion to dismiss for lack of personal jurisdiction. Boyle's motion is

A. valid, because jurisdictional objections may be asserted in the answer under the Federal Rules.
B. valid, since she asserted it before removal.
C. invalid, because Boyle responded to the merits in state court, thereby waiving her objection to personal jurisdiction.
D. not waived by removal. The court should dismiss if there is no personal jurisdiction over Boyle in Oregon, even though the case was properly removed.

ANALYSIS. This example assumes that Oregon follows the common law special appearance rule, under which a defendant waives her objection to personal jurisdiction if she appears and raises any issue in addition to her objection to jurisdiction. Boyle did that here — she answered the complaint on the merits as well as objecting to jurisdiction — so she waived her jurisdiction objection before removing. Removal will not revive it, since state court procedures apply to the case until it is removed. Thus, it is irrelevant that she could have included her objection in her answer under the Federal Rules. Thus, **A** is wrong; **C** is the right answer.

H.   Procedural requirements and motions to remand

The removal statute provides that "all defendants who have been properly joined and served as defendants must join in or consent to the removal." 28 U.S.C. §1446(b)(2)(a). If Akila sues Redstone and Cianci in state court on a federal claim, and Redstone wants to be in federal court, but Cianci doesn't, the case cannot be removed. Well, that's not quite true. Redstone could file a notice of removal, but if Cianci wants the state forum, he would then move to remand to the state court on the ground that he did not agree to removal. And that motion would be granted. If the defendants don't agree to federal court, the case will stay in state court.

If a case is removable, it must be removed within thirty days. 28 U.S.C. §1446(a). But there's another thirty-day rule in the removal statutes, and it's trickier than the first. Section 1447(c) provides in part: "A motion to remand the case on the basis of any defect other than lack of subject matter jurisdiction must be made within 30 days after the filing of the notice of removal under section 1446(a)." This section requires that, if any party has an objection to removal, other than lack of subject matter jurisdiction, she must raise it within thirty days after removal, or the objection is waived. For example, if the plaintiff claimed the case wasn't removed within thirty days, she could seek remand on this ground, but only within thirty days after removal. The rationale for this short window for most motions to remand is the same as the rationale for the *first* thirty-day period for removing the case: Both courts need to know where the case is going to be litigated. The section seeks to avoid belated procedural objections from disgruntled litigants that would disrupt the litigation.

This question illustrates the operation of §1447(c)'s waiver provision.

QUESTION 9. Removal malpractice. Tyrgyz, from New Jersey, sues Dr. Boch, from Maryland and Dr. Ivens, from Delaware in state court in New Jersey, for negligence in an operation. He seeks $120,000 (a supportable amount) in damages, claiming that either Boch or Ivens was the cause of his injuries. Ivens answers the complaint ten days later. Boch files a notice of removal to federal court ten days after Ivens answers. Two months later, Ivens moves to remand the case to state court on the ground that he did not agree to removal. The motion should be

A. granted, because the amount-in-controversy requirement is not met. Tyrgyz seeks $120,000, which only works out to $60,000 each. This objection does not come too late, since objections to subject

matter are not covered by the thirty-day limit on most objections to removal.
B. granted, because Ivens did not join in the notice of removal and removal requires agreement of all the defendants.
C. denied, because the court has original jurisdiction over the case and Ivens's objection has been waived.
D. denied, because removal was proper, since the case is within the federal diversity jurisdiction.

ANALYSIS.   A is very tempting. It is true that objections to federal subject matter jurisdiction don't have to be raised within the thirty-day period for objections to removal. See §1447(c) (objections "other than lack of subject matter jurisdiction" must be made within thirty days after filing of the notice of removal). But the amount-in-controversy requirement is met here. Tyrgyz claims that either Boch or Ivens caused his injury, he doesn't know which. So there is a legitimate claim for that amount against each. See Chapter 2, pp. 21-22. If the jury concludes that Boch caused the harm, he could be held liable for $120,000. If it concludes that Ivens caused it, she will. If it concludes that neither is liable, Tyrgyz will lose. But he still has asserted a claim for $120,000 against each defendant, and might recover that amount from either. So **A** is wrong.

B is also quite credible. Ivens didn't join in the notice of removal, and under §1446(b)(2)(a) the case can't be heard in federal court if Ivens doesn't agree to the removal. The problem is that no one moved to remand the case within the thirty-day window for motions to remand based on objections other than lack of subject matter jurisdiction. Ivens' failure to join is a defect, but not a *jurisdictional* defect. The case is a proper diversity case, whether Ivens joins in the notice of removal or not. So Ivens has waived her objection to removal if she doesn't move to remand within thirty days. That's the effect of §1447(c)'s requirement that a motion to remand based on any problem with the removal — other than lack of subject matter jurisdiction — be made within thirty days. If no motion is made, the objection is waived. So **C** takes the prize. (**D** isn't a bad second choice, but removal really isn't proper without Ivens joining in the notice of removal, which she didn't do.)

I.   The Closer: Permutations

Here's a challenging Closer that involves removal under §1441(a), supplemental jurisdiction under 28 U.S.C. §1367(a), and the §1441(b)(2) limit on removal of diversity cases. Good luck!

QUESTION 10. Removing all doubt. Rasmussen, an employee of Apex Welding Corporation who lives in Ohio, sues Apex for breach of contract, for firing him. Apex is a New York corporation with its principal place of business in Pennsylvania. He brings the action in state court in Pennsylvania. He seeks $300,000 in damages. Apex answers the complaint, and discovery proceeds.

Three months later, Rasmussen moves to amend his complaint to add a claim that the same firing violated the Federal Age Discrimination in Employment Act. The motion is granted. Twenty days later, Apex files a notice of removal to federal court. The action is

A. properly removed, because Rasmussen's case became removable after the motion to amend to add the federal claim was granted.
B. not properly removed, because there is an in-state defendant.
C. not properly removed, because Rasmussen should have removed the case initially based on diversity.
D. not properly removed as a whole. The federal claim is removable, but not the breach of contract claim, because Apex is from the forum state.

ANALYSIS. C is wrong here, because the action was not removable as originally filed. It was a diversity case, and Apex is an in-state defendant, from Pennsylvania, so §1441(b)(2) barred removal of the case as originally filed.

However, when Rasmussen's motion to amend his complaint was granted, allowing him to add his claim under federal law, the case became removable. The court has jurisdiction over it under 28 U.S.C. §1331 and has supplemental jurisdiction over the state law claim under 28 U.S.C. §1367. The bar on removal of a case with an in-state defendant does not apply to cases arising under federal law, just to diversity cases. So the case has now "become removable" (28 U.S.C. §1446(b)(3)) and Apex will get its thirty days to do so.

The last choice suggests that the case is removable only in part, that the claim arising under federal law can be removed, but not the state law claim, since there's an in-state defendant. Not so. Once Rasmussen amends to assert a claim arising under federal law, this becomes a federal question case. Because the court has jurisdiction based on the federal claim, the entire case can be removed, including the supplemental state law claim for breach of contract arising from the same events. Thus, D fails.

B also is wrong, because the case is no longer a diversity case, once the federal law claim is added. So it is irrelevant that Apex is a citizen of the forum state. A takes the prize: the entire action became removable when

Rasmussen added the claim arising under federal law, and is properly removed by Apex on that basis.

Suppose that we change just one fact in this example, making Apex's principal place of business Virginia instead of Pennsylvania. Which of these two answers would be right on those facts?

A. Removal is proper, because the case became removable when Rasmussen added the claim under federal law.

B. Removal is not proper, because the case was removable when it was originally filed.

B is right. On these facts, the original case would have been removable: It was a diversity case and there was no in-state defendant. Having had one shot at removal, Rasmussen would not get another under §1446(b)(3). That subsection only allows removal of cases that *become removable* by a change in the plaintiff's case. It does not authorize removal if a case that was removable on one ground to begin with (but the defendant didn't remove it) later becomes removable on another ground.

 ## Glannon's Picks

1. Patent medicine	D	
2. My state, or yours?	B	
3. Professor's delight	B	
4. Return to sender	D	
5. Jurisdictional asymmetry	C	
6. Your court or mine?	D	
7. A switch in time	D	
8. Another switch	C	
9. Removal malpractice	C	
10. Removing all doubt	A	

5

Personal Jurisdiction: Myth and Minimum Contact

~

There once was a sharp western lawyer
Whose client was a real annoyer.
So he sued for his fee,
Posted notice on a tree,
And started much grief for Pennoyer!

~

CHAPTER OVERVIEW
A. The jurisdictional premise of *Pennoyer v. Neff*
B. In-state contacts as an alternative basis for exercising jurisdiction
C. The nexus requirement: The myth of miscellaneous contacts
D. The difference between foreseeability and purposeful availment
E. The role of reasonableness in minimum contacts analysis
F. The erratic stream of commerce
G. The Closer: Stream of consciousness
⟡ Glannon's Picks

Many civil procedure teachers spend more time on personal jurisdiction than on any other subject in the first-year procedure course. I do myself. Yet I find at the end that students still misunderstand a number of basic points about personal jurisdiction. The next three chapters will address some of the issues that create confusion.

This chapter will address the basics of personal jurisdiction, primarily the minimum contacts analysis of *International Shoe*. The next chapter deals with two related issues: general in personam jurisdiction, and the complexities of in rem and quasi in rem jurisdiction. Statutory authority to exercise jurisdiction, the "long-arm jurisdiction" problem, is covered in Chapter 7.

A.   The jurisdictional premise of *Pennoyer v. Neff*

The early law of personal jurisdiction, represented by *Pennoyer v. Neff*, 95 U.S. 714 (1877), based personal jurisdiction on physical power over the defendant, at least in cases against individuals. The logic was that a court had the authority to exert physical power over a defendant within the territory of the state where the court sat. The court could order a sheriff to seize and detain the defendant if he found her within the state. So, the logic proceeded, if the sheriff asserted that authority symbolically, by serving the defendant with process in the state, rather than actually arresting her, the court would acquire jurisdiction to adjudicate the claim and could enter a judgment against her if she were found liable.

Here's a quick example to illustrate *Pennoyer's* "presence theory" of personal jurisdiction.

QUESTION 1. Gone, but not forgotten.   Neff hired Mitchell, a lawyer, in Oregon to sue Jones for breach of contract. Neff agreed to pay Mitchell $300 for his services. Mitchell did the work, but Neff left the state for California and didn't pay Mitchell's fee. Mitchell sues Neff for his fee in an Oregon state court, and has Neff served with process in Oregon while Neff was visiting there on unrelated business. Neff promptly departed once more for California and has not returned to the state since. Under personal jurisdiction theory as expounded in *Pennoyer,* the Oregon court

A. has personal jurisdiction over Neff.
B. does not have personal jurisdiction over Neff, because he was served while he was there for a purpose unrelated to the fees claim.
C. does not have jurisdiction over Neff, because he is no longer physically present in Oregon.
D. has jurisdiction over Neff for the fees claim, but would not have jurisdiction over him if Mitchell had sued him for a claim that arose in another state.

ANALYSIS.   This question makes the basic point about *Pennoyer:* that jurisdiction was acquired by the symbolic act of in-state service of process, and that once in-state service was made, the court acquired the power to adjudicate the case for which process was served. The distractors reflect various misconceptions about this principle.

C suggests that, for the court to litigate the case, the defendant must not only have been served with process in the state, but remain in the state while the case proceeded. Not so. The logic of *Pennoyer* was that a defendant within the state was subject to the sheriff's (and the court's) power to arrest. Under early English practice, the local sheriff may actually have arrested the defendant and held her pending resolution of the case, or at least had the power to do so. Later, actual arrest of the defendant gave way to symbolic seizure, through personal delivery of the court papers in the suit. However, the premise was that this symbolic seizure subjected the defendant to the court's authority, not just at the moment of service, but on an ongoing basis. The court's power, once properly asserted by service of process within the forum state, continued throughout the litigation. Neff could leave after he was served if he wanted, but that would not prevent the court from proceeding with the case once it had acquired jurisdiction.

B fails as well. It suggests that Neff could only be subjected to jurisdiction through in-state service if he was in the state for some reason connected to the plaintiff's claim. But the logic of *Pennoyer* was that a defendant present within the forum state was subject to the authority of that state's courts, without regard to *why* he was there. Jurisdiction was based on symbolic arrest, not on any relationship between Neff's reason for being in Oregon and the law suit. He could be there to play the lottery, to visit the zoo, or to be inaugurated as governor; it wouldn't matter. His presence when served was the key, not the reason for that presence.

D also comes up short. It suggests that jurisdiction could be based on service of process in the state, but that the court would only acquire jurisdiction by in-state service to adjudicate claims that arose within the state. This is another misconception. If Mitchell filed suit in Oregon, and served Neff with the papers for that suit in Oregon, it didn't matter what the claim was for. It could be for an auto accident in Maine, a property dispute in Texas, or lies told about him in Minnesota. Jurisdiction was not based on any relation between the claim and the state; it was based on the premise that the court could exert judicial power over a person physically present there. (After all, if Neff never came back to Oregon, Mitchell would have to sue him in California under *Pennoyer's* approach, and the California court would then exercise jurisdiction over Neff, even though the claim Mitchell sued upon arose in Oregon.)

So **A** is the winner. If Mitchell managed to serve Neff with the papers initiating the suit in Oregon, under *Pennoyer* the Oregon court obtained jurisdiction over Neff for that suit, and leaving wouldn't deprive the court of authority to proceed. Once jurisdiction attached, it continued, even though the sheriff, after "catching" Neff in the state, let him go.

B.   In-state contacts as an alternative basis for exercising jurisdiction

To some extent, the logic of *Pennoyer* persists. In *Burnham v. Superior Court*, 495 U.S. 604 (1990), the Supreme Court reaffirmed that an individual defendant who is served with process in the state will usually be subject to personal jurisdiction in the action for which service was made. But the *Pennoyer* framework for jurisdiction never worked very well for corporations. Ultimately, the Supreme Court, in *International Shoe v. Washington*, 326 U.S. 310 (1945), held that another basis, "minimum contacts . . . such that the maintenance of the suit does not offend 'traditional notions of fair play and substantial justice'" (326 U.S. at 316), would also support personal jurisdiction over a defendant. Subsequent cases have made clear that such "minimum contacts" jurisdiction applies to individual defendants as well as corporations.

The rationale underlying minimum contacts jurisdiction is different from that underlying *Pennoyer*. *International* Shoe recognized that the "due process" required by the Constitution could be based not only on the formalistic concept of physical arrest, but also on the idea that a defendant, by choosing to engage in activities in a state, submitted to litigation there if claims arose out of those voluntary activities in the state. The idea is that it is fair to make the defendant take the bitter with the sweet. If she chooses to engage in activities focused on a state, that state may require her to answer there for claims that arise from those activities she chooses to conduct in the state. She may not be sued there for *any* claim based on limited in-state activities, however, only for claims arising out of the in-state activities.

Here's a question that highlights the shift in the jurisdictional rationale from *Pennoyer* to *Shoe*.

> **QUESTION 2. Contact sports.**   Neff went to Oregon and met with Mitchell, a lawyer, about a claim Neff had against Jones. Mitchell did some work on the problem and sent Neff, a Californian, a bill for $3,000. After consulting Mitchell, Neff left Oregon, has not been back since, and has never paid Mitchell's bill. Mitchell sues Neff in an Oregon state court for his fee. He has the papers initiating the suit served on Neff in California.
>
> **A.** Jurisdiction based on in-state service was reaffirmed in *Burnham v. Superior Court*. Consequently, Neff is not subject to jurisdiction in the Oregon suit, since he was not served with process in Oregon.
> **B.** Under *International Shoe*, Neff's contacts in Oregon suffice to support personal jurisdiction over Neff for Mitchell's fees claim. If Neff returns

to Oregon, Mitchell may serve him there with the papers in the action and then proceed with the suit.

C. Under *International Shoe,* Neff's contacts in Oregon suffice to support personal jurisdiction over him in any state for Mitchell's fees claim.

D. Under *International Shoe,* Neff's contacts in Oregon suffice to support personal jurisdiction over Neff in the Oregon action for Mitchell's fees claim, even if he is not served in Oregon.

ANALYSIS. **A** is a real head scratcher. In *Burnham,* the Supreme Court did reaffirm that a court can still obtain personal jurisdiction over an individual defendant if she is served with process in the action in the forum state. So, if *Pennoyer* is still the law, **A** must be right . . . right?

The flaw in this logic is that, while *Burnham* said that jurisdiction may still be asserted over an individual defendant served with process in the state, it did not say that this was *the only basis* on which such a defendant is subject to personal jurisdiction. It's true, if Neff showed up in Oregon, Mitchell could still get jurisdiction over him by serving him with process in the action while he was there. But *International Shoe* says that, if he does *not* return to Oregon, there's another basis on which he may be forced to defend an action there: If it arises out of voluntary contacts Neff made in Oregon. *Shoe,* in other words, added an alternative way to obtain personal jurisdiction over a defendant. If the claim arises out of in-state contacts, those contacts will support jurisdiction, even if the defendant (like Neff here) isn't served with process in the state. On the other hand, if the defendant is served in the state, that provides a basis for jurisdiction, even if the claim did not arise there.

B suggests that, when the defendant bases jurisdiction on minimum contacts, the defendant must still be served with process in the forum state. If that were true, *International Shoe* wouldn't be much help to plaintiffs: They'd still have to catch the defendant in the state. On the contrary, the beauty of *Shoe* is that, if the claim arises out of the defendant's in-state activities, the defendant is subject to jurisdiction on that claim, even if she assiduously stays away to avoid service. The court still has a basis for exercising jurisdiction — the defendant's voluntary contacts there. As long as she is notified of the action in a reasonable manner — as here, by being served with process in California — she is subject to jurisdiction under *Shoe,* not *Pennoyer.*

C isn't right either. The logic of *International Shoe* is that a defendant should realize that his activities in a state may give rise to claims and that it would not be unfair, would not violate due process, if suits that arise from the activities in that state are brought there. This means that a defendant with Oregon contacts should anticipate suits from those contacts in Oregon, but not in Montana, or Kansas. This concept is often referred to as "specific in personam jurisdiction," that is, jurisdiction limited to claims that arise from the contacts the defendant has voluntarily made in the state. A corollary is that, if you conduct limited activity in Oregon, you subject yourself to suit there only for claims that arise from your acts there. You can't be sued there for North Dakota contacts, nor in North Dakota for these Oregon contacts. At some point, a defendant's contacts may become so substantial as to support "general in personam jurisdiction" for any claim, but limited or sporadic contact will only support specific in personam jurisdiction.

So **D** is the best answer. Neff, though long gone, may be required to return and defend this claim, because it arises from his deliberate activity in Oregon — hiring Mitchell there to represent him and agreeing to pay him for his services.

C.   The nexus requirement: The myth of miscellaneous contacts

International Shoe established the proposition that a defendant's deliberate contacts in a state could support jurisdiction over her, even if she could not be served with process there in the action. But, where the defendant's contacts with the state are limited, *Shoe* established an important limitation on such jurisdiction: The plaintiff may only assert claims against the defendant that arise from those voluntary contacts.

The idea is that the defendant, by establishing limited in-state contacts, submits to jurisdiction there for claims that arise from those contacts, but not for other, unrelated claims. Recall that, under *Pennoyer,* the "contact" of being served with process in the state subjected the defendant to suit for whatever claim the plaintiff had filed. But "minimum contacts" jurisdiction is limited: It is only as broad as the defendant's in-state voluntary contacts themselves.

A corollary of this is that a defendant can have contacts in a state, but not be subject to suit there on a particular claim. The following example illustrates this fundamental point. It may seem too simple, but I find that even after considerable repetition, a good many students have not fully grasped the meaning of "specific" in personam jurisdiction.

QUESTION 3. Minimum, or miscellaneous?   Cartwright is a carpenter who lives in Vermont and works out of his home there. In addition to his Vermont customers, he has some customers across the border in New York, and some in Massachusetts. Last year, he built a garage for a New York customer and put an addition on another New Yorker's house. This was about 5 percent of his construction business for the year, which is about the average for his New York business each year.

> While driving to a job in Massachusetts, Cartwright has an accident, in
> Massachusetts, with Morales, from New York. Morales brings suit against
> Cartwright for his injuries in a New York state court.
>
> A. Cartwright is subject to personal jurisdiction in New York for this
>   claim because he has minimum contacts in New York.
> B. Cartwright is subject to personal jurisdiction in New York based
>   on minimum contacts if New York has a long-arm statute that
>   authorizes jurisdiction in tort cases.
> C. Cartwright is not subject to personal jurisdiction in New York, because
>   the claim does not arise out of Cartwright's New York contacts.
> D. Cartwright is not subject to personal jurisdiction in New York
>   because his work in New York is a small percentage of his yearly
>   construction business.

ANALYSIS. The real culprit here is **A**. Too many students have trouble
with the basic point that, where jurisdiction is based on limited in-state
contact, the claim *must arise out of the contact* to support personal
jurisdiction. Miscellaneous contacts are not minimum contacts! Cartwright
can't be sued in New York for *any* claim because he has purposely chosen to
do limited construction activity there. If his contacts in New York are
limited, he is only subject to specific in personam jurisdiction in New York,
that is, jurisdiction for claims that arise out of his New York activities. Since
Morales' claim does not arise out of those New York activities, *Shoe* does not
support personal jurisdiction for Morales' claim. If Morales sued Cartwright
in Massachusetts for this claim, jurisdiction would be proper under *Shoe*,
since the claim arises out of Cartwright's driving in Massachusetts. Or if a
New York customer sued Cartwright in New York for doing shoddy
carpentry on her garage, minimum contacts jurisdiction would also be
proper, since the claim arises out of contacts in New York.

　　B represents another ever-so-common confusion about minimum
contacts jurisdiction. I wish I had a nickel for every time a student has
written that "if the defendant doesn't have minimum contacts with the state,
he may be sued there if the long-arm statute authorizes jurisdiction." It is
true that, for a state court to exercise personal jurisdiction over a defendant,
a statute of the state (for example, a section of a "long-arm" statute) must
authorize that exercise of jurisdiction. But the fact that a statute authorizes
jurisdiction is not enough. It must *also* be constitutionally permissible for the
state to require the defendant to return and defend the particular suit that is
brought there. No matter what the New York long-arm statute says, the
New York court could not exercise jurisdiction over Cartwright if it would
exceed due process limits to do so. For more on the relation of long-arm
statutes to constitutional analysis, see Chapter 7, pp. 118-122.

Here, suing Cartwright in New York for a claim that arose in Massachusetts based on his unrelated contacts in New York would not be constitutionally permissible, unless the New York contacts were so extensive as to support general in personam jurisdiction. Any exercise of personal jurisdiction must pass both tests: it must be authorized by statute *and* be consistent with constitutional standards. Just satisfying the long-arm statute will not do.

The last answer, **D**, is also wrong. It suggests that, in deciding whether the defendant's contacts in a state support jurisdiction, the court should consider the defendant's in-state activity relative to his total activity, and, if his in-state contact is a small percentage of his overall activity, refuse jurisdiction. But that isn't so. For example, suppose that Cartwright drove to Massachusetts to look at a job, and had an accident with Morales on the way. Suppose he didn't get the job, and that he had no other business in Massachusetts. He could still be sued in Massachusetts for Morales' accident, even if it represented .01 percent of his total economic activity for the year. He would still have deliberately entered the state and engaged in risk-creating activity there that gave rise to the claim. His contact would not be an unrelated, miscellaneous contact, but a minimum contact that gave rise to the claim. The analysis is not relative; it asks whether the defendant has engaged in purposeful activity in the state that gave rise to the claim, not whether he has engaged in more activity somewhere else.

So, the fact that Cartwright's New York activity is a small part of his total business isn't the point. If Morales' claim arose out of that limited New York activity, he would be able to sue Cartwright for the claim in New York. But it doesn't arise out of those contacts. So **C** takes the prize.

D.   The difference between foreseeability and purposeful availment

The basic premise of minimum contacts jurisdiction is that the defendant who chooses to relate to a state — who "purposely avails" herself of the opportunity to conduct activities there — can expect to be sued there for claims that arise from that relationship. A suit there shouldn't come as a surprise to her since she chose to relate to the state and can foresee this consequence of her conduct there. So foreseeability certainly has some role to play in determining whether minimum contacts jurisdiction exists. But there is a difference between foreseeing the possibility of injury in a state and the type of "purposeful availment" that supports minimum contacts jurisdiction.

In *World-Wide Volkswagen v. Woodson*, 444 U.S. 286 (1980), the Supreme Court distinguished between foreseeability that a product would go to a state and foreseeability that the defendant would be sued there based on deliberate contacts. In *World-Wide,* the dealership, Seaway, sold an automobile to the plaintiffs. Certainly, nothing is more foreseeable than that a car will travel; that's what it's for. But the Court held that this did not support jurisdiction over the New York seller in Oklahoma, where the plaintiffs drove it and had an accident. Instead, said the Court, the foreseeability that is relevant to personal jurisdiction is the foreseeability that "the defendant's conduct and connection with the forum State are such that he should reasonably anticipate being haled into court there." 444 U.S. at 297. Jurisdiction, then, must be based, not on the fact that a defendant could foresee that events might happen there that would lead to a claim against her, but rather on purposeful availment. When the defendant makes the conscious, voluntary, avoidable decision to interact with people in a state, she assumes the risk that suits that arise from that purposeful interaction will be filed in the state where she chose to act.

Here are two examples that illustrate this distinction.

QUESTION 4. Rolling risks. Ace Truck Bodies builds gasoline tanks in Minnesota for installation on trucks that deliver gas to gas stations. It sells a replacement tank to Deuce Petroleum Company in Kansas, which has it mounted on the bed of its delivery truck and places it in service. As Ace was aware, Deuce delivers petroleum products to customers throughout the midwest.

While making a delivery in Illinois, the tank explodes, injuring Jack. Jack sues Ace Truck Bodies in Illinois for his injuries. Ace Truck has no contacts with Illinois other than those described in this question. The Illinois long-arm statute authorizes the exercise of personal jurisdiction over a defendant who "commits a tortious act in Illinois." The Illinois Supreme Court has held, in *Gray v. American Standard Radiator,* that this language is met if the defendant's product causes injury to a person within the state.

Ace is probably

A. subject to personal jurisdiction in Illinois because it was aware that the tank it sold to Deuce would be used in Illinois.
B. subject to personal jurisdiction in Illinois, because it could foresee that its tank, if it was defective, would cause injury in Illinois.
C. subject to personal jurisdiction in Illinois, because it committed a tortious act in Illinois under the long-arm statute.
D. not subject to personal jurisdiction in Illinois, because its contacts with Illinois are insufficient to support jurisdiction over it under the minimum contacts test.

ANALYSIS.   In this case, Ace makes a product and sells it to a buyer in Kansas, who—as Ace knows—plans to use it in other states. The question is whether the act of selling the tank into Iowa, with knowledge or foreseeability that it would be used in nearby states, supports jurisdiction when its buyer proceeds to do so. Even if Ace had not known that Deuce would use the tank in Illinois, it certainly would not be surprised to learn that it did, since the very *raison d'être* of such a tank is to transport gasoline from place to place.

C takes the position that Ace is subject to personal jurisdiction in Illinois, because it committed a tortious act there, when its tank exploded there. It may be true, under Illinois's interpretation of its long-arm statute, that Ace "committed a tortious act" there, but Ace still may only be sued there if it would be fair, under due process analysis, to make it appear and defend in Illinois. Personal jurisdiction in a state must be authorized by a statute, but it also must be within constitutional constraints. (Chapter 7 explores this theme in more detail.)

It is unlikely that such knowledge, or foreseeability, would satisfy due process standards for jurisdiction over Ace in Illinois for this claim. **A** and **B** are inadequate answers, because Ace has not reached into Illinois to conduct activities there; Deuce has. *World-Wide* suggests a distinction between subjecting a seller to jurisdiction in states where it sells its product to an end user and states where that buyer *uses* them. Allowing jurisdiction wherever a buyer or third party took the product, *World-Wide* suggests, would make the chattel the seller's "agent for service of process," allowing suit in states where the defendant had not established deliberate contacts. Just as Seaway, in *World-Wide*, could foresee that the car it sold would travel to Oklahoma, Ace could foresee that its tank would be used by Deuce in Illinois. But it must itself engage in activities focused on Illinois in order to be subject to jurisdiction there. **D** is the best answer.

––––––––––––

Here's another case that involves foreseeable harm in the forum state. Has the defendant purposely availed herself of the opportunity to conduct activities in the state this time?

QUESTION 5. Contracts and contacts.   Boyarin is the vice-president of an Illinois company, Compu-Drive, that does software design for medical applications. She learns that Mercy Hospital, a major research facility in Virginia, is planning to contract with MediSoft, Compu-Drive's main competitor, a Virginia company with its offices in Virginia, to design software to support its genetic research facility. Boyarin calls Mercy's vice president for operations and explains in livid detail the shortcomings of

MediSoft's products. Mercy backs out of the MediSoft agreement, and MediSoft, when it learns why, sues Boyarin for interference with advantageous business relations. It sues in Virginia. Boyarin moves to dismiss for lack of personal jurisdiction.

A. The motion will likely be denied, if Compu-Drive has extensive contacts in Virginia.

B. The motion will likely be denied, because Boyarin's contacts suffice to support jurisdiction over her for this claim.

C. The motion will likely be granted. Boyarin has not acted in Virginia and has no physical presence in the state.

D. The motion will likely be granted. Although MediSoft has extensive contacts in Virginia, the plaintiff's contacts in the state do not suffice to support personal jurisdiction.

ANALYSIS. There's a certain diabolical pleasure in writing distractors. **D** is bewitching; it is true that the plaintiff's contacts do not suffice to support personal jurisdiction over a defendant. The focus must be on the contacts of the defendant. In *International Shoe*, for example, the plaintiff, a state agency, certainly had plenty of contacts in Washington. But the *defendant had contacts too* that supported jurisdiction over it. In determining whether jurisdiction is proper, we look at the defendant's contacts. If she has none, she's not subject to jurisdiction. If she has established deliberate contacts in the forum state, she may be sued there, whether the plaintiff has contacts there or not. So **D** simply focuses on the wrong issue.

   C is also wrong. It suggests that the defendant must physically enter the state and act there to be subject to personal jurisdiction. This isn't always necessary. A defendant may establish sufficient contacts with a state in various ways. In *McGee v. International Ins. Co.*, 355 U.S. 220 (1957), for example, the defendant sent a letter to a Californian offering to reinsure him. That sufficed to support jurisdiction for a claim arising from that solicitation. In *Calder v. Jones*, 465 U.S. 783 (1984), the defendant researched and wrote an article about a Californian to be published in California. That, too, was held sufficient to support jurisdiction, even if the defendant never entered the state in connection with the story. These and other cases establish that a defendant may purposely relate to a state — without going there — in a way that can lead her to anticipate the risk of litigation there.

   Here, Boyarin's contacts would meet that test. Boyarin deliberately contacted Mercy Hospital, in Virginia, in order to interfere with a contract between the hospital and the Virginia plaintiff. **B** is right, because Boyarin should not be surprised that her act had an adverse effect on MediSoft in Virginia, and that MediSoft would sue her there for this claim. Unlike Ace in the previous question, Boyarin initiated a contact with a Virginian, for the purpose of affecting a business decision involving Virginia commerce. Boyarin could hardly argue that she had never deliberately reached into Virginia. She did, for her own purposes, and could foresee that her Virginia-oriented act would have the kind of impact there that would lead to litigation.

It is relevant, but not dispositive, that MediSoft is a Virginia company. That fact makes it clear to Boyarin that her call will have an impact in Virginia. Compare *Calder v. Jones,* 465 U.S. 783 (1984), in which the Supreme Court noted that the defendant wrote an allegedly defamatory article about a California citizen whose career was centered there, so that the brunt of the harm would be suffered there. However, it is likely that MediSoft's loss of the contract in Virginia would support jurisdiction even if MediSoft were not a Virginia company, since Boyarin reached into the state to interfere with the contract there, and caused the loss of the contract with a Virginia customer by this deliberate act.

A suggests that Boyarin can be sued in Virginia if Compu-Drive, the company she works for, has extensive contacts there (thus presumably supporting general in personam jurisdiction). However, the contacts of the company will not all be attributed to Boyarin just because she works for it. Her contacts in the course of Compu-Drive's business *will* be attributed to the corporation, because in making those contacts she acts as an agent for the corporation. (How can a corporation have contacts in a state, other than through people who work for it?) But it doesn't work the other way around: the contacts of the corporation will not always be attributed to its officers and employees. Suppose, for example, that another division of Compu-Drive, dealing with military software, has extensive business in Utah. It would not make sense to attribute those contacts to Boyarin, who did nothing in Utah and has nothing to do with this branch of Compu-Drive's business.

E.   The role of reasonableness in minimum contacts analysis

There is a good deal of discussion in the Supreme Court's personal jurisdiction cases about the reasonableness of asserting personal jurisdiction over a defendant. In *McGee v. International Insurance Co.,* 355 U.S. 220 (1957), for example, the Court noted that the increased ease of transportation and communication has reduced the inconvenience of defending an action in another state. In *World-Wide Volkswagen v. Woodson,* 444 U.S. 286, 292 (1980), the Court stated that the burden of defending in a foreign state will be considered in light of other factors, including the plaintiff's interest in obtaining a remedy, the forum state's interest in adjudicating the dispute, and shared interests of the states in furthering substantive policies. And, in *Asahi*

Metal Industry v. Superior Court, 480 U.S. 102 (1987), the Court rejected jurisdiction over the impleaded Japanese defendant on reasonableness grounds, concluding that, even if it had minimum contacts with California (a point disputed among the Justices), it would be unreasonable to assert jurisdiction over Asahi on the facts of the case.

Thus, *Asahi* stands for the proposition that in some cases, even if the defendant has established deliberate contacts in the state that gave rise to the plaintiff's claim, it will be unreasonable for the court to exercise jurisdiction over the defendant. In assessing reasonableness, a court should consider the plaintiff's interest in obtaining a convenient remedy, the forum state's interest in providing it, the extent of the inconvenience to the defendant, and other factors.

But the opposite is also true: Sometimes, even if the interests of the state and the plaintiff would support taking jurisdiction, and even if it would not significantly inconvenience the defendant to do so, it may still be impermissible.

> Even if the defendant would suffer minimal or no inconvenience from being forced to litigate before the tribunals of another State; even if the forum State has a strong interest in applying its law to the controversy; even if the forum State is the most convenient location for litigation, the Due Process Clause, acting as an instrument of interstate federalism, may sometimes act to divest the State of its power to render a valid judgment.

444 U.S. at 294. If the defendant has *not* established contacts in the state, these other interests cannot substitute for contacts. First, the defendant must establish deliberate contacts focused on the forum state. If she has, the interests of the plaintiff and the forum state become relevant on the second prong of the test, whether it would be fair and reasonable to exercise jurisdiction. If she has not, these factors cannot in themselves support jurisdiction.

Consider the following case.

QUESTION 6. A matter of convenience. Fein, from Wisconsin, meets Lonergan, a college classmate of her sister, while Fein is visiting her sister in Minnesota. Lonergan is a Minnesota auto salesman. They talk. Fein tells Lonergan that she is from Wisconsin. She agrees to buy an expensive Maserati from Lonergan, who deals in used cars out of his home in Minnesota, about 20 miles from the Wisconsin border. After returning home, Fein sends him a deposit check. Lonergan cashes the check, but does not buy the car, and never contacts Fein again.

Fein sues him for fraud in Wisconsin. She chooses to sue at home in part because Wisconsin has a tough fraud statute, authorizing treble damages for fraud in auto sales transactions. The Wisconsin court

A. will have personal jurisdiction over Lonergan if, as a matter of choice of law, it would apply the Wisconsin fraud statute to the transaction.

B. will probably have personal jurisdiction over Lonergan, because Wisconsin has a strong interest (reflected in the statute) in protecting Wisconsin citizens from fraud.

C. will probably have personal jurisdiction over Lonergan, because Fein has a strong interest in obtaining a remedy, Lonergan knew that Fein was from Wisconsin, and he will not be inconvenienced by litigation in Wisconsin, since he lives close to the border.

D. will probably not have personal jurisdiction over Lonergan.

ANALYSIS. This question illustrates a case in which it would be reasonable for the court to exercise jurisdiction, considering the convenience of the parties and the interests of the plaintiff and the forum, but in which the court probably could not require the defendant to defend in Wisconsin. Fein has a strong interest in obtaining a remedy, and Wisconsin has an interest in protecting its citizens from fraud (though less interest than it would have if the fraud were perpetrated in Wisconsin). Wisconsin has established a powerful cause of action to redress such claims, and the Wisconsin court might, under choice-of-law principles, apply its statute to this transaction, which involved a Wisconsin buyer. Nor can Lonergan argue that he will be seriously inconvenienced by litigation in Wisconsin, since he lives and works fairly close by.

However, it is unlikely that the Wisconsin court could exercise jurisdiction over Lonergan for this claim. It arises from negotiations in Minnesota for the purchase of a car in Minnesota. Although Lonergan knew Fein was from Wisconsin, he has not reached into Wisconsin to do business there. He has simply solicited a sale from a Wisconsin citizen in Minnesota. Thus **C** is probably wrong, since Lonergan never established "affiliating circumstances" (*World-Wide*, 444 U.S. at 295) that represent a deliberate choice to engage in activities focused on Wisconsin.

A suggests that Wisconsin would have personal jurisdiction over Lonergan if it would apply Wisconsin law to the transaction. However, the standards for applying a state's substantive law, under "choice-of-law" rules, are distinct from the standards for exercising personal jurisdiction. *Hanson v. Denckla*, 357 U.S. 235, 254 (1958). The fact that a defendant has entered into a transaction expecting forum law to apply would at least bolster the case for "purposeful availment," *Burger King Corp. v. Rudzewicz*, 471 U.S. 462, 481-482 (1985), but that didn't happen here — the parties never discussed the matter. Yet, in some cases, a state could apply its own law to a case, but not have the power to assert jurisdiction over the defendant. For example, Oklahoma, as the place of the accident, might well apply its law to the accident in *World-Wide*, if it heard the case, yet the Supreme Court concluded that it lacked jurisdiction over Seaway, the New York dealership.

B suggests that Wisconsin's interests in affording Fein a remedy, and in policing sales transactions, supports jurisdiction over Lonergan. These interests would enter into the reasonableness calculus, if this claim arose out of contacts by Lonergan with Wisconsin, but they cannot support jurisdiction in the absence of minimum contacts. This disposes of **C** as well, which suggests that Wisconsin has jurisdiction because it would be a reasonable place to litigate the case. It is hard to see any basis for concluding that Lonergan availed himself of the opportunity to conduct activities focused on Wisconsin. Thus, since Lonergan fails the first prong, purposeful availment, **D** is the best answer.

F.   The erratic stream of commerce

No one ever said that minimum contacts is simple. In fact, it continues to give rise to a great deal of fact-specific litigation, applying *Shoe's* general principles to the myriad facts of human experience. But the real kicker for my students has been the stream-of-commerce problem addressed — or obfuscated — in *Asahi Metal Industry Co. v. Superior Court*, 480 U.S. 102 (1987) and revisited by the Court in *J. McIntyre Machinery Ltd. v. Nicastro*, 131 S. Ct. 2780 (2011). This section probes the meaning of so-called stream-of-commerce jurisdiction.

"Stream of commerce" is a phrase that refers to the entry of a defendant's products into the forum state through commercial channels of distribution. For example, suppose that Snoflake Incorporated makes snowblowers in Nevada and sells them to a wholesaler in Oregon, which resells them to retail stores in ten states, including Wyoming. If Wakimoto buys a Snoflake snowblower at a hardware store in Wyoming and is injured using it in Wyoming, will a Wyoming court have personal jurisdiction over Snowflake for his claim? Snoflake did not sell the snowblower in Wyoming itself. It may or may not have known that the wholesaler would resell its product there. But it did sell its product into the stream of commerce with the hope that it would be sold widely, and with knowledge that, if it was defective, it could injure a user wherever it was bought and used. And, of course, it cheerfully accepted the profits derived, ultimately, from sales in Wyoming.

The stream-of-commerce question is whether Snoflake's sale of the product to the wholesaler in Oregon, with the hope and expectation that it would be resold to consumers in other states, establishes a sufficient contact with the final purchaser's state to support personal jurisdiction where Wakimoto buys and uses it and is injured by it.

This is an important question, to which the Supreme Court has given only an equivocal answer. In *World-Wide Volkswagen v. Woodson*, the Court appeared to suggest that selling into the stream of commerce in one state, which leads to resale to consumers in a different state, would support jurisdiction there if the consumer was injured where she bought it (*not* where she took it, as *World-Wide* holds). See *World-Wide*, 444 U.S. at 297 (jurisdiction appropriate where injury results from manufacturer or distributor's efforts to "serve, directly or indirectly, the market for its product in other states").

But the Court later divided on this issue in *Asahi*. In *Asahi*, the defendant made a component that was incorporated into a final product in another country and resold into California. The question was whether the component maker had sufficient contacts with California to support jurisdiction, when a consumer bought the product there and was injured by it there. Justice O'Connor's opinion suggested that a defendant that merely sold its product to another company, without controlling where that other company would redistribute it as part of its final product, was not subject to jurisdiction where the finished product was ultimately sold. Jurisdiction, Justice O'Connor suggested, is based on purposeful availment, and the mere sale of a part — or 100,000 parts — from Japan to Taiwan did not establish minimum contacts with California. Instead, she would require that a defendant like Asahi actually establish direct contacts in the consumer's state to subject it to suit there for injuries caused by its products sold in the state. She would find such "purposeful availment" if the defendant establishes sales agents in the state, advertises there, has dealership networks there, or makes other deliberate efforts, *itself,* to market its goods in the state of ultimate sale to the consumer.

Justice Brennan's concurring opinion in *Asahi*, however, appeared to accept the principle that sales of large quantities of the defendant's product in an American state, *even* indirectly through the stream of commerce, would support jurisdiction in that state, if the plaintiff suffered injury there from the product. Justice Stevens, while finding it unnecessary to reach the minimum contacts question, also appeared inclined to find jurisdiction based on indirect sales in a state, depending on the nature and quantity of those sales. However, while the Justices could not agree on what constitutes "purposeful availment" in a stream-of-commerce case, eight did agree that, *even if minimum contacts existed,* it would be unreasonable on the facts of the case for the California court to exercise jurisdiction over Asahi, since the dispute remaining after the plaintiff settled was a claim for indemnification between two Asian corporations.

We Civil Procedure wonks waited long and anxiously — for twenty-four years — for the Court to clarify this vexing problem. Finally the Court took certiorari in *J. McIntyre Machinery Ltd. v. Nicastro*, 131 S. Ct. 2780 (2011), and we looked forward to further wisdom on stream-of-commerce jurisdiction. Alas, fooled again. The case involved a machine made in England, imported to a distributor in Ohio, and resold into New Jersey. Nicastro was injured there using the machine and brought suit against the English manufacturer in New Jersey. It argued, predictably, that it was not subject to personal jurisdiction for this claim in New Jersey, since it had done nothing in New Jersey at all; it had just made machines in England and sold them to a distributor in Ohio.

In *Nicastro* the Court again split badly on the reach of stream-of-commerce jurisdiction. Justice Kennedy's plurality opinion, joined by three other justices, concluded that J. McIntyre had not "engaged in conduct purposely directed to New Jersey" (131 S. Ct. at 2790) and therefore could not be sued in New Jersey for Nicastro's claim. Two justices filed a concurring opinion saying, essentially, "no jurisdiction on these facts but we might rule differently if there were a regular course of sales into New Jersey, or deliberate efforts to cultivate the New Jersey market." And three dissenters argued, vociferously, that J. McIntyre had sought to cultivate the United States market, had succeeded in doing so, and ought to defend the product in a state where it was resold to the ultimate user and caused injury.

So, neither *Asahi* nor *McIntyre* provides clear guidance on the stream-of-commerce problem. There will be a lot of unclear cases, and expensive litigation of the jurisdiction issue in such cases will continue. Perhaps this is inevitable; perhaps the Justices have not given us a clear answer because there never can be one for a problem with so many possible variations. But the following questions may help you to at least define the parameters of the problem.

QUESTION 7. One end of the spectrum. Atlanta Precision Drill Corporation makes drill presses in Georgia. It sells them to several wholesale distributors, including Emporia Distributors in Pennsylvania. It sells five hundred drill presses to Emporia in 2011. Emporia resells three of them to Modern Tool and Die Company in Maryland. A local machine shop buys one from Modern, and Edwards, an employee, is injured using it in Maryland. He sues Atlanta Precision in state court in Maryland for his injuries. Atlanta Precision has no other contacts in Maryland. After the *Nicastro* decision the Maryland court will probably conclude that it

A. has jurisdiction over Atlanta Precision, because it is an American company, unlike Asahi and J. McIntyre.
B. has jurisdiction over Atlanta Precision, because it could foresee that Emporia, which is based in Pennsylvania, would resell Atlanta Precision's machines into nearby Maryland.

C. has jurisdiction over Atlanta Precision, because it sold its machines in large quantities to a distributor which it expected to resell in other states.

D. cannot exercise jurisdiction over Atlanta Precision, because its contacts with Maryland are insufficient under the minimum contacts test.

ANALYSIS. This question explores the current state of stream-of-commerce jurisdiction after the Court's split decision in *J. McIntyre*. **A** is not right. The logic of Justice Kennedy's opinion in *J. McIntyre* (echoing Justice O'Connor's approach in *Asahi*) is that the defendant did not purposely direct its sales activities to New Jersey, not that it was a foreign manufacturer. And Justice Breyer's concurring opinion in *J. McIntyre* relied on the minimal nature of the sales in New Jersey and the absence of other purposeful activity by J. McIntyre, not on the fact that J. McIntyre was a foreign manufacturer. In fact, both the plurality and concurring opinions expressed concern about the consequences for small domestic manufacturers if jurisdiction could be based on such minimal in-state sales. 131 S. Ct. at 2790, 2793.

B also fails. In both *Asahi* and *J. McIntyre* the manufacturer could foresee resales into the forum state, but that did not convince the Court to uphold jurisdiction. In both, the plurality opinions called for a deliberate effort by the defendant to serve the market *in that state*, not just knowledge that its products might be resold there. And **C** is also dubious; the *Asahi* and *J. McIntyre* Courts did not base their opinions on the volume of sales from the manufacturer to the distributor. Both courts focused on the relation (or lack thereof) between the manufacturer and the state where the product was resold and caused injury. So **D** is the winner, Very likely, the Court — or, at least, a solid majority of six Justices — would find this case governed by the decision in *J. McIntyre*, which is actually pretty close on its facts to this example.

Consider whether this variation on Edwards' case would lead to a different ruling on personal jurisdiction.

QUESTION 8. A distinction with a difference? Atlanta Precision Drill Corporation makes drill presses in Georgia. It sells them to several wholesale distributors, including Emporia Distributors in Pennsylvania. It sells five hundred drill presses to Emporia and agrees to give them a price rebate on any presses resold into Maryland, a state in which it has no distributor. Emporia resells five presses to Modern Tool and Die Co. in Annapolis,

Maryland. A local machine shop buys one from Modern, and Edwards, an employee, is injured using it in Maryland. He sues Atlanta Precision in state court in Maryland for his injuries. Atlanta Precision has no other contacts in Maryland. After the *J. McIntyre* decision the Maryland court will probably conclude that it

A. has jurisdiction over Atlanta Precision, because it has purposely engaged in conduct calculated to serve the market for its products in Maryland.

B. has jurisdiction over Atlanta Precision, because five of its presses were resold in Maryland.

C. lacks jurisdiction over Atlanta Precision, because only five of its presses were resold in Maryland.

D. lacks jurisdiction over Atlanta Precision, because it has not reached into Maryland to promote its products.

There is a significant difference here that would likely lead to a different outcome. In this example Atlanta Precision has focused on Maryland sales and has taken action to promote them. It has not cast its products into the stream to flow wherever they will; it has encouraged their resale in Maryland by its price break to Emporia. I think this would meet Justice O'Connor's requirement that the defendant deliberately focus on promoting sales of its product in the forum state. I go with **A**.

B is dubious because the minimal sale of five machines in Maryland (leaving aside the rebate, which this distractor does) would not likely convince either the plurality or the concurring Justices in *J. McIntyre* to find jurisdiction over Atlanta Precision, since this minimal resale would not constitute a "regular . . . flow" or "regular course" of sales in New Jersey or represent a deliberate effort by Atlanta Precision to cultivate buyers in Maryland. **C** also seems unlikely. Where Atlanta Precision has focused on the Maryland market, through its price rebate program, this contact will likely support specific in personam jurisdiction for a claim that arises out of that program, even if that plan only minimally succeeded. See the plurality opinion in *J. McIntyre*, 131 S. Ct. at 2788 ("The defendant's transmission of goods permits the exercise of jurisdiction only where the defendant can be said to have targeted the forum . . ."). And I would reject **D** on the ground that Atlanta Precision *has* reached into Maryland by its sales promotion program.

So, let's try one more variation.

QUESTION 9. Between two extremes.   Atlanta Precision Drill Corporation makes drill presses in Georgia. It sells them to several wholesale distributors, including Emporia Distributors in Pennsylvania. It sells about five hundred drill presses a year to Emporia. Emporia resells in ten states, including Maryland, where it typically resells about one hundred presses a year. It sells one of them to Modern Tool and Die Co. in Annapolis, Maryland. A local machine shop buys one from Modern, and Edwards, an employee, is injured using it in Annapolis. He sues Atlanta Precision in state court in Maryland for his injuries. Atlanta Precision has no other contacts in Maryland. After the *J. McIntyre* decision the Maryland court will probably conclude that it

A. definitely lacks personal jurisdiction over Atlanta Precision, because it did not sell into Maryland or encourage Emporia to do so.
B. lacks personal jurisdiction over Atlanta Precision, because exercising jurisdiction on these facts would make its presses Atlanta Precision's "agent for service of process," allowing a user to sue it wherever its presses were sold.
C. lacks personal jurisdiction over Atlanta Precision in this case, because Emporia resold its products in ten states, not just Maryland.
D. may exercise personal jurisdiction over Atlanta Precision in this case, because it is regularly serving the market for its product in Maryland.
E. Glannon doesn't have any idea whether the Court would find personal jurisdiction proper on these facts, so why should I?

ANALYSIS.   E is not right. Glannon thinks he does know the best answer here (as always!) and your professor will think she does as well.

A might be right, but it probably reads Justice Breyer's concurring opinion in *J. McIntyre* too narrowly. That opinion rejected jurisdiction on the facts of the case but suggested that in other circumstances a regular flow of goods into the state would support jurisdiction. Here, a significant number of Atlanta Precision presses are sold in Maryland each year, which would likely influence Justice Breyer to find jurisdiction proper. At the least, we can't say that he (and Justice Alito, the other concurring Justice) would "definitely" find no jurisdiction where the manufacturer's goods are being resold in significant quantities in the state on a regular basis.

B provides a nice turn of phrase, but it pushes the concept of the product as "agent for service of process" too far. The question is whether the manufacturer somehow has affiliated itself with the forum state in a way that makes jurisdiction fair. It seems likely that at least the three *J. McIntyre* dissenters and the two concurring Justices would find that this can be true based on resale of goods into the state by a distributor, if it sells a significant amount of the defendant's goods into the state over a period of time. And C is a pretty dippy distractor; the question is not how many states Emporia resells the presses to, but whether Atlanta Precision has established a deliberate affiliation with Maryland, either through direct efforts to sell in Maryland or, perhaps, through substantial resales of its products there. So **D** seems the best choice, though it is certainly less than certain that the Court will find jurisdiction on these facts if it gets this case . . . in another twenty-four years![1]

So the three cases represent two ends of the spectrum and a point in between. The first case is much like *J. McIntyre*, in which a majority of the Justices rejected jurisdiction. The second illustrates (I think) a case that is likely to satisfy the purposeful availment requirement in a stream-of-commerce case, because the defendant has deliberately sought to promote sales of its product in the state. And the third is a case that is a "pure" stream-of-commerce case, but one in which a majority of the Court might be willing to find jurisdiction proper based on significant ongoing sales in the forum state. There, take it for what it's worth.

G.   Inconvenience and unconstitutionality: A hard case

Let's consider one more example that concerns the relation between minimum contacts and litigation convenience.

> **QUESTION 10. Cold cruel world.** Mary Smith, a divorced, working-class woman of fifty-five, lives in Massachusetts. She doesn't have enough money to travel ordinarily but saved her pennies to attend her daughter's wedding in California. While there, she rented a car to get to the ceremony and had an accident with an Exxon Mobil oil truck. Exxon Mobil, a huge multinational corporation, does business in all states and has a large corporate office in Massachusetts.
>
> After Mary returns to Massachusetts, Exxon Mobil sues her in a California state court for the damage to its truck. Mary

---

1. I find Justice Kennedy's avuncular comment below a tad ironic:

> The defendant's conduct and the economic realities of the market the defendant seeks to serve will differ across cases, and judicial exposition will, in common law fashion, clarify the contours of that principle.

131 S. Ct. at 1790. Really? We waited twenty-four years for the Court to clarify the contours of *Asahi*, and we got *J. McIntyre*!

A. will not be subject to personal jurisdiction in the California action, because she was only in California for a few days.
B. will not be subject to personal jurisdiction in the California action, because it would greatly inconvenience Mary, a woman of limited means, to defend the case in California.
C. has minimum contacts with California that gave rise to the claim, but it would not be reasonable to force her to defend the action in California, given Exxon Mobil's ample resources to bring suit in Massachusetts.
D. will be subject to personal jurisdiction in California in this action, even though it will be inconvenient for her to defend the case there.

ANALYSIS. **A**, of course, is a throwaway. A defendant can establish contacts that give rise to litigation in the course of a short visit to a state or without visiting it at all. Consider a defendant who makes a single defamatory phone call to a newspaper in Tennessee, leading to a story in a Tennessee newspaper that damages a Tennessee resident's reputation. This act would clearly support specific in personam jurisdiction for claims for the defamation.

C suggests that a defendant can avoid personal jurisdiction in a state by arguing that it would be more convenient for the plaintiff to come to her than for her to go to the defendant. This comparative balancing analysis isn't supported by the Supreme Court's cases on personal jurisdiction, although occasionally "inconvenience" goes into the analysis. The Court's cases ask whether the plaintiff has chosen a forum that is acceptable under due process analysis, given the defendant's contacts and a number of reasonableness factors, not whether an alternative forum would be more convenient for the defendant than the one the plaintiff has chosen.

Wouldn't we all like to choose **B** in this example? It will be massively inconvenient for Mary to defend this action in California, so doesn't it offend due process to make her do so? Almost certainly not. Mary went to California, engaged in risk-creating conduct there by driving, and that conduct gave rise to Exxon Mobil's claim against her. As to the reasonableness of the California forum, most factors favor suit in California: Most of the evidence and the witnesses will probably be in California; the plaintiff is there; the truck is there. Although it will be inconvenient for Mary to litigate in California, she did choose to go there and caused the accident there (allegedly). A procedure that requires her to defend her California conduct in a California court hardly reflects a lack of due process under the *International Shoe* line of cases. Although one has sympathy for Mary and perhaps little for her opponent, this worthy sentiment is almost certainly insufficient to defeat California jurisdiction under minimum contacts analysis.

It is indeed a cold, cruel world. With a sigh I choose **D**.

H.   The Closer: Stream of consciousness

Real personal jurisdiction cases come with their own unpackaged, unique facts. It isn't always easy to fit them into the framework of the Supreme Court's cases. You have to fall back on the underlying rationale of minimum contacts jurisdiction and do your best. Here's a chance to try it on a tough case.

QUESTION 11. Close to the line. Dispos-All Waste Corporation collects hazardous wastes from manufacturers in Delaware and Virginia, and stores them in a landfill in Delaware, within a mile of the Maryland border. The landfill is lined to prevent chemicals from leaching into the groundwater. This is important, because groundwater studies show that the groundwater runs under the landfill toward an aquifer across the Maryland border. The aquifer is used to supply water to nearby homes.

As long as the truckers are careful to deposit the wastes in the lined area, the landfill is safe. However, on several occasions Marquette, a Dispos-All driver, got sloppy and tipped his truck along the edge of the lined area. Some of the waste slid off onto the ground.

Wasnowski, who lives near the border in Maryland and has a well drawing from the aquifer, develops cancer. Investigation indicates that Wasnowski's well contains contaminants that may have spread from Dispos-All's landfill. He sues Dispos-All in a Maryland state court.

A. Dispos-All is not subject to personal jurisdiction in Maryland, because it has not advertised in Maryland, established a service network there, or done the other deliberate acts in Maryland that would suffice to support personal jurisdiction in a stream-of-commerce case.
B. Dispos-All is not subject to personal jurisdiction in Maryland, because it does not do business in Maryland and has not reached into Maryland by any purposeful act.
C. Dispos-All is subject to personal jurisdiction in Maryland, because it can foresee that negligent disposal at its Delaware facility would cause harm to persons and property in Maryland.
D. Dispos-All would be subject to personal jurisdiction in Maryland, since the stream of commerce has carried its wastes into Maryland.

ANALYSIS.   I would probably not give this question on an exam. A valid multiple-choice question should have one — and only one — clearly right or best answer. Not just one your professor thinks is best, but one that is clearly better supported by the law. I have a clear favorite here, but I can't say that it is definitively "right."

A is the weakest answer. (I could make the question work, I suppose, by asking, "which of the following is the weakest response?") **A** looks at this problem, as many of my students did, as a stream-of-commerce case, and rejects jurisdiction because Dispos-All doesn't deliberately send its goods into Maryland. But stream-of-commerce analysis doesn't apply here. Here, it's the flow of water, not of markets, that injects the pollutants into Maryland. Cases like *Asahi* involve the distribution of quantities of the defendant's product into a state through channels of commercial distribution, not a situation like this.

Instead, we need to ask whether the defendant has done anything relating to Maryland that it can expect to have an effect in Maryland that might lead to a law suit. When I gave this as an essay problem on an exam, many students said that it had not. All it did was maintain a landfill in Delaware, with no intent to take advantage of the benefits and protections of Maryland law. I think that's a reasonable argument, which would lead to choosing **B**. Dispos-All doesn't have customers in Maryland, doesn't have a landfill there, doesn't have any intent to engage in activities in Maryland.

However, I think a court would almost certainly rule otherwise. What Dispos-All has done is to establish a hazardous waste facility right near the border, with knowledge that improperly dumped wastes could infiltrate the groundwater and injure persons and property "downstream" in Maryland. They have chosen to impose a risk on Marylanders from outside the state that they know could have serious adverse effects in Maryland. I can't really see the court declining jurisdiction where that deliberate choice leads to an injury in Maryland. I vote for **C**.

Suppose Dispos-All burned toxic wastes at the facility, with knowledge that if they do it in the wrong conditions, the fumes would blow over the border. Would a court conclude that it was not subject to jurisdiction for injuries in Maryland from breathing the toxic fumes? I doubt it. The court would likely conclude that the defendant had, for its own purposes, created a risk that it could foresee causing injury nearby in Maryland, and that that choice should subject it to jurisdiction when it does. See *Illinois v. Milwaukee*, 599 F.2d 151 (7th Cir. 1979) (en banc), *overruled on other grounds*, 451 U.S. 304 (1981), which upheld jurisdiction in one state over a city in a neighboring state, for allegedly discharging pollutants into Lake Michigan.

Certainly, the argument can be made that allowing suit in Maryland in this case bases jurisdiction on foreseeability of the wrong kind, that is, the mere foreseeability that an act in one state may cause harm in another. But I don't think so. Unlike the situation in *World-Wide Volkswagen*, Dispos-All has deliberately chosen to locate near the border, with knowledge that failure to adequately control its wastes would cause serious impacts in Maryland.

That is an act sufficiently related to Maryland to support jurisdiction for a claim that arises from it.

But I don't know that this is how the court would rule. I have a view, based on considered judgment, but I really *don't know*. I probably wouldn't give the question based on that state of mind (especially since a respected colleague disagrees with my analysis). However, I think a lot of professors *would* give a question like this, arguing that multiple-choice questions can fairly require the student to make close calls based on educated judgment developed from studying a complex principle.

 ## Glannon's Picks

1. Gone, but not forgotten	A
2. Contact sports	D
3. Minimum, or miscellaneous?	C
4. Rolling risks	D
5. Contracts and contacts	B
6. A matter of convenience	D
7. One end of the spectrum	D
8. A distinction wtih a difference?	A
9. Between two extremes	D
10. Cold, cruel world	D
11. Close to the line	C, but . . .

More Personal Jurisdiction: General In Personam Jurisdiction and In Rem Jurisdiction

~

There once was a first-year named Stu
Who struggled with International Shoe.
Though he weathered Asahi
And gave Goodyear a fair try,
He never did fathom Quasi, Type Two.

~

CHAPTER OVERVIEW

A. The meaning of general in personam jurisdiction
B. What contacts suffice for general in personam jurisdiction?
C. A perennial confuser: General in personam jurisdiction and principal place of business
D. The historical role of in rem jurisdiction
E. The three types of in rem jurisdiction
F. The impact of *Shaffer v. Heitner*
G. The Closer: What did *Shaffer* hold?
◈ Glannon's Picks

A. The meaning of general in personam jurisdiction

The previous chapter iterates, and reiterates, that jurisdiction based on a defendant's "minimum contacts" with the forum is limited to claims that arise out of those contacts. If a defendant conducts limited activities directed to the forum state, it is subject to "specific" personal jurisdiction for claims arising out of those contacts, but not for other claims that arise in other states.

However, in *International Shoe* the Court suggested that a defendant's contacts in the state may sometimes be so extensive that it could be sued there for any claim against it, no matter where it arose. "[T]here have been instances in which the continuous corporate operations within a state were thought so substantial and of such a nature as to justify suit against it on causes of action arising from dealings entirely distinct from those activities." 326 U.S at 318. The premise behind general in personam jurisdiction is that, where a defendant's contacts are sufficiently extensive in the forum state, it is neither unfair nor inconvenient to require it to defend any lawsuit there, including ones that arise in other states. Thus, if International Shoe is subject to general in personam jurisdiction in Missouri, it could be sued there for unemployment taxes due in Washington, or breach of a contract in Colorado. This is analogous to general in personam jurisdiction over an individual defendant based on her domicile in the state. In *Milliken v. Meyer*, 311 U.S. 457 (1940), the Supreme Court affirmed that a person's domicile is such an important connection to a state, and confers sufficient benefits, that an individual domiciled in a state may fairly be required to defend any claim in that state.

Let's start by distinguishing assertions of general in personam jurisdiction from other exercises of jurisdiction. Consider the following question.

QUESTION 1. Line-up. In which of the following cases could the court rely on general in personam jurisdiction as the basis for exercising judicial authority over the defendant?

A. Johnston brings an action in New Mexico against Moreno, a Texas citizen, for breach of a contract they entered into in Texas, in which Moreno agreed to sell Johnston a painting. He obtains jurisdiction by attaching a time share Moreno owns at a condominium complex in the New Mexico mountains.

B. Truscott sues Mancini Motors, a Texas corporation that sells antique cars at its dealerships in Texas and California. Truscott sues in New Mexico, for injuries he suffered in New Mexico while driving a 1964 Ford Mustang that Mancini had advertised in New Mexico, sold to

Truscott, and shipped to him in New Mexico. Truscott serves Mancini with process in the action at the Texas dealership. Mancini has no place of business in New Mexico, but sells three or four cars a year there.

C. Truscott sues Mancini Motors, the Texas antique car company, in Texas. He seeks damages for misrepresentations a Mancini salesperson made to him at a Mancini dealership in California, which led him to purchase a car at the California dealership.

D. Cartwright sues Skilful Electric Tool Company in Michigan for injuries he suffered there using a Skilful saw he bought in Michigan. Skilful, incorporated in Delaware, manufactures its tools in Tennessee, and sells them to wholesalers around the United States. The wholesalers resell Skilful products in all states. Skilful advertises its saws in Michigan. About thirty Skilful saws are sold there every year.

ANALYSIS. In **A**, jurisdiction is not based on general in personam jurisdiction. Indeed, it is not based on in personam jurisdiction at all. It is an exercise of in rem jurisdiction, based not on bringing the defendant before the court, but upon the seizure of his property by attachment to satisfy an unrelated claim. More on this later in the chapter. Note too, that the defendant in this case is an individual. General in personam jurisdiction based on extensive contacts (as opposed to domicile) may not apply to individual defendants at all, but only to corporations. See *Burnham v. Superior Court*, 495 U.S. 604, 610 n.1 (1990).

B involves an exercise of specific in personam jurisdiction. Surely, selling a few cars a year in New Mexico is insufficient to support general in personam jurisdiction, which rests on the premise that the defendant conducts continuous, extensive activity in the forum state. However, Truscott's claim here arises out of a minimum contact of Mancini in New Mexico: advertising the car there and subsequently selling it to Truscott there. This would support specific in personam jurisdiction, since Truscott's claim arises out of a sale actively solicited by Mancini in New Mexico.

D is also a specific in personam case. Here, Cartwright sues for a claim that arises out of indirect sales of Skilful's products into Michigan. Even after the *Asahi* and *J. McIntyre* cases, Skilful would likely be subject to personal jurisdiction in Michigan for this claim since, unlike those cases, Skilful directly cultivated the Michigan market for its products by advertising in Michigan, and the claim arises from a product sold there. But Skilful's contacts would not support general in personam jurisdiction in Michigan. Although we don't know exactly how to assess general jurisdiction based on ongoing contacts, the indirect sale of thirty saws in the state each year may be continuous, but is not substantial enough to support general jurisdiction. See *Goodyear Dunlop Tires Operations, S.A. v. Brown*, 131 S. Ct. 2846 (2011), in which the Supreme Court held that a foreign corporation that sold "tens of thousands" of tires (131 S. Ct.

at 2852) in North Carolina was not subject to general in personam jurisdiction in that state. Nor would Cartwright need to invoke general in personam jurisdiction, since the claim arises out of a Skilful contact in the forum.

C is different. Here, Truscott sues Mancini in Texas for a claim that arose from its activity in California. Mancini has plenty of contacts in Texas, but this claim does not arise from them. If the court is to exercise jurisdiction in the case, it will have to do so based on the fact that Mancini, which is incorporated in Texas and has a permanent place of business there, has extensive contacts in Texas that support general in personam jurisdiction, that is, jurisdiction over any claim against the corporation, even if it arose in another state.

B.   What contacts suffice for general in personam jurisdiction?

The real problem with general jurisdiction is that no one really knows what activities suffice to support it. The Supreme Court has decided three general in personam jurisdiction cases, *Perkins v. Banguet Mining Co.*, 342 U.S. 437 (1952); *Helicopteros Nacionales de Columbia S.A. v. Hall*, 466 U.S. 408 (1984); and *Goodyear Dunlop Tires Operations, S.A. v. Brown*, 131 S. Ct. 2846 (2011). *Perkins* was an oddball, because the corporation had fled the Philippines during the Second World War and was conducting skeletal operations from its temporary Ohio headquarters, pending return to the Philippines. Effectively, there wasn't any place else to bring the action. The Court held that jurisdiction in Ohio was proper, even though the claim arose elsewhere, but did not elucidate what other contacts would suffice to allow jurisdiction over a claim that did not arise in the forum.

In handwritten margin note: Perkins - Exceptional circumstances

In *Helicopteros*, the defendant bought helicopters from Texas and had entered Texas for related training and to negotiate a contract to provide transport services using the helicopters. But it provided those services in South America, and the crash that gave rise to the plaintiffs' claims took place there. The Court held that the defendant's Texas contacts were insufficient to support general in personam jurisdiction.

Goodyear is somewhat more helpful, though still enigmatic. In *Goodyear*, the Court addressed a case in which the defendants, foreign tire manufacturers, were sued in North Carolina by the families of two boys killed in an accident outside Paris, France. Clearly there was no basis for the North Carolina court to exercise specific in personam jurisdiction over these defendants for this accident, since the suit did not arise out of any activity of the manufacturers in North Carolina. The plaintiffs argued, however, that the defendants were subject to general in personam jurisdiction, because thousands of their tires were resold by distributors in North Carolina. The

Supreme Court held that such resales in the forum state do not support jurisdiction over unrelated claims such as the ones at issue in *Goodyear*. Otherwise, the Court noted, "any substantial manufacturer or seller of goods would be amenable to suit on any claim for relief wherever its products are distributed." 131 S. Ct. at 2856.

The *Goodyear* opinion included some helpful dicta about general in personam jurisdiction, noting that "the paradigm case" for general jurisdiction is the plan "in which the corporation is fairly regarded as at home" and citing an article suggesting that the state of incorporation and the state of a corporation's principal place of business satisfy this criterion. 131 S. Ct. at 2853-2854. Thus, after *Goodyear*, it is very likely that a corporation is subject to general in personam jurisdiction in the state in which it is incorporated and in the state of its principal place of business.

The unsettled question, however, is whether a corporation is subject to general jurisdiction in any other states as well. Suppose, for example, that an oil refining company is incorporated in Delaware, has its principal place of business in California, but also has a huge production facility in Texas. Is it subject to general in personam jurisdiction in Texas as well as California and Delaware? We don't know. A good many cases prior to *Goodyear* based general in personam jurisdiction on such extensive in-state activity, but *Goodyear* certainly suggests the possibility that a corporation is only "at home"—and subject to general in personam jurisdiction—in the states of incorporation and principal place of business. It is even unclear what period of time a court should consider in assessing general jurisdiction. The concept of ongoing "presence" suggests that it should be based on in-state activity over a period of years, not solely when the plaintiff's claim arises.

Let's try a question that considers both specific and general in personam jurisdiction, and both individual defendants and corporate defendants.

QUESTION 3. Weight of authority. Marathon Crane Company, a Canadian company, sold small cranes to Partlett Construction Company, a South Dakota corporation. Marathon knew that Partlett did road construction throughout the midwestern states. Marathon also sold cranes occasionally in Minnesota; it had sold fifteen cranes there over the five years before the accident.

Partlett took a Marathon crane to Minnesota, where it collapsed, injuring Perez. Perez brought suit in Minnesota against Marathon for his injuries. In the same action, he asserted a claim against Francis, a Partlett supervisor who had advised the crane driver, in South Dakota, that the crane would lift 10,000 pounds, though it was actually rated for 3,000 pounds. Francis *Defendant* is a Minnesota citizen who works in Partlett's central offices in South Dakota. The Minnesota court

A. has personal jurisdiction over Marathon based on general jurisdiction.
B. has personal jurisdiction over Marathon based on specific jurisdiction, since Marathon knew that Partlett used Marathon cranes in all midwestern states.
C. has jurisdiction over Marathon because, unlike *Asahi*, it would not be unreasonable to require Marathon to come from Canada to nearby Minnesota.
D. lacks personal jurisdiction over either defendant.
E. has general in personam jurisdiction over Francis, but probably does not have general in personam jurisdiction over Marathon.

ANALYSIS. Let's go through the choices in order. It is quite clear that **A** is wrong. General jurisdiction — that is, jurisdiction that does *not* arise out of the defendant's in-state contacts — must be based on substantial and continuous contacts in a state. Usually, it will be based on the corporation's principal place of business or state of incorporation. So clearly, selling a few cranes each year in Minnesota does not give Marathon the kind of in-state presence that would make it fair to sue it there for unrelated claims. It has no on-going presence in the state, just occasional sales there. If it could be sued in Minnesota for Perez's claim, based on general in personam jurisdiction, it could be sued there for a breach of contact in Idaho or a traffic accident in Texas. This doesn't seem to be a fair quid pro quo for its very limited conduct in Minnesota.

It is also doubtful that Marathon would be subject to specific jurisdiction for this claim. While it knew that Partlett would use its cranes in other states, it sold this one into South Dakota. If it could be sued in any state where Partlett used the crane, that would make the crane Partlett's "agent for service of process." Taking the crane to Minnesota was a deliberate contact of Partlett with Minnesota, not Marathon. So **B**, while perhaps arguable, is not the best choice.[1]

C also fails. While it would be less onerous to bring Marathon to Minnesota than it would be to bring Asahi to California, personal jurisdiction analysis must start with some connection of the defendant with the forum state that supports jurisdiction. Here, Marathon's contacts are insufficient to support general jurisdiction and the claim does not arise out of the contacts it has there. Very likely, it lacks sufficient contacts to support jurisdiction. If that is true, the court would not reach the reasonableness prong of the analysis. Lack of inconvenience, or the interest of the forum

---

1. The best argument here would be that this was an out-of-state act that caused in state injury, and that marathon was doing other similar business in Minnesota. Some long-arm statutes assume that this is proper. See, e.g., Uniform Instate and International Procedure Act, §1.03(a)(4). But it seems like too little business to support jurisdiction under Fourteenth Amendment analysis.

and the plaintiff in bringing suit in Minnesota, will not support jurisdiction there if the defendant does not have a relationship with the state that supports jurisdiction. *World-Wide Volkswagen v. Woodson*, 444 U.S. 286, 294 (1980).

D is wrong, because the court has jurisdiction over Francis based on his domicile in Minnesota. In *Milliken v. Meyer*, 311 U.S. 457 (1940), the Supreme Court upheld jurisdiction over a domiciliary of a state, even for unrelated claims. Thus, Francis is subject to jurisdiction in Minnesota, whether or not the claim arose out of any act he directed to Minnesota. One might argue that his mistake in advising about the weight limit would support specific jurisdiction if he knew the crane would be used in Minnesota. But we needn't resolve that question, since Francis can be sued in Minnesota for any claim.

So **E** is the best answer. Francis could be sued in Minnesota for any claim, but Marathon very likely could not and almost certainly could not be sued there based on general in personam jurisdiction.

C. A perennial confuser: General in personam jurisdiction and principal place of business

Because the standard for general in personam jurisdiction is unsettled, it is hard to test on it, especially through multiple-choice questions. Who really knows what is right and what isn't? But there is one source of confusion that is reflected in my procedure exams every year. It involves the relation of general in personam jurisdiction to corporate citizenship for purposes of diversity (subject matter) jurisdiction. As Chapter 2 explains, for purposes of diversity jurisdiction, a corporation is deemed a citizen of the state in which it is incorporated and the state where it has its principal place of business. 28 U.S.C. §1332(c)(1).

In *Hertz Corp. v. Friend*, 559 U.S. 77 (2010), the Supreme Court held that a corporation's principal place of business *for diversity purposes* is, in all cases, the state of its headquarters. After *Hertz*, a corporation is citizen, under 28 U.S.C. §1332(c)(1), of the state in which its headquarters are located, even if all of its actual manufacturing or service activities take place elsewhere. The Court emphasized the importance of having a relatively clear rule that will avoid uncertainty and litigation about whether diversity jurisdiction is met in cases involving corporate parties. And in *Goodyear*, the Court suggested that general in personam jurisdiction will be proper in a corporation's state of incorporation and its principal place of business. However, we don't know that the Court will use the *Hertz* test as the test for "principal place of business" for purposes of general in personam jurisdiction! Perhaps it will look, in this different context, to the state where the most productive activity takes place. It seems somewhat unlikely that it would simply borrow the *Hertz* standard, since the policies underlying diversity and personal jurisdiction analysis are different.

It is important to keep this diversity analysis separate from the issue of general in personam jurisdiction. General in personam jurisdiction will likely be proper in the states where a corporation is a "state citizen" under §1332(c)(1), but it is important to recognize that the reason for that has nothing to do with the diversity statute.

Consider the following, slightly wacky question.

QUESTION 3. The quality of contacts. Pontes, an Ohio citizen, is injured in an accident with Swedenbourg, who is driving a truck for her employer, Quality Auto Parts, Inc. The accident takes place in South Dakota.

Quality Auto Parts is incorporated in Delaware. Its corporate headquarters are in Indiana. Its sales are spread around the Midwest: 35 percent of its sales are in Ohio, 28 percent are in Indiana, 21 percent are in Illinois, and the rest are scattered among six other states, including South Dakota. It manufactures $50 million worth of auto parts each year at its factory in Ohio.

Pontes sues Quality for her injury in a federal court in Ohio. The Ohio court will

A. have personal jurisdiction over Quality under the *Hertz* case.
B. have personal jurisdiction over Quality under the *Goodyear* case.
C. have subject matter jurisdiction over the case under the *Goodyear* decision.
D. have subject matter jurisdiction over the case based on diversity. It may also have personal jurisdiction over Quality for this claim, but we don't know for sure.

ANALYSIS. The point of this question is that the standard for determining whether a corporation's contacts in a state will support general in personam jurisdiction is *not the same* as determining its state citizenship for purposes of diversity jurisdiction. For purposes of *subject matter jurisdiction* based on diversity of citizenship, a corporation is a citizen of the state where it is incorporated and the state where its principal place of business is located. 28 U.S.C. §1332(c)(1). And a corporation's principal place of business *for diversity purposes* is its home office, under *Hertz Corp. v. Friend*, 559 U.S. 77 (2010). But §1332(c)(1) has nothing to do with where a corporation is subject to general in personam jurisdiction.

True, after *Goodyear*, it appears that a corporation's activities in the state of its principal place of business will support general in personam jurisdiction. However, that does not mean that courts will use the *Hertz* test to determine a corporation's principal place of business for purposes of general in personam jurisdiction, or that a corporation cannot have sufficient activity in *additional states*, beyond these two, to support general jurisdiction. These concepts are confusingly similar, but not identical.

So let's consider the choices. **A** just has to be wrong, because the *Hertz* test is used to determine a corporation's principal place of business under 28 U.S.C. §1332(c)(1), for purposes of diversity jurisdiction, which is *subject matter jurisdiction*. Maybe the Supreme Court will one day endorse the same test for a corporation's principal place of business for general in personam jurisdiction. But it hasn't done that yet and may never do that.

B may or may not be true. *Goodyear* did not tell us whether extensive instate activity would support general in personam jurisdiction, even if that state is not the principal place of business of the corporation. Nor did it tell us how to determine what state *is* a corporation's principal place of business for general in personam jurisdiction purposes. So it's a considerable stretch to say that *Goodyear* establishes a test for a case like Quality's. The case is too Delphic to resolve this one.

C is the real loser. *Goodyear* says nothing whatsoever about subject matter jurisdiction, even though it discusses two concepts — incorporation and principal place of business — that apply in diversity analysis as well. This distractor mixes apples with oranges and will only be chosen by the (understandably) confused.

D is the best answer. Under 28 U.S.C. §1332(c)(1) Quality is a citizen of its state of incorporation — Delaware — and of its principal place of business. And *Hertz* tells us that its principal place of business, *for diversity purposes*, is the state of its home office, which is Indiana. So it is diverse from Pontes, an Ohio citizen, even though Quality has a huge manufacturing presence in Ohio. But we don't know if it is subject to general in personam jurisdiction in Ohio. *Goodyear* tells us that it is almost certainly subject to general in personam jurisdiction in Delaware and in the state of its principal place of business. Perhaps, for general in personam jurisdiction purposes, the Court would look to Ohio, the state where Quality makes millions of dollars worth of goods, as its principal place of business. Or, perhaps not — we don't know. If it were to adopt the *Hertz* test for a corporation's principal place of business for *general in personam jurisdiction purposes* (which would mean Indiana on these facts) perhaps it would *also* endorse general in personam jurisdiction in a state with the massive contacts that Quality has in Ohio. Don't know . . . stay tuned.

D.   The historical role of in rem jurisdiction

Unlike jurisdiction "in personam," that is, over the person of the defendant, "in rem" jurisdiction refers to jurisdiction over a thing, an item of property. As *Pennoyer v. Neff* explains, for many years courts proceeded on the premise that their authority to exercise jurisdiction was based on physical power. A court could exercise jurisdiction over a person within the territory of the state ("in personam jurisdiction") if he was symbolically arrested there through service of process. Or the court could exercise jurisdiction over property within the state ("in rem jurisdiction") if the property was seized through attachment.

The process for seizure of property through attachment varied from state to state, and for different types of property. Usually, land was (and still is) attached by obtaining a writ of attachment from the court and filing it in the registry of deeds or other office for recording titles, and perhaps posting notice of the attachment on the property as well. This gives notice to the world that the court has assumed jurisdiction over the property and might enter an order affecting its title. For tangible personal assets, the property may be taken into custody by the sheriff pursuant to a writ of attachment issued by the court, or a keeper appointed to retain control of the property pending further order from the court.

Attachment provided an alternative means to satisfy claims of local citizens when the defendant could not be sued there in personam. Suppose, for example, that Neff hired Mitchell, an Oregon lawyer, to represent him in a divorce case in Oregon, but moved to California without paying Mitchell's fee. Under the jurisdictional principles of *Pennoyer v. Neff,* Neff could not be sued in personam in Oregon, since he could not be served with process there. However, if he left property in the state, the court could assert jurisdiction over that property by attaching it. It could then adjudicate Mitchell's fees claim, and if it concluded that Neff owed the fee (or if Neff defaulted), it could order Neff's property sold to satisfy Mitchell's claim. Thus, in rem jurisdiction provided an alternative means of satisfying a claim, if the defendant had obligingly left property subject to attachment in the forum state.

Often, however, the in rem alternative would not be fully satisfactory. Because the court's authority to adjudicate was based on its seizure of property, not power over the defendant personally, it could only dispose of the property before it. If the court determined that Mitchell was owed $300, but Neff's attached property sold for $200, the court could not enter an order requiring Neff to pay the other $100. To do so would be to exercise jurisdiction over Neff personally, but Neff wasn't before the court; only the property was. So, the in rem remedy was limited to the value of the property the court had attached at the outset of the case.[2]

Even if the property was worth less than the plaintiff's claim, however, an in rem action placed the defendant in a difficult position. Consider the following example.

QUESTION 4. Hostage-taking. In the era before *International Shoe* and *Shaffer v. Heitner,* Mitchell sues Neff in Oregon for a $20,000 legal fee. Neff claims that he had already paid the fee, but Mitchell claims that his payment was for other services. Neff lives in California and cannot be served with process in Oregon. However, he had left his Model T in the garage at his brother's house in Bend, Oregon. Mitchell obtains a writ of attachment and has the Model T, worth $6,000, seized by the sheriff. Neff receives notice of the suit and the attachment, and consults you for advice on how to respond to the suit and the attachment. Which advice would be most appropriate?

A. Neff should ignore the action, since he is not subject to personal jurisdiction in Oregon.
B. Neff should ignore the action, and resist enforcement of any resulting judgment in California.
C. Neff should file a special appearance in Oregon claiming that he is not subject to personal jurisdiction there.
D. Neff should appear and defend the underlying claim, to avoid losing his Model T.

ANALYSIS. Let's work through the consequences to Neff of making each choice. If he chooses **A**, and ignores the action, the Oregon court will enter a default judgment for Mitchell, and order his Model T sold. Mitchell will get the proceeds of the sale. It probably won't be a full $6,000, because buying at a sheriff's sale always carries some risk that the procedure may not have been proper, which could give rise to a claim by the prior owner — that's what gave rise to Pennoyer's troubles. But Neff will be out one Model T. If, as the question indicates, he has a viable defense to the underlying fees claim, he would be ill-advised to take that course.

B is dreadful advice, because there wouldn't be any action brought in California to enforce the Oregon judgment. An in rem judgment operated only against the property, not against Neff personally. So it could only be executed by sale of the attached property in Oregon. Mitchell could not seek further

---

2. The problem in *Pennoyer,* of course, was that Mitchell hadn't attached *any* property at the outset of the case, only later after getting a judgment for his fee. Thus, when the court purported to exercise jurisdiction, by entering a default judgment, it had no jurisdiction, either in personam or in rem.

satisfaction from Neff based on the in rem judgment. Here again, Neff loses his Model T.

C would also be pointless, because the Oregon court is not exercising personal jurisdiction over Neff. It is exercising in rem jurisdiction over his property instead. Prior to *Shaffer v. Heitner*, this was conceptually different, and could be done even if Neff was not subject to personal jurisdiction. In fact, that was frequently *why* it was done. So it makes no sense for Neff to come in and object to personal jurisdiction.

So **D** seems like the only sensible course. If Neff has a viable defense to the underlying fees claim, and he doesn't want to lose the Model T, he will have to appear and defend the action. This illustrates the potential power of an in rem action under traditional practice: Property left in the state could serve as a hostage to force the defendant back into the forum.

Suppose that Neff did return to defend the Oregon action, to avoid losing his Ford. Would he, by doing so, submit to full personal jurisdiction? Not necessarily. A good many states allowed a defendant in Neff's position to enter a "limited appearance" to protect his property from sale. He could appear and defend the fees claim on the merits without submitting to personal jurisdiction. Consequently, if he lost on the fees claim, the court could order sale of the attached assets, but it could not enter a personal judgment against Neff for any remaining balance. If local state law authorized such a limited appearance, his exposure was limited to the value of the attached property.

E.   The three types of in rem jurisdiction

As if these matters aren't complex enough, courts have recognized several different types of in rem jurisdiction.

Let's start with "true" in rem jurisdiction. A true in rem proceeding is one that seeks to adjudicate the title to specific property, as against all possible claimants, known and unknown. Two examples are an action to clear the title to real property, and a probate proceeding to settle an estate. In each of these situations, the court is asked to determine the ownership of specific property, "to reach a conclusive determination of all claims to the thing so that it may be transferred to, or confirmed in the hands of, a person who will then hold it free and clear of all claims." Restatement (Second) of Judgments, §6, cmt. b. Suppose, for example, that the title to a piece of real estate is disputed, and the owner wishes to sell it. She might bring an action to determine title to the property, give notice to known claimants individually, and publish notice to unknown claimants (the best notice possible to unknown parties who might hold an interest in the property). The court would then determine all interests in the property, so that it could be conveyed with a clear title. Any other claims to the property, known or unknown, would be extinguished by the court's decree.

Another example of a "pure" in rem action is an action to forfeit property to the government. Forfeiture is used by the federal government, for example, to obtain title to goods imported illegally, and, more recently, property used in or purchased with the proceeds of drug transactions. In forfeiture actions, the property itself is "the defendant." These cases end up in the reporters with names like "*United States v. 23 Cases of Jack Daniels Whiskey*," or, to cite an actual case, *United States v. Cadillac Sedan Deville*, 933 F.2d 1010 (6th Cir. 1991). Here again, the purpose of the action is to confirm the government's title to the subject property. The property is both the subject of the action and the source of the court's authority to adjudicate. The court proceeds even if it lacks personal jurisdiction over some or all claimants to the property, since it has power over the property based on its presence in the district. Such in rem forfeiture actions remain common today. See generally M. Harrington, "Rethinking *In Rem:* The Supreme Court's New (and Misguided) Approach to Civil Forfeiture," 12 Yale L. & Pol'y Rev. 281 (1994).

A second type of in rem jurisdiction is often referred to as "quasi in rem jurisdiction," or "quasi in rem type I jurisdiction." See *Shaffer v. Heitner*, 433 U.S. 186, 199 n.17 (1977). This type also involves disputes as to title to property. Unlike pure in rem jurisdiction, however, the action only seeks to "secure a preexisting claim in the subject property and to extinguish or establish the nonexistence of similar interests of particular persons." Id. In other words, in this type of action the party bringing the action asserts that, "as to this particular parcel of land, or this automobile, Smith, my interest is superior to yours." It does not affect *other* potential claimants' interests in the property, but simply seeks a declaration that, as between the party bringing the action and a particular other contender, the plaintiff's claim is superior. An example is an action to foreclose a mortgage. In a foreclosure action, the bank does not seek to have all other interests in the property determined or extinguished. It simply seeks a decree that its interest in the mortgaged property is superior to the mortgagor's, due to nonpayment, and an order for sale of the property to satisfy its superior claim. As in "true" in rem cases, the parties to a type I action assert *preexisting* claims to the property before the court, and ask the court to sort those preexisting claims out.

The third type, called "quasi in rem type II jurisdiction," or "attachment jurisdiction," is analytically different. In a case commenced by attachment, the party bringing the action has a claim against the defendant *having nothing to do with the property attached.* "In attachment jurisdiction, the basis of jurisdiction is the existence of property owned by the defendant. Attachment jurisdiction is also to be contrasted with in rem jurisdiction, where the purpose of the action is to resolve conflicting claims to the property; in attachment jurisdiction both parties accept that the property is owned by defendant but plaintiff wants to expropriate it to pay his [unrelated] claim." Ehrenzweig, Louisell & Hazard, *Jurisdiction in a Nutshell, State and Federal* 40-41 (4th ed. 1980).

For example, Mitchell might bring a quasi in rem type II action against Neff in Oregon to recover the legal fees for his work on Neff's divorce. Unable to obtain jurisdiction over Neff personally, he might attach land Neff owned in Oregon. He does not seek the attachment to assert any preexisting interest in the land; indeed, the very reason to attach it is that Neff does own it. Instead, Mitchell asks the court to exert jurisdiction over the property to establish a basis for the court to adjudicate the unrelated fees claim. The seizure of the land through attachment gives the court a jurisdictional base and an asset to sell to satisfy Mitchell's fees claim. Similarly, Ortiz, seeking contract damages for Neff's failure to deliver goods under a contract, might sue and attach Neff's property, to give the court a basis to adjudicate the unrelated contract claim. In these cases, the party bringing the action, unable to sue the defendant in personam, resorts to the alternative illustrated by Question 4. He sues the defendant and seeks seizure of her property, to give the court a basis to adjudicate a claim unrelated to the attached property. The property is not the subject of the action, it is a hostage for the defendant. Consider the following example on the three types of in rem jurisdiction.

QUESTION 5. Quasi-distinctions. Which of the following cases involves an exercise of quasi in rem type II jurisdiction?

A. Ohora is injured when she falls in a hole while crossing the lawn in front of Roux's house in Iowa. She brings an action against Roux in Iowa for her injuries and serves him personally with notice of the action.

B. Ohora is injured in Iowa in a collision with Roux, from Iowa. She brings an action against Roux in Nebraska for her injuries, and obtains a writ of attachment in the action on a Nebraska farm owned by Roux.

C. Ohora, a Nebraska lawyer, is hired by Roux, from Iowa, to represent him in acquiring a farm in Nebraska. Roux leaves the state and fails to pay Ohora for her services. Ohora sues him for her fee in Nebraska and has him served with notice of the action in Iowa.

D. Consolidated Equipment Company sells Roux a construction crane in Iowa, on an installment contract, subject to a right of repossession for nonpayment. Roux fails to pay. Consolidated brings an action in Nebraska to repossess the crane, and obtains a writ from the court attaching the crane while it is at a job site in Nebraska.

ANALYSIS. This question requires you to apply the basic distinction between quasi in rem type II jurisdiction and other exercises of jurisdiction. The case in **A** arises out of Roux's ownership of property, but it is not an in rem action of any type. Ohora has simply brought an in personam action against Roux for her personal injury claim. The fact that the claim arises out of the ownership of real property does not mean that the action must be brought by attachment, and here it has not been.

The third case, **C**, is also an action in personam against Roux. It arises out of legal services related to the Nebraska farm, but the farm is not attached in connection with the action as an asset from which to satisfy Ohora's claim. There is a difference between bringing an action against Roux personally for a claim that relates to a piece of property, which Ohora has done here, and proceeding by seizure of an asset to provide the court a basis for adjudicating an unrelated claim.

D involves an assertion of quasi in rem type I jurisdiction. Consolidated claims that it has an interest in the crane under the installment contract that takes priority over Roux's interest. It asks the court to confirm this claim and its entitlement to repossess the crane.

The action in **B** is an exercise of quasi in rem type II jurisdiction. Ohora sues Roux in Nebraska for an injury in Iowa. There would probably not be specific in personam jurisdiction over Roux in Nebraska for this claim. Instead, Ohora attaches Nebraska real estate owned by Roux. The property attached is not the subject matter of the suit. Ohora doesn't claim that she has any preexisting interest in the farm, or that the claim relates to it. She merely invokes the court's power to seize and sell it to satisfy Ohora's unrelated claim against Roux, should it find her claim valid. So, **B** is right.

F.   The impact of *Shaffer v. Heitner*

Over the years from *Pennoyer v. Neff* to *Shaffer v. Heitner*, attachment jurisdiction was widely invoked to support jurisdiction over unrelated claims. It was routinely used, for example, to attach intangible assets, such as bank deposits. This expanded the doctrine beyond its traditional roots, which involved physical control of physical assets. It is harder to think of a bank account, which is a contractual right to repayment of the deposited amount, as physically "present" in a particular place.

Harris v. Balk, 198 U.S. 215 (1905), was an extreme example of the use of attachment jurisdiction to seize an intangible asset. In *Harris,* Epstein, a Maryland citizen with a claim against Balk, learned that Harris, who owed money to Balk, was coming to Maryland. Epstein sued Balk in Maryland, and obtained a writ of attachment for the seizure of Harris's debt to Balk. He then served the writ on Harris while he was in Maryland. The Supreme Court concluded that Harris's debt to Balk traveled with him, so that it could be "seized" in Maryland while Harris was there, and disposed of by order of the Maryland court. This was an exercise of attachment, or quasi in rem type II jurisdiction, because Harris's debt to Balk was completely unrelated to

Epstein's claim against Balk. It simply provided an unrelated asset that could be seized by the court and used to satisfy Epstein's claim.

Shaffer involved a similarly extreme exercise of quasi in rem jurisdiction. Heitner sued officers and directors of Greyhound Company in Delaware, asserting a claim arising out of alleged mismanagement of the company's business in Oregon. Many of the defendants had not acted in Delaware, and had no other connection to Delaware that would support personal jurisdiction over them there. But many of them owned Greyhound stock. And Delaware had a statute that declared all shares of stock in Delaware corporations to be present in Delaware. Del. Code Ann., Tit. 8, §169 (1975). So, Heitner sought — and was granted — a court order seizing ("sequestering") the Greyhound stock owned by the defendants.

Here, as in *Harris v. Balk,* Heitner did not claim any preexisting ownership interest in the stock itself. Rather, he sought to adjudicate an unrelated claim that arose in Oregon based on the court's seizure of these intangible assets. Like the plaintiff's ploy in *Harris,* this was an exercise of quasi in rem jurisdiction — very type II.

In *Shaffer,* the Court held that the artificial distinction between exercising jurisdiction over the defendant and over his property in quasi in rem type II cases "supports an ancient form without substantial modern justification." 433 U.S. at 212. Because taking the defendants' property was merely an "elliptical way" of asserting jurisdiction over the defendants themselves, the Court broadly concluded that it could only be asserted under the same standards: "We therefore conclude that all assertions of state-court jurisdiction must be evaluated according to the standards set forth in *International Shoe* and its progeny." 433 U.S. at 212. If this broad language from *Shaffer* means what it says, it would allow the assertion of attachment jurisdiction only when the defendant could personally be sued in the state for the underlying claim, under in personam jurisdiction standards.

For the moment, let's take the broad holding quoted above at face value. On that assumption, consider the following example.

QUESTION 6. *Shaffer* survivors?   In which of the following cases could the court properly assert jurisdiction, after the Supreme Court's decision in *Shaffer v. Heitner?*

A. Ohora is injured when she falls in a hole while crossing the lawn in front of Roux's summer house in Nebraska. She sues Roux in Nebraska for her injuries and asserts jurisdiction by obtaining a writ of attachment on the property on which she was injured.

B. Ohora brings an action to quiet title to her Nebraska farm in a Nebraska court. She gives notice of the action by mail to Roux, who lives in

New York but claims a one-third interest in the farm inherited from a great aunt. She also gives notice by publication to unknown claimants to the property.

C. Consolidated Equipment Company sells Roux a construction crane in Iowa, on an installment contract, subject to a right of repossession for nonpayment. Roux fails to pay. Consolidated brings an action in Nebraska to obtain clear title to the crane, and obtains a writ from the court attaching the crane while present on a job in Nebraska.

D. All of the above.

E. None of the above.

ANALYSIS.   In his majority opinion, Justice Marshall suggested that exercises of in rem jurisdiction would have to be measured by the same standards as exercises of in personam jurisdiction. Thus, attachment jurisdiction is not dead. It is constitutionally permissible for a court to exercise jurisdiction based on an attachment . . . if it could assert jurisdiction over the defendant personally for the claim plaintiff seeks to adjudicate. So, to decide whether the above in rem cases are still permissible, we must ask whether the plaintiff could have sued the defendant for the same claim in an in personam action.

In **A**, the plaintiff was injured on the defendant's property and seeks to recover for the injury. This claim arises out of the ownership and maintenance of real property in the state. Since it arises from a significant in-state contact of Roux in Nebraska — maintenance of his property there — he could be sued for it in Nebraska based on specific in personam jurisdiction. Thus, this exercise of jurisdiction meets *International Shoe* jurisdictional standards, and Ohora may proceed by attaching the property under an attachment statute if she chooses to do so. Justice Marshall notes that the minimum contacts test will usually be met in such cases. See 433 U.S. at 208.

One might legitimately wonder why Ohora would choose to proceed by attachment, which only brings the defendant's property before the court, rather than suing Roux in personam, which would support a personal judgment for the full amount of Ohora's injuries. Presumably, Ohora *would* sue in personam in most cases. She might proceed by attachment, however, if the state long-arm statute did not authorize personal jurisdiction under the circumstances, yet the attachment statute authorized attachment of the defendant's in-state assets. For an example of such a case, see *Intermeat Inc. v. American Poultry Inc.,* 575 F.2d 1017 (2d Cir. 1978).

B is a "pure" in rem action to quiet title to real property. Under the broad holding of the *Shaffer* majority, such actions would have to meet the personal jurisdiction standards *of International Shoe*. And they usually would, since the suit involves title to property within the forum state. Because it arises from ownership of an interest in land in Nebraska, claimants to the property will have a minimum contact in Nebraska that gives rise to the claim. Since the court could proceed in personam, it may proceed based on jurisdiction over the property instead. This one is OK.

The trend seems pretty clear here, doesn't it. **C** is an exercise of quasi in rem type I jurisdiction. Here again, the claim is to property present in the forum. Since the case involves conflicting ownership interests in property in Nebraska, the court would quite likely have jurisdiction over the claimants under the minimum contacts test. Thus, **D** is the best answer. Each of these exercises of in rem jurisdiction is permissible, even after *Shaffer v. Heitner*.

G.   The Closer: What did *Shaffer* hold?

Here's one more bemusing *Shaffer* question.

> **QUESTION 7. Barely reasonable.**   In *Shaffer v. Heitner,* the United States Supreme Court held that
>
> **A.** the exercise of all three types of in rem jurisdiction is unconstitutional.
> **B.** the exercise of quasi in rem type I and type II jurisdiction is unconstitutional.
> **C.** the exercise of quasi in rem type II jurisdiction is unconstitutional.
> **D.** None of the above is accurate.

ANALYSIS.   In *Shaffer,* the Supreme Court rejected Heitner's effort to base quasi in rem jurisdiction on the fictitious "presence" of the defendant's stock in Delaware. The Court held that exercising jurisdiction on this basis, even if limited to the value of the sequestered property, is effectively the same as exercising jurisdiction over the defendant's interests in the property. 433 U.S. at 207. There is little constitutional difference, in terms of the effect on the defendant, between entering a judgment ordering sale of the defendant's property worth $2,000 and entering a personal judgment for $2,000 against the defendant. Since both significantly affect the defendant's interests, the Court held that both should be based on the same standard: that the defendant have contacts with the forum that make the particular exercise of jurisdiction fair and reasonable.

However, the Court did not hold that in rem jurisdiction was unconstitutional. Rather, it held that exercises of such jurisdiction should be measured against the standard for exercising *personal* jurisdiction over the defendant under the minimum contacts test *of International Shoe*. 433 U.S. at 212. And, the Court suggested that this standard would generally be met in "true" in rem cases. In true in rem cases, the plaintiff asks the court to determine title to property within the forum state. Thus, the claim arises out of a contact of all claimants to the property with the forum court, claiming an interest in property located there. Thus, the minimum contacts test will likely be satisfied. So **A** is not right.

B isn't right either. As Justice Marshall suggested in *Shaffer*, most, perhaps all, quasi in rem type I cases will satisfy the minimum contacts standard in *International Shoe*. "When claims to the property itself are the source of the underlying controversy between the plaintiff and the defendant, it would be unusual for the State where the property is located not to have jurisdiction." 433 U.S. at 207. By definition, such cases involve claims to particular property within the forum state. (If it were not in the forum state, the court could not obtain jurisdiction over the property by seizing it.) Having an interest in property (such as the crane in the last question, or a home in the state subject to a mortgage) is a contact that supports jurisdiction over claims to the property itself.

C is closer. The Court did suggest that most exercises of quasi in rem type II jurisdiction would fail the minimum contacts test, since they usually involve seizure of property completely unrelated to the plaintiff's claim against the defendant. 433 U.S. at 208-209. However, this will not be true in every case. Consider the case in which the plaintiff sues for an injury suffered on land of the defendant, and brings the action by attachment, rather than seeking personal jurisdiction over the defendant. This would be an exercise of quasi in rem type II jurisdiction, but the Court certainly implied that it would meet the minimum contacts test, since the claim arises out of the ownership of the property in the forum state. See 433 U.S. at 208, n.29 (describing such a case as an exercise of quasi in rem type II jurisdiction). Thus, *Shaffer* does not hold that the exercise of quasi in rem type II jurisdiction is always unconstitutional, just *usually*.

So this is a pretty tough question. Fair enough as a Closer, perhaps, but awfully subtle to give on a first-year exam. **D** is probably the best answer, but I'd feel a little guilty refusing credit for **C**.

We might conclude, then, by asking what *Shaffer* changed, if anything? Well, the case — read broadly based solely on the majority opinion — bars the use of quasi in rem type II jurisdiction based on attachment of assets unrelated to the plaintiff's claim. However, even this may not be accurate. *First*, the two concurring opinions in *Shaffer* both hedged, suggesting that they might uphold more traditional exercises of quasi in rem jurisdiction based on attachment of real property or a bank account. *Second*, in *Burnham v. Superior Court*, 495 U.S. 604 (1990), the Court reaffirmed the power of a court to exercise personal jurisdiction based on personal service of process within the forum state. This endorsement of the time-honored practice of basing jurisdiction on service in the state suggests that the Court may take a more lenient approach to jurisdiction based on property in the state as well.

Justice Scalia's opinion in *Burnham* also read *Shaffer* quite narrowly, suggesting further support for "traditional" exercises of quasi in rem type II jurisdiction.

A number of *post-Shaffer* courts have asserted jurisdiction in circumstances that would seem impermissible under the broad language of Justice Marshall's majority opinion in *Shaffer*. For example, in *Feder v. Turkish Airlines*, 441 F. Supp. 1273 (S.D.N.Y. 1977), the federal district court in New York upheld jurisdiction over a claim arising out of an airline crash in Turkey, based on the attachment of a bank account that Turkish Airlines maintained in the Southern District of New York. This seems like the type of claim rejected by the majority in *Shaffer:* a claim that did not arise out of contacts with the forum, brought based on attachment of unrelated assets of the defendant present in the federal district. The judge in *Feder* relied on Justice Stevens's concurring opinion in *Shaffer*, distinguishing this more traditional exercise of quasi in rem type II jurisdiction from the more attenuated assertion of jurisdiction in *Shaffer* based on the fictional presence of the defendants' stock in Delaware.

So, while the holding in *Shaffer* is broadly stated, its impact may be less drastic than the majority's language suggests.

✵ Glannon's Picks

1. Line-up	C	
2. Weight of authority	E	
3. The quality of contacts	D	
4. Hostage taking	D	
5. Quasi-distinctions	B	
6. *Shaffer* survivors?	D	
7. Barely reasonable	D	

7

More than an Afterthought: Long-arm Statutes as a Limit on Personal Jurisdiction

A long-arm can reach the limits of due process
Or the pols can decide to confer less,
        But the statute can't grope
        Beyond the constitutional scope,
Or there'd be no end to the jurisdictional mess.

CHAPTER OVERVIEW

A. The need for a constitutional and a statutory basis for personal jurisdiction
B. Statutes that "exceed the bounds of due process"
C. Long-arm statutes and specific jurisdiction
D. A perennial confuser: "Tortious acts within the state"
E. Another confuser: Constitutional and statutory limits on personal jurisdiction in the federal courts
F. Double Closer: "Going to the limits of due process"
    Glannon's Picks

I
t is hard enough to understand the limits that the United States Constitution imposes on a court's power to exercise personal jurisdiction over a defendant. But even when students have made some headway in understanding these constitutional constraints, they are frequently mystified

by the other prong of the analysis: the need for statutory authority for a court to exercise in personam jurisdiction. The problem is aggravated by the fact that class coverage of long-arm and other personal jurisdiction statutes is frequently tacked on as an afterthought, often in a single class, when professor and students have about reached their limits of personal jurisdiction endurance.

Most states have "enumerated act" long-arm statutes that authorize their courts to exercise jurisdiction over a defendant for claims that arise from specific types of contacts with the state, such as transacting business, contracting to supply goods or services in a state, committing a tort, owning property, or insuring a risk in a state. See, e.g., Uniform Interstate and International Procedure Act, 13 ULA 355 (West 1980). To exercise jurisdiction, the court must determine that the defendant has engaged in one of the enumerated contacts. Usually, courts will start by considering whether there is a statutory basis to exercise jurisdiction, since, if there isn't, the court can avoid deciding the further constitutional question: whether exerting jurisdiction would be consistent with due process.

A.   The need for a constitutional and a statutory basis for personal jurisdiction

Let's start with the role of the United States Constitution in defining the limits of a court's power to subject a defendant to jurisdiction. The Fourteenth Amendment bars a state from depriving a person of life, liberty or property "without due process of law," that is, without a basically fair procedure. If it's a court that's doing the depriving — by entering a judgment against a person and forcing her to pay it — basic fairness requires that the defendant have some relationship to the state where the court sits that will make it fair to conduct the litigation there. In civil procedure terms, that means that the court must have "a basis to exercise personal jurisdiction" over the defendant.

In the major personal jurisdiction cases, such as *International Shoe, World-Wide Volkswagen, Goodyear, Asahi*, and *Burnham v. Superior Court*, the United States Supreme Court has provided some guidance as to the types of relations to a state that will support the exercise of jurisdiction. Some relations that satisfy due process under the Fourteenth Amendment include domicile in a state,[1] continuous and substantial contacts with it,[2] minimum contacts that give rise to the claim,[3] and service of process on an individual in the forum state.[4] That's not an exhaustive list, and of course there are

---

1. *Milliken v. Meyer*, 311 U.S. 457 (1940).
2. *Goodyear Dunlop Tires Operations, S.A. v. Brown*, 131 S. Ct. 2846, 2853 (2011).
3. *International Shoe v. Washington*, 326 U.S. 310 (1945).
4. *Burnham v. Superior Court*, 495 U.S. 604 (1990).

refinements and ambiguities, but the point is that the Supreme Court has upheld certain relations to a state as sufficient under the Fourteenth Amendment to support personal jurisdiction over a defendant there.

However, it is not enough that a defendant has a contact with the state that is sufficient under the Due Process Clause to allow the state to exert jurisdiction over him. The state must also have a statute that authorizes the court to exercise that jurisdiction. This is confusing; if the exercise of jurisdiction is constitutionally permissible, why does the legislature have to authorize it in a statute too?

The reason is that the Fourteenth Amendment does not actually confer jurisdiction on courts. It sets *limits* on the exercise of jurisdiction. ("No state shall deprive any person of life, liberty, or property without due process of law.") It says to the states, "go ahead, define your courts' jurisdiction as you like, but in doing so, don't overreach." It is the state legislatures that define the power of their courts to exercise personal jurisdiction. So, when a defendant is sued in the courts of California, the California court must ask whether a California statute authorizes it to assert jurisdiction over that defendant. If the suit is in Wisconsin, the court will look to Wisconsin personal jurisdiction statutes, and so on.[5]

Thus, two requirements must be met before the court can proceed to adjudicate the defendant's rights. The court must be authorized to exercise jurisdiction by statute, and it must be constitutionally permissible, under due process analysis, for the court to exercise that statutory authority. Thus, courts address challenges to personal jurisdiction in two steps. *First*, they ask whether a statute of the state (such as a long-arm statute) authorizes the court to exert jurisdiction over the defendant. *Second*, if there is statutory authority to exercise jurisdiction, the court proceeds to the second question: whether applying the statute, in the particular circumstances of the case, would assert jurisdiction beyond the bounds permitted by the Due Process Clause.

Consider the following example on the relation between statutory requirements and constitutional constraints.

> **QUESTION 1. Bad words.** Perrone, an Acadia resident, sues Margules, a Montanan, in an Acadia state court, for defamation. He claims that Margules called Acme Corporation, an Acadia company that was planning to hire Perrone, and made false and defamatory statements about his professional abilities that led Acme to decide not to hire him. Margules placed the call from her office in Montana. Assume that Acadia has a long-arm statute that authorizes personal jurisdiction over a defendant who

---

5. In some states, jurisdiction may be based on court rules adopted pursuant to a statutory authorization to adopt jurisdictional rules.

"causes personal injury in this state by a tortious act or omission while physically present within this state." Assume that this is the only statute that might authorize the Acadia court to exercise personal jurisdiction over Perrone for this claim.

A. The Acadia statute authorizes the court to exercise jurisdiction over Margules in this case. However, it would be unconstitutional under the Fourteenth Amendment for the court to exercise jurisdiction over her on the facts of this case.

B. The Acadia statute does not authorize the court to exercise jurisdiction over Margules in this case. In addition, it would be unconstitutional under the Fourteenth Amendment for the court to exercise jurisdiction over her on the facts of this case.

C. The Acadia statute does not authorize the court to exercise jurisdiction over Margules in this case. However, it would be constitutional under the Fourteenth Amendment for the court to exercise jurisdiction over her on the facts of this case.

D. Although the Acadia statute does not authorize the court to exercise jurisdiction over Margules in this case, the court may do so because the claim arises out of her deliberate contacts with Acadia that gave rise to Perrone's claim.

ANALYSIS. It shouldn't be too hard to narrow down the choices here. The statute requires that the defendant, when she commits the tortious act, be physically present in Acadia. Margules wasn't, so the statute does not authorize the Acadia court to exercise personal jurisdiction over Margules. That eliminates **A** right off the bat.

B asserts that the statute does not authorize the court to hear the case, and that, if it did, it would exceed constitutional bounds to exercise jurisdiction over Margules on these facts. This is almost certainly not so. Margules deliberately reached into Acadia to cause a substantial adverse effect on Perrone in Acadia, and did. A person need not physically enter a state to establish a minimum contact there that will support personal jurisdiction over her. She need only purposely engage in conduct focused on the state that she can foresee might cause adverse effects there and lead to litigation there. Margules certainly did that, and it would not be unreasonable to require her to defend this Acadia-focused act in Acadia. Compare *Calder v. Jones,* 465 U.S. 783 (1984) (Florida defendant who wrote defamatory article about California actress published there subject to personal jurisdiction in California, even if he did not travel to California in connection with the article).

How about **D**, which suggests that the court can exercise jurisdiction because Margules' minimum contacts in Acadia would constitutionally allow the court to do so? This dangerously misconstrues the relation of jurisdictional statutes and constitutional constraints. Although it would be consistent with due process for Acadia to require Margules to defend this case in Acadia, it has *chosen not to require him to.* Instead, it has written a long-arm statute that does not "reach to the limits of due process." In this long-arm provision, Acadia has granted its courts less personal jurisdiction authority than it constitutionally could, by excluding cases like Perrone's, in which communications from outside the state defame a plaintiff in the state. Maybe it just doesn't want to hear all these cases. For whatever reason, it has not given its courts statutory authority to hear this claim, even though it could have. **C** is the best answer.

This point is fundamental, so let's try again.

QUESTION 2. Gone, but not forgotten. Nhan, a resident of North Carolina, purchases a life insurance policy from United Assurance Company, a Georgia company that sells insurance only in the southeastern states. Three years later, he dies in North Carolina. His mother, McGee, the beneficiary of the policy, lives in Utah. She brings suit against United Assurance in a state court in Utah to collect the policy proceeds. Assume that a Utah jurisdictional statute authorizes Utah courts to hear "any suit by a resident of this state on a contract of insurance if the resident is either the insured or a beneficiary of the contract."

A. The Utah statute authorizes jurisdiction in McGee's suit, but it would likely exceed the bounds of due process for the court to exercise jurisdiction over United Assurance in this case.

B. The Utah statute authorizes jurisdiction in McGee's suit, and it would likely be constitutionally permissible for the court to assert jurisdiction over United Assurance.

C. The Utah statute authorizes jurisdiction in McGee's suit, but it would likely exceed the bounds of due process for the state court to exercise jurisdiction over United Assurance in this case. McGee should sue in a Utah federal court instead based on diversity jurisdiction.

D. The Utah statute does not authorize jurisdiction in McGee's suit. Consequently, the court cannot exercise jurisdiction even if it would be constitutionally permissible for the court to exercise jurisdiction over United Assurance in this case.

ANALYSIS. Those of you who have read *McGee v. International Ins. Co.,* 355 U.S. 220 (1957), will recognize this question as a twist on the facts of *McGee.* But the resemblance is superficial.

D can't be right. It asserts that the Utah statute doesn't authorize jurisdiction, but by its terms it does. It authorizes a policy beneficiary residing in

Utah to sue on the policy in Utah. McGee's a beneficiary, she's suing in Utah, she's suing on the policy. The statute authorizes the court to exercise jurisdiction. The real question is whether Utah could constitutionally exercise jurisdiction over the company based solely on the residence of a beneficiary in the state. (The statute is hypothetical.)

C provides a preview of a point covered in more detail below. It suggests that the reach of personal jurisdiction in this case would be broader if the suit were brought in a Utah federal court. This is a common, understandable misconception about personal jurisdiction. Generally, the federal courts do not exercise wider personal jurisdiction than the courts of the state in which they sit. Rule 4(k)(1)(A) of the Federal Rules, effectively a long-arm statute for the federal courts, provides that, in most cases (including diversity cases) the federal court will exercise jurisdiction over a case only if the courts of the state in which it sits could do so. There are some exceptions to this (see Fed. R. Civ. P. 4(k)(1)(B), (C), (D)), but in most cases Rule 4(k)(1)(A) restricts the Utah federal courts to the same reach of personal jurisdiction as the state courts of Utah. So, McGee would fare no better by filing in a Utah federal court than she would in Utah state court. So C loses.

B asserts that the Utah statute authorizes jurisdiction, and that it would likely be constitutional for the court to exercise it. This is very dubious. United Assurance only does business in the southeastern states. It sold a policy to Nhan in North Carolina. Nhan's decision to designate his mother from Utah as a beneficiary is a contact of Nhan with Utah, not "purposeful availment" by United Assurance of the opportunity to conduct activities in Utah. I haven't researched the cases, but this seems like overreaching under basic minimum contacts principles. Otherwise, insurance companies would effectively be subject to nationwide jurisdiction based on the residency of the beneficiaries chosen by the insured. That might be a good thing but doesn't reflect current personal jurisdiction doctrine.

So A survives the process of elimination. The question illustrates the situation — not as atypical as one might expect — in which the legislature has authorized jurisdiction that, in at least some cases, would exceed the bounds of due process.

B.   Statutes that "exceed the bounds of due process"

Suppose the legislature does write a statute that authorizes jurisdiction in some cases that exceed the bounds of due process, that is, authorizes jurisdiction in circumstances that would be impermissible under the Supreme Court's Fourteenth Amendment cases. If a plaintiff sues a defendant in the state, and the statute authorizes jurisdiction, but the court determines that exerting jurisdiction over the defendant would exceed the bounds of constitutional due process, what will it do? And what is the effect of that holding in a later case? Here's a question to illustrate the point.

QUESTION 3. **Not gone, and not forgotten.** Nhan, a resident of North Carolina, purchases a life insurance policy from United Assurance Company, a Georgia company that sells insurance throughout the southeastern states. Three years later, he dies in North Carolina. His mother, McGee, the beneficiary of the policy, lives in Utah. She brings suit against United Assurance in a state court in Utah to collect the policy proceeds. Assume that a Utah jurisdictional statute authorizes Utah courts to hear "any suit by a resident of this state on a contract of insurance if the resident is either the insured or a beneficiary under the contract." The Utah court holds that it would be unconstitutional to exercise jurisdiction over United Assurance in McGee's case, and dismisses the action.

Two years later, Poretto, a Utah resident, dies. She had an insurance contract with National Life Insurance Company, an Oregon company, which she had bought through the mail from National, in response to a phone solicitation from a National telemarketer. She had renewed the policy from year to year. Her husband, Frank, who also lives in Utah, is her beneficiary. He sues in Utah, invoking the Utah statute just quoted as the statutory basis for exercising jurisdiction over National. Assume that National does no other business in Utah.

A. The Utah statute was declared unconstitutional in McGee's case. The court in Poretto's case will reach the same conclusion under the principle *of stare decisis*.
B. Although the court had held that the Utah statute could not be applied to McGee's case, under due process analysis, it would be constitutional to apply the statute on the facts of Poretto's case. The court will entertain the action.
C. Although the court had held that the Utah statute could not be applied to McGee's case, under due process analysis, the court will consider whether it may be applied in Poretto's. However, because it would be unconstitutional to apply it here as well, the court will dismiss the action.
D. Because the Utah statute was declared unconstitutional in McGee's case, it is defunct and irrelevant to Poretto's.

ANALYSIS. The question illustrates a basic point. The statute has been declared, in a prior case, to go too far, to authorize jurisdiction which exceeds due process limits. What role can the statute play in later cases?

D takes the position that the statute has been declared unconstitutional, and thus is defunct, has been stricken from the books. But this isn't the effect of the holding in McGee's case. The McGee court held that it would be unconstitutional to apply the statute in McGee's case, because, on those facts, United Assurance had no sufficient relation to Utah to support jurisdiction over it for McGee's claim. However, the court did not hold that the statute could never be applied in *any* case, only that it would exceed due process bounds to apply it to McGee's.

When a court holds that a particular application of a long-arm statute would exceed constitutional bounds, it does not strike down the statute itself. It simply refuses to apply it to circumstances in which the exercise of jurisdiction would be unconstitutional. The statute remains on the books; it has not been held unconstitutional on its face, that is, invalid for all applications. It has been held unconstitutional as applied to a particular set of facts. It remains in effect, and may be applied in other cases where doing so would not exceed constitutional bounds. So **D** is wrong. The statute isn't defunct, and the court in Poretto's case will consider whether it may assert jurisdiction under it without violating due process standards.

But wouldn't *stare decisis* require the court in Poretto's case to hold the same way as the court did in McGee's? No, because the question in McGee's case is different from the question in Poretto's. The question in McGee's case was whether it would be constitutional to apply the statute *on the facts of McGee's case.* If the exact same case arose again, then *stare decisis* would support ruling the same way. But Poretto's case is not the same; the relation of the defendant to the state is quite different; the question in her case is whether the statute could be used to exercise jurisdiction *on the facts in Poretto's case.* That's a new question on which the Utah court will rule anew.

The court will likely conclude that the statute authorizes jurisdiction over National Insurance, and that it would be constitutional to exercise jurisdiction. Certainly, the statute applies: Just as in McGee's case, it's a claim brought by a Utah beneficiary to collect on the policy. And here, constitutional constraints are likely satisfied as well. The claim arises out of purposeful activity initiated by the insurer in Utah, soliciting a policy from a Utah resident. Although that's a single contact (or, perhaps, a series of yearly contacts) it is a deliberate contact that should lead the insurer to anticipate a suit in Utah arising out of that contact. Jurisdiction on this basis was held constitutional in *McGee v. International Ins. Co.,* and would be upheld here as well. So **B** prevails.

C. Long-arm statutes and specific jurisdiction

So, whenever a court exercises personal jurisdiction over a defendant, it must have statutory authority to do so. This is true not just when jurisdiction is based on minimum contacts, but for any exercise of jurisdiction. If Smith sues Jones in Florida, and serves her with process while she is attending a convention there, that is probably constitutionally sufficient to support jurisdiction over Jones. *Burnham v. Superior Court*, 495 U.S. 604 (1990). But the court likely would not have jurisdiction unless Florida also had a statute authorizing its courts to exercise personal jurisdiction based upon service of process on the defendant in the state.

The typical long-arm statute, such as the Uniform Interstate and International Procedure Act,[6] and most state long-arm statutes reproduced in the casebooks, are "enumerated act" long-arm statutes. That is, they list types of contacts with the state, and authorize the courts of the state to hear claims that arise out of such contacts. These contacts often include transacting business in the state, contracting to supply goods or services in the state, committing a tortious act in the state, owning property in the state, and others. If the defendant did one of these things in the state, and that conduct gives rise to a claim, the plaintiff is authorized to bring the claim in the courts of the state. These statutes, in other words, authorize the state's courts to exercise "specific" in personam jurisdiction over claims that arise out of the defendant's purposeful acts focused on the state. *International Shoe* held that such jurisdiction, arising out of acts focused on the state, is constitutional. So most states have responded with statutes that authorize their courts to exercise such "minimum contacts" jurisdiction.

This seems straightforward, but it can throw students (and lawyers) off. Consider this example.

QUESTION 4. Here and there. Quantus Software Company, based in Massachusetts, designs specialized software for law firms and sells it throughout New England. Most of its customers are in Massachusetts and Connecticut, but it has a few in Maine, Vermont, and New Hampshire as well. Recently it installed two systems in law offices in Vermont, one for a small firm, Marshall & Story, and another for a larger firm, Tawney and Hughes, which has a small office in Vermont and its main office in Connecticut.

Quantus negotiated a separate contract with Tawney & Hughes's managing partner, in Connecticut, to build a system for their main office in Connecticut. The Connecticut system never worked right. Tawney & Hughes sues Quantus for breach of contract, seeking damages for the faulty system, in a Vermont state court. Assume that the Vermont long-arm statute authorizes suits that "arise out of (1) transacting any business in the state; (2) contracting to supply goods or services in the state; or (3) committing a tortious act in the state."

---

6. 13 U.L.A. 355 (1980).

A. The Vermont court would have jurisdiction over Quantus under the "transacting business" provision.

B. The Vermont court would have jurisdiction over Quantus because it contracted to supply services in Vermont.

C. The Vermont court lacks jurisdiction over Quantus under the Vermont long-arm statute.

D. The Vermont court would have jurisdiction over Quantus under the long-arm statute if Quantus's Vermont sales were sufficient to support general in personam jurisdiction over it in Vermont.

ANALYSIS. This isn't a tough question, especially after the introductory discussion, but I would catch some students with it on an exam. The key to it is that long-arm statutes like this one authorize specific in personam jurisdiction, that is, jurisdiction over claims that *arise out of* the in-state contact. *International Shoe* holds that a court may exercise jurisdiction over a defendant who does limited acts in the state, but only for claims that arise out of that activity. State legislatures have crafted their long-arm statutes accordingly, to authorize jurisdiction based on limited contacts only if the plaintiff's claim arises from those contacts. Too often, students lose sight of the requirement in the long-arm statute itself that the claim arise out of the defendant's in-state contacts.

Both **A** and **B** reflect this oversight. Quantus did transact business in Vermont — it sold two computer systems there. It even sold one of them to Tawney & Hughes. It did contract to supply services in Vermont as well. However, Tawney & Hughes's claim does not arise out of Quantus's transaction of business or supplying services in Vermont; it arises from the sale of a system in Connecticut. The long-arm statute limits the Vermont court's authority to hear claims to those that *arise out of* the defendant's Vermont contacts, and the claim here doesn't.

There's a simple reason why the statute includes this limitation: Otherwise, the statute would authorize a great deal of jurisdiction that was beyond constitutional bounds. Here, for example, if the Vermont court exercised jurisdiction over Tawney & Hughes's claim for the Connecticut work, it would essentially be basing jurisdiction over Quantus on unrelated Vermont contacts. That is, it would be exercising *general* in personam jurisdiction over Quantus. Two sales in Vermont is a very dubious basis on which to assert general in personam jurisdiction. Thus, the arising-out-of limitation in the statute prevents it from authorizing jurisdiction over many cases that it could not hear under due process constraints.

How about **D**? **D** suggests that the court can hear this case if Quantus's contacts in Vermont are sufficient under due process analysis to permit it to be sued there. But meeting constitutional standards merely means that it would be permissible for the legislature to authorize jurisdiction. There still must be a statute authorizing jurisdiction. If there isn't, the fact that exerting jurisdiction would be constitutionally permissible is no substitute. And here the statute does not authorize jurisdiction: It requires the claim to arise out of the in-state transacting or contracting, and here it does not. So **C** prevails.

When a court exercises general in personam jurisdiction — like any other type — it still needs a statutory basis to do so. The long-arm statute in this question doesn't authorize general in personam jurisdiction, that is, jurisdiction over any claim against the defendant, whether or not it arose out of in-state acts. The Vermont statute here is limited to claims that arise out of the acts done in the state.

Many states have statutes that allow jurisdiction over a defendant that is "doing business" in the state. These are usually interpreted to authorize general in personam jurisdiction, that is, jurisdiction over the defendant, even for claims that arose outside the forum state. Such jurisdiction is constitutionally permissible if the defendant has ongoing, extensive in-state contacts. See *Helicopteros Nacionales de Colombia v. Hall*, 466 U.S. 408, 414 (1984). These "doing business" statutes, unlike the typical long-arm provision, do not specify that the claim asserted must arise out of the defendant's in-state acts.

D. A perennial confuser: "Tortious acts within the state"

Some procedure teachers assign *Gray v. American Radiator & Standard Sanitary Corp.*, 176 N.E.2d 761 (Ill. 1961), as an example of a court grappling with a long-arm statute. In *Gray*, the defendant Titan Valve Company made a water heater valve in Ohio and sold it to American Radiator in Pennsylvania, which incorporated the valve into a water heater that was sold through the "stream of commerce" into Illinois. The Illinois long-arm statute authorized jurisdiction if the defendant "commits a tortious act within this state." The *Gray* court held that Titan had "committed a tortious act" in Illinois, because the valve had caused *an injury* in Illinois, and an act does not become a "tortious act" until the plaintiff suffers injury. Thus, Titan was subject to suit in Illinois under this long-arm provision, although it had not actually done any act in Illinois.

This is a mighty broad interpretation of the commits-a-tortious-act phrase. The New York Court of Appeals rejected this extravagant interpretation shortly after the *Gray* decision. It held that, under similar language in New York's statute, the defendant must do the negligent act in the state to "commit a tortious act" there. See *Feathers v. McLucas*, 21 App. Div. 2d 558 (N.Y. App. Div. 1964). But the Illinois courts are the final word on the meaning of the Illinois statute. If the Illinois Supreme Court says that the tortious act happens where the injury occurs, that's where it happens . . . for purposes of applying Illinois's statute.

But, of course, the question still remains whether, assuming a case falls within a long-arm statute that has been broadly construed by the state's courts, it would be constitutional to apply that statute in a particular case. No matter how Illinois chooses to construe its own statute, the *constitutional* question remains.

So let's try an example applying the Illinois long-arm statute in a tort case.

QUESTION 5. Shades of Gray.   Robertson buys an Audi from Jackson's Audi, a Florida car dealership. He drives it to Illinois, where he has an accident, and the driver's air bag fails to deploy, aggravating his injuries. Robertson believes the dealership was negligent in preparing the air bag before selling him the car. He sues Jackson's in an Illinois state court, basing jurisdiction on the provision of Illinois's long-arm statute that authorizes jurisdiction if the defendant "commits a tortious act in Illinois." The Illinois Supreme Court, as we know, has interpreted this statute broadly in *Gray v. American Radiator*.

A. The long-arm statute does not authorize jurisdiction over Robertson's case, because Jackson's negligent act took place in Florida.

B. The long-arm statute authorizes jurisdiction in Robertson's case, but it would be unconstitutional for the court to require Jackson to defend this case in Illinois.

C. The long-arm statute authorizes jurisdiction over Robertson's case, because Robertson's injury took place in Illinois. Because the suit is brought in the Illinois court, and satisfies Illinois's long-arm statute, the suit is proper.

D. The long-arm statute authorizes jurisdiction in Robertson's case, and it will not offend due process for the court to exercise jurisdiction.

ANALYSIS.   This is a thinly disguised reprise of *World-Wide Volkswagen v. Woodson*, in which the Robinsons bought their Audi in New York and were injured using it in Oklahoma. Let's see how the analysis works out in a state with a long-arm statute as broad as Illinois's.

Hopefully, **C** did not catch much interest. It implies that, if the state's long-arm statute applies, jurisdiction is proper. However, that isn't enough to support jurisdiction. Even if a long-arm statute authorizes jurisdiction (and broad long-arm statutes make good politics, since they favor residents), the court still must ask whether it would exceed constitutional limits to apply the statute, given the defendant's contacts with the state. **C** would only be right if we repealed the Due Process Clause, which imposes constitutional limits on the assertion of jurisdiction over an out-of-stater.

A isn't right either. Common sense may tell us that Jackson committed its tortious act in Florida, not Illinois. But the Illinois Supreme Court is the last word on the meaning of Illinois statutes, and it has construed its statute to mean that an actor commits a tortious act in Illinois if she commits the act elsewhere but the resulting injury takes place in Illinois. See *Gray v. American Radiator*. That may seem like a stretch, but that's how Illinois reads its statute. If the Illinois legislature thinks it should mean something other than the *Gray* court's reading, it can always change it. It hasn't changed the substance of this provision in the fifty-odd years since *Gray* was decided.

So that leaves **B** and **D**. Both affirm that the statute authorizes jurisdiction, but differ on whether it would be constitutional for the court to exercise jurisdiction over Jackson. B has the better of the argument: *World-Wide Volkswagen* holds that it is unconstitutional for a state to exercise jurisdiction based solely on the fact that the plaintiff took the product to another state and was injured using it there. Jackson, like Seaway in *World-Wide*, has not purposely availed itself of the opportunity to conduct activities in Illinois; it just sells cars in Florida. To exercise jurisdiction over it on these facts would indeed make the chattel [the Audi] its "agent for service of process," that is, it would allow suit wherever Robertson chooses to take the car. The Illinois statute may authorize jurisdiction here, but the court could not constitutionally exercise it. **B** wins.

E. Another confuser: Constitutional and statutory limits on personal jurisdiction in the federal courts

Most of the personal jurisdiction cases you read in civil procedure concern the constitutional limits on a *state* court's exercise of personal jurisdiction over an out-of-state defendant. But federal courts exercise personal jurisdiction over defendants too. Thus, it's important to understand the limits on their power to force defendants to defend in a particular district as well.

The constitutional limits on a state court's power to exercise jurisdiction are rooted in the Fourteenth Amendment's Due Process Clause, which provides, "nor shall any *State* deprive any person of life, liberty or property, without due process of law" (emphasis supplied). The Fourteenth Amendment applies to the states; it does not apply to the federal government.

The Fifth Amendment contains a similar due process clause that does apply to the federal government and its courts. However, it has been interpreted somewhat differently from the Fourteenth. Generally, the Fifth

Amendment Due Process Clause has been held to allow a federal court to exercise jurisdiction over a defendant if she has an appropriate relation to the United States as a whole, not to a particular state. See, e.g., *Busch v. Buchman, Buchman & O'Brien Law Firm*, 11 F.3d 1255, 1258 (5th Cir. 1994); see generally Wright & Miller, *Federal Practice & Procedure* §1068.1. Thus, a defendant with a contact anywhere in the country can probably be required to defend an action arising from that contact in any federal court (just as a defendant with appropriate contacts anywhere in California is subject to jurisdiction in a California court in any part of the state, under the Fourteenth Amendment). Under this analysis, if McGee bought insurance in North Carolina, he could sue the insurer on the policy in a Utah federal court, and it would be constitutional under the Fifth Amendment Due Process Clause for the Utah federal court to entertain the case, since it arises out of contacts in the United States.[7]

Even if contacts anywhere in the country will support "nationwide jurisdiction" over a defendant, federal courts seldom exercise such broad jurisdiction. In the federal courts, as in the state courts, jurisdiction must not only be within constitutional limits, but must also be authorized by statute, or, in this case, by court rule.[8] In most cases, the reach of personal jurisdiction in the federal courts is governed by Fed. R. Civ. P. 4(k)(1)(A): "Service of a summons or filing a waiver of service is effective to establish jurisdiction over the person of a defendant (A) who could be subjected to the jurisdiction of a court of general jurisdiction in the state in which the district court is located. . . ." Under this provision, the federal court sitting in Utah is authorized to exercise personal jurisdiction if the courts of Utah could do so. A federal court sitting in Texas could exercise personal jurisdiction over a defendant if the courts of Texas could, and so on. Clearly, this rule restricts federal jurisdiction in many cases in which the Fifth Amendment would allow much wider jurisdiction. The rule has the great virtue, however, of making the reach of personal jurisdiction the same (in most cases) in the federal and state court systems. This neutralizes personal jurisdiction as a forum shopping factor: Under Rule 4(k)(1)(A), the plaintiff won't be able to obtain jurisdiction over a defendant in federal court unless she could in the local state courts.

---

7. Some of the cases hold that this would not be permissible if the case had no connection with Utah and it would be unreasonable to conduct the litigation in Utah. *Peay v. Bellsouth Medical Assistance Plan*, 205 F.3d 1206, 1211-1213 (10th Cir. 2000). But others take the broader position that, constitutionally, any federal court would have the power to hear McGee's case. See, e.g., *Busch v. Buchman, Buchman & O'Brien, Law Firm*, 11 F.3d 1255, 1258 (5th Cir. 1994) (relevant inquiry is whether defendant has minimum contacts with United States); *United Elec. Radio & Mach. Workers of America v. 163 Pleasant St. Corp.*, 960 F.2d 1080, 1085 (1st Cir. 1992) (same).

8. Why can a *rule* authorize jurisdiction in the federal courts, if jurisdiction has to be conferred by the legislature (i.e., by Congress, in the federal system)? Congress has delegated the authority to the Supreme Court to promulgate federal procedural rules. See 28 U.S.C. §§2072-2074. Congress may intercept any rule before it takes effect. So, in essence, the Rules are authorized by Congress.

There are some situations in which federal courts do exercise broader jurisdiction than the state courts. Congress may authorize nationwide jurisdiction in particular types of cases. See, e.g., 28 U.S.C. §1361 (authorizing nationwide service of process in interpleader cases). But such statutes are the exception. In most cases, including most cases based on federal law, Rule 4(k)(l)(A) provides the applicable "long-arm statute" for the federal courts.

Here's a question to illustrate the point.

QUESTION 6. Dueling amendments.   Argo, from Arizona, sues Jason, from New Mexico, in an Arizona state court on a breach-of-contract claim, arising from Jason's alleged failure to complete a landscaping job in New Mexico. Jason removes the action to federal court, based on diversity jurisdiction. Jason then moves to dismiss the action for lack of personal jurisdiction.

A. The federal court should deny the motion if the courts of Arizona would have personal jurisdiction over Jason under the Fourteenth Amendment and the Arizona long-arm statute.

B. The federal court should deny the motion if the Arizona long-arm statute authorizes jurisdiction, and it would be constitutional under the Fifth Amendment for the federal court to require Jason to defend the suit in Arizona.

C. The federal court should deny the motion if exercising jurisdiction over Jason would be constitutional under Fourteenth Amendment analysis.

D. The federal court should deny the motion, because a federal court has the constitutional power to hear claims against a defendant who has contacts anywhere in the United States.

E. The federal court should deny the motion, because Jason waived his objection to personal jurisdiction by removing to federal court.

ANALYSIS.   Rule 4(k)(1)(A) applies to cases removed to federal court as well as to cases filed there originally. Generally, under that rule, the court may exercise jurisdiction if the courts of the state in which the federal court sits could do so.

As was pointed out in the removal chapter (see pp. 64-66), removing a case to federal court does *not* waive the right to object to personal jurisdiction. It simply changes the court in which the objection will be raised. Jason may remove and then move to dismiss for lack of personal jurisdiction. The Arizona federal court will then determine whether it has statutory and constitutional authority to exercise jurisdiction over him. So **E** here is a nonstarter.

Choice **C** is tempting but incorrect. Under Federal Rule 4(k)(1)(A) the court indeed will ask whether it would be constitutional under the Fourteenth Amendment to exercise jurisdiction over Jason. But it will *also* ask whether Arizona's long-arm statute has authorized its courts to exercise jurisdiction in the circumstances of Argo's case. So this choice is incomplete.

D is a nonstarter as well. It takes the broad position that, because the federal court could constitutionally exercise jurisdiction based on minimum contacts *anywhere* in the United States, the court has jurisdiction here. But, not to beat a dead myrmidon,[9] the fact that the federal court has constitutional power to exercise personal jurisdiction over Jason is only one step of the analysis. Jurisdiction must also be authorized by statute (or, in this case, by a Rule promulgated pursuant to statutory authority). We still have to look at Rule 4(k)(1)(A) to determine whether the federal court has been authorized to hear the case.

Here, the statute (Rule, actually) says that the federal court can exercise jurisdiction over Jason if the state court could. What determines if the state court could? The Arizona long-arm statute and the *Fourteenth* Amendment (not the Fifth). The federal judge has to ask herself, "If I were sitting in the Arizona state court, could I force Jason to come in and defend this action here?" The answer to that depends on whether an Arizona statute authorizes jurisdiction over Jason and whether it would be consistent with due process of law under the Fourteenth Amendment to exercise it. Those are the two constraints on the exercise of jurisdiction by an Arizona court. Rule 4(k)(1)(A) makes those same two constraints applicable in an Arizona federal court. Consequently, **A**, not **B**, is right.

F. Double closer: "Going to the limits of due process"

No verbiage is more common in personal jurisdiction cases than the shibboleth that "our long-arm statute goes to the limits of due process." But what does this verbiage *mean*? It would seem to mean, "in our state, if it would be constitutional to exercise jurisdiction, the long-arm statute authorizes the court to do so." Or, put another way, that the scope of jurisdiction under the statute is the same as the scope of the court's constitutional reach under the Due Process Clause.

In some states, this is true. California, for example, has a simple long-arm statute, which provides that its courts can exercise jurisdiction "on any basis not inconsistent with the Constitution of this state or of the United States." Cal. Civ. Proc. Code §410.10. Here, the statute really does "go to the

---

9. See Glannon, *Civil Procedure: Examples & Explanations* 542 n.1 (7th ed.).

limits of due process," in that it authorizes all jurisdiction that is constitutionally permissible.

But many states don't have long-arm statutes like California's. Instead, they have "enumerated act" long-arm statutes that authorize jurisdiction if the defendant has done certain acts in the state, such as transacting business, contracting to supply goods, insuring a risk, or committing a tortious act in the state. In these states, it's a little unclear what a court means when it says that the long-arm statute "goes to the limits of due process." Yet, it just *can't mean* that anything constitutional goes. If it did, the specific provisions of the statute would simply be irrelevant, wouldn't they?

Consider the following question, which illustrates the problem with interpreting all long-arm statutes to "go to the limits of due process."

QUESTION 7. The limits of *"the limits of due process."*   Perrone, an Acadia resident, sues Margules, from Montana, in an Acadia state court for defamation. He claims that Margules called Acme Corporation, an Acadia company that was planning to hire Perrone, and made false and defamatory statements about his professional abilities that led Acme to decide not to hire him. Margules placed the call from her office in Montana. Assume that Acadia has a long-arm statute that authorizes personal jurisdiction over a defendant who "causes personal injury in this state by a tortious act or omission while physically present within this state." Assume that this is the only statute that might authorize the Acadia court to exercise personal jurisdiction over Perrone. Assume also, however, that the Acadia Supreme Court has held that "our long-arm statute goes to the limits of due process."

A. The court has jurisdiction over Margules, since Acadia interprets its long-arm statute to authorize all constitutionally permissible exercises of personal jurisdiction.

B. Because the Acadia Supreme Court has held that the long-arm statute goes to the limits of due process, it will likely hold that Margules "cause[d] personal injury by a tortious act while physically present in this state."

C. The court will probably conclude that Margules cannot be sued in Acadia for this claim, even though it would be within due process constraints for it to hear the case.

D. The court will probably hold that Margules cannot be sued in Acadia for this claim, because it would exceed due process limits to do so.

ANALYSIS.   The legislature clearly wrote this statute to restrict tort cases to ones in which the defendant was physically in the state when she committed the tortious act. Consequently, **A** just can't be right. If the court, by pronouncing that lofty "limits of due process" language, could eliminate the requirement that the defendant do the act in the state, it would be substituting a California-type statute for the one the Acadia legislature wrote. The Acadia legislature didn't want its courts to hear all the cases it constitutionally could. It deliberately wrote a statute that did not authorize certain cases to be heard in its courts, even if it would be constitutional for the court to hear them. Surely, the courts can't construe away that limitation under the guise of broad statutory construction.

The logic of **B** appears to be that, since the court has held that its statute reaches to the limits of due process, the court will have to interpret the statute to apply. So, it will have to hold that Margules was physically present in the state when he uttered the defamatory statements! This really is putting the cart before the horse. "The statute has to apply, so we have to interpret it, in the face of obviously contrary language, to reach this case." This can't be the law, or Dickens's famous comment would be definitively confirmed.[10] The statute clearly doesn't apply, *and wasn't meant to apply*, to defamatory statements made from Montana.

No, the Acadia courts may interpret their long-arm statutes expansively, but they won't rewrite them to exercise constitutionally permissible jurisdiction that the legislature obviously did not grant. The exercise of jurisdiction over Margules is not allowed by the statute, because he did not do what the statute requires: commit the tortious act while in Acadia. So the court can't hear the case, despite that "limits-of-due-process" language in its previous cases, and despite the fact that it would be constitutional to hear the case. **A** is wrong, too, for the same reason; the Acadia court could not reasonably interpret the statute to apply on these facts. And **D** is wrong because it clearly would be constitutional to exercise jurisdiction over Margules in Arcadia for this act. He has reached into Acadia by calling there to defame Perrone, a deliberate contact that gives rise to this claim.

So, **C** is right, because this is a case that could constitutionally be heard in Acadia (see the discussion on pp. 120-121 following Question 1), but that the legislature has not authorized the Acadia courts to hear.

So what does this "limits of due process" language mean, if it doesn't mean that the court will take jurisdiction over any case that it constitutionally can? Appropriately understood, it means that the court will construe the specific provisions of its long-arm statute as broadly as possible without overreaching constitutional bounds. If language in the statute might be interpreted one way to support jurisdiction, and another to deny it, the court will opt for the broadest interpretation consistent with due process constraints.

---

10. "The law is an ass." Charles Dickens, *Oliver Twist*, Chapter 51, p. 489 (1970).

A second example may help to make the distinction.

QUESTION 8. Double trouble. Ausable Motors Corporation manufactures motors for industrial machinery. It makes its motors in Louisiana, and sells them to various wholesalers, including Sunday River Distributors in Kentucky. Ausable's contract with Sunday River requires Sunday River to solicit sales of Ausable motors in Tennessee, Ohio, Indiana, and Kentucky, and allows Ausable to cancel the contract if Sunday River fails to sell at least one hundred motors in each of these states each year. Sunday River resells a substantial quantity of Ausable motors into Tennessee each year. Twelve of them are sold to Delta Retooling, a company in Nashville, Tennessee. While Lemmon is using an Ausable motor at Delta's Nashville shop, a belt flies off the flywheel and injures his eye. He sues Ausable in Tennessee.

Assume that the Tennessee long-arm statute authorizes jurisdiction for a claim "arising out of the transaction of business within the state," and that the Tennessee courts interpret the Tennessee long-arm statute to "go to the limits of due process."

Ausable moves to dismiss Lemmon's suit for lack of personal jurisdiction.

A. The court will likely conclude that Ausable is subject to personal jurisdiction under the "transacting business" provision of the long-arm statute, and that it would be constitutional to exercise jurisdiction over Ausable.
B. The case will likely be dismissed for failure to satisfy the long-arm statute.
C. The case will likely be dismissed because it would be unconstitutional to exercise personal jurisdiction over Ausable in this case.

ANALYSIS.   C here is very likely wrong. It would probably be constitutionally permissible to sue Ausable in Tennessee in this case. True, it's a stream-of-commerce case, like *Asahi* and *J. McIntyre,* but here Ausable has *required* their buyer to resell in Tennessee. This deliberate effort to serve the Tennessee market would satisfy Justice O'Connor's understanding of purposeful availment. See 480 U.S. at 112 (marketing through a distributor in the state is one example of deliberate efforts to serve the market). And Justices Kennedy (who wrote the plurality opinion in *J. McIntyre Machinery, Ltd. v. Nicastro*) and Breyer (who concurred in *J. McIntyre*) would almost certainly distinguish this case from *J. McIntyre* on the ground that Ausable has deliberately targeted the market for its products in Tennessee by requiring its distributor to resell in that state.

That leaves us to consider whether the "transacting business" provision of Tennessee's long-arm statute is satisfied here. "Transacting business" is hardly a self-defining concept. Ausable has not sold its motors directly in Tennessee. A court that construes this language narrowly might conclude that the legislature meant only to reach defendants who sold goods directly in the state. But that's not the only possible interpretation. Ausable has made active efforts to serve the market for its motors in Tennessee, by requiring Sunday River to solicit sales there. This conduct would suffice under a broad interpretation of the term "transacting business." See, e.g., *Stabiliserungsfonds fur Wein v. Kaiser Stuhl Wine Distrib., Inc.*, 647 F.2d 200 (D.C. 1981) (interpreting "transacting business" statute to authorize jurisdiction over foreign seller that sold in the forum through distributor). And, because the Tennessee courts interpret their long-arm statute to go to the limits of due process, it will interpret the statute as broadly as it can without exceeding constitutional bounds.

Here, such a broad interpretation would be within the constitutional bounds, as discussed immediately above. So the Tennessee court, which interprets the provisions of its jurisdictional statutes as broadly as constitutionally permissible, would conclude that Ausable had "transacted business" in Tennessee. That, I think, is what it means to interpret a long-arm statute to "go to the limits of due process": to choose, where the statute might be interpreted narrowly or broadly, the broadest interpretation that is consistent with constitutional limits. Thus, the most likely answer here is **A**.

✵ Glannon's Picks

1. Bad words	C
2. Gone, but not forgotten	A
3. Not gone, and not forgotten	B
4. Here and there	C
5. Shades of *Gray*	B
6. Dueling amendments	A
7. The limits of "the limits of due process"	C
8. Double trouble	A

8

Home and Away: Litigating Objections to the Court's Jurisdiction

~

There once was a nudist named Clarence
Who was caught out in public quite bare once.
When brought in for exposure
He sought to bring closure
By making . . . a special appearance!

~

CHAPTER OVERVIEW

A. Methods of challenging jurisdiction: The special appearance and the motion to dismiss
B. Defendant's dilemma: Appealing jurisdictional objections
C. Another way to go: Challenging jurisdiction in the enforcing court
D. Double dipping: Direct and collateral challenges to jurisdiction
E. A Killer Closer: Personal jurisdiction in the enforcing court
✦ Glannon's Picks

Given the generality of tests like "minimum contacts" and "fair and reasonable," it will frequently be less than obvious that the court has personal jurisdiction over the defendant. In such cases, the defendant will likely object to personal jurisdiction, and the court will have to hear and determine the issue. This chapter discusses the procedures the defendant may use to raise objections to jurisdiction, either in the court where she has been sued, or in a court that is asked to enforce another court's judgment that may have been rendered without proper jurisdiction.

A. Methods of challenging jurisdiction: The special appearance and the motion to dismiss

The natural inclination of the defendant who thinks she's been sued in the wrong court is to protest. You'd feel the same way. "Hey, wait! This case doesn't belong here; throw it out." All court systems provide a procedure for defendants to appear at the outset of the case and object to the court's exercising jurisdiction over them. The older, common law approach was the "special appearance." The defendant would "appear specially" for the sole purpose of objecting to the court's jurisdiction. The court would hear the objection, and dismiss if it agreed that it lacked personal jurisdiction over the defendant. If it disagreed, of course, it would proceed with the case.

However, when the defendant made a special appearance, she had to be careful not to raise any issue other than personal jurisdiction. Even before *Pennoyer*, courts held that a defendant may waive her objection to personal jurisdiction. Many courts held that a defendant who appeared to object to jurisdiction had to confine her appearance to that purpose. If she strayed beyond arguing jurisdiction, she was deemed to be litigating the case on the merits, which implied that she accepted the court's authority to adjudicate it. For example, if the defendant appeared and objected to personal jurisdiction and also argued that the complaint failed to state a claim on which relief could be granted, she had joined issue on the merits, and that implied submission to the court's jurisdiction. She would be deemed, by adding the failure-to-state-a-claim objection (or any objection other than to jurisdiction) to have "appeared generally," waiving her special appearance and accepting the court's power to hear the case.

Thus, a good many older (and some recent) cases conclude, based on some ill-considered argument by defense counsel, that the defendant had fallen over the line and consented to jurisdiction. See, e.g., *Davis v. Eighth Judicial Dist. of Nevada*, 629 P.2d 1209 (Nev. 1981) (defendants waived special appearance by opposing plaintiff's motion to amend complaint). Some states even held that a defendant who failed to specifically designate its appearance as a "special appearance" had forfeited the objection and consented to suit in the state.

A hundred years ago, the special appearance was the standard procedure for challenging personal jurisdiction at the outset of a case. However, the federal courts, in the Federal Rules of Civil Procedure, and an increasing number of states, have adopted a more flexible approach. Under the Federal Rules, and in states that have modeled their procedural rules on them, a defendant who objects to personal jurisdiction may raise her objection to jurisdiction before answering the complaint, by moving to dismiss for lack of personal jurisdiction. Alternatively, she may raise the objection in her answer to the complaint instead.

The Federal Rules approach is more flexible because, when the defendant asserts the objection, she may combine it with other objections or defenses without waiving her objection to the court's jurisdiction. For example, she might move to dismiss for lack of personal jurisdiction and also for failure to state a claim. She would not lose her objection to jurisdiction by raising it with the objection that challenges the case on the merits. Similarly, in a jurisdiction that uses this approach, she could answer the complaint, raising *all of her defenses on the merits,* and include her objection to personal jurisdiction in her answer. Combining the challenge to personal jurisdiction with other defenses would not waive the objection to personal jurisdiction.

However, there's a trap for the unwary under the Federal Rules too. While objections to jurisdiction may be combined with others, they must be raised in the defendant's *first response* to the complaint. She may move to dismiss for lack of personal jurisdiction and for other reasons. She may answer, raising defenses to the merits of the claim and objecting to personal jurisdiction. But she may not, for example, respond first by moving to dismiss for failure to state a claim, and later answer the complaint, including an objection to personal jurisdiction. By failing to include the jurisdictional objection in her first response to the complaint (here, her motion to dismiss for failure to state a claim), she would waive the objection to jurisdiction. Similarly, if she answers the complaint without including her jurisdictional objection, she waives it as well. (The technicalities of this are explored more fully in Chapter 17 on pre-answer motions.)

This rule, that the defendant waives the objection by failing to assert it right away, prevents the defendant from gaming the system. If she could raise the objection to jurisdiction at any time, she might keep the objection in her back pocket, and see how the litigation goes. If her case turns sour on the merits, she might then assert her objection to jurisdiction, in an effort to get the case dismissed after substantial litigation has taken place. The raise-it-or-lose-it rule assures that, if no personal jurisdiction objection is raised at the outset, the court will have authority to hear the case.

In many states today, the rules of civil procedure are modeled on the Federal Rules. In these states, the more flexible motion to dismiss for lack of personal jurisdiction has replaced the common law special appearance. Students frequently believe that a defendant has a choice to use either procedure within a single state. That isn't right; a state will either continue to use the common law special appearance approach, or have changed its procedural rules to adopt the Federal Rules approach. If it has adopted the more flexible federal approach, the defendant should raise the objection by moving to dismiss for lack of jurisdiction, or put it in her answer. If the state continues to follow the common law approach, the defendant should — very carefully — enter a special appearance to challenge personal jurisdiction.

Here's a question to test the point. I've tried to make it a little tricky, but if you've read the discussion above it should be easy.

QUESTION 1. Something special. Ito, a stockbroker, lives and works in Massachusetts, a state that has modeled its rules of procedure after the Federal Rules. He is served in Massachusetts with the complaint and summons in an action Ervin has brought against him in a Nevada court, seeking recovery for misrepresentation in the sale of stock. Assume that Nevada requires a defendant to challenge jurisdiction through the traditional special appearance. Ito's attorney files a special appearance in the Nevada court objecting to the court's jurisdiction. A week later, while the objection is pending, he files a motion to dismiss claiming that the case was not filed within the applicable statute of limitations. The court would

A. hear and decide the jurisdictional objection, since Ito has properly raised the objection by making a special appearance.
B. conclude that Ito had waived his objection to personal jurisdiction by raising the limitations issue.
C. consider both objections, since it would apply the Massachusetts approach to raising jurisdictional objections.
D. conclude that Ito had improperly raised his jurisdictional objection, but still consider it and dismiss if it appears that there is no proper basis for jurisdiction over him.

ANALYSIS. By the way, here's a quick point on exam-taking strategy, which I may already have made but is worth repeating. The question asks you to assume that Nevada follows the special appearance approach. Suppose that you happen to know that Nevada *doesn't* follow that approach anymore? What would you do in answering the question?

Remember that the professor is the boss in writing her exam. If she asks you to assume that under Nevada law the court orders the immediate execution in the public square of a defendant who objects to jurisdiction, you should answer the question on that assumption. I wouldn't recommend answering on the basis of personal knowledge that Nevada actually uses a different rule. This isn't the real world, it's a constructed hypothetical and should be answered on its own terms.

The real loser here is **C**. The Nevada court will, of course, apply its own rules concerning the procedure for raising jurisdictional objections in a Nevada law suit. And, the question indicates, its rule is that a defendant waives her objection to personal jurisdiction, even if she comes into court and raises it, if she also raises other arguments. That is just what Ito did here; he objected to jurisdiction, but then raised a defense on the merits as well. True, he raised the objection to personal jurisdiction first, but under (the assumed) Nevada law any response that appears to litigate the substantive issues in the case waives the special appearance and consents to the jurisdiction of the court. So **A** isn't quite right; although Ito properly made a special appearance, his later motion raising the limitations issue waives his objection to jurisdiction. Ito should have waited to make his second motion until the personal jurisdiction issue was resolved.

D is interesting. Might the court agree that Ito had made a procedural misstep, but still consider the jurisdictional issue, if it appears that the court lacks a basis for requiring Ito to defend in Nevada? Almost certainly not. The point of the special appearance rule is that an appearance that contests any issue other than jurisdiction is a consent to the court's jurisdiction. Thus, even if Ito has no minimum contacts with Nevada, and there is no other basis for suing him there, his counsel's in-court conduct of arguing to the merits constitutes a voluntary submission to the court's jurisdiction. Unlike an objection to the court's subject matter jurisdiction, the personal jurisdiction objection may be waived. The very point of the special appearance rule is that the defendant waives it by combining it with other objections. Consequently, the court need not consider whether there is some other basis for exercising jurisdiction over Ito. **B** is the best answer. By the procedural faux pas of asserting the limitations objection, Ito has waived his objection to personal jurisdiction and the court will proceed to hear the case.

It is true that, if Ito's lawyer had filed the same two objections in a state that uses the Federal Rules approach, his objection to personal jurisdiction would not be waived. But he didn't. The special appearance approach is more restrictive, and when in Nevada, you have to do as the Nevadans do.

B. Defendant's dilemma: Appealing jurisdictional objections

So, the defendant, if he does it right, can come into the court where the case is filed and object to jurisdiction. Ito, for example, if he navigates the special appearance rules carefully, could raise his objection in the Nevada court and have the judge decide it before considering the merits of the case. Suppose that he does, and the court rules that it has jurisdiction over him. What should Ito do next?

If the court holds that Ito is subject to jurisdiction, it will naturally proceed to litigate the claim. If Ito stalks off in a huff and refuses to participate — "defaults," in the language of civil procedure — the court will enter a default judgment for the plaintiff, which will very likely be enforceable in that state or in others. (More on that later.) You wouldn't advise Ito to do that. Instead, you might suggest that he take an immediate appeal of the judge's finding that he is subject to jurisdiction there. If he could get the Nevada appellate court to reverse the trial judge's ruling, and order the case dismissed, he would at least avoid litigating the merits of the underlying claim in Nevada.

Thinking of a law suit as a time line, Ito would rather obtain review of the jurisdictional finding at Point **A** rather than having to litigate the case on the merits and then appeal (if he loses on the merits) at the much later Point **B**. If he can't take an immediate appeal, he will end up doing exactly what he believes he shouldn't have to: litigating in the Nevada court. In many cases, this could take several years, and involve expensive discovery and a full trial on the merits.

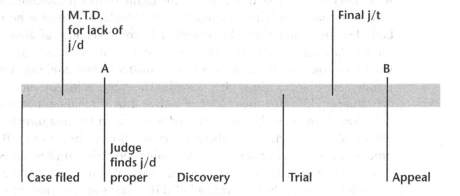

Some states do allow a defendant to immediately appeal the trial court's decision that it has personal jurisdiction over the defendant. But other states, and the federal courts, take the view that this decision is "interlocutory" — part of an ongoing process in the trial court — that cannot be reviewed until the case is litigated to a final judgment in the trial court. See, e.g., *IHT Corp. v. Paragon Cutlery Co.*, 794 A.2d 651, 653 (Me. 2002). There's a good argument for this no-interlocutory-appeal approach. A trial judge makes many decisions in the course of a case. One of the parties — the one who loses on the issue — probably objects to most of these. If the loser could appeal each such decision, the case would bounce back and forth between the trial and the appellate courts repeatedly, causing delay and expense to the parties. And remember that many of those decisions along the way will not end up being crucial to the outcome of the case. After all, most cases settle. And the party who loses on one issue may still win the case on another. For example, the court might hold that it has jurisdiction over Ito, but later accept his argument that the limitations period for the claim had passed. If so, he would have no reason to seek review of the jurisdictional decision. For a variety of reasons, many contested issues fall by the wayside before the case is resolved, so it may not be wise to allow immediate review.

So, the answer here is that the answer varies from jurisdiction to jurisdiction. In some states, Ito could obtain immediate review of the trial judge's decision that he is subject to jurisdiction, without having to litigate the merits of the case in the trial court first. In others, and in the federal courts, he would have to litigate the case on the merits in the trial court and then appeal the jurisdictional finding if he loses. In these courts, however, he does not waive his objection by litigating the case in the trial court. (That would be a tough rule, wouldn't it, since once the trial court finds that it has jurisdiction, Ito really has no choice but to stay and litigate the case.) If he loses the case on the merits, he may still appeal the jurisdiction question at Point **B**, after the case reaches final judgment.

Let's see if we can illustrate this with a thorny question.

QUESTION 2. Appealing options.   Assume that Ervin brings his action for fraudulent misrepresentation against Ito in Emporia, a state that follows the Federal Rules approach to jurisdictional objections and does not allow interlocutory appeals of jurisdictional rulings. Ito, believing that the court lacks personal jurisdiction over him, answers Ervin's complaint, denying the allegations of fraud, raising a statute of limitations defense, and objecting to the court's exercise of personal jurisdiction over him for the claim.

The court holds a hearing on Ito's jurisdictional objection, and rules that he is subject to jurisdiction for Ervin's claim. Consequently, it refuses to dismiss the case. Ito therefore defends the case on the merits. After trial, the jury concludes that his representations were fraudulent, that the suit was not barred by the statute of limitations, and awards damages to Ervin. Final judgment is entered for Ervin.

A. Ito may not appeal the jurisdictional ruling. He waived his objection to personal jurisdiction by raising it in the answer with other defenses on the merits.

B. Ito may not appeal the jurisdictional ruling. He waived his objection by litigating the case on the merits. He should have defaulted, allowed a final default judgment to enter for Ervin, and appealed on the ground that the court lacked jurisdiction to render it.

C. Ito may appeal the jurisdictional ruling. If the appellate court concludes that he was not subject to jurisdiction in Emporia for Ervin's claim, it will order the case dismissed. Ervin will have to bring a new action

> in a state that does have jurisdiction over Ito for the claim, and relitigate the case.
>
> **D.** Ito may appeal the jurisdictional ruling. If the appellate court concludes that he was not subject to jurisdiction in Emporia, it will order the case dismissed. However, the parties will not relitigate the case. Ervin will sue Ito in a state that does have jurisdiction over him. That court will enter a judgment based on the findings by the jury in the Emporia suit.

ANALYSIS.   Let's take the options in order. **A** is wrong, because Emporia follows the Federal Rules approach to jurisdictional objections. Under that approach, the defendant need not file a special appearance *or* a pre-answer motion to dismiss for lack of personal jurisdiction. She may choose to answer the complaint, raising all of her defenses and jurisdictional objections together. She does not waive the jurisdictional defense by asserting it in the answer along with defenses on the merits.

   B is wrong too. It reflects the position that the defendant should either abandon her objection to jurisdiction, or stake her whole case on it, by defaulting on the merits, allowing a final judgment to enter, and hoping to convince the appellate court that the trial judge was wrong on jurisdiction. This would put the defendant in a very tough position. Most lawyers would advise their clients not to default, even if it meant abandoning their jurisdictional objection. Losing the chance to litigate the real case — whether Ito committed fraud and injured Ervin — is too great a price to pay for the chance to appeal the objection to jurisdiction. But the courts don't require the defendant to pay that price. After the trial judge refuses to dismiss, Ito may stay, defend the merits of the fraud allegations in the trial court, and (if he loses on the merits) appeal after final judgment, claiming that the court had no power to make him litigate in Emporia.

   So Ito may appeal, even though he stayed and litigated the fraud case after the judge decided that he was subject to jurisdiction in Emporia. But what will the appellate court do if it determines that the trial judge was wrong? It will have to dismiss the case. If Ito was not subject to jurisdiction, then the court below had no authority to hear the case. If the court had no power to proceed, its proceedings are invalid. The appellate court will order the case dismissed for lack of personal jurisdiction over the defendant.

   So **C** is right; Ervin will have to start over from scratch (risking, of course, statute of limitations problems). The court in the new action will not fashion a judgment based on the findings in the Emporia suit (as **D** suggests). To do so would be to treat them as valid findings. If the court had no authority to render them they are not valid, and cannot bind Ito in the new action.

C. Another way to go: Challenging jurisdiction in the enforcing court

A defendant sued away from home has another option if she believes that the court lacks jurisdiction to adjudicate the claim. She may ignore the suit entirely. Suppose that Ito, sued by Ervin in Emporia, never moves to dismiss, never appears specially, simply ignores the law suit. What will happen?

The court will very likely assume that Ito has no defense to the claim, and enter a default judgment for Ervin on the claim. But who cares? If Ito has no property in Emporia, and no plans to go there personally, Ervin won't be able to collect the judgment there. He will have to come to Ito's state to enforce the judgment. This is often done by bringing an action for a "judgment on the judgment" in the enforcing state, to convert the Emporia judgment into a judgment of the enforcing state. Once Ervin obtains such a judgment in the state where he seeks to enforce the judgment, he can invoke its judgment-collection procedures to collect the judgment from Ito.

Suppose, for example, that Ito lives in the state of Acadia, and has property there that could be sold to satisfy Ervin's judgment. An Acadia court would not order "execution" on an Emporia judgment, that is, the use of its court procedures to collect the Emporia judgment from Ito's assets. Acadia courts only enforce Acadia judgments. So, Ervin would have to bring a suit in the courts of Acadia, asking the court to enter an Acadia judgment on the Emporia judgment. This is a new law suit; Ervin's the plaintiff, Ito's the defendant. Ito will be served with process in the enforcement action and have an opportunity to raise any defenses he may have. States generally have to honor each other's judgments, under the Full Faith and Credit Clause of the United States Constitution. Acadia would be bound, under the Full Faith and Credit Clause, to recognize the Emporia judgment by entering an Acadia judgment recognizing it. Once that has been done, Ervin has an Acadia judgment against an Acadia defendant, and can use local court procedures to have Ito's assets sold to satisfy his judgment.[1]

However, states do not automatically honor all judgments of other states under the Full Faith and Credit Clause. A defendant in Ito's position can raise certain narrow defenses to enforcing the Emporia judgment ... including the defense that the court that rendered the judgment lacked the power to do so. Even before *Pennoyer v. Neff,* courts allowed judgment debtors to resist enforcement of judgments on the ground that the court that rendered the judgment lacked personal jurisdiction.

---

1. Many states have adopted statutory procedures for registering judgments of other states, as a simpler alternative to an action on the foreign judgment. See generally Friedenthal, Kane & Miller, *Civil Procedure* 750-751 (4th ed. 1999). Registration statutes still allow a judgment debtor like Ito to raise the same defenses to enforcement that he could raise to an action for judgment on the out-of-state judgment.

In the earlier cases, it was supposed that the [full faith and credit] act gave to all judgments the same effect in other States which they had by law in the State where rendered. But this view was afterwards qualified so as to make the act applicable only when the court rendering the judgment had jurisdiction of the parties and of the subject-matter, and not to preclude an inquiry into the jurisdiction of the court in which the judgment was rendered, or the right of the State itself to exercise authority over the person or the subject-matter.

Pennoyer v. Neff, 95 U.S. 714, 729 (1877).

So, Ervin may bring his Emporia judgment to Acadia to enforce, and Ito may try to convince the court not to enforce it because the Emporia court lacked personal jurisdiction over him. In light of this black letter law, consider the following question.

QUESTION 3. Default positions. Ervin sues Ito, from Acadia, for fraud in a sale of stock. He brings the action in an Emporia court. Emporia uses the common law special appearance approach to challenging personal jurisdiction. Ito is served in Acadia with the complaint and summons in the action. On counsel's advice that he is not subject to jurisdiction in Emporia for this claim, Ito ignores the suit.

After obtaining a default judgment in the action, Ervin brings suit in Acadia, seeking a judgment on the Emporia judgment. Ito is served with the complaint and summons in this enforcement action in Acadia. He appears, and raises the defense that the Emporia court lacked personal jurisdiction over him for Ervin's claim. Consequently, Ito argues, the Emporia judgment is not entitled to full faith and credit.

A. If the Acadia court concludes that the Emporia court had personal jurisdiction over Ito, it will order judgment entered on the Emporia judgment.

B. If the Acadia court concludes that the Emporia court had personal jurisdiction over Ito, it will order Ito to appear and defend the original action in the Emporia court.

C. The Acadia court will not consider whether the Emporia court had personal jurisdiction over Ito, because Ito failed to make a special appearance to challenge jurisdiction in the Emporia court.

D. If the Acadia court concludes that the Emporia court lacked personal jurisdiction over Ito, it will proceed to adjudicate the merits of Ervin's fraud claim.

ANALYSIS. This question illustrates the consequences of the tactical decision to default in the original court (we'll call it the "rendering court," since it renders the original judgment for Ervin) and resist enforcement in another state. The enforcing state — Acadia here — has very few options in this scenario. It may hear evidence and argument on the issue of the rendering court's jurisdiction, and refuse to enter a judgment on the judgment if it concludes that the rendering court lacked the power to render it, that is, if it lacked personal jurisdiction over Ito. But if it concludes that the rendering court did have jurisdiction over Ito, the Full Faith and Credit Clause requires the Acadia court to enforce the judgment. It cannot reopen the merits, or simply refuse to help Ervin collect his judgment against a local resident.

D is again a dog. If the Acadia court concludes that the Emporia court lacked jurisdiction to adjudicate the merits of the fraud claim, it will not proceed to adjudicate that claim itself. Ervin hasn't asked the Acadia court to do that. His action seeks a judgment recognizing his Emporia judgment. If that judgment is entitled to full faith and credit, the Acadia court will award him an Acadia judgment recognizing the Emporia judgment, so that Ervin can use Acadia enforcement procedures to collect it. If that judgment is not entitled to full faith and credit, the Acadia court will refuse to enter a judgment on it. But the Acadia suit is not about the merits of the fraud claim; it's about the validity of the Emporia judgment.

C is highly seductive. It is true that, in Emporia, a defendant challenges the court's jurisdiction by filing a special appearance. Since Ito failed to do that, hasn't he waived his objection to the Emporia court's jurisdiction? No. A defendant who *stays away entirely* does not waive his objection to personal jurisdiction. He may still raise it "collaterally" when Ervin obtains a default judgment in the rendering court and brings it to Acadia to enforce. That judgment is only entitled to full faith and credit in other states if the rendering court had the power to render it. And it only had that power if it had personal jurisdiction over the defendant. So here, Ito may challenge the validity of the judgment in the Acadia court by arguing that the Emporia court lacked personal jurisdiction over him.

B suggests that, if the Acadia court concludes that the Emporia court had jurisdiction, it will order Ito to appear in the Emporia court and defend the action on the merits. This won't happen either. The Emporia suit is over. Final judgment has entered for Ervin. If the judgment is valid, the Acadia court must enforce it. If it isn't, it won't. But it cannot do what **B** suggests, tell Ito that he made a mistake, and give him the chance to undo it in the rendering court. If the Emporia court had jurisdiction over Ito, its judgment is valid, even though rendered by default, and Acadia must enforce it. **A** is the right answer.

Imagine what would happen if **B** were right. Defendants sued in another state would simply default, and wait for the plaintiff to bring the judgment to their home state for enforcement. Then, they would object on jurisdictional grounds. If the court agrees, great; if it disagrees, they would simply have to appear belatedly in the rendering court to litigate the merits. That would be nice for defendants, but frustrating for plaintiffs and an intolerable waste for courts.

So the question illustrates the great risk that the defendant takes by choosing to challenge jurisdiction collaterally, in the enforcing court, rather than directly in the rendering court. If her guess about personal jurisdiction turns out to be wrong, she will have lost her chance to defend the case on the merits. The default judgment will be valid, and the enforcing court will have no choice but to honor it.

Let's try a variation on the last scenario.

QUESTION 4. Late, or never? Ervin sues Ito, from Acadia, for fraud in a sale of stock. He brings the action in an Emporia court. Assume that Emporia uses the Federal Rules approach to challenging personal jurisdiction. Ito is served in Acadia with the complaint and summons in the action. He answers the complaint, denying that his representations were fraudulent and denying that they injured Ervin. The case is litigated, and ultimately tried to a jury, which finds for Ervin. The judge enters a judgment for $50,000 for Ervin. However, Ito has no assets in Emporia, and does not pay the judgment.

Ervin now brings suit in Acadia, seeking a judgment on the Emporia judgment. Ito appears and raises the defense that the Emporia court lacked personal jurisdiction over him for Ervin's claim.

A. The Acadia court may consider whether the Emporia court had jurisdiction over Ito, since Ito did not litigate the issue in the Emporia court.

B. The Acadia court may consider whether the Emporia court had jurisdiction over Ito. Under the Federal Rules approach, Ito could have raised the issue in the Emporia court, but didn't have to.

C. The Acadia court may not consider whether the Emporia court had personal jurisdiction over Ito, because Ito waived his objection to jurisdiction in the Emporia court.

D. The Acadia court may consider whether the Emporia court had personal jurisdiction over Ito. Although Ito waived the issue in the Emporia court, he has not waived it in the Acadia court.

ANALYSIS. In this example, Ito appeared and litigated the case on the merits in Emporia. He lost. Ervin then brings his judgment to Acadia to enforce, and Ito argues that it is not entitled to full faith and credit since the Emporia court lacked jurisdiction over him. **A** takes the position that this is all right, since Ito never litigated personal jurisdiction in Emporia.

But consider what a waste it would be to allow the parties to litigate the entire case and reach a resolution, only to have it undermined in the enforcing court for lack of jurisdiction. If there's a problem with jurisdiction, it ought to be raised and decided in the rendering court before litigating the merits, not in the enforcing court *after* litigating the merits. This is why courts have such strict rules about raising objections to personal jurisdiction or losing them. Here, Ito answered the complaint and litigated the fraud claim without objecting to personal jurisdiction. When he did that, he *waived his objection* to personal jurisdiction. Under the Federal Rules approach, that objection may be raised in the answer to the complaint (if no pre-answer motion is filed) or in a motion to dismiss before answering. But if it isn't raised at the outset by one of these responses, the objection is waived. **B** is wrong; the Federal Rules may be a bit more flexible about the methods for raising a jurisdictional objection, but they still require that the defendant raise it at the outset of the suit, or waive it by the failure to assert it. Fed. R. Civ. P. 12(h).

Once waived, the objection is lost. So **A** is wrong. Ito can lose his personal jurisdiction objection by *not* litigating it, as well as by litigating it. And once lost, it is lost not only in the Emporia court, but in any enforcing court as well. So **D** is wrong too. Once Ito waives the objection, it can't be resuscitated to resist enforcement later in another state. If this were not so, Ito could litigate the merits in Emporia, and hold his objection to jurisdiction to litigate later in Acadia. This would prove extremely wasteful, should the Acadia court conclude that the Emporia court that rendered the judgment (after full litigation) lacked personal jurisdiction to do so. Better to force the objection out at the outset, in the rendering court, in this situation, by applying the principle that a failure to raise it constitutes a waiver of the objection. **C** rules the roost.

Here's another variation.

> **QUESTION 5. Variation.** Ervin sues Ito, from Acadia, for fraud in a sale of stock. He brings the action in an Emporia court. Assume that Emporia uses the Federal Rules approach to challenging personal jurisdiction. Ito defaults.
>
> Ervin now brings suit in Acadia, seeking a judgment on the Emporia judgment. Ito is served with the complaint and summons in the action in Acadia. He appears, and argues that the Emporia court lacked personal jurisdiction over him, and that he never made false representations to Ervin about the stock.
>
> **A.** Ito may raise both defenses in the Acadia enforcement action, since he did not litigate them in the Emporia court.

B. Ito may raise both defenses in the Acadia enforcement action, but the court will only hear the substantive defense to the fraud claim if it determines that the Emporia court lacked jurisdiction over Ito.

C. Ito may not raise either defense in the Acadia enforcement action, because he waived them by defaulting in the Emporia action.

D. Ito may raise the personal jurisdiction defense in the Acadia enforcement action, but not the substantive defense to the fraud claim.

ANALYSIS.   This is more a recap than anything else. Here, Ito defaulted in the original action, and now raises jurisdictional and substantive defenses in the enforcing court. He may assert the defense of lack of personal jurisdiction, because the judgment isn't valid if the Emporia court lacked jurisdiction over him. And he hasn't waived that defense, because he never appeared in the Emporia action. So he's preserved his right to object in the enforcing court based on lack of jurisdiction.

But he won't be able to litigate the merits of the fraud claim in the Acadia enforcement action. Thus, **A** and **B** are wrong, because the only issue Ito can litigate in the Acadia action is whether the Emporia judgment is valid. If Ito wanted to raise the defense that his statements were not fraudulent, there was only one place to do it: in the original action. His default there waives all defenses in the action, other than jurisdictional ones.[2] So **D** is the best answer; Ito may resist enforcement based on lack of jurisdiction in the rendering court, but not based on any defense to the underlying fraud claim.

It's still possible, however, that he will get a chance to defend the claim on the merits. If the Acadia court determines that there was no jurisdiction to render the original judgment, and refuses to enforce it, Ervin will likely bring a new action — probably in Acadia, since Ito's assets are there. Ervin would be able to bring a new suit on the merits, because the first one, in which the court lacked jurisdiction, is viewed as a nullity. Ervin can't enforce it, and Ito isn't bound by his default in that suit. It has no legal effect. Ervin will have to start over, if the limitations period hasn't passed and he can find a court that does have jurisdiction over Ito. If he does, Ito will presumably appear and answer the fraud allegations, and the parties will end up litigating the merits of the claim in this later action.

Here's another, fairly tricky twist on Ito's troubles. You actually don't have enough information (from this chapter, anyway) to answer it, but consider what the answer *ought to be* based on common sense.

---

2. This is a bit of an overgeneralization. Ito might be able to raise certain other limited objections to enforcement that could be asserted in the rendering court as well, such as fraud on the court in obtaining the judgment.

> **QUESTION 6. Procedural blasphemy.** Ervin sues Ito, from Acadia, for fraud in a sale of stock. He brings the action in Emporia. The Emporia Rules, which are modeled on the Federal Rules of Civil Procedure, provide that "[w]henever it appears, by suggestion of the parties or otherwise, that the court lacks jurisdiction over the subject matter, the court shall dismiss."
>
> Ito answers Ervin's fraud complaint, and the parties litigate the merits. Ervin wins, obtaining a jury verdict for $50,000.
>
> Ervin now brings suit in Acadia, seeking a judgment on the Emporia judgment. Ito is served with the complaint and summons in the action in Acadia. He appears, and argues that the Emporia court lacked subject matter jurisdiction over the action, because the claim was really for an accounting, and therefore had to be brought in the Emporia equity court, not the superior court.
>
> A. Ito may raise this defense, because he did not litigate subject matter jurisdiction in the original action.
> B. Ito may raise this defense, because objections to subject matter jurisdiction are never waived.
> C. Ito may raise this defense because, as *Pennoyer* held, full faith and credit only requires the Acadia court to enforce the judgment if "the court rendering the judgment had jurisdiction of the parties and of the subject-matter, and [does not] preclude an inquiry into the jurisdiction of the court in which the judgment was rendered. . . ."
> D. Ito may not challenge subject matter jurisdiction in the Acadia enforcement action.

ANALYSIS. The quote from *Pennoyer v. Neff* makes it clear that subject matter jurisdiction, like personal jurisdiction, may be attacked "collaterally." But we saw in Question 4 that where the plaintiff appears and litigates the case on the merits in the original action, he waives his objection to personal jurisdiction. Here, Ito appeared and defended on the merits in the Emporia court. By doing so, did he waive his objection to *subject matter* jurisdiction?

It is basic, almost religious dogma in civil procedure that subject matter jurisdiction is never waived, that the parties or the court can always raise it, and that a court that lacks jurisdiction must always dismiss. So the answer here may seem blasphemous. Courts do not usually allow a collateral attack on subject matter jurisdiction, if the defendant litigated the merits in the original suit. If the defendant appears and litigates the case through final judgment in the rendering court, she will almost always be precluded from resisting enforcement of the judgment elsewhere on the ground that the rendering court lacked subject matter jurisdiction over the case. *Chicot County Drainage Dist. v. Baxter State Bank,* 308 U.S. 371, 376-378 (1940);

Restatement (Second) of Judgments, §12. Even with subject matter jurisdiction, enough is enough. Ito could make a direct attack on subject matter jurisdiction at any time during the litigation in the Emporia trial court. Or, he could appeal to the Emporia appellate court, arguing that the trial court lacked subject matter jurisdiction. But he may not litigate the merits in Emporia (hoping for a favorable verdict) and then try to undo the judgment in the Acadia enforcement action on the ground that the Emporia court lacked subject matter jurisdiction.

So we should qualify that broad language from *Pennoyer*. The enforcing court may inquire into the jurisdiction of the rendering court, but generally only if the defendant didn't waive the issue by litigating the case on the merits in the rendering court. **D** takes the Full Faith and Credit prize here.

D.   Double dipping: Direct and collateral challenges to jurisdiction

So, we've seen that the defendant has several options in challenging the jurisdiction of the rendering court. She may challenge it at the outset of the action, by special appearance or an objection in the rendering court. Or, if she's a risk taker, she can ignore the action in the rendering court and resist enforcement of the resulting default judgment when the plaintiff tries to enforce it in another state.

So, why not try them both? Consider the following example.

QUESTION 7. If at first you don't succeed. . . . Ervin sues Ito, from Acadia, for fraud in a sale of stock. He brings the action in an Emporia court. Ito appears specially in the Emporia court to argue that the Emporia court lacks personal jurisdiction over him for Ervin's claim. The court holds a hearing on Ito's objection and rules that he is subject to jurisdiction in Emporia for the claim. Ito, unconvinced, defaults, and the court enters a default judgment for Ervin.

Ervin now brings suit in Acadia, seeking a judgment on the Emporia judgment. Ito appears, and raises the defense that the Emporia court lacked personal jurisdiction over him for Ervin's claim.

A. The court will not determine whether Ito was subject to jurisdiction in Emporia, but Ito will be able to take an appeal on that issue in Acadia, since he defaulted on the merits in the Emporia trial court.
B. The court will enforce the judgment without allowing Ito to relitigate the jurisdictional defense.

C. The court will consider whether Ito was subject to jurisdiction in Emporia, because Ito made a proper special appearance in Emporia and defaulted on the merits in the Emporia action.

D. None of the above is true.

ANALYSIS.   Although the introduction doesn't give you the black letter on this, you must have had an uncomfortable feeling that this tactic wasn't going to work for Ito. It shouldn't, should it? He already had his "bite at the apple" on personal jurisdiction. He litigated the issue in the Emporia court and lost on it. This looks like sour grapes, or an effort to try again in a forum that may be more favorably disposed towards a local resident.

A has a slight patina of credibility. We saw earlier that a party who litigated and lost on jurisdiction has a right to appeal that issue and try to get it reversed. But that right allows Ito to appeal the Emporia trial judge's ruling to an *Emporia* appellate court, not save it up and appeal it in the enforcing court. If a judge in an Emporia court makes an incorrect finding, the Emporia court system is the one to correct it; the Acadia appellate courts have no authority to review rulings of the Emporia trial courts. (Imagine what a mess it would be if New York appellate judges started reviewing the rulings of California trial judges. We'd have just the type of internecine strife that the Full Faith and Credit Clause was meant to avert.)

C isn't right either. While it is generally true that a defendant may challenge jurisdiction "collaterally" in the enforcing court, she may not do so if she appeared and litigated the issue in the original action, as Ito did in this example. Civil procedure has a vexing doctrine called "collateral estoppel" that bars parties from relitigating issues that were litigated and resolved between them in a prior proceeding. See Chapter 24 for some vexing analysis of this vexing doctrine. **B** is right; since Ito appeared and litigated whether the Emporia court had jurisdiction over him in the Emporia action, the Acadia court will estop him from litigating that issue again when Ervin sues to enforce the judgment. Once is enough; if Ito really wants to litigate the jurisdiction issue in an Acadia court, he's going to have to default in Emporia—a huge price to pay—to preserve his right to do so.

E.   A Killer Closer: Personal jurisdiction in the enforcing court

Closers are designed to be tough. So a "Killer Closer" should be even worse. Closers are optional. You have no one to blame but yourself.

QUESTION 8. Impersonal jurisdiction. Ervin sues Ito, from Acadia, for fraud in a sale of stock. He brings the action in an Emporia court. Ito defends the case on the merits and loses; the case ends in a judgment for Ervin for $50,000.

Ervin now brings suit in New Mexico, where Ito (who lives in Acadia) owns a valuable two-week time share at a resort. Ervin seeks a judgment on the Emporia judgment, so that he can obtain a New Mexico court order for sale of the time share to satisfy his judgment. Ito appears and objects to the New Mexico court exercising personal jurisdiction over him for Ervin's claim. He argues that he has no minimum contacts with New Mexico that gave rise to this claim, and that he is not subject to general in personam jurisdiction in New Mexico based on owning a time share there. If the judge agrees that the New Mexico court has no basis to exercise personal jurisdiction over Ito for Ervin's underlying fraud claim, she will likely

A. dismiss the enforcement action.
B. enter a judgment on the judgment, and allow Ervin to invoke its procedures for collecting on the judgment by selling Ito's property there.
C. attach the time share, and require Ervin to bring an action on the judgment in Acadia (where Ito is subject to personal jurisdiction based on domicile) ordering its sale to satisfy the Emporia judgment.
D. transfer the enforcement action to a state in which Ito would be subject to personal jurisdiction on the fraud claim.

ANALYSIS. First, **D** is clearly wrong. A New Mexico court cannot transfer cases to the courts of other states; they are independent court systems that don't take orders from the New Mexico judges.

Just to focus the analysis, let's recap the problem. The suit is brought in Emporia, leading to a final judgment for Ervin. He takes his judgment to New Mexico, and asks the New Mexico court to recognize it and assist him in collecting from Ito's assets there. But Ito himself is not subject to personal jurisdiction in New Mexico for the fraud claim, which arose out of conduct somewhere else. Should we care?

No, due process of law does not require that Ito have minimum contacts that give rise to the fraud claim in the state *where Ervin goes to collect.* Due process requires that Ito have some appropriate relation — minimum contacts, or some other basis for jurisdiction — to the court that *adjudicates his liability on the fraud claim itself.* If he does, and the court fairly adjudicates the claim and enters a valid judgment for Ervin on that claim, the judgment then becomes enforceable wherever Ito has assets that can be sold.

There need not be personal jurisdiction over Ito for the fraud claim in the enforcing state as well as the rendering state.

> Once it has been determined by a court of competent jurisdiction that the defendant is a debtor of the plaintiff, there would seem to be no unfairness in allowing an action to realize on that debt in a State where the defendant has property, whether or not that State would have jurisdiction to determine the existence of the debt as an original matter.

Shaffer v. Heitner, 433 U.S. 186, 210 n.36 (1977). See also *Lenchysyn v. Pelko Electric Inc.,* 723 N.Y.S.2d 285 (2001).

Thus, Ervin may take his judgment to any state where Ito has assets, and seek enforcement under the Full Faith and Credit Clause. Ito will have to be given notice of the action, so that he can raise any defenses to the enforcement action that are proper, such as lack of jurisdiction in the original suit. But Ervin need not limit the states where he collects on the judgment to those where he could have sued Ito on the original claim under personal jurisdiction analysis. **B** is the best answer to this important, though perhaps befuddling, example.

 Glannon's Picks

1. Something special	B
2. Appealing options	C
3. Default positions	A
4. Late, or never?	C
5. Variation	D
6. Procedural blasphemy	D
7. If at first you don't succeed . . .	B
8. Impersonal jurisdiction	B

9

Due Process and Common Sense: Notice and Service of Process

There once was a young lady named Jessie
Whose divorce from her ex turned quite messy.
When she tried to serve papers
He used all sorts of capers,
And proved harder to find than Loch Nessie.

CHAPTER OVERVIEW

A. Constitutional standards for adequate notice: *Mullane v. Central Hanover Bank*

B. *Pennoyer* perplexities: The separate requirements of notice and personal jurisdiction

C. Some technicalities: What gets served and who does it

D. More technicalities: Serving process on individual defendants in federal cases

E. Service of process on a corporation under Federal Rule 4

F. Waiver of service

G. A modest Closer: Practice for the perplexed

H. Glannon's Picks

W hilethe law — especially civil procedure law — often seems arcane, it usually echoes common sense. It makes sense, for example, for a court that is going to adjudicate a party's rights to let her know it is going to do so. This chapter considers this sensible requirement of adequate notice to a defendant that a lawsuit has been filed against her.

A. Constitutional standards for adequate notice: *Mullane v. Central Hanover Bank*

The Due Process Clause of the Fourteenth Amendment prohibits a state from depriving a person of life, liberty, or property without due process of law. When a court enters a civil judgment against a person, it begins the process of taking the person's property (usually in the form of money). Consequently, the due process clause requires the court to use a fair procedure in entering judgment. Certainly, one component of a fair procedure is to *tell the defendant* that the court is going to adjudicate her rights. Hence, the Due Process Clause requires a court to use a constitutionally adequate means of notifying the defendant that a lawsuit has been commenced against her.

Typically, it is the plaintiff who does the legwork of serving process on the defendant. The statutes or court rules in every state contain detailed provisions governing how this notice of a lawsuit is provided to the defendant. Court rules may authorize various means of serving process. The most obvious is to deliver the initiating papers in the case to the defendant in person, called "personal service of process." Other methods are often authorized as well, though they are less certain to actually inform the defendant about the suit. The service rules may provide, for example, that the papers may be left with someone at the defendant's home or place of business or slipped under the door. Some authorize service to the defendant by certified or ordinary mail. In some circumstances, court rules or statutes may authorize service by publication, by printing a notice of the suit in the legal notices in the local newspaper for several weeks. Such publication notice is sometimes referred to as "constructive service," as opposed to actual delivery of the papers to the defendant.

Which of these methods is constitutionally adequate under the Due Process Clause? Justice Jackson's wise opinion in *Mullane v. Central Hanover Bank & Trust Co.*, 339 U.S. 306 (1950) does not provide a mechanical answer to that question, but instead establishes broad standards for constitutionally adequate notice.

Mullane involved a device called a common trust fund, which allowed a bank to pool a group of small trusts into one common fund, which could be managed more efficiently. Income (or losses) from the trust would then be shared by each smaller trust in proportion to their contributions to the fund. Periodically, the trustee of the fund would file accounts with the court. If the court approved the accounts, its judgment would bar investors from suing the bank for mismanagement. Since this judicial accounting could deprive trust beneficiaries of property — the right to sue the bank for mismanagement — due process required adequate notice to them of the proceeding.

The problem in *Mullane* was that it was difficult to ascertain who all the beneficiaries were. Beneficiaries currently entitled to receive income from the trust were known, and the bank had their addresses in its files. But most trusts have contingent beneficiaries, such as the children or heirs of a beneficiary if the primary beneficiary dies. The bank might not know who these beneficiaries were, and they could change periodically. Perhaps, with a large investment of time by lawyers and investigators, the bank could identify most them, but doing so would eat up the profits of the common trust fund. Many were contingent beneficiaries; that is, they had no current right to receive income from the fund but might later under the terms of the individual trusts. So who did the bank have to tell about the suit and how?

Mullane held that "an elementary and fundamental requirement of due process in any proceeding which is to be accorded finality is notice reasonably calculated, under all the circumstances, to apprise interested parties of the pendency of the action and afford them an opportunity to present their objections." 339 U.S. at 314. What is reasonable in one circumstance would not necessarily satisfy due process in another. On the facts of *Mullane*, several factors reduced the risk of error if notice failed to reach all beneficiaries. First, the statute provided for the appointment of a guardian in the settlement proceeding to represent the interests of all beneficiaries. Second, even if all beneficiaries did not receive notice of the proceeding, many would, and would likely share and represent the interests of all beneficiaries in the settlement of the accounts.

Consequently, the Court in *Mullane* did not require that each individual with an interest in the fund be given personal notice of the action. The question below probes what it *did* require.

QUESTION 1. Unnoticed notice.   In *Mullane v. Central Hanover Bank & Trust Co.*, the Supreme Court held that

A. every person whose interests may be affected by a judicial proceeding is entitled to at least mail notice of the proceeding.

B. every person whose name and address could be ascertained through reasonable investigation must be given individual notice of the proceeding.

C. any person whose interests might be affected by the proceeding must be given notice by in hand service of process.

D. due to the large number of persons whose interests might be affected by the proceedings, notice by publication was sufficient on the facts of the case.

E. None of the above is true.

ANALYSIS.   **A** takes the position that everyone who might be affected by the settlement of the accounts must receive individual notice. If that were true, it would be impossible to settle the accounts of the trust. Even some beneficiaries with a current right to income may be impossible to find; if due process required individual notice to them it couldn't be done. Other people have contingent interests: They might get income in the future, for example, as the heir of a current beneficiary. The bank may not know who these contingent beneficiaries are, though it might be able, with research, to find some of them. Justice Jackson viewed due process as a flexible concept that involves a balance of the importance of the right involved, the risk of an erroneous decision, the cost of providing individual notice, and the likelihood that the absentee's interest would be protected by other parties. He rejected the view that everyone with some interest in the action must be individually notified for it to proceed.

B would impose a lesser burden: to notify the persons whose interests could be ascertained with reasonable investigation. This could be done, but it would be costly, involving legal review of 113 trusts and factual research on the whereabouts of all identified beneficiaries. This would more effectively reach affected persons, but the cost of doing so would likely impose such a severe burden on the plan as to "dissipate its advantages." 339 U.S. at 318. Under the circumstances — including the presence of the guardian appointed to represent the interests of beneficiaries and the actual notice to many of them — the Court held that due process did not require that. Consequently, a beneficiary might never learn of the proceeding, have her right to object to the accounts foreclosed by it, and have no constitutional complaint.

C is also a loser. *Mullane* held that notice by mail is sufficiently likely to actually inform a person of the proceeding to be constitutionally sufficient under most circumstances. In fact, *Mullane* did not hold that anyone had to be notified of the suit by personal service of process — that is, by in-hand delivery of the papers. And **D** fails as well. The Court required at least mail notice of the action to those beneficiaries whose names and addresses were known to the bank, since they could easily and inexpensively be informed of the action. So **E** is right. None of the prior statements is quite true.

With *Mullane's* constitutional standards in mind, consider the following enigma.

QUESTION 2. **Mailing it in.** LeCompte brings suit against Wilkins for battery in state court. His counsel looks up the service of process rules and finds that the rule authorizes service of process by first class mail. He serves the complaint and summons on Wilkins by mailing them, first class, to Wilkins at his home address. If Wilkins raises the objection that service of process was improper, the court will likely

A. reject the argument, because LeCompte used a form of service that was authorized by the state's service of process rules.
B. uphold his objection, because service by first class mail is not constitutionally proper.
C. uphold his objection if LeCompte could have arranged for in-hand service on Wilkins.
D. reject the argument, because service of process by first class mail is constitutionally sufficient.

ANALYSIS. **A** is a great wrong answer, and it is important to recognize why it is wrong. As a lawyer, it is always comforting to argue that you followed the rules, and LeCompte has followed the rule here, which authorized service by mail. But states can't write any rules they want: Their rules for service of process must meet constitutional standards. After all, the bank followed the state service statute in *Mullane*, but the Supreme Court held that, as to some beneficiaries, its method of service was inadequate. So it is never a complete answer that the rule authorizes the method used.

B reflects the position that service of process by first class mail is constitutionally insufficient under *Mullane*. In almost all cases, however, service by first class mail will be upheld under *Mullane*, which described the mails as "an efficient and inexpensive means of communication." 339 U.S. at 319. Indeed, *Mullane* required notice by mail to persons with interests in the trusts whose addresses were within the bank's files. Mail service will almost certainly be upheld. And, if it is constitutionally sufficient, and authorized (as it is here) by the state service rule, it will be upheld, even if LeCompte could have done something even better, such as in-hand service. So **C** also fails. Choose **D**.

Let's try one more question that illustrates the difference between service of process and actual notice. To answer this, look at Rule 60(b) of the Federal Rules of Civil Procedure, and consult your common sense.

QUESTION 3. **Service, but not notice.** LeCompte brings suit against Wilkins for battery in state court. His counsel looks up the service of process rules and finds that the rule authorizes service of process by first class mail. He serves the complaint and summons on Wilkins by mailing them, first class, to Wilkins at his home address. Wilkins brings in his mail, including the mailing from LeCompte's lawyer, and places it unopened on his cluttered kitchen table. Later in the afternoon, his mother mistakenly throws it in the recycling along with a bunch of advertising circulars.

Because Wilkins does not file an answer to the complaint, LeCompte obtains a default judgment against Wilkins. Three months later he begins post-judgment proceedings to sell Wilkins' house to satisfy the judgment. Wilkins now learns of the case and moves for relief from judgment under the state's rule governing relief from judgment, which is substantially the same as Fed. R. Civ. P. 60(b).

A. The court cannot grant the motion, because service of process was made in compliance with the state rule, which provided for a constitutionally sufficient form of notice.

B. The court must grant the motion, because Wilkins never found out about the suit. Thus, the judgment is void, and relief from judgment is required under Rule 60(b)(4).

C. The court would have the authority to grant relief from judgment, under Rule 60(b)(1), and probably would.

D. The court would have the authority to grant relief from judgment, under Rule 60(b)(1), but probably would not.

ANALYSIS.   In this case LeCompte complied with the state rule governing service of process, and as we saw from the last question, the method prescribed by that rule is constitutionally sufficient. However, in this case a satisfactory method of *service* still did not provide actual *notice* to the defendant that he had been sued. When he finds out later, he is surprised, and wants to reopen the default judgment that has entered against him.

The first answer takes the position that there is nothing the court can do for Wilkins. "LeCompte properly sued and served you, you didn't answer, so we defaulted you. Deal with it, Wilkins." I suppose the system could give this heartless answer to Wilkins's plea, "but I didn't defend because I didn't know!" But it would be a callous and impractical answer, wouldn't it? It is true that LeCompte did everything by the book, and that mail is a constitutionally adequate means to serve process. Consequently, the default judgment he received is a valid judgment, and potentially enforceable. But the fact is that Wilkins never learned of the case and never had a chance to present his defenses. Rule 60(b) allows a trial judge in appropriate circumstances to reopen cases, for any of the reasons set forth in the rule. Thus, **A** is not accurate; even if the service was proper and the judgment was validly obtained, it may be reopened in circumstances like this.

B asserts that the judge must grant relief from judgment, because Wilkins never learned of the case. But this isn't true either. The judgment is not void, because LeCompte properly sued and served Wilkins, and the court was authorized to enter a default judgment when he failed to defend. It is a valid judgment, which, if it is not reopened, may be enforced. A party is entitled to have service made by a proper method, but if it is and it still does not reach the defendant the judgment is still valid. Proper service does not always assure *actual notice*; it may support a valid judgment nonetheless.

So, the choices boil down to whether the judge would be likely to exercise her authority under Rule 60(b) to reopen the case or would not. Isn't it clear that **C** is right, that the judge would grant relief from judgment for "inadvertence" under Rule 60(b)(1)? Wouldn't you do that, if you were the judge? Wilkins never knew he was sued, and wasn't at fault in failing to respond. Little time has gone by, and no one has relied on the judgment to their detriment (as might be the case if a third party had bought his house in execution of the judgment). All the equities cry out to allow Wilkins his opportunity to be heard. Given this possibility lurking behind every default judgment, it will likely be in the plaintiff's interest to make every effort to assure that the defendant actually learns of the case. Meeting constitutional minima is nice, but giving actual notice may be in everyone's best interest.

B. *Pennoyer* perplexities: The separate requirements of notice and personal jurisdiction

Because *Pennoyer* based jurisdiction on service of process, it tended to blur the distinction between two constitutional requirements — adequate *notice* to the defendant and a *basis to adjudicate*. But these are separate requirements, each of which must be met. Personal jurisdiction requires that the defendant have some relationship to the state that makes it fair to require her to defend the action there. The distinct constitutional requirement of notice of the action assures that the defendant is adequately informed that a court is going to adjudicate a claim involving her rights. As *Mullane* mandates, every court system requires careful procedures to inform the defendant of the commencement of a lawsuit. This constitutional requirement is satisfied if the initial papers in the action are served on the defendant by a means reasonably calculated to actually inform her of the pendency of the action.

Pennoyer v. Neff creates confusion about these requirements for three reasons. *First*, under *Pennoyer*, the same act — personal service of the papers in the action on the defendant — provided both notice of the action and a basis for the court to exercise personal jurisdiction. Notice was sufficient under the *Pennoyer* regime, because handing the papers to the defendant in person is more likely than any other method to actually inform her that she has been sued. And the court acquired jurisdiction, under *Pennoyer's* reasoning, if service was made while the defendant was in the forum state, because the court had authority over persons and property "seized" within the forum state.

Second, the *Pennoyer* opinion suggests that giving the defendant notice by publication, that is, publishing notice of the commencement of an action in a newspaper, satisfies the constitutional due process requirement to give notice of the action, at least in cases commenced by attachment. This is no longer good law. Under *Mullane,* publication is not sufficient to "reasonably inform [the defendant] of the pendency of the action" (*Mullane,* 339 U.S. at 315) unless no other type of notice more likely to reach her is possible. See *Mennonite Board of Missions v. Adams,* 462 U.S. 791, 796 (1983). Generally, there are better alternatives, such as personal service or delivery through some form of mail to the defendant's last known address. In cases against corporations, service on an officer or managing agent of the corporation will provide adequate notice to the corporation that suit has been filed against it.

A third source of confusion arises from *Pennoyer's* suggestion that service of process outside the state was always improper. "Process from the tribunals of one State cannot run into another State, and summon parties there domiciled to leave its territory and respond to proceedings against them [in another state]." 95 U.S. at 727. However, this language from *Pennoyer* means that such service would not provide a *basis for jurisdiction.* It did not mean that serving the papers on the defendant in another state would not constitute adequate *notice* that the law suit had been filed. Today, courts commonly exercise personal jurisdiction over defendants located in other states, based on minimum contacts in the state where the suit is brought. In such cases, personal delivery of the papers notifying the defendant of the action, or some form of mail notice, provides constitutionally adequate notice of the action, even though delivered outside the forum state (the state in which the action is brought).

This example may help to sort out these two constitutional touchstones.

QUESTION 4. Served, but not satisfied. Carnahan, from New Hampshire, has an accident with Perkins, from Missouri, in New York. After the accident, they exchange papers and leave. Carnahan decides to sue Perkins for his injuries. In which of the following cases are constitutional standards for both notice and personal jurisdiction likely to be satisfied? Assume that current standards for personal jurisdiction apply.

A. Carnahan sues Perkins in New Hampshire, for the accident. He sends a process server to Perkins's house in Missouri to serve him with the summons and complaint. Perkins answers the door and the process server delivers the papers to Perkins, with an explanation of the lawsuit and the process for responding to it.

B. Carnahan sues Perkins in New York for the New York accident. He publishes notice of the action four weeks in a row in the New York Times.

C. Carnahan sues Perkins in New York for the New York accident. Carnahan serves the summons and complaint on Perkins by mailing them, certified mail, return receipt requested, to Perkins at his home in Missouri.

D. Carnahan sues Ace Tool & Die Company, Perkins's Missouri employer, for the New York accident, since it occurred while Perkins was making a delivery for Ace. He sues in a New Hampshire state court. He delivers the summons and complaint to Walker, president of Ace Tool & Die, while she is at a convention in Manchester, New Hampshire.

ANALYSIS. In **A**, Carnahan's method of service of process is constitutionally sufficient. Carnahan has delivered the papers directly to Perkins, with an explanation of what they are and what he must do to respond. Notice doesn't get any better than this. Perkins can hardly argue that Carnahan has failed to give notice by a means reasonably calculated to actually inform him of the law suit. However, there is no basis for the New Hampshire court to exercise personal jurisdiction over Perkins. He doesn't live in New Hampshire. The action doesn't arise out of New Hampshire contacts. Nor was he served with process in New Hampshire. The facts don't suggest any basis for the New Hampshire court to exercise personal jurisdiction over Perkins for this claim. Constitutionally adequate notice is necessary, but not sufficient to allow the New Hampshire court to proceed. The court must also have a basis for requiring Perkins to defend in New Hampshire before it can proceed.

In **B**, the claim arises out of conduct by Perkins — driving in the state where the suit is brought. It is certainly foreseeable that driving in a state may give rise to injury and that the injured party would sue where the accident took place. Under *International Shoe*, this is a contact that gives rise to specific in personam jurisdiction over Perkins. But notice by publication in the Times is not likely to be found constitutionally sufficient. Publication is generally viewed as a last resort, permissible only where no means of notice more likely to actually reach the defendant is feasible. As long as Carnahan has an address for Perkins — and he should, since they exchanged papers at the scene of the accident — a more viable means of giving notice to Perkins is possible, through in-hand service at his home in Missouri or some form of mail notice to that address. Thus, publication is hardly the type of notice "one desirous of actually informing the absentee might reasonably adopt to accomplish it." *Mullane*, 339 U.S. at 315.

D is a little tricky. Serving Walker, the president of Ace, "in hand" (that is, by handing the papers to her personally) is surely a sufficient means of informing the corporation of the action. Service of process on a corporate officer is commonly authorized by statutes governing service of process on corporations. See, e.g., Fed. R. Civ. P. 4(h)(1)(B) (service may be made on corporation by delivery of summons and complaint to an officer of the corporation). And, such service is constitutionally adequate because it is very likely to make the officers — who must respond to the suit on behalf of the corporation — aware of the pendency of the action. However, service on Walker, even in New Hampshire, does not give the New Hampshire court personal jurisdiction over the corporation. The Supreme Court has reaffirmed that *an individual defendant* is usually subject to personal jurisdiction in a state if she is served with process in the action within the forum state. *Burnham v. Superior Court*, 495 U.S. 604 (1990). However, in-state service on an employee or officer of a corporation does not establish personal jurisdiction over the corporation itself. Otherwise, a corporation could be sued wherever its officers traveled. Although *Burnham* reaffirmed that an individual is subject to jurisdiction based on symbolic "seizure" in the state, a corporation cannot be.

That leaves **C**, which is the best choice. Certainly, there is a basis for the New York court to exercise jurisdiction over Perkins for this claim, since it arises out of the New York accident. And, constitutionally adequate notice is provided as well. Sending the summons and complaint to Perkins by certified mail at his home is a method very likely to actually reach Perkins and inform him of the pendency of the action. Many service statutes authorize service by various forms of mail and have been held constitutionally sufficient. So, assuming that the service statute authorizes mail notice, both due process requirements are met here.

C.   Some technicalities: What gets served and who does it

So you get that elusive first job, start work, and you are asked to sue somebody. (Oh my goodness! What do I actually do?) Well, start by doing what my students always resist doing: look at the rules. If you're in federal court, the rule is Rule 4, governing service of process in the federal courts. And you will probably start by figuring out what you have to deliver to the defendant and figuring out who should do it.

The relevant provisions are in Rule 4(a) - (c); I'm not going to repeat them here, but go right to a question to test whether you took my advice and read them.

> **QUESTION 5. Dim prospects for partnership.** In which of the following service of process situations is the boss likely to roll her eyes and say, "What did we hire this kid for?"
>
> **A.** Neophyte drafts a complaint against Gates for breach of a contract to design software for the plaintiff. She serves the complaint by delivering it herself to Gates at his office.
> **B.** Neophyte drafts a complaint against Gates for breach of a contract to design software for the plaintiff. She prints out a form summons from the office files containing the information called for in Rule 4(a)(1)(A) to (E) and serves both documents on Gates by a method authorized by Rule 4(e).
> **C.** Neophyte drafts a complaint against Jobs and Gates for breach of a contract to design software for the plaintiff. She files the complaint, has the clerk sign and seal the summons, and serves the documents on Gates by a method authorized by Rule 4(e).
> **D.** Neophyte drafts a complaint against Gates for breach of a contract to design software for the plaintiff. She delivers two copies of the complaint and two summonses to be signed and sealed by the clerk and then served by the clerk on Gates.
> **E.** All of these methods are insufficient.

ANALYSIS. **E** is right, because none of these efforts complies with the requirements of Rule 4(a)-(c). In **A**, Neophyte served the complaint herself, which is authorized by Rule 4(c)(2) (any person 18 or over who isn't a party). But she did not serve a summons with the complaint, as required by Rule 4(c)(1). In **B**, she drafted a proper summons, but did not have it signed and sealed by the clerk,[1] as required by Rule 4(a)(1)(F) and (G). The summons is a document issued by the court, the official document by which the court formally commands the defendant to appear and defend the suit. It's not "official" without the signature and seal of the court.

In **C**, Neophyte followed Rule 4 to the letter in serving Gates, but didn't serve Jobs at all. Surely, Jobs has just as much right to notice of the action as Gates. *Mullane* certainly stands for that proposition, doesn't it? Rule 4 does not flatly say that a summons and complaint must be served on each defendant, but Rule 4(b) does say that a summons must be issued "for each defendant to be served." Thus, service is inadequate in **C** for failure to serve process on the second defendant.

D is also improper, because it is not the clerk's job to serve the papers on the defendant. This is the plaintiff's job under Rule 4(c)(1), which states that

---

1. In some districts, the court may issue summonses, signed and sealed, in blank, to be filled in by counsel before service. In others, however, the clerk will sign and seal a summons submitted by plaintiff's counsel when the complaint is filed.

"the plaintiff is responsible for having the summons and complaint served." While, technically, service represents the command of the court to appear and defend, the plaintiff's lawyer carries the laboring oar in making sure that the defendant gets the proper papers.

D.   More technicalities: Serving process on individual defendants in federal cases

So, Rule 4(c) mandates delivery of the summons and complaint to the defendant in federal cases, as do most state rules of civil procedure. Now, *how* should the papers be delivered? For federal cases, the Federal Rules specify proper methods for serving process on different types of defendants, such as individuals, corporations, and political subdivisions. This section will focus on the methods for serving individuals.

- Rule 4(e) authorizes service on an individual defendant — that is, a person — by delivering the summons and complaint to her personally. Fed. R. Civ. P. 4(e)(2)(A). This is fairly straightforward — you take the papers to the defendant and physically give them to her.
- Alternatively, you may deliver them to the individual's home and leave them with a person of "suitable age and discretion" who lives there. Fed. R. Civ. P. 4(e)(2)(B).
- You may also serve an individual defendant by delivering the summons and complaint to an agent authorized to receive process for the defendant. Fed. R. Civ. P. 4(e)(2)(C). It must be a person the defendant has specifically authorized to receive process in a lawsuit or who is designated by statute as authorized to receive service, not just a person who works for the defendant or is a general agent in her business. (A defendant might have appointed an agent for service of process in a contract, for example.)
- Alternatively, Rule 4(e)(1) allows you to *use state service of process methods* for the courts of the state in which the case is pending *or* for the state in which service of process is made. So, if you sue in the Eastern District of Michigan, and you are serving process on a defendant in the Eastern District of Washington, you may use the methods of service of process authorized by Michigan law for the state courts of Michigan or those authorized by Washington law for the state courts of Washington. Frequently, these state rules will allow methods not authorized by the Federal Rules, such as service by mail. See, e.g., Michigan Civil Rules 2.105(A)(2) (authorizing service by registered or certified mail). If so, a plaintiff may use these methods instead of one of the methods authorized by Rule 4(e)(2).

So, let's try a question on proper methods of service.

QUESTION 6. Details, details. Skelton sues Larry, Moe, and Curley, three funny guys, on a claim for unfair competition, in federal court in Virginia. West, from California, is also named as a defendant. Skelton's lawyer has a private investigator from her office serve Larry by delivering the summons and complaint to Larry's home in Virginia, where the investigator hands them to Fields, the New York booking agent for Larry, Moe, and Curley, who had flown down for the weekend to discuss business. She serves Moe several weeks later, by having the investigator deliver the summons and complaint to Fields at his office in New York. She serves Curley by mailing the summons and complaint to Curley at his home in Michigan by first class mail. All three move to dismiss for improper service of process under Rule 12(b)(5). She serves West by having a constable in Los Angeles deliver the summons and complaint to West at her office. When West says she does not want the papers, the constable places them in front of her on the desk.

A. Service is proper on all four defendants.
B. Service is proper only on Larry and Moe, but not on Curley or West.
C. Service is proper on West and Curley only.
D. Service is only proper on West.
E. Service is not proper on any of the defendants.

ANALYSIS. Service on Larry is improper in this case, because, no matter how suitable Fields's age and discretion may be, he does not live with Larry, he's a visitor. I suppose you could argue that he is "residing" there for the weekend, but that is probably stretching the rule beyond the breaking point. There's a difference between residing and visiting. While I haven't researched the cases, I'll guess that they make that distinction because a visitor is less likely to remember to give the papers to the defendant and less likely to care that the defendant learns of the court proceeding. You might find a judge who would hold this service sufficient, but why take the chance? Scratch A . . . and B, since service is improper on Larry.

Service on Moe is insufficient because nothing in the question indicates that Moe has appointed Fields his agent for service of process; he is only his business agent. Service is only proper under Rule 4(e)(2)(C) on an agent specifically designated to receive service of process in a lawsuit.

Service is not proper on Curley either, though Skelton's lawyer came close this time. Although Federal Rule 4(e) does not expressly authorize service of process by mail, Rule 4(e)(1) allows service under the service of process rules for the state in which service is made, which in this case is

Michigan. As noted above, Michigan allows service of process by mail . . . but only by registered or certified mail. Close, but no cigar; drop **C**.

How about West? Rule 4(e)(2)(A) authorizes Skelton to deliver the papers to West personally. But here, Skelton delivered them in California for a law suit in Virginia. Does that satisfy the rule? Sure it does. The point of service of process is to *let the defendant know* that she has been sued, and handing the summons and complaint to West is just as effective to do that, whether they are delivered in L.A. or in Richmond. Rule 4(e)(2)(A) doesn't say anything about *where* the papers must be delivered. But here West refused to take them; is service still proper? Yes it is. Skelton delivered them to her, made her aware of them, and left them with her. Surely, West can't prevent valid service by refusing to put out her hand. So **D** is the best answer.

E. Service of process on a corporation under Federal Rule 4

Rule 4(h) provides several options for serving process on a corporation, when service is made in a judicial district of the United States.

- Service may be made by delivering a copy of the summons and complaint to an officer of the corporation, for example, the president, vice-president, or secretary of the corporation. Fed. R. Civ. P. 4(h)(1)(B). The phrase "delivering a copy" means physical delivery, not mailing.
- Alternatively, service may be made by delivering a copy to a managing or general agent of the corporation. Fed. R. Civ. P. 4(h)(1)(B). This provision is the most ambiguous part of Rule 4(h), because it is unclear who will qualify as a "managing or general agent" of a corporation. In deciding whether a person is a managing or general agent, the court will consider how much authority the person served has in the general management of the business at the place where service is made. The logic is that a person with broad responsibilities will more likely recognize the importance of the papers and feel a responsibility to see that the proper people find out about them and defend the case.
- Service may also be made on an agent authorized by law or appointment to receive service of process for the corporation. Fed. R. Civ. P. 4(h)(1)(B). Many states have statutes providing that a corporation registered to do business in the state appoints the state's Secretary of State as its agent for service of process in actions brought against the corporation. These statutes typically require the plaintiff, if he serves process on the Secretary as agent for the corporation, to give notice by mail directly to the corporation as well.

- Fed. R. Civ. P. 4(h)((1)(A) authorizes service "in the manner prescribed by Rule 4(e)(1) for serving an individual." This is confusing, because Fed. R. Civ. P. Rule 4(e)(1), allows service *on an individual* by the methods of service authorized by the state where the action is pending or the state where process is actually served. Read literally, this seems to suggest that the plaintiff in a case against a corporation can use the state law methods *for serving an individual*. However, this reference is clearly intended to authorize a plaintiff to serve process on a corporation under state rules for serving *a corporation*.

Well, let's probe the limits of these provisions with another question. Be sure to consult the Rule itself in testing what was done against the requirements of the Rule.

QUESTION 7. Special delivery. PourPack is a Delaware corporation that sells dairy products to retailers. Its headquarters, offices, and freezers are in California. Girardi, a sales representative for PourPack in Utah, sues PourPack for firing him from his job, claiming age discrimination and seeking damages under the Federal Age Discrimination in Employment Act. His lawyer, Perini, files the action in federal district court in Utah. In which of these cases is service of process most likely to be upheld?

Perini serves PourPack by

A. delivering the summons and complaint to Suares, a member of the board of directors of Pourpack.
B. delivering the papers to the Utah Secretary of State, based on a Utah statute that authorizes such service in actions against a corporation arising out of its activities in Utah and mailing a copy of the papers (as required by the statute) to PourPack at its corporate address. PourPack argues that this is improper because Girardi's claim arises under federal law.
C. having a process server deliver the summons and complaint to Riggins, the vice-president of PourPack. Riggins is not home when the process server knocks, so he leaves the papers with Riggins's roomate, Schwartz.
D. delivering the summons and the complaint to Porado, a biochemist who is in charge of testing PourPack's products for spoilage.

ANALYSIS. In **D**, Perini apparently relies on Fed. R. Civ. P. 4(h)(1)(B), claiming that he has delivered the papers to "a managing or general agent" of PourPack. This phrase properly applies to an employee with broad supervisory responsibilities, who is likely to act generally for the corporation in the management of its business, at least at the office where he or she works. Porado is very much a specialist, with narrow responsibilities for product testing. Perhaps a mellow federal judge would find her to be a "managing agent," but most probably would not. See, e.g., *Street v. Steel Valley Industrialized Center*, 2006 W.L. 2172550 (W.D. Pa) (service on "Intake Eligibility Specialist" did not satisfy Rule 4(h)). So this is not the choice "most likely to be upheld."

In **C**, Perini appears to rely on the subsection dealing with service on an individual, Fed. R. Civ. P. 4(e)(2)(B). But she is not serving Riggins as a defendant in the action, she is serving PourPack. So she has to follow the procedure for serving a corporation in Rule 4(h)(1). Subsection (B) of that rule authorizes service on the corporation by delivering the papers to an officer of the corporation, not leaving them with someone else. But wait, how about Rule 4(h)(1)(A), which allows service in a manner prescribed by Rule 4(e)(1) for serving an individual? Rule 4(e)(1) allows use of state service or process methods, but the reference in Rule 4(h)(1)(A) almost certainly means state methods for serving process on a corporate defendant, not an individual defendant. So, unless state law allows service on a corporation by leaving the papers with someone else at the home of a corporate officer (very unlikely), service here is probably insufficient.

Service in **B** is proper, however. Here, Perini has used a method of service authorized by Utah state service of process rules for serving a corporate defendant. Rule 4(h)(1)(A) authorizes Perini to use the service rules of the state in which the suit is filed, and she has properly looked to the Utah rules for serving a corporation. However, what about PourPack's argument that she has used state service of process rules in an action based on federal law? So what? Nothing in Rule 4(h)(1)(A) suggests that service can only be made under the state rules if the case is based on state law. Rule 4(h) prescribes general methods for service in federal actions,[2] without regard to the type of claim the plaintiff asserts and authorizes by reference what Perini has done here.

A is wrong here, because there is a difference between an officer of a corporation and a *director* of a corporation. Rule 4(h)(1)(B) authorizes service on an officer, because officers are almost always involved in the daily operation of the corporation and hence likely to take the steps necessary to present a defense to an action. Directors, by contrast, sit on a board that meets periodically to provide broad oversight and strategic direction, may not live near the corporate offices, frequently do not participate in the day to day management of the corporation, and are not as likely to be familiar with the dispute and take appropriate steps to defend the case.

---

2. The rule does have a tricky proviso, "unless federal law provides otherwise." Congress has prescribed special methods of service of process for some specialized federal claims. There is no hint here of such a twist, however.

F.   Waiver of service

All of this is fairly technical, though important. But in many cases the defendant already knows that suit is being filed or can easily be given notice without the formality of service under the Federal Rules. So Rule 4 provides a method for a defendant to waive compliance with formal service requirements. Rule 4(d) authorizes a plaintiff to send the defendant a notice of the action and request that she waive service of process. A request for waiver must be addressed to the defendant (or, for a corporate defendant, an appropriate officer or managing agent or other agent authorized to receive process), and provide the name of the court in which the suit is pending, a copy of the complaint, two copies of the waiver form, and a stamped envelope to send it back. It must inform the defendant of the consequences of waiving service and of not waiving it, state the date of the request, give at least 30 days to return the waiver, and be sent by "first-class mail or other reliable means." Fed. R. Civ. P. 4(d)(1).

Rule 4(d)(1) provides that the defendant has a duty to avoid unnecessary costs of service, and Rule 4(d)(2) tells her what will happen if she fails to fulfill that duty: She will have to pay the costs of formal service and any motion necessary to collect those costs. That isn't too scary, because the cost of service is not going to break the bank. But the rule makers cleverly provided a carrot as well as a stick: Rule 4(d)(3) provides that a defendant who waives formal service gets 60 days to file an answer, rather than the usual 21. For busy lawyers, that's a real incentive.

So waiver is a genteel alternative to formal service and will frequently happen, but not always. Rule 4(d) does not expressly tell us what a plaintiff should do if the defendant does not waive service. But it provides that the penalty for failure to waive is to pay the cost of formal service (Rule 4(d)(2)), clearly implying that if the defendant does not waive service, the plaintiff must serve her with a copy of the summons and complaint through one of the formal methods provided in Rule 4. So, consider these scenarios.

> **QUESTION 8. Technical fouls.**   Eban brings suit against Lorenzo for interference with business relations. Eban's lawyer, Darrow, calls Lorenzo's lawyer, Sadecki, and tells her that he is filing suit that afternoon. In which of the following scenarios may the case proceed without formal service of process?
>
> **A.** Darrow files the complaint with the district court clerk with an affidavit swearing that he informed Sadecki of the case and mailed her a copy of the complaint.

B. Darrow files the complaint and mails a copy of it by first class mail to Lorenzo with two copies of a proper request for waiver. He files an affidavit with the court attesting to those acts.

C. Darrow files the complaint and mails a copy of it by certified mail to Lorenzo with two copies of a proper request for waiver. He does not send a summons, signed and sealed by the court, with the waiver request. He receives the signed waiver form back and files it with the court.

D. Darrow files the complaint and mails a copy of it by certified mail to Lorenzo with two copies of a proper request for waiver. He receives the green postal receipt back in the mail. Darrow files the postal receipt with the court.

E. In each of these scenarios, there is no proper waiver and formal service must be used.

ANALYSIS. Interestingly, in each of these cases the defendant, or his counsel, *has been informed of the filing of the case.* But actual notice is not a substitute for proper service of process or waiver of the requirement of service. Many cases have been dismissed for lack of proper service, even though the defendant knew that she had been sued or even received a copy of the complaint. See Moore's Federal Practice §4.03[3][a]. Service is a formal act by which a court asserts its authority over the defendant. The cases require that it be done by the book in order to acquire that authority. Knowledge of the action by the defendant or someone who works for it will not substitute for formal submission to the court's authority through service (or a proper waiver). So we have to see if the defendant has properly waived service in any of these cases.

In **A**, Darrow has attested to telling Lorenzo's counsel about the case. But he hasn't served him with process, and he hasn't complied with the Rule 4(d) procedure for waiving it. The court has not acquired jurisdiction over Lorenzo. He has been sloppy in **B** as well. A waiver is not obtained by sending a request for it, even if it includes all the information required in Rule 4(d)(1). A waiver is obtained when the defendant signs and returns the waiver form. Nothing indicates that Lorenzo did that in **B**. And in **D**, Darrow gets back the post office receipt showing that Lorenzo got the form, but that doesn't constitute a waiver by Lorenzo. It only means that he received the request to waive service.

In **C**, Darrow sent a proper request for waiver, with the complaint, and got it back signed. But he didn't send a formal summons from the court. That's all right. A formal summons, signed and sealed by the clerk, is required for proper service (see Rule 4(c)(1)), but is not required for a proper waiver. The whole point is that defendant waives this formality. See

Rule 4(d)(1), which provides in part that "the plaintiff may . . . request that the defendant waive service of a summons." So Lorenzo has waived service in C, and it, not E, is the best answer.

G. A modest Closer: Practice for the perplexed

This Closer introduces no new material; it just provides a question that requires you to apply the various concepts covered in the chapter, including the separate requirement of personal jurisdiction.

> **QUESTION 9. Problems, problems.** Preferred Metalworks, Inc. is incorporated in Delaware and has its principal place of business in Kentucky. It also has a factory in Ohio, where Stamski worked. One day Donitz, president of Preferred, called Stamski into his office at the Ohio plant and fired him. Stamski sues Preferred and Donitz in federal court for breach of contract. In which of the following situations is service of process proper on both defendants and is personal jurisdiction proper over both defendants?
>
> A. Stamski serves process by mailing a summons, addressed to Preferred Metalworks, Inc., and a copy of the complaint to Donitz by first class mail, at his home in Indiana. The Ohio service of process statute authorizes service on any defendant by first class mail and authorizes sending the summons and complaint to a corporate officer if the defendant is a corporation.
> B. Since Donitz does not live in Ohio, and no corporate officer can be served there, he serves Donitz and Preferred by publication of notice of the action in a newspaper of general circulation in the area where the case is filed for four successive weeks.
> C. Stamski sues in federal court in Indiana, where Donitz lives. He serves process by having the process server deliver a summons addressed to Donitz and another addressed to Preferred, with two copies of the complaint to Donitz at his home in Indiana.
> D. Stamski sues in federal court in Kentucky. He serves Preferred by mailing the summons and complaint, first class mail, to Prosnitz, secretary of the corporation, at her home in Ohio. Ohio state law authorizes service on a corporation by mail to a corporate officer, but Kentucky law

> does not. He serves Donitz by having a process server deliver his summons and the complaint to him at his home in Indiana.
>
> **E.** Service and personal jurisdiction are not both proper in any of the cases above.

Let's start in the middle and nibble up and down. In **C**, service of process is proper on both Donitz and the corporation. Stamski delivered the papers personally to Donitz, which is a proper means of serving an individual defendant under Fed. R. Civ. P. 4(e)(2)(A). Delivering the summons and complaint for Preferred to Donitz personally also constitutes proper service on the corporation under Fed. R. Civ. P. 4(h)(1)(B), because he is an officer of the corporation. But nothing indicates that Preferred is subject to personal jurisdiction in Indiana for this claim — there are no facts suggesting that it has any presence in Indiana. Its president lives there, but this contact will not be attributed to the corporation, and the events giving rise to the claim took place in Ohio.

In **D**, Stamski served process on Preferred using a method authorized by Ohio law for service on a corporation, but one that was not authorized by Kentucky service rules, the state where the action is pending. But that's alright; Fed. R. Civ. P. 4(e)(1) authorizes service under the state rules for the state in which the action is pending *or* those of the state where service is made. So, service is proper on the corporation, and it is almost certainly subject to general in personam jurisdiction in the state of its principal place of business, even though the claim arose out of acts in another state. So he's nailed Preferred. And service is proper on Donitz, since the summons and complaint were delivered to him personally. See Fed. R. Civ. P. 4(e)(2). However, there is nothing to suggest that Donitz is subject to personal jurisdiction in Kentucky for this claim, which arises out of events in Ohio. Since he is domiciled in Indiana, it is highly unlikely that he is subject to general in personam jurisdiction in Kentucky; the fact that Preferred is does not mean that its president is.

B suggests that, since the officers of Preferred are not in Ohio, service by publication is proper. No way! First, there is no provision in Federal Rule 4 that authorizes service by publication. However, state service of process rules often provide that, if the defendant cannot be served through the usual methods, the court may authorize service in another way such as publication. See, e.g., Alaska Rules of Civil Procedure 4(e). So, in an appropriate case, a plaintiff may obtain a court order for service by publication, by looking to such a state service provision. See Rule 4(h)(1)(A) (incorporating state service rules for corporations). But this is not an appropriate case, since, while Donitz and other officers of Preferred are not physically present in Ohio, Stamski knows where they are and can use other methods of service much more likely to inform them of the action, such as mail or personal delivery in some other state. Publication is a last resort, and there are several more effective options here.

In **A**, service is proper on Preferred, because the summons commanding Preferred to respond was delivered to Donitz, an officer of Preferred, together with a copy of the complaint. But no summons addressed to Donitz was served on him. Even though Donitz received *a summons*, as well as a copy of the complaint, service here is technically deficient. See Fed. R. Civ. P. 4(a)(1)(B) (summons must be "directed to the defendant"). Donitz will know, from the complaint, that he is also a defendant, but he has not received an order from the court to appear and defend. His objection is a tad technical, but if there is one area in which the courts require dotting the "i"'s and crossing the "t"'s, it is likely to be initial service of process. So the best answer is **E**, service and jurisdiction are not both proper in any of the other choices.

 # Glannon's Picks

1. Unnoticed notice	E
2. Mailing it in	D
3. Service, but not notice	C
4. Served, but not satisfied	C
5. Dim prospects for partnership	E
6. Details, details	D
7. Special delivery	B
8. Technical fouls	C
9. Problems, problems	E

10

Venue and Transfer: More Limits on the Place of Suit

~

When Jill's limited credit was outspent
The bank sued her in court for money lent.
Since Jill couldn't pay it,
She asked the court to stay it
Since the action was clearly inconvenient.

~

CHAPTER OVERVIEW

A. The basic federal venue provisions
B. Venue in cases involving corporate defendants
C. Corporate "residence" in multidistrict states under §1391(c)
D. Forum non conveniens and transfer
E. Complications, complications: Transfer under 28 U.S.C. §1406(a)
F. The Closer: The professor outsmarts himself
◈ Glannon's Picks

It's confusing enough to sort out all the intricacies of personal and subject matter jurisdiction. But court systems impose a third constraint on choosing a court. Every court system has statutory venue rules, in addition to limits on personal and subject matter jurisdiction. These statutes restrict suit to a court that has some sensible relationship to the parties or to their dispute.

State court venue rules usually restrict suit to a county within the state where one of the parties resides or has a place of business, or where the claim arose. But there are myriad specialized state venue provisions as well, which vary from state to state. This chapter analyzes the federal venue statute, which restricts venue to particular federal judicial districts, as an example of venue rules in action.

A.   The basic federal venue provisions

Venue in most federal actions is governed by 28 U.S.C. §1391(b), which provides:

> (b) Venue in general. A civil action may be brought in —
>   (1) a judicial district in which any defendant resides, if all defendants are residents of the State in which the district is located;
>   (2) a judicial district in which a substantial part of the events or omissions giving rise to the claim occurred, or a substantial part of property that is the subject of the action is situated; or
>   (3) if there is no district in which an action may otherwise be brought as provided in this section, a judicial district in which any defendant is subject to the court's personal jurisdiction with respect to such action.

Note that subsections 1 and 2 are alternatives. Venue is proper in a district where *either* a defendant resides (if they are all residents of the state where the action is brought) *or* a district in which a substantial part of the events giving rise to the claim took place. Section 1391(b)(3) is a "fallback" venue provision that is only available in unusual circumstances: when there is *no district*, anywhere in the United States, where venue would be proper under subsection (b)(1) or (b)(2). If the defendants all reside in the state where suit is brought, or if a substantial part of the events giving rise to the claim occurred in some federal judicial district, or if property that is the subject of the action is found in a district, §1391(b)(3) cannot apply, because there will be at least one district in which venue is proper under §1391(b)(1) or (b)(2).

Note also that there is a nasty proviso in 28 U.S.C. §1391(a) that poses a trap for the unwary: The first sentence of that subsection provides that the venue options in §1391(b) apply "except as otherwise provided by law." Section 1391 is a general venue statute that applies *unless* there is a special venue statute for the type of claim the plaintiff brings. The United States Code has many specialized venue provisions for particular types of actions. See, e.g., 28 U.S.C. §1402 (tort action against the United States must be brought in the district where the plaintiff resides or wherein the act or omission complained of occurred). If there is a special venue statute, it, rather than §1391, applies.

To sort out the basics of §1391(b), try the following question. Assume for all examples in the chapter that no special venue statute applies. In answering these questions, please *do refer to the venue statutes.* Once again, my questions are based on the assumption that you have the Federal Rules book available, so you can refer to relevant statutes and rules, rather than memorizing them. I want to test my students' ability to apply provisions like the venue statutes or Federal Rules, rather than their memory of them. Needless to say, you should find out *your professor's* policy on bringing materials into the exam before you prepare for it. If she doesn't allow you to refer to the rules book, you obviously need to spend more time memorizing statutes and rules.

QUESTION 1. Redistricting. Dziezek, who resides in the Southern District of Indiana, sues Torruella and Hopkins. Torruella resides in the Western District of Kentucky. Hopkins resides in the Western District of Tennessee. Dziezek sues them both for damages arising out of a business deal for the financing of a subdivision Dziezek planned to build in the Southern District of Ohio. His claim against Torruella is for fraud, his claim against Hopkins is for fraud and for violation of the Federal Truth in Lending Act. The negotiations between the parties for the financing took place in the Western District of Tennessee. Dziezek claimed that, after the defendants had provided the first installment of financing for the project, and he had commenced construction, they refused to provide subsequent payments needed to complete the project. Venue in Dziezek's action would be proper in

A. the Western District of Kentucky.
B. the Southern District of Indiana.
C. the Southern District of Ohio.
D. Both **A** and **C** are true.

ANALYSIS. Let's see. Under §1391(b)(1), venue is proper in a district where all defendants reside. But here they don't all reside in the same district. Nor do they reside in different districts within the same state (in which case the district where either resides would be a proper venue). So §1391(b)(1) doesn't provide any venue options for Dziezek. He'll have to look to §1391(b)(2) or (b)(3).

Section 1391(b)(2) is more fruitful. It allows venue in a district where a substantial part of the events or omissions giving rise to the claim took place, or where property that is the subject of the action is located. Here, you might argue that the property in the Southern District of Ohio, where the subdivision is being built, is the subject of the action. This is doubtful, since the action is for fraud, not to establish an interest in the real estate. However, venue is proper in the Southern District of Ohio anyway, since a substantial part of the events giving rise to Dziezek's claim — the partial construction of the subdivision — took place there. Or, arguably, an omission that gave rise to the claim took place there, the failure to provide the second financing installment. So **C** is a correct answer. But **B** is clearly not: the *plaintiff's* residence is not one of the venue options in §1391(b).

So the remaining question is whether the Western District of Kentucky, where Torruella resides, is a proper venue. Venue isn't proper there under §1391(b)(1), which only applies if all defendants reside in districts within the same state. Here, only Torruella resides in Kentucky.

Section 1391(b)(3) authorizes jurisdiction — in some cases — in "a judicial district in which any defendant is subject to personal jurisdiction with respect to such action." Here, Hopkins presumably is subject to personal jurisdiction in the Western District of Kentucky, since he resides there and could be served with process there. However, §1391(b)(3) is not available in this case. That section only applies if there is *no other district* where the case can be brought under subsection (1) or (2). Here, the Southern District of Ohio is proper. The Western District of Tennessee, where the parties negotiated the contract, would also be proper under §1391 (b)(2). Since Dziezek could choose either of those districts under subsection 2, and both defendants would be subject to jurisdiction there based on their involvement in the subdivision project, §1391(b)(3) never comes into play. Consequently, **C** is the right answer.

B. Venue in cases involving corporate defendants

The venue provisions in §1391(b) also apply in cases involving corporate defendants. Such cases may still be brought in a district in which all defendants reside, or where a substantial part of the events giving rise to the claim took place. And subsection (3) is solely a fallback provision in cases involving corporate defendants, as in all other cases. But there is a confusing twist in cases involving corporate defendants.

The twist arises from the definition of where a corporation "resides" for purposes of applying the venue provisions. Two subsections of §1391 deal with this. The first, 28 U.S.C. §1391(c)(2), provides that in cases where a corporation is the defendant, it shall be deemed to reside "in any judicial district in which such defendant is subject to the court's personal jurisdiction with respect to the civil action in question. . . ." The second, §1391(d), defines what district a corporation resides in if a state has more than one judicial district. It is even more perplexing:

> For purposes of venue under this chapter, in a State which has more than one judicial district and in which a defendant that is a corporation is subject to personal jurisdiction at the time an action is commenced, such corporation shall be deemed to reside in any district in that State within which its contacts would be sufficient to subject it to personal jurisdiction if that district were a separate State, and, if there is no such district, the corporation shall be deemed to reside in the district within which it has the most significant contacts.

These two provisions are admittedly a little grim. Basically they provide (§1391(c)(2) for a single-district state and §1391(d) for a multi-district state) that a corporate defendant resides in any judicial district in which its contacts would support personal jurisdiction over it. Why do we care where the corporation resides? Because §1391(b) allows venue in a district where all defendants reside. Section 1391(c) defines the residence of a corporate defendant *for purposes of applying §1391(b)(1)*.

Let's do an example; maybe it'll help. Imagine that Sampson Corporation is incorporated in Delaware (a single-district state). Sampson has its principal place of business in Richmond, in the Eastern District of Virginia, but no other contacts in Virginia. Teller (a driver for Sampson, who lives in Delaware) has an accident with Rimini in the Eastern District of Pennsylvania. What venues would be proper in Rimini's action against Sampson Corporation for her injuries? Well, she could sue in the Eastern District of Pennsylvania, basing venue on §1391(b)(2), right? Certainly the accident in that district is a substantial part of the events giving rise to her claim. But she could also choose to sue Sampson in any district in which it resides; §1391(b)(1) tells us that. And §1391(c)(2) tells us that Sampson resides in Delaware, since it could be sued in that district based on general in personam jurisdiction. See *Goodyear Dunlop Tires Operations, S.A. v. Brown*, 131 S. Ct. 2846, 2853-2854 (2011) (place of incorporation a paradigm case for general in personam jurisdiction). And §1391(d) tells us that Sampson resides in the Eastern District of Virginia, since its principal place of business is there. See *id.* (citing principal place of business as another paradigm case for general in personam jurisdiction). So Sampson's "residences" offer two additional venues for Rimini's action.

Just for contrast, suppose that Rimini sues Teller along with Sampson Corporation. The Eastern District of Pennsylvania is still a proper venue under §1391(b)(2). And the District of Delaware is also a proper venue under §1391(b)(1), because both defendants reside in Delaware: it is Teller's domicile and Sampson resides there under §1391(c)(2). But the Eastern District of Virginia is not a proper venue under §1391(b)(1), because only one of the defendants resides there.

Here's a question that allows you to grapple with these confusing provisions in §1391.

QUESTION 2. Venue exercises. Chu, a Californian, went skiing at Aspen, in Colorado, which has only one federal judicial district. After he discovered that he was somewhat out of shape, he bought an exercise machine from Jackson, a friend from Kansas with a two-week time share in Aspen, who had brought the machine with him to Aspen from his home in Texas. The machine was made by Sweda-Trak, a Texas company that sells its products only in Texas, and with its only place of business in the Western District of Texas. Chu brought the machine back to Los Angeles, California, where he was injured using it.

Chu brings a diversity action against Jackson and Sweda-Trak in federal court, alleging that Jackson was negligent in maintaining the machine, and Sweda-Trak in designing it. Venue in Chu's action would be

A. proper in the Southern District of California (which includes Los Angeles) under §1391(b)(2), because property that is the subject of the action is located there.
B. proper in the District of Colorado under §1391(b)(1), because both Jackson and Sweda-Trak reside there for venue purposes.
C. proper in the Southern District of California under §1391(b)(2), because a substantial part of the events giving rise to the claim took place there.
D. improper in the Southern District of California, because, while a substantial part of the events giving rise to the claim took place there, the defendants do not "reside" there under the venue statute.

ANALYSIS. This question didn't give my students much trouble. **A** is pretty clearly wrong. Although §1391(b)(2) allows suit in a district where property that is the subject of the action is located, the exercise machine is not "the subject of the action." This provision of §1391(b)(2) addresses cases in which an interest in property, such as a parcel of real estate or a bank deposit, is disputed, not a situation like this, in which the claim is for injury caused by a piece of personal property. This is not a suit about an interest in property; the "subject of the action" is the personal injury to Chu.

B is another loser. First of all, Jackson doesn't "reside" in Colorado based on a two-week time share. Courts have usually equated an individual's "residence" with her domicile, and the venue statute was recently amended to confirm this interpretation. See §1391(c)(1) (natural person's residence for venue purposes is the district of her domicile). (Remember that basing "residence" on being subject to personal jurisdiction in a district doesn't apply to individuals, just corporations, under §1391(c)(1) and (d).) In addition, Sweda-Trak doesn't reside in Colorado either. Section 1391(d) tells us that it "resides" for venue purposes in districts where it would be subject to personal jurisdiction for the plaintiff's claim. Sweda-Trak does no business in Colorado that would support general in personam jurisdiction. Nor would it be subject to specific in personam jurisdiction there based on Jackson's act of selling the exercise machine to Chu there. That's a contact of Jackson's. He took the machine there and sold it there. Sweda-Trak did nothing in Colorado at all, and its machine is not its "agent for service of process," subjecting it to jurisdiction wherever a third party takes it. So Colorado is not a proper venue under §1391(b)(1).

The Southern District of California is proper, however, under §1391(a)(2), since Chu suffered his injury there. Surely that is a "substantial part of the events . . . giving rise to the claim." So **C** is correct. Note, by the way, that Chu probably couldn't actually sue Sweda-Trak in the Southern District of California. It does business only in Texas, and did not sell the exercise machine into California, so (under the logic of *World-Wide Volkswagen v. Woodson,* 444 U.S. 286 (1980)), it would not be subject to personal jurisdiction there for Chu's claim. But *venue* would be proper in the Southern District of California, which is what the question asks.

D reflects the misconception that venue is only proper if *both* subsection (b)(1) and (b)(2) are met. Not so; venue is proper if the district satisfies one subsection or the other. Thus **C** prevails.

C. Corporate "residence" in multidistrict states under §1391(d)

Section 1391(d), which defines the residence of a corporation that has contacts in one district within a state but not others, is confusing. Suppose, for example, that Omni-Plex Corporation has its principal place of business in the Northern District of California, sufficient contact to support general in personam jurisdiction over the corporation, that is, jurisdiction for a claim that arises anywhere. Assume further that Omni-Plex has no contacts in any other federal district within California. Under §1391(d), Omni-Plex "resides" in the Northern District of California, because, if the Northern District were a state, its contacts there would be sufficient to support personal jurisdiction over it there. But it would not "reside" in the Eastern District of California. It has no contacts there, so that, if the Eastern District were a state, it would not be subject to personal jurisdiction there.

This is confusing because a defendant that has substantial and continuous contacts in a state is subject to personal jurisdiction *anywhere in the state,* not just in the part of the state where the contacts exist. But §1391(d) tells us that, for venue purposes, we should look at the contacts in each district within the state separately. The corporation will be deemed to "reside" only in the districts where its contacts would support personal jurisdiction if that district were a state.

Here's a question to illustrate the operation of this vexing provision.

QUESTION 3. Manufacturing venue. Arthur wishes to bring a diversity action in federal court against Cleveland Manufacturing Company. Cleveland has its factory and principal place of business in the Northern District of Illinois, but no other contacts with Illinois. The claim is based on alleged negligence in making a toaster at the Illinois factory, which caused a fire in Arthur's home in the Middle District of Georgia.

A. The Southern District of Illinois is a proper venue under §1391(b)(2) because a substantial part of the events giving rise to the claim took place in Illinois.

B. The Southern District of Illinois is a proper venue under §1391(d) because Cleveland Manufacturing is subject to general in personam jurisdiction in Illinois and therefore "resides" in the Southern District.

C. The Southern District of Illinois is not a proper venue under §1391 because no events giving rise to the claim took place there and Cleveland does not reside there under the venue statute.

D. The Northern District of Illinois is not a proper venue under §1391(b)(2), because a more substantial part of the events giving rise to the claim took place in the Southern District of Georgia.

ANALYSIS. Here, Cleveland has contacts in the Northern District of Illinois, but none in the Southern District. Therefore, under §1391(d), it "resides" in the Northern District, but not the Southern District. **B** is wrong. Although Cleveland Corporation, based on its principal place of business in the Northern District of Illinois, would be subject to personal jurisdiction *anywhere* in Illinois, that does not determine the venue analysis. Under §1391(d), Cleveland "resides" only in the districts where its contacts would support personal jurisdiction if that district were a separate state. Its contacts in the Southern District would not support personal jurisdiction over it if the Southern District were a state, since it has no contacts there at all.

A is also dead on arrival. It relies on §1391(b)(2), which provides that venue is proper in a district where a substantial part of the events giving rise to the claim took place. But again, under §1391(b)(2) we have to focus on the *district* where the events took place, not the state. Arthur cannot obtain venue in the Southern District based on the fact that events giving rise to the claim took place in the Northern District.

How about **D?** The accident that injured Cleveland in the Middle District of Georgia may be a "more substantial" event giving rise to his claim than the manufacture of the toaster in Illinois . . . or, it may not be. It's hard to say that one event is particularly more substantial than the other. But **D** is wrong because venue is proper in *any* district where a substantial part of the events giving rise to the claim took place, even if substantial events also took place in other districts. We don't have to choose which events are most substantial; the statute clearly contemplates that more than one district may be proper under §1391(b)(2). If important events giving rise to the claim take place in five districts (as, for example, large sales of a product that infringes a trademark in five districts), there may be five proper venues under subsection (b)(2).

So, **C** is the right answer. The Southern District of Illinois is not a proper venue.

How about one more example that involves both individual and corporate defendants?

QUESTION 4. Places of business. Excelsior Rubber Company brought a diversity action against Chem-Pro Company, for delivering adulterated chemicals to Excelsior that ruined a large production run of rubber. It also sued Compagna, the salesperson who had come to Excelsior's factory in Minnesota and misrepresented the purity of the chemicals, as a codefendant. Excelsior is incorporated in Delaware, with its principal (and only) place of business at its factory in Minnesota. Chem-Pro is incorporated in Florida with its principal place of business in the Western District of New York, and large factories in the Eastern District of Michigan and in the Northern District of Iowa. Compana lives in the Northern District of New York and regularly visits Chem-Pros' Michigan factory. The adulterated chemicals were manufactured at Chem-Pro's Iowa plant.

Venue in the action is probably proper in

A. the Southern District of New York.
B. the Eastern District of Michigan.
C. the Northern District of New York.
D. the District of Minnesota only, since the events giving rise to the claim took place there.

ANALYSIS. To answer this question, put the choices through the hoops of §1391(b). **A** doesn't cut the mustard. Nothing that gave rise to the claim took place in the Southern District of New York, and no defendant resides there. Compagna, the individual defendant, resides in the Northern District of New York. Under §1391(d), Chem-Pro resides in any New York district in which its contacts would suffice to support personal jurisdiction. But as far as the question reveals, Chem-Pro has no contacts in the Southern District, so it does not reside there under 28 U.S.C. §1391(d).

It is true that Chem-Pro would very likely be subject to general in personam jurisdiction in the Southern District of New York based on its principal place of business in the Western District. And a defendant that is subject to personal jurisdiction in a state is subject to jurisdiction in *any court within that state*, not just in a particular district. But even if Chem-Pro is subject to personal jurisdiction in the Southern District based on having its principal place of business in the state, that does not mean that it "resides" in the Southern District *for venue purposes* under §1391(d). For a multi-district state, §1391(d) focuses on the defendant's contacts *in the particular district.* We must ask whether those contacts would suffice to support personal jurisdiction over it if that district were a state. Here, Chem-Pro has no contacts in the Southern District, when viewed as a state, so it does not "reside" there under the venue statute.

Chem-Pro does "reside" in the Western District of New York, because its contacts there — having its principal place of business there — would almost certainly support general in personam jurisdiction over it if the Northern District were a separate state. Under §1391(b)(1), venue is proper in "a judicial district in which any defendant resides, if all defendants are residents of the State in which the district is located." Since Compagna resides in the Northern District of New York, both she and Chem-Pro "reside" in New York. Thus, venue is proper in a judicial district within New York where *either* resides. Either the Northern or Western District of New York is a proper venue. So **C** is right.

B is not right. It might be argued that Chem-Pro "resides" in the Eastern District of Michigan for venue purposes, since it would be subject to general in personam jurisdiction there based on its large factory in the Eastern District. It is not clear, after the *Goodyear* case, whether this would support general in personam jurisdiction in Michigan. But even if it would, Compagna, the other defendant, does not reside in Michigan. She visits there but lives in New York. An individual "resides" for venue purposes in the district of her domicile, not other districts that she visits. 28 U.S.C. §1391(c)(1). So venue is not proper in the Eastern District of Michigan under §1391(b)(1), even if Chem-Pro "resides" there. Nor is it proper under §1391(b)(2), since no events giving rise to Excelsior's claim took place in the Eastern District of Michigan.

D is wrong, because, while the District of Minnesota would be a proper venue under §1391(b)(2), it is not the *only* proper venue. The Northern District of New York is also a proper venue, under §1391(b)(1). Frequently there will be more than one proper venue in a case. In fact, the Western District of New York would also be proper in this case, since both defendants reside in New York, and one of them (Chem-Pro) resides in the Western District of New York.

D.   Forum non conveniens and transfer

So, venue is the "third ring" in choosing a proper court, along with personal jurisdiction and subject matter jurisdiction. If all three rings are satisfied, the court has the power to hear the case. However, it doesn't always do so. Sometimes a case is filed in a court that has subject matter jurisdiction over the case, personal jurisdiction over the defendant, and is a proper venue under the venue statutes, yet the court concludes, as a matter of common sense, that it should be litigated somewhere else.

Suppose, for example, that Robinson has an accident driving an Audi in Oklahoma, and wants to sue Audi, a German corporation, for his injuries. After the accident, Robinson moves to Arizona, but contacts a personal injury lawyer in Texas. The lawyer files suit on Robinson's claim in the Western District of Texas, where Audi has a large distribution facility. The federal court has subject matter jurisdiction, because the case is between a citizen of a state and an alien. 28 U.S.C. §1332(a)(2). It has personal jurisdiction, we will assume, based on Audi's extensive corporate operations in Texas. And venue is proper, since the only defendant, Audi, "resides" in the Western District, where its Texas operations are located. So Robinson has jumped through the hoops. The court has the authority to hear the case. But it doesn't make any sense for it to do so. The events giving rise to the claim took place in Germany and Oklahoma, the plaintiff was hospitalized in Oklahoma and now lives in Arizona. Why Texas for this case?

In *Gilbert v. Gulf Oil Co.*, 330 U.S. 501 (1947), the Supreme Court held that a federal district court could "dismiss for forum non conveniens" in cases like this, on the ground that, even though it had jurisdiction to adjudicate the case, practical factors suggest that it should be litigated somewhere else. The *Gulf Oil* court noted a number of factors a judge should consider in deciding whether to dismiss for forum non conveniens. One set of factors, the so-called "private interest factors," relate to the convenience of litigating the case. Such factors include the location of the events giving rise to the case, the ability to implead other parties in the court, the ability to take a view of premises involved in the dispute, and the location of relevant witnesses and documentary evidence. *Gulf Oil* also noted several "public interest" factors, including (among others) whether the dispute involves local people or events, and is likely to be decided under local law. In the Robinson example, both the private interest factors and the public interest factors point to litigating elsewhere — probably Oklahoma — rather than in Texas, since the events took place in Germany and Oklahoma, evidence is likely to be in those places, Oklahoma law is likely to govern, and Oklahomans — not Texans — would likely have an interest in observing the litigation and taking part (as jurors) in deciding it.

In response to the *Gulf Oil* decision, Congress enacted 28 U.S.C. §1404(a), the federal transfer-of-venue statute. Under this section, a judge may *transfer* a case filed in her court that should be litigated elsewhere to the more appropriate federal district, instead of dismissing it for forum non conveniens.

> (a) For the convenience of parties and witnesses, in the interest of justice, a district court may transfer any civil action to any other district or division where it might have been brought or to any district or division to which all parties have consented.

This statute makes good administrative sense. Because the federal district courts are all units of the same system, Congress has the authority to provide for transfer of cases among them to promote efficiency.[1] And, because the case is transferred rather than dismissed, the plaintiff need not file a new complaint, serve the defendant with process again or face statute of limitations problems. The case is simply passed on to the more appropriate federal district, where the litigation goes on.

Although the standard for transfer ("for the convenience of parties and witnesses, in the interest of justice") is as broad as a barn, case law interpreting §1404(a) makes clear that the factors outlined in *Gulf Oil* continue to govern the trial judge's discretionary decision whether to transfer a case to another district. However, since the consequences of transfer are less drastic, the presumption in favor of the plaintiff's chosen forum is somewhat weaker under §1404(a) than it would be under the common law forum non conveniens principle.

Today, §1404(a), rather than the common law forum non conveniens doctrine, governs most cases that are brought in a federal court. If the case should be litigated in another district, (and if it "might have been brought" in that district), the federal court will transfer it to that district under §1404(a) rather than dismiss for forum non conveniens. However, if the proper forum under the *Gulf Oil* analysis is in *another country*, the transfer statute does not apply; Congress could not enact a statute requiring courts in another country to accept transferred cases. Thus dismissal for forum non conveniens is the court's only option in cases like *Piper Aircraft Co. v. Reyno*, 454 U.S. 235 (1981), in which the court concluded that the case should be heard in Scotland. Forum non conveniens is also applied in state courts, which have no power to transfer cases to the courts of another state. If Jones files a case in a North Dakota state court that really ought to be litigated in Wisconsin, the North Dakota court will dismiss for forum non conveniens, leaving Jones to pursue his remedy by filing a new action in Wisconsin.

Note that §1404(a) allows transfer of a case to a district "where it might have been brought." The Supreme Court has interpreted this phrase to mean

---

1. States often have similar provisions allowing transfer from a state court in one county to the state court in another county of the same state. See, e.g., Mass. Gen. Laws ch. 223, §13.

that the case can only be transferred to a district where it could have been filed originally, that is, one that would be a proper venue and where the defendants would be subject to personal jurisdiction for the claim.[2] *Hoffman v. Blaski*, 363 U.S. 335 (1960). This substantially limits the court's options. For example, in *World-Wide Volkswagen v. Woodson*, 444 U.S. 286 (1980), Oklahoma would certainly be an appropriate place of trial for the plaintiff's claim against Seaway, the New York dealership that sold the car. It would even be a proper venue under §1391(a)(2), since a substantial part of the events took place in the Oklahoma district where the accident happened. But, if the case were filed in a New York federal court, the *Hoffman* rule would bar transfer to an Oklahoma federal district, since it could not have been brought there, for lack of personal jurisdiction over Seaway.

Here's a §1404(a) question that requires a basic application of these principles.

QUESTION 5. The federal shuffle. Connors, a computer programmer living in the Northern District of Texas, did some contract work for Ace Corporation, which is incorporated in Delaware with its principal place of business in the Northern District of Illinois. Ace has an office in the Northern District of Texas, but no other offices in Texas. It has large operations in three other states. Connors negotiated the contract by phone and e-mail from his home, dealing with Ace employees in the Texas office and the Illinois office. He did the programming work, which was to be used for Ace's Texas operation, at his home. Ace Corporation claimed that Connors had only done half the work, and refused to pay. Connors, believing that he had completed all the work called for under the contract, brought a diversity action against Ace for the contract price ($200,000) in federal court in the Northern District of Texas.

A. If Ace moves to transfer to the Southern District of Texas, the judge would have the authority to grant the motion, but probably wouldn't.

B. If Ace moves to transfer to the Northern District of Illinois, the court would not have the authority to do so, since the action could not have been brought there.

C. The court would have the authority to transfer to the Northern District of Illinois, but probably would not.

D. If Ace prefers to litigate the case in a Texas state court, it should move to dismiss for forum non conveniens. Section 1404(a) does not authorize transfer to a state court, but the common law doctrine would authorize dismissal.

---

2. A 2011 amendment to §1404(a) also allows transfer if all parties consent to the transfer.

ANALYSIS. A good place to start in analyzing a transfer question is with the *Hoffman v. Blaski* limitation: the federal court cannot transfer to a district unless the plaintiff could have filed the case there. In this case, Connors could not have filed suit in the Southern District of Texas, because it would not be a proper venue for the action. Ace does not "reside" there based on its operations in the Northern District. Remember, §1391(d) requires that we look at each district and ask whether the defendant's contacts in that district would support personal jurisdiction over it for the plaintiff's claim. Ace has no contacts in the Southern District, so it does not "reside" there under §1391(b)(1) and (d). Even though Ace would presumably be subject to personal jurisdiction in a court in the Southern District, based on its contacts with Connors that led to the suit in Texas, the action could not have "been brought" there under the venue statute, since Ace does not reside there under §1391(d) and no events giving rise to the claim took place there. Scratch **A** from the list.

The court would have the authority to transfer to the Northern District of Illinois under *Hoffman v. Blaski*. Ace, the sole defendant, would be subject to general in personam jurisdiction there, since its principal place of business is there. Consequently, it "resides" in that district under §1391(b)(1) (as elucidated by §1391(d)). So Connors' action could have been brought in the Northern District of Illinois. Scratch **B** as well.

Although the court would have authority under 28 U.S.C. §1404(a) to transfer this case to the Northern District of Illinois, why would it? Most of the events giving rise to the claim took place in the Northern District of Texas. The plaintiff did the work there, dealt with Ace employees there, and suffered the damages there. The programming was to be used in Ace's Texas office. The defendant, a corporation with a local office, would not be greatly inconvenienced or put to great expense to litigate this case in Texas. Some witnesses and evidence may be in Illinois, but it seems very doubtful that more would be there than in Texas. It seems highly unlikely that the convenience of witnesses and the interests of justice require transfer of this case to Illinois. So **C** takes the cake.

The last choice is a real spaceshot. It suggests that a defendant who is sued in federal court but prefers state court could move to dismiss for forum non conveniens, arguing that state court is more appropriate. This effort to use forum non conveniens as a forum shopping tactic is not going to work. The federal court in Texas is not "inconvenient" because the defendant prefers state court. Forum non conveniens does not authorize a federal court to dismiss so that a party can litigate in state court instead. That would provide a form of "reverse removal" that is not authorized by the federal removal statutes.

If the defendant's real argument is that a court in another state is preferable, the court can—if it agrees—transfer to a *federal* court in the other state under §1404(a). Forum non conveniens will not allow the defendant sued in a federal court to avoid the federal court system, unless the proper forum is in another country. If that is the case, the federal court will dismiss the case even though it was properly filed in federal court.

Here's a nice little question that requires you to consider removal, personal jurisdiction, transfer, and forum non conveniens. It flummoxed a good many of my students.

QUESTION 6. Any port in a storm. Cullen, a Vermont citizen, has an accident with Barnabas, a citizen of California, and Tecumseh, a New Yorker, in California. She sues Barnabas and Tecumseh for negligence in state court in Albany, New York, alleging negligence. She serves Barnabas with process in the action while he is visiting Albany.

Barnabas's best argument for getting the case out of the New York state court would be to file

A. a motion to transfer the case to a California court under 28 U.S.C. §1404(a).
B. a motion to dismiss for lack of personal jurisdiction under the Fourteenth Amendment.
C. a motion to dismiss for forum non conveniens.
D. a notice of removal, removing the action to federal court.

ANALYSIS. This question provides a nice little recap of various jurisdiction and venue issues. Barnabas wants out of the New York state court. What motion is likely to do the trick?

Removal seems like an option, though of course he'd still have to litigate in New York. Remember that you can only remove to the federal court that encompasses the place where the state court action was filed. But, you can't remove a diversity case (as this negligence case would be) if there is a defendant from the forum state. 28 U.S.C. §1441(b)(2). Since Tecumseh is a New Yorker, option **D** isn't available.

How about personal jurisdiction? Barnabas is from California, and the accident took place in California. But Barnabas was served with process in the action in New York. The Supreme Court suggested, in *Burnham v. Superior Court*, 495 U.S. 604 (1990), that a court can usually obtain personal jurisdiction over an individual defendant by service of process within the state. So **B** fails; his motion to dismiss for lack of personal jurisdiction would likely be denied.

A isn't right either. Section 1404(a) is a federal statute, authorizing a federal court to transfer a case to another federal court. It does not govern the state courts. There is no transfer statute allowing state courts in one state to transfer cases to courts in another. No state could constitutionally write a statute authorizing transfer to the courts of another state, which is a separate sovereign for most purposes. Congress probably couldn't either, and it hasn't.

Barnabas's best argument would be that, since he is from California, the accident took place there, and much of the evidence regarding the accident is likely to be there, the New York court should dismiss, leaving Cullen to refile in California. The argument for **C** is not a sure winner: Two of the parties live in the Northeast, and the evidence may be primarily the testimony of the parties, all of whom are before the New York court. But at least there would be an argument that the case should be litigated in a California court. Barnabas could try, and the New York court would have to think about it. It's a colorable argument. The other three fail as a matter of law.

E. Complications, complications: Transfer under 28 U.S.C. §1406(a)

So, when a plaintiff files suit in a district that is proper under the venue statute, the court may hear the case. However, it might also transfer it if the *Gulf Oil* factors suggest that it should be litigated in another federal district. But suppose a plaintiff files in a district that is *not* a proper venue under 28 U.S.C. §1391?

Naturally, the defendant may move to dismiss such a case for improper venue, under Fed. R. Civ. P. 12(b)(3). And, the court would be within its rights to grant the motion. But could it *transfer* the case instead, to a federal district in which venue is proper? This is the scenario addressed by 28 U.S.C. §1406(a). Section 1404(a) applies to cases in which the plaintiff chooses a proper venue and the court considers transferring the case elsewhere. Section 1406(a) applies when the plaintiff files in an improper venue and the court considers curing the problem by transfer.

Section 1406(a) provides that, if the case is filed in an improper venue, the court "shall dismiss, or if it be in the interest of justice, transfer such case to any district or division in which it could have been brought." Note several things about the statute: first, it gives the federal district judge the authority to dismiss rather than transfer. Second, it allows the judge to transfer, even though the case is not properly before her (because venue is improper). And third, it limits the districts the case can be transferred to: It may only be moved to a district where it might have been brought. The cases interpret this limitation in §1406(a) the same as the similar language in §1404(a), that is, to limit transfer to a district that would be a proper venue and have personal jurisdiction over the defendants.

A striking virtue of section 1406(a) is that it allows a court to save a plaintiff's cause of action if she files in the wrong venue shortly before the limitations period passes. Section 1404(a) would not authorize transfer: It applies to cases that are properly filed in the transferor district. But §1406(a) allows the court to transfer the case to a proper district rather than dismissing. Thus, the suit is not re-started in the transferee forum, but continued. As long as it was filed in the wrong venue before the limitations period ran, the judge can send it to a district that is proper under the venue statute, and it will continue on, even though it only reached the proper court after the passage of the limitations period. It also saves the plaintiff the trouble of drafting a new complaint, refiling it in the new district, and serving the defendants with process. Here's an illustration.

QUESTION 7. A venue medley. Zirkhov brings a diversity action against Pardee, a truck driver from Ohio, and Lugo Enterprises, his employer, for injuries in an accident that took place in the Western District of Kentucky. He files the action in the federal district court for the Northern District of Illinois, where Lugo's principal place of business is located. Pardee, who lives in Ohio, moves to dismiss the action for improper venue.

A. The court would grant the motion to dismiss. Although the Western District of Kentucky would be a proper venue, the court has not been asked to transfer the action there, so it must dismiss.

B. The court would have the authority to transfer the action to the Western District of Kentucky under 28 U.S.C. §1406(a) or to dismiss it.

C. The court must transfer the action to the Western District of Kentucky under 28 U.S.C. §1406(a), since it is a proper venue.

D. The court will have to dismiss, since 28 U.S.C. §1406(a) only allows transfer to a district in which the case might have been brought.

E. The court could transfer the action under 28 U.S.C. §1404(a) if doing so would be in the interest of justice.

ANALYSIS. A good place to start is to ask whether venue is proper in the Northern District of Illinois. If it is, then §1406(a) is irrelevant, and that eliminates three answers off the bat. Venue is not proper under §1391(b). Section 1391(b)(2) is not satisfied, since no events giving rise to the claim took place in the Northern District of Illinois. And §1391(b)(1) is not satisfied, since only one defendant resides in Illinois. Scratch E from the list, and focus on the answers that deal with application of §1406(a).

A is interesting. It suggests that the court can't transfer on its own motion to save Zirkhov's case. Practically, however, the defendant is unlikely to move to transfer; she wants to get rid of the case, not send it somewhere else. And she has a perfectly good motion to dismiss under Rule 12(b)(3). So she's not going to ask to transfer. And the plaintiff filed the suit; why would she ask to transfer it (other than to save her derriere if it looks like the court may dismiss). It is well established that the court may invoke §1406(a) on its own motion to transfer the case instead of granting Pardee's motion to dismiss it. That's why Congress enacted the section.

Nibbling away at the edges, consider **D**, which takes the position that the Illinois federal judge can't transfer, since the case could not have been filed in the Western District of Kentucky. But it could have been. Because a significant part of the events giving rise to the claim — the accident — took place there, the Western District is a proper venue under §1391(b)(2), and both defendants would be subject to personal jurisdiction in Kentucky.

C suggests that the judge must transfer under §1406(a) if there is another proper venue. The language of the statute leaves the decision whether to dismiss or transfer to the judge in the transferor district. Even if dismissing instead of transferring would croak the plaintiff's case, the court may dismiss under §1406(a). This would hardly be "in the interest of justice" in most cases, but it might be in some. So **B** reigns; the decision whether to dismiss is within the judge's discretion. Zirkhov should throw himself on the mercy of the court and plead for a transfer.

F.   The Closer: The professor outsmarts himself

One of the dangers of multiple-choice testing is that the professor may know less than she thinks she does. Here's a question that struck me as fair, even straightforward, when I wrote it. However, only *9 percent* of my students got it right. As it turns out, there's an ambiguity in the law that I never saw until I wrote this chapter. I'll never know whether that ambiguity led to the large number of "wrong" answers, but it makes an interesting study in the perils of multiple-choice testing.

QUESTION 8. International incident.   Tiant sues Lenoir, who lives in the Southern District of New York, and Sorrel, who lives in the Western District of Pennsylvania, for negligence in causing an auto accident in the province of Ontario, Canada. Tiant, a pedestrian from Ontario, was injured when cars driven by Lenoir and Sorrel collided and swerved off the road. He alleges that Lenoir was negligent in running a red light at the time of the accident, causing the collision with Sorrel. He claims that Sorrel was negligent in improperly repairing his brakes himself at his home in Pennsylvania, so he couldn't avoid hitting Tiant after the collision. He brings suit in the federal district court for the Southern District of

> New York, and serves Sorrel with process in the action while Sorrel is visiting New York City.
>
> A. Venue is proper in the Southern District of New York under 28 U.S.C. §1391(b)(3) since the defendants are subject to personal jurisdiction in New York.
> B. Venue is proper in the Southern District of New York under 28 U.S.C. §1391(b)(1) because both defendants "reside" in the Southern District of New York for purposes of the venue statute.
> C. Venue is not proper in the Southern District of New York; it is only proper in the Western District of Pennsylvania.
> D. Venue is not proper in any federal district.

GLANNON'S INITIAL ANALYSIS.   First, let's go through the analysis as I understood it when I wrote — and graded — the question.

B concludes that the defendants both "reside" in the Southern District of New York. But Sorrel doesn't reside there. For individual defendants, "reside" means the district where the defendant is domiciled. Perhaps some of the 91 percent who got this question wrong confused the meaning of "reside" in subsection (1) with the definition of where a *corporation* resides in §1391(d). Under that subsection a corporation does "reside" in a district where it is subject to personal jurisdiction. Not so individuals, however; for them, most courts have equated the term "reside" with the concept of domicile. The venue statute now states this explicitly. 28 U.S.C. §1391(c)(1).

A states that venue is proper in the Southern District of New York because the defendants are subject to personal jurisdiction there. However, while they are both subject to jurisdiction there, this doesn't mean that venue is proper in the Southern District, *unless* §1391(b)(3) applies; (b)(3) does not apply if there is *any district* in the United States where the action may be brought under subsection (1) or (2). Here, there is such a proper district: the Western District of Pennsylvania. Surely, Sorrel's negligent repair in that district was "a substantial part of the events . . . giving rise to the claim" (although, arguably, only to the claim against Sorrel), so that district would be proper under §1391(b)(2). So venue cannot be premised on where the defendants are subject to personal jurisdiction.

So, **C** is right. . . . I thought (and it may even *be* right, though it's not so clear to me now). Venue is proper in the Western District of Pennsylvania, under §1391(b)(2), since a substantial part of the events giving rise to the claim took place there. This is *almost* a case in which there is no proper venue under subsections (1) and (2), but not quite.

A MORE EDUCATED ANALYSIS.   While writing this chapter, I stumbled on a case that interprets §1391 differently. *F.S. Photo, Inc. v. Picture Vision, Inc.*,

48 F. Supp. 2d 448 (D. Del. 1999) interpreted the language "if there is no district in which the action may otherwise be brought" to apply if there is no district that would be a proper venue *and in which the defendants would be subject to personal jurisdiction.* This interpretation, although it had never occurred to me in ten years of teaching the statute, makes a lot of sense. After all, the statute doesn't say, "if there is no other district that would be a proper venue." And a case cannot be brought in a district unless the defendants are subject to personal jurisdiction there. And it makes sense that Congress would intend the statute to be interpreted in a way that assures at least one venue where the action really *could* be litigated, not just one where venue would be satisfied but the action still couldn't be litigated (due to lack of personal jurisdiction).

Assuming that this is what §1391(b)(3) means, Tiant's case *is* one where "there is no other district in which the action may otherwise be brought," because there is no basis for exercising personal jurisdiction over Lenoir in the Western District of Pennsylvania. And, if that is so, then **A** is the best answer to this question. And I owe some students—who knows how many—some retroactive extra points.

Actually, there may be an even more basic problem with this question. It is clear that venue is proper *as to the claim against Sorrel,* in the Western District of Pennsylvania. That's where he repaired the brakes, which is surely a "substantial part of the events . . . giving rise to the claim" 28 U.S.C. §1391(a)(2). But Lenoir didn't do anything in the Western District of Pennsylvania. If Lenoir were sued alone for this claim, venue would presumably not be proper in that district, because none of the events giving rise to the *claim against him* took place there. So, the interpretive question is, if venue is proper on the claim against one defendant, is it also proper as to other defendants who did not act in that district?

The answer to this is, unfortunately, unclear. A few cases have applied a concept of "pendent venue," under which venue is proper as to all claims if it is proper as to one. See, e.g., *Pacer Global Logistics, Inc. v. National Passenger R.R. Corp.,* 272 F. Supp. 2d 784 (E.D. Wis. 2003). But it is not clear that this is the proper interpretation of 28 U.S.C. §1391. So this question was doubly dubious.

There's a lesson in this. Writing a good multiple-choice question, one that is reasonably clear and has a single clearly best answer, is a sophisticated enterprise that can go awry. Although we usually do OK, professors aren't infallible. Some of us aren't even all that smart.

Now that you've waded through the entire chapter, you've no doubt noticed that all but one of the answers were "**C**"s. Can you imagine how berserk you would be if you worked your way through a multiple-choice exam and had the same choice for every question! Your professor would have to be unusually diabolical to do this to you. But there's a strategic point here: In answering a question, it is utterly, totally, completely irrelevant what the answers to the other questions were. Ignore them completely! So what if they're all Cs; that's the professor's problem. If they're your best choices, go with them.

Glannon's Picks

1. Redistricting	C
2. Venue exercises	C
3. Manufacturing venue	C
4. Places of business	C
5. The federal shuffle	C
6. Any port in a storm	C
7. A venue medley	B
8. International incident	C, er . . . A?

11

State Law in Federal Courts: Basics of the *Erie* Doctrine

There once was a railroad named Erie
Whose doors on its freight cars were weary.
When Tompkins got hit
The Court took a fit
And tossed out the Swift/Tyson theory.

CHAPTER OVERVIEW

A. The bad old days: The rule of *Swift v. Tyson*
B. The Great Divide: *Erie Railroad Co. v. Tompkins*
C. Federal courts determining the content of state law
D. The precedential effect of an *"Erie"* guess
E. The impact of change in the state law on federal diversity cases
F. The Closer: Which state's law?
◆ Glannon's Picks

When the plaintiff sues in federal court, and asserts a claim arising under federal law, such as a claim under a federal civil rights statute or the federal copyright statute, the federal court will obviously apply federal law in deciding the case (or, at least, in deciding the *federal claim* on which its jurisdiction is based). But if the plaintiff sues in federal court based on diversity jurisdiction, the case, by definition, does *not* arise under federal law . . . if it did, it would be a federal question case.

So, it seems axiomatic that the federal court will apply state law in diversity cases. If Bergin, from Oregon, sues Pollard, from Washington, for breach of contract, it seems that state contract law should apply. However, for over a hundred years, under the rule of *Swift v. Tyson*, 41 U.S. 1 (1842), federal courts did *not* apply the law of any particular state in a diversity case. Instead, they looked to something called "general common law" to determine the appropriate contracts principle to apply to cases like Bergin's.

This chapter explores the rule of *Swift v. Tyson*, and the meaning and application of *Erie Railroad Co. v. Tompkins*, 304 U.S. 64 (1938), which overruled it. The next chapter struggles with the more complex "substance/procedure" cases following *Erie*.

A.   The bad old days: The rule of *Swift v. Tyson*

The First Congress recognized and addressed the problem of the substantive law to be applied in diversity cases in 1789. They passed the Rules of Decision Act, which has remained in effect, with almost no textual change, ever since. Today it reads:

> **28 U.S.C. §1652. State Laws as Rules of Decision**
> The laws of the several states, except where the Constitution or treaties of the United States or Acts of Congress otherwise require or provide, shall be regarded as the rules of decision in civil actions in the courts of the United States, in cases where they apply.

This would seem to settle the matter. If a federal statute, constitutional provision, or treaty applies, it will provide the governing law. Otherwise, the federal court should apply relevant state law. In a federal question case, of course, federal law *would* apply, by definition. But in diversity cases and some others within the federal judicial power, state law should govern.

Although this may have been the First Congress's intent, Justice Story interpreted the Rules of Decision Act (which I will refer to as "the RDA") more narrowly in *Swift*. Justice Story concluded that the phrase, "the laws of the several states" in the RDA referred only to state statutes, not to the common law decisions of state courts. If the Pennsylvania legislature enacted a statute providing that "The only duty of care owed to a trespasser on a railroad right-of-way is the duty to avoid wilful and wanton conduct," *Swift* recognized that a federal court would be bound, under the RDA, to apply that state "law" in a diversity case. However, if there were no such statute, but Pennsylvania Supreme Court had held that railroads owe trespassers a duty to avoid wilful or wanton conduct, *Swift* concluded that the RDA did not require the federal court—even in Pennsylvania—to follow that decision.

If it didn't apply Pennsylvania law to such a case, what law was it to apply? Story thought the federal court should apply *the common law* to the case. He, and perhaps all judges at the time, thought of the common law as a general body of legal principles, carried over from English law and adapted to American conditions, to govern common types of disputes such as contract, commercial, and tort cases. They didn't think of it as "Pennsylvania common law," or "Georgia common law," but as *the common law*, which every court applied and had the duty to apply correctly. Thus a Pennsylvania judge, a Florida judge, or a federal judge would examine all the authorities on an issue—such as the duty of care owed to a trespasser—and determine what the proper rule should be. All common law judges looked to the same broad sources for insight into the "true rule" of duty of care to trespassers, and applied the true rule as they deduced it from those authorities.[1]

Proceeding from this premise, Justice Story concluded in *Swift* that the federal judge should look at relevant authorities, not just from New York (where the *Swift* case arose) but all jurisdictions, and secondary materials such as treatises as well, to determine the proper answer to the commercial law issue posed in that case. The question was not, "What is the New York rule on consideration for cancellation of a debt," but rather, "what is the proper common law rule with regard to consideration for cancellation of a debt?"

So, under *Swift*, federal courts in diversity cases routinely reached their own conclusions about the proper rule in common law cases, even if those conclusions contradicted the governing case law of the state in which they sat.

Consider the following illustration of life under the *Swift* regime. Assume that pre-Erie law, that is, the *Swift* doctrine, applies.

> **QUESTION 1. Life before Erie.** Thomas is injured while walking along the railroad right of way in Pennsylvania in 1910, during the heyday of *Swift v. Tyson*. He is hit by something protruding from the train, perhaps a door. He sues the Erie Railroad Company in federal court for his injuries, basing federal jurisdiction on diversity. He alleges that the Railroad owed him a duty of due care, since it was aware that trespassers routinely used the right-of-way. Pennsylvania had no statute covering the duty of care owed to a railroad trespasser, but Pennsylvania cases had held that railroads owed trespassers only a duty to avoid willful or wanton conduct. Assume that no federal statute or constitutional provision applies.

---

1. Of course, a state *trial* court judge would only do this if there were no governing precedent from the state's appellate courts. If there were, the trial judge would be bound to follow such "mandatory authority."

A. The Rules of Decision Act, as interpreted by Justice Story in
   Swift v. Tyson, would require the federal court to apply Pennsylvania
   law to Thomas's claim.
B. Under *Swift v. Tyson*, the federal court would apply Pennsylvania
   common law to Thomas's claim, because its jurisdiction was based on
   diversity.
C. The Rules of Decision Act, as interpreted by Justice Story, would require
   the federal judge to apply federal law to Thomas's claim.
D. None of the above is true.

ANALYSIS.   Actually, none of the above is true, except **D**. Each mistakes
the holding of *Swift v. Tyson* in one way or another.

   A fails because Justice Story held that the Rules of Decision Act did not
require federal courts to apply common law rules of the state in which they
sat. Instead, *Swift* held that the federal court should make its own judgment
as to the proper common law rule, based on its review of all relevant cases
and secondary authorities. It might conclude that the willful/wanton rule
was appropriate, and choose to apply it, but it might also conclude that the
Pennsylvania cases did not represent the correct approach to trespasser
liability, and apply a different rule under *Swift's* "general common law"
approach.

   B also contains a fatal flaw. It states that *Swift* required the federal court
in a diversity case to apply Pennsylvania common law in deciding Thomas's
case. *Swift's* holding was quite the contrary: The point of *Swift* was that the
federal judge in a diversity case (even a Pennsylvania federal judge) did *not*
have to apply Pennsylvania common law — the decisions of the Pennsylvania
state courts — in deciding the appropriate standard of care owed to Thomas.
Under *Swift*, the federal judge was to apply the "general common law,"
looking at relevant authorities from Pennsylvania, from other states, from
English cases, and secondary authorities as well, in determining what the
"true rule" of duty of care to a trespasser should be. Indeed, the mindset
was, in a sense, that there was no such thing as "the common law of
Pennsylvania," but rather a general body of law called *the* common law, that
judges from all state and federal courts attempted to perceive and apply
correctly.

   C also misstates the holding of *Swift*. The RDA, even in the heyday of
Swift, required federal courts to apply federal law where a federal statute or
constitutional provision applied. Or, if a state statute or "local usage"
applied, it should be applied in a diversity case. If there were no state statute
or local usage involved, and no federal statute or constitutional provision at
issue, the RDA did not dictate the governing law at all. Instead, *Swift v. Tyson*
itself held that the federal court should apply "general common law," based
on its reading of all the authorities, not just the holdings of the local state

courts. So, if one of the choices had been "Under *Swift v. Tyson*, the federal court would look to the general common law to determine the applicable duty of care," that would have taken the prize.

The case usually given as a perfectly horrible example of the application of *Swift* is *Black & White Taxicab Co. v. Brown & Yellow Taxicab Co.*, 276 U.S. 518 (1928). In that case, Brown & Yellow ran a taxi business in Kentucky, but reincorporated in Tennessee, to create diversity between it and Black & White Taxicab Company. It then brought a diversity action in federal court — in Kentucky — to enforce its exclusive contract with the railroad for conveyance of passengers at the Bowling Green, Kentucky, railroad station. Federal courts, under *Swift*, enforced such exclusive contracts, but Kentucky's courts did not. Brown & Yellow, having manipulated the case into federal court, argued that the federal court could enforce the contract.

Consider this variation on the *Black & White* case.

QUESTION 2. The out-of-state advantage. In 1920, before *Erie*, Black & White Taxicab sought to do business at the Bowling Green railroad station. However, Brown & Yellow Taxicab, a Tennessee cab company, had an exclusive contract with the railroad to pick up and discharge passengers there. Since Kentucky courts held such contracts against public policy, Black & White sued Brown & Yellow in a Kentucky court, to enjoin it from enforcing the contract. Brown & Yellow removed the case to federal court in Kentucky (the only court it could remove to — see now 28 U.S.C. §1441(a)) on the basis of diversity jurisdiction. Assume that diversity exists and the amount-in-controversy requirement is met.

The federal court would

A. apply Kentucky law, because the case was brought originally in a Kentucky court.
B. apply Kentucky law under the Rules of Decision Act.
C. apply Kentucky law, because the disputed events took place in Kentucky.
D. apply general common law, under *Swift*.

ANALYSIS. This question isn't too hard, but it nicely illustrates the reach of the *Swift* doctrine. Here, the federal and state courts differ in their approach to exclusive contracts. The Kentucky company shops for Kentucky law, which is more favorable to its position, by suing in state court. But the diversity defendant seeks to displace Kentucky law with "general common law," by removing to federal court *in Kentucky,* and arguing that the federal court should ignore Kentucky's rule.

Under *Swift*, the federal court would make its own judgment whether to enforce an exclusive contact, so long as no state statute applied. Under Justice Story's rationale, that state and federal judges both looked to the same sources to ascertain the proper rule, the federal judge would make an independent judgment on the enforceability of the exclusive contract. **A** fails because the federal court, under *Swift*, would have the authority to apply "general common law," whether the case was filed in federal court or removed to it. Either way, the federal court was not bound by the state's approach to the issue. **B** is wrong, because *Swift* held that the RDA did not require federal courts to follow state decisions on common law issues. **C** is also wrong; under *Swift*, the federal court did not apply the local law of the state in which it sat (though it would respect certain "local usages," such as property and water rights rules). Under Justice Story's worldview, the law could not be "one thing in Rome and another in Athens." See *Swift*, 41 U.S. at 19. If enforcing exclusive contracts was the proper rule, the federal court would apply it to a Kentucky case, whether Kentucky judges disagreed or not. Thus **D** is the best answer; the federal court would very likely make its own judgment whether to enforce the contract, under general common law principles.

Note the options this provided to the out-of-state party in a diversity case. If Kentucky law favored Brown & Yellow, the out-of-state party, it could sue in Kentucky state court. Because in-state defendants may not remove in diversity cases (see 28 U.S.C. §1441(b)), Black & White would be stuck in the state court, with the state rule. If federal courts applied a more favorable rule under *Swift*, the out-of-state party could sue in federal court. In that scenario, Black & White would be stuck in *federal* court, since there's no right to "remove" from federal court to state court. See Chapter 4, p. 62. Thus, the out-of-state defendant had a choice of different contracts rules, because it had a choice of two court systems.

B.   The Great Divide: *Erie Railroad Co. v. Tompkins*

The decision in *Erie* really was the great divide, between the era of *Swift v. Tyson* and a new approach to determining the applicable law in diversity cases. In *Erie*, the Supreme Court held that *Swift's* interpretation of the RDA, restricting its scope to state statutes and local usages, led to an unconstitutional assumption of power by the federal courts. Under the Constitution, the federal government is a government of limited powers. It can legislate on those subjects delegated to it in Article I of the Constitution, but power to legislate on subjects *not* within that delegation is left to the states. United States Constitution, Amendment X. However, under *Swift*, the federal courts were "making" law in many substantive areas the Constitution leaves to the states. Congress has no general power to make law in areas such as contracts, torts, commercial law, and wills and trusts. But under *Swift* the federal courts *were* making law in these areas in diversity cases.

It was this undelegated assumption of law-making power that the Supreme Court declared unconstitutional in *Erie.* Instead, the *Erie* Court held, the RDA must be interpreted to require federal courts to apply not only the state statutes, but also the common law of the state in a diversity case.

Under *Erie*, the federal court in a diversity case cannot apply federal law, or its own perception of the "proper" rule under "general common law." Instead, it must apply the law of the relevant state, whether that law is found in a state statute or established by the state's courts through case law. If Pennsylvania has a statute proclaiming that trespassers are owed only a duty to avoid willful and wanton negligence, a federal court sitting in diversity must apply that statute (if the appropriate state law is Pennsylvania law). If there is no relevant statute, but the Pennsylvania Supreme Court has held that trespassers are owed a duty to avoid willful and wanton negligence, a federal diversity court must apply that judicial rule. A federal diversity court, after *Erie*, is not a law-making court. It is instead a law-applying court, and the law it applies is the law of the relevant state.

Consider the application of the *Erie* principle in the following case.

QUESTION 3. The state of the law. Thompson, a trespasser, is injured while walking along the Erie Railroad's Pennsylvania right-of-way in 1973. He sues the Railroad for his injuries in a Pennsylvania state court. Assume that, at the time his suit is filed, most states have held that railroads owe a duty of due care to trespassers on a lateral right-of-way. Assume further that no Pennsylvania statute applies, but the Pennsylvania Supreme Court had held, in *Estrada v. Corrault*, in 1921, before *Erie*, that the only duty of care owed to the trespasser was to avoid willful or wanton conduct. It has not revisited the duty-of-care issue since, or suggested in analogous cases or dictum that it would decide the issue differently today. However, a good many other states have (please assume) adopted a due care standard for such cases.

The Railroad removes Thompson's suit to federal court based on diversity jurisdiction. The federal court will apply

A. general common law on the duty-of-care issue, since the case has been removed to federal court.
B. Pennsylvania's willful-or-wanton conduct rule established in the *Estrada* case.

C. general common law on the duty-of-care issue, since no Pennsylvania statute applies and the only Pennsylvania case on point was decided before *Erie*.

D. its own conclusion about the preferable duty of care, since there is no Pennsylvania statute on the point or recent Pennsylvania case.

ANALYSIS.   If you kept your eye on the ball, this question should not have given you trouble. **A** is likely to distract only those who haven't understood the basic issue. This case is a diversity case. Consequently, under *Erie*, the federal court must apply state law to it, not "make up" the law. The fact that this diversity case comes to federal court by removal, rather than by Thompson's filing it directly in the federal court, does not change the fact that the federal court must apply state law to it. It would make no sense to allow federal courts to make up "general common law" in diversity cases removed to federal court, but require them to apply state law to those filed there directly. This would simply introduce a new type of discrimination, between cases filed initially in federal court and those removed to it. And it would contradict the *Erie* Court's fundamental premise: that the federal court has no constitutional authority to make the law in a diversity case. That's equally true whether a diversity case starts in federal court or is removed to it.

D suggests that the federal court could apply its own views about the preferable duty-of-care rule, since no Pennsylvania statute applies and only an old, pre-Erie Pennsylvania case covers the point. But what difference does it make that *Estrada*, which held that the duty is to avoid willful and wanton conduct, pre-dates *Erie*? It's still a case from Pennsylvania's highest court establishing Pennsylvania law. Unless that court has given clear indications that it would overrule *Estrada*, which the question indicates it has not, that case represents Pennsylvania law on the issue. *Erie* requires the federal court to apply it, whether it is out of step with the "modern" cases or the federal judge's views or not. Thus, **D** and **C** are both wrong. **B** is correct. The federal court must apply the law of Pennsylvania to this case, and the willful/wanton rule is Pennsylvania law.

So, the federal courts can't make state law in diversity cases. But how about this case?

QUESTION 4. Supplementing the *Erie* doctrine.   Zandrow, from Texas, sues Beta Corporation (a Texas corporation) in federal court. In his first claim for relief, he alleges that Beta violated the Federal Age Discrimination in Employment Act, by firing him due to his age. In his second claim, he asserts that Beta violated his contract of employment by firing him without cause. (The federal court has supplemental jurisdiction over this claim, because it arises out of the same events as the federal claim.) Assume that, under the law of Texas, where Zandrow was hired, worked, and was fired, the employer can fire a worker at any time without cause. However, in many states (please assume) an employee may sue for "bad faith discharge," if fired without cause.

In deciding the breach of contract claim, the federal court should

A. apply federal law, since this is not a diversity case. The court has subject matter jurisdiction over the case based on federal arising-under jurisdiction.
B. create "general common law" to govern the claim, since it is not a diversity case.
C. apply Texas law to the claim.
D. dismiss the state law contract claim in its discretion, because it arises under state law.

ANALYSIS.   Zandrow's case is not a diversity case. It's a federal question case, or, as I prefer to call it, an "arising-under" case, because Zandrow asserts a claim against Beta that arises under a federal statute. However, Zandrow has also asserted a second claim, arising from the same facts, under state law. This, in modern parlance, is a "supplemental" claim, a claim arising under state law that could not have been brought in federal court on its own, but is asserted along with another jurisdictionally sufficient claim.

As noted in the question, the federal court has supplemental jurisdiction over the state breach of contract claim, since it arises out of the same case or controversy as the main federal claim. 28 U.S.C. §1367(a). **D** implies that federal courts should always dismiss such related state law claims in federal cases. But the grant of supplemental jurisdiction in §1367 clearly authorizes federal courts to hear related state law claims in federal cases. Section 1367(c) gives the federal court discretion to decline supplemental jurisdiction, but the very existence of that discretion to decline jurisdiction in limited circumstances reaffirms that federal courts generally will hear supplemental state law claims in federal question cases.

So what law should the court apply to the contract claim? Clearly, the court must apply state law to it. The basic premise of *Erie* is that federal courts cannot displace state law just because they have jurisdiction to hear a dispute. This logic applies equally to state law claims that are litigated in federal court based on either supplemental jurisdiction or diversity jurisdiction. In the one context, as in the other, the federal courts don't have the power to make general contract law. Since the federal court has the power to hear the contract claim, but not to create the law to govern it, the federal court must apply state law to it. Although this isn't a diversity case, the logic of *Erie* applies. So **A** and **B** are also wrong. The court must apply Texas law to the state law claim. **C** is the best answer.

C.   Federal courts determining the content of state law

The *Erie* case established the basic proposition: A federal court hearing a state law claim — whether in a diversity case or a federal question case with supplemental state law claims — must apply the law of the relevant state to the state law claim, not make "general common law." That, of course, provides a fresh problem for the federal judge in such cases: how is she to determine what the law of the state *is*?

Sometimes this is easy. If the Pennsylvania Supreme Court has recently decided a case on the duty of care to a trespasser on a railroad right of way, and reaffirmed the willful/wanton rule, the federal judge knows her course. But how often will that be true? More often, there will be an older state supreme court decision on point, or on an analogous point. Perhaps there's a Pennsylvania Supreme Court case from 1963 that reaffirms the willful/wanton rule for railroad trespassers, or a 1982 case that *abandons* that rule for trespassers on residential property . . . or both! Or, perhaps there is dicta in a 1998 Pennsylvania intermediate appellate court opinion suggesting that the early case establishing the willful/wanton rule is inconsistent with modern tort principles of the state, including the 1982 case on residential trespassers.

Suppose that all three of these cases are on the books, the 1963 decision reiterating the willful/wanton rule, the 1982 state supreme court decision changing the rule for residential property, and the 1998 appellate court decision doubting whether the willful/wanton rule would be followed by the Pennsylvania Supreme Court today. What should the federal court do?

Early post-Erie cases suggested that the federal court had to follow any state precedent on point, whether the state supreme court would be likely to decide differently today. Under this approach, the federal court, sitting in diversity and adjudicating a railroad trespasser case, would have to apply the 1963 case affirming the willful/wanton rule. That case is on point, and has not been overruled. Thus, it is "good law," even if it might — or even probably — would be reconsidered by the Pennsylvania Supreme Court if the issue reached that court today. The Supreme Court's early decisions suggested that the same would be true if the only case on point were from an intermediate appellate court, or even from a trial court. See *West v. American*

Tel. & Tel. Co., 311 U.S. 223 (1940); *Fidelity Trust Co. v. Field*, 311 U.S. 169 (1940).

This approach, however, is unnecessarily rigid. Under it, the federal judge would have to apply a rule even though she is firmly convinced that it would not be applied in the state court system, if the case got up to the state supreme court. Later, the Supreme Court recognized this and provided a more flexible approach for federal judges applying state law. Under this approach, the federal judge is to apply the state law as she concludes that it would be applied today by the supreme court of the relevant state. Under this "supreme court predictive" approach, the federal judge has more latitude to conclude, even though older precedents are still on the books, that they would be swept away if the issue reached the state supreme court again. If she is firmly convinced, for example, that the Pennsylvania Supreme Court would overrule the willful/wanton rule, the federal judge could refuse to apply it, even though that 1963 case is still, as a matter of precedent, "good law." The federal judge would not lightly make the prediction that a state supreme court case would be overruled, however, since this would lead to application of a rule in federal court that is not yet — and perhaps never will be — the law of the state. See, e.g., *Carleton v. Worcester Ins. Co.*, 923 F.2d 1, 3 (1st Cir. 1991) (warning that litigants should not expect that new [state law] trails will frequently be blazed in diversity cases).

This question considers the dilemma of a post-Erie judge trying conscientiously to fulfill her law-applying role.

QUESTION 5. Predicting the present. Laurel and Hardy are both injured in an accident in the State of Emporia, when their car is involved in an accident with Fields's and Connors's cars. Laurel sues Fields for his injuries in state court. Hardy sues Fields for his injuries in federal court., based on diversity jurisdiction. Laurel alleges, in the state suit, that Fields is jointly and severally liable for all of his damages, even if Connors was partly at fault as well. Fields argues, however, that he is only "severally" liable for his percentage of fault, that is, that if the jury finds he was 40 percent at fault, and Connors 60 percent, he should only be liable for 40 percent of Laurel's damages, instead of 100 percent.

In the federal suit, Hardy alleges that Fields is jointly and severally liable for his full damages, and Fields raises the same defense, that under Emporia law he is only liable for his own percentage of fault. Both suits are filed in 2012.

The state of Emporia law is as follows. The Emporia Supreme Court held, in 1911, in *Powers v. Hall,* that tortfeasors are jointly and severally liable for a plaintiff's full damages, even if another actor was also at fault in causing the injury. Over the years, the rule has been applied numerous times. In 1998, in *Sholto v. Dickens,* the Emporia Supreme Court refused to change to several liability, but there was a vigorous dissent from two justices (out of the seven on the court). Since then, one of the judges who was in the majority in *Sholto* has left the bench and been replaced. Also, a neighboring state switched to several liability in 2000. Assume further that in 1995, a draft of the Third Restatement of Torts, promulgated by the prestigious American Law Institute, endorsed several liability as the appropriate rule. In 2001, it issued the final draft of the Third Restatement, which also favors several liability rather than joint and several liability. In Laurel and Hardy's cases

A. both the federal and state judges will probably rule that joint and several liability applies.

B. the state judge will probably rule that joint and several liability applies, but the federal judge will probably rule that several liability applies.

C. the state judge will probably rule that several liability applies, but the federal judge will probably rule that joint and several liability applies.

D. both judges will probably rule that several liability applies.

ANALYSIS.   This question is a little dicey, because it requires an exercise of judgment, which means there is room for debate. But I think one choice is clearly the best.

To assess the choices, let's first ask what the state trial judge will do in Laurel's case. Will it apply the 1911 *Powers* case (reaffirmed in *Sholto*), or will it conclude that the Emporia Supreme Court will overrule *Powers*? There is little question that the state trial judge will apply *Powers* and *Sholto*. A federal judge, under the "state supreme court predictive approach," has some flexibility to predict that the Emporia Supreme Court would overrule *Powers*, if the issue came before it today. But an Emporia state trial court cannot do that. It is bound by the current precedents from higher Emporia courts; that's what the system of precedent means. The Emporia Supreme Court is the supervisory, law-making court for Emporia. The law it makes must be applied by Emporia trial judges until it is overruled, whether the Emporia trial judge likes it or doesn't, whether she predicts that it is fated for the scrap heap or not. So you can scrap choices **C** and **D**, which both assume that the state judge would apply several liability.

That reduces the options to **A** and **B**, and the choice between them depends on whether the federal judge would conclude, based on the precedents described in the question, that *Powers* would be overruled if the Emporia Supreme Court decided the issue today. Only if the federal judge is convinced that Emporia's highest court would overrule *Powers* could it apply several liability, ignoring *Powers*.

On these facts, that is extremely unlikely. True, there has been change in a neighboring state, and the ALI (the question assumes) has formally endorsed several liability. But the ALI had already indicated that it favored several liability in the draft of the Restatement *before* the *Sholto* decision. Thus, the Emporia Court was aware of the ALI's position when it reiterated its commitment to joint and several liability in *Sholto*. One of the judges who voted not to change Emporia law five years earlier is gone. But that leaves four from the *Sholto* majority . . . and who knows how the new justice will vote.

In the end, perhaps the Emporia Supreme Court will revisit the issue, and maybe it will adopt several liability. But a federal judge sitting on a diversity case is not likely to conclude that it will on such mixed evidence. Only in the clearest case is she likely to hold that the rule that appears to be Emporia law, and that clearly would bind an Emporia trial judge, is not "really" Emporia law. **A** is the best answer.

D.   The precedential effect of an *"Erie"* guess

So, after *Erie* the federal court cannot make the law in a diversity case. Instead, it must apply the law of the relevant state. Consider, in light of this, what precedential effect a state trial judge should give to a federal diversity court's holding on the content of that state's law.

QUESTION 6. Deference due?   Red & Orange Taxicab Company has a contract with the Tennessee Southern Railway, allowing it exclusive access to the Railway's grounds to pick up and discharge passengers at the Memphis station. In 1942, after *Erie Railroad v. Tompkins* was decided, Blue & Green Taxicab Company starts picking up passengers at the station, arguing that Red & Orange's contract is unenforceable because such exclusive contracts are against public policy. Red & Orange brings a diversity action in federal court, seeking to enjoin Blue & Green from using the station grounds.

The federal judge, under Erie, is bound to apply Tennessee law, but assume that Tennessee has never decided the issue. The federal district judge concludes, after reviewing Tennessee cases in related areas, that Tennessee would hold such exclusive contracts enforceable. She therefore grants the injunction, barring Blue & Green from interfering with the contract. This decision is affirmed by the federal Court of Appeals.

Later, in an unrelated case, Pazzolla sues Wren in a Tennessee state court to enjoin him from interfering with a similar exclusive contract. Assume that, at the time of Pazzolla's action, Tennessee appellate courts still have not addressed the issue. In determining the validity of the contract,

A. the Tennessee trial court judge would follow the Court of Appeals' holding in *Red & Orange Taxicab,* since the federal court was applying Tennessee law to the case.

B. the Tennessee trial court judge would follow the Court of Appeals' holding in *Red & Orange Taxicab,* since it is the only precedent available on the point and the Court of Appeals is an appellate court.

C. the Tennessee trial court judge would not be bound by *Red & Orange Taxicab,* but would consider it for whatever persuasive value its reasoning may have.

D. None of the above is true.

ANALYSIS. This question analyzes the precedential effect of a federal court's holding, after Erie, as to the content of state law. Here, since there was no Tennessee case directly ruling on the validity of exclusive contracts, the federal judge had to look at holdings in related areas to predict how the Tennessee Supreme Court would view them. After doing so, she concluded that the Tennessee courts would enforce the contract. So she did. And the Sixth Circuit Court of Appeals, looking at the same suggestive, but tangential evidence about how the Tennessee Supreme Court would rule, reached the same conclusion. Now, a Tennessee state court judge has to decide the same issue. Is she bound by the federal Court of Appeals' holding on the point? How should she regard it?

The Tennessee trial judge is not bound by the Court of Appeals' decision in *Red & Orange Taxicab,* even though it was decided by the august federal appeals court. The federal court does not oversee Tennessee trial judges, nor can it overrule their decisions. In addition, the federal court is *not making law* when it decides a diversity case, it is simply applying Tennessee law as it understands it to be. **A** is wrong. Although the federal court's opinion about the content of Tennessee law will certainly be of interest to the Tennessee trial judge, she is not bound by the federal court's "*Erie* guess" about it, since the federal court neither oversees the Tennessee trial courts nor makes the law of Tennessee. **B** is wrong as well; the trial judge is not bound to follow federal cases that have decided the exclusive-contract point, even from a federal appellate court. She is bound only by authority from courts above her in the Tennessee court system, which do indeed make the law of Tennessee.

C, however, is accurate. The federal Court of Appeals' opinion, reflecting the considered judgment of three federal appellate judges about how the Tennessee Supreme Court would rule on the point, is certainly worthy of the trial judge's consideration, as *persuasive* precedent, even though she is not bound by it. If unpersuaded, however, the Tennessee judge would be free to rule otherwise.

E. The impact of change in the state law on federal diversity cases

State law is not static. It may change while a federal diversity case is being litigated, before it is litigated, after it is litigated, or while it is on appeal. If it changes during the litigation, should the federal court conform to the state law as it existed when the case arose, when it was filed, when it was tried, or as of some other point in the litigation?

Here's a question that illustrates the problem. The basic premises of *Erie* should help you to choose the best answer.

QUESTION 7. Comedy of errors.   Laurel and Hardy are injured when they are traveling in Fields's car in the State of Emporia and Fields collides with Gleason. Laurel and Hardy bring a diversity action against Fields and Gleason in federal court. Under Emporia case law, it is unclear whether, if Gleason and Fields were both negligent, they would be liable for their percentages of fault (several liability) or each liable for the plaintiff's full damages (joint and several liability).

The federal district judge, making her best guess at the law of Emporia on the liability of joint tortfeasors, concludes that the Emporia Supreme Court would apply joint and several liability. Consequently, after the jury finds both Fields and Gleason negligent, she holds each defendant liable for Laurel and Hardy's full damages, rather than for reduced damages based on each defendant's percentage of negligence. Fields appeals her ruling to the federal Court of Appeals. Gleason does not appeal.

While Fields's appeal is pending, the Emporia Supreme Court holds, in an unrelated case, that several liability is the proper rule in joint tortfeasor cases.

Fields's federal appeal is heard after the Emporia Supreme Court's decision comes down. Fields argues that the Court of Appeals should apply several liability to his case, even though the trial judge had applied joint and several liability. Gleason, the other defendant, moves for relief from the judgment against him in the federal district court, on the ground that the judgment was based on a mistake concerning the applicable law. The federal Court of Appeals will

A. affirm the decision in Fields's case, if the trial court's reading of Emporia law was a reasonable reading of Emporia law at the time of trial. It will deny Gleason's motion for relief from judgment.

> **B.** reverse the decision in Fields's case, and remand it for entry of a
>   new judgment based on several liability. The federal district court will
>   grant Gleason's motion for relief from judgment.
> **C.** reverse the decision in Fields's case, and remand it for entry of a new
>   judgment based on several liability. The federal district court will
>   probably deny Gleason's motion for relief from judgment.
> **D.** None of the above is accurate.

ANALYSIS.   In this example the federal judge did her best to ascertain the content of Emporia law. However, her prediction of Emporia law on joint and several liability turned out to be wrong. The Emporia Supreme Court has now made it clear that several liability is the law of Emporia. What should the federal diversity court now do about Laurel and Hardy's cases?

There's an argument for **A**. The federal trial judge conscientiously performed her role under *Erie:* She made her best guess at the content of Emporia law, based on the precedents at the time, and applied it to the case. If Fields's appeal is decided under a "new" liability rule, it might have to be remanded for retrial, even though it was fairly tried under the law as the judge understood it at the time. This seems wasteful. On the other hand, by taking his appeal, Fields has challenged the trial judge's ruling that joint and several liability applies in Emporia. When the Court of Appeals reviews that ruling, shouldn't it consider all the data concerning the content of Emporia law? And what better data could there be on the point than a new decision from the Emporia Supreme Court? It seems artificial to uphold the trial judge's conclusion about Emporia law on the ground that it was reasonable at the time, when we now know that it was wrong.

On this reasoning, the Court of Appeals will reverse the judgment against Fields and remand the case for entry of a new judgment based on several liability. The Court of Appeals, like the federal district court, must make its best guess at the content of Emporia law at the time it reviews the case, and it is now clear that several liability is the law of Emporia. Thus **A** is wrong.

But what will the federal trial court do about Gleason's motion for relief from judgment? Now that it is clear that Gleason's liability should be "several" under Emporia law, shouldn't he get relief from the judgment, which was entered based on joint and several liability?

There's an argument for Gleason's position, but it will very likely be rejected. Gleason's case is over. If he were allowed to challenge that judgment based on a later change — or clarification — of the law, judgments could be reopened whenever the law changed. This would place a large burden on the system, and undermine the finality of judgments. "There is nothing in *Erie* that suggests that consistency must be achieved at the expense of finality, or that federal cases finally disposed of must be revisited any time an unrelated state case clarifies the applicable rules of law." *DeWeerth v. Baldinger*, 38 F.3d 1266 (2d Cir. 1994). Fields's case is distinguishable, since he took an appeal, which was still pending at the time the state law changed. He had persisted in claiming that several liability applies and was still litigating the question in the original case when the Emporia court clarified its position. So, **B** is wrong. **C** is the best answer.

F.   The Closer: Which state's law?

The message of the *Erie* case is clear: "federal court: apply state law in a diversity case." But there was an interesting twist in *Erie* that the Supreme Court didn't discuss. Tompkins's accident took place in Pennsylvania, but he brought suit against the railroad in New York. *Erie* clearly requires the federal court to apply state law to his claim, but *which* state's law, Pennsylvania's — where the accident happened — or New York's, where the case was filed? Because the case has connections with both states, each would have a basis for applying its own law to it. How is the federal court to choose between the two bodies of state tort law?

Every state has "choice-of-law" rules to deal with this problem, which arises frequently in state cases as well as federal diversity cases. For example, for many years the states used the "lex loci delicti" choice-of-law rule in tort cases, which looked to the tort law of the place of injury, even if the suit were filed in a different state. Similarly, in contracts cases, traditional choice-of-law doctrine looked to the contract law of the place where the contract was formed.

After *Erie* established that federal diversity courts had to apply state law, federal courts faced the further problem of choosing *which* state's law to use in a case like *Erie*. Should federal courts develop their own "choice-of-law" rules for diversity cases, or borrow from the states? Three years after *Erie*, the Supreme Court addressed this issue in *Klaxon Co. v. Stentor Mfg. Co.*, 313 U.S. 487 (1941). *Klaxon* held that a federal diversity court should use the choice-of-law rules of the state in which it sits. Thus, a New York federal court should apply whatever state substantive law the New York state court would apply to the case. If a New York court, under its choice-of-law rules, would apply New York tort law to Tompkins's accident (even though it took place in Pennsylvania), the New York federal court should do so as well. On the other hand, if a New York court would, under its choice-of-law rule for torts, apply Pennsylvania law to Tompkins's case, the New York federal court should similarly look to Pennsylvania law.

Klaxon reasoned that *Erie* required that the case come out the same way in federal court that it would in the state courts *of the state where the federal court sat.* To further that uniformity goal, the federal court should choose whatever body of tort law (or contract law or other state law) the local state court would. When *Erie* was decided, most courts applied the *lex loci delicti* choice of law rule to tort cases, which looked to the tort law of the place of the injury. Under the *lex loci* rule, there was little doubt that, if a New York state court heard Tompkins's case, it would apply Pennsylvania tort law to it. So a federal court in New York would also look to Pennsylvania tort law to decide the case.

Today, however, states use widely divergent choice-of-law rules. One state might use the place-of-the-injury rule in a tort case, another might look to the interests of the various states connected to the case, and another state might apply its own law as long as the case has some connection to it. It is entirely possible, under this balkanized approach to choice of law, that a New York court would apply New York law to a case, even though, had the case been filed in Pennsylvania, that court would have chosen its law — or that of a third state — to govern the same case.

Since New York courts and Pennsylvania courts might apply different bodies of tort law to a case, it follows, under *Klaxon,* that federal courts in those states might also end up applying different tort rules to the same dispute. If the New York federal court uses New York's choice of law rules to select the proper tort law (as it must under *Klaxon*), it might select New York law in a case like Tompkins's, because a New York state court would, under its choice-of-law rules. But, if Pennsylvania uses different choice of law rules, a Pennsylvania federal court using Pennsylvania choice of law rules might apply Pennsylvania law, if Tompkins sued there. So Tompkins's lawyers might find, even now, that by selecting a federal court in one state rather than another, *they can still shop for more favorable law,* since the federal court in each state will use local choice-of-law rules to select the applicable substantive law. The *Klaxon* Court recognized that its holding posed this risk, but shrugged it off as inevitable:

> Whatever lack of uniformity this may produce between federal courts in different states is attributable to our federal system, which leaves to a state, within the limits permitted by the Constitution, the right to pursue local policies diverging from those of its neighbors.

313 U.S. at 496.

So, the bottom line is that a federal diversity court must apply whatever state law the courts of the state in which it sits would apply. In cases with connections to more than one state, this adds a second layer to the *Erie* analysis.

QUESTION 8. Your law or mine? Whitney, a Rhode Island citizen, goes skiing at a ski area in Vermont. When he purchases his lift ticket, he quickly signs a release of liability, waiving his right to sue, should he be injured due to negligence of the operator. While coming down an expert trail, he comes suddenly upon a bare spot full of rocks. He falls and is injured. He brings a diversity action against the operator in federal court in Rhode Island, basing personal jurisdiction on the fact that it had sent him an offer there for a weekend ski package that induced him to go to Vermont to ski.

Assume that Rhode Island tort law refuses to enforce advance waivers of liability for negligence, unless they were individually negotiated. Assume further that Vermont tort law holds such waivers enforceable. Assume further that Rhode Island's choice-of-law rule for tort cases is to apply the law of the place of the injury, while Vermont's choice-of-law rule involves an assessment of the interests of the parties and states involved. It is less predictable under this balancing approach to choice of law whether the court would apply Rhode Island or Vermont law. The Rhode Island federal district judge would probably apply

A. Vermont law to Whitney's case, because the accident happened in Vermont.
B. Rhode Island law to Whitney's case, because Rhode Island has an interest in providing compensation to a Rhode Island plaintiff.
C. Rhode Island law, because the action is brought in Rhode Island.
D. whatever state's tort law would have been applied if the case had been brought in a Vermont state court.

ANALYSIS. *Klaxon* holds the key to this question. It requires the Rhode Island federal judge to do what a Rhode Island state judge would have done, had the case been filed in a Rhode Island state court. If it had been, the Rhode Island judge would have used Rhode Island's choice-of-law rules to choose between Vermont tort law (which would uphold the release) and Rhode Island tort law, which probably would not.

B appears based on the premise that the Rhode Island court would apply whatever body of law would favor the resident plaintiff. But that isn't Rhode Island's choice-of-law rule. Instead, it applies the law of the state of the injury, which is Vermont in this case. Consequently, the plaintiff's rights will be decided under Vermont law, even though the case is litigated in Rhode Island. **C** suggests that the federal judge should use the law of the state in which the federal court sits. This also isn't accurate under *Klaxon*. A more accurate statement is that the Rhode Island federal judge should apply the same body of substantive law to the case *that a Rhode Island state judge would apply*. Often, that will be Rhode Island law. But in cases with connections to several states (which is likely to be true in many diversity cases), the federal judge must choose the law of another state, under *Klaxon,* if a Rhode Island judge would.

So the judge in Whitney's case must look at Rhode Island's choice-of-law rule. It calls for (the question assumes) application of the law of the place of injury. That was Vermont, so we look to Vermont tort law, which enforces waivers. So **A** is the best answer.[2] Although Rhode Island wouldn't enforce this waiver in a domestic case, its choice-of-law rule calls for application of the law of the place of injury, and that means Vermont law rather than its own.

Whitney was pretty clearly ill-advised to sue at home. The combination of Rhode Island's *lex loci* choice of law rule and Vermont's enforcement of liability waivers leaves her client out in the cold (no pun intended). If she had sued in Vermont, Vermont might have chosen its own law under "interest analysis," but at least *might* have found Rhode Island's interests greater. Thus, *Erie* and *Klaxon* together suggest that lawyers should carefully consider the choice-of-law implications of the forum they choose in diversity cases.

 Glannon's Picks

1. Life before *Erie*   D
2. The out-of-state advantage   D
3. The state of the law   B
4. Supplementing the *Erie* doctrine   C
5. Predicting the present   A
6. Deference due?   C
7. Comedy of errors   C
8. Your law or mine?   A

---

2. In some circumstances, a state may refuse to apply the law of another state, even though its choice-of-law rules point to that state's law, if the other state's law violates a fundamental public policy of the forum. It seems doubtful that this applies here, however, since Rhode Island (the question assumes) enforces waivers if they are clearly bargained for.

Two Ways to Run a Railroad: Substance and Procedure After *York, Byrd,* and *Hanna*

∼

Cox's first case seemed a hummer,
But the outcome couldn't have been glummer.
The judge quickly saw
Cox had followed state law
'Cause he didn't know his Hanna from his Plumer!

∼

CHAPTER OVERVIEW

A. *Guaranty Trust Co. v. York:* First efforts at drawing a line
B. *Byrd v. Blue Ridge:* A caveat based on countervailing federal policies
C. Second track: *Hanna v. Plumer*
D. Direct conflicts with the Federal Rules
E. The power of Congress to write procedural rules
F. Another Closer: Another shot at *Hanna* analysis
◈ Glannon's Picks

E*rie Railroad Co. v. Tompkins* established a fundamental proposition, that federal courts sitting in diversity should apply state substantive law, not "general common law." The Court hasn't questioned that proposition since, but it has faced some devilish complexities in adhering to it. The problem (or, at least, one of them) is to distinguish which rules are "substantive," so that state law applies, and which are "procedural," so that the federal court can apply its own rules or practices, even if the court procedures of the relevant state are different.

For example, no one doubts after *Erie* that a federal court hearing a modern clone of Tompkins's case would have to apply state law on the question of the duty of care owed to a trespasser on the railroad's right of way. This is purely a matter of substance, a rule concerning the duty that applies to conduct in the real world outside the courtroom. But would a federal court hearing Tompkins's claim today have to apply the state's statute of limitations, rather than a federal limitations period? Would it have to use the state court's rules for pleadings, amendments and burden of proof, or discovery? These are rules for the conduct of litigation rather than primary rights and duties that govern the parties' relationships before becoming litigants. Very likely, the Justices who handed down the *Erie* decision had no intention to mandate use of state *procedural* rules in diversity cases. Indeed, the Court adopted the Federal Rules of Civil Procedure the *same year* that it decided *Erie*. The new Rules established uniform rules of practice and procedure for federal courts nationwide, for the first time in the history of the federal courts. It hardly seems that they would have promulgated the Rules, intending that they be ignored in diversity cases.

After *Erie*, the Supreme Court encountered a series of cases probing the limits of its broad state-law-in-diversity-cases pronouncement. The most important of these are *Guaranty Trust Co. v. York*, 326 U.S. 99 (1945); *Byrd v. Blue Ridge Rural Electric Cooperative, Inc.*, 356 U.S. 525 (1958); and *Hanna v. Plumer*, 380 U.S. 460 (1965). There have been others,[1] and they continue to come along periodically. But these three are the intellectual cornerstones of current *Erie* analysis.

This chapter will discuss each of these cases, with a question or two to illustrate their holdings. Then, it will illustrate how these key cases establish a framework for analysis of substance-procedure problems in diversity cases.

A. *Guaranty Trust Co. v. York:* First efforts at drawing a line

Guaranty Trust Co. v. York, decided seven years after *Erie*, considered whether a federal court had to apply a state statute of limitations in a diversity case,

---

1. Other important cases include: *Walker v. Armco Steel Co.*, 446 U.S. 740 (1980); *Burlington Northern R.R. Co. v. Woods*, 480 U.S. 1 (1987); *Stewart Organization, Inc. v. Ricoh Corp.*, 487 U.S. 22 (1988); *Gasperini v. Center for Humanities, Inc.*, 518 U.S. 415 (1996); *Semtek Int'l Inc. v. Lockheed Martin Corp.*, 531 U.S. 497 (2001); *Shady Grove Orthopedic Assocs., P.A. v. Allstate Ins. Co.*, 559 U.S. 3931 (2010).

instead of the "laches" doctrine previously applied by federal courts in equity cases. Certainly, the question of what limitations period to apply to a case is a step closer to "procedure" than the duty-to-a-trespasser issue in *Erie*. It involves the issue of how long a party has to file suit, which relates to the litigation process, rather than the duty owed between parties outside of litigation. It was not at all clear that *Erie* meant that the Rules of Decision Act required a diversity court to apply such procedural rules in diversity cases.

In *Guaranty,* the Court refused to resolve the issue by labeling a limitations period as "substantive" or "procedural." Instead, the Court looked to the underlying policy *Erie* sought to achieve, that the choice of state or federal court in a diversity case should not affect the outcome of the case.

> The intent of that decision [*Erie*] was to insure that, in all cases where a federal court is exercising jurisdiction solely because of the diversity of citizenship of the parties, the outcome of the litigation in the federal court should be substantially the same, so far as legal rules determine the outcome of a litigation, as it would be if tried in a State court.

326 U.S. at 109. Under this rationale, if federal practice differs from state practice, the court should determine whether the case would come out differently if it applied its own rule. If it would, a federal diversity court should use the state rule instead. Since York's case might go forward if the federal court applied the federal laches doctrine, but was barred under the state limitations period, *York* held that the federal court should apply the state limitations period.

Thus, *York* established an "outcome-determinative test" for determining the reach of the Rules of Decision Act. The federal court should defer to a state rule if ignoring it could lead the case to come out differently in federal court than it would "in a State court a block away." Consider how the following case would be resolved under this approach.

QUESTION 1. Service without a smile. Barnstable brings an action against Noriega in federal court, based on diversity jurisdiction. The claim is for damages under the Minnesota Consumer Protection Act. The Minnesota Act provides that service of process in actions under it must be made in hand on the defendant, before the passage of the statute of limitations. The relevant Federal Rule, however, allows the summons and complaint initiating the action to be left at the plaintiff's home with a person of suitable age and discretion (but not necessarily the defendant).

Barnstable's counsel has service made under the federal approach, by leaving it at Noriega's home with her husband, on the day before the state limitations period expires. Noriega does not receive it until after the period has passed.

If this case arose shortly after *York* was decided, but before *Byrd* and *Hanna*, the court would probably

A. apply state law, since to do otherwise would lead the case to come out differently in federal court than it would in state court.

B. apply federal law, because the method of service of process is clearly a matter of procedure rather than substantive law.

C. apply federal law, because the federal approach is established in a Federal Rule of Civil Procedure.

D. apply state law, because the state rule is found in a statute.

ANALYSIS. If you're up on your *Erie* line of cases, you will recognize this as close to the facts of *Hanna v. Plumer*. But the question asks you to assume that the case takes place well before *Hanna* was decided, so you need to ask how it would be decided under the reasoning of *York*. That case, and the other early *post-Erie* cases, did not clearly distinguish conflicts between state law and a Federal Rule from conflicts between state law and federal judicial practices unguided by the Rules. Under *York's* approach, the cases asked whether ignoring the state rule was likely to make the case come out differently in federal court than it would in state court. If it would, the state rule would be followed.

So, **C** is wrong. It appeared, after *York*, that the federal courts would not analyze a conflict involving a Federal Rule any differently than other conflicts. The issue was whether using the state rule could lead to a different outcome than using the federal approach. Under *York's* outcome determinative test, it appeared that the federal courts would defer to state law, even if the issue were arguably controlled by a Federal Rule in federal court. Indeed, the Court applied state law in several cases after *York* that arguably were controlled by a Federal Rule.[2]

B is also a weak answer, because *York* refused to choose between state and federal law based on labels. *York* suggested that a federal court should defer to state law in a diversity case, even on an issue that is arguably procedural — or, presumably, clearly procedural — if ignoring the state rule would lead to a different outcome in federal court than the litigants would obtain in state court.

D is wrong too, because *York's* deference to state law did not turn on the fact that the state approach was embodied in a statute. Rather, it turned on the fact that the outcome could differ if the state's practice were ignored. This logic suggests that a federal diversity court should defer to the state rule, whether that rule was statutory, established by a state rule of procedure, or a

---

2. See, e.g., *Ragan v. Merchants Transfer & Warehouse Co.*, 337 U.S. 530 (1949); *Cohen v. Beneficial Industrial Loan Co.*, 337 U.S. 541 (1949).

matter of state judicial practice, if failing to do so would lead to a different outcome in federal court.

A is the best answer. Very likely, in the era after *York,* the Court would have held, based on *York's* policy of conforming to state practice to assure uniform outcomes, that the federal diversity court should apply the state in-hand service rule, even if it directly conflicted with a practice mandated by a Federal Rule of Civil Procedure. Under Minnesota's approach, the claim would be barred, since Noriega was not served in hand within the limitations period. Under the Federal Rule, however, the limitations statute would be deemed satisfied, and the case would go forward. Since using the Federal Rule would lead to a different outcome, *York* appeared to require the court to use the state procedure instead.

B.   *Byrd v. Blue Ridge:* A caveat based on countervailing federal policies

Fundamentally, *Erie* was a constitutional decision, based on the premise that areas of law not delegated to the federal government remained with the states. The *Erie* Court rejected the idea that federal courts could "make up" the law of contracts, torts or property simply because they had jurisdiction to hear diversity cases.

But *York* mandated deference to state law even in areas where there *was constitutional authority to make a separate federal rule.* This was a big step, taken without much discussion of its implications by Justice Frankfurter in *York.* For example, Article III, §2 of the Constitution, together with the Necessary and Proper Clause (Article I, §8), provide constitutional authority for federal courts to apply their own rules on matters of procedure, like the method of service of process. A federal court would hardly be a court if it couldn't organize itself (or be organized by Congress) and provide basic procedures for the conduct of judicial business. Yet Justice Frankfurter's outcome-determinative test required deference to state law even in such matters of litigation procedure. This broadened considerably the area in which federal courts deferred to state law. *Erie* had not suggested that such deference to state law would be required in procedural matters.

York, in other words, expanded *Erie* from a constitutional doctrine, under which federal courts applied state law in diversity cases because there was no other constitutional possibility, to a broader doctrine based on the policy of promoting uniform outcomes in diversity cases in the two court systems. Since the purpose of diversity jurisdiction was merely to provide an alternative, presumably neutral forum, it should provide just that, a different forum that applied the same rules. That way, diverse plaintiffs would obtain no litigation advantage by virtue of their right to choose a federal court, only an unbiased forum applying the same law.

This difference between deferring to state law for constitutional reasons and doing so for policy reasons, is important in understanding *Byrd v. Blue Ridge.* Where deference to state law is *constitutionally* mandated, it is not "balanced" against other policies. The court applies state law because "there can be no other law." *Hanna v. Plumer,* 380 U.S. at 472. But where the federal court could, constitutionally, apply its own rule, and is making a discretionary policy decision whether to apply state law to ensure uniform outcomes, the court may balance that uniformity policy against other policies. Sometimes, those other policies may be sufficiently strong to outweigh *York's* emphasis on uniform state/federal outcomes in diversity cases.

That is the basic holding of *Byrd.* While *Byrd* is sometimes thought of as breaking with the *York* analysis, *Byrd* actually reaffirms both *Erie* and *York.* In *Byrd,* Justice Brennan reaffirmed that diversity courts must "respect the definition of state-created rights and obligations," as well as state rules "bound up with rights and obligations of the parties." This restates the core constitutional holding of *Erie,* that the federal court must apply state law governing primary rights, because it has no constitutional power to substitute its own rules, as the Court had done under *Swift v. Tyson.*

Justice Brennan then noted that the cases following *Erie* — notably *York* — had "evinced a broader policy" of conforming to state law where failure to do so might lead to a different result in federal court. In other words, *York* mandated deference to state law, as a matter of policy, even where such deference was *not* required by the Constitution. Thus, diversity courts had applied state rules "even of form and mode" (that is, matters having to do with procedure in conducting the litigation, rather than primary rights like the duty of care owed to a trespasser) under the outcome-determinative test, although they would have constitutional authority to follow a separate federal practice. For example, on the facts of Question 1, a federal court would presumably follow the state service rule under *York,* although this is not a substantive matter as to which it is constitutionally bound to follow state law.

Byrd expressed no general dissent from this outcome determinative test, even in matters of "form and mode." However, Justice Brennan suggested that in matters of litigation procedure, where state practice is followed as a policy choice rather than as a constitutional imperative, the *York* policy of uniform outcomes should be considered along with other policies, which might sometimes outweigh the uniformity policy. In *Byrd* itself, the division of functions between the judge and jury in federal cases, under the "influence" of the Seventh Amendment, was an important consideration supporting the use of federal procedure in federal court. Since the state law was not "bound up with rights and obligations of the parties" (in which case the federal court would have to defer to it), the Court could consider "affirmative countervailing considerations." In *Byrd,* the federal priority given to the role of the jury outweighed the policy in favor of uniform state/federal outcomes in diversity cases.

So *Byrd* did not overrule *York's* deferential approach in diversity cases or question its central premise. Rather, it noted that in cases involving procedural differences between state and federal law, this policy-based deference could be outweighed by important policies concerning the integrity of the federal court system. Such balancing would only be appropriate, however, for matters of "form and mode," issues of court procedure in processing cases, not for matters closely related to substantive rights. As to matters bound up with substantive rights, *Erie* and *York* continued to mandate use of state law.

Transport yourself back to 1960 and consider how the following case would be analyzed shortly after *Byrd* was decided.

QUESTION 2. Pocketbook policies. The state of Fredonia has a Consumer Protection Act that authorizes suits for unfair practices in consumer transactions. The statute authorizes plaintiffs who prevail on their claims to recover attorneys' fees in litigating the case as well. The purpose of the fees statute is to promote enforcement of consumers' rights by encouraging aggrieved parties (and their lawyers) to sue. Awarding fees to prevailing plaintiffs significantly increases recoveries, since they must otherwise pay their lawyers out of their damage awards. Assume that there is no provision in the Federal Rules of Civil Procedure for prevailing plaintiffs to recover their attorneys' fees, nor do federal judges allow them as a matter of judicial practice.

In 1960, Bartholomew sues Abelard in federal court, based on diversity, for damages under the Fredonia Consumer Protection Act. She recovers damages, and moves for an award of attorneys' fees as well. In deciding whether to award fees to Bartholomew, the federal court should

A. follow the state statute unless it concludes that federal procedural interests outweigh the policy of uniform outcomes in state and federal court.

B. follow the state statute because it is bound up with the rights and obligations of the parties, without regard to balancing the federal procedural interest in applying its no-fees policy.

C. follow federal practice because this involves a matter of form and mode rather than substantive law.

D. follow federal practice because doing so does not affect whether Bartholomew will recover, but only the amount of his recovery.

ANALYSIS. The key to this question is to understand how much of *York* was reaffirmed by *Byrd.* Justice Brennan did not suggest a general balancing test for *Erie* problems. Nor did he suggest that a state rule could be ignored as long as it was labeled "procedural." Rather, he reaffirmed that "state-created rights and obligations" (like duty of care, or enforcing exclusive contracts), or matters closely "bound up" with such substantive rights must be applied in federal diversity cases. He went further. He affirmed that even in matters of "form and mode," that is, matters of procedure in the court enforcement of substantive rights, a federal diversity court should generally defer to state practice, to ensure uniform outcomes. Only if important federal policies would be compromised by following state rules might the federal court choose to follow a federal procedural rule in the face of a contrary state rule.

D is an interesting choice. It suggests that the difference between the federal and state approaches is not outcome-determinative, because Bartholomew can still win if the federal court uses its own approach to fees . . . he would just recover less. That is true, but it certainly leads to significantly different outcomes in state and federal court, if the plaintiff cannot recover fees in federal court. Ignoring the state fees statute would drastically reduce the plaintiff's recovery. In many civil cases, the fees award will exceed the plaintiff's damages, and the award of fees means that the plaintiff retains the entire compensatory award, instead of paying a significant part of it to her lawyer. If federal courts ignored this state fees statute, plaintiffs would virtually always sue in state court, and any defendant who could would remove, to avoid paying fees. So, though Bartholomew could still recover, denying fees would affect the outcome dramatically. Thus, *York* would lead to application of state law, unless *Byrd* balancing tips the scales toward federal law.

C is wrong, because the fees statute is not fairly characterized as purely a matter of form and mode. The right to fees significantly enhances the substantive remedy for violations of the statute, and is either a "state-created right" or at least "bound up with" the state-created right to recover for consumer protection violations. Justice Brennan reaffirmed that in such cases state law applies, without regard to balancing federal procedural policies. Thus, A is wrong too, since it suggests that such balancing would be appropriate. B, then, is the best answer. For a matter so closely akin to state substantive law as this, *Byrd* would not change the analysis. State law would be applied.

C.   Second track: *Hanna v. Plumer*

That is how matters stood until 1964, when the Supreme Court decided *Hanna v. Plumer*. But *Hanna* changed the landscape, by fracturing the analysis for state/federal conflicts in diversity cases into two parts.

In *Hanna,* Chief Justice Warren recognized that conflicts between state and federal practice arise in two different contexts. The first is a conflict between state law and federal judicial practices, that is, procedural rules developed by federal judges but not mandated by a federal statute or a Federal Rule. *York* and *Byrd* both involved such conflicts. *York* involved a conflict between a state statute and the *judicial practice* of applying the equitable laches doctrine. And *Byrd* involved a conflict between a state judicial practice of having the judge decide employee status and federal *judicial practice* of having the jury decide all factual issues. The federal approach in these cases was judge-made; no Federal Rule was involved.

In these "relatively unguided" *Erie* conflicts, *Hanna* reaffirmed that the question is whether the policy of uniform outcomes requires deference to state law. Of course, the federal court must defer on matters of pure substance, like the duty of care to a trespasser, or the validity of an exclusive contract. On such matters, or those (in *Byrd's* language) bound up with substantive rights, state law must apply, because "there can be no other law." *Hanna,* 380 U.S. at 472. But in the grey area between substance and procedure, questions like whether the judge or jury decides a particular question, or the standard for reviewing a jury's verdict, the problem is one of policy, not constitutional command. Here, the decision whether to defer to state law should be approached with sensitivity to the policy *Erie* sought to further—uniform administration of state law in the state and federal courts—but also with sensitivity to other policies.

So, in the first part of the *Hanna* opinion (see pp. 466-469), Chief Justice Warren suggested a more focused version of *York's* outcome-determinative test to decide between state law and federal judicial practices which are *not* prescribed by the Federal Rules of Civil Procedure. The court should consider whether applying the federal approach rather than the state rule would lead to forum shopping and "inequitable administration of the laws," that is, significantly different litigation opportunities for diversity litigants than for those who must proceed in state court. And, the Court suggested, this question should be viewed prospectively; that is, the judge should ask whether the litigant, before filing suit, would have significantly greater litigation opportunities in federal court if that court followed its own practice instead of state law on the disputed issue.

Applying this test, Chief Justice Warren concluded that, if the last-and-usual-place-of-abode service rule were a matter of federal judicial practice rather than prescribed in a Federal Rule of Civil Procedure, the *Erie-York* line of cases would *not* require the judge to apply state law. Following the federal approach would only require the plaintiff to serve process in a slightly different manner, a difference too slight to affect her choice of forum or provide unfair advantages to diverse plaintiffs over nondiverse plaintiffs. So, if the federal approach were a matter of judicial practice, the federal court could follow that practice, even though state law was different. (Notice the difference between this analysis and the analysis following Question 1.)

That's *Hanna* Part I. It's dicta, actually, because Warren went on to note that in *Hanna*, unlike in *York* or in *Byrd*, the conflict was between state law and a Federal Rule of Civil Procedure. Conflicts between state practice and the Federal Rules must be analyzed differently, he concluded, for some fairly sophisticated reasons. The Federal Rules are adopted by the Supreme Court, under authority delegated to it by Congress in the Rules Enabling Act, 28 U.S.C. §2072ff (REA). Consequently, when a Federal Rule is challenged in a diversity case, the issue is whether Congress had the power to enact such a Rule itself, and whether it has delegated that power to the Court in the REA. If Congress has the power to write such a rule, and has validly delegated that authority to the Court, the Rule is valid and will apply, even if it contradicts state procedure.

Hanna construed Congress's power to write procedural rules for the federal courts very broadly indeed:

> [T]he constitutional provision for a federal court system (augmented by the Necessary and Proper Clause) carries with it congressional power to make rules governing the practice and pleading in those courts, which in turn includes a power to regulate matters which, though falling within the uncertain area between substance and procedure, are rationally capable of classification as either.

380 U.S. at 472. This suggests that Congress could constitutionally mandate any procedure in the federal courts that is "rationally capable of classification" as procedural . . . even if it is also rationally capable of classification as substantive. Under such a broad test, Congress would have the power to write many procedural rules for the courts that would fail the "outcome-determinative" test of *York*, or the more refined outcome-determinative test of *Hanna* Part I.

But the rule involved in *Hanna* wasn't written by Congress; it was adopted by the Supreme Court, pursuant to the Rules Enabling Act, in which Congress delegated to the Court authority to "prescribe general rules of practice and procedure" for the federal district courts. 28 U.S.C. §2072(a). In *Hanna*, the Supreme Court interpreted this delegation of Congress's power to regulate procedure in the federal courts very broadly as well. In the second part of *Hanna*, Chief Justice Warren interpreted §2072 to authorize the Court to adopt any rule that

> "really regulates procedure, — the judicial process for enforcing rights and duties recognized by substantive law and for justly administering remedy and redress for disregard or infraction of them."

380 U.S. at 464 (quoting from *Sibbach v. Wilson & Co.*, 312 U.S. 1, 14 (1941)). This wide-ranging test suggests that Congress's delegation to the Court to write the Rules is virtually as broad as Congress's own expansive power to write rules to govern federal procedure.

However, the second subsection of the Rules Enabling Act circumscribes the Court's rule-making power: 28 U.S.C. §2072(b) provides that the Rules "shall not abridge, enlarge, or modify any substantive right." Even if a Rule satisfies 28 U.S.C. §2072(a), because it addresses a procedural matter, §2072(b) bars the Court from adopting Federal Rules that interfere with substantive rights.

So, for conflicts involving a Federal Rule, the question to ask is not whether applying it might lead to a different outcome than state law. Rather, the question is whether the Court had the power to adopt the Rule. It must be broadly procedural, under the *Sibbach* test, and — even if it is — it must not alter substantive rights. If it meets this two-part test, it is valid, and will apply, even if it leads to a different outcome than the plaintiff would obtain in state court.

The bottom line after *Hanna* is that deciding whether the federal court must follow state practice requires a different analysis depending on the source of the conflicting federal practice. If the conflict involves a federal judicial practice, the "modified outcome-determinative test" of *Hanna* Part I applies. If it involves a conflict between state law and a Federal Rule of Civil Procedure, the question under *Hanna* Part II is whether the Court had the power to write the rule. If it did, it applies, since valid federal law is the "Supreme Law of the Land." United States Constitution, Article VI.

This is heavy sledding. I hope the questions will help. Always start by classifying the problem: Is it modified outcome-determination problem, which the court must decide under *Hanna* Part I, or a Rules Enabling Act problem, to be addressed under *Hanna* Part II?

QUESTION 3. Branches of the decision tree. The State of Emporia has a statute that bars introduction of evidence that a party in a motor vehicle case was not wearing a seatbelt at the time of an accident. This statute prevents use of such evidence to show that the plaintiff was negligent, which, under Emporia negligence law, would reduce her recovery by whatever percentage of negligence the jury ascribes to her. In federal court, assume that no Federal Rule applies, but that judges generally hold that evidence is admitted if it is relevant to an issue in the case. The no-seatbelt evidence would be relevant to the issue of the plaintiff's negligence.

Tancredi sues Maguire for injuries in an accident. At trial, Maguire offers evidence that Tancredi was not wearing his seatbelt. The federal judge should

A. admit the evidence, since admission of evidence is a matter of trial procedure.

B. admit the evidence, because the question of admissibility of evidence is "rationally capable of classification" as procedural.

C. admit the evidence, because the question of admissibility of evidence is part of "the judicial process for enforcing rights and duties recognized by substantive law and for justly administering remedy and redress for disregard or infraction of them. . . ."

D. exclude the evidence, because admitting it when the state court would not would lead to forum shopping and inequitable administration of the laws.

E. admit the evidence, because doing so would not lead to forum shopping and inequitable administration of the laws.

ANALYSIS. A seeks to resolve this problem by labeling it. That's not going to work. The crux of the problem is that "substance" and "procedure" are overlapping categories. We have to use some more refined test — or, rather, *two* tests — to decide between state and federal law.

How about the test suggested in **B**, that federal law applies if the issue is "rationally capable of classification" as procedural? This is the test *Hanna* offered for *Congress's* power to enact statutes governing the federal courts. It is not the test for choosing between a federal *judicial practice*, like the federal practice here, and state law.

How about the test suggested in **C**, that the federal court can use its own approach because the issue is part of "the judicial process for enforcing rights and duties recognized by substantive law and for justly administering remedy and redress for disregard or infraction of them. . . ." This is the standard *Hanna* describes for the Supreme Court's power to promulgate a Federal Rule of Civil Procedure under §2072(a) of the Rules Enabling Act. That's not involved here either, since the competing federal approach is not embodied in a Federal Rule.

Instead, we have a "relatively unguided *Erie* choice" (*Hanna*, 380 U.S. at 471) between a federal judicial practice and state law. For such conflicts, *Hanna* Part I provides the framework of analysis. The court must ask whether ignoring state practice would lead to the "twin evils" that *Erie* was aimed at: forum shopping and inequitable administration of the laws. So the winner must be **D** or **E**. It should be **D**. The seat-belt evidence could make a big difference to Tancredi's case, since a jury might ascribe a large percentage of negligence to her for failing to wear a seatbelt. Thus, this difference between federal and state practice would significantly affect the choice between the two systems — plaintiffs would choose state court, but defendants would very likely remove to get this evidence in front of the jury — and the litigation opportunities in each. Consequently, under *Hanna* Part I, the federal court should follow the state practice.

Here's another question to probe the relationship of the two *Hanna* tests.

QUESTION 4. Replay. Assume that a case similar to *Guaranty Trust Company v. York* arose today, in which the plaintiff sued for restitution, an equitable remedy for the defendant corporation's conversion of certain notes. The local state statute of limitations had passed. The federal district court, however, decides to apply the equitable laches doctrine (which is not embodied in a Federal Rule) instead, allowing the action to proceed. The federal judge's decision would be

A. reversed, under the modified outcome determinative analysis in the first part of *Hanna v. Plumer*.

B. affirmed, because limitations issues are "arguably procedural."

C. reversed, because it "abridges, modifies or enlarges" substantive rights under 28 U.S.C. §2072, the Rules Enabling Act.

D. affirmed, because *Guaranty Trust Company v. York* was overruled in *Hanna v. Plumer*.

ANALYSIS. This one is fairly straightforward for an *Erie* question. Again, start by asking which branch of the decision tree to pursue: *Hanna* Part I or *Hanna* Part II. To choose the right branch, look at the nature of the federal procedure involved. Here, the federal laches doctrine is a matter of judge-made practice, not required by a federal statute or Federal Rule of Civil Procedure. So, to decide whether to use the state approach instead of the laches doctrine, we examine the factors discussed in *Hanna* Part I, whether using the federal approach instead would lead to forum shopping or inequitable administration of the laws. If it would, the court should apply state law, absent some federal "countervailing consideration" not mentioned in the question.

D is a poor answer, because *Hanna* did not overrule *York*. *Hanna* accepted the fundamental policy goal of *York*, that federal courts should use state law if ignoring it would lead to greater litigation opportunities for diversity litigants. *Hanna* Part I refined this analysis by creating the "twin aims" test, but did not overrule *York*.

C is wrong, because the Rules Enabling Act is irrelevant to this case, which does not involve a Federal Rule. As *Hanna* Part II indicates, this question would be relevant if the federal approach were found in a Federal Rule of Civil Procedure. But it isn't.

B is also dubious. Even if a federal judicial practice is "arguably procedural," *York*, even as modified in *Hanna* Part I, requires the federal court to use state law instead if using the federal approach would lead to forum shopping and inequitable administration of the laws. Under *Hanna* Part I, as under *York*, the choice must turn on the policy of uniformity of outcomes, not on whether the federal court's practice can be broadly dubbed a matter of procedure. This "arguably procedural" phrase was used in *Hanna* to describe the power of *Congress* to govern practice in the federal courts, not to set a standard for choosing between a federal judge-made practice and state rules.

So, **A** is the best answer. Today, as in 1945, a federal court would apply the state limitations period in this situation, to further the policy of uniform outcomes in diversity cases in state and federal court.

D.   Direct conflicts with the Federal Rules

After *Hanna*, a crucial first step in solving *Erie* problems is determining whether the case involves a conflict between a Federal Rule of Civil Procedure and state practice, or a "relatively unguided" conflict between federal judicial practice and state practice. One would think this fairly straightforward, but the Supreme Court hasn't found it easy to decide when a Federal Rule directly conflicts with state practice. For example, in *Walker v. Armco Steel Corp.*, 446 U.S. 740 (1980), state practice provided that the plaintiff must file suit within the limitations period and serve process in the action on the defendant within sixty days, to avoid being barred. Under Fed. R. Civ. P. 3, however, an action is "commenced by filing a complaint with the court." If Rule 3 provides that filing the complaint satisfies the limitations period, an action (like the one in *Walker*) might be barred under state law—because service of process was not made in time—but timely under the Federal Rule (because the complaint was filed within the limitations period).

In *Walker*, the Court avoided the problem by holding that Federal Rule 3 did not address the issue of meeting the limitations period. Instead, the Court held that Rule 3 establishes the date for computing various time limits under the Rules—such as the time to answer the complaint—but "does not affect state statutes of limitations." Id. at 751. Thus, the conflict was a *Hanna* Part I conflict, since there was no "direct collision" between the Federal Rule and the state statute. Consequently, the *Walker* Court looked to the modified outcome-determination analysis *of Hanna* Part I, and concluded that the state limitations statute should apply, since the case otherwise could go forward in federal court but would be barred in state court.

Since *Walker*, several other Supreme Court cases have narrowly construed Federal Rules to avoid a "direct collision" (*Walker* at 749) with state law. See, e.g., *Semtek International Inc. v. Lockheed Martin Corp.*, 531 U.S. 497, 502-505, 1024-1027 (2001). Others, however, have found a direct conflict where a narrower reading seemed possible. In *Burlington Northern R.R. Co. v. Woods*, 480 U.S. 1 (1987), for example, the Court concluded that Federal Rule of Appellate Procedure 38, which allows but does not require an award of fees to a prevailing appellant, conflicted with an Alabama statute that imposed a mandatory penalty for unsuccessful appeals. Id. at 6-8. Since it found a direct conflict, the Court held that Federal Rule 38 would apply, despite the contrary Alabama provision.

This question, whether there is a conflict between a Federal Rule and state procedural provision, is basically one of statutory construction. There's a lot of play here, and not too much help to be offered in predicting whether the court will find an irreconcilable conflict between the state rule and the Federal Rule. It seems likely, however, that where a logical limiting construction is possible that avoids a direct conflict, the court will lean towards that construction.

Try this example for some "direct collision" practice.

QUESTION 5. Part I or Part II?   Assume that Rule 4(q) of the Federal Rules of Civil Procedure provides that a civil action in federal court is commenced, for purposes of satisfying the relevant statute of limitations, upon filing of the complaint with the clerk's office. However, cases in the state of Emporia have held that the limitations period is only satisfied if the complaint is actually served on the defendant within the statutory period.

Tubby brings a diversity case against Muhammed in Emporia, and files it with the clerk on the last day of the limitations period. A week later, he has the summons and complaint served on Muhammed. The federal court should

A. apply the Federal Rule, since the Supreme Court had the authority to promulgate it under the Rules Enabling Act.

B. apply the Federal Rule, because Congress could enact this provision, which is "rationally capable of classification as procedural."

C. apply the state approach, because ignoring it would lead to forum shopping or inequitable administration of the laws.

D. apply the state approach, because there is no "direct conflict" between the two rules.

ANALYSIS.   Once again, the crux of the matter is which *Hanna* analysis to pursue, the refined "twin-aims" analysis of Part I or the Federal Rule analysis of Part II. If the Federal Rule governs the issue before the court, and conflicts with the state approach, *Hanna* Part II mandates application of the Rule, as long as it does not modify or abridge substantive rights. Here, the (imaginary) Fed. R. Civ. P. 4(q) does apply, and does conflict with state practice. Federal Rule 4(q) expressly provides that filing suffices to meet the limitations period. This is directly contrary to Emporia practice, because the action may proceed in federal court if it is filed with the court before the passage of the limitations period, even if it is served on the defendant later. Under state practice, the case would be dismissed if the defendant was not served by that time.

Thus **D** is wrong, because there is a direct conflict between the federal and state approaches. The two provisions are irreconcilable, since the one allows what the other does not. And, because it is a conflict between a Federal Rule and state practice, the "twin aims" test of *Hanna* Part I, referred to in **C**, is also irrelevant. Even if applying the Federal Rule would lead to forum shopping or inequitable administration of the laws, it applies in federal court if it is valid.

B is also a little off, because the question isn't whether Congress could enact Rule 4(q), but whether *the Court* could adopt it under the Rules Enabling Act. The REA allows promulgation of "arguably procedural" rules, but bars any rule that would abridge or modify substantive rights. 28 U.S.C. §2072(b). Thus, the Court's power under the REA is narrower than Congress's power under Article III, §1 and the Necessary and Proper Clause.

So, **A** is the best answer. Because the Federal Rule directly covers the point, it will be applied, as long as doing so does not modify substantive rights. 28 U.S.C. §2072(b). There is an argument that the Rule hypothesized here would be invalid because it modifies a substantive right, but the Court would likely conclude that this minor difference in the method of satisfying the limitations period only "incidentally" affects the parties' rights (see *Burlington Northern*, 480 U.S. at 5), so that the Rule is valid under the REA. Compare the federal service provision in *Hanna*, which the Court upheld, though it called for a different method of service from state law. Note also the difference between this example, in which the Federal Rule covers the point and trumps state law, and *Walker*, in which the Court concluded that Rule 3 did not conflict with the state rule, and deferred to state practice under *Hanna* Part I.

E.   The power of Congress to write procedural rules

In *Hanna*, the Court addressed the power of Congress to promulgate rules that govern procedure in the federal courts. See 380 U.S. at 464. Analytically, it had to do so, because the power to write the Federal Rules of Civil Procedure is granted by Congress to the Court, in the Rules Enabling Act. Surely, Congress could not delegate to the Court any broader rule-making power than it possesses itself. In *Hanna*, the Court describes Congress's rule-making authority as follows:

the constitutional provision for a federal court system (augmented by the Necessary and Proper Clause) carries with it congressional power to make rules governing the practice and pleading in those courts, which in turn includes a power to regulate matters which, though falling within the uncertain area between substance and procedure, are rationally capable of classification as either.

380 U.S. at 472. That's a mighty broad test for Congressional power over federal court procedure: If the provision can rationally be viewed as regulating procedure, Congress may enact it, even if it will affect the outcome of litigation.

Consider, however, how the Court would rule if Congress enacted a statute that impinges on state law rights that can reasonably be classified as "substantive."

QUESTION 6. Limits on limitations.   Congress, in an effort to avoid complex and time-consuming litigation on the proper time for filing diversity cases in the federal courts, enacts the Federal Diversity Limitations Act (FDLA), establishing a two-year limitations period for diversity cases in the federal courts, regardless of the applicable state limitations period for the claim.

Sanchez brings a diversity action against Bernstein in federal court for fraud arising out of a real estate transaction. The relevant state limitations period for fraud claims is four years. Sanchez's suit is brought two years and five months after the alleged fraud was committed. The federal court should

A. dismiss the claim under the FDLA, unless it concludes that doing so would "abridge, enlarge or modify" a substantive right under the REA.
B. entertain the claim, because dismissing it would lead to forum shopping and inequitable administration of the laws.
C. dismiss the claim, because the FDLA applies and bars it.
D. entertain the claim, because the limitations period is "bound up with the rights and obligations" of the parties.

ANALYSIS.   This is a tough case. It assumes that Congress has enacted a statute of limitations for diversity cases. *York* held that the federal court must apply a state statute of limitations instead of the more flexible laches doctrine of federal equity practice. But does *York* control where the federal approach is mandated by Congress in a federal statute?

Let's work our way through the options. **A** improperly applies the REA proviso that Rules promulgated under the REA must not abridge, enlarge, or modify substantive rights. The REA address *the Supreme Court's authority* to write procedural rules, not that of Congress. So this choice focuses on the wrong analytical framework.

So does **B**, which rejects the federal statute because it would lead to the "twin evils" of forum shopping and inequitable administration of the laws. It undoubtedly would affect the plaintiff's choice of forum, though in this case it would lead her to choose *state* court rather than federal.[3] However, the validity of a federal statute governing federal court procedure is not tested under *Hanna* Part I, which addresses conflicts between state procedures and federal judicial practices not mandated by either Federal Rule or federal statute.

D, quoting language from *Byrd*, suggests that the limitations period is so closely related to substance that state law would have to apply. There's an argument for this, that it is a situation in which the basic constitutional command of *Erie* mandates adherence to state law. But a limitations period is not definitively "substantive," as a duty-to-a-trespasser rule would be, nor indisputably "procedural." Very likely, it falls "within the uncertain area between substance and procedure, [where the rule is] rationally capable of classification as either." *Hanna*, 380 U.S. at 472. If so, this passage from *Hanna* suggests that the statute is valid, even though it preempts a state rule that has substantive as well as procedural purposes. *Hanna's* endorsement of congressional power to enact rules for the federal courts that have substantive ramifications suggests that such interference with state policy is permissible in this "gray zone" between substance and procedure.

Thus, **C** is the best of the available answers. While this limitations period would not apply if it were a matter of federal judicial practice (see *York*), and probably could not be validly adopted as a Federal Rule (see 28 U.S.C. §2072(b)), there's a strong argument, under *Hanna's* description of congressional power over procedure, that this statute could be enacted by Congress. After all, under *Hanna*, Congress has very broad authority to regulate procedure in the federal courts. You could imagine that Congress might seek to protect those courts from expending limited judicial resources on state claims by imposing a limitations period on diversity cases. It is very likely within its power to do so, and should be. Of course, it hasn't, and probably won't pass such a limitations statute, since such a statute would interfere significantly with the administration of state causes of action. The members of Congress do, after all, represent the states.

---

3. What would the federal court do if the plaintiff filed in state court, after the two-year federal period had passed, and the defendant removed? The action would be timely under state law, but would the two-year federal statute apply on removal? Nice question, but luckily academic, since no such federal limitations period exists.

F.   Another Closer: Another shot at *Hanna* analysis

All of the questions in this chapter are hard. The *York/Hanna* doctrine is hard. So the Closer here is just another Closer. Consider again the two prongs of the *Hanna* analysis in choosing the best answer.

QUESTION 7. A matter of procedure? Columbus sues Moriarty in federal court, based on diversity jurisdiction. Her claim is for an injury she suffered in Tennessee, when she was hit by a bullet fired by one of a group of hunters. Her injuries are grievous, so her damages evidence will be graphic and moving. There is a significant question in the case as to whether it was Moriarty who shot her. Moriarty moves to bifurcate the trial, that is, to try the issue of whether his bullet hit Columbus first — and have the jury decide it — before trying the damages issues. Fed. R. Civ. P. 42(b) authorizes federal courts to order a separate trial of one or more issues "in furtherance of convenience or to avoid prejudice." However, Tennessee has a state constitutional provision that has been interpreted to require a single, unified trial of all the issues in a suit.

The federal judge grants the motion for a separate trial, and the jury finds that it was not Moriarty's bullet that hit Columbus. Judgment therefore enters for Moriarty. Columbus appeals, arguing that the court should have applied the state unified-trial approach. The Court of Appeals should

A. affirm the judgment, because Moriarty might have won in a unitary trial as well, so the Rule 42(b) decision to bifurcate is not outcome-determinative.
B. affirm the judgment, because the Federal Rule applies and is valid.
C. reverse the judgment, because the Tennessee provision requiring unified trial is found in its Constitution, not a procedural rule.
D. reverse the judgment, because the Rule abridges a substantive right and is therefore invalid under the second subsection of the REA.

ANALYSIS.   With this question, as with all the others, the trick is to put the conflict through the hoops of the *Hanna* analysis. First, determine the nature of the conflict, then apply the relevant standard.

If Fed. R. Civ. P. 42(b) directly conflicts with the state constitutional provision for unified trial, we ask whether it is valid. If it directly conflicts, and if it is valid, then the federal court must apply it.

There seems little question that Rule 42(b) directly conflicts with Tennessee's approach. It authorizes the judge to order a separate trial of the identity issue, while Tennessee law bars a Tennessee judge from doing so. It is hard to see how the Federal Rule and the state approach can coexist. One has to be applied instead of the other. Under *Hanna* Part II, if Rule 42(b) is valid, it will apply in federal court.

C here is tempting. How can a mere rule of procedure, even a Federal Rule of Civil Procedure, preempt a constitutional provision? The answer is that federal law, if it is valid, preempts state law that contradicts it, under the Supremacy Clause, whether the preempted provision is found in a state court rule, a state statute, or a state constitution. So the question remains, is Rule 42(b) a valid exercise of the Court's rule-making power? If it is, and if it conflicts with the state approach, it will prevail.

To determine whether it is valid, we apply the *Hanna* Part II analysis, because the federal approach is found in a Federal Rule of Civil Procedure. **A** is wrong, because the use of federal procedure here doesn't turn on the outcome-determinative test. It turns on the Court's authority to write the rule. So, it's either **B**, which states that the Rule is valid and applies, or **D**, which indicates that it would fail under the "substantive rights" proviso of the REA.

Very likely, Rule 42(b) would be upheld.[4] Certainly, it passes the "procedural" test — whether it "really regulates procedure — the judicial process for enforcing rights and duties recognized by substantive law and for justly administering remedy and redress for disregard or infraction of them" — since it pertains directly to the conduct of trials. And it seems doubtful that the Court would conclude that it abridges a substantive right, since it is a general provision dealing with the trial process, not a regulation of primary rights and duties outside the courtroom. I go with **B**.

Glannon's Picks

1. Service without a smile	A
2. Pocketbook policies	B
3. Branches of the decision tree	D
4. Replay	A
5. Part I or Part II?	A
6. Limits on limitations	C
7. A matter of procedure?	B

---

4. Indeed, it has been. See *Moss v. Associated Transport, Inc.*, 344 F.2d 23 (6th Cir. 1965) (upholding Rule 42(b) in face of Tennessee constitutional provision requiring unified trial).

13

The Scope of the Action: Joinder of Claims and Parties Under the Federal Rules

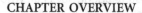

There once was a young man named Jules
With degrees from a great many schools.
He thought he'd add Law
'Til a prof stuck out her paw
And handed him the Federal Rules.

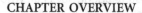

CHAPTER OVERVIEW
A. Joinder of claims under Rule 18(a)
B. Joinder of parties under Rule 20(a)
C. Back and forth: Counterclaims
D. Another layer of complexity: Crossclaims against coparties
E. Piling rules upon rules
F. Rule 14: An introduction
G. The fur flies: Claims asserted by third-party defendants
H. The Closer: Distinguishing crossclaims, counterclaims, and Rule 14 claims
◈ Glannon's Picks

How do litigants get named as plaintiffs or defendants in a lawsuit? Who decides who will be in and who will be out, and who will be on the defendants' side of the "v" and who will be on the plaintiff's side?

Basically, *the plaintiff decides* whom she will sue, whom she will join with as coplaintiffs, and what claims she will assert in the suit. But her choices are constrained by the court's rules for "joinder of claims" and for "joinder of parties." These rules vary somewhat from state to state, and between the federal courts and some states, but the Federal Rules provide a good introduction to the concepts of joinder. In addition, many states have modeled their joinder rules after the Federal Rules, so understanding the federal approach will help considerably in mastering state joinder rules as well.

It's hard to cope with these rules with only an image in your head of what parties are asserting what claims against what opponents. Thus, in analyzing the questions in the chapter, be sure to draw a diagram of the claims and parties before evaluating the answers.

A.   Joinder of claims under Rule 18(a)

Let's start with the easiest question: if a plaintiff wants to sue a defendant on a claim, can she also assert other claims against the defendant? If so, which claims? The governing rule in federal court is simple:

> **Fed. R. Civ. P. 18(a): Joinder of Claims.** A party asserting a claim, counterclaim, crossclaim, or third-party claim may join, as independent or alternate claims, as many claims, as it has against an opposing party.

This is clear and comprehensive: When Amos sues Boris in federal court for a fraud claim, Boris is an "opposing party"; that is, he's on the other side of the "v." So Amos can assert "as many claims . . . as [he] has" against Boris. Consider the application of Rule 18(a) in the following example.

> **QUESTION 1. Potpourri.** Felina, a real estate agent, sues Pai, who owns the real estate agency where she worked. She sues in federal court, for violation of the Age Discrimination in Employment Act. She claims that Pai discharged her from the agency because of her age, and seeks $100,000 in money damages. She also asserts, in the same complaint against Pai, a claim that she and Pai were informal partners in a venture to buy a large piece of open land, and that Pai took title to the land in her own name only, in violation of their contract. She seeks specific performance of the contract, through an order to convey a half interest in the property to her. Last she seeks compensatory and punitive damages from Pai for breach of her fiduciary duty as a partner in the land deal.

A. Joinder of the two money damages claims is proper, but the claim for specific performance is an equitable claim that should be brought in a separate action.

B. Joinder of the two claims arising out of the land purchase venture is proper, but the unrelated ADEA claim would have to be brought in a separate action, because it does not meet the same-transaction-or-occurrence test.

C. Joinder of the three claims is improper, because there will be no efficiency achieved by litigating the contract claims with the unrelated ADEA claim.

D. Joinder of the three claims is proper.

ANALYSIS. Rule 18(a) says that a party may join "as many claims as it has" against the opposing party. It doesn't say anything about suing for the same type of relief. It doesn't say that the plaintiff can only join claims if they arise from the same underlying transaction or occurrence. It says *anything* may be joined . . . so why shouldn't you believe it? **D** is right.

B is tempting, because so many of the joinder rules do limit the right to join claims to those arising from the same transaction or occurrence. See, e.g., Fed. R. Civ. P. 20(a); 13(g). It is also tempting because it would seem to make sense to allow Felina to litigate related claims together, but not to allow her to throw in the kitchen sink. But that's just what the rule does. The rule-makers took the view that, as long as the parties are going to have a lawsuit, they might as well drag out any claims they have and resolve them all. Under the Federal Rules, the court can hear and determine both legal and equitable claims, and can grant almost any type of relief the plaintiff seeks. In addition, most cases aren't tried, they are compromised through settlement, and the settlement is likely to be more effective if it encompasses all the claims the parties have against each other rather than just some. If the various claims do go to trial, the unrelated ones can be separated for trial. Fed. R. Civ. P. 42(b).

So the rule-makers opted for the broadest possible scope of joinder of claims. They did not require that they arise from the same events, as both **B** and **C** suggest. They didn't limit joinder to claims that seek the same type of relief, as **A** would. Whatever you've got, Felina, go for it. Would that all the rules were so clear.

One caveat should be noted, however. Even if Rule 18(a) (or any other rule) authorizes joinder, the court must still have a basis for subject matter jurisdiction over each claim a party asserts. The fact that Rule 18(a) authorizes joinder should always be read as if it included the following phrase: "assuming that the court would have a basis for exercising jurisdiction over the added claims." Often, such jurisdiction will be proper in federal court under 28 U.S.C. §1367, the supplemental jurisdiction statute.

B.   Joinder of parties under Rule 20(a)

Rule 18(a) governs which *claims* the plaintiff may assert when she brings a suit against a defendant. Rule 20(a) governs joinder of parties by the plaintiff in her complaint, that is, when the plaintiff may sue more than one defendant in the action and when she may join with other plaintiffs as coplaintiffs in a suit. First, the rule deals with joinder of multiple plaintiffs in an action:

> **Rule 20.**
>   (a) Persons Who May Join or Be Joined.
>   (1) *Plaintiffs*. Persons may join in one action as plaintiffs if:
>   (A) they assert any right to relief jointly, severally, or in the alternative with respect to or arising out of the same transaction, occurrence, or series of transactions or occurrences; and
>   (B) any question of law or fact common to all plaintiffs will arise in the action.

Under Rule 20(a)(1), the plaintiff decides whether to sue with one or more coplaintiffs or to go it alone. The rule sets the outer parameters: to join as coplaintiffs, the plaintiffs' claims against the defendant must arise from the same underlying events (or series of events), and involve litigation of at least one common question of either law or fact. The Rule 20(a)(1) test encourages efficient litigation. If Felina and Pai each have claims against Amory arising from the same accident, it will be more efficient to depose the witnesses once, to produce records relevant to the accident once, to try the common issue of the cause of the accident once, than to do it twice. So the rule encourages (but does not require) Felina and Pai to sue together.

Rule 20(a)(2) establishes the same standard for joining multiple defendants in a single action, and does so for the same reason. It will be more efficient, and avoid inconsistent outcomes, if the plaintiff litigates her claims against different defendants together when this two-part standard is met. If some complication arises (such as a different legal standard for recovery, or defenses unique to the claim against one of the defendants), the court can always order separate trials under Rule 42(b).

Here's a question that applies the Rule 20(a) standard.

> **QUESTION 2. Separation anxiety.**   Lutsky and Patrick (a passenger in Lutsky's car), both from Arizona, are injured in a three-car collision involving Lutsky's car and cars driven by Rowe and Bailey, both from New Mexico. Lutsky and Patrick sue Rowe in federal court, each seeking $200,000 for his injuries. The jury finds Rowe liable, and awards Lutsky $110,000, and Patrick $68,000. Rowe declares bankruptcy and does not pay. Lutsky now sues Bailey for the same injuries.

A. Lutsky's claim is not barred, because it could not have been joined in the first suit. There is not likely to be a common question of law or fact in his claims against Rowe and Bailey.

B. Lutsky's claim against Bailey is not barred. Although he could have joined his claim against Bailey in the first action, he was not required to do so.

C. Lutsky's claim against Bailey is not barred. A party can join with other plaintiffs or sue multiple defendants under Rule 20(a), but not both.

D. Lutsky's claim is barred because he failed to join Bailey as a codefendant in his suit against Rowe. Both requirements of the rule were met, so Bailey had to be joined.

ANALYSIS. The four choices here probe several points about the rule. You should be able to put the distractors aside by reading and thinking about the rule.

D, concluding that the action against Bailey is barred, fails because Rule 20(a) *does not require joinder if the two criteria are met*. The rule says that the plaintiff "may" make Rowe and Bailey codefendants in a single suit if his claims against them arise out of the same transaction or occurrence, and will involve a common question of law or fact. He doesn't have to. If he prefers to sue them separately — perhaps in different states, due to personal jurisdiction problems, or in different courts, due to complete diversity problems — he may do so.

A is off the mark, because Lutsky's claims against Bailey and Rowe will certainly raise at least one common question of fact: Whose negligence caused the accident? I suppose you could argue that this is actually three questions: (1) Did Lutsky's negligence cause it? (2) Did Rowe's? and (3) Did Bailey's? But I doubt that the court would parse the common-question requirement quite that closely. In fact, I don't think I've ever seen a case in which the same-transaction-or-occurrence test was met but joinder was denied on the ground that there was no common question. Even if you wanted to be a stickler, wouldn't the question of whether *Lutsky's* negligence caused the accident be common to both claims? If it did, it would likely reduce or bar his recovery against both defendants. Lutsky's damages would also be a question of fact common to both claims.

Rule 20(a) doesn't explicitly say that plaintiffs can both join as coplaintiffs *and* sue multiple defendants in one suit if the two-part test is met. But it clearly authorizes joinder of plaintiffs if the test is satisfied, (Rule 20(a)(1)) and of defendants under the same test (Rule 20(a)(2)). It's a fair inference — and established black letter law — that both may be done in the same action. So **C** doesn't wash, which leaves **B**. While Lutsky could have sued Bailey with Rowe, he may sue Bailey separately if he chooses not to make him a codefendant in his action against Rowe.

C.   Back and forth: Counterclaims

Rule 13, which governs "counterclaims," allows defending parties to assert claims against parties who bring claims against them. For example, if Lutsky sues Rowe for his injuries in the three-car collision, Rule 13 allows Rowe, the defendant, to assert a claim for his own injuries in the collision against Lutsky.

Under Rule 13, a counterclaim is either compulsory or permissive. Rule 13(a) governs compulsory counterclaims:

> **Fed. R. Civ. P. 13.**
>> (a) Compulsory counterclaim.
>>> (1) *In General.* A pleading must state as a counterclaim any claim that — at the time of its service — the pleader has against an opposing party, if the claim:
>>>> (A) arises out of the transaction or occurrence that is the subject matter of the opposing party's claim; and
>>>> (B) does not require adding another party over whom the court cannot acquire jurisdiction.

Rowe's counterclaim for his injuries in the collision would be compulsory, since it arises from the same accident as Lutsky's claim against him. Rule 13 (b) allows a defending party (like Rowe) to assert any claims he has against the opposing party that do *not* arise out of the same events. Between the two, they cover the ground: Any claim that a defending party has against her opponent may be included. But some of them — compulsory counter-claims — must be. This ensures efficiency, since the same issues are likely to arise on the counterclaim, and the same witnesses to be called to testify if the counterclaim is compulsory. And litigating the opposing claims together will avoid inconsistent verdicts on the issues, which could result if the claim and counterclaim are submitted to different juries.

However, litigants, like other people, don't always follow the rules. What will happen if Rowe has a claim against Lutsky, but does not assert it as a counterclaim? (Consider Rule 13(h) in analyzing this question.)

QUESTION 3. Gone, but not forgotten. Lutsky and Bailey, both from Arizona, are injured in a three-car collision involving Lutsky's car, Rowe's, and Bailey's. Rowe is from New Mexico. Lutsky sues Rowe in federal court, seeking $200,000 for his injuries. The case is tried and Rowe wins, since the jury finds that he was not negligent.

Three months later, Rowe sues Lutsky and Bailey, to recover $30,000 for his own injuries in the accident, also in federal court.

> **A.** Rowe's claim against Lutsky is barred. He should have asserted this
>   claim as a compulsory counterclaim under Rule 13(a)(1) in the
>   prior federal suit and waived it by failing to do so. His claim against
>   Bailey is not barred.
> **B.** Rowe's claims against both Lutsky and Bailey are barred. He should
>   have asserted his claim against Lutsky in the prior action as a
>   counterclaim and added Bailey as a codefendant on the claim,
>   under Rule 13(h).
> **C.** Rowe's claim is not barred. He could not have asserted it in the
>   prior action since it does not meet the amount-in-controversy
>   requirement.
> **D.** Rowe's claim is not barred. The claim could have been joined in
>   the prior action but did not have to be, under Rule 13(b).

ANALYSIS. Here again, the question comes at the joinder issue by
indirection, by considering what happens if a counterclaim is *not* asserted.
Let's eliminate **C** first, which takes the position that the claim could not have
been joined in the first action, because it did not meet the amount-in-
controversy requirement. Even if Rowe's claim against Lutsky would have
been proper under Rule 13(a)(1), it would still have had to meet subject
matter jurisdiction requirements. But supplemental jurisdiction authorizes
subject matter jurisdiction over compulsory counterclaims, so it could have
been brought even though it does not meet the amount requirement. See
Chapter 14, p. 265.[1]

   D is a hopeless throw-away. If this claim does not meet the test for a
compulsory counterclaim, I don't know what would. Lutsky sues for his
injuries in the collision; now Rowe sues for his injuries in the same collision.
Both claims arise out of the same underlying occurrence — the accident. So
Rowe's claim was compulsory under Rule 13(a), not permissive under Rule
13(b).

   B is half-right. It takes the position that Rowe's claim against both
Lutsky and Bailey is barred, because Rowe was required to assert both claims
as compulsory counterclaims in the first action. Rowe's claim is a
compulsory counterclaim, and Rule 13(a)(1) requires that it be asserted in
the original suit . . . against Lutsky (defending party "must state as a
counterclaim" any claim the party has *against an opposing party* arising from
the same events). And the consequence of failing to assert the claim is to
waive it . . . against Lutsky. But joinder of a party *in addition to* the plaintiff
as a party on the defendant's counterclaim (which is what **B** suggests that
Rowe should have done, adding Bailey as a codefendant on the counterclaim

---

1. Although jurisdiction over the main claim is based on diversity, and 28 U.S.C. §1367(b) limits
supplemental jurisdiction over certain claims in diversity cases, it does not apply to claims asserted
by defendants (as Rowe's would have been, had he joined it in the first suit).

he should have asserted against Lutsky) is governed by Rule 13(h). That Rule incorporates the joinder provisions of Rule 20, which allow joinder but do not compel it. So **B** doesn't quite cut it. **A** is right: Rowe waives his counterclaim against Lutsky by omitting it from the first action. After all, what would it mean to call the counterclaim "compulsory" if there were no sanction for failing to join it? The usual sanction is that the defendant will be barred from suing the plaintiff on the omitted claim later. Use it, Rowe, or lose it . . . against the opposing party. But the claim against Bailey did not have to be added in the earlier action, so it may proceed.

D. Another layer of complexity: Crossclaims against coparties

There are further permutations on the joinder problem. Rule 13(g) authorizes another variation, the crossclaim. A crossclaim is a claim against a coparty, for example, a claim by one defendant against a codefendant, or by one plaintiff against another plaintiff. Crossclaims are authorized by Fed. R. Civ. P. 13(g):

> A pleading may state as a crossclaim any claim by one party against a coparty if the claim arises out of the transaction or occurrence that is the subject matter of the original action or of a counterclaim, or if the claim relates to any property that is the subject matter of the original action. The crossclaim may include a claim that the coparty is or may be liable to the crossclaimant for all or part of a claim asserted in the action against the crossclaimant.

The basic point is simple: If you're sued along with another defendant, and you have a claim against the other defendant that arises from the same underlying dispute, you may assert it as a "crossclaim" in the same action. Suppose, for example, that Hammer hires Milsap to build a house for him, and Milsap subcontracts the wiring work to Rosov. The wiring fails, and Hammer sues Milsap, the general contractor, and Rosov, the wiring subcontractor, for damages. Milsap and Rosov are codefendants. Rule 13(g) allows either one to assert claims against the other codefendant arising out of the wiring work. This promotes efficiency in resolving the entire dispute among the parties. It also avoids the potential for inconsistent factual findings, which could happen if claims between Milsap and Rosov arising from this job were litigated separately: If two juries considered the issue of the cause of the failed wiring, one might attribute it to Milsap, and the other to Rosov.

Here's a slightly more complex example building on the Milsap/Rosov hypothetical.

QUESTION 4. Marital discord. Hammer sues Milsap and Rosov for damages, due to alleged faulty wiring in the house they built for him. Milsap then asserts a claim against Hammer and Ainsley (Hammer's estranged wife) for the balance due on the contract to build the house. Ainsley then asserts a claim against Hammer, claiming that they signed the contract for the house shortly before they separated, and that he later agreed to be responsible for the full cost of construction. She demands indemnification from Hammer if she is held liable to Milsap for the contract price, under their subsequent agreement.

A. Milsap's claim against Ainsley is improper under Rule 13, so the claim against her and her claim against Hammer will be dismissed.

B. Milsap's claim against Hammer and Ainsley is a crossclaim, because Hammer and Ainsley are coparties on the claim.

C. Milsap's claim against Hammer and Ainsley is a counterclaim with an added party. Ainsley's claim against Hammer is a crossclaim.

D. Milsap's claim against Hammer and Ainsley is a counterclaim. Ainsley's claim against Hammer is a crossclaim, but is improper, because she claims that Hammer is liable to her for Milsap's claim against her. This type of "derivative liability" claim should be asserted under Rule 14(a).

ANALYSIS. A diagram should help considerably in analyzing this scenario.

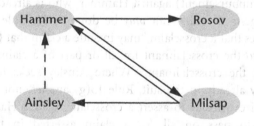

Let's start with Milsap's claim against Hammer, which asserts a claim against Ainsley as well. Hammer is the plaintiff who sued Milsap, so a claim by Milsap back against him is a counterclaim, and a compulsory one at that, since it arises out of the same construction work as Hammer's claim against him. Rule 13(h) allows Milsap to add a second defendant to the counterclaim if the standards in Rule 20(a) are met. This is a little confusing. It means that he can add Ainsley as a codefendant on the counterclaim if he seeks relief from her arising out of the same transaction or occurrence as his claim against Hammer, and if there will be some question of law or fact common to his claim against Hammer and Ainsley. This dual standard is certainly met: His claim against both arises from the work on the house, and there will be a common question of fact as to whether the work was defectively performed. So **A** isn't right; Milsap's claim against Ainsley is proper.

B is calculated to confuse. (Such infernal choices show up with regularity in multiple-choice distractors, so they are useful practice.) Although Hammer and Ainsley are codefendants on Milsap's claim, that doesn't make *Milsap's* claim a crossclaim. A claim *between* Hammer and Ainsley would be a crossclaim, but Milsap's claim against the two of them is a counterclaim with an added defendant under Rule 13(h). Enticingly wrong.

Skip to **D**. It starts out well; Milsap's claim against the two of them is a counterclaim. And Ainsley's claim against Hammer, her husband and codefendant on the counterclaim, is a crossclaim, because it is a claim by one party on the counterclaim against a coparty on the counterclaim. The posture of these parties isn't quite the same as the typical one-defendant-on-the-main-claim-sues-the-other crossclaim, but Rule 13(g) says a crossclaim is a claim between "coparties," and Hammer and Ainsley fit this definition; they are codefendants on Milsap's counterclaim.

So far so good, but **D** goes astray at the end. Here, Ainsley's claim against Hammer is "derivative," that is, she's saying, "Hey, Hammer, if I'm held liable to Milsap, I want you to reimburse me for that liability." If you've studied Rule 14(a), you know that it allows a defendant to *bring in a new party* to a suit on this type of claim, that is, to pass on liability to the "impleaded" third-party defendant for "all or part" of the plaintiff's claim against the defendant. Here, Ainsley asserts the claim for indemnification (full reimbursement) against Hammer, who is already a party to the action. **D** suggests that this can *only* be done under Rule 14(a). But Rule 13(g) provides that a crossclaim "may include a claim that the coparty is or may be liable to the crossclaimant for all or part of a claim asserted in the action against the crossclaimant." Where Ainsley seeks indemnification from a coparty already in the suit, Rule 13(g) applies, not Rule 14(a). Rule 13(g) authorizes Ainsley to assert a crossclaim against Hammer for indemnification — to pass on all "of a claim asserted in the action against the crossclaimant [Ainsley]" — should she be held liable to Milsap under the contract. **C** rules.

E. Piling rules upon rules

We've plumbed four rules dealing with different joinder situations. Here's an example that involves the use — or is it misuse? — of a number of these rules in a single case.

QUESTION 5. A case for dissection. Edstrom and Ling perform surgery on Arshad. Things don't go well, and Arshad sues them for medical malpractice in federal court. After the suit is filed Ling asserts a claim in the action against Edstrom for contribution, that is, claiming that if they are both found negligent and Ling pays, Edstrom should reimburse him for part of the judgment. He also asserts a claim against Edstrom for a share of the profits in their professional corporation, which Edstrom had withheld. In the same pleading, he asserts a claim against Schuman (another surgeon involved in the surgery), claiming that Schuman was also negligent, and should contribute to paying the judgment. Edstrom asserts a claim against Arshad for medical bills Arshad owed him for a previous operation. Assume that there are no subject matter jurisdiction problems with joining these claims.

A. Edstrom's claim against Arshad is properly joined under Rule 18(a), because, once Edstrom is in the action, Rule 18(a) allows him to assert whatever claims he has, related or unrelated to the main claim.

B. Ling's contribution claim against Edstrom is proper under Rule 13(g) and Schuman is properly joined to the claim as well. Ling's unrelated claim for the profits withheld by Edstrom is also properly joined in the action.

C. Ling's contribution claim against Edstrom is proper under Rule 13(g), and Schuman is properly joined to the claim as well. However, Ling's unrelated claim for the profits withheld by Edstrom may not be joined in the action.

D. Ling's contribution claim against Edstrom is properly joined under Rule 13(a), because it arises out of the same transaction or occurrence as the main claim.

E. None of the above is correct.

ANALYSIS. Here again, a quick diagram will help:

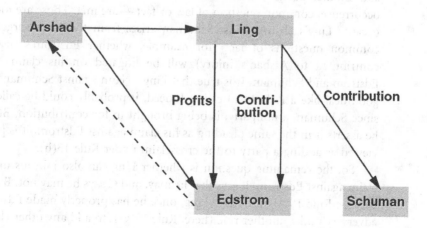

This is another of those nasty "none of the above" questions. They can be excruciating. "None of the above" is probably the right answer in these questions more often than it statistically should be. The professor trots out a bunch of misstatements, to see if you recognize that they are all wrong. But you can't bank on them all being wrong . . . not this time, anyway.

Three of them are wrong. **A**, though tempting, misconstrues Rule 18(a). That rule doesn't say any party can assert any claim against any other party. If it did, why would we need any of the other joinder rules? No, Rule 18(a) says (though not so clearly) that, once a claimant has properly asserted a claim against another party, she may add on any other claims she has against that party. If Amos asserts a proper claim against Boris under one of the other joinder rules, Rule 18(a) kicks in, authorizing Amos to add on any other claims she has against Boris. Or, suppose that Xerxes, a defendant, asserts a proper crossclaim against Zelda, a codefendant, that is, a claim arising from the same occurrence as the main lawsuit. Once he has properly made Zelda an adversary under Rule 13(a), Rule 18(a) says Xerxes may add on other claims he has against Zelda. But Rule 18(a) is not itself authority to assert an initial claim against another party. (Edstrom's claim against Arshad is, however, properly joined under Rule 13(b) as a permissive counterclaim.)

D is wrong as well, because Ling's claim against Edstrom is not a counterclaim. A counterclaim is a claim back against a party who is claiming against you. Edstrom has not asserted a claim against Ling; they were not adversaries before Ling asserted his claim. Rather, they are codefendants. A claim by one coparty against another is a crossclaim, not a counterclaim. So strike **D** and keep on looking.

That brings us to **B** and **C**. Both state that Ling's claim against Edstrom is a crossclaim and that Schuman is properly added to it. That's true; Ling's claim for contribution is a claim by one defendant against another, a crossclaim. And it is a proper crossclaim under Rule 13(g) because it arises from the same events as the main claim, Arshad's surgery. And Schuman can be joined as a party on the crossclaim under Rule 13(h), which says you can add another party to a crossclaim if the standards of Rule 20(a) — same occurrence, common question of law or fact — are met. Those are met here, because Ling's claim against Schuman arises from the same surgery, and common questions of fact (for example, whether Edstrom's negligence contributed to Arshad's injury) will be litigated on his claims against Edstrom and Schuman. It is true that Ling's claim against Schuman looks a good deal like a Rule 14(a) claim. Indeed, it probably could be called that, since Schuman, a nonparty, is being brought in for contribution. But since he asserts it in the same pleading as his claim against Edstrom, it is properly viewed as adding a party to the crossclaim under Rule 13(h).

So, the remaining question is whether Ling can also join his unrelated claim against Edstrom. **B** says that he may, and **C** says he may not. **B** is right, because Rule 18(a) authorizes Ling, once he has properly made Edstrom an adversary under another rule (here, Rule 13(g)), to add any other claims he has against Edstrom, related or unrelated.

F.   Rule 14: An introduction

Now let's tackle Rule 14. Remember that basically, the plaintiff designs her lawsuit. She decides whom she will sue and with whom she will join as co-plaintiffs. The federal rulemakers have generally accepted this premise that the "plaintiff is master of her claim." But Rule 14 is an exception. It gives defending parties a limited opportunity to bring in a new party to the action, to redesign the suit. But the opportunity really is limited: Under Rule 14(a), a defending party may only bring in a "third-party defendant" in order to pass on all or part of her liability to the party seeking relief from her:

> **Fed. R. Civ. P. 14. Third Party Practice**
>   (a) When a Defending Party May Bring in a Third Party.
>   (1) . . . A defending party may, as third-party plaintiff, serve a summons and complaint on a nonparty who is or may be liable to it [i.e., to the third-party plaintiff, that is, the original defendant!] for all or part of the claim against it.

Under Rule 14(a)(1), a defendant cannot bring in a person who might be liable to the plaintiff only. Nor can she bring in a person who might be liable to her (the defendant) for some related damage that she has suffered. She may only bring in a third-party defendant who may be responsible to reimburse her for part, or all, of the judgment the plaintiff recovers from her.

This usually arises in two situations. First, it frequently occurs where a party is liable for an injury but has a right of reimbursement for the damages from another party. For example, a retailer who sold a defective product to a consumer is frequently liable for injuries from the defective product, but can demand indemnification from the manufacturer. If the retailer is sued, it can bring in the manufacturer under Rule 14(a), claiming that the manufacturer is liable to reimburse the retailer for the entire damages awarded against it.

Second, Rule 14(a) applies where one defendant has a right to force another party to share in a judgment the plaintiff recovers. Suppose that two drivers cause an accident, and the injured party sues one of the drivers. In many states, that driver, if negligent, would be liable to the injured plaintiff for her full damages, but would have a right to recover "contribution"— part of the damages she pays to the plaintiff—from the other driver if the second driver was negligent too. So Driver 1 could implead Driver 2 under Rule 14(a) for contribution. In this common scenario, the primary defendant is trying to recover from the third-party defendant part of the plaintiff's claim against the third-party plaintiff [the defendant].

Consider the following example. Recall that supplemental jurisdiction under 28 U.S.C. §1367(a) generally allows the court to hear proper Rule 14(a) claims.

254 The Glannon Guide to Civil Procedure

> **QUESTION 6. Feeling the heat.** Firenze, a tenant in Smith's apartment building, sues his landlord Smith, for injuries suffered in a fire in the building. Suit is brought in federal court based on diversity jurisdiction. He claims that Smith negligently maintained the building leading to the fire, and seeks $150,000 in damages for serious personal injuries. Smith brings in Carlson, a firefighter, as a third-party defendant, claiming that Carlson is liable to him (Smith) because, while fighting the fire, he negligently sprayed water over Smith's computer equipment, stored in the basement, which wasn't threatened by the blaze.
>
> **A.** The claim is properly joined, and the court could hear it regardless of Carlson's citizenship.
> **B.** The claim is properly joined, but the court could only hear it if Smith and Carlson are diverse.
> **C.** The claim is not properly joined, but the court may hear it anyway, under supplemental jurisdiction.
> **D.** The claim is not properly joined and could not be heard in the action.

ANALYSIS. We'll analyze supplemental jurisdiction in the next chapter, but you should be aware from class that it allows proper third-party claims to be heard in diversity cases, because they arise out of the same "case or controversy" as the main claim. So **A** is only partly right; since the claim arises out of the same fire as the main claim, the court would likely have supplemental jurisdiction over it. However, the other part of **A** is wrong, because Smith's claim against Carlson is not properly joined under Rule 14(a)(1). Smith is not claiming that he can pass on all or part of the damages he has to pay Firenze, if he is held liable to Firenze. He simply asserts a separate claim against Carlson for his own, independent losses suffered in the same occurrence, the fire. Same-transaction-or-occurrence is the standard for joinder under a number of the rules, but *not under Rule 14(a)*. Rule 14(a)(1) only allows a defendant to expand the lawsuit, by bringing in a new party whom the plaintiff did not choose to sue, if she (the defendant) is seeking to pass on some or all of the liability she (the defendant) incurs to the plaintiff. She must show that the impleaded party "is or may be liable to [the third-party plaintiff] for all or part of the claim" the plaintiff had asserted against the third-party plaintiff. Here, Smith doesn't allege that Carlson is liable to reimburse Smith for Firenze's injuries, if Smith has to pay them. Rather, he alleges that Carlson is independently liable to Smith for separate harm to Smith, the damage to his computers.

The failure to meet the Rule 14(a) standard eliminates **A** and **B**. **C** suggests that, even though the claim doesn't satisfy the Rule, it can still be heard in federal court under supplemental jurisdiction. This suggests that, if there's a basis for jurisdiction, the joinder rules don't have to authorize the claim. This is a common misconception, but a misconception nonetheless. Supplemental jurisdiction provides a basis for subject matter jurisdiction over a claim *if it is properly joined.* But if the claim cannot be joined under the Rules, the fact that the court would have supplemental jurisdiction over it doesn't cure the joinder problem. **D** is the winner here.

G. The fur flies: Claims asserted by third-party defendants

Let's consider the joinder question from the point of view of the third-party defendant. Once brought in, she may have some claims of her own. Of course, the rulemakers considered this possibility, and dealt with it in Rule 14(a). The preceding discussion, and the various subsections of Rule 14(a) itself, should provide all the information you need to address the following tidbit.

QUESTION 7. **More slings and arrows.** Clear Code Software agreed to create a litigation-support computer program for Holmes, a lawyer. It contracted out the writing of the code to Jasper, a Caltech grad student. Jasper wrote the code using a computer he rented from High Tech Rentals, Inc. He delivered the code to Clear Code, which put the program together and delivered it to Holmes, who claimed that it never worked properly and didn't pay for it.

Holmes sued Clear Code for breach of contract in federal court. (Assume that there are no subject matter jurisdiction problems with the action.) Clear Code in turn asserted a claim against Jasper, claiming that (while it was liable for Jasper's work) the problem resulted from his faulty programming, so that he should end up absorbing the loss.

Jasper then asserted five claims. His first claim was a quantum meruit claim against Holmes for the value of the services he rendered in preparing the computer program. The second was a claim for defamation against Holmes, for claiming to Clear Code that his programming work was "abominable." His third claim was against High Tech, claiming that a glitch in the computer they rented to him caused the problem in the code, causing the Holmes program to fail. Jasper alleged that, if he was liable to Clear Code, then High Tech, as the cause of the defect in the program, should end up absorbing the damages. Fourth, he asserted a claim against Clear Code, the defendant, for the fee he had been promised for preparing the Holmes code, and another for his fee for an unrelated job.

A. All the claims in the action are proper under the federal joinder rules.
B. Of Jasper's two claims against Clear Code only the one for the Holmes job is proper under the rules.
C. Of Jasper's claims against Holmes, one is permissive, the other compulsory.
D. Jasper's claim against High Tech is not a proper impleader claim, because Jasper is not the original defendant.

ANALYSIS.   This one desperately needs a diagram to sort out the claims:

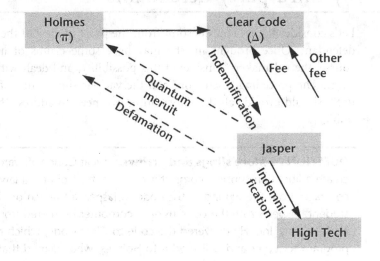

As the diagram shows, Holmes sued Clear Code, which impleaded Jasper. Jasper asserted two claims against the plaintiff, two back against Clear Code, and one against High Tech, which, until then, was not a party to the action. **D** suggests that Jasper can't assert this claim against High Tech, because only an original defendant can implead a party. However, Rule 14(a)(5) authorizes a third-party defendant to implead another party (called a fourth-party defendant) who may be liable to him for all or part of the defendant's claim against him. Again, the rule restricts the right to implead to derivative liability situations, but that's what Jasper has alleged: that if he is held liable because the code was defective, he can pass on the liability to High Tech.

   B asserts that Jasper's first claim against Clear Code, for the contract price for the job, is a proper claim, but that his other claim, for the fee on an unrelated job, is improper. This isn't right. Both claims are counterclaims, the first, compulsory, the second, permissive. Rule 13(a)(1) requires Jasper to assert claims he has against an opposing party (here, the defendant/third-party plaintiff, Clear Code) if they arise from the same events as the main claim. The claim for Jasper's fee clearly does, so it is a compulsory counterclaim. His claim for his fee on another job is a permissive counterclaim under Rule 13(b) (though it might also be characterized as an added claim under Rule 18(a)). There could be jurisdictional problems with it, but there's none under the joinder rules. An unrelated claim against an opposing party may be asserted under Rule 13(b).

C is tricky. Jasper's claim for the value of his work on the code arises from the same events as the main claim. His other claim, for defamation based on Holmes's complaints about his work, is less clear, though it arguably could be held to arise from the same events. It's close; it doesn't arise directly from the contract, but from the partners' reaction to the quality of the contract work. But we don't have to decide whether it arises from the same transaction or occurrence or not. Even if both do, *Jasper doesn't have to assert them in this action.* Rule 14(a)(2)(D) allows, but does not require a third-party defendant to assert claims he has against the plaintiff, even if they do arise from the same events. Neither of Jasper's claims is compulsory.

That leaves **A** as the right choice. Jasper's claims against Clear Code are counterclaims; His claims against Holmes are proper, though not compulsory, under Rule 14(a)(2)(D);[2] and his impleader of High Tech is also proper under Rule 14(a)(5). If you got that one, you're on your way to mastering the joinder rules.

H.   The Closer: Distinguishing crossclaims, counterclaims, and Rule 14 claims

Now remember, this is the Closer. Don't blame me if it's technical, the *rules* are technical.

My students always confuse crossclaims, counterclaims, and Rule 14 claims. They call one the other, refer to the wrong rule numbers, and get very frustrated. Well, it is confusing, but the best antidote is to simply remember the basic distinctions and apply them systematically. A counterclaim is a claim asserted by a defending party—someone who is on the receiving end of a claim—back against the party who has asserted a claim against him. A crossclaim is a claim asserted against a coparty, that is, a codefendant or coplaintiff on a claim. However, be careful about situations where a party asserts a claim against a coparty (a crossclaim) and the defending party on that crossclaim has a claim back against the claimant. For example, Parker, a codefendant in a case with Spanogle, asserts a claim against Spanogle for contribution, and Spanogle then asserts a claim back against Parker for his

---

2. If the defamation claim does not arise out of the same transaction, it would still be proper under Rule 18(a).

own injuries in the accident. In this situation, Spanogle's claim is a counterclaim. Once Parker asserted a crossclaim against him, he became a "defending party." Any claim he has against Parker, who asserted the claim against him, is therefore a counterclaim.

Once we add Rule 14(a) to the mix, this becomes even more elegant, because Rule 14(a)(3) and (2)(D) allow the plaintiff to assert claims against the third-party defendant and vice versa. For example, if Moretti sues Parker and Spanogle, and Spanogle impleads Adair for contribution, Rule 14(a)(3) allows Moretti to assert a claim directly against Adair, the third-party defendant. But this claim is not a counterclaim. Why not? Because a counterclaim is a claim against an opposing party, and, until Moretti asserts a claim against Adair, they are not opposing parties. They are both litigants in the case, but no claim runs between them, until Moretti (or Adair) asserts one.

Here's a stubbornly technical question that asks you to sort all this out. (A diagram is a must here to sort out these complex variations.)

QUESTION 8. Wrong turn.   Iannotti was driving a tractor-trailer down the interstate when a tire blew out. He swerved toward the breakdown lane to stop. Nickles was parked in the breakdown lane arguing with his girlfriend on his cell phone. Skolnick, driving on Iannotti's right, tried to speed up to get out of the way, but was unable to do so because Erskine, in the car in front of him, didn't speed up or turn. The swerving truck forced him into the breakdown lane, where he crashed into Nickles' car. The truck and Erskine's car collided as well.

Skolnick sued Iannotti and Erskine in federal court for his injuries, claiming that their negligent acts led to the accident. He also sued Maria, Erskine's mechanic, because Erskine maintained that he had tried to avoid the accident but his accelerator, which had just been repaired by Maria, did not respond.

Erskine asserted a claim against Iannotti for contribution, in the event that he was held liable to Skolnick. Iannotti then asserted a claim against Erskine for contribution, and for his own injuries in the accident. Maria brought a claim against Nickles for contribution, claiming that Nickles was negligent in parking in the breakdown lane to argue with his girlfriend. Not to be outdone, Nickles asserted a claim against Skolnick for his injuries. Skolnick then asserted a claim for *his* injuries against Nickles.

A. Erskine's claim against Iannotti is a crossclaim, Iannotti's claims against Erskine and Skolnick's claim against Nickles, are counterclaims. Nickles' claim against Skolnick is neither a crossclaim nor a counterclaim.

> **B.** Skolnick's claim against Nickles, Erskine's claim against Iannotti, and both of Iannotti's claims are counterclaims.
>
> **C.** Skolnick's claim against Nickles and Iannotti's first claim against Erskine are counterclaims, Iannotti's second claim against Erskine is a crossclaim.
>
> **D.** Erskine's, and Nickles' claims are crossclaims. So is Skolnick's claim against Nickles.

ANALYSIS.   Here's what the case looks like:

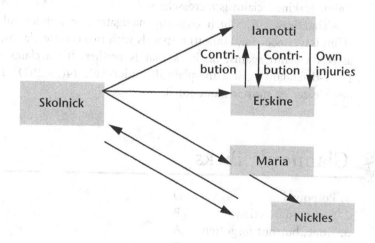

O.K., let's consider the options. **D** can be eliminated, because a claim by Nickles, the third-party defendant, against Skolnick, the plaintiff, is not a crossclaim. A crossclaim is a claim against a coparty, and Skolnick, the plaintiff, and Nickles, the third-party defendant, are not coparties — that is, they are not jointly on the receiving end of the same claim. Erskine, Maria, and Iannotti are coparties (codefendants) but not Nickles and the plaintiff.

C fails as well. Both of Iannotti's claims against Erskine are counterclaims. Why, for goodness sake? Aren't they coparties on the main claim? Yes, they are, but once Erskine asserts a claim against Iannotti, they become opposing parties as well. Now Iannotti's claims (which otherwise would have been crossclaims) are claims he has against an opposing party. The characterization matters, because if they are counterclaims, and if they arise out of the same transaction or occurrence as the main claim, Iannotti must assert them or lose them, while crossclaims are permissive. In this case, both of Iannotti's claims against Erskine (for contribution and for his own injuries) arise out of the accident, which gave rise to Erskine's claim against him, so he must assert them under Rule 13(a).

B is wrong too. Parts of it are right, but parts are not. Skolnick's claim against Nickles is a counterclaim. Why? Because Nickles first asserted a claim against Skolnick, making him an opposing party. Once Nickles does that, the counterclaim rules click in. Rule 13(a) does not refer solely to claims by a defendant against a plaintiff." It applies to a claim "the pleader has against any opposing party." The rule is written generally to apply generally, to any party on the receiving end of a claim, including, in this case, a plaintiff.

However, while Skolnick's claim is a counterclaim, as B states, Erskine's claim against Iannotti is not. At the time he asserted this claim, he and Iannotti were not opposing parties, they were codefendants on the main claim. Erskine's claim is a crossclaim.

That leaves **A**, which correctly navigates the joinder rules. Erskine's claim is a crossclaim, Iannotti responds with two counterclaims, and Nickles asserts a claim against Skolnick that is neither. It's a claim-by-the-third-party-defendant-against-the-plaintiff-under-Rule 14(a)(2)(D). I don't know any clearer or shorter name for it.

✦ Glannon's Picks

1. Potpourri	D
2. Separation anxiety	B
3. Gone, but not forgotten	A
4. Marital discord	C
5. A case for dissection	B
6. Feeling the heat	D
7. More slings and arrows	A
8. Wrong turn	A

14

Of Hooks and Nuclei: Supplemental Jurisdiction over State Law Claims

If an interest in procedure you've lacked
And on the exam you're afraid you'll get whacked,
Here's some advice elemental
About questions supplemental:
Just keep mouthing "common nucleus of operative fact."

CHAPTER OVERVIEW
A. The constitutional and statutory reach of supplemental jurisdiction
B. Supplemental jurisdiction over claims subsequent to the complaint
C. Limits on supplemental jurisdiction in diversity cases: Section 1367(b)
D. "Pendent party" jurisdiction
E. The Closer: Section 1367(b) and the amount in a controversy requirement
⬧ Glannon's Picks

I f you've studied federal subject matter jurisdiction, the joinder rules, and the supplemental jurisdiction statute, then you're ready to tackle this chapter. To understand the problem, reading *United Mine Workers v. Gibbs*, 383 U.S. 715 (1966), and *Owen Equipment & Erection Co. v. Kroger*, 437 U.S. 365 (1978), will help. I also recommend my chapter in *Civil Procedure: Examples & Explanations* for a review of the historical background to the supplemental jurisdiction statute. However, I'll try to provide enough background in the text to allow you to tackle the questions.

A.   The constitutional and statutory reach of supplemental jurisdiction

The most basic point to understand about supplemental jurisdiction is that it allows federal courts to entertain entire disputes, rather than single theories or claims. Cases seldom come as single claims for relief. Usually, the plaintiff sues on multiple claims, some that support federal jurisdiction under Article III, §2 and others that don't. For example, if Tolman has a pay dispute with his employer, he might bring suit in federal court against it for violation of the Federal Fair Labor Standards Act (FLSA), but also sue, based on the same events, for breach of contract. Maybe he has a claim under a state unfair labor practices statute as well. The federal court would have arising-under jurisdiction over the FLSA claim, but not over the state law contract or statutory claims (assuming the parties are not diverse). But, since all three claims are part of the same dispute, it certainly would be nice if the federal court could hear and resolve them all together.

In *United Mine Workers v. Gibbs*, the Supreme Court held that, if the federal court has a basis for subject matter jurisdiction over one of the plaintiff's claims, it may hear other claims that arise out of the same "nucleus of operative fact." In Tolman's case, the court has jurisdiction under 28 U.S.C. §1331 over the FLSA claim, so it would have constitutional power, under Article III, §2, as interpreted in *Gibbs*, to hear other claims arising from the same events as well. The Court's logic was that cases have long involved multiple claims, that the Framers understood this, and that they must have contemplated that the federal court would hear the entire dispute, as long as there was a "federal hook"—here, the FLSA claim—from which to append the other, jurisdictionally insufficient claims.

So *Gibbs* recognized a constitutional basis for federal courts to hear related state law claims like Tolman's contract claim. But in *Kroger*, the Court reminded the lower federal courts that they can't hear claims just because they are within the constitutional scope of Article III, as expounded in *Gibbs*. Congress must authorize them to hear the claims as well, by statute. Even if a state law claim arises from the same underlying facts as a proper federal claim, so that *Gibbs* provides constitutional power to hear the state law claim, and even if it would make sense for the federal court to resolve all the claims in the case, it cannot do so unless a federal statute authorizes the federal court to hear the related claims.

Unfortunately, most federal statutes say nothing one way or the other about the authority to hear related state-law claims. Consequently, *Kroger*, and especially *Finley v. United States*, 490 U.S. 545 (1989), nine years later, created considerable confusion as to when a federal court could exercise jurisdiction over such related claims in federal cases. So Congress reacted to those cases by enacting 28 U.S.C. §1367(a), which broadly authorizes federal courts to exercise "supplemental jurisdiction" over related claims in proper federal cases. Here's the basic provision granting supplemental jurisdiction:

> **Section 1367(a).** Except as provided in subsections (b) and (c) or as expressly provided otherwise by Federal statute, in any civil action of which the district courts have original jurisdiction, the district courts shall have supplemental jurisdiction over all other claims that are so related to claims in the action within such original jurisdiction that they form part of the same case or controversy under Article III of the United States Constitution. Such supplemental jurisdiction shall include claims that involve the joinder or intervention of additional parties.

What does this mean? It means that where the federal court has "original jurisdiction," because the case presents a claim that the plaintiff could properly file in federal court, the court can hear not only that claim, but all other claims arising out of the "same case or controversy." And, the legislative history of §1367, as well as case law, make clear that all claims that meet the *Gibbs* "common nucleus of operative fact" test are part of the same "case or controversy." So, as long as the court has a federal "hook"—a claim properly within the federal court's original jurisdiction—it can hang all the related state law claims from it, and resolve the entire dispute between the parties.

There's more to §1367, but for now let's focus on this basic purpose of §1367(a).

QUESTION 1. This and that. Garabedian, an Arkansas developer, sues Ellis, a local Arkansas official, under 42 U.S.C. §1983, for deprivation of his First Amendment rights, for refusing to allow him to speak at a local zoning meeting concerning a proposal by a competitor. He adds a second claim against Ellis for defamation, a state tort claim, based on statements Ellis made to the local newspaper about the quality of the construction on several houses Garabedian had built in town. The federal court

A. has constitutional authority to hear Garabedian's defamation claim under *Gibbs*, but does not have statutory authority to do so under §1367(a).

B. has statutory authority to hear Garabedian's defamation claim under §1367(a), but it would be unconstitutional, under *Gibbs*, for the court to do so.

C. has both constitutional and statutory authority to hear Garabedian's defamation claim.

D. has neither constitutional nor statutory authority to hear Garabedian's defamation claim.

ANALYSIS. This is pretty straightforward, but there's no harm in building a little self-confidence as we wade into a difficult subject.

Here, the §1983 claim arises under federal law. The federal court has "original jurisdiction" over it. That is, it is a claim that, on its own, may be brought in federal court under arising-under jurisdiction. So it provides that necessary federal hook from which to hang related state law claims. Since there is a proper federal claim, *Gibbs* holds that it is *constitutionally* permissible to hear jurisdictionally insufficient claims (like Garabedian's defamation claim) if they arise out of the same nucleus of operative fact as the proper federal claim. And, in §1367(a), Congress authorized federal courts, where there is a claim within the federal court's "original jurisdiction," to hear other, jurisdictionally insufficient claims if they are part of the "same case or controversy."

These two tests basically require the same thing: that the state law claim arise out of the same underlying dispute as the federal claim. The cases indicate that Congress, in using the phrase "same case or controversy" in §1367(a), meant to give supplemental jurisdiction to the full reach that *Gibbs* held constitutionally permissible under the "nucleus of operative fact" test. So, since the constitutional test under *Gibbs* and the statutory test under §1367(a) are the same, both **A** and **B** have to be wrong. If the defamation claim satisfies the *Gibbs* test, it satisfies the statute; if it doesn't satisfy *Gibbs*, it doesn't satisfy the statute. The question primarily tests whether you've got that basic point down.

If you do, it only remains to decide whether the defamation claim arises from the same set of facts as the First Amendment claim. **C** is wrong, because it pretty clearly doesn't. Even if Garabedian and Ellis have a long-running local feud going, and both claims arise from the bad blood between the parties, these appear to be separate incidents that took place at different times and involve different issues. Thus, *Gibbs* would not support sweeping in the jurisdictionally insufficient claim, just because Garabedian can sue on the First Amendment claim in federal court. There has to be a limit on this inferential extension of federal jurisdiction to claims not expressly authorized in Article III, §2. The limit is the scope of a single dispute, and this one looks like two distinct disputes, though perhaps linked by ongoing animosity. So **D** is the best choice here.

B. Supplemental jurisdiction over claims subsequent to the complaint

Question 1 dealt with the simplest example of supplemental jurisdiction, joinder by the plaintiff, in the initial complaint, of a claim that satisfies federal jurisdiction with another that does not. Prior to the statute, this situation was analyzed under the rubric of "pendent" jurisdiction. Visually, this basic case looks like this:

$$\pi \text{ (CA)} \quad \xrightarrow[\text{State claim}]{\text{Federal claim}} \quad \Delta \text{ (CA)}$$

But supplemental jurisdiction doesn't just apply to the plaintiff's joinder of jurisdictionally sufficient and insufficient claims. It also extends to claims joined later in the action, such as counterclaims, cross-claims, and impleader claims. Section 1367(a) authorizes supplemental jurisdiction over "all other claims that are so related to claims in the action within such original jurisdiction that they form part of the same case or controversy," not just claims asserted by the plaintiff.

So, if the federal court has original jurisdiction over the main claim, §1367(a) authorizes the court to hear a wide variety of claims added later as well. True, §1367(b) imposes some limits on this broad authority, in diversity cases. We'll get to that. But before we do, try this example, focusing again on §1367(a).

QUESTION 2. **This, that, and the other.** Jilbert, from Colorado, hires Pope, from Wyoming, to do some plantings in his yard. Pope hires Vaughan, a Utah citizen who runs a backhoe business, to come in and dig the necessary holes for the plantings. They do the work and leave. But the new shrubs die, and Jilbert claims that Vaughan ran over his underground sprinkler system and his septic system, ruining both. He sues Pope and Vaughan in federal court, based on diversity jurisdiction, for $90,000 in damages based on the faulty yard work.

After the suit is filed, Pope asserts (in the same suit) a crossclaim against Vaughan for contribution, for half of any damages Jilbert recovers, on the ground that he was negligent as well as Pope in causing the yard damages. He also asserts a claim against Vaughan for $5,000 in damages that resulted when Vaughan hit his riding mower while working on another job.

A. The court has supplemental jurisdiction over Pope's contribution claim against Vaughan, but not his mower claim against him.

> **B.** The court has supplemental jurisdiction over both of Pope's claims against Vaughan, under the *Kroger* case.
> **C.** The court has supplemental jurisdiction over both of Pope's claims against Vaughan, under §1367(a).
> **D.** The court lacks jurisdiction over either of Pope's claims against Vaughan. Even adding together the $5,000 in damages for the mower and $45,000 (contribution for half of Jilbert's damages) on the contribution claim, Pope does not satisfy the amount in controversy requirement, so there is no "original jurisdiction" over his claims against Vaughan.
> **E.** The court cannot exercise supplemental jurisdiction under §1367(a), because the main claim is based on diversity, not arising-under jurisdiction.

ANALYSIS. If you understand the basics of §1367(a), this question shouldn't throw you off. It illustrates the point just made, that, if the basic nucleus-of-operative-fact test is met, the court can exercise supplemental jurisdiction over related claims asserted later in the litigation, including those asserted by parties other than the plaintiff. Prior to the enactment of §1367, this exercise of jurisdiction over later claims in the action was referred to as "ancillary jurisdiction," and was generally approved for related claims until *Kroger* introduced a more complex analysis.

Now, however, analysis of subsequent claims, such as counterclaims, crossclaims, and third-party claims, is governed by §1367(a), which has superseded the Supreme Court's analysis in *Kroger* and *Finley*. So **B** is wrong here: In determining whether supplemental jurisdiction exists, we have to look to §1367, not to *Kroger*. While *Kroger* helps us to understand supplemental jurisdiction (much as history helps us to understand the present), it no longer directly governs the court's authority to hear related state law claims. Congress can, and did, supersede the Court's common law limits on that authority when it enacted §1367.

So §1367 determines whether the court has the power to hear the two claims against Vaughan, not the foregoing cases. **E** suggests that, under §1367, supplemental jurisdiction doesn't apply if the main claim is based on diversity. No, no, not so! Supplemental jurisdiction does apply in diversity cases, though §1367(b) creates some exceptions to supplemental jurisdiction in diversity cases. But the basic grant in §1367(a) simply requires that the federal court have a basis upon which to exercise original jurisdiction, and diversity is a perfectly satisfactory basis upon which to do so. Many claims appended to a diversity suit will come within supplemental jurisdiction, because a proper diversity claim provides a "federal hook" to hang them from.

D is one of those great distractors that sounds so plausible that it begs to be chosen. But this analysis is drastically wrong. It's true that Pope's claims against Vaughan, even if we aggregate the damage amounts, would not support diversity jurisdiction if Pope sued Vaughan on these claims as a separate action in federal court. But he didn't. Instead, he has added them as later claims in a case that is already properly before the federal court. So the question is not whether the claims come within the court's "original jurisdiction"; it's whether they come within its *supplemental* jurisdiction.[1] Original jurisdiction is based on Jilbert's diversity claim against Pope and Vaughan. Since that claim provides a basis for original jurisdiction, we look to §1367(a) to determine whether the court has jurisdiction over Pope's crossclaims as well. The very point of supplemental jurisdiction is to allow the court to hear claims that are *not* within its original jurisdiction.

By the way, note that **D** is the longest choice. It's not unusual for the longest choice to be right, because it often takes more words to say something that is accurate than something that isn't. I suppose, if I had no clue as to which of two choices was right, I might opt for the longer one on this rationale. But **D** is living proof that it isn't always so.

We're getting there; we've eliminated **B**, **D**, and **E**. That leaves **A**, which takes the position that the court has supplemental jurisdiction over Pope's contribution claim only, and **C**, which asserts that there is supplemental jurisdiction over both of his claims against Vaughan. The test for supplemental jurisdiction is whether the added claim arises out of the same underlying events as the main, jurisdictionally proper, claim. The contribution claim certainly does; it asks for contribution because Vaughan's negligence was partly responsible for causing the plaintiff's yard damages. But the mower claim arises out of other events on another job. It does not arise from the "same case or controversy" as the yard damage claim, and therefore is not within the grant of supplemental jurisdiction in §1367(a). **A** rules.

Let's do a quick twist on the last question, to nail this down before we complicate matters. Don't consider §1367(b) in answering this question.

QUESTION 3. This, that, and another other. Jilbert (CO) hires Pope (WY) to do some plantings in his yard. Pope hires Vaughan, who runs a backhoe business, to come in and dig the necessary holes for the plantings. They do the work and leave. But the new shrubs die, and Jilbert claims that Vaughan (UT) ran over his underground sprinkler system and his septic system, ruining both. Jilbert sues Pope in federal court, based on proper diversity of citizenship, for $90,000 in damages based on the yard work.

---

1. Of course, if these claims would themselves support *original* federal jurisdiction (for example, if Pope's two claims together sought recovery of more than $75,000 from Vaughan, a diverse party), there would be no need for supplemental jurisdiction.

> After the suit is filed, Pope brings Vaughan in as a third-party defendant. He claims that, if he is found liable to Pope, Vaughan should contribute one-half to the judgment, since he was negligent as well as Pope in causing the yard damages. He also asserts a claim against Vaughan for $12,000 in damages that resulted when Vaughan, while digging holes for the plantings, backed into Pope's dump truck.
>
> The court probably
>
> A. has supplemental jurisdiction over both of Pope's claims against Vaughan, under §1367(a).
> B. has supplemental jurisdiction over Pope's contribution claim against Vaughan, but not his truck damage claim against him.
> C. has supplemental jurisdiction over Pope's truck damage claim, but it is not properly joined under the federal joinder rules.
> D. has supplemental jurisdiction over Pope's truck claim, because it is compulsory under the joinder rules.

ANALYSIS. If you chose **D** you should go back and study the joinder rules some more. First, the claim for damage to the truck *isn't* compulsory . . . at least, it isn't compulsory under the rules. Once Pope brought in Vaughan for contribution, Rule 18(a) allows him to add other claims he has against Vaughan. Rule 18(a) provides that a party "may" add other claims once she has asserted one proper claim against an adversary. Visually, the case looks like this:

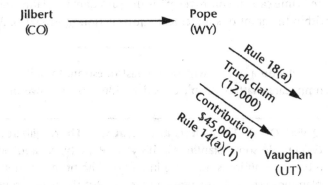

It is true that, if Pope failed to assert the truck damage claim along with his Rule 14(a) impleader claim, he would probably lose it. Because it arises out of the same underlying "transaction"—the yard work—as Pope's contribution claim, res judicata would probably bar a second action by Pope against Vaughan if, after asserting his contribution claim against Vaughan in this case, he didn't add his truck damage claim as well. See Chapter 23, pp. 472-478. But it still isn't compulsory under the joinder rules.

More importantly, the test for supplemental jurisdiction under §1367(a) is not whether the added claim is compulsory. Section 1367(a) simply provides that, if it arises from the same "case or controversy" (that is, the same "nucleus of operative fact"), the court has the power to hear the claim. So **D** is the weakest of the choices.

C is wrong as well, because Rule 18(a) authorizes joinder of this claim. Once Pope has properly asserted a claim against Vaughan, Rule 18(a) allows him to pile on any other claims he has against Vaughan. In Question 2, Pope cross-claimed against Vaughan, a codefendant, and added an unrelated claim under Rule 18(a). That's fine under the Rules, though, as the example illustrates, there was no supplemental jurisdiction over the unrelated Rule 18(a) claim. Here, Pope impleaded Vaughan under Rule 14(a) and added a *related* claim against him under Rule 18(a). That's fine under the Rule too, and there probably will be supplemental jurisdiction over it, since there's a strong argument that it arises from the same set of facts as the main claim—the work on Jilbert's yard. So **A** rather than **B** is the strongest answer here. The court would likely conclude that the truck claim is part of the same "case or controversy" as the main claim and take supplemental jurisdiction over it as well as the contribution claim.

C.   Limits on supplemental jurisdiction in diversity cases: Section 1367(b)

The grant of supplemental jurisdiction in §1367(a) is broad; indeed, it probably reaches to the outer limit of constitutional power to hear added claims, as defined in *Gibbs*. However, after granting supplemental jurisdiction very broadly in §1367(a), Congress pulled back a bit in §1367(b), which bars jurisdiction—even if the test in §1367(a) is satisfied—over certain claims in diversity cases. Thus, the best way to analyze a §1367 problem is to ask first, whether the added claim comes within the broad grant in §1367(a). If it does, then ask whether it is one of the narrow set of claims that §1367(b) excepts from supplemental jurisdiction.

Section 1367(b) was drafted with *Kroger* in mind. *Kroger* had suggested that the federal courts shouldn't always exercise jurisdiction over related claims to the full extent of the power delineated in *Gibbs*. *Kroger* held that the federal courts should not hear claims by plaintiffs against third-party defendants in diversity cases, even if they arose out of the same nucleus of operative fact as the main claim, if doing so would be inconsistent with the long-standing complete diversity rule of *Strawbridge v. Curtiss*, 7 U.S. 267 (1806).

In 28 U.S.C. §1367(b), Congress sought to preserve the *Kroger* limit on supplemental jurisdiction in diversity cases.

Section 1367(b). In any civil action of which the district courts have original jurisdiction founded solely on section 1332 of this title, the district courts shall not have supplemental jurisdiction under subsection (a) over claims by plaintiffs against persons made parties under Rule 14, 19, 20, or 24 of the Federal Rules of Civil Procedure, or over claims by persons proposed to be joined as plaintiffs under Rule 19 of such rules, or seeking to intervene as plaintiffs under Rule 24 of such rules, when exercising supplemental jurisdiction over such claims would be inconsistent with the jurisdictional requirements of section 1332.

This provision is the source of most student confusion concerning supplemental jurisdiction. Basically, it provides that in *diversity cases only,* the federal court will not have supplemental jurisdiction over certain *claims by plaintiffs* or persons sought to be joined as plaintiffs. Not all claims, just *some* claims, defined in §1367(b) by reference to the rules used to join them.

The purpose for this exception to the broad grant of supplemental jurisdiction in §1367(a) is to prevent parties from evading the *Strawbridge* complete diversity rule. Under that rule, a plaintiff in a diversity case can't sue defendants from her own state. If she could achieve the same result by suing a diverse defendant and then using supplemental jurisdiction to add a claim against one who is not diverse, *Strawbridge* would be a dead letter. Some think it should be a dead letter, but Congress evidently doesn't. So §1367(b) enumerates certain situations in which a plaintiff in a diversity case cannot rely on supplemental jurisdiction to assert additional claims, even if they arise out of the same case or controversy under §1367(a).

Section 1367(b) isn't too bad if you approach it in steps.

- *First,* ask if jurisdiction over the main claim is based solely on diversity. If it isn't, stop! Section 1367(b) does not apply, because the first phrase in the subsection says "in any civil action of which the district courts have original jurisdiction founded solely on section 1332. . . ."
- *Next,* if jurisdiction over the original case is based solely on diversity, ask if the claim you are analyzing was asserted by a plaintiff. If it isn't, stop! Section 1367(b) does not apply, because it only excepts certain "claims by plaintiffs" (or persons being joined as plaintiffs under Rules 19 or 24). And the word "plaintiff" means the original plaintiff, not a third-party plaintiff or a "plaintiff" on a counterclaim.
- *Then,* if the case is based on diversity, and the added claim is asserted by a plaintiff, you have to ask if it is a claim "against persons made parties under Rule 14, 19, 20, or 24" of the Federal Rules. If so, supplemental jurisdiction is barred.
- *Or,* if the case involves Rule 19 or Rule 24, consider whether the person would be joined as a plaintiff under Rule 19 or intervene as a plaintiff under Rule 24. If so, §1367(b) bars supplemental jurisdiction.

- *Last,* just to be thorough, ask whether there is a basis for *original jurisdiction* over the added claim. If there is, the claim should be fine even though it is one of the claims described in §1367(b). If the claim could have been asserted in federal court on its own, there is no need for supplemental jurisdiction. For example, if Luis, a plaintiff from Maine, asserts a claim against DeVoto (a third-party defendant in the case who is also from Maine) under a federal statute, who cares that there's no diversity, and who cares that §1367(b) bars supplemental jurisdiction. This is a case that Luis could have asserted in federal court in a stand-alone suit, so the court has jurisdiction over it without regard to supplemental jurisdiction.

An example should help. In analyzing it, ask first whether the federal court has original jurisdiction based on a proper federal court claim, then whether the broad grant of supplemental jurisdiction in §1367(a) applies, and then whether §1367(b) bars supplemental jurisdiction over it.

QUESTION 4. **Exceptions, exceptions.**   Cavers, from Wisconsin, sues Pariah Corporation, an Iowa corporation with its principal place of business in Iowa, for damages for defamation. He sues in federal court, for $100,000, based on diversity jurisdiction. Pariah impleads Donnelly, a former supervisor for the company who allegedly made the actual statements on which Cavers's claim is based. It seeks indemnification (a state law theory of recovery) from Donnelly, an Iowa citizen, for any damages it is ordered to pay to Cavers. Donnelly moves to dismiss the claim against him for lack of subject matter jurisdiction.

A. The court has supplemental jurisdiction over the claim against Donnelly under §1367(a), but jurisdiction over it is barred by §1367(b).
B. The court does not have supplemental jurisdiction over the claim under §1367(a).
C. The court has supplemental jurisdiction over the claim under §1367(a), and §1367(b) does not bar the court from hearing the claim.
D. The court does not have supplemental jurisdiction, because Donnelly and Pariah are both from Iowa.

ANALYSIS.   This question is pretty easy if you understand the statute. **D** is clearly wrong. The fact that both of the parties to the impleader claim are from the same state means that there is no independent basis for subject matter jurisdiction over this state law claim. But that does not mean that there can't be a basis for supplemental jurisdiction. The whole point of supplemental jurisdiction is to authorize a federal court to hear claims that it cannot hear under original jurisdiction. So don't confuse standards for original jurisdiction, based on diversity or a claim arising under federal law, with standards for supplemental jurisdiction.

B is also wrong. The court has supplemental jurisdiction over the claim under §1367(a) if it arises out of the case or controversy (same nucleus of operative fact) as the main claim. Pariah's claim against Donnelly meets this test. Pariah claims that, if it is liable for its employee's tort, Donnelly should ultimately pay the damages, since he actually made the defamatory statements. Since the impleader claim arises from the same events as the main claim, the broad grant in §1367(a) is satisfied.

The further question is whether one of the exceptions in §1367(b) bars the claim. None of them do, since this a claim by a defendant rather than a plaintiff. Thus, **A** is wrong, since §1367(b) does not apply. One might argue, I suppose, that Pariah is a "plaintiff" on the impleader claim. But if the drafters had intended that construction, they would almost certainly have used more general language to indicate that. (Compare, for example, Rule 8(a), which, in prescribing the contents of pleadings, refers to "a pleading that states a claim for relief," because it applies to plaintiffs, defendants, and other parties.) The cases affirm that the word "plaintiff" in §1367(b) refers to an original plaintiff only. See, e.g., *Viacom International, Inc. v. Kearney*, 212 F.3d 721, 726-727 (2d Cir. 2000). Since the claim here is not asserted by a plaintiff, or an intervenor, or a person being joined as a plaintiff under Rule 19, the exceptions in §1367(b) don't apply. The court has supplemental jurisdiction over it, as **C** concludes.

——————————————

Let's tackle another example that probes the limits of §1367(b).

QUESTION 5. **The exception that proves the rule.** Cavers, from Wisconsin, sues Pariah Corporation, an Iowa corporation with its principal place of business in Iowa, for damages for defamation. He sues in federal court, based on diversity jurisdiction. He claims $50,000 in compensatory damages and $50,000 in punitive damages.

Pariah impleads Pelosi, a former supervisor who allegedly gave it inaccurate information that led to publication of the defamatory statements. It seeks contribution, a state tort theory, from Pelosi, a Wisconsin citizen. After Pariah impleads Pelosi, Cavers asserts a claim directly against her, seeking $50,000 in compensatory damages for the defamation. (Assume that only the publisher may be liable for punitive damages.) Pelosi moves to dismiss Cavers's claim against her for lack of subject matter jurisdiction.

A. The court has supplemental jurisdiction over Cavers's claim against Pelosi under §1367(a), but jurisdiction over it is barred by §1367(b). Congress could have granted jurisdiction over this claim but didn't in the supplemental jurisdiction statute.

B. Jurisdiction over the claim is not authorized by the supplemental jurisdiction statute. If it were, it would exceed the permissible constitutional scope of jurisdiction under Article III, §2.

> **C.** The court has supplemental jurisdiction over the claim under §1367(a), and §1367(b) does not bar the court from hearing the claim.
> **D.** This claim is barred by the *Kroger* case, because, as in *Kroger,* the plaintiff here seeks relief from a nondiverse third-party defendant.

ANALYSIS. Perhaps you noticed, as **D** points out, that this claim involves the same configuration of claims as the *Kroger* case: Plaintiff sues a diverse defendant, who impleads a third-party defendant from the plaintiff's state, and then the plaintiff fires off a direct claim against the third-party defendant. Here's a quick diagram:

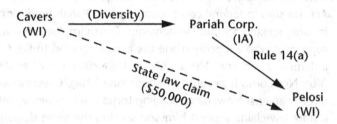

Kroger rejected ancillary jurisdiction over a similar claim by a plaintiff against a third-party defendant, on the ground that the plaintiff should not be able to assert such a claim indirectly, since she couldn't sue Pelosi on it directly under *Strawbridge.* If a plaintiff in this scenario could wait for parties like Pelosi to be impleaded, and then claim against them, they could, effectively, sue one diverse defendant and another who is not.

But, as noted earlier, *Kroger* is no longer the governing law: 28 U.S.C. §1367 is. So the question isn't whether the *Kroger* Court would approve Cavers's claim, but whether it is authorized by §1367. So **D** is misguided, though it is true that *Kroger* rejected a similar claim.

So let's turn to the statute. There's little doubt that §1367(a) authorizes jurisdiction over this claim. It arises out of the same defamation as Cavers's claim against Pariah, so it is part of the same "case or controversy." But is jurisdiction over this claim denied by §1367(b)? It is. This is a claim by a plaintiff, Cavers, against a person made a party under Rule 14(a) — Pelosi, the third-party defendant. The express language of §1367(b) bars supplemental jurisdiction over it, codifying the holding in *Kroger.*

That eliminates **C**, so we only need choose between **A** and **B**. Both acknowledge that §1367(b) bars the court from hearing Cavers's claim. **A** says that Congress could constitutionally authorize jurisdiction over it; **B** says that it couldn't. So you need to ask, "What is the constitutional standard for jurisdiction over supplemental claims?" The answer is, the *Gibbs* common-nucleus-of-operative-fact test, which is essentially the same as the same-case-or-controversy test of §1367(a). Since Cavers's claim against Pelosi does arise out of the same underlying facts, it is part of the same "constitutional case" under *Gibbs.* Congress could have authorized jurisdiction over it, but chose instead to limit supplemental jurisdiction in diversity cases more narrowly, just as the Court did in *Kroger.* So **A** takes the cake.

———————————————

We aren't quite done with §1367(b). Here's one more question to make a particular point.

———————————————

QUESTION 6. Wish I had a nickel. Cavers, from Wisconsin, sues Pariah Corporation, an Iowa corporation with its principal place of business in Iowa, for damages under the Federal Age Discrimination in Employment Act. He sues in federal court, claiming that Pariah fired him based on his age, seeking $50,000 in damages. Pariah impleads Newcomb, a former supervisor who allegedly made the actual decision to fire Cavers. It seeks indemnification from Newcomb, an Iowa citizen, for her illegal act. After Newcomb is brought in under Rule 14(a), Cavers asserts a claim directly against Newcomb, alleging tortious interference with the contract, a state law claim, against him and seeking the same damages. Newcomb moves to dismiss Cavers's claim against her for lack of subject matter jurisdiction.

A. The court has supplemental jurisdiction over the claim against Newcomb under §1367(a), but jurisdiction over it is barred by §1367(b).
B. The court lacks supplemental jurisdiction over the claim, but may hear it because Cavers and Newcomb are diverse.
C. The court lacks supplemental jurisdiction over the claim, but may hear it since it satisfies the *Gibbs* test for a single constitutional case.
D. The court has supplemental jurisdiction over the claim under §1367(a), and §1367(b) does not bar the court from hearing the claim.

ANALYSIS.   I really do wish I had a nickel for every time I've tripped up a student with this fact pattern. First let's dispose of **C**, which is based on the misconception that the court can hear a claim, whether or not it is authorized by the supplemental jurisdiction statute, if it meets the *Gibbs* test for a single constitutional case. This doesn't pass muster. For the court to hear the claim, it must be within the constitutional grant of jurisdiction over related claims, expounded in *Gibbs, and* Congress must convey that jurisdiction to the federal district courts by statute. Both *Kroger* and *Finley* reminded us of that. For statutory authorization, we look to §1367. If it doesn't authorize the court to hear the claim, it can't be heard (absent some special statute authorizing it).

B is interesting. It suggests that the court *may not need supplemental jurisdiction* to entertain the claim ... there may be direct jurisdiction over the claim. Supplemental jurisdiction, as its name suggests, is there to fill in the gaps, to provide a basis for the federal court to hear related claims that it can't hear under diversity or arising-under jurisdiction. If a claim has its own basis for jurisdiction, there's no need to consider whether it meets the §1367 standards for supplemental jurisdiction. That's true, but this one doesn't quite have its own basis for jurisdiction. While the parties are diverse, the amount-in-controversy requirement isn't met. Thus, Cavers's claim against Newcomb meets the Article III, §2 test for a diversity case, but the basic diversity statute, 28 U.S.C. §1332(a) does not authorize the federal courts to hear it. Consequently, the federal court does not have "original jurisdiction" over it. So jurisdiction will have to be based on §1367 or the court won't have it.

Certainly, jurisdiction over Cavers's claim is authorized by §1367(a), since it arises from the same set of facts — his discharge — as the main claim. But is it barred by the §1367(b) exceptions? No, it isn't, because this is *not a diversity case*. Section 1367(b) limits certain claims by plaintiffs in diversity cases. That subsection is irrelevant if the federal court has "original jurisdiction" over the main claim (Cavers's claim against Pariah) based on some other category of federal jurisdiction, as it does here. This case arises under federal law, so, even though Cavers's claim, like Mrs. Kroger's against Owen Equipment, is brought by a plaintiff against a party brought in under Rule 14, the exceptions in §1367(b) are simply irrelevant.

This is so, even though Cavers and Pariah (the original parties to the case) are diverse. The limits in §1367(b) only apply to cases in which the federal court's original jurisdiction is "founded solely on §1332." That provision doesn't apply in this case, since the federal court has original jurisdiction based on the federal ADEA claim. Thus, **A** is wrong, and **D** is, after all is said and done, the right answer.

D. "Pendent party" jurisdiction

Before §1367 was enacted, the federal courts decided a number of cases involving "pendent party jurisdiction." In *Finley v. United States*, for example, the California plaintiffs sued the United States under the Federal Tort Claims Act (FTCA), seeking damages from a plane crash in California. The federal court had jurisdiction, because the case was against the United States. Cases in which the United States is a party are authorized by Article III, §2 of the Constitution, and the FTCA authorizes, indeed, requires tort claims against the United States to be filed in federal court. See 28 U.S.C. §1346(b).

But the Finleys also had claims against other parties — California citizens — arising out of the same accident. They asserted those claims in the federal suit as well, and asked the court to take "pendent party" jurisdiction over them. The argument for this is based on *Gibbs*. The federal court had original jurisdiction in *Finley* based on the proper federal claim against the United States. And the plaintiffs' claims against the California defendants arose out of the same set of facts, the plane crash. So the plaintiffs argued that the court could hang the jurisdictionally insufficient claims against the California defendants from the other, jurisdictionally proper claim against the United States. It's just another exercise of pendent jurisdiction, they argued, except that the jurisdictionally insufficient claim is asserted (unlike typical pendent jurisdiction cases like *Gibbs*) against a different party. Visually, it looks like this:

```
                        (FTCA)
    Finley    ──────────────────▶    United States
    (CA)      ──────────────────▶    Defendant #2
                      State law              (CA)
```

In *Finley,* the Supreme Court suggested that pendent party jurisdiction might be constitutionally permissible under *Gibbs,* since the claims against the added parties arose from the same underlying facts as the FTCA claim. But the Court then looked to the second requirement, whether Congress, in the FTCA, had authorized jurisdiction over the related state law claims. Since it saw no indication that Congress had done so, it rejected pendent party jurisdiction in that case.

In the supplemental jurisdiction statute, Congress responded to the Court's reminder in *Finley* that Congress must authorize such exercises of federal jurisdiction. In the second sentence of §1367(a), Congress expressly authorized supplemental jurisdiction over claims by or against added parties: "Such supplemental jurisdiction shall include claims that involve the joinder or intervention of additional parties." So, if the basic standard for jurisdiction over an added claim is met — that it arises from the same case or controversy as the main claim — it may be asserted even if it is asserted against a new party. Of course, §1367(b) must still be consulted, since it limits the broad scope of §1367(a) in certain diversity cases.

Here's a nice little mind-bender to help you sort out the limits of pendent party jurisdiction under §1367.

QUESTION 7. **Added, but not authorized.** In which of the following cases would the federal court have jurisdiction over the last-mentioned claim? In each, assume that Richards Corporation is incorporated in Delaware and has its principal place of business in New York. Ortega is a citizen of New Jersey.

1. The Richards Corporation sues Ortega, a former engineer for the company, for misappropriating trade secrets. The suit is brought in federal court, based on diversity jurisdiction, and seeks $100,000 in damages. Ortega counterclaims for patent infringement, based on the company's decision, unrelated to the trade secret dispute, to market a device on which he claimed to hold a patent. He demands $60,000 in damages on the counterclaim.

2. The Richards Corporation sues Ortega, a former engineer for the company, for misappropriating trade secrets, which led to his discharge. The suit is brought in federal court, based on diversity jurisdiction, and seeks $100,000 in damages. Ortega counterclaims for breach of contract, based on the same events that led the company to discharge him. He seeks $40,000 in damages. Richards then brings in Suriyama, a former vice president for personnel, under Rule 14(b). It claims that Suriyama, a New Yorker, misled the company about Ortega's conduct, leading it to dismiss Ortega. Richards seeks indemnification for any damages it must pay Ortega on the counterclaim.

3. The Richards Corporation sues Ortega, a former engineer for the company, for misappropriating trade secrets. The suit is brought in federal court based on diversity jurisdiction, seeking $100,000 in damages. Richards also makes Carson, a New York employee, a codefendant in the case, claiming damages for fraud. The claim against Carson arises out of the same events as the claim against Ortega and also seeks $100,000 in damages.

4. The Richards Corporation sues Ortega for trademark infringement, a federal claim. In the same action, it asserts a claim against Sheindienst, an employee from New York, for fraud, arising from the same events as the claim against Ortega.

   A. 1, 2, and 3.
   B. 2 and 3 only.
   C. 1 only.
   D. 1 and 4 only.

ANALYSIS. This question is traumatic enough to make a Closer, unless you've figured out how §1367 works. Once you have, it's not too bad.

Let's go through the cases in turn. In the first, the plaintiff brings a diversity case, and the defendant asserts an unrelated counterclaim. That's permissible under Rule 13(b), but there still has to be a basis for subject matter jurisdiction over the counterclaim. And supplemental jurisdiction won't provide it, since the claim arises from a different set of facts. This fails both the *Gibbs* constitutional test and the case-or-controversy test of §1367(a).

But who cares? The counterclaim arises under the federal patent laws. It has its own basis for federal jurisdiction. Ortega could have sued Richards on this claim in a stand-alone federal suit, and the federal court would have had jurisdiction over it. He doesn't need supplemental jurisdiction. The court has independent arising-under jurisdiction over the claim.

In the second case, Ortega counterclaims against Richards, which then impleads Suriyama. Rule 14(b) allows a plaintiff to implead a third party under the same circumstances that Rule 14(a)(1) allows a defendant to do so. Here, the impleader is proper, since Richards seeks to pass on "all" of its liability to Ortega on the counterclaim. But there still must be a basis for jurisdiction over the claim.

Section 1367(a) grants jurisdiction, since the impleader claim arises from the same events as the claim that supports original jurisdiction, the diversity claim against Ortega. So the only question is whether §1367(b) bars the claim. It probably does, since this is a claim by a plaintiff against a party brought in under Rule 14.[2] This was probably a drafting mistake. The drafters probably meant to limit claims like the plaintiff's in *Kroger,* not claims in which the plaintiff herself, as a defendant on the counterclaim, brings in the third party. But it's hard to ignore the plain language of the statute, even if it was a mistake. See *Guaranteed Systems, Inc. v. American National Can Co.,* 842 F. Supp. 855, 857 (M.D.N.C. 1994) (rejecting supplemental jurisdiction over a Rule 14(b) impleader claim on this reasoning).

In the third case, the plaintiff asserts a claim against one diverse defendant and tries to hang a second claim against a nondiverse defendant from this federal hook. Remember, §1367(a) contemplates claims against added parties. "Such supplemental jurisdiction shall include claims that involve the joinder or intervention of additional parties." However, this one fails under §1367(b), which bars jurisdiction, in diversity cases, over claims by plaintiffs against persons made parties under Rule 20, if they are inconsistent with the requirements of §1332. If it weren't for this provision in §1367(b), *Strawbridge v. Curtiss* would be a dead letter: Plaintiffs would simply sue one diverse defendant for the proper jurisdictional amount, and add other, nondiverse parties, under the last sentence of §1367(a).

The fourth case is a proper exercise of "pendent party" jurisdiction under §1367. It is authorized by §1367(a), even though the supplemental claim is against a new party, since it arises from the same events as the proper federal claim against Ortega. And §1367(b) is irrelevant, since the claim that provides "original jurisdiction" is not a diversity claim. Note that, on the

---

2. There's an argument that, even though this is a claim by a plaintiff against a party brought in under Rule 14, it is not "inconsistent with the jurisdictional requirements of section 1332," since the *original parties* to the case are diverse. But Richards' is not diverse from Suriyama, so on a straightforward reading it appears to be barred.

same logic, the pendent party claims in *Finley v. United States* would be proper if that case were filed today.

The first case is a "yes," the second and third are "no's," and the fourth is a "yes." So **D** is the right answer to the question, which asks in which cases the court *has* jurisdiction over the last claim.

E.   The Closer: Section 1367(b) and the amount in controversy requirement

Before the supplemental jurisdiction statute was enacted, the case law had held that in a diversity case, each plaintiff had to meet the amount in controversy requirement independently against each defendant. Suppose that Currier and Ives were injured in an accident, and sued Hochstein. If Currier's damages were $120,000, and Ives's were $25,000, Currier would satisfy the amount in controversy requirement in 28 U.S.C. §1332(a)(1), but Ives would not. Ives could not add his damages together with Currier's, and argue the case was for $145,000: he had to assert a claim *himself* for more than $75,000.

Similarly, if a plaintiff sued multiple defendants, she had to assert a colorable claim for more than $75,000 against each defendant. Suppose Currier sued Hochstein for $60,000 in business losses, and claimed that he was entitled to double damages under an unfair business practices statute. He might recover a total of $120,000 on these claims, so he met the amount requirement. Now suppose that Currier made Faust a second defendant, seeking recovery of the same business losses, but the double damages statute did not apply to Faust. Because Currier only had a $60,000 claim against Faust, he did not satisfy the amount requirement against her. Again, he had to meet the amount in controversy requirement separately against each defendant.

When Congress enacted the supplemental jurisdiction statute, it probably did not intend to change either of those rules. However, the *text* of §1367 appears to change one of them. The question below illustrates the problem, which the Supreme Court addressed at length in *Exxon Mobil Corp. v. Allapattah Services*, 545 U.S. 546 (2005). In analyzing the problem, focus ruthlessly on the language of the statute.

QUESTION 8. Supplementing supplemental jurisdiction. Cavers, from Wisconsin, sues Pariah Corporation, an Iowa corporation with its principal place of business in Iowa, for damages for breach of contract, after he is fired by Pariah on the ground that he, along with Westford, had embezzled funds from Pariah. Cavers sues in federal court, for $100,000, based on diversity jurisdiction. Westford, another Wisconsin citizen, was also fired for the embezzlement, and joins as a coplaintiff in the suit, seeking $40,000 in damages. Under the language of 28 U.S.C. §1367 in the suit, the court would

A. have jurisdiction over Westford's claim under §1367(a), but it is barred by §1367(b).
B. not have jurisdiction over Westford's claim under §1367(a).
C. have supplemental jurisdiction over the claim under §1367(a) and it would not be barred by §1367(b).
D. have jurisdiction over Westford's claim under §1367(a), but his claim is barred because it is inconsistent with the diversity requirements of §1332, since it does not meet the amount in controversy requirement.

ANALYSIS.   This is a fairly simple case, in which one plaintiff sues the defendant on a proper diversity claim, but the other plaintiff's claim does not meet the amount in controversy requirement. The case looks like this:

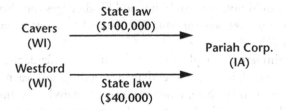

We know that, under the traditional "aggregation rules" courts have used in assessing the amount in controversy, each plaintiff was required to meet the amount requirement individually, so that Westford's claim would not be proper. The question is whether, in enacting §1367, Congress has changed the traditional rule.

Let's start with **B**, which suggests that Westford's claim cannot be added under supplemental jurisdiction, because it is not part of the same case or controversy under §1367(a). This is clearly wrong: Both plaintiffs were fired at the same time for the same conduct, so these would surely be treated as arising out of a common nucleus of operative fact.

A is also off the mark. It states that §1367(a) authorizes supplemental jurisdiction, but that §1367(b) takes it away. But none of the exceptions in §1367(b) expressly applies. Westford's claim is a "claim by [a] plaintiff," but it is not "against persons made parties under Rule 14, 19, 20, or 24." Rule 20 *would* apply if there were multiple defendants, since it applies to joinder of claims against parties joined under Rule 20. But it doesn't seem to apply where there is only one defendant. So none of the exceptions in §1367(b) bars this claim, on a plain reading of the statute. If Congress meant to perpetuate the rule that each plaintiff must meet the amount in controversy requirement separately, it could have included an exception in §1367(b) for "claims by plaintiffs joined under Rule 20 that do not meet the amount in controversy requirement," or similar language. It didn't.

But it is true, isn't it, as **D** suggests, that allowing it would be inconsistent with the established rules for determining the amount in controversy in a diversity case, which have always required each plaintiff to meet the amount requirement separately? Well, that is true, but Congress may change the established rules, and probably did so inadvertently by granting broad supplemental jurisdiction over related claims in 28 U.S.C. §1367(a), and failing to exclude claims such as Westford's in §1367(b). In *Exxon Mobil*, the Supreme Court parsed the statute carefully, and concluded that — whatever the drafters may have intended — the text of sections 1367(a) and (b) is clear: section 1367(a) authorizes jurisdiction over all other claims that arise out of the same case or controversy. That would include Westford's claim here. And no exception to that broad grant in §1367(b) bars Westford's claim. **C** takes the cake.

Question. Ok, if you've got that down, consider this case: Suppose that Cavers, from Wisconsin, sues Pariah Corporation for $200,000 in damages in an industrial accident, and Rolvaag joins as a coplaintiff, seeking $120,000 in damages for his injuries in the same accident. Rolvaag is from Iowa. The case looks like this:

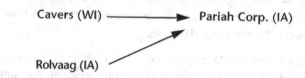

Cavers (WI) ⟶ Pariah Corp. (IA)

Rolvaag (IA)

How about this argument for supplemental jurisdiction over Rolvaag's claim? The court has original jurisdiction over Cavers's claim against Pariah, since it is a diversity claim for more than $75,000. Rolvaag's claim arises out of the same "case or controversy," since he is suing for the same accident. So §1367(a) authorizes supplemental jurisdiction over his claim. And nothing in §1367(b) excludes the claim, since it is not one brought against a person made a party under one of the stated rules. Pretty good argument, isn't it?

Perhaps, but if this argument were accepted, §1367 would overrule the complete diversity requirement of *Strawbridge v. Curtiss*. Justice Kennedy managed to avoid that conclusion in *Exxon Mobil* by holding that, in a diversity case, the court does not have original jurisdiction of *any claim* unless there is complete diversity between all plaintiffs and defendants. So, in Cavers's and Rolvaag's case, the court has no original jurisdiction from which to hang the added claim. Note, however, that in considering the amount in controversy requirement, the *Exxon Mobil* court analyzes the case *claim by claim*, concluding that, where one plaintiff met the amount requirement, others did not have to. By this awkward parsing of the statute, Justice Kennedy managed to perpetuate the complete diversity rule.

Let's try to tie this all up with a Super-Closer. Remember, Closers are optional.

QUESTION 9. Pushing the limits. In which of the following cases would the federal court have subject matter jurisdiction over all claims?

Case #1. Kae and Lindstrom, both from Missouri, sue Smirnov, from Colorado, for injuries suffered in an auto accident. Kae suffered $150,000 in damages from the accident. Lindstrom was unhurt, but her car, worth $25,000, was totalled.

Case #2. Kae (MO) sues Smirnov (CO) for $150,000 in damages from an auto accident. After the accident, Toby's Towing Company arrived to tow Kae's car, but ran into it, causing $10,000 in additional damages to the car. Kae makes Toby's (incorporated in Colorado with its only place of business there) a codefendant in the action, seeking recovery of $10,000.

Case #3. Kae (MO) sues Smirnov (CO) for $150,000 in damages from an auto accident. Lahiri, a passenger in Kae's car, suffered $30,000 in damages and joins as a coplaintiff in her action against Smirnov. Lahiri is from Colorado.

Case #4. Kae (MO) sues Smirnov (CO) for $150,000 in damages from an auto accident. In the same action, she sues Plotkin, a third driver, from Missouri, for the same damages.

Case #5. Kae and Lindstrom, both from Missouri, sue Smirnov, from Colorado, for injuries suffered in an auto accident. Kae suffered $50,000 in damages from the accident. Lindstrom was unhurt, but her car, worth $35,000, was totalled.

A. Case #1 and Case # 2.
B. Case #1 and Case #3.
C. Case #1 only.
D. Case #1 and Case #5.
E. The court does not have jurisdiction over all claims in any of these cases.
F. The court has jurisdiction over all the claims in all of these cases.

ANALYSIS. Really, this is excruciating. It's even excruciating *to me*, and I wrote the darn thing.

There's no way around it, we have to work our way through each case to see if the court has supplemental jurisdiction. In Case #1, the parties are diverse, but only one meets the amount in controversy requirement. However, *Exxon Mobil* held that, where the parties are completely diverse, and Kae asserts a claim that meets the amount requirement, the court has original jurisdiction. Lindstrom's claim arises from the same facts, so it is within the court's supplemental jurisdiction under 28 U.S.C. §1367(a). And there is no exception in §1367(b) that takes away jurisdiction. So both claims in this case are properly before the federal court. So, we can eliminate **E**, since we have found a case in which the court has jurisdiction over all claims.

In Case #2, Kae sues one defendant on a claim that meets the amount requirement, and sues a second defendant on a claim that does not. Under *Exxon Mobil*, Kae's claim against Smirnov gives the court original jurisdiction, since there is complete diversity and her claim against Smirnov meets the amount requirement. And her claim against Toby's arises out of the same series of occurrences, the accident and its aftermath, which I think most courts would construe as a single case or controversy under §1367(a). If that section provides jurisdiction, we have to ask whether an exception in §1367(b) applies. It does, because Kae's claim against Toby is a claim by a plaintiff against a person made a party under Rule 20, and it does not meet the amount in controversy requirement in the diversity statute. Although, under *Exxon Mobil*, a plaintiff who does not meet the amount requirement may tag along, a claim against a defendant that does not meet it is excepted by the language of §1367(b). This case fails. So, **A** is wrong, and **F**, which says that all the cases are jurisdictionally proper, is wrong too.

In Case #3, there is no complete diversity, because the added plaintiff is from the same state as the defendant. In *Exxon Mobil*, the Court held that the federal court lacks diversity jurisdiction over any of the claims if there is not complete diversity among the parties. So this case fails entirely. Scratch **B**. Similarly, in Case #4, the amount requirement is met against each defendant, but one of them is from the same state as the plaintiff. There is no complete diversity, and the court therefore has no jurisdiction over the case. Scratch **D**.

In Case #5 there is complete diversity, but no party meets the amount requirement. There is no jurisdictionally proper claim to serve as an anchor for other claims, so there is no jurisdiction over either claim. The parties cannot add their claims together to meet the amount requirement. So this case fails. Scratch **D** and crown **C** the winner.

✤ Glannon's Picks

1. This and that	D
2. This, that, and the other	A
3. This, that, and another other	A
4. Exceptions, exceptions	C

5. The exception that proves the rule   **A**
6. Wish I had a nickel   **D**
7. Added, but not authorized   **D**
8. Supplementing supplemental jurisdiction   **C**
9. Pushing the limits   **C**

15

Sufficient Allegations: Pleading Under the Federal Rules

Plaintiff has a great deal to say,
But it seems he skipped Rule 8(a).
His Complaint is too long,
Which renders it wrong,
Please rewrite and refile today.[1]

CHAPTER OVERVIEW

A. Stating a claim under the Federal Rules
B. The new era: *Bell v. Twombly* and *Ashcroft v. Iqbal*
C. Allegations of fact and conclusions of law
D. Pleading alternatively or inconsistently
E. Admissions and denials in the defendant's answer
F. Pleading multiple defenses and objections . . . with an early Closer
G. Rule 11 limits on legal allegations
H. Rule 11 limits on factual allegations . . . and a caveat
◈ Glannon's Picks

---

1. Federal Judge Ronald Leighton, in *Presidio Group, LLC v. GMAC Mortg., LLC*, 2008 WL 2595675, in dismissing the plaintiff's complaint for failure to comply with Fed. R. Civ. P. 8(a).

T he plaintiff starts a federal lawsuit by filing a complaint. Usually, the defendant responds by filing an answer to the complaint. These "pleadings" apprise the court and the opposing party of the nature of the claims and defenses, the positions of the parties about the dispute. The Federal Rules take a very flexible approach to pleadings. But there are requirements and limits as well as ethical constraints on both factual and legal allegations in the pleadings. Both the pleading rules and the ethical constraints of Rule 11 are explored below.

A.   Stating a claim under the Federal Rules

The plaintiff starts the ball rolling by filing a complaint, but what has to be in it? Federal Rule 8 says it must contain (1) a statement of the basis for the court's jurisdiction, (2) a statement of the relief the plaintiff is seeking, and most perplexingly, (3) "a short and plain statement of the claim showing that the pleader is entitled to relief." Fed. R. Civ. P. 8(a). The purpose of pleading under the Federal Rules is *notice* to the opposing party: notice of the events that gave rise to the claim, and the general nature of the legal right the plaintiff asserts. The idea is to do away with technical requirements, to allow the plaintiff to proceed to discovery based on a simple, general statement of the legal claims she has against the defendant.

This "short and plain statement" requirement is probably met even if the plaintiff does not specifically allege each element she must establish to prove the claim she asserts.

For example, in a negligence case, the court and the defendant may be able to understand the nature of the plaintiff's claim, even if she does not specifically allege each of the elements of a claim for negligence: duty, breach, causation, and damages. Similarly, it is clear that the plaintiff need not allege every fact she plans to rely on to prove her allegations. For example, she may plead generally that the defendant drove negligently, without specifying the exact conduct that was negligent. Similarly, she may plead generally that she suffered medical expenses as a result of the defendant's negligence, without specifying in the complaint the medical procedures she required or the cost of those procedures. In addition, judges are to construe the complaint liberally, taking all reasonable inferences in the plaintiff's favor in deciding whether an adequate claim has been alleged. The details will be explored through discovery and at trial; they need not be in the pleadings. The forms accompanying the Federal Rules give a sense of just how spare a complaint can be and still pass muster under Rule 8(a)(2). See Fed. R. Civ. P. Forms 10-11, 15, 17, 21. See also *Swierkiewicz v. Sorema, N.A.*, 534 U.S. 506, 513 and 513 n.4 (2002).

While usually very general pleading suffices, even if it does not allege every element of a legally recognized claim, practice will vary. Judges who are sticklers for good pleading may find a complaint that fails to allege each element of a claim insufficient, while others will find a complaint adequate so long as the plaintiff asserts facts that, if proved, would support relief. Practice also varies with the type of case: Judges may be less exacting for simple types of cases, such as negligence or contract cases, but expect pleading of all the requirements of more complex claims, such as civil rights or securities cases. While Rule 8 suggests that a minimalist approach will survive a motion to dismiss, it will often make sense, to avoid challenges to the complaint and for strategic reasons, to plead in more detail.

Here's a quick example.

QUESTION 1. Too short and too plain?   Carstairs is injured when he is hit by Noble's car. He sues Noble in federal court, alleging that the court has jurisdiction on the basis of diversity, that "the defendant hit me while driving down Main Street on June 14, 2002," and that he suffered physical injuries as a result. He demands $100,000 in damages.

Which of the following is the best argument that the complaint is insufficient under Rule 8(a)(2)?

A. The quoted allegation is inadequate because it does not give Noble notice of the events that are the basis of the suit.

B. The quoted allegation is inadequate because it provides insufficient detail concerning the location and time of the accident.

C. The quoted allegation is inadequate because it does not allege that Noble owed Carstairs a duty of care.

D. The quoted allegation is inadequate because it does not suggest that Noble has violated a legal right that gives Carstairs a right to relief from him.

ANALYSIS.   Carstairs' complaint here is darned minimal . . . but so are the examples in the Forms accompanying the Federal Rules. We can eliminate two of the choices easily. Both **A** and **B** take the position that more detail about the facts is needed. The court is unlikely to agree. The complaint provides the date and the place of the accident (and, or course, the name of the victim, since the plaintiff's name is in the caption of the complaint — see Rule 10(a)). This is probably enough to give Noble notice of the events he is being sued for. After all, how many accidents did he have with Carstairs on Main Street on June 14? Noble has enough information about the source of Carstairs' claim that he can begin to investigate it and form a defense. He can get the additional detail he needs through discovery.

C takes the position that Carstairs' complaint is insufficient under Rule 8(a)(2) because it does not expressly allege that Noble owed him a duty of care. In a simple case, it is probably sufficient to allege the claim generally, or perhaps even to allege facts that show that the plaintiff may be able to prove those elements. See, e.g., Form 11 after the Federal Rules, which does not include an allegation that the defendant owed the plaintiff a duty of care. The plaintiff will of course have to *prove* every element in order to recover, but it is unlikely that the judge would require Carstairs to amend to add an allegation that Noble owed him a duty of care.

If, in a complex case, the plaintiff has not alleged an element, and the defendant doubts that the plaintiff has grounds to plead it under the constraints of Rule 11, he will likely challenge the plaintiff's complaint by filing a motion to dismiss for failure to state a claim. In this situation, the motion challenges whether the plaintiff can allege each element necessary to establish her claims, and may lead the judge to require the plaintiff to amend to include the disputed allegation. See *Crawford-El v. Britton,* 523 U.S. 574, 598 (1998) (authorizing trial judges to require specific allegations where plaintiff's ability to make them is challenged). In a straightforward negligence case, however, it is very doubtful that a judge would deem the complaint insufficient for failure to expressly allege that Noble owed Carstairs a duty of care.

However, though the complaint may be very spare, it ought to provide an indication that "the pleader is entitled to relief." Fed. R. Civ. P. 8(a)(2). A plaintiff cannot recover from a driver simply because the driver hit him on Main Street. Something more is needed to show that Carstairs is entitled to damages from Noble: a violation of the plaintiff's legal rights. This complaint doesn't allege that Noble did anything wrong, simply that he hit him. Contrary to public belief, an accident victim isn't entitled to damages just because he was hurt; he must prove that the driver was at fault. The word "negligently" after "driving" would put the court and Noble on notice that Carstairs alleges that the accident resulted from Noble's *fault,* which would show an entitlement to relief. Absent some suggestion of carelessness by Noble, the complaint arguably doesn't "state a claim upon which relief can be granted."

On the other hand, the logic of Rule 8(a)(2) is to provide an informal description of the claim, not a mechanical black letter pronouncement of every element required in order to recover. It seems that a judge, who is supposed to take all inferences in the pleader's favor in determining whether he has stated a claim, could reasonably infer that Carstairs alleges that Noble was driving negligently. After all, he has sued him for damages.

Well, maybe so, but I think the better view is that the complaint should contain some indication that the claim alleged *entitles the pleader to relief,* and that means that the complaint should suggest a legal right of the plaintiff that the defendant has violated. See, e.g., Fed. R. Civ. P. Forms, Form 11 (including the word "negligently" in the allegation of a claim). On this reasoning, **D** represents the best argument that the complaint is insufficient. Some judges would likely so rule; others would probably let it go forward.

For many years, federal courts applied the standard of *Conley v. Gibson*, 355 U.S. 42 (1957), in determining the sufficiency of a complaint. In *Conley*, the Supreme Court held that "a complaint should not be dismissed for failure to state a claim unless it appears beyond doubt that the plaintiff can prove no set of facts in support of his claim which would entitle him to relief." Id. at 45-46. This standard was very indulgent toward the plaintiff. If the court, looking at the allegations in the complaint, could imagine facts consistent with the pleading that would establish a violation—any violation—of the plaintiff's legal rights, the complaint should not be dismissed. The plaintiff should get her shot at discovery to establish those facts. Consider this question applying the *Conley* standard before we turn to those nasty new pleading decisions from the Supreme Court.

QUESTION 2. A sense of outrage. Dahlal is fired from his city job three weeks after Curley, the new mayor, takes office. He sues Curley *pro se* (without counsel). He pleads that he worked for the city and was fired after Curley took office, and that "that rascal Curley had it in for me. I want damages." Curley moves to dismiss. If the court applies the *Conley v. Gibson* standard it will probably

A. dismiss the action, because Dahlal has provided insufficient factual detail in support of his claim.
B. dismiss the action, because Dahlal has not pleaded the elements of any recognized cause of action.
C. dismiss the action, because Curley could have had legitimate reasons for firing Dahlal.
D. allow the action to proceed.

ANALYSIS. Very likely, a court following *Conley v. Gibson* would allow this action to proceed, especially given that the plaintiff is proceeding without a lawyer. **A** suggests that the complaint needs more factual detail. That would be nice; Dahlal's complaint provides a very skeletal picture of his real problem. But it does contain a kernel from which a judge could divine a possible claim. The new mayor came in and fired Dahlal. This *might* violate various discrimination statutes or be based on constitutionally suspect grounds such as political retaliation. The complaint doesn't allege that, but it may be that Dahlal can prove a set of facts based on these allegations that would state a legitimate claim, even a compelling one.

B suggests that the complaint should be dismissed because it does not plead the elements of a recognized claim. But Rule 8(a)(2) does not require that. For a dramatic example of a complaint that was upheld even though it lacked reference to legal theories, see *Dioguardi v. Durning*, 139 F.2d 774 (2d Cir. 1944). It is usually good practice to allege specific legal theories — doing so goes a long way to "show that the pleader is entitled to relief." But case law under *Conley* has not required it, especially from *pro se* litigants.

The argument for **C** is that the complaint does not eliminate the possibility that Curley fired Dahlal for some legitimate reason. But a complaint need not do that, if it adequately alleges that he was fired for a reason which is not legitimate. So very likely this complaint would have survived a Rule 12(b)(6) motion before a patient judge in the *Conley* era. **D** is the best choice. Very likely, the court would have let Dahlal's case go forward, and sorted out the validity of the claim through discovery, pre-trial motions or trial.

B.   The new era: *Bell v. Twombly* and *Ashcroft v. Iqbal*

The Supreme Court's decisions in *Bell v. Twombly*, 550 U.S. 544 (2007), and *Ashcroft v. Iqbal*, 556 U.S. 662 (2009), draw back considerably from this indulgent approach to adequate pleading. In *Bell*, the plaintiffs sought recovery from local telephone companies. They claimed that the companies had conspired to restrain competition in the telecommunications area, in violation of the Sherman Act, 15 U.S.C. §1, by agreeing to allocate the market for telecommunications services and to stay out of each others' market areas. The complaint flatly alleged that the defendants had conspired. But the details of their pleading indicated that they (the plaintiffs) had inferred a conspiracy from the parallel conduct of all the defendants in *not* seeking to enter each others' market areas. Under federal antitrust law, the mere fact that entities try to discourage competitors, or engage in parallel anti-competitive conduct, does not amount to a conspiracy. They must agree to engage in conduct in restraint of trade, not just engage in it. The plaintiffs' complaint did not allege any meetings, memos, or other evidence of such an agreement. However, it did allege that they conspired.

In *Bell*, the Supreme Court, explicitly rejecting the oft-quoted language from *Conley*, held the complaint insufficient under Rule 8(a)(2). The court noted that the complaint "does not set forth a single fact in a context that suggests an agreement." 550 U.S. at 561-562. The Court held that the plaintiffs must allege enough to show that their claim is "plausible," not just conceivable. Where the facts alleged might reflect either illegal conduct or simply parallel conduct, the plaintiff's claim was not "plausible."

In *Iqbal*, the Court reaffirmed its commitment to stricter pleading standards. The Court held that a plaintiff cannot state a sufficient claim under Rule 8 based on conclusory allegations about the defendant's conduct. The Court held Iqbal's complaint insufficient even though the plaintiff alleges that the defendant discriminated against him "solely on account of [his] religion, race and/or national origin." See 556 U.S. at 669. Such general allegations are too conclusory to open the door to discovery. To "plausibly establish" a violation of rights, the plaintiff must allege facts that, if proved, would demonstrate a legal violation.

Bell and *Iqbal* have created a lot of uncertainty as to what is sufficient to plead a proper claim under Fed. R. Civ. P. 8(a)(2). Arguably, these cases require "fact pleading," under which a plaintiff must not only plead that the defendant has violated her rights, but must also allege supporting evidence of the violations. About all that can be said with certainty is that the rules for pleading have changed — at least in some contexts — but it is unclear how much supporting factual material is needed. It seems fair to say that a plaintiff will have to allege facts that, if established, would support a finding that the defendant had violated her rights rather than acting for some legitimate purpose. If the allegations do not suggest that an impermissible reason is likely, the complaint will fail.

The question below may help you to at least understand what the Court held with regard to the case it had before it. That's a start.

QUESTION 3. A plausible sense of outrage?   Dahlal is fired from his city job three weeks after Curley, the new mayor, takes office. He sues Curley, represented by counsel. Counsel pleads that Dahlal "worked for the city and was fired by Curley because he belongs to the political party that lost the election." Curley moves to dismiss. After the *Bell* and *Iqbal* decisions, the court will probably

A. grant the motion, because the complaint does not show that Dahlal has a plausible right to relief.

B. deny the motion, because Dhalal's complaint alleges a recognized legal theory: discrimination based on his political affiliation.

C. deny the motion, because the plaintiff has not yet had a chance to conduct discovery to determine whether the defendant violated his rights.

D. deny a motion to dismiss the complaint, because Dahlal has alleged facts that may represent a violation of his rights.

ANALYSIS. You probably had no problem concluding that **A** takes the cake after *Bell* and *Iqbal*. **D** suggests an indulgent approach to pleading that appears to be overruled by these cases. Under *Bell* and *Iqbal*, the court will not allow the case to go forward simply because the pleaded facts *might* support some legal cause of action. They call for specific factual allegations that make it "plausible"—whatever that means—that such a violation actually took place. Mere conclusory allegations won't do.

B is wrong as well. In *Iqbal*, the plaintiffs did allege recognized constitutional violations—discrimination based on race, religion and national origin. But the Court held that it does not suffice to allege even clearly established claims in general terms. It now demands enough factual context to allow the federal judge to make an assessment—based on the complaint alone—whether the plaintiff has a plausible claim.

C also fails. The very premise of *Bell* and *Iqbal* is that plaintiffs will not get a chance to do discovery unless the plaintiff's complaint indicates that she has a plausible claim. And that showing requires supporting facts that suggest a violation of her legal rights. A general complaint like that in the question might have done the trick under *Conley*, but the new pleading regime demands more—factual plausibility that the plaintiff *will* establish a violation.

C.   Allegations of fact and conclusions of law

The *Iqbal* case clearly distinguishes between purely conclusory statements and allegations of fact. The Court characterized Iqbal's allegations that Ashcroft and Mueller had exposed them to harsh conditions of confinement based solely on their race, religion or national origin as "a formulaic recitation of the elements" of a cause of action, rather than assertions of fact. Such allegations "are conclusory and not entitled to be assumed to be true." 556 U.S. at 681, quoting from *Bell*, 550 U.S. at 554-555. This distinction echoes the era of code pleading, which required a plaintiff to plead "the facts constituting a cause of action" rather than legal conclusions.

This is a crucial distinction. It is still true, after *Bell* and *Iqbal*, that the court in passing on a Rule 12(b)(6) motion will assume the truth of the *facts* alleged. So we need to decide what are facts and what are legal conclusions in order to predict how a court will treat the allegations in a complaint. Consider this question.

QUESTION 4. Fine distinctions. Which of the following allegations in a complaint will be assumed to be true in passing on a Rule 12(b)(6) motion?

A. On or about May 5, 1959 . . . the defendants, without cause or just excuse, maliciously came upon and trespassed upon the premises occupied by the plaintiff as a residence, and by the use of harsh and threatening language and physical force directed against the plaintiff assaulted the plaintiff and placed her in great fear, and humiliated and embarrassed her by subjecting her to public scorn and ridicule, and caused her to be seized and exhibited to the public as a prisoner, and to be confined in a public jail, all to her great humiliation, embarrassment, and harm.

B. That on or about July 1, 1956, on Amherst Street in the City of Buffalo, New York, the defendant assaulted, battered, and beat plaintiff without any provocation or just cause.

C. The defendants discriminated against the plaintiff solely on account of his race, religion, and national origin.

D. The defendant is indebted to the plaintiff for $1,000, which is now due.

E. I give up.

ANALYSIS.   Remarkably, the allegations in **A** were held to set forth merely conclusions of law. *Gillespie v. Goodyear Serv. Stores,* 128 S.E.2d 762 (N.C. 1963). **B** was held to adequately state "facts sufficient to state a cause of action." *D'Auria v. Niemiec,* 182 N.Y.S.2d 378 (Sup. Ct. 1950). But doesn't **B** come perilously close to mere legal conclusions without supporting facts? **C** was held to reflect mere conclusions in *Iqbal.* **D** sounds pretty conclusory, but isn't it also a statement of fact?

I would never give this question as anything but an illustration, because it leaves one bewildered as to the true distinction between law and fact. I can't even begin to choose here, though, truthfully, **A,** which was held inadequate in *Gillespie,* strikes me as the most fact-specific in explaining what events support recovery. Choosing **E** is okay with me.

The point, of course, is that by requiring pleading of facts to demonstrate a plausible claim, the Supreme Court has waded back into the metaphysical morass that requires distinguishing between law and fact.

D.   Pleading alternatively or inconsistently

Under early English pleading, from which our own pleading rules evolved, a plaintiff was required to stake his case on one version of the facts and law. He could not, for example, plead in one count that the defendant breached a contract with him, and in another that he could recover for fraud. He could not proceed in assumpsit, for breach of contract, and plead replevin, based on a different writ, in the same action. He had to choose a particular theory. Similarly, he had to take one position from the outset about the facts, and stick with it through trial. He couldn't plead in one count that the defendant acted as an employee of Ace Motor Company at the time of the events in suit, and plead in another claim that he acted as an independent contractor. Common law pleading demanded ruthless efficiency and tough tactical choices. Even if the plaintiff wasn't sure when he pleaded what the evidence would ultimately show on the issue — and couldn't be at the time of pleading — he had to commit himself at the outset.

> A party was required to elect a particular set of facts and a legal theory at the pleading stage. Unfortunately, this forced a litigant to set forth his allegations with a degree of certainty that often was not warranted in terms of the state of his knowledge at that point in the case. If the facts he asserted in the pleadings were not confirmed by later proof, his action would fail even if his proof demonstrated a right to relief on some other theory.

Wright & Miller, *Federal Practice and Procedure* §1282.

The Federal Rules rebel against such rigid constraints at the pleading stage. Under Rule 8(d)(3), the plaintiff may assert as many alternative versions of the claim as he has evidence to support, may include both legal and equitable claims in the same complaint, and may assert different versions of a claim "regardless of consistency." The Rules recognize that, when the plaintiff drafts the complaint, he may not be able to predict what facts will ultimately be found by the jury at trial. For example, it may be impossible at the outset of a case, without discovery, for the plaintiff to know whether a defendant acted as an independent contractor or as an employee. That's a complex factual issue, which is governed by a fairly ambiguous, multifactor test. See Restatement (Second) of Agency, §220. Ultimately, if the issue must be determined in the case, the jury will decide it based on the evidence presented at trial. The plaintiff's lawyer isn't required to stake his case on the prediction of what that determination will be. Under Rule 11, he may allege different versions of his claim, alleging one basis for recovery if the defendant is found to be an employee, and another if he is found to be an independent contractor, so long as he has evidentiary support for each position. Similarly, he may demand different relief, depending on which claim he proves at trial. As the case unfolds, the plaintiff may abandon one version or another of his claim if it becomes clear that one is unsupported. If, however, he has support for multiple versions of his claim after discovery, he may attempt to prove each version of his claim for which he has supporting evidence at trial.

Here's a thought-provoking question that considers the meaning of Rule 8(d)(3).

QUESTION 5. Pleading for relief. Giscard sues Munson and Bigby, who both own separate property abutting Giscard's. In Count One he claims that construction work Munson has done on his lot has altered the drainage on his property, causing water to flow onto Giscard's property and making his lawn soggy. In Count Two, he makes the same allegations against Bigby. He seeks damages from Munson and Bigby for the past interference. He also seeks an injunction against each of them, requiring them to regrade their property to prevent further drainage problems on his.

A. Giscard has pleaded inconsistently by alleging in one count that Munson caused damage to the lawn, and in the other count that Bigby has.

B. Giscard has pleaded inconsistently by seeking damages for the past interference, but an injunction against future interference.

C. Giscard has pleaded inconsistently both with regard to the defendant who caused the harm and with regard to the type of relief, but this is permissible under Rule 8(d)(3).

D. Giscard has not pleaded inconsistently.

ANALYSIS. This question's a bit droll, but makes a point. There's nothing inconsistent about this pleading. Giscard has alleged that Munson damaged his property by altering the drainage pattern, and that Bigby did. It's entirely possible that he will prove that they both did. Liability here isn't an "either/ or" proposition, in which, if he recovers against one defendant he will definitely lose against the other. Both may have contributed to Giscard's soggy lawn problem, and both may be liable to him if they did.

Giscard's demands for relief aren't inconsistent either. There's nothing inconsistent about demanding damages for past interference and protection from future interference. In fact, these demands are utterly "consistent," aren't they? **D** is right, because Giscard is not "talking out of both sides of his mouth" in this pleading, that is, alleging "X" in one count and "not X" in the other, so that one count can only be proved if the other is not. In fact, he *could do that too* under Rule 8(d)(3), within the ethical limits of Rule 11. But he hasn't pleaded inconsistently here, because the jury could find for him against both defendants, and it could award him both damages for past interference and an injunction against future interference.

Here's another question on inconsistent pleading under Fed. R. Civ. P. 8(d)(3).

QUESTION 6. The consistency hobgoblin. Singh sues Nuclear Processing Corporation, his former employer, for exposing him to radiation during his employment at its plant for processing nuclear power plant wastes. In the first claim for relief in his complaint he alleges that Nuclear negligently failed to recognize the risk that its employees were exposed to dangerous levels of radiation that could cause leukemia, because it had never adequately tested for elevated radiation levels. In the second claim for relief, he asserts that Nuclear was aware at the time of his employment that its facility exposed employees to elevated radiation levels that could cause leukemia, but failed to warn him of that risk or take steps to reduce it. In the third claim for relief, he alleges that after he had left Nuclear's employ, it learned of the risk of leukemia from the radiation levels its employees encountered at the facility, but failed to warn him so that he could obtain proper medical treatment and monitoring.

A. Singh has pleaded inconsistently, because the three counts assert different versions of the facts regarding Nuclear's knowledge of the risk. This is permissible under Rule 8(d)(3), even if they can't all be true.

B. Singh has pleaded inconsistently, under Rule 8(d)(3), but it is not permissible here, because there is no way that Singh could prove all three counts at trial.

C. Singh hasn't pleaded inconsistently, since a jury might find any one of these three versions of his claim to be true.

D. Singh has pleaded inconsistently, which is permissible under Rule 8(d)(3) unless he has substantially more evidence that one version of the claim, rather than the others, is true.

ANALYSIS. **C** is clearly wrong here; so wrong that I just threw it in to distract. The fact that any one of these may be true hardly shows that Singh's three counts are not inconsistent. Singh's allegations in Counts One, Two, and Three can't all be true. Count One alleges that they never knew of the risk from exposure at the facility, but should have. Count Two alleges that they knew about the risk when he worked there, but failed to take precautions against it. And Count Three alleges that they learned of the risk later. Certainly, all three versions can't be true, and probably only one of them can. But Singh may not be aware of which it is when he files his complaint. He may have some evidence to support each version, and hope to develop a clearer understanding of "what did they know and when did they know it" through discovery. After all, Nuclear isn't likely to *tell* him which version is true without being compelled to reveal information through discovery.

Perhaps the most tantalizing distractor is **D**, which suggests that Singh can't plead all three versions of his claim if he has significantly more evidence for one of them than the others. If this choice were right, it would mean that

Singh would have to choose the version of his claim that he thinks is most likely true at the time of pleading, even if his investigation suggests that one of the others might be. Rule 8(d)(3) is meant to relieve the pleader from having to make that choice among possible versions of his claim, by allowing him to plead whatever versions have evidentiary support. Singh's counsel is not required to pre-judge the strength of these three theories, and abandon two because the preliminary evidence is stronger for the third. By pleading all three, he puts these allegations in play. The parties will proceed to discovery. Perhaps one or more will prove untenable, and be voluntarily withdrawn, or dismissed on summary judgment. Or, perhaps, at the time of trial, it will remain unclear what the true facts are, in which case all three theories will be tried, and the jury will decide what Nuclear knew, and when.

B, then, is also wrong. Pleading three theories is permissible, even if only one of them can ultimately be true. Singh doesn't plead these alternative versions of his claim because he expects to prove them all, but because he doesn't know which one the jury will ultimately accept. Even though, logically, only one can be true, Singh can pursue them all through discovery and, if he still has evidentiary support for more than one, at trial as well. So **A** is the best response; pleading the three counts is proper under Fed. R. Civ. P. 8(d)(3).

E. Admissions and denials in the defendant's answer

Rule 8 contains simple, sensible provisions governing the defendant's responses to the allegations in the complaint. First, Rule 8(b) requires the defendant to admit or deny each of the allegations in the complaint. Usually, this is done paragraph by paragraph. Rule 10(b) requires that averments in the complaint be set forth in separate paragraphs. The defendant, in answering, must take a position on each of these allegations, by admitting those that are true, and denying those that aren't. Under Rule 8(b)(2), a "denial must fairly respond to the substance of the allegation." If the defendant means to deny only a part of an allegation, she must specify what is true and deny only the parts that are not. Failing to deny an allegation constitutes an admission of it. Fed. R. Civ. P. 8(b)(6). The idea is that, if the parties plead conscientiously by the Rules, the parties and the court can compare the allegations in the complaint and the responses in the answer, and determine which issues are contested and which are agreed upon (and therefore need not be litigated). If all goes right, this simple pleading process can narrow the scope of the dispute considerably.

The Rule also recognizes that the defendant may not know whether some allegations in the complaint are true or not. If she has grounds to deny them, she may do so, but if she just doesn't know, or doesn't have the information necessary to admit or deny at the time of pleading, she may respond that she "lacks knowledge or information sufficient to form a belief about the truth of an allegation." Fed. R. Civ. P. 8(b)(5). Under the rule, this response to an allegation "has the effect of a denial."

To determine what issues remain in dispute, of course, the plaintiff — and the court — have to read the defendant's answer in light of the provisions of the pleading rules. Consider, for example, what the plaintiff should make of the defendant's answer in the following case.

QUESTION 7. Yes, no, and maybe. Patterson sues Applied Electronics, Inc., for injuries suffered in an accident with Adair, one of AE's delivery drivers. Patterson alleges in Paragraph 4 of his complaint that Adair was an employee of AE at the time of the accident, that Adair was acting in the scope of employment at the time of the accident (which Patterson must prove in order to recover from the employer), that Adair was talking on his cell phone at the time of the accident, and that Adair's negligent driving caused the accident.

AE answers Paragraph 4 as follows: "The defendant admits that Adair was its employee at the time of the accident, denies that Adair was negligent, but is without sufficient information to form a belief as to the truth of the allegation that Adair was talking on his cell phone at the time of the accident." Under Federal Rule 8,

A. the allegation that Adair is AE's employee is admitted. The allegation that he acted in the scope of employment is admitted. The allegation that Adair was talking on his cell phone is treated as denied.
B. AE has admitted that Adair was its employee and that he acted in the scope of employment. The allegation that Adair was talking on his cell phone is treated as admitted.
C. the allegation that Adair is AE's employee is admitted. Everything else is treated as denied.
D. AE has admitted that Adair was its employee, but not that he acted in the scope of employment. The allegation that Adair was talking on his cell phone is treated as denied.

ANALYSIS. If you read the rule (or even my preface to the question), this question simply requires you to compare Patterson's allegations with the defendant's responses, and apply the provisions of Rule 8 as to the effect of a denial, failure to deny, or allegation that the pleader is "without sufficient facts to form a belief." (Remember, my questions assume that you have the Rule in front of you. I'm not testing whether you remember the provisions of the rule, though your professor might. Rather, the questions test whether you can apply the rules to these allegations and responses.)

Naturally, AE has admitted that Adair was its employee, by admitting it! (Sometimes even the pleading rules are commonsensical.) The allegation that Adair was talking on his cell phone is treated as denied: Under the Rule 8(b)(5), the "without sufficient information" response is treated as a denial. Adair hasn't responded at all to the allegation that Adair acted in the scope of employment at the time of the accident. Frequently, defendants would like to ignore allegations in the complaint, if they aren't sure of their truth, or it would be awkward to admit them. But this head-in-the-sand strategy doesn't work under the Rules: Rule 8(b)(6) provides that allegations that are not denied are deemed admitted. So, effectively, AE has admitted that Adair was its employee and that he acted in the scope of employment, but denied negligence and that Adair was chatting on the cell phone.

So, **A** is right.

As we saw in the first part of this chapter, the Federal Rules allow the plaintiff to present as many claims as she has evidence to support, even if they can't all be true. The idea is to put the defendant on notice of the positions that you may seek to establish, not a single one you have settled on irrevocably.

The same goes for the defendant. Under Rule 8, the defendant is allowed to plead whatever defenses she has to the plaintiff's claim. She may take inconsistent positions about the facts or the law, and may raise multiple defenses without choosing among them. The defendant might, for example, deny that she was negligent, but also allege that the plaintiff was more negligent than she was and is therefore barred from recovery. She might deny that she had a contract with the plaintiff, raise as a second defense that she did not breach, and raise as a third defense that the statute of limitations bars recovery. Under Rule 11, she must have evidentiary support for the defenses she asserts, but isn't required to stake her case on one of them.

Although Rule 11(b)(3) requires support for affirmative defenses as well as factual allegations in the original complaint, it is unfortunately common for defendants to "overplead" affirmative defenses. Given the short period for filing an answer, and the potential for malpractice exposure for failing to raise a defense, many answers include a long list of "boilerplate" defenses, many clearly irrelevant to the case. Doubtless, counsel view the risk of sanctions for overpleading defenses as less grievous than the risk of waiving a defense by failing to assert it. The unfortunate side effect of this, however, is that such answers do not fully serve the purpose the rule-makers envisioned: to reveal the parties' real positions and to narrow the scope of controverted issues.

Here's a question that explores the defendant's options.

> **QUESTION 8. Sufficient information?** Patterson sues Applied Electronics, Inc., for injuries suffered in an accident with Adair, one of AE's delivery drivers. Patterson alleges in Paragraph 4 of his complaint that Adair was acting in the scope of employment at the time of the accident (which is necessary in order to recover from the employer). When it answers the complaint, AE has some information suggesting that Adair was acting in the scope of employment at the time, but also some information suggesting that he was not.
>
> **A.** AE should admit and deny that Adair acted in the scope of employment at the time of the accident, since it has some information that would support both positions.
> **B.** AE should not answer this allegation, since it doesn't know whether Adair acted in the scope of employment or not.
> **C.** AE should answer that it is "without knowledge or information sufficient to form a belief as to the truth of [the] allegation in Paragraph 4." This will constitute an admission of the allegation, but AE could move to amend its answer if it learns through discovery that Adair did not act in the scope of employment.
> **D.** AE should deny the allegation.

ANALYSIS. This is a nice question. Clearly, AE doesn't want to admit that Adair acted in the scope of employment, but it does have some evidence tending to support that position. What should it do?

C is "wrongest." Rule 8(b)(5) provides that, where a party pleads that it doesn't have enough information to admit or deny, that response "has the effect of a denial." (If this "I dunno" response were treated as an admission, parties would rarely use it.) Basically, this response keeps the defendant's options open to develop evidence that Adair was not in the scope of employment, without having to explicitly take that position in the answer before it has fully developed its case. Because the Rules treat this response as a denial, C is wrong. AE has not admitted the allegation, and may still try to disprove the scope-of-employment allegation.

B also falls short. Rule 8 requires the pleader to admit or deny the allegations, or state that she is without sufficient information. Further, Rule 8(b)(6) provides that allegations that are not denied in the answer are admitted. So ignoring the allegation would be ill advised.

A is an interesting suggestion. The rules expressly allow the parties to take different positions — where they don't know the true facts — "regardless of consistency." So, if you have some evidence suggesting that the allegation is true, and some suggesting that it is false, why not admit and deny? It's hard to plead more honestly than that! Of course, the defendant presumably does not *want* to admit that Adair acted in the scope of employment. So the fact that it would be permissible to take inconsistent positions isn't the end of the matter . . . *must* the defendant do so?

Certainly not. A pleader decides what defenses she wishes to raise, from those permissible under the rules. Because AE has evidentiary support for the position that Adair did not act in the scope of his employment, a denial is proper. AE has grounds to admit it too, since they have some evidence of that as well, but clearly doesn't want to raise that as a "defense" and isn't required to. **D** is the best answer. If you work in a defense firm, I wouldn't suggest that you recommend admitting a damaging allegation, simply because you have some information suggesting that it is true. Ordinarily, an admission removes the issue from contention (though perhaps not if admitted *and* denied!), and this one is still very much an open question. Where the defendant has grounds to deny a damaging allegation such as this, it may do so under the rules, and certainly will.

An alternative would be to respond that AE is without knowledge or information sufficient to form a belief as to the truth of the averment in Paragraph 4. This is permissible if you really don't know, and leaves the issue open, since this response "has the effect of a denial." Fed. R. Civ. P. 8(b)(5). However, given its obligation under Rule 11 to conduct a reasonable investigation before answering, it seems likely that AE would know enough about Adair's meanderings to take a position on the scope of employment issue. Even if it could reply that it was "without sufficient knowledge," **C** would still be wrong, since it states that this response is treated as an admission.

Here's another interesting question on denials under Rule 8(b).[2]

> **QUESTION 9. Defendant in denial.** Cardozo is in an accident on Main Street with two other cars, driven by Hooper and Lopes. Cardozo brings a suit in federal court against Hooper and Lopes for his damages. Paragraph 21 of Cardozo's complaint alleges that Hooper had signaled before he turned onto Main Street. The police report on the accident states that, according to a bystander, Hooper had signaled before turning onto Main Street. Lopes, who was coming from Hooper's left, had no view of the right side of Hooper's car, and did not see whether he signaled or not. At the time an answer is due, Lopes's counsel has seen the police report, but has not yet been able to locate other witnesses to obtain their testimony.

---

2. This question is inspired by one in Yeazell, *Civil Procedure* 463 n.5 (5th ed. 2000).

The most appropriate response for Lopes to Paragraph 21 of Cardozo's complaint would be to

A. admit the allegation, since the only evidence he has suggests that is true.
B. deny the allegation, to preserve the option to dispute it at trial.
C. state that he is without sufficient information to form a belief as to the truth of the allegation.
D. make no response to paragraph 21.

ANALYSIS. In this example, Lopes's counsel has some information on the allegation that suggests that it is true, but hasn't yet had the opportunity to test the truth of that information or develop other evidence concerning the allegation. Is he required to admit it, on the ground that he lacks evidence that it is false?

Let's start by asking whether **B** is right, whether Lopes may deny the allegation, to keep his options open. Under Rule 11(b)(4), denials of factual contentions must be "warranted on the evidence." Fed. R. Civ. P. 11(b)(3). Here, Lopes has no reason to take the position that the turn-indicator allegation is false. The only information he has about it suggests that it's true.

It would be troubling, however, if the rules required Lopes to admit this allegation. One witness has apparently stated that it is so, but why must Lopes adopt the testimony of this witness at this early stage of the case, by admitting the truth of the allegation? The effect of an admission is to take that issue out of contention, to remove it from dispute, because the parties agree that it is true. Thus, Lopes would effectively waive the opportunity to seek out opposing evidence, just because *someone* has said that it's true.[3] That wouldn't make a whole lot of sense. It isn't as though Lopes *knows* it to be true just because someone has said so. Lopes doesn't know that it's true; he only knows that his very preliminary information supports it. In light of the short window for filing an answer, the pleading rules allow him to keep his options open here. Lopes should plead that he is without sufficient information to form a belief as to the truth of the allegation, which, under the Rules, will be treated as a denial. **C** is the best answer.

What's the difference between this question and the last? In the last, the defendant had an evidentiary basis to deny the allegation, though she wasn't sure that it was false. So, the Rules allow her to take that position. In this one, Lopes has no grounds to deny the allegation, yet has little information on which to form a conviction that it's true. Consequently, the Rules allow her to stand on her lack of information, by pleading insufficient information to form a belief, and keep the question open for discovery and proof at trial.

---

3. He could, I suppose, admit it and move to amend later, if he finds evidence that it isn't true. But this introduces another layer of procedure, and the possibility that the motion would be denied.

F.   Pleading multiple defenses and objections ...with an early Closer

At common law, the defendant could take a number of positions regarding the case. She could "traverse the allegations," that is, deny the truth of the facts. If she did that, the case would go to trial to resolve the dispute of fact. Or the defendant could "demur to the complaint," that is, assert that the facts alleged, if proved, would not entitle the plaintiff to relief. This challenged the sufficiency of the averments in the complaint to support recovery under the law, not the factual truth of those averments. Or, the defendant could assert that, despite the validity of the plaintiff's prima facie claim, she loses anyway, due to some additional fact, such as the passage of the statute of limitations, or a release of the claim by settlement. Last, the defendant could raise various objections to the court's going forward, such as improper venue or lack of subject matter jurisdiction.

Strict common law pleading did not allow the defendant to raise all of these defenses. If the defendant "traversed," she couldn't demur as well. If she raised new matter to avoid liability (called a "confession and avoidance"), she had to admit the truth of the plaintiff's allegations and rely solely on the defense to it — she had to "confess" in order to "avoid." For example, if she wanted to raise the statute of limitations as a defense to a contract claim, she couldn't *also* deny that she ever made the contract: to raise the limitations defense ("the avoidance") she had to confess the validity of the plaintiff's basic claim.

Through this ruthless insistence that the defendant put all her eggs in one basket, the common law pleading system boiled cases down to single issues. A demurrer reduced it to the single question of law, "does the plaintiff's complaint state a claim upon which relief can be granted?" Traversing the allegations reduced it to a dispute over the truth of the factual allegations. And a confession and avoidance reduced it to the validity of the affirmative defense (since the defendant, by raising one, admitted the truth of the plaintiff's case-in-chief).

Maitland declared that "the forms of action we have buried, but they still rule us from their graves."[4] The old pleading rules are largely gone, but much of their substance remains. As under the common law, federal pleading recognizes traverses — they are denials under Rule 8(b). It recognizes demurrers — now challenges to the legal validity of the plaintiff's claim under Rule 12(b)(6) or 12(c). Similarly, federal pleading allows parties to avoid liability by raising affirmative defenses under Rule 8(c). Last, a defendant may also interpose procedural objections to the case, such as

---

4. F.W. Maitland, *The Forms of Action at Common Law* 2 (A.H. Chaytor and W.J. Whittaker eds., 1965) (1909).

improper venue or lack of personal or subject matter jurisdiction. See Rule 12(b)(1), (2), (3).

Plus ça change, plus c'est la même. . . .[5] But there is an important difference from the common law. Under the Federal Rules, the defendant (much like the plaintiff in her complaint) may raise multiple objections to the plaintiff's case; she is not required to stake her case on one. She may deny that the parties made a contract, but also raise the affirmative defense that the limitations period bars enforcing it. See Fed. R. Civ. P. 8(c)(1), which gives a (non-exhaustive) list of affirmative defenses that may be included in an answer. She may deny that she caused emotional distress to the plaintiff, but also claim that there's no cause of action for infliction of emotional distress and that the court lacks jurisdiction over her. And so on. Once again, the Rules flexibly allow the pleader to state whatever positions she has evidentiary support for, "regardless of consistency." But the various positions are, basically, recognizable descendants of common law devices: the traverse, the demurrer, the confession and avoidance, or pleas to the court's jurisdiction.

It's useful to be able to classify defenses appropriately under these four categories. This question offers a chance to do that. I know, the Closer is supposed to come at the end, but this one just belongs here. So face it now, and then you can coast through the rest of the chapter.

QUESTION 10. **An early Closer.**   Patterson sues Applied Electronics, Inc. in federal court, for injuries suffered in an accident while he was a passenger in a truck with Adair, one of AE's delivery drivers. He bases jurisdiction on diversity. Patterson's complaint alleges that he is an employee of AE, that Adair is also an AE employee, that Adair was acting in the scope of employment at the time of the accident, and that Adair was negligent in causing the accident. The jurisdiction applies joint and several liability.

In its answer, AE asserts the following defenses (among others):

1. "Adair was not negligent, because he acted reasonably in a sudden emergency."
2. "The court lacks power to hear the case, because Patterson is from the same state as AE."
3. "The plaintiff cannot recover, because he is covered by the workers compensation statute, which bars suits by a covered employee against his employer. She may only recover statutory benefits from the workers' compensation insurer."

---

5. I can't abide authors who quote in other languages without giving a translation, as if every educated person knows seventeen languages. This French adage means "The more things change, the more they stay the same."

    4. "The plaintiff cannot recover from the defendant because the injury resulted solely from the negligence of Chang, the other driver involved in the accident."

    5. "The plaintiff cannot recover, because in riding in the open bed of the truck, he was more negligent than Adair." (Under the relevant comparative negligence statute, a plaintiff who is more negligent than the defendant is not entitled to recover.)

    A. AE's answer contains a denial, a jurisdictional objection, one defense of failure to state a claim, and two affirmative defenses.

    B. AE's answer contains two denials, a jurisdictional objection, one defense of failure to state a claim, and one affirmative defense.

    C. AE's answer contains two denials, two defenses of failure to state a claim, and one affirmative defense.

ANALYSIS. This is a hard question. I probably wouldn't give it on an exam, because first-year students are just getting a feel for pleading, so classifying these isn't easy. But it illustrates how subtly the different positions the defendant may take resemble each other. And, it may be important to analyze which is which for various reasons, such as the burden of proof at trial, or whether the defense can be resolved by a motion rather than at trial.

    The first defense is clearly a denial. The plaintiff alleges that Adair was negligent, and the defendant says that he wasn't, that he acted reasonably in responding to an emergency situation. That raises a dispute of fact to be litigated and tried.

    The second defense is also straightforward: It challenges the court's subject matter jurisdiction. It isn't as explicitly pleaded as it might be. A tidier statement of the objection would be, "The court lacks subject matter jurisdiction based on diversity of citizenship under 28 U.S.C. §1332(a), because the parties are both citizens of Minnesota." But it clearly goes to the authority of the federal court to hear the case.

    The third defense is tougher. It takes the position that Patterson can't recover because the legislature has barred employees from suing their employers for injuries on the job. This defense asserts that Patterson's complaint fails to state a claim on which relief can be granted, that there's no right to recover in negligence from the employer for injuries suffered on the job. Therefore, Patterson's negligence complaint — which itself alleges that Patterson was an employee of AE — seeks recovery that the court can't grant. Suppose that AE, instead of filing an answer, had filed a motion to dismiss under Rule 12(b)(6), for failure to state a claim upon which relief can be granted. If the workers comp statute bars negligence recovery in the circumstances Patterson has alleged, that motion would be granted, because the complaint makes clear that Patterson seeks recovery for an injury on the job due to the negligence of another employee, and that right doesn't exist.

The fourth defense takes the position that the negligence claim will fail, because the accident resulted from the other driver's negligence. Analytically, this is just another way of denying that Adair was negligent. Patterson has alleged that Adair was negligent, and that Patterson can recover for that negligence. This defense says, "No, he wasn't; you may have alleged a negligence cause of action but you can't prove that." While the third defense asserts that negligence law doesn't apply, because of the workers compensation statute, the fourth defense says, "even if negligence law applies, and we would be liable for Adair's negligence, we aren't liable because he wasn't negligent; the other driver was." This defense could not be resolved on a Rule 12(b)(6) motion: It requires a decision of the factual question whether Adair's negligence contributed to Patterson's injury. If the jury finds that only the other driver was negligent, AE would win, not because another driver's negligence is an affirmative defense to Patterson's claim,[6] but because Adair was *not* negligent, so Patterson cannot prove the prima facie negligence case he has alleged.

How about the fifth defense? AE alleges that negligence law applies, but that under relevant negligence law a plaintiff can't recover if he was more negligent than the defendant, and that is what happened here. This is an affirmative defense. Patterson claims he is entitled to recover from AE because Adair, its employee, negligently caused the injury. If he proves that (and if negligence law applies) he could recover. But AE raises new facts, not pleaded by the plaintiff, that alter the situation. "Patterson, you may have stated a negligence claim by alleging that Adair was negligent and that his negligence led to the accident, but we say that you were more negligent, which bars recovery even if Adair was negligent." This defense doesn't say that there's no right to recover for negligence. Rather, it says that, even if Patterson proves his prima facie case, his right to recover is undermined by additional facts.

Just to highlight the difference between #5 and #3, imagine that AE moved to dismiss Patterson's complaint for failure to state a claim upon which relief can be granted, on the ground that Patterson was more negligent than Adair. The motion would be denied. Patterson's complaint states a good cause of action (if workers comp doesn't apply): he *could* recover if he proves that Adair's negligence was the primary cause of his injuries. AE's comparative negligence defense does not show that Patterson hasn't asserted a legally recognized claim. Rather, it asserts that AE has a defense to it. The judge would deny the motion, stating "that's a matter of proof. If we try the case and you establish that Patterson was more negligent, then Patterson

---

6. In jurisdictions with joint and several liability, it would not be. It would simply make the other driver liable as well.

loses, not because his complaint fails to state a legally recognized claim, but because you have proved additional facts that avoid recovery anyway." That's an affirmative defense.

So, let's see. #1: Denial. #2: Jurisdictional objection. #3: Failure to state a claim. #4: Denial. #5: Affirmative defense. The tally is two denials, one jurisdictional objection, one Rule 12(b)(6) defense, and one affirmative defense. **B** wins.

G. Rule 11 limits on legal allegations

Previous sections emphasize the parties' right to take different, even contradictory positions about the facts and the law. But there are limits to this liberality under the Rules. A party can't plead whatever she pleases without some support for it or, in some cases, at least an anticipation of finding support for it. Rule 11 establishes ethical parameters on both the factual and legal positions a party presents to the court.

Under Rule 11, a party presenting a pleading or motion certifies several things to the court. To begin with, she certifies that she has *made an inquiry*, reasonable under the circumstances, before taking the position asserted in the pleading or motion. See Fed. R. Civ. P. 11(b), first sentence (attorney or party certifies "to the best of the person's knowledge, information, and belief, formed after an inquiry reasonable under the circumstances"). You can't just go off half-cocked; you have to look into the matter, usually by doing legal research on legal positions taken in a pleading, or factual investigation with regard to factual assertions.

A person asserting a *legal position* in a pleading or motion also certifies that the position is "warranted by existing law or by a nonfrivolous argument for extending, modifying, or reversing of existing law or for establishing new law." Fed. R. Civ. P. 11(b)(2). What does *that* mean? It means that there is a colorable argument that the position taken should be accepted by the court. It certainly doesn't mean that the position must represent current law in the jurisdiction: Rule 11(b)(2) specifically authorizes a pleader to argue for reversal or modification of existing law. It doesn't require that the weight of authority — in the courts of the relevant jurisdiction or more widely — accepts the argument being advanced: Rule 11(b)(2) authorizes a pleader to argue for "the establishment of new law," including, presumably, law that currently doesn't exist anywhere.

It's easy to see the dilemma the rule makers faced in drafting Rule 11(b)(2). They wanted to rein in promiscuous pleading of unsupported legal positions, without chilling counsel from making creative arguments from analogy, which have always caused the common law to grow. The key to complying with the Rule is to have a basis in authority or logic for predicting that the position might be accepted by the court, even if it hasn't been yet.

Sheer obstinacy won't do, but reasoned argument based on recognized authority, or analogous precedent, is very likely permissible.

Fundamentally, Rule 11(b)(2) requires that the party asserting a legal position have a rational argument for the position, and that it has not been definitively rejected by the courts of the jurisdiction so recently that nothing but obstinacy would lead a lawyer to try again. When you start drafting pleadings, think of it this way:

> Assume that you take a legal position in a complaint, and the defendant moves for sanctions under Rule 11, arguing that the allegation violates Rule 11(b)(2). The judge schedules a hearing on the motion. She leans down over the bench, scowling, and asks, "Counsel, what grounds do you have to make that allegation?"

What will you say? Will you stammer and stutter and wish you were anywhere else but in court? Or will you have an answer to hand, because you *thought about it* (as the rule requires you to) before making the allegation, and have rational support for the position asserted? You might say, "Your Honor, I recognize that the state supreme court rejected this position in 1962, but since then it has decided four cases in related areas indicating that it is changing its approach to torts cases." That sounds like "a nonfrivolous argument for . . . modifing . . . existing law." Or, you might say, "Your Honor, I know our courts have not accepted this position, but four states that have similar approaches to contract enforcement have accepted it. Our supreme court hasn't considered the issue since those cases have come down, but has used similar reasoning in these two analogous areas." That also sounds like a nonfrivolous argument.

Consider this question on the point.

QUESTION 11. Try, try again. In 2001, Hu witnesses an accident in West Dakota in which his son John is injured. He sues Olsen, the driver of the car that hit John, for the emotional distress he suffered from witnessing the accident.

In 1982, the West Dakota Supreme Court had held, in *Smith v. Jones*, that there is no right to recover for indirect infliction of emotional distress, unless the plaintiff on the distress claim was also injured in the accident. (Hu was not.) The *Smith* court concluded that allowing recovery without a physical injury would open the door to too many fraudulent claims. It has not addressed the issue since. In 1990, the Supreme Court of East Dakota, a neighboring state, held that a bystander may recover for emotional distress. It rejected the reasoning of *Smith*, concluding that recent experience in other states shows that juries can adequately distinguish between genuine and fraudulent emotional distress claims. Two other nearby states have accepted bystander emotional distress claims during the 1990s, but one, citing *Smith*, has rejected them.

Coincidentally, Hu's counsel had sued for emotional distress on behalf of another client in 1999, two years before Hu's case. In that case, *Pogulski v. Tripp*, the trial court had dismissed the case, holding that the *Smith* case was binding authority in West Dakota, and that Hu's client could not recover, since she was not injured in the accident. Hu's counsel did not appeal that ruling.

A. Hu's counsel has violated Rule 11(b)(2) by asserting Hu's claim for emotional distress, because *Smith v. Jones*, which refused to allow recovery for emotional distress, has not been overruled.

B. Hu's counsel has violated Rule 11(b)(2) by asserting Hu's claim for emotional distress, since the trial judge in the *Pogulski* case had ruled, just two years earlier, that the right does not exist.

C. Hu's counsel has not violated Rule 11(b)(2), because he always has the right to argue for a change in the law.

D. Hu's counsel has not violated Rule 11(b)(2), because he has support for an argument that *Smith* should be overruled. The trial court's rejection of the argument in *Pogulski* does not make the argument frivolous.

ANALYSIS. In this example, Hu's counsel, by filing a complaint seeking recovery for indirect infliction of emotional distress, asserts that there is a legal right to recover on such a claim. But *Smith*, from the state supreme court, rejected that position. *Smith* is several decades old, and the more recent decisions from other states have been mixed, several neighboring states recognizing the right and one rejecting it. When Hu's counsel made the argument two years before, the trial court dismissed his complaint on the merits.

Let's start with **A**, which asserts that Hu's counsel violates Rule 11(b)(2), because *Smith* is on point and rejected recovery for bystander emotional distress. Surely this can't be the law, can it? That you can't argue for overruling a case on point? Rule 11(b)(2) doesn't say that; indeed, it clearly suggests that you may argue for reversal of current law if you have a colorable argument for it. The important point is to have a colorable basis on which to renew the fight. If Hu's counsel has a "nonfrivolous argument" for reversal of *Smith v. Jones*, he has the right to make it, even if it didn't convince the court back in 1982.

B is more befuddling. The trial court in *Pogulski* considered the same legal position two years ago, and rejected it. So Hu's counsel has made the argument recently and lost on it. Can he persist in the face of that recent ruling? Well, the trial judge dismissed *Pogulski* because she was bound by the state supreme court's opinion in *Smith*. She had no choice, whether she agreed with *Smith* or not, and whether she thought the state supreme court would decide the same way in 1999 or not. So the *Pogulski* ruling doesn't mean that there's no credible argument for recovery for bystander emotional distress. It simply means that the trial judge was not free to accept that argument in the face of a binding precedent from West Dakota's highest court. If Hu's counsel wants to get the law changed, he's going to have to argue for it in the trial court, lose, take an appeal, and convince the West Dakota Supreme Court to overrule *Smith v. Jones*.

C is a clear overstatement. Hu does not have an *unlimited* right to argue for change in the law. He must have a credible ground to support the argument, and one that has not been clearly and recently rejected by the court. So **D** is the best answer. The fact that the trial court rejected his argument in *Pogulski* should not foreclose him from making the argument again, since the trial court did not reject his argument because there was no credible argument for it. Instead, it followed mandatory precedent from a higher court. And Hu's counsel has a viable argument that the West Dakota Supreme Court should overrule *Smith*. It's a thirty-year-old decision and three neighboring states have since recognized the claim, one expressly rejecting the reasoning in *Smith* based on more recent experience of courts dealing with emotional distress claims. Even if no West Dakota case has suggested that *Smith* was wrongly decided, this seems like a credible basis for making an argument that it was.

H.   Rule 11 limits on factual allegations ...and a caveat

Rule 11 also imposes constraints on the factual allegations made in a pleading or motion. Under Rule 11(b)(3), the party making factual allegations certifies that "after an inquiry reasonable under the circumstances," those allegations "have evidentiary support or, if specifically so identified, are likely to have evidentiary support after a reasonable opportunity for further investigation or discovery." This establishes two standards, actually. For "regular" factual allegations — those not "specifically so identified" — the pleader must have "evidentiary support." Other allegations, specifically identified in the pleading as made on information and belief, may be made if they are "likely to have evidentiary support after a reasonable opportunity for further investigation or discovery." This is an odd standard. Effectively, the pleader admits that she doesn't have much supporting evidence at the time of pleading, but sanguinely certifies that she expects to find more.

Here again, the rule-makers attempt to walk a thin line. They don't want to allow groundless allegations made without evidentiary support. But they also don't want to discourage parties from making allegations that may turn out to be true once the pleader has a full opportunity to develop her case. Much of the factual development of a case takes place through formal discovery. Often, information crucial to the plaintiff's case can only be obtained from the defendant through discovery. Yet discovery comes after pleading, not before. So the system needs to build in some leeway for parties to make allegations they believe are valid, and then to try to unearth the supporting proof.

Rule 11(b)(3)'s "likely-to-have-evidentiary-support-after-a-reasonable-opportunity. . . ." provision allows a party the flexibility to make such allegations, which they expect to be able to prove, even if they have little evidentiary support prior to filing suit. The plaintiff may make allegations at the outset for which she lacks adequate proof, as long as she identifies them appropriately. She may then use the tools of discovery to dig for the proof. However, Rule 11 also limits such allegations. Under Rule 11(b), a party may not continue to advocate a position once she has had a reasonable opportunity to develop the facts, if she hasn't developed evidentiary support for that position. If she does the digging and the hole comes up dry, she can't "later advocate" those allegations.

Here's a question to probe these Rule 11(b)(3) requirements.

QUESTION 12. Alleged allegations. Tolliver sues Acme Company. In one count of her complaint, she alleges on information and belief that Acme discharged her based on her sex, and that this allegation is likely to have evidentiary support after a reasonable opportunity for further investigation or discovery. At the time that she files the complaint, Tolliver has done preliminary investigation, and has some reason to believe the allegation is true, but expects to develop her proof through discovery from Acme's employees. Tolliver engages in full discovery, but fails to unearth any evidence that the discharge was based on her sex. After discovery is complete

A. Tolliver is in violation of Rule 11, because she has not discovered any support for the sex discrimination allegations in her complaint.

B. Tolliver is required under the Rules to withdraw her allegation of sex discrimination.

C. Tolliver need not withdraw her allegation of sex discrimination, but may not attempt to prove this allegation at trial.

D. Tolliver may continue to advocate this claim as long as Acme does not serve her with a "safe harbor" motion under Rule 11(c)(2).

ANALYSIS.   A is wrong here, because Tolliver did not violate Rule 11 by making the allegation with little admissible evidence. Here, she revealed in her pleading that she made the allegation on information and belief, identifying the allegation appropriately in the complaint as required by Rule 11(b)(3). If, despite her conviction that she would find sufficient evidence of sex discrimination, she turns out to be wrong, she isn't in violation of Rule 11. The Rule clearly contemplates that she may identify this allegation as made on information and belief, and go ahead and do the investigation and discovery. It doesn't say, "We'll let you take a shot at it but if you don't turn anything up we will sanction you for unfounded allegations." Even if she fails to find the proof she suspected was out there, she hasn't violated the Rule's certification requirement by making the allegation and searching for support for it.

Nor does Rule 11 require Tolliver to affirmatively withdraw the allegations once she's finished looking and hasn't found supporting evidence. See Advisory Committee Note to 1993 Amendment, Subdivisions (b) and (c). Under Rule 11(b) she is only barred from "later advocat[ing] it" once she has taken her full shot at developing the evidence and hasn't found any. (The rule leaves unclear, as perhaps it must, when she will have reached that point.) So **B** fails too. Since Tolliver need not withdraw the allegation, how will Acme *know* if she is still advocating this position? One way it may find out is to send Tolliver a Rule 11(c)(2) motion, demanding that she withdraw the unsupported allegation. If Acme doesn't do that, it may remain unclear at least until a pretrial conference whether the allegation is still in play.

D is wrong too. Acme could send Tolliver a motion under Rule 11(c)(2), to induce her to withdraw the allegation. But even if Acme doesn't do that, Tolliver may not continue to advocate the sex discrimination claim once discovery is complete, if she has not developed an evidentiary basis for it.

So **C** is the right answer. Once Tolliver has had the full opportunity to find supporting evidence for the allegation, and hasn't found any, the Rule bars her from "later advocating" that position. To take the sex discrimination claim to trial, after discovery is complete and she has found no support for it, would violate the certification requirement in Rule 11(b)(3).

The Caveat ... And now, the caveat to this question. Is the answer affected by *Bell v. Twombly* and *Ashcroft v. Iqbal?* The cases appear to require factual support for a pleading that demonstrates that the plaintiff's allegations "plausibly" set forth a claim for relief. Yet Rule 11(b)(3) appears to allow the plaintiff to sue without knowing the facts necessary to establish a claim, so long as she has reason to believe that she will develop them. Suppose the *Bell* plaintiffs had pleaded that "on information and belief, the defendants met and entered into a deliberate agreement not to compete in each other's markets, as will be established by further information and discovery." Could they so plead, and then argue that, having alleged the supporting facts on information and belief, Rule 11(b)(3) allows them to go forward to develop those facts through discovery? It is hard to see how this would be any different from the actual allegations the plaintiffs made in *Bell*, except that the allegation *admits* to not yet having the evidence needed to substantiate the allegation. It is very hard to see how *Bell's* plausibility standard can coexist with the license apparently extended to plaintiffs by Rule 11(b)(3).

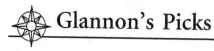 ## Glannon's Picks

1.	Too short and too plain?	**D**
2.	A sense of outrage	**D**
3.	A plausible sense of outrage?	**A**
4.	Fine distinctions	**E**
5.	Pleading for relief	**D**
6.	The consistency hobgoblin	**A**
7.	Yes, no, and maybe	**A**
8.	Sufficient information?	**D**
9.	Defendant in denial	**C**
10.	An early Closer	**B**
11.	Try, try again	**D**
12.	Alleged allegations	**C**

16

Change over Time: Amending the Pleadings Under Rule 15

Whatever Smith may have intended,
His complaint Rule 8 sore offended;
When the trial judge dismissed it
Smith tried to twist it,
But it weren't any better as amended.

CHAPTER OVERVIEW

A. Quick fix: Amendments "as a matter of course"

B. Amendments with leave of court

C. Relation back of amendments

D. Pre-Closer: Amendments to add parties under Rule 15(c)(1)(C)

E. The Closer: Amendments under Rule 15(b) to conform to the evidence

◈ Glannon's Picks

T he plaintiff's complaint and the defendant's answer are the opening volleys in a lawsuit. Certainly, the parties investigate their claims before filing these "initial pleadings." But the devil is often in the details, and development of the details tends to come after pleading, through discovery and preparation for trial. As preparation proceeds, it isn't unusual for parties to learn that their initial understanding of their claims or defenses was wrong, or incomplete, and to wish to amend their pleadings to reflect their evolving understanding of their claims. In federal court, the right to amend is governed by Fed. R. Civ. P. 15. State procedural systems, many closely modeled on the Federal Rules, have similar provisions governing amendments.

A.   Quick fix: Amendments "as a matter of course"

The Federal Rules give all parties one free shot at amending their pleadings. "As a matter of course" means without leave of court or consent of the adverse party. You have a *right* to do it. You just file the amended pleading and it supersedes (or supplements) the first. If you're a defending party, and your answer "closes the pleadings" (that is, no further pleading is allowed in response to your answer), you may amend your answer once within twenty-one days after serving it. Fed. R. Civ. P. 15(a)(1)(A). If the pleading is one to which a responsive pleading is required — typically, the original complaint, but also an answer that asserts a counterclaim or crossclaim — the pleader may amend as a matter of course within twenty-one days after service of the opposing party's responsive pleading (usually, the answer) or a responsive motion under Rule 12. Fed. R. Civ. P. 15(a)(1)(B).

Just to illustrate: Maxim serves a complaint for defamation on Ruggiero, who files an answer to the complaint and serves it on Maxim. Maxim may amend his complaint without leave of court within twenty-one days after Ruggiero serves the answer (or a motion to dismiss) on Maxim. That's governed by subsection (a)(1)(B). Ruggiero can amend his answer without leave of court within twenty-one days after he serves it on Maxim. That's governed by subsection (a)(1)(A).

Actually, this is so simple that it is totally confusing. I confused myself in trying to write this. But hopefully working through the two questions below will help.

QUESTION 1. **Late, or too late?**   Farrell, a potter, sues Malone for negligence, seeking to recover for personal injuries she suffered in an accident while a passenger in Malone's car driving to a crafts fair. She sues in federal court based on diversity jurisdiction on January 2 and serves the complaint on Malone on January 4. On January 22, twenty days after receiving it, Malone moves to dismiss the complaint under Fed. R. Civ. P. 12(b)(2) for lack of personal jurisdiction. On February 9, Farrell amends the complaint to add a second claim against Malone for damage to seven boxes of pots that were in the car and broken due to the accident. Farrell's amendment.

> **A.** is too late to be filed as of right, since it is served more than twenty-one days after she filed the complaint.
> **B.** is too late, because it is filed after Malone has responded to the complaint.
> **C.** is timely under Fed. R. Civ. P. 15(a)(1)(B).
> **D.** is improper, because it adds a claim for different damages not mentioned in the original complaint.

ANALYSIS. **D** is a real woofer. Nothing in Rule 15 says that the claims added by amendment must be for the same damages or for the same events as the original complaint. The amendment may add different damages, different legal theories, different facts, whatever. Rule 15 places no limit on the substantive nature of the changes that are allowed. Farrell could add a claim for shooting her pet rhinoceros in Piccadilly Circus if she likes.

A is also off the mark. The twenty-one day limit on the original plaintiff's right to amend runs from service of the responsive pleading or motion, not from the filing of the original complaint. Fed. R. Civ. P. 15(a)(1)(B). And **B** is similarly a dud, because Fed. R. Civ. P. 15(a)(1)(B) allows Farrell twenty-one days after Malone serves the Rule 12 motion to amend as of right. So **C** is right; Farrell may amend as of right because the twenty-one day period for doing so has not run.[1]

So here's another one, a little more complex. . . .

> **QUESTION 2. Later, or too late?** Farrell, a potter, sues Malone for negligence, claiming she was injured while a passenger in Malone's car driving to a crafts fair. She sues in federal court based on diversity jurisdiction and serves her complaint on Malone on January 2. Malone answers the complaint twenty days after receiving it, on January 22, denying negligence. At the end of her answer, under a separate heading entitled "Counterclaim," she asserts a counterclaim against Farrell, claiming that Farrell agreed to deliver forty pots to Malone for sale in her shop, and didn't do so. Farrell files an answer to the counterclaim on January 29, asserting that she never agreed to deliver the pots and that the contract is not enforceable because it was not in writing.
>
> After receiving Farrell's answer to the counterclaim, Malone's counsel realizes that Farrell's second argument is valid: The contract for the pots is not enforceable under the applicable statute of frauds because it was not in

---

1. Actually, for Farrell, the period for amendment is more than twenty-one days, right? She could amend during the twenty days after serving her complaint but before Malone serves the responsive motion. And she gets an additional twenty-one after that. From January 4 to February 12, I think! That's like forty-one days altogether, isn't it? (For details on counting days, see the delicious technicalities of Fed. R. Civ. P. 6.)

writing. Consequently, on February 16, Malone serves an amended counterclaim on Farrell, changing her theory to misrepresentation, a tort claim, based on Farrell's statements promising prompt delivery of the pots.

A. The amendment is proper without leave of court, since the amended counterclaim was filed within twenty-one days after Farrell's answer to the counterclaim.

B. The amendment will need leave of court, since Farrell has already served a responsive pleading to the counterclaim.

C. The amendment is not proper without leave of court, since it was filed more than twenty-one days after Malone filed her answer to the original complaint.

D. The counterclaim cannot be amended, since the period for amendments as of right has passed.

ANALYSIS.   No one chose **D**, I hope. Rule 15(a)(1) sets strict time limits for amendments *as a matter of course*—that is, without the court's permission. But amendments may still be sought with "leave of court"— that is, with the judge's assent—after those deadlines have passed. Fed. R. Civ. P. 15(a)(2). So Malone may seek an amendment months, or perhaps even years, after filing her counterclaim, even though the period for amendments as a matter of right has gone by. She'll just need to convince the judge to allow it.

Rule 15(a)(1)(A) provides that, if Malone's answer is the last pleading allowed, she has twenty-one days after serving the pleading to amend as of right. **C** says the amendment is too late, evidently based on this reasoning. However, in this example Malone's answer is not the last pleading allowed; Farrell must still answer the counterclaim Malone included in the answer. See Fed. R. Civ. P. 7(a)(3). So Malone's right to amend without leave is governed by Fed. R. Civ. P. 15(a)(1)(B). That devilish subsection provides that Malone may amend as of right within twenty-one days after Farrell serves her responsive pleading on Malone. She answered the counterclaim on January 29, so the amendment on February 16 is timely. So **B** is wrong; Malone can still amend as of right. **A** is the right choice here.

If you grasp the reasoning for this provision allowing the party to amend after receiving the responsive pleading, you are more likely to remember it. When Malone got Farrell's answer to the counterclaim, she realized that Farrell's no-contract defense was right, so she could not recover on a contract theory. Having been educated by Farrell's counsel, she will either drop her counterclaim or want to change her theory to one that will support recovery—here, misrepresentation. Allowing amendment as of right *after* receiving the responsive pleading gives the pleader a chance to fix a pleading *in light of the defenses raised by the other side*. That's what Malone did here.

B. Amendments with leave of court

Usually, the occasion to seek an amendment arises later in the action, as parties review documents, depose witnesses, prepare testimony, and research their legal claims and defenses. Thus, the time for amendment as of right will have passed, and the party who wants to amend will have to seek leave of court — that is, the judge's permission — or consent of the other party, to amend the pleading. Fed. R. Civ. P. 15(a)(2).

Under Rule 15(a)(2), the judge should generally grant amendments, so that cases can proceed based on the parties' educated understanding of the facts and theories of recovery. If a party has learned that the facts are not what she initially pleaded, or that she should have alleged a different legal claim or defense than she did at the outset, she should be allowed to amend the pleadings to conform to her evolving understanding of her case. The goal is to have the trial reflect the true state of the evidence, not the parties' initial understandings when they filed the complaint and answer. If parties were stuck with the positions in the complaint and answer, they would frequently have to try the case based on allegations or defenses that appeared correct at the time, but were not borne out by further research and discovery. The whole thrust of the Federal Rules is to avoid such calcification of legal procedure. Consequently, Rule 15(a)(2) provides that the court should "freely give leave [to amend] when justice so requires." The presumption, especially early in the litigation, is that amendments will be allowed, so that the issues framed for trial will reflect the parties' fully developed understanding of the case.

However, while amendments are liberally allowed, they are not always granted. A common reason to deny leave to amend is that the amendment is offered too late, when the opposing party will be unable to develop the evidence or arguments to meet the new allegation. As trial approaches, the tension increases between the premium the Federal Rules place on flexibility to reframe the issues and the due process right to an adequate opportunity to meet the claim. A change of position that might be fair in the first weeks of a case would be manifestly unfair a week before trial.

The grant or denial of an amendment is a discretionary decision, which means it's committed to the judge's good judgment, and in many cases either granting or denying the amendment would be reasonable. That makes multiple-choice questions on amendments with leave of court a bit dicey, since it isn't always clear that one answer is "right." Yet many professors will give questions that involve a certain amount of judgment, on the theory that a major goal of the first year is to develop legal judgment, and that questions may fairly probe whether you have acquired some. Here's an example of one I've used on my own exams. While it calls for judgment, I think one answer is clearly best.

QUESTION 3. The latest news. Quarles sues the City of Decatur for injuries caused by its employee, Fred, driving a City of Decatur Parks Department pickup truck. In her complaint, she alleges that Fred was acting in the scope of his employment as a parks employee for the City at the time of the accident. The City's counsel checks the time sheets for the day of the accident, which indicate that Fred was working that day, and the accident report, which indicates that the truck involved was a City vehicle. The City then answered the complaint, admitting that Fred acted in the scope of his employment at the time of the accident.

Five months later, one month prior to the date for finishing discovery, the City's lawyer meets with Barbara, Fred's immediate supervisor, to prepare for her deposition. Barbara explains that, while Fred did come to work that day, she had let Fred go an hour before the accident to visit his sick mother, and let him take the truck to drive to the hospital. Barbara had known this all along, but had not volunteered this awkward bit of information until directly interviewed by the City's counsel. Upon learning this, the City's lawyer moves to amend its answer to deny that Fred acted in the scope of employment. The amendment will probably

A. be denied, because Barbara was aware when the complaint was filed that Fred was not on the job at the time of the accident.

B. be denied, because it attempts to change the defendant's position as to the facts, not add or change a legal claim or defense.

C. be allowed, because discovery is not yet complete and Quarles will still be able to prepare to meet the amended allegation at trial.

D. be denied, because it comes shortly before the close of discovery.

ANALYSIS. Note that in this question it is the defendant who took one position in its answer and later wants to change its position. Rule 15's standards for amendment apply equally to parties asserting claims and parties defending against them.

The City's amendment attempts to change its position on a crucial issue in the case: If Fred did not act in the scope of employment, the city isn't liable for his negligence. Needless to say, the plaintiff will oppose the amendment vigorously.

Certainly, the rules favor trying that issue on the merits, rather than foreclosing the issue because the city admitted that Fred acted in the scope of employment when it first filed its answer. But time has gone by, the parties are supposed to be almost through with discovery, and this raises a new issue that formerly appeared to be settled by the City's answer, and that Quarles would now have to prepare to meet at trial. So there are values to be balanced on both sides, which is what exercises of discretion are all about.

Let's look at the options. **B** suggests that the amendment should not be allowed, because it attempts to change the City's position about the facts, not its legal contentions. However, Rule 15 makes no distinction between factual and legal changes to the pleadings. Very frequently, the parties' understanding about the facts will evolve, especially as they take discovery from nonparty witnesses and from opposing parties. The philosophy behind the rule is to allow the parties, where consistent with fairness, to change the pleadings to reflect their evolving understanding of both the facts and their legal positions based on the facts. Here, for example, if the amendment were allowed, and it looked as though the City would probably prove that Fred didn't act in the scope of employment, Quarles might wish to change her allegations too. For example, she might seek to amend to add a claim for negligent entrustment of the truck to Fred.

A takes the position that the amendment should be denied because a city employee — though not counsel for the city — knew all along that Fred had not been working at the time of the accident. This suggests that, if the true facts could have been discovered by the City's lawyer, but weren't, the amendment should be denied. If this were so, counsel would have to do exhaustive investigation before pleading, and would be bound by what they knew when they filed the complaint or answer, without a right to amend if they learned later that what they pleaded was wrong. This is a heavy burden, heavier than the rule-makers chose to impose on litigants. Instead, under Rule 15(a) leave to amend should be freely given "when justice so requires."

Even if counsel might have discovered her error by more exhaustive pre-pleading investigation, the rules don't give first priority to punishing lawyers' lapses. Rather, first priority goes to trying cases on the merits. Here, trying the dispute on the merits would clearly be facilitated by allowing the amendment, even if the need for an amendment might have been averted by more intensive pre-pleading investigation. So the view reflected by **A**, that "you could have known this, so you should stew in your own juice," is unlikely to decide the amendment motion. The answer might be different if the amendment had been sought immediately before trial, or if it was clear that the City's lawyer had done no investigation of the facts before filing its answer.

C and **D** are closer options. The amendment is sought fairly far down the line towards trial. But discovery is not complete yet; there's some time to do more. And, the judge could extend the time for discovery if the amendment is allowed, to give Quarles an opportunity to meet the City's denial of the acting-in-the-scope allegation. On the other side of the ledger, whether Fred acted in the scope of employment is fundamental to the plaintiff's right to recover. To deny this amendment is to bar the City from raising a complete, possibly valid defense to liability. Judges don't like to do that. And here, the City's counsel had investigated before answering and had reasonable grounds to admit the allegation. Absent evidence of bad faith, or deliberate delay in offering the amendment, the judge in this situation would likely allow the amendment, so that this issue can be tried on the merits, rather than foreclosed by an early misimpression. **C** is the best choice.

Here's another example, again calling for judgment concerning the discretionary decision whether to grant an amendment. Note that here the amendment seeks to change the legal claims rather than the factual allegations.

QUESTION 4. Hedging bets. Jhala is injured while riding an off-road vehicle over the dunes. He retains a lawyer, Pope, to bring a suit against Adventure Vehicles, Inc., the company that manufactured the vehicle. Pope files suit, seeking recovery on a theory of strict products liability, that is, that the defendant is liable, without fault, for selling a defective vehicle that injured Jhala. His theory is that the ORV was built with too narrow a wheelbase, making it dangerously prone to rolling over.

At a discovery conference, the federal judge sets a schedule for discovery that calls for completion of discovery in nine months, and trial several months thereafter. Six months later, Pope remembers what is basic black letter law in his state: that conscious misuse would be a complete defense to Jhala's products liability claim, but misuse would only reduce recovery (under comparative negligence) if he sued on a negligence theory. He moves to amend to assert a second claim for relief, alleging that Adventure was negligent in designing the vehicle with too narrow a wheel base.

The judge will likely

A. deny the amendment, because it would add an additional theory of recovery, rather than changing the theory asserted in the initial complaint.
B. deny the amendment, if she concludes that Pope should have thought of this theory when he filed the initial complaint.
C. deny the amendment, because Jhala can still proceed on a strict products liability theory, and may recover on this ground.
D. allow the amendment, because it facilitates a decision on the merits, even if Jhala's counsel should have asserted it in the initial complaint.

ANALYSIS. This example is quite similar to the previous one. Here, as there, the amended pleading could have been the original pleading if counsel's preparation had been a bit more aggressive. Had Pope reviewed basic theories of tort recovery, this difference in defenses to negligence and strict liability would have been clear to him. Indeed, if he regularly does personal injury work, he probably should simply have known it. But he didn't, or he forgot, or was in a rush when he drafted the complaint, so now he wants to fix things by adding the negligence claim.

The argument for allowing the amendment is a little weaker here, though. In the first example, the City's counsel was under an understandable misimpression about the facts, which were later clarified by further discovery. In Jhala's case, Pope didn't need any additional facts to realize the need to plead the additional claim, he only needed to think a bit harder about the legal issues, or do some further legal research to realize that he should include a negligence claim.

A suggests that Pope can't amend because he would be adding a new theory of recovery. However, nothing in Rule 15(a) suggests that amendments that add new theories of recovery — or new defenses — are off-limits. They aren't. Very frequently, parties will seek to add additional claims for relief or defenses, based on newly developed facts or further legal research and analysis. Once again, the priority of the rules is presentation on the merits, so these are commonly allowed, as long as the defendant isn't prejudiced due to an unreasonable delay in seeking the amendment, or the fact that trial is imminent.

B argues that the amendment should be denied if Jhala's lawyer should have thought of it initially. But the test isn't whether counsel made a mistake; it is whether justice would be furthered by allowing the party to litigate a position rather than foreclosing it. Justice to the client will frequently support amendments, even if they do stem from counsel's negligence.

I wouldn't want to state this as an ironclad rule. Certainly, one factor in rejecting an amendment is that there is no reason why it couldn't have been included in the original pleading. Sometimes it will be clear that the omission reflects egregious sloppiness — or deliberate tactical delay — that should not be tolerated, at least if the amendment comes close to trial. But more often, amendments are likely to be granted to correct oversights, even if they might have been avoided by more careful pre-filing analysis.

C suggests that the amendment should be denied because Jhala might still win on the products liability theory, even if barred from asserting the additional negligence claim. But Rule 15(a)(2) favors allowing the parties to present all their claims and defenses, even if belatedly invoked. See also Fed. R. Civ. P. 8(d)(3) (pleading may assert as many claims or defenses as the party has). It would be cold comfort to Jhala to be told that he can't present his strongest claim because he can still proceed with a weaker one. It is unlikely that the court would do so. Given the fact that the amendment comes while there is still three months for further discovery, the judge would very likely allow the amendment, as **D** indicates.

There's another reason why "justice" would support allowing the amendment here. Doubtless, the parties were *already investigating Jhala's conduct*, since misuse of the vehicle would be a complete defense to the original products liability claim. Adding a negligence claim means that his conduct will be assessed against an additional standard, but the parties were very likely already developing the factual evidence about that conduct before the amendment. Consequently, allowing the amendment will not likely prejudice Adventure's ability to present a full defense.

Despite the last two questions, I don't want to leave the impression that amendments are always granted. They aren't. As the case gets close to trial, the prejudice to the opposing party, who must gear up to meet an unexpected claim or defense, is likely to counterbalance the policy in favor of amendments, especially if a court-established deadline for amendments has passed. Other factors that may overcome the presumption in favor of amendment include the absence of any reason for delay in asserting a claim or defense, and the fact that the amended claim or defense would be legally insufficient anyway.

C. Relation back of amendments

Special problems arise when the plaintiff seeks to amend to add additional claims, or change the nature of her claims, after the statute of limitations has expired. The rule-makers addressed this problem in Rule 15(c). Let's start with Rule 15(c)(1), which deals with the most common situation, in which the plaintiff files the complaint within the limitations period, the limitations period passes, and later the plaintiff wants to amend her complaint to add another claim. Rule 15(c)(1) provides:

> *When an Amendment Relates Back.* An amendment to a pleading relates back to the date of the original pleading when . . . (B) the amendment asserts a claim or defense that arose out of the conduct, transaction, or occurrence set out — or attempted to be set out — in the original pleading . . .

What does it mean that the amendment "relates back" if it arises from the same underlying events alleged in the original pleading? It means that the amended complaint, containing the new claim, will be treated as though it had been filed when the original complaint was filed. What's the point of this? It is intended to make clear that the statute of limitations is not a defense to the amended complaint, any more than it was to the original claim.

A diagram should help. Assume that Roberts sues Morales for breach of contract, based on the sale of a quantity of men's suits to him on March 15, 2008. He files suit on March 1, 2011, just before the three-year limitations period for contract claims in the relevant jurisdiction runs out. Four months later, he moves to amend his complaint to add an allegation that the sale constituted the tort of fraud, a claim that also has a three-year limitations period.

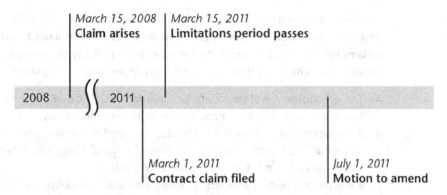

March 15, 2008 | March 15, 2011
Claim arises | **Limitations period passes**

2008   2011

March 1, 2011 | July 1, 2011
Contract claim filed | **Motion to amend**

If Roberts had brought *no suit* until July of 2011, and then sued Morales for fraud, the fraud claim would be barred by the statute of limitations. But here, Roberts *did* sue Morales for this sale of goods before the passage of the limitations period. All he wants to do now is to add to his complaint another theory of recovery for the sale. Under Rule 15(c)(1)(B), if the amendment is allowed, the fraud claim will be treated as though it had been filed on March 1, 2011, before the statute of limitations passed.

Why does the rule allow this bit of legal fiction? The purpose of a statute of limitations is to ensure that the defendant has notice of a claim within a given period of time, so she can adequately prepare to defend that claim. Here, Roberts put Morales on notice that he would have to defend his conduct involving the March 15, 2008 sale when he sued him on March 1, 2011, within the limitations period. Morales should realize, as of that date, that he will have to defend that sale, and gather the evidence to do so before it disappears. True, he thinks he has to defend a *contract claim* based on the sale, not a fraud claim. But Rule 15(c)(1)(B) reflects the rule-makers' conclusion that, once a defendant has been put on notice that particular conduct will be litigated — the March 15, 2008 sale — the purpose of the limitations period is satisfied. Consequently, since Roberts sued Morales for the sale before the limitations period ran, Roberts should be allowed to assert whatever claims or theories he has arising from that sale, even if he thinks of additional theories later. Otherwise, Roberts would have to develop his whole case before March 15, 2011, not just sue Morales by that date.

Here's an example to illustrate the point.

QUESTION 5. Better late than never? Roberts runs a clothing store and regularly buys suits from Morales, a clothing wholesaler. He buys a batch of men's suits from Morales on March 15, 2008. On June 15, 2008, he buys a batch of women's dresses from Morales.

On March 1, 2011, Roberts sues Morales for breach of contract, claiming that the men's suits were not Armani suits, as represented, but Brand X.

> The relevant limitations period for contract claims is three years. Six months later, on September 7, 2011, he amends his complaint to add a claim for breach of contract for the June 2008 delivery of women's dresses. He claims that they were irregulars rather than first quality.
>
> A. The amendment will not relate back under Fed. R. Civ. P. 15(c)(1)(B). The dress claim will be barred by the statute of limitations.
> B. If the amendment is allowed, Morales may add this claim, and it will relate back to March 1, 2011, the date of original filing, since, like the initial claim, it is based on breach of contract.
> C. If the amendment is allowed, Morales may add this claim, and it will relate back to June 15, 2011, the date on which the limitations period for the dress claim would have run.
> D. The amendment will not relate back under Fed. R. Civ. P. 15(c)(1)(B), but the claim will not be barred by the statute of limitations if the judge grants leave to amend to add this claim.

ANALYSIS. The key to this question is that the dress claim does not arise out of the same transaction as the suit claim. These are two separate sales at different times. Rule 15(c)(1)(B) can't help Roberts here, because it says, "If you sued Morales for one set of events, you can amend the complaint to assert different theories or facts based on that set of events without encountering limitations problems." It doesn't say, "If you sued Morales for one set of events, you can sue him later for a separate transaction at a different time, even though the statute of limitations has passed on that separate claim." Here, Roberts's original suit put Morales on notice that he must defend the sale of men's suits, but did not put him on notice of a claim arising from the sale of dresses. Roberts must put him on notice of a claim arising from *that sale* within the limitations period. He can't argue, "Well, I sued you for the suit claim within the limitations period, so I'm just amending to add another claim and it relates back." That's not what Rule 15(c)(1)(B) says, and it would undermine a state's limitations statute if it did. (Indeed, interpreting the rule to allow this would likely fail under *Erie*/Rules Enabling Act analysis, since it would abridge Morales' substantive right to be protected by the statute of limitations. See 28 U.S.C. §2072(b).)

B reflects the position that an amendment will relate back if it is based on the same legal theory as the original pleading. But Rule 15(c)(1)(B) requires that the amended claim arise from the *same events* as the original claim, not assert the same legal theory. So this choice is wrong, as is **C**, which also asserts that this amendment would relate back.

How about **D**, which suggests that the dress claim can be added if the judge grants the motion to amend? It is true that Rule 15(a)(2) encourages judges to allow amendments; in fact, it tells them to bend over backwards to allow them "where justice so requires." So can't the judge just allow Roberts to amend his complaint to assert this claim, so that it can be heard on the merits?

Well, the judge could allow Roberts to amend to assert this claim. But she certainly could not bar Morales from asserting a statute of limitations defense to it. Rule 15(c)(1)(B) says that a claim relates back if—and, by implication *only* if—it arises from the same events as the original claim. This one doesn't, so the fact that Roberts filed suit on the suit claim does not affect any limitation defense to the dress claim. If the judge were to allow the amendment, Morales would plead the limitations period as a defense to the dress claim. The period ran on the dress claim on June 15, 2011. Whether filed as an independent suit or added to Roberts' initial action, the limitations period bars the claim.

So **A** is the right answer here. Roberts cannot use Rule 15(c)(1)(B) to avoid the limitations defense on this separate claim.

Let's try a second relation-back problem.

QUESTION 6. Amendment rights? In March 2009, shortly after a new mayor takes office, Harcourt is fired from her job as a City administrator. She sues the City for breach of contract in February 2011, one month before the two-year limitations period passes. The parties conduct discovery over the course of seventeen months. In July 2012, just before the pre-trial conference, Harcourt moves to amend to add a federal civil rights claim to her complaint, alleging that she was fired because she belonged to the outgoing mayor's party, and that the firing violates her First Amendment rights. A three-year limitations period applies to the civil rights claim.

The judge holds a hearing on the motion to amend, and indicates reluctance to allow the motion, because it comes late in the litigation.

A. Even if the judge allows the amendment, it will not relate back under Rule 15(c)(1)(B), because her new claim is based on a different legal theory.

B. If the judge denies the amendment, Harcourt will be barred by the statute of limitations from recovering on her civil rights claim.

C. If the judge denies the amendment, Harcourt can bring a separate action, which will relate back for limitations purposes to the date of filing of her breach of contract claim.

D. The judge must allow the amendment, because it arises out of the same events as the original contract claim.

ANALYSIS. I like this question, because it highlights the effect of the judge's discretionary decision to grant or deny an amendment.

The first issue is whether, if the judge grants the amendment, the civil rights allegation will "relate back" to the original filing, that is, be treated as though it had been contained in the original complaint, which was filed before the three-year limitations period had passed. **A** is wrong, because, if the amendment were allowed, it *would* relate back, since it arises out of the same events — Harcourt's dismissal from her job — as the claim in the original complaint. Don't be fooled by the fact that the new claim is based on a different legal theory from the first. Amendments very commonly add new theories. Under Rule 15(c)(1)(B), the amendment will relate back as long as it is based on the same conduct, transaction, or occurrence as the original claim. Consequently, if the judge grants the motion, the claim can proceed, and the limitations defense will not bar it.

D takes the position that the judge must grant the motion to amend, since the claim to be added by amendment arises out of the same events as the original claim. But nothing in Rule 15 says that an amendment must be allowed because it arises out of the same events as the original claim. Rule 15(c)(1)(B) says that, *if the amendment is allowed*, and the amended claim arises from the same events as the original claim, it will "relate back." But the judge still has a discretionary decision to make, considering the various factors discussed earlier, whether to allow the amendment at all. She is not compelled to grant an improvident amendment just because it asserts a claim arising from the same underlying events as the original claim. The judge will first ask whether, given the circumstances, it is appropriate to allow the amendment, under the discretionary analysis of Rule 15(a)(2). If the answer is "yes," then the "same-transaction-or-occurrence" standard of Rule 15(c)(1)(B) determines whether it will relate back for limitations purposes.

But suppose the judge denies the amendment? Then, of course, Harcourt's only recourse would be to file a separate suit on it. **C** takes the position that, if she does, the claim will relate back to the date of filing of the breach of contract complaint in her first suit. I suppose the argument for this would be that the City was put on notice (by the filing of her first suit) of her claim arising from the dismissal, so the limitations period should be deemed satisfied.

Nice try, Harcourt, but this argument misreads Rule 15(c)(1)(B), which only allows amendments in the first suit to relate back, not separate actions Harcourt might bring against the defendant. The rule doesn't say that Harcourt can bring a separate action against the City and adopt the date of filing of her previous suit to avoid a limitations defense! She can't. If Harcourt's amendment is denied, and she then files a separate action on the civil rights claim, the limitations period will bar it, since her new action will have been filed after the three-year limitations period has expired.

So **B** is right. If the judge allows Harcourt's amendment, she will be allowed to litigate the civil rights claim. If the judge denies the amendment, that claim is lost. Harcourt better have a darn good argument why she didn't offer this amendment sooner. The question highlights the importance of the judge's discretionary decision whether to allow an amendment — and one reason why judges have a natural, human inclination to grant them.

D. Pre-Closer: Amendments to add parties under Rule 15(c)(1)(C)

There are some subtle problems in the amendment area. So we have a pre-closer and a closer.

A party who sues a defendant on a claim within the limitations period may change theories, add new damages, or recast the factual basis of the claim through amendments, assuming that the amended allegations still are based on the same underlying facts, and that the judge allows the amendment. The amended allegations will "relate back" to the date the original complaint was filed. If the claim asserted in the amended complaint would have been timely on that date, Rule 15(c)(1)(B) avoids any limitations problem.

But suppose the amendment adds a *new defendant* to the case? Rule 15 has a separate, more abstruse provision, Rule 15(c)(1)(C), that deals with this twist. As an example, assume that Leroy sues Tele-Sell, a telemarketing firm, under a statute barring telemarketing calls to consumers who have placed their names on a state do-not-call list. After he sues, the limitations period passes. Several months later, he learns that he was mistaken, that the calls actually came from Tel-Connect, a different firm. Consequently, he moves to amend to substitute Tel-Connect as the defendant. Allowing relation back for an amendment like this, adding a new party, requires a more stringent standard than others, because the new claim is against a different defendant, who was not sued before the limitations period expired.

Under Rule 15(c)(1)(C) three requirements must be met before an amendment changing the party against whom a claim is asserted will "relate back" to the date the original complaint was filed.

- *First,* the amended pleading must arise out of the same events as the original pleading. Rule 15(c)(1)(C).
- *Second,* the defendant being added must have "received such notice of the action that it will not be prejudiced in defending on the merits."

Rule 15(c)(1)(C)(i). This notice must have been received within the period of time it would have been received had the new defendant been sued originally.

- *Third*, the plaintiff must show that the new defendant brought in by the amendment "knew or should have known that the action would have been brought against it, but for a mistake concerning the proper party's identity." Rule 15(c)(1)(C)(ii).

The first requirement is met in Leroy's case. He is suing Tel-Connect for the same harassing calls that were the basis of his initial suit against Tele-Sell. But Rule 15(c)(1) requires more than that. It also requires that Tel-Connect was aware, within the period for suing and serving the complaint on Tele-Sell, that the suit had been brought, and that it — Tel-Connect — was actually the intended target of the suit.

What's the point of this complex provision? It is meant to ensure that Tel-Connect, the party Leroy brings in late, had actual notice within the limitations period (plus the additional 120 days that Fed. R. Civ. P. 4(m) gives for serving the complaint[2]) that Leroy intended to sue it. If it had such notice, the purpose of the limitations period has been satisfied: The added defendant was aware of the need to preserve evidence and prepare a defense, within the limitations period prescribed by the legislature.

Perhaps the following question will help to sort out the requirements of Rule 15(c)(1)(C).

QUESTION 7. Black and White. Williams is roughed up during an arrest by a police officer and suffers a broken wrist that doesn't heal right. Williams consults Darrow, a lawyer, who brings a federal civil rights action for his injury. Darrow obtains the police report of the arrest, which lists Officer Black as the arresting officer. Darrow names Black as the defendant. Suit is filed one month before the limitations period runs.

In fact, it wasn't Black who arrested Williams, it was Officer White. The report, filled out by the booking officer, was simply mistaken. Within a few days, every officer in the precinct, including White, became aware that Black had been sued by an arrestee for excessive force, though they were

---

2. This refinement in the rule is confusing. A party sued in federal court — at least, one sued on a federal claim — might not actually *find out* about the case within the limitations period. Filing the complaint with the court within the limitations period satisfies the statute of limitations. Rule 4(m) then gives the plaintiff 120 days to serve the complaint on the defendant. So the defendant might not actually find out about the suit until 120 days after the limitations period has passed, and yet have no limitations defense, since the claim was *filed* in time. Rule 15(c)(1)(C) requires that the added defendant must get notice of the case within the same period (limitations period plus 120 days) within which the original defendant must.

not aware of the specific circumstances of the case or the identity of the plaintiff.

Six months later, Black answers interrogatories sent to him by Williams, denying that he was the arresting officer. Darrow investigates, confirms from other witnesses that White was the arresting officer, and moves to amend to name White as the defendant in the action. The amendment, if allowed, will likely

A. not relate back, because it was filed after the limitations period had passed.
B. not relate back, because it was filed after the limitations period had passed and White was not on notice that he was the intended target of Williams's suit.
C. relate back, because White was aware, before the passage of the limitations period, that Black had been sued.
D. relate back, because it arises out of the same arrest alleged in the initial complaint.

ANALYSIS. Here, Darrow has sued one defendant and discovers, after the time to sue the proper defendant has passed, that he sued the wrong officer. The limitations period for suing White has now passed. Darrow's only hope is to amend the timely-filed complaint against Black to make White the defendant. Darrow will doubtless reread Fed. R. Civ. P. 15(c)(1) in a cold sweat when he realizes the problem. This could croak his client's case. Even if he wasn't negligent in suing Black, he won't look forward to telling Williams if the case is thrown out.

   D takes the position that the amended complaint will relate back, since it arises from the same arrest. This is wrong, because Rule 15(c)(1)(C) provides that the amendment will only relate back if that is true *and* the two further requirements in Rule 15(c)(1)(C)(i) and 15(c)(1)(C)(ii) are met. **C** suggests that the amendment to add White will relate back, because White knew, within the limitations period for Williams's claim, that Black had been sued. But that isn't enough under Rule 15(c)(1)(C) either. The rule requires that White receive, within the limitation period (plus the 120 days for service of the complaint), "such notice of the action that [White] will not be prejudiced in defending on the merits. . . ." Rule 15(c)(1)(C)(i). Knowledge that someone has sued Black for excessive force is hardly the equivalent of notice that Williams had mistakenly sued Black for the arrest made by White. The question indicates that other officers were not aware of the particular circumstances, so it is unlikely that White was on notice that Black had been sued for an arrest he (White) had made. Unless Williams could show that it would be clear to White that the suit must be for his arrest of Williams, so that, "but for a mistake concerning the identity of the proper party" he would have been the defendant, White doesn't have the notice called for by Rule 15(c)(1)(C)(i).

So **A** or **B** is the proper answer. **A** is very close. It is true that the amendment will not relate back because it was filed after the limitations period had passed. But it is not the best answer. It's a bit sloppy, because it suggests that an amendment to add a party can't relate back if it is filed after the limitations period has passed. That isn't so: If the requirements of Rule 15(c)(1)(C) are met, it would be treated as though it had been filed at the time of the original complaint. **B** is the better answer. While the amendment could relate back, it doesn't here, because White was not on notice that the action should have been filed against him. He knew that Black had been sued, but the question does not indicate that he understood that the suit was by Williams, or that it was for an arrest White had made. Thus, he is unaware, as Rule 15(c)(1)(C)(ii) requires, that, "but for a mistake concerning the proper party's identity," the action would have been brought against him.

This is a nice example of the difference between the "best" answer and the "right" answer. **A** is arguably right — the amendment will not relate back — but **B** is tighter, more precise in reflecting the logic for that result. A good many professors would consider this question fair for that reason.

E.   The Closer: Amendments under Rule 15(b) to conform to the evidence

While the pleadings are meant to define the scope of the issues litigated at trial, in practice it is not unusual for parties to litigate issues, both in discovery and at trial, that were never pleaded. For example, in a breach of contract case, Smith might try to develop evidence that, if the contract was not enforceable, the defendant had been unjustly enriched, so that Smith should recover in quantum meruit. Even though Smith hadn't pleaded quantum meruit, the course of the parties' discovery, the manner in which they presented their evidence at trial, their cross-examination of the other side's witnesses, and their requests for jury instructions might make it clear that they were actually trying the case on both contract and quantum meruit theories. If so, the fact that the quantum meruit claim was never added to the complaint should not prevent consideration of a quantum meruit claim.

Similarly, the depositions and cross-examination in a negligence case might show that the defendant relied on the plaintiff's negligence as a defense (or a partial defense, in a comparative negligence jurisdiction), and that the plaintiff had tried to controvert the defense. Even if the defendant's answer to the complaint did not raise comparative negligence as a defense, it might be evident to everyone that the parties were litigating that issue.

Where this is the case, Rule 15(b) provides that the court may acknowledge the reality that the parties have litigated the issue by allowing an amendment to formally place that issue in contention. Rule 15(b)(1) addresses the situation in which a party objects to evidence at trial on the ground that her opponent is trying to litigate issues at the trial that were not raised in the pleadings.

(b) Amendments During and After Trial.

(1) *Based on an Objection at Trial.* If at a trial, a party objects that evidence is not within the issues raised in the pleadings, the court may permit the pleadings to be amended. The court should freely permit an amendment when doing so will aid in presenting the merits and the objecting party fails to satisfy the court that the evidence would prejudice that party's action or defense on the merits. The court may grant a continuance to enable the objecting party to meet the evidence.

This subsection addresses the situation in which evidence is offered at trial to establish a claim or defense that is not in the pleadings. The rule permits the judge, if the parties have consciously been litigating the issue to which the offered evidence is relevant, to allow an amendment to the pleadings — at the trial itself — to expressly assert the claim or defense the evidence supports. Of course, if the judge concludes that the objecting party really did not understand that the issue was being litigated, the judge may exclude the evidence and deny an amendment raising the new issue (or allow the amendment and grant a continuance for the objecting party to prepare to litigate the new issue).

Rule 15(b)(2) addresses the similar situation in which the parties actually try an issue that is not in the pleadings. If the parties have treated the issue as actually in dispute (such as the plaintiff's comparative negligence), and presented their evidence on the point, and the jury is instructed on it and decides the issue, Rule 15(b)(2) confirms that the issue is properly tried, even though it was not in the initial pleadings and no amendment raising it was sought during the trial. In either case, the thrust of the rule is to make the pleadings reflect the issues that the parties are really litigating, rather than forcing the parties to litigate only the issues originally pleaded. As with Rule 15(a), the goal is to allow the parties every opportunity, consistent with fair notice to the other side, to try the issues as they are, not as they were initially framed.

That does not mean that parties will always convince a judge to hold that issues that were not pleaded are fairly in contention at trial. The key is fairness, and fairness requires notice to the opposing party. Where parties clearly understand that issues are in contention, and are prepared to meet them, the court will allow amendments to the pleadings to confirm that those issues are in the case (or simply act as though they were pleaded without requiring a formal amendment). However, Rule 15(b) does not allow a party to inject a new issue into the case at trial that was not "tried by the parties' express or implied consent."

Sometimes, of course, it can be a subtle question whether the parties were consciously litigating an issue, especially where evidence produced at trial is relevant to more than one claim or defense. Here's a tough question to illustrate the application of Rule 15(b).

QUESTION 8. Ups and downs. Jhala is injured while riding an off-road vehicle over the dunes. He retains a lawyer, Pope, to bring suit against Adventure Vehicles, Inc., the company that manufactured the ORV. Pope files suit, seeking recovery on a theory of strict products liability, that is, that the defendant is liable without fault for selling a defective vehicle that injured Jhala. His theory is that the ORV was built with too narrow a wheelbase, making it dangerously prone to rolling over. He also asserts a negligence claim against Adventure, on the theory that it negligently designed the ORV.

Adventure answers the complaint, denying that the ORV was defectively designed, denying that it was negligently designed, and alleging as an affirmative defense that Jhala was negligent for driving it too fast on a steep slope.

After discovery based on these pleadings, the case goes to trial. To support its comparative negligence defense, Adventure presents evidence about Jhala's route at the time of the accident, his speed, and the slope of the hill where the accident occurred. Jhala introduces opposing evidence on these issues.

After both parties have rested their cases, Adventure seeks a jury instruction on the theory of assumption of the risk. In the state where the action arose, assumption of the risk provides a complete defense to a product liability claim if the plaintiff fully understood a risk posed by a defective product and deliberately chose to encounter the risk anyway.

Adventure moves to amend its answer under Rule 15(b)(1) to add a defense of assumption of the risk, so the jury can consider this defense. The judge should

A. allow the amendment, since evidence concerning Jhala's conduct in using the ORV was introduced at trial by both parties.
B. hold that the defendant waived this defense by failing to plead it in its answer.
C. treat the assumption-of-risk issue as though it had been pleaded, and instruct the jury on it.
D. deny the amendment, since the parties did not impliedly try the issue of assumption of the risk.

ANALYSIS.   The rationale for Rule 15(b) is that, if the parties knew they were trying an issue, and did, then the pleadings filed months or years earlier shouldn't serve as a straitjacket that bars resolution of that issue. The premise for Rule 15(b) is, however, that the parties really did understand that the issue to be added by amendment was in the case and was being tried. Not just the party — like Adventure here — who wants to add the issue to the pleadings, but *both* parties must have understood that, to make such an amendment at trial fair.

In this case, nothing suggests that Jhala expressly agreed that the assumption-of-risk issue was in contention. So the question is whether, when the parties introduced evidence about his conduct, they both understood that they were litigating assumption of the risk. There is no reason to believe that Jhala's counsel did understand that: The evidence about Jhala's route, his speed, and the slope of the hill were all relevant to a different issue that was already in the case: the defense that he was comparatively negligent in the way he used the ORV. Comparative negligence only requires that the plaintiff have acted unreasonably under the circumstances. By contrast, assumption of the risk requires that the plaintiff be fully aware of the defect in the ORV and choose to take his chances. The fact that Adventure introduced evidence about Jhala's conduct, which was relevant to an issue already in contention (negligence), would not put his counsel on notice that a different issue (assumption of the risk) with a different standard (actual knowledge and choice to encounter the risk) was being litigated. Thus, **A** and **C** are wrong. Jhala's natural inference would be that the evidence was introduced to prove Jhala's negligence, not his knowing assumption of the risk of a defective product. It would be unfair to spring this on him after the parties had rested their cases. The Rule 15(b) motion should be denied. **D** is the best response.

There is an argument for **B**. If Adventure is not allowed to amend, I suppose it has, in a sense, waived the defense. But it didn't waive it just by leaving it out of the answer. Parties can frequently raise new issues that they left out of their initial pleadings — that's what the liberal amendment rules are all about. Adventure could have raised it by an amendment as of right, or a later amendment with leave of court, or perhaps even by seeking an amendment at trial, though, as the question illustrates, if it is offered at trial, the court would have to grant a continuance to allow Jhala to meet the new defense.

 ## Glannon's Picks

1. Late, or too late?   **C**
2. Later, or too late?   **A**

3. The latest news   **C**
4. Hedging bets   **D**
5. Better late than never?   **A**
6. Amendment rights?   **B**
7. Black and White   **B**
8. Ups and downs   **D**

17

Technicalities, Technicalities: Pre-answer Motions Under the Federal Rules

Should you ever be seized by the notion
To respond with a pre-answer motion,
Just be warned you can waive stuff
So if you want to hang tough
You must study Rule 12 with devotion.

CHAPTER OVERVIEW
A. Starting with the basics
B. Rule 12(g): Limits on multiple pre-answer motions
C. Driving students to distraction: Rule 12(g)(2) and waiver distinguished
D. Waiver under Rule 12(h)
E. Waiver without a pre-answer motion
F. Raising Rule 12(b) objections after answering the complaint
G. Curable objections to process, service, and joinder of indispensable parties
H. Another double Closer: Rule 12 and the notorious "special appearance"
Glannon's Picks

Admittedly, Rule 12 is a little grim. It is full of technical distinctions hidden in out-of-the-way places. Basically, it deals with several fundamental objections to the plaintiff's suit, the time for raising such objections, and the consequences of failing to raise them. We'll deal with it one step at a time, focusing first on Rule 12(b), then Rule 12(g) and then Rule 12(h).

A.   Starting with the basics

When a plaintiff files a complaint in federal court, the defendant must file a response to it. Fed. R. Civ. P. 12(b) describes her options. The rule provides, in the first sentence, that the defendant should put every defense that she has to a claim in her answer to the complaint. *However,* if the defendant has certain objections to the case, she may raise them by a "pre-answer motion" before pleading, that is, before answering the complaint. If the defendant makes a pre-answer motion, it suspends the time for answering the complaint until the court addresses the objections raised in the motion. See Rule 12(a)(4)(A), (B).

Rule 12(b) provides that the following objections may be made by a pre-answer motion:

1. lack of subject matter jurisdiction;
2. lack of personal jurisdiction over the defendant;
3. improper venue;
4. insufficient process (that is, a defect in the summons required to be served on the defendant along with the complaint);
5. insufficient service of process (that is, the method used to deliver the summons and complaint to the defendant);
6. failure to state a claim upon which relief can be granted; and
7. failure to join a party under Rule19 (that is, a person who must be made a party to the action to fairly adjudicate the case).

One further pre-answer motion is squirreled away in Rule 12(e), the motion for a more definite statement. A Rule 12(e) motion asserts that the plaintiff's claim is so incomprehensible that the responding party cannot meaningfully respond to it, and asks the court to require the plaintiff to file a clearer complaint.

A crucial point about Rule 12 pre-answer motions is that the defendant *never has to make one.* Making a pre-answer motion to assert these defenses is allowed, but not required. If the defendant prefers, she may raise any of these seven objections — or all of them — in her answer instead. I always snare a reasonable percentage of students on this basic point. Here's a question that illustrates the point.

QUESTION 1. Answers and objections.   Creasey sues Trinh in federal court in Florida for injuries suffered in an accident in Alabama. Trinh files an answer to the complaint, including in the answer an allegation that the court lacks personal jurisdiction over her. The objection to personal jurisdiction

A. is proper, and will be considered and decided by the court.
B. is proper, as long as it was also asserted in a pre-answer motion under Fed. R. Civ. P. 12(b)(2).
C. should be stricken, because the objection must be raised by a motion, not in a responsive pleading.
D. should be stricken. Trinh waived it by failing to file a pre-answer motion under Fed. R. Civ. P. 12(b)(2) asserting the objection.

ANALYSIS. This question shouldn't detain us long. **A** is right. It is perfectly appropriate for the defendant to respond by answering the complaint, and to include in that answer any objections she has, including those listed in Rule 12(b). A responding party *never* has to make a pre-answer motion to raise these objections. **B**, which states that Trinh's objection must be raised in a pre-answer motion, is wrong. So is **D**, because a defendant does not waive any Rule 12(b) objections by failing to make a pre-answer motion. She would waive certain Rule 12(b) objections by making a pre-answer motion and leaving them out; but you don't forfeit any of these defenses by choosing to answer instead of moving to dismiss. **C** is also wrong, because it states that an objection to personal jurisdiction cannot be raised in the answer, that it must be asserted by motion. That's not true; it's fine to put personal jurisdiction objections, or other Rule 12(b) objections, in the answer to the complaint.

B. Rule 12(g): Limits on multiple pre-answer motions

The seven preliminary objections singled out in Rule 12(b) involve problems that might prevent the court from proceeding, or that need to be resolved at the outset of the case. Consequently, Rule 12 allows them to be raised immediately, and limits the defendant's ability to raise them later if they are *not* raised in a pre-answer motion or in the answer.

First, let's consider what happens if the defendant *does* make a pre-answer motion, and leaves some objections out of it. Contrary to popular belief, Rule 12(g) does not provide that Rule 12(b) objections are waived if the defendant makes a pre-answer motion and leaves one out. All it says is that, if a party makes a pre-answer motion, and leaves out a preliminary objection that could have been included in the motion (was "available" to the moving party), the party can't *make another pre-answer motion* based on the omitted objection. Rule 12(g)(2).

For example, suppose that Cox moves to dismiss under Rule 12(b)(3) for improper venue, and the judge denies the motion. Rule 12(g)(2) provides that he cannot file a second pre-answer motion to dismiss under Rule 12(b)(5) for insufficiency of service of process. Because he made a pre-answer motion based on one of these objections, and left out the insufficiency-of-service objection, Cox "must not make another motion under this rule raising a defense or objection" that was omitted from the first. Fed. R. Civ. P. 12(g). In other words, Cox, don't harass the plaintiff with successive motions, each delaying the proceedings. If you have multiple Rule 12(b) objections, put them all in the first motion, so the judge can deal with them together.

Note again that Rule 12(g) *doesn't say that an omitted objection is waived.* It only says that the defendant can't make another pre-answer motion based on it. It is Rule 12(h) that does the dirty work. Rule 12(h)(1)(A) provides that four of these preliminary objections — personal jurisdiction, venue, sufficiency of process, and sufficiency of service of process — are waived if the defendant makes a pre-answer motion and leaves them out of the motion. I call these the "four disfavored defenses," because the Rule pronounces them waived if they are not asserted in a timely manner. Failure to join a party under Rule 19, failure to state a claim upon which relief can be granted, and lack of subject matter jurisdiction, however, are treated differently. Under Rule 12(g)(2), they may not be raised by a second pre-answer motion, if they were available and left out of the first. However, they may be asserted later in the litigation. Rule 12(h)(2).

The following question illustrates the effect of Rule 12(g). It will help if you read Rule 12(g) carefully before you attempt it.

QUESTION 2. Dispelling the fog. McMahon brings an action, pro se (without counsel), against Advanced Fabricators, Inc., claiming "outrageous conduct in manufacturing inverse rototurnbuckles." Advanced, unable to discern the legal basis for the claim, moves for a more definite statement under Rule 12(e). The judge grants the motion, and McMahon (now represented by counsel) files a clearer complaint alleging that Advanced's product infringes on a patent McMahon holds on a similar device. Advanced responds to the amended complaint by filing a motion to dismiss under Rule 12(b)(3), arguing that under 28 U.S.C. §1400(b), the special venue provision for patent cases, venue is improper. Advanced's objection to venue

A. is waived under Rule 12(g)(2), because it was omitted from Advanced's first pre-answer motion.

B. is not waived under Rule 12(h)(1)(A), but Advanced cannot make a second pre-answer motion based on it.

> **C.** is not barred by Rule 12(g)(2). Advanced can make a second pre-answer motion based on it.
>
> **D.** is improper, because it cannot be made by pre-answer motion.

ANALYSIS. The key to this question is the subtle proviso in Rule 12(g)(2), that a party can't make a second pre-answer motion based on an objection that was "available to the party" when she made the first. The spirit of the rule is, "if you have several of these objections when you file your pre-answer motion, file a combined motion based on all of them." But the available-to-the-party phrase creates an exception: If you couldn't have asserted the objection in your first motion, you may file a second.

Here, when Advanced received the complaint, it couldn't understand the claim. It didn't know that it was being sued for patent infringement, so it couldn't know that the special venue statute for patent claims applied. Thus, the venue objection wasn't "available" to Advanced when it filed its first pre-answer motion, and it may therefore file a second on this ground. **C** is the winner here.

A is badly wrong. First it is wrong because it talks about an objection being "waived under Rule 12(g)." Rule 12(g)(2) doesn't say anything about waiving objections! It merely says that a party can't make a second *pre-answer motion* in certain circumstances. Second, it is wrong because Rule 12(g)(2) doesn't bar *all* repeat pre-answer motions, as the previous paragraph explains. It only bars a second pre-answer motion raising an objection that could have been included in the first.

B is wrong, because a defendant *can* make a second pre-answer motion to raise an objection unavailable when she made the first. And **D** is just pure filler: Under Rule 12(b) improper venue obviously is one of the objections that may be raised by pre-answer motion.

C. Driving students to distraction: Rule 12(g)(2) and waiver distinguished

There's an important difference between the effect of Rule 12(g)(2), which bars repeat pre-answer motions (usually), and Rule 12(h), which provides that the four disfavored defenses — personal jurisdiction, venue, sufficiency of process, and sufficiency of service of process — are waived if not raised in a timely manner. A defendant might be barred from raising an objection by a second pre-answer motion, although it could still be raised in the answer or later.

Here's an illustration of the point that has driven many of my students to distraction.

QUESTION 3. Repeat performance.   Tedeschi sues LaFleur for negligence, alleging that he suffered emotional distress from witnessing injury to a close friend in an accident with LaFleur. LaFleur responds by moving to dismiss under Rule 12(b)(3). After the court denies the motion, but before answering, LaFleur moves to dismiss under Rule 12(b)(6).

A. The motion is improper because LaFleur cannot make a second pre-answer motion under Rule 12 to assert a defense that was available when the first motion was made.

B. The motion is improper, because LaFleur's failure to assert his Rule 12(b)(6) motion in his first pre-answer motion waives the objection of failure to state a claim.

C. The motion is proper because the objection is not waived by making a motion on other grounds, and may be raised at any time.

D. The motion is proper because the motion to dismiss under Rule 12(b)(6) is not one of the four "disfavored defenses."

ANALYSIS.   This is a good question, because it requires careful parsing of the rule. If you understand the point of the rule you should get it right.

The point of Rule 12(g) is to force a defendant to file one consolidated pre-answer motion, asserting all available Rule 12 objections, if she files one at all. "If ya have 'em, use 'em." LaFleur didn't do that. He nickel-and-dimed the plaintiff with successive motions where he could have filed one, delaying the proceedings unnecessarily. Rule 12(g)(2) is meant to avert such conduct. It is true, as **D** suggests, that the Rule 12(b)(6) objection is not "disfavored." That is, it is not waived if left out of a pre-answer motion. But the question doesn't ask whether it is waived; it asks whether LaFleur *can raise it in a second pre-answer motion.* Although the Rule 12(b)(6) objection is not waived if left out of a pre-answer motion, a second pre-answer motion based on it may be barred under Rule 12(g)(2). And it is here; **A** is right, because LaFleur could have raised the failure-to-state-a-claim objection in his first pre-answer motion, but didn't. Rule 12(g)(2) says he can't make a second pre-answer motion based on it.

True, Rule 12(h)(2) says he can still raise it later. He can, which is why **B** is wrong. LaFleur does not lose the objection by leaving it out of the pre-answer motion. But he cannot make another pre-answer motion based on it. See Rule 12(g)(2). Thus, **C** is wrong. It's not quite true that the Rule 12(b)(6) objection may be raised at *any* time. While it may be raised later in the case, it may not be raised by another pre-answer motion.

That said, it seems likely that many judges would blink at this limit in Rule 12(g) and hear the motion anyway. If there really is no claim upon which relief can be granted, it seems a waste to require an answer or proceed further. So, while **C** is wrong under the Rule, I wouldn't be surprised if it reflected actual practice in some courts.

D.   Waiver under Rule 12(h)

Now let's consider the intricacies of Rule 12(h), which specifies the circumstances in which an objection is lost for failure to assert it in a prior response to the complaint. The two subparts of Rule 12(h)(1) address two distinct situations. Rule 12(h)(1)(A) applies where the defendant had made a pre-answer motion. It provides that, if the defendant left one of the four disfavored defenses out of that motion, she has waived that defense (assuming that the omitted objection was "available" to her when she made the first motion).

Rule 12(h)(1)(B) applies where no pre-answer motion was made. It provides that if the defendant answers, without including one of the disfavored defenses, that the omitted defense is waived as well (unless added by a motion to amend the answer as a matter of course under Rule 15(a)). The cumulative effect of these two subsections is that the defendant must include these defenses (once again, objections to personal jurisdiction, venue, sufficiency of process, and insufficient service of process) in her first response to the complaint — be it a pre-answer motion or an answer — or lose it.

To imprint these technicalities on your brain, keep in mind the reason for the rule: to force the defendant to bring up these defenses immediately, so that the court can consider and dispose of them.

Here's an easy question to illustrate the operation of Rule 12(h)(1).

> **QUESTION 4. Late, or never?**   Cain files a complaint against Able for breach of an implied contract. Able moves to dismiss the complaint under Rule 12(b)(6) for failure to state a claim upon which relief can be granted. The court denies the motion. Able then files an answer to the complaint, including in his answer the defense that venue is improper, and the defense that Cain gave him a written release of the claim as part of a previous settlement.
>
> **A.** Able has waived both defenses by failing to include them in his pre-answer motion.
> **B.** Able may include these defenses in his answer or an amendment allowed as of right under Rule 15(a).

> **C.** Able may assert the release defense in his answer and may include the venue defense in his answer because the Rule 12(b)(6) objection is not one of the "disfavored defenses."
> **D.** Able may include the release defense in his answer but has waived his objection to venue.

ANALYSIS.   The third choice here is demonic. It sounds quite credible. It's true that the Rule 12(b)(6) defense is not one of the disfavored defenses. If Able had left it out of a pre-answer motion, he could have asserted it in the answer anyway. Fed. R. Civ. P. 12(h)(2). But that's not what happened! Instead, Able left out the venue objection, and the question is whether he has waived that. He has, because he made a pre-answer motion, could have included the venue objection but didn't. Rule 12(h)(1)(A) says it's lost. So **C** isn't right, and neither is **B**.

How about the release defense? He left that out of his pre-answer motion too; has he waived that? No. This isn't one of the objections that can be raised by a pre-answer motion under Rule 12; it is an affirmative defense to the claim on the merits. So it could not properly have been raised in Able's pre-answer motion. Don't lose sight of the language at the beginning of Rule 12(b): "Every defense to a claim for relief . . . must be asserted in the responsive pleading if one is required [except for those that may be raised by pre-answer motion]." So he certainly hasn't waived his affirmative defense by failing to put it in a pre-answer motion. **A** is wrong. So **D** is the winner; Able waived the venue defense but may include the release defense in his answer . . . which is the only appropriate place for it.

E.   Waiver without a pre-answer motion

Rule 12 lays several traps for the unwary defendant. She may waive the disfavored defenses by filing a pre-answer motion and leaving some out. But she may also waive them by answering, without filing a pre-answer motion at all, and leaving them out. See Rule 12(h)(1)(B).

Consider whether Goliath has waived his objection in this example.

> **QUESTION 5. Among the missing.**   Goliath sues David for slander. David answers on the merits, denying that he made the offending statement. Six weeks later, he realizes that Goliath has filed suit in an improper venue.

> **A.** David should move to amend his answer to raise the defense of improper venue. Under Rule 15(a), the judge may grant the motion in her discretion.
> **B.** David may file a motion for judgment on the pleadings, claiming that venue is improper, since he did not raise any of the four disfavored defenses in either a pre-answer motion or his answer.
> **C.** David may file a motion to dismiss for improper venue, since he did not make a pre-answer motion.
> **D.** David has waived the defense of improper venue.

ANALYSIS.   In this example, David answered the complaint on the merits. He didn't raise any of the Rule 12(b) objections. If he had raised some of them in the answer and left others out, he would have waived the omitted objections. Rule 12(h)(1)(b), read very carefully, says that.

But he also waives the disfavored four if he answers the complaint and raises none of them. The point of the rule is that he must raise these defenses in his first response to the plaintiff's complaint, or lose them. His answer is a response to the complaint, and the disfavored four must be in there or are waived. **D** is the right choice.

The most distracting distractor is **A**. Suppose that David answers, raising none of the disfavored defenses, but later realizes that he should have asserted one. We all know that under the liberal federal rules, amendments are freely granted. Fed. R. Civ. P. 15(a). The idea is to allow cases to be decided on the merits, not on the basis of mistakes of counsel. So why not cure this mistake by amending the answer to add the venue objection?

If this worked it would undermine the goal of Rule 12, which is to determine at the outset whether these preliminary problems exist, and to dispose of them promptly. A party who had run afoul of the rule would simply amend later — perhaps months or years later — to add the omitted defense to the answer. (Of course, this would not work if the party had made a pre-answer motion and left the defense out.)

The rule-makers saw this one coming, and averted it by the language in Rule 12(h)(1)(B). That subsection provides that the defense is waived if it is omitted from "a responsive pleading or an amendment allowed by Rule 15(a)(1) as a matter of course." Under Rule 15(a)(1), an amendment as a matter of course (i.e., without leave of court) to a responsive pleading must be made within twenty-one days after serving it (if no further pleading is allowed). The clear implication of this reference is that an omitted defense may *only* be added by an amendment as of right. David's motion is too late, since the time for an amendment without leave of court has passed. Under Rule 12(h)(1)(B), he has waived his venue objection, and cannot revive it, even if the judge is willing to grant leave to amend to raise it.

F.   Raising Rule 12(b) objections after answering the complaint

We've dealt with the pre-answer motion and with putting Rule 12(b) objections in the answer. The third possibility is that a defendant would try to raise them after answering the complaint. Here's an example that illustrates this variation.

QUESTION 6. Now, or never?   Knauss brings an action against Vrabel for negligent misrepresentation. He alleges that Vrabel made negligent misrepresentations to him in connection with a sale of real estate, and seeks damages. Vrabel moves to dismiss for lack of personal jurisdiction. The motion is denied. Vrabel then answers, denying that he was negligent in his representations concerning the transaction.

Three months later, after researching the tort of negligent misrepresenta-tion, Vrabel's lawyer realizes that the tort requires reliance: A defendant is only liable if the plaintiff relied on the misrepresentation in entering into the transaction. Knauss's complaint does not allege reliance. Vrabel files a motion seeking dismissal of the complaint for failure to state a claim upon which relief can be granted.

A. Vrabel has not waived this objection. If the court agrees that the complaint fails to allege an essential element of misrepresentation, it will likely allow Knauss to file an amended complaint.

B. Vrabel has not waived this objection. If the court agrees that the complaint fails to allege an essential element of misrepresentation, it will likely dismiss the case.

C. Vrabel has waived this objection because he made a pre-answer motion under Rule 12(b) and left it out.

D. Because objections based on failure to state a claim may be raised in the answer, Vrabel should move to amend his answer under Rule 15(a).

ANALYSIS.   Rule 12(h)(2)(B) provides that the defense of failure to state a claim may be raised in a motion for judgment on the pleadings. A motion for judgment on the pleadings under Rule 12(c) asserts that, given what the plaintiff has pleaded, and the defenses raised in the answer, that the complaint fails as a matter of law. The motion is very commonly used as a way of challenging the legal sufficiency of the plaintiff's complaint—the same failure-to-state-a-claim challenge raised by a Rule 12(b)(6) motion before answering—after the answer. It is, basically, a delayed motion to dismiss for failure to state a claim.

Rule 12(h)(2) specifically allows this objection to the plaintiff's claim to be raised after answering the complaint. It is not waived, even if omitted from a pre-answer motion or the answer. The rationale for this is that it would be silly to take a case to trial where there's no legal remedy for the plaintiff's claim, just because the defendant didn't realize that until after answering the complaint. That would exalt procedure over substance, something the Rules seek to avoid.

So **C** is wrong; under Rule 12(h)(2), the objection is not waived. And **D** is wrong too. There is no need for Vrabel to amend the answer to assert the Rule 12(b)(6) objection, since it can be asserted in a motion for judgment on the pleadings. So Vrabel hasn't waived the failure-to-state-a-claim objection, and the court should consider it. But what should it do if it agrees with the objection? The real battle here is between **A** and **B**. Should the judge dismiss the case, or allow Knauss to replead?

No reasonable judge would dismiss a case simply because the complaint failed to include the reliance allegation, even if it is essential to recovery. That would *really* exalt procedure over substance. The judge would allow the plaintiff at least one opportunity to file an amended complaint setting forth the required allegations, if she can make such allegations consistent with Rule 11. If she can, then the case can go forward. If she can't allege reliance, because in fact she has no basis to claim reliance, then the case could be dismissed when that becomes clear. **A** is the best choice.

G.   Curable objections to process, service, and joinder of indispensable parties

As earlier sections point out, the Rules allow some pre-answer objections to be raised because they may obviate the need for the court to go any further with the case. If the court lacks subject matter jurisdiction, personal jurisdiction over the defendant, or is not a proper venue, the case will be dismissed, since the court lacks the authority to hear it. Several of the Rule 12(b) objections, however, are not necessarily fatal.

Consider how the judge should rule in the following case.

> **QUESTION 7. Procedural defects.** Hovenkamp sues Remoso in federal court for negligence arising out of an auto accident. He has the complaint delivered (without a summons) to Remoso's house, where the process server slips it under the door. Remoso moves to dismiss for insufficient service of process (claiming that Hovenkamp did not serve properly under Fed. R. Civ. P. 4(e)(2)), and for insufficient process, claiming

that Hovenkamp violated Rule 4(c)(1), since he did not serve the summons with the complaint. The judge should

A. deny the motion, because Remoso asserted two separate grounds for the motion.
B. deny the Rule 12(b)(5) motion, because service was proper under Fed. R. Civ. P. 4(e)(2).
C. order Hovenkamp to serve process again in compliance with the rules.
D. dismiss the case for lack of compliance with the Rule 4 requirements for proper service of process.

ANALYSIS.   In this example, Remoso files a pre-answer motion to dismiss based on defects in the process and in the method of service of process. Both of these objections may be raised by a pre-answer motion. See Rule 12(b)(4), Rule 12(b)(5). The question, however, is what the judge should do if she agrees with Remoso's objections.

A is clearly wrong. Nothing in Rule 12 suggests that Remoso must confine himself to one Rule 12(b) objection. In fact, the Rule says the opposite: "No defense or objection is waived by joining it with one or more other defenses or objections in a responsive pleading or in a motion." Rule 12(b), last sentence. A defendant may raise as many Rule 12(b) defenses as she has, either by motion or in her answer.

B fails as well. The method of service was not proper under Rule 4(e)(2), since the complaint was simply slipped under Hovenkamp's door; the rule requires that it be left with a person of suitable age and discretion who resides there.[1] So the real issue is, if the judge agrees that service was improper, should she dismiss the case, or order service to be made properly under the rules?

Clearly, good sense suggests that **C** is the proper answer. There is no reason to throw the case out simply because the defendant has not been properly notified. Remoso obviously found out about the suit — otherwise he wouldn't have moved to dismiss it. There is no reason to dismiss the case, forcing Hovenkamp to refile, pay a new filing fee, and risk statute of limitations problems. Proper service is a preliminary matter to be cleared up at the outset . . . that's why it is included among the Rule 12(b) objections that may be raised before answering. But it isn't a fatal defect; it's a housekeeping matter that needs to be taken care of before the suit proceeds.

Your humble author filed a pre-answer motion objecting to service of process in federal court once. The court scheduled the motion for a hearing, and the very experienced federal judge glared down at me from the bench and said, "Why don't you just go down to the clerk's office and accept

---

1. Service might be proper under Rule 4(e)(1), which allows service under state methods of service of process. But that's not one of the choices in the question.

process in the action, so we can get on with the business of the case?" What could I say, other than "O.K."? The defect is basically formal. It ought to be cleared up, but where notice has been given, it ought not delay the proceedings or lead to dismissal.

H.   Another double Closer: Rule 12 and the notorious "special appearance"

My students perennially confuse the special appearance with the objection to personal jurisdiction under Fed. R. Civ. P. 12(b)(2). That's understandable. In studying personal jurisdiction, we read common law cases in which the defendant "appears specially" to object to jurisdiction. Then we study pleadings and motions under the Federal Rules, and along comes a different approach to jurisdictional objections. It's easy enough to mix them up.

The special appearance was the common law's rather formalistic approach to raising objections to personal jurisdiction. A defendant who claimed that the court in which suit was filed lacked jurisdiction over her would "appear specially" to contest the court's jurisdiction. The defendant making a special appearance had to do so before answering the complaint on the merits, and she had to confine her argument to the lack of jurisdiction. If she raised any other issue, the court would hold that she had entered a "general appearance" by litigating issues other than jurisdiction. Any reference to the merits, or even to other types of preliminary objections, could lead the court to conclude that, by appearing to litigate other issues, the defendant had submitted to the jurisdiction of the court and waived her objection to personal jurisdiction.

In the federal courts, and in the many states that have modeled their procedural rules after the Federal Rules of Civil Procedure, objections to personal jurisdiction are governed by Rule 12. The common law special appearance *does not apply.* But Rule 12 bears some resemblance to its common law ancestor. It still requires that the objection be asserted in the first response to the complaint, either a pre-answer motion or answer. And it still provides that the objection is waived if it isn't raised in a timely manner. The major difference, however, is that a defendant who moves to dismiss in federal court under Rule 12 for lack of jurisdiction may, in the same motion, assert other pre-answer defenses. She could, for example, move to dismiss for lack of personal jurisdiction and for failure to join an indispensable party. If she raised those two objections in a jurisdiction that adheres to the older special appearance approach, she would be deemed to waive her objection to personal jurisdiction by also raising an issue that is presumably only relevant if the court *has* jurisdiction.

Here are two examples to help sort these matters out. They both involve cases removed to federal court. Keep in mind that in a removed case, state procedure applies until removal. Federal procedure applies once the case has been removed to federal court. Fed. R. Civ. P. 81(c)(1).

QUESTION 8. Something special. Goloupolos sues Hue in state court, in a state that uses the special appearance approach to objections to personal jurisdiction. Hue responds by filing an objection in the state court to personal jurisdiction, and a motion to dismiss the case for failure to state a claim. Five days later, before the court rules on his objections, he removes the action to federal court. After removal, he moves to dismiss, on the ground that the court lacks personal jurisdiction over him. Goloupolos argues that the defense has been waived. The court will probably rule that Hue

A. has waived the objection to personal jurisdiction, because he invoked the federal court's jurisdiction by removing the case.
B. has waived the objection to personal jurisdiction, because his state court response constituted a general appearance.
C. has not waived the objection to personal jurisdiction, since under Federal Rule 12 it can be combined with other objections in an answer.
D. has not waived the personal jurisdiction objection, because under Federal Rule 12(b) these two defenses may be asserted together in a pre-answer motion.

ANALYSIS. Let's deal first with a *major* source of confusion illustrated by **A**. A defendant does not waive objections to personal jurisdiction by removing a case to federal court. When sued in a state court, the defendant has only thirty days to remove. He can't wait for the state court to rule on an objection to personal jurisdiction, and then remove if he loses on it. He has to remove right away, before the issue is likely to be decided by the state court. Suppose the defendant reasons as follows: "I think the Utah court lacks personal jurisdiction over me for this claim. I'd like to get the case dismissed on that ground. But if the court doesn't agree that it lacks jurisdiction, I'd rather litigate this case in federal court." If this is the defendant's thinking, he has to remove, doesn't he, since the state court is unlikely to rule on the personal jurisdiction question in the first thirty days? It would be a tough rule that tells this defendant: "remove if you like, but if you do you are consenting to suit in this state."

The rules don't put a defendant to this choice, because he does not waive his objection to personal jurisdiction in Utah by removing; he simply changes the court in which the question will be decided. After removal, the

Utah federal court, instead of the state court, will decide whether the defendant is subject to jurisdiction in Utah. So **A** is wrong.

C is another loser. It suggests that the objection is still valid because under federal procedure it can be asserted in the answer. But *state* procedure applies until removal, and under this state's procedure (the example indicates) you waive your objection by appearing in the action and failing to confine your objection to the lack of personal jurisdiction. And that's what Hue did here. He appeared, in a state that uses the special appearance approach to jurisdictional objections, and raised a defense of failure to state a claim along with his objection to personal jurisdiction. Big mistake! In states that adhere to the traditional special appearance approach, this constitutes a general appearance and waives the objection to jurisdiction.

So **B** is probably right. Hue waived the objection before removing. Since the objection was waived before removal, it can't be revived by removal. It makes no difference that he could have raised both defenses together in federal court (**D**). He certainly could have done that, if he had responded in federal court under Rule 12. But he didn't respond in federal court; he responded in state court, and state procedure applies until the case is removed.

A caveat is in order here. I've had some battles with a colleague over this one. He argues that the objection is not waived, since no decision was made in state court before removal that Hue had waived his objection. In his view, when the motion is renewed in federal court, the federal court should apply federal standards. Send me your thoughts.

––––––––––––––––––––

Here's another question to clarify the point.

––––––––––––––––––––

QUESTION 9. Removing the objections.   Goloupolos sues Hue in state court, in a state that uses the special appearance approach to objections to personal jurisdiction. Ten days later, before an answer is due in the state court, Hue removes the case to federal court. After removing, Hue answers the complaint, responding on the merits to the allegations in the complaint and also raising the objection that the court lacks personal jurisdiction over him and that the complaint fails to state a claim upon which relief can be granted.

A. Hue has waived his objection to personal jurisdiction, because he did not include it in his first response to the complaint, the notice of removal.

B. Hue has waived his objection to personal jurisdiction, because he answered on the merits as well as raising the two Rule 12(b) objections in his answer.

> **C.** Hue's objection to personal jurisdiction is properly raised in his answer.
> **D.** Hue's objection to personal jurisdiction is waived, because the state court from which it was removed applies the special appearance rule.

ANALYSIS. A illustrates a common confusion about the relation between Rule 12 and removal. Rule 12 requires that the four "disfavored defenses" must be raised in the first response to the complaint, either the pre-answer motion or, if none is made, the answer. But suppose the defendant's first response to the complaint is to remove it to federal court? Does he waive the right to raise these defenses?

No, no, no, no . . . NO! Removal does not affect the right to raise these objections; it only changes the forum in which they will be raised. While Rule 12 requires these objections to be asserted in the defendant's first response to the complaint, a notice of removal is not a response to the complaint, in the sense that an answer is, or a motion to dismiss. It's a response to the case itself, moving it to another court system. Nor does the language of Rule 12 state that removal waives these objections. Rule 12(h)(1) says these defenses are waived if they are left out of a pre-answer motion, or out of the answer (when no pre-answer motion is made). There's no mention of waiving them by removal.

In the example, Hue hasn't done anything that would waive his objection to personal jurisdiction. Under the Federal Rules, putting the objection in the answer along with the failure-to-state-a-claim objection doesn't waive it. A defendant who chooses to answer instead of moving to dismiss in federal court must put all of his defenses in the answer, and he can raise as many as he has in that answer. He could put all seven of the Rule 12(b) defenses in there if he likes; he doesn't have to choose one over another. So **B** is wrong.

Nor is **D** correct. Hue has not waived his objection by failing to make a special appearance in the state court before removing. Removal must be done within thirty days, but can be done either before or after answering. Since Hue never responded in state court, he didn't make a general appearance. Instead, he bumped the case into the federal court system. Since he did not do anything that would waive his objection in state court, and his case is now in federal court, federal law governs the manner in which he must raise that objection. Fed. R. Civ. P. 12(b) says he may raise it in the answer. So what he did is fine, and **C** is the right stuff.

Glannon's Picks

1.	Answers and objections	A
2.	Dispelling the fog	C
3.	Repeat performance	A
4.	Late, or never?	D
5.	Among the missing	D
6.	Now, or never?	A
7.	Procedural defects	C
8.	Something special	B
9.	Removing the objections	C

Probing to the Limits:
The Scope of Discovery
Under the Federal Rules

The judge ruled Jack's claim was pure puffery
That didn't state any ground for recovery.
Jack said, "Judge, please don't nix it,
I know I can fix it,
If you just give me a shot at discovery."

CHAPTER OVERVIEW
A. Rule 26(b)(1): The scope of discovery
B. The court's role in limiting discovery: Relevance and burden
C. Another limit: Objections based on privilege
D. Another exception: The meaning of "work product"
E. The Closer: *Hickman* and the limits of Rule 26(b)(3)
◈ Glannon's Picks

Discovery is the process of compelled exchange of information between parties to a law suit. Under the federal discovery rules (Fed. R. Civ. P. 26-37), parties may use six devices—automatic disclosure, requests for production of documents, interrogatories, depositions, requests for admissions, and physical or mental examinations—to obtain information about the case from other parties, and in some cases from nonparty witnesses as well. The Federal Rules not only create these discovery devices; they require the parties to respond to requests for information made through them. Discovery, no matter how intrusive, is mandatory. The parties may object to burdensome or inappropriate discovery requests, and the court may limit discovery, but the parties must still respond to requests for discovery by producing a wide range of information about their claims and defenses in the action.

A.   Rule 26(b)(1): The scope of discovery

A good place to start is with the basic question of the scope of discovery, that is, what issues the parties may inquire about through the discovery process. The answer is in Fed. R. Civ. P. 26(b)(1), which governs the scope of discovery through each of the discovery devices. Whether information is sought through a deposition, an interrogatory, or production of documents, the Rule 26(b)(1) standard applies.

> **Discovery Scope in General**. Unless otherwise limited by court order, the scope of discovery is as follows: Parties may obtain discovery regarding any nonprivileged matter that is relevant to any party's claim or defense — including the existence, description, nature, custody, condition and location of any documents or other tangible things and the identity and location of persons who know of any discoverable matter. . . .

As broad as this limit on discovery may seem, it used to be broader. Prior to an amendment in 2000, Rule 26(b)(1) allowed discovery of "any matter, not privileged, relevant to the subject matter involved in the pending action." In an effort to rein in discovery, the relevant-to-the claim-or-defense-of-any-party language was substituted. Thus, some information relevant to "the subject matter of the pending action," but not relevant to any claim or defense asserted by a party in that action, was discoverable before 2000 and now is not. But the standard is still remarkably broad. And if a party demonstrates a need for broader discovery, the court may expand discovery to the parameters allowed under the prior rule, any matter relevant to the subject matter of the action. Fed. R. Civ. P. 26(b)(1), second sentence.

Rule 26(b)(1) expressly provides that information is *discoverable* even though it isn't admissible as evidence at a trial. "Relevant information need not be admissible at the trial if the discovery appears reasonably calculated to lead to the discovery of admissible evidence." For example, statements that are "hearsay," that is, statements made by one person concerning statements by another, are not generally admissible at trial. If Smith says he heard Jones say that Chen ran the red light, that statement is hearsay. Unless a hearsay exception applies, Smith cannot testify to that at trial, at least if Chen can be brought into court to testify himself. But the information would be subject to discovery, if it is relevant to a claim or defense in the action.

Here's a first question on the scope of discovery under Rule 26(b)(1).

QUESTION 1. Time past and time future.   Karim sues Precision Machine Company after she suffers a serious injury to her hand using a stamping machine manufactured by Precision. Her suit is brought after the statute of limitations on a strict products liability claim has expired, so her complaint alleges negligence by Precision in the design of the machine. Karim's counsel sends an interrogatory to Precision asking whether, at any time between the accident and the present, it has added a safety guard to the machine that injured Karim (which it has).

Under the relevant rules of evidence, evidence of such "subsequent remedial measures" is not admissible in an action to establish that the defendant was negligent in failing to take a similar precaution before the plaintiff's injury. The purpose of this rule of evidence is to encourage defendants to eliminate unsafe conditions, without fear that such safety measures will be introduced at trial to establish liability for not taking those measures before. The information sought in the interrogatory

A. is not within the scope of discovery, because evidence of subsequent remedial repairs is inadmissible at trial under the relevant rules of evidence.

B. is not within the scope of discovery, because it concerns events taking place after Karim's injury, and is thus irrelevant to her claim in the action.

C. would be within the scope of discovery under the earlier standard in Fed. R. Civ. P. 26(b)(1), but is not subject to discovery under the 2000 amendment to that rule.

D. is within the scope of discovery under the current standard in Fed. R. Civ. P. 26(b)(1).

ANALYSIS.   **A** is pretty much a throwaway. Rule 26(b)(1) explicitly provides that information is discoverable, even if it could not be used at trial, if it meets the broad relevance standard in the rule. The idea is that information might assist a party in developing her case, even though it could not be presented at trial. This is manifestly true in many cases. For example, the hearsay statement "I heard Smith say that a Federal Express delivery man drove away after the accident" might be inadmissible hearsay. But this information could clearly assist the plaintiff in finding an important witness. Similarly, in an assault case, evidence that a witness had heard of instances of violence by the defendant would likely be inadmissible hearsay, yet could lead to the discovery of evidence of violent conduct that could be used to impeach the defendant's testimony about who started a fight.

B rests on the assumption that events taking place after a claim arises are irrelevant to the issues in a law suit. However, such evidence frequently leads to admissible evidence relevant to the plaintiff's claim. For example, in the assault case, evidence of later assaults by a defendant would be relevant to impeach him if he testifies that the plaintiff started the quarrel. Evidence that a company consistently promoted men over women — before and after the plaintiff was passed over — would assist a sex discrimination plaintiff to show a pattern of discriminatory conduct. Evidence that a company had disciplined an employee after the date of an accident might assist the plaintiff in discovering that the employee had a long record of accidents before the one that injured her.

Here, evidence that the company made its stamping machine safer after the accident is certainly relevant to the case. It suggests that the machine *can* be made safer, which may mean that they were aware of that before Karim's accident but decided, for whatever reason, not to improve it. If Karim's counsel discovers that they have added a guard, she can take depositions of Precision's engineers, to determine when they developed the design for the guard, and why it was not added before. This could lead to evidence suggesting that Precision was negligent, because it was aware of the need for the guard but delayed introducing it. Surely, this information is not only "relevant to the subject matter in the action" (the Rule 26(b)(1) standard before the 2000 amendment), but also "relevant to the claim" of a party (the current standard in Rule 26(b)(1)). It is relevant to Karim's claim that Precision negligently failed to act with reasonable care in designing the stamping machine. Thus, **C** fails; **D** is the best answer.

Because the standard for relevance in Rule 26(b)(1), as amended in 2000, is tied to the claims and defenses in the case, the parties' pleadings play an important role in determining the scope of discovery. By raising issues in the pleadings, the parties lay themselves open to discovery on issues which otherwise might remain free from inquiry. Prior to the amendment, the pleadings were less central to the scope of discovery, since any information relevant to "the subject matter of the action," rather than the "claims or defenses" raised by the parties was subject to discovery.

In the following question, consider whether the information sought is relevant to the claims and defenses of the parties.

QUESTION 2. Issues and answers. Apex Health Care, a health care corporation, terminates the admitting privileges of Sanchetti, a surgeon at Medway General Hospital. Sanchetti sues Apex in federal court, claiming that her privileges were terminated based on sex discrimination. She claims that she has been unable to find an equivalent position, and has lost income as a result of the termination. In its answer, Apex denies that it discriminated against Sanchetti, claiming that the termination was based on poor patient care instead. It also denies that she has lost income as a result of the dismissal.

Which of the following is least likely to be subject to discovery under Rule 26(b)(1)?

A. Apex requests Sanchetti's tax returns for the three years before and the three years since her termination.

B. Apex requests a copy of a letter Sanchetti sent to other staff doctors, complaining about medical staff salaries, and suggesting a job action to force improvements.

C. Sanchetti requests detailed information on the computer operating system and access methods for Apex's files on patient treatment.

D. Sanchetti seeks the names and addresses of all doctors and nurses at Medway General who have been disciplined over the last seven years.

ANALYSIS. When parties send requests for discovery, they don't include a citation or an argument as to why the requested material is within the scope of discovery under Rule 26(b)(1).[1] The party receiving the discovery request will have to assess independently whether the requested information is relevant to a claim or defense in the case, and object if she concludes that the information is not relevant. Of course, there's nothing to prevent Apex's counsel from giving Sanchetti's counsel a call to ask why she thinks she is entitled to information that seems beyond the scope of discovery. That would frequently be the sensible thing to do. Compare Fed. R. Civ. P. 37(a)(1) (party seeking to compel discovery must certify that she has conferred with the opposing party to resolve the issue before moving to compel discovery).

So let's consider why the various items here might be discoverable, starting with **A.** Sanchetti's tax returns should be discoverable. She has placed her income in issue by claiming that she has lost income as a result of the termination of her admitting privileges. Consequently, her income is relevant to an issue in the case, and should be subject to discovery, even though this is otherwise confidential information. Sanchetti may regard this as intrusive. It is. That's one of the prices she must pay to litigate this claim, under the broad access to information authorized by the federal discovery rules. She might convince the court to limit production to records of her *earned* income (since that is what she claims was affected by the defendant's conduct), but income information is going to be discoverable.

---

1. Would it make sense to amend Rule 26(b)(1) to require the requesting party to do that? Perhaps not. It might eliminate some disputes over relevance, but probably, for the vast majority of discovery requests, there is little doubt that the material is relevant, given the breadth of the standard. So it would make a lot of unnecessary work for lawyers, and expense for clients.

The information sought in **C** is also relevant under Rule 26(b)(1). The rule allows discovery of the "existence, description, nature, custody, condition and location of any books, documents or other tangible things . . ." that may contain relevant information. This is broad enough to include the computer systems used for storage of relevant records. Here, at least some patient treatment records—those concerning Sanchetti's patients—are placed in issue by Apex's defense that Sanchetti's privileges were terminated due to poor patient care. And information about the "nature" of those records—how they are kept and how to access them—should be discoverable.

The information sought in **D**, concerning disciplinary actions at Medway, is also likely discoverable, even though Sanchetti has sought disciplinary files on nurses as well as doctors. It would certainly assist Sanchetti in establishing sex discrimination if she learned that Apex had frequently disciplined or discharged women but not men. Such evidence could assist Sanchetti in unearthing discriminatory actions or statements by Apex administrators that would demonstrate a policy of sex discrimination.

B is the most doubtful item under the narrower standard in Rule 26(b)(1), as amended by the 2000 amendment. This letter might be "relevant to the subject matter of the action"—Sanchetti's termination. Perhaps Apex really fired her because she was fomenting discontent among the staff. The letter would surely be relevant to that defense. But under the current standard in Rule 26(b)(1) the information must relate to the claims and defenses the parties *have* pleaded. It is at least questionable whether this letter has any relevance to Sanchetti's claim that her privileges were terminated based on her sex, or to Apex's defense that it was based on poor patient care. I choose **B**.

This suggests that the change in the relevance standard has enhanced the importance of pleading in federal cases. Had Apex pleaded its defense more generally, say, by a simple denial that it fired her based on her sex, it might have a right to broader discovery. If it simply denied the allegation of sex discrimination, it would arguably be asserting that it fired her for *some other reason*. This would presumably make other reasons for her termination relevant. By specifying poor patient care as the reason for termination in its answer, Apex has arguably limited its discovery to information relevant to that "defense."

B. The court's role in limiting discovery: Relevance and burden

One problem with the relevance standard is that it is a matter of degree. "The boundaries defining information that is relevant to the subject matter involved in the action are necessarily vague and it is practically impossible to state a general rule by which they can be drawn." Wright & Miller §2008. Some information may be urgently relevant, some pretty relevant, and some marginally relevant, but still arguably useful in preparing a case. Without a bright-line test, there is a great deal of room for disagreement between the parties.

For example, if an accident victim claims chronic back pain, his medical treatment by a back surgeon, or a chiropractor, is certainly relevant. His records of treatment by an internist probably are as well, since they may suggest other reasons for his condition. The defendant might seek discovery of the plaintiff's psychiatric records as well, on the theory that the pain may be psychosomatic rather than a result of the accident. One could even make an argument for access to the plaintiff's last five years of performance reviews at work, on the theory that job stress is the real source of his trouble. Relevance is not a yes/no proposition, but a slippery slope.

Partly because of this ambiguity in the standard, Rule 26(b)(1) authorizes the court to restrict access to information even if it is relevant: Under the rule, discovery extends to relevant information "unless otherwise limited by order of the court." Thus, the broad relevant-to-claims-or-defenses standard makes material *presumptively* discoverable, but the court has discretion to limit discovery for various reasons. For example, under Fed. R. Civ. P. 26(b)(2)(C), the court may limit discovery because it is cumulative, of marginal relevance, obtainable in another way, or if the burden of production outweighs the likely value of the information, in light of various practical realities about the case. And these bases for restricting discovery are not exhaustive. For example, the court may also restrict discovery of information that would be unduly intrusive on the privacy of a party, or that is sought for an improper purpose such as harassment of an opposing party.

Because the relevance limit is vague, and cogent arguments can frequently be made for protecting relevant information from discovery, much is left to negotiation between counsel for the parties. If they cannot agree on the information to be produced, the party making the discovery request may move to compel production of the information, on the ground that she is entitled to it under the Rule. However, Fed. R. Civ. P. 37(a)(1) requires the moving party to certify that she has conferred with the objecting party, in an effort to resolve the discovery dispute without involving the court.

Conversely, the party opposing production of information may take the initiative, by moving for a protective order under Rule 26(c), barring production of the disputed information. The judge presiding over the case will then have to decide what must be produced. If she orders production of the information, she may also impose conditions to protect confidentiality of information, to avoid intimidation, or to limit the burden of responding. See Fed. R. Civ. P. 26(b)(1). Generally, the model is one of broad presumptive access to information, constrained (ideally) by the common sense of counsel, and discretionary limits imposed by the judge where they are not negotiated by the parties.

QUESTION 3. Relevance and discretion. In which of the following cases is the requested discovery *least* likely to be ordered by the court?

A. *P* brings an action against *D* alleging that she contracted a sexually transmitted disease from him. *D* asks *P* an interrogatory seeking the names of all other sexual partners *P* had during the six-month period when she must have contracted the disease. *P* resists on the basis the request unduly intrudes on her privacy.

B. *P* sues *D*, who has only $10,000 in auto liability insurance, for $100,000. *P* seeks discovery of *D's* financial assets, in order to determine whether it is worth prosecuting the action to judgment. *D* resists on the ground that the information is not within the scope of discovery under Rule 26(b)(1).

C. *P* sues *D*, claiming that it discharged her in violation of her contract, to save money, because she was making more money than *D's* other managers. She seeks discovery of the salaries of all other managers in the company. *D* resists on ground that the information is confidential and will invade the privacy of the other managers.

D. *P* brings a products liability action against *D*, a car manufacturer, based on failure of the brakes on a 1998 van made by *D*. *P* seeks all reports from dealers concerning brake problems on vans of that model sold between 1994 and 1998. *D* resists the request on the ground that it is too burdensome because complaints are not segregated by the type of complaint, and it sold 125,000 vans of that model during the requested period.

E. *P*, a prisoner, sues the Department of Corrections for deprivation of his constitutional rights under the First Amendment, claiming the Department promulgated a policy requiring prisoners to shave their beards. *P* argues that the policy is based on hostility to his religion, which requires him to wear a beard. *P* suffered no monetary damages, but seeks nominal damages of $1 and an injunction ordering the warden to change the policy. *P* seeks all written complaints by prisoners at his facility over a five-year period that assert the deprivation of rights of religious expression. *D* resists production on the ground that it is too burdensome in light of the monetary value of the case.

ANALYSIS. As indicated before, a good multiple-choice question should have one clearly superior answer. Questions that involve matters of degree (as here, "least likely" to be discoverable) are chancy, because they involve close exercises of judgment. But the important points about the scope of discovery *are* frequently matters of degree rather than black and white.

E is a very weak answer. It suggests that little effort should be invested in discovery, because the plaintiff is only seeking nominal damages. While Rule 26(b)(2)(C) allows the court to limit discovery where the expense of discovery outweighs the benefits, and the amount in controversy is a relevant factor under Rule 26(b)(2)(C), the rule itself refers to the "importance of the issues at stake in the litigation." Here, the plaintiff is seeking something much more important than money — vindication of a constitutional right through an injunction requiring the defendant to allow a form of religious expression. The case challenges a systemic practice, and the requested discovery seeks information about that practice. It will very likely be allowed.

The discovery sought in **D** is also likely to be allowed. Information concerning complaints about other vans with the same brakes would be extremely useful to the plaintiff in making her case. It would establish that the defendant was on notice of the problem with the brakes, suggesting that it was negligent for failing to redesign them. Finding those complaints may be burdensome, but should be possible. In addition, the rules authorize the defendant to cast that burden on the plaintiff, by producing the records as kept in the course of business. Fed. R. Civ. P. 34(b)(2)(E). The four-year period and limit to models using the disputed brakes are also reasonable. Consequently, the court will very likely allow this discovery.

The information about other managers' salaries requested in **C** will also likely be allowed. *P* has alleged that she was dismissed because of her high salary relative to the other managers, so the information is relevant to her claim. It may reveal confidential information, but the court should be able to limit the intrusion in several ways. It might, for example, order production without the other managers' names. Or, it might enter a confidentiality order barring any party from revealing the information beyond its use in the litigation.

If the salary information in **C** invades privacy, the request in **A** *really* requests intimate information. Yet it will likely be allowed. *P* has placed her sexual relations in issue by suing *D* for causing the disease. Information that *P* had relations with two other partners with the disease during the relevant period would certainly be relevant to disprove those allegations. This evidence is central to the issue in the case, yet only accessible from the plaintiff. As private as it is, the court is likely to allow the discovery, though it would almost certainly impose strict limits on its use.

B is the least likely to be granted. While the information is very important to *P*, indeed, in a sense, life or death to the case, it is not relevant to a claim or defense in the action, only to whether there's a pot of gold at the end of the lawsuit to make it worth proving the claim. Most courts have denied discovery of a defendant's assets in these circumstances, though they have allowed such discovery where punitive damages are sought. See *Moore's*

Federal Practice §26.41[8]. Ironically, the Rules now require disclosure of insurance that may cover a claim (Fed. R. Civ. P. 26(a)(1)(A)(iv)), but do not authorize this kind of inquiry into the defendant's assets.

C.   Another limit: Objections based on privilege

Although discovery usually extends to all evidence relevant to claims and defenses in the action, Rule 26(b)(1) expressly carves out one limit on this: "Parties may obtain discovery regarding any nonprivileged matter...." Thus, a privilege bars production of information even though it is relevant to issues in the case.

The term "privilege" in the context of litigation refers to information that is protected from disclosure under the rules of evidence. The decision to recognize a privilege represents a policy judgment that maintaining the confidentiality of certain communications is so important that society is willing to sacrifice the evidentiary value of those communications to preserve that confidentiality. There are lots of privileges out there, some recognized by all states, some by most, some by a few.[2] The best known are probably the attorney-client privilege and the constitutionally based privilege against self-incrimination. For a discussion of these and other privileges, such as the physician/patient privilege, priest/penitent privilege, psychotherapist privilege, and others more arcane, see *Moore's Federal Practice* §26.48ff.

If information is privileged, the party holding the privilege may refuse to testify about that communication, either in discovery or at a trial. The very meaning of privilege in this context is that the information need not be disclosed at all; obviously this purpose would be undermined if privileged information could be demanded through discovery.

However, the existence of a privilege does not protect *factual* information simply because it was communicated in a privileged conversation. "The privilege only protects from disclosure of communications; it does not protect disclosure of the underlying facts by those who communicate with the attorney." *Upjohn Co. v. United States*, 449 U.S. 383, 395 (1981). Suppose, for example, that Mavroules admits to his priest in a counseling session that he felt guilty, because he knew his brakes were malfunctioning before a recent accident. If Mavroules were sued by the accident victim, and asked to answer an interrogatory concerning the condition of the brakes, he could not refuse to answer, even if the jurisdiction recognizes a priest/penitent privilege. The privilege protects the *communication itself*. Here, if Mavroules were asked

---

2. Generally, the existence of a privilege is a matter of state law, even in federal court, in cases governed by state law. However, in federal question cases, federal common law governs. See generally Fed. R. Evid. 501.

whether he had told his priest that he knew his brakes were malfunctioning, he could refuse to answer if the jurisdiction recognizes a priest/penitent privilege. But the privilege does not protect facts about the litigation events themselves, simply because they were the subject of a privileged communication.

If talking about the facts of a case in a privileged conversation would shield those facts from discovery, clients in litigation would be very forthcoming with their counsel: they would immediately tell their counsel everything about the case, bringing everything they know about the case within the scope of the attorney-client privilege. Of course, this would eviscerate the discovery system. Nor is a privilege this broad necessary to serve the public policy goal of encouraging the protected communication. Protecting the communication itself suffices to further that policy. Thus, the privilege does not protect the underlying facts, or even the fact that a party has consulted counsel; only the content of the discussions between counsel and client is protected.

Consider the application of the attorney-client privilege in the following troubling example.

> **QUESTION 4. Confidential chat.** Shag, a budding rock star with no business experience, enters into a five-year exclusive contract with Fringe Records, after recording his first album with them. The album turns out to be a smash hit, and Big Money Records offers him a contract at fifteen times the paltry income called for by his contract with Fringe.
>
> Shag contacts Rivera, a lawyer, for advice. He asks Rivera if their discussion is confidential, and Rivera assures him that it is. Shag then explains the situation, and indicates that he plans to repudiate the Fringe contract, on the ground that Fringe had misrepresented the terms of the contract. Rivera asks what the misrepresentation was, and Shag admits that there wasn't any. He admits that Jewell, Fringe's vice president, told him that the agreement was binding for five years, but that he will testify that Jewell told him it was terminable by either party at will. Rivera advises him that the contract is binding, and that he will be liable for damages if he reneges on the Fringe contract.
>
> Shag does back out, signs with Big Money, and is sued by Fringe for damages, including punitive damages for deliberately repudiating the contract. Fringe sends interrogatories to Shag (now represented by new counsel) asking (1) whether he consulted a lawyer before repudiating the contract, (2) whether he ignored his lawyer's advice when he repudiated the contract, and (3) whether Jewell told him, when he signed the Fringe contract, that it bound him to perform exclusively for Fringe for five years.

A. Shag will have to answer all three interrogatories, because they are all relevant to Fringe's claim that he deliberately repudiated the contract, which would support punitive damages liability.

B. Shag will have to answer the first interrogatory, but not the other two.

C. Shag will have to answer the first and second interrogatories, but not the third.

D. Shag will not have to answer any of the interrogatories, because all three were discussed in confidence with Rivera in the course of his representation.

E. None of the above is accurate.

ANALYSIS. Let's start by eliminating **A**. It proceeds on the premise that all three items are subject to discovery, because all three are relevant to a claim in the action. If Shag contacted a lawyer, was advised that he was bound by the Fringe contract, and ignored it, that's a deliberate breach that would bolster Fringe's argument for punitive damages. It's true that all three items are relevant, but that doesn't mean they are all subject to discovery. Under Rule 26(b)(1), all relevant information is not discoverable. That rule contains an express exception for privileged communications, *even if relevant.* Thus, a privilege bars production of information even though it is relevant. (The privilege would not be of much use if it only protected irrelevant privileged communications from disclosure!) So it is no answer to a claim of privilege that the information sought is relevant to issues in the case.

D, which asserts that Shag may refuse to answer all three interrogatories, fails as well. There is no general privilege to refuse to answer discovery responses simply because you have discussed the case with counsel "in confidence." As noted above, the privilege is limited to the substance of communications with counsel; the first and third interrogatories here don't call for such communications.

B states that Shag will have to answer the first interrogatory. That is true. The cases have held that the attorney-client privilege protects the content of attorney-client communications, but not the fact that a lawyer was consulted. See, e.g., *Howell v. Jones*, 516 F.2d 53 (5th Cir. 1975), *cert. denied*, 424 U.S. 116 (1976). But **B** still isn't the right answer, because it states that Shag won't have to answer either of the other two interrogatories. Shag will have to answer the third interrogatory. It calls for Shag's personal knowledge about his discussions with Jewell. Although Shag described that conversation to Rivera, that does not provide any privilege for facts within Shag's personal knowledge.

Shag may be upset when his new counsel tells him that he has to answer the third interrogatory. Shag thought he spoke to Rivera in confidence, and probably thought that whatever he told Rivera would be protected from disclosure. Not quite. The fact that he and Rivera discussed the negotiations is protected by the attorney-client privilege. Suppose that Fringe asked Shag, "Did you tell your lawyer that Jewell told you the contract was exclusive for five years?" Shag could refuse to answer, because that question calls for the substance of the communication between Shag and Rivera. But if he is asked, "Did Jewell tell you that the contract was exclusive for five years?" he has to answer that, whether he discussed it with Rivera or not. And, if he decides to bend the facts and answer "No," his new counsel (if aware of the true facts) will have to tell him he can't be a party to untruthful discovery responses, since that would perpetrate a fraud on the court. See, e.g., ABA Model Rules of Professional Conduct, Rule 3.3(a)(3) (lawyer may not offer evidence the lawyer knows to be false). Thus, the limits of the attorney-client privilege can lead to awkward problems between client and counsel.

C states that Shag must answer the first interrogatory about consulting a lawyer and the second, which asks whether he ignored advice of counsel in repudiating the contract. This isn't right either, because the second interrogatory asks for privileged information. There's no way he could respond to the second interrogatory without revealing the substance of the advice Rivera had given him. This is a lawyer/client communication protected by the privilege.

So **E**, that nasty none-of-the-above, takes the prize.

Administering discovery objections based on privilege can be problematic. The very point of the privilege is to protect the communication from revelation. Yet how can a requesting party evaluate claims that an item is privileged without knowing the content of the document or conversation? Rule 26(b)(5) attempts to deal with this problem by requiring parties who object to production of information based on privilege to provide enough detail about the protected material to allow the requesting party to evaluate the privilege objection. The party claiming a privilege must

(1) expressly make the claim; and
(2) describe the nature of the documents, communications, or tangible things not produced or disclosed — and do so in a manner that, without revealing information itself privileged or protected, will enable other parties to assess the claim.

Fed. R. Civ. P. 26(b)(5)(A).

This provision is meant to facilitate assessment of claims of privilege, by requiring the objecting party to provide sufficient information to allow the requesting party to determine whether a privilege applies to it, or at least whether the issue is sufficiently doubtful to justify moving to compel production of the information. If the applicability of the privilege is challenged, the court can decide whether it is privileged based on the information required under Rule 26(b)(5)(A). In doubtful cases, the court can review documents in camera (privately, rather than in open court) to determine whether the privilege applies. If it does not, of course, discovery will be ordered.

Consider the appropriate response to the requested discovery in the following question.

QUESTION 5. Tricks of the trade. Loman, a salesman, is involved in difficult negotiations with Sanders Abrasives, his employer, concerning his commissions on future sales. Loman meets with the president of Sanders, and afterward dictates a memo describing the statements made at the meeting.

Subsequently, a dispute arises concerning Loman's commissions, and he sues Sanders. Loman retains Barlow, a lawyer, to represent him, and, at Barlow's request, sends a copy of his memo to Barlow.

Sanders sends a Request for Production of Documents under Rule 34 to Loman. Its Third Request demands production of "all notes, documents, memoranda or other records, in whatever form, relevant to the negotiations between the parties relating to the plaintiff's entitlement to commissions under the contract." Loman does not want to produce the memo describing his meeting with Sanders' president. Which of the following responses is appropriate under the rules of discovery?

A. "The plaintiff objects to the Defendant's Third Request for Production under Rule 26(b)(1)."

B. "The plaintiff objects to the Defendant's Third Request for Production under Rule 26(b)(1) on the ground that the information sought is protected from discovery under the attorney-client privilege."

C. "The plaintiff denies the Defendant's Third Request for Production. The only document which is responsive to the request is a memorandum dictated by the plaintiff to the file on April 7, 2001, after the meeting with the defendant's president on that date, concerning the negotiations at that meeting. This memorandum is exempt from discovery based on the attorney-client privilege, as it was communicated to Robert W. Barlow, counsel for the plaintiff, for purposes of seeking legal advice concerning this litigation."

D. Either B or C is proper.

E. None of the above is a proper response.

ANALYSIS. The "trick of the trade" here is not a lawyer's trick, but a trick of the professorial trade. The "distractors" in this question tend to distract attention from the basic point of the question.

Even if a requested item is within the scope of the attorney-client privilege, that privilege must be properly asserted. General responses like "the plaintiff objects, not discoverable" are inadequate under the discovery rules. Under Fed. R. Civ. P. 26(b)(5)(A) and 34(b)(2)(C), the reasons for the objection must be stated, so that other parties and the court can assess the validity of the objection. The response in **A** would be insufficient, since it simply claims that the information is not subject to discovery, without any explanation of the ground of the objection.

Nor would **B** suffice. It merely asserts the privilege, without the supporting details necessary to evaluate the claim. Rule 26(b)(5) requires specificity with regard to claims of privilege — such as who created the document, its nature, when it was created, and who it was sent to — to allow the requesting party to determine whether the claim of privilege is justified. **C** probably contains sufficient detail to comply with Rule 26(b)(5). It states the nature of the document, who made it, when it was made, and that it was communicated to Barlow during the representation.

The problem, however, is that the memo is not privileged. It was made by Loman for his own records prior to retaining Barlow. It was not a communication to counsel for the purpose of seeking legal advice or engaging in litigation. It is a business record, a document relevant to the claims in the action and properly subject to discovery. Sending it to Barlow in the course of representation doesn't change that. So, while the distractors tend to focus you on the adequacy of Loman's response, the real point is that the privilege, no matter how elegantly asserted, does not apply. **E** is the proper, though tricky, answer.

D.   Another exception: The meaning of "work product"

When the Federal Rules were adopted in 1938, they contained no provision dealing with discovery of "work product," or "trial preparation materials." However, as the federal courts gained experience with the broad right to discovery introduced by the Rules, they were frequently called upon to protect documents developed in the course of representation by lawyers or their agents. For example, a lawyer might be asked to produce a statement she had taken from a witness to the events in suit, or an index she had made of a file containing large numbers of documents in a client's possession, or a memo to a partner stating which documents in the client's files were relevant to the opposing party's claim. Such documents, created in the course of representation and for the purpose of preparing the case, are clearly relevant to the issues in the case, under Rule 26(b)(1). Yet allowing discovery of these materials would severely impact lawyers' practices, since they could reveal counsel's case evaluation and trial strategy to the opposing party.

In *Hickman v. Taylor*, 329 U.S. 495 (1947), the Supreme Court held that such "attorney work product" should be protected from disclosure, at least absent a showing of a particular need for the information, and inability to obtain it through other means. The Court was concerned that discovery of trial preparation materials would interfere with lawyers' ability to develop their case strategy in private, and lead lawyers to build their cases through opposing counsel's efforts rather than their own. Thus, the Court created a limited objection to shield work product materials from discovery. This is an additional limit on access to materials, even if they satisfy the broad relevance standard in Rule 26(b)(1).

In 1970, Rule 26(b)(3), entitled "Trial Preparation: Materials" was added to the Federal Rules. That Rule partially codifies the protection *Hickman* provided to work product materials. Under Rule 26(b)(3), trial preparation materials are protected from discovery if three criteria are met. The materials must be "documents or tangible things." They must be "prepared in anticipation of litigation or for trial," and they must be prepared "by or for another party or its representative. . . ." If these criteria are met, the materials need not ordinarily be produced in discovery.

So, the first issue to consider in analyzing a claim of work product protection is whether the materials are presumptively protected. That depends on the three criteria in Rule 26(b)(3)(A). Not all documents in the possession of a lawyer are trial preparation materials. Suppose, for example, that Jackson is defending the City police department on a charge of unlawful arrest, and the chief of police sends him a copy of the booking sheet concerning the arrest and the arresting officer's report about the incident that gave rise to the arrest. These are not trial preparation materials. They are "documents or tangible things," and they are prepared by or for another party (the police department) but they are not "prepared in anticipation of litigation or for trial." They are simply the general business records of the police department, made as a matter of routine in every case, whether litigation may follow or not. Although they were sent to counsel in the course of defending the case, that is not enough to make them work product. If it were, all documents would be shielded from discovery simply because they were sent to counsel.

The next issue to consider under Rule 26(b)(3) is whether this presumptive protection for such materials is overcome in the circumstances. Under the rule, the court may order production of protected materials if the party seeking them shows that it has "substantial need for the materials to prepare its case" and cannot obtain their substantial equivalent by other means. Fed. R. Civ. P. 26(b)(3)(A)(ii). However, even if the requesting party cannot otherwise obtain the material, it may not be discoverable under Rule 26(b)(3). Work product need not be produced, even if a substantial need is shown, if it would reveal "the mental impressions, conclusions, opinions, or legal theories of a party's attorney or other representative concerning the litigation." Fed. R. Civ. P. 26(b)(3)(B).

It may be helpful to think of Rule 26(b)(3) in terms of a decision tree:

Step #1: Is the material a document or tangible thing?
> Was it prepared by or for another party?
> Was it prepared in anticipation of litigation?
> > If the answer to these questions is "yes," the document enjoys presumptive protection under Rule 26(b)(3). Then go on to Step #2.

Step #2: Does the requesting party have a substantial need for the material in preparing its case?
> Is it unable to obtain equivalent information by other means?
> > If the answer to both questions is "yes," it will have to be produced despite presumptive work product protection.
> > . . . unless . . .

Step #3: Would the material reveal the mental impressions, conclusions, opinions, or legal theories of counsel?
> If yes, it will be protected from discovery in almost all cases, despite surviving Steps #1 and #2.

This protection for trial preparation materials in Fed. R. Civ. P. 26(b)(3) is usually referred to as the "work product doctrine," or the "protection for trial preparation material," rather than as a privilege. This reflects in part the fact that work product protection, unlike a privilege, can be outweighed, under *Hickman* or under Rule 26(b)(3), by a sufficient showing of need. But the doctrine is loosely referred to as a privilege in a good many opinions, and in at least some situations it is treated as one.

Consider, in the following example, whether the material requested satisfies the Rule 26(b)(3) standard for "trial preparation materials."

QUESTION 6. Eager anticipation. Leahy Pharmaceuticals receives a series of complaints about its "Nasa-Clean" nasal spray. One letter, from counsel for Wallace, demands compensation for injuries Wallace allegedly sustained from using the spray, and threatens suit if compensation is not provided. Leahy officers doubt that Nasa-Clean caused Wallace's injuries. In order to determine whether to settle or litigate the claim, they ask Friedan, a chemist who works for the company, to review relevant records regarding the spray to determine whether it had caused similar injuries to other users. Friedan submits a written report on her investigation to Leahy.

Four months later, Wallace brings suit in federal court against Leahy for his injuries and requests production of all documents and reports in Leahy's possession concerning problems with Nasa-Clean. Friedan's report

A. is protected from discovery under Rule 26(b)(3), unless Wallace makes a showing of substantial need and inability to obtain equivalent information through other means.
B. is not protected under Rule 26(b)(3), since it was prepared before Wallace filed suit.
C. is not protected under Rule 26(b)(3), because it was requested by Leahy, not by its counsel.
D. is not subject to discovery under Rule 26(b)(1), because it concerns injuries to other patients, not to Wallace.

ANALYSIS. In this case, the client sought information to evaluate a claim, and asked an in-house employee to review the company's records to determine whether there was a pattern of problems that might suggest that Wallace has a valid claim. Surely, Friedan's report is relevant to Wallace's claim, so it is within the broad scope of discovery in Rule 26(b)(1). The crucial question, then, is whether it is protected under the three-part standard for protection of "trial preparation materials" under Rule 26(b)(3).

D takes the position that we don't have to decide whether the report is work product, because the report is irrelevant, since it concerns problems experienced by other patients, not by Wallace. This clearly won't fly. Surely, it will be relevant to Wallace's claim to establish that the spray did, or did not, cause problems to other patients who used it. This would tend to establish that the problem was frequent enough to suggest an unreasonable danger, or sufficiently rare that Leahy would not have anticipated it or been required to withdraw the spray from the market.

B would deny work product protection because the report was requested and produced before suit was filed. However, Rule 26(b)(3) does not limit protection to materials created after suit is filed. It is enough if they are created "in anticipation of litigation." Since Leahy has received a letter from Wallace's lawyer demanding compensation and threatening suit, it seems reasonable that they would anticipate that Wallace will sue if they don't settle his claim. In fact, Wallace's claim is the very reason for preparing the report. This would almost certainly suffice to demonstrate anticipation of litigation.

C would deny work product protection on the ground that the report was produced for the client, not the lawyer, presumably before Leahy's counsel even entered the picture. But this too will not defeat a claim of work product protection. The Rule applies if the material is created "by or for another party," which this report clearly was. Arguably, this protection is broader than *Hickman* envisioned. *Hickman* relied heavily on the importance of protecting counsel's trial preparation, but Rule 26(b)(3) extends to materials produced during the investigatory phase and by agents for the client as well as for its counsel. The Rule extends confidentiality to the entire process of claims investigation, so long it is in anticipation of litigation.

So, **A** is the best answer. The report is protected under Rule 26(b)(3), so long as the court concludes that it was prepared in anticipation of litigation.[3] Unless Wallace makes the showing of special need and inability to obtain the material in other ways, the report need not be produced.

That does not, however, protect the underlying material that Friedan examined in investigating the claim. For example, Leahy could not raise a work product objection to a Request for Production of Documents seeking "all complaints received by the defendant concerning Nasa-Clean" for a reasonable period of time. Indeed, such a request would likely be a reasonable alternative way of getting the information in Friedan's report, which suggests that Wallace would be unable to overcome the presumptive protection of Rule 26(b)(3).

Here's another question that requires careful application of Rule 26(b)(3).

QUESTION 7. Presumptuous presumptions. Mason sues Drake in federal court for negligently causing a fire in her warehouse in Boston. A week after the fire, Mason's attorney locates and interviews Collins, who was drinking wine behind the warehouse at the time of the fire. Collins says he and Engels saw someone who looked like Drake speed away from the fire just after it began. Mason's counsel made an audio recording of the interview with Collins. Collins lives in Boston, within the district in which the suit is pending. Drake's attorney had asked Collins to come in to discuss the case informally with him, but Collins refused.

Drake serves interrogatories on Mason asking Mason to "state the names of any witnesses who may have knowledge of the events giving rise to this action." He also sends a request for documents, which requires Mason to "produce any statements you or your attorney have from any witness regarding the cause of the fire." Mason's counsel responds by objecting to both the interrogatory and the request on the ground of "work product." Which of the following statements is true?

---

3. The cases show considerable reluctance in concluding that documents are created in anticipation of litigation if counsel have not been retained to defend a claim. See, e.g., *APL Corporation v. Aetna Casualty & Surety Co.*, 91 F.R.D. 10, 16-18 (D. Md. 1980). However, the question here makes it hard to argue that the report was not prepared "because of the prospect of litigation." 8 Wright & Miller, *Federal Practice and Procedure* §2024.

A. Mason may refuse to answer the interrogatory and to produce the tape, based on the work product doctrine.

B. Mason must answer the interrogatory, and will have to produce the tape of the interview, since Drake can make the showing required under Rule 26(b)(3) for production of work product materials.

C. Mason must answer the interrogatory, but the request for production of the tape is probably protected from disclosure under Rule 26(b)(3).

D. Mason must produce the tape under Rule 26(b)(3)(C), because it contains the statement of a witness.

ANALYSIS.   Drake has requested two items: the names of witnesses to the litigation events and the statement of one witness taken by opposing counsel. Let's consider the witness list first.

Mason's counsel cannot protect the names of witnesses he is aware of simply because he learned them in the course of trial preparation. But why not? Isn't this "work product," in the sense that he unearthed the names of these witnesses through his trial preparation efforts?

Well, in a sense this is "trial preparation material"; it is information Mason's counsel has learned in the course of preparing the case. However, the protection does not apply to everything an attorney knows or learns. It applies, under Rule 26(b)(3) to "documents and tangible things" created during trial preparation, and attorneys' strategic musings, but not to the facts those documents contain.

Even though Mason's counsel discovered these facts himself while developing his case, this will not shield the information from discovery. Mason's lawyer is his agent, and his knowledge of facts about the case will be attributed to Mason. Thus, when Mason answers the interrogatory (and it is the client, not the lawyer, who signs the answers), he will have to include responsive information developed by his lawyer about the case. So **A** is wrong; Mason must answer the interrogatory requesting the names of relevant witnesses.

The other choices consider whether Rule 26(b)(3) protects the witness statement from discovery. **D** takes the view that it must be produced under Rule 26(b)(3)(C), which deals specifically with witness statements. This is too loose a reading of the subsection, however. This provision allows a party to obtain *her own* statement about the case. It also allows a nonparty to obtain *her own* statement. It does not apply where a party seeks a statement of a nonparty.

So is it **B** or **C**? Since Collins's statement was taken during the course of trial preparation by Mason's counsel, it enjoys protection under the work product doctrine, unless that presumptive protection is overcome under Rule 26(b)(3). The presumption is not likely to be overcome here. Drake will not likely be able to show that he could not obtain substantially equivalent information in another way. Collins lives in Boston. Although he refused an informal interview, he presumably can be subpoenaed for a deposition to obtain his testimony. Thus, the presumptive protection of the Rule is not overcome. **C** is the better answer.

E. The Closer: *Hickman* and the limits of Rule 26(b)(3)

Rule 26(b)(3) governs work product objections to production of "documents and tangible things." However, it has been clear since *Hickman* that a party may object to production of work product that is not embodied in a document or tangible thing. For example, in *Hickman*, opposing counsel sought production of Fortenbaugh's recollections of his interviews with witnesses, as well as his notes of other interviews. Rule 26(b)(3) would not protect this information, since it is not a "document or tangible thing."

It isn't clear why the rulemakers, in Rule 26(b)(3), chose to address only work product objections to production of documents and tangible things. It might be argued that, since they chose to protect these from disclosure (unless the appropriate showing is made), by implication, other work product — that is, intangible work product like Fortenbaugh's recollections of witness interviews — are *not* protected. However, this has not been the reading of the courts. Most courts have held that intangible work product continues to enjoy protection under standards established in the *Hickman* case itself. Thus, they need not be produced absent some showing of extraordinary need. See, e.g., *Sporck v. Peil*, 759 F.2d 312 (3d Cir. 1985). And "opinion work product" — the mental impressions of counsel — is probably protected from disclosure in almost all cases.

So, consider the following worthy Closer.

> **QUESTION 8. Exceeding the limits?** Sorenson sues Marathon Corporation in federal court for the fee he had earned as the broker after he had assisted Marathon in acquiring a family business. He seeks his commission, damages for fraud, and statutory damages under a state statute.
>
> DeMarco, Sorenson's counsel, takes the deposition of Sanchez, an independent accountant who audited Marathon's business, and had been involved in the negotiations and planning for the acquisition. At the outset of the deposition, DeMarco asks Sanchez whether the company's lawyers, in preparing him for his deposition, had noted any particularly

problematic issues they expected to come up at the deposition, and what areas of inquiry they had spent most of their time discussing. Marathon's counsel objects based on the work product doctrine and attorney-client privilege.

The objection should probably be

A. sustained, based on the attorney-client privilege.
B. sustained, because the material is protected as trial preparation material under Rule 26(b)(3).
C. sustained, since the material is protected from discovery unless DeMarco has a substantial need for this information and cannot obtain equivalent information through other means.
D. sustained under *Hickman v. Taylor*, even if Rule 26(b)(3) does not apply and Sorenson demonstrates a substantial need for the information.
E. overruled, since Rule 26(b)(3) does not protect the information from discovery.

ANALYSIS. **A** is not right. The attorney-client privilege extends to communications between lawyer and client, but here the witness is not the client or even the employee of a client. If the information sought is protected, it will have to be under the work product doctrine, not attorney-client privilege. But Rule 26(b)(3), by its terms, does not provide such protection. It extends work product protection to "documents and tangible things." The questions here seek oral testimony concerning Sanders's conversations with Marathon's counsel, so the rule does not apply. **B** is wrong.

Although Rule 26(b)(3) doesn't apply, **E**, which takes the position that the objection should be overruled, is not the best answer either. The case law has held that Rule 26(b)(3) has *partially* codified the work product protection recognized in *Hickman*. It governs where the material sought to be protected is found in documents or tangible things. But, where similar work product information *not* included in a document or tangible thing is sought, the cases look back to *Hickman* and extend similar protection to the material. In other words, Rule 26(b)(3) is not the exclusive source of work product protection. Attorneys' mental processes can still be protected under the common law protection stemming from *Hickman* as well.

So, we're down to **C** and **D**. **C** asserts that the material is protected, but that the protection can be overcome if DeMarco makes a showing similar to that required under Rule 26(b)(3): that he really needs it and can't get equivalent information any other way. This is likely wrong as well. Here, the material sought is true "opinion work product," that is, it seeks the mental impressions of counsel about what the major problems are with the case. This type of evaluative judgment by counsel enjoys almost complete protection under *Hickman* and Rule 26(b)(3). See *Hickman v. Taylor*, 329 U.S. 495, 510-514 (1947) (noting damage to the legal profession from requiring production of counsel's mental impressions); compare Rule 26(b)(3)(B) (even if requesting party makes the required showing, "the court must protect against disclosure of the mental impressions, conclusions, opinions or theories of a party's attorney or other representative"). Thus, **D** is the best answer; it is very doubtful that any showing could be made to support an order that these questions be answered.

 Glannon's Picks

1. Time past and time future   D
2. Issues and answers   B
3. Relevance and discretion   B
4. Confidential chat   E
5. Tricks of the trade   E
6. Eager anticipation   A
7. Presumptuous presumptions   C
8. Exceeding the limits?   D

19

The Basic Tools of Discovery in Federal Court

The rulemakers set the goal forth in Rule One,
To achieve simple and speedy resolution.
If this be their intendment
How about an amendment,
To call an interrogatory a question?

CHAPTER OVERVIEW
A. Automatic disclosure under the Federal Rules
B. Supplementation of initial disclosures
C. Interrogatories to parties under Rule 33
D. Requests for production of documents under Rule 34
E. Problems posed by electronic discovery
F. Depositions
G. The Closer: Instructions not to answer at a deposition
⟐ Glannon's Picks

The previous chapter addressed the scope of discovery under Federal Rule 26(b)(1), including the scope of information that can be obtained and several basic limitations on discovery. This chapter segues from *what* may be obtained to *how* it may be sought.

American court procedure offers the most comprehensive process for pre-trial exchange of information in the world. Many procedure systems in other countries use an "inquisitorial" model, under which the compelled production of evidence is controlled by the judge. In American courts, by contrast, the rules of discovery authorize the parties (usually through their counsel) to develop the evidence by using discovery devices to compel disclosure of information in the hands of adversaries and non-party witnesses. This chapter discusses the four most common devices parties use to obtain discoverable information: automatic disclosure, interrogatories, requests for production of documents and depositions.

A.   Automatic disclosure under the Federal Rules

Most discovery is initiated by counsel for the litigants, who send interrogatories and requests for production of documents to opposing parties and schedule depositions of witnesses. However, in 1993 the Federal Rules introduced "automatic disclosure" under Fed. R. Civ. P. 26(a), which requires parties to exchange basic information about the case without a request from another party. Rule 26(a) requires three categories of disclosures: initial disclosures (Rule 26(a)(1); disclosure of expert testimony (Rule 26(a)(2)), and pre-trial disclosures (Rule 26(a)(3)). We will focus on initial disclosure under Rule 26(a)(1), which takes place at the outset of the case.

Under Rule 26(a)(1), parties in most federal cases[1] are required to exchange four categories of information at the outset of the case, without a request from the other side. They must disclose

- the identity of individuals "likely to have discoverable information — along with the subjects of that information — that the disclosing party may use to support its claims or defenses"
- copies or descriptions of documents (including electronically stored information) and things in the possession, custody, or control of the disclosing party that the party may use to support its claims or defenses
- a computation of damages claimed, making available for inspection and copying the documents and other materials on which the computation is based
- any insurance agreement under which an insurer may be liable to satisfy all or part of a judgment in the action

The parties are also required to meet and confer about these disclosures and other discovery issues and to file a written report with the court outlining their plans for discovery. Fed. R. Civ. P. 26(f). Until this meeting takes place, the

---

1. The disclosure requirements do not apply to certain specialized types of cases listed in Rule 26(a)(1)(B). They may also be modified by a stipulation of the parties or by court order. Fed. R. Civ. P. 26(a)(1)(A).

parties are barred from taking discovery by other means (such as interrogatories, requests for documents, or depositions). Fed. R. Civ. P. 26(d)(1).

Note several points about the disclosure requirements. They do not require a party to reveal all witnesses she knows of, but only those likely to have information *that the disclosing party may use* to support its claims or defenses. If a party knows of a witness she will definitely not use, that witness need not be listed. Of course, if the party has any doubt as to whether she will use the witness's testimony, she would likely disclose the witness. If she does not, Rule 37(c)(1) will likely bar the party who failed to make the disclosure from using that witness's testimony at trial.

The same principle applies to automatic disclosure of documents and things. The rule requires production of documents the party "may use to support its claims or defenses." Here again, the Rule requires a party to reveal *supporting* evidence, but not adverse evidence. This avoids placing counsel in the position of having to review all known evidence, locate all documents that might support the *other party's* case, and hand them over without a request.

Consider this example.

QUESTION 1. Missing in action. Fremont Publishing Company sues New Era Press for publishing a story about a shipwreck that it claims duplicated a copyrighted story from one of its books. New Era denies that Fremont held the copyright to the story. Shortly after the parties make their disclosures under Rule 26(a)(1), New Era's lawyers learn that Fremont had received a letter from an individual claiming that he held the copyright on the shipwreck story and demanding compensation from Fremont for using it. Fremont had not disclosed the existence of this letter in its Rule 26(a) disclosures.

New Era

A. should move for sanctions under Rule 37(c)(1) for Fremont's failure to disclose the letter in its Rule 26(a) disclosures.

B. should move to require supplemental disclosure of the letter, under Rule 26(a)(1) and 26(e)(1).

C. should send Fremont a Rule 34 Request for Production of documents to obtain the letter.

D. cannot obtain the letter, because it is not subject to disclosure under Rule 26(a).

ANALYSIS. In this example, Fremont evidently had the document but failed to include it in its initial disclosure. New Era learns that it exists and was left out. What should it do?

B seems like a sensible course, to move for further disclosure, since the letter was not produced. This isn't likely to be granted, however, because the letter probably does not have to be disclosed. Rule 26(a)(1)(A)(ii) requires disclosure of documents the disclosing party "may use to support its claims or defenses." It hardly seems that Fremont will use this letter, challenging the validity of its copyright, to support its claim against New Era for infringing that copyright. If the letter was not subject to disclosure under Rule 26(a)(1)(A)(ii), the court is not going to order it disclosed in response to New Era's motion. For the same reason, the motion for sanctions suggested in **A** isn't going to be granted: Fremont would not be sanctioned for failure to disclose the letter if it was not required to disclose it.

D suggests that New Era cannot obtain the letter, since it is not within the scope of disclosure under Rule 26(a). While the letter very probably is not subject to disclosure under Rule 26(a), that does not mean that New Era cannot obtain it through discovery. It only means that Fremont does not have to *disclose it automatically* at the outset of the case. It is still discoverable under Rule 26(b)(1), which allows parties to obtain discovery of information "relevant to the claim or defense of any party" in the action. Surely, the letter is relevant to New Era's defense that Fremont did not have a copyright on the story. Consequently, it is subject to discovery under the broad standard of relevance in Rule 26(b)(1). So **C** is the best answer: New Era is entitled to obtain this letter through the traditional discovery devices and may send Fremont a request for production of the letter under Rule 34.

This illustrates that a party cannot rely on disclosure as a substitute for discovery. Disclosure will only reveal information favorable to the other party (that it may "use to support its claims or defenses"). To obtain information that is unfavorable to Fremont, New Era must ask for it using the traditional discovery devices.

In some cases, Rule 26(a)(1) may call for disclosure of a document as to which a party claims a privilege or that constitutes work product. Rule 26(a) does not expressly authorize a disclosing party to object to disclosure based on the attorney-client privilege or work product protection. What should a party do if she has information subject to disclosure under Rule 26(a)(1) but arguably subject to such protection?

In analyzing the question below, consider Rule 26(a)(1)(A)(ii) and Rule 26(b)(5)(A). The latter requires a party who objects to discovery based on a "privilege or protection" to "describe the nature of the documents, communications, or tangible things not produced or disclosed — and do so in a manner that, without revealing information itself privileged or protected, will enable other parties to assess the applicability of the privilege or protection."

QUESTION 2. Disclosure and protection. Roberge sues Casteneda for injuries in an auto accident. Casteneda meets with her defense counsel, Darrow, and explains that Roberge caused the accident by running a red light. She indicates that Quinn, a bystander who witnessed the accident, will corroborate her version of the facts.

Darrow interviews Quinn and drafts an affidavit for Quinn to sign, stating under oath his testimony that Roberge ran the light and drove into Casteneda. He obtains the affidavit in order to use it in support of an early motion for summary judgment. A week later Darrow's Rule 26(a) disclosures are due.

A. Darrow will violate Rule 26(a)(1)(A)(ii) if he fails to disclose Quinn's affidavit.
B. Darrow need not disclose the affidavit, because it is not within the definition of documents to be disclosed under Rule 26(a)(1).
C. Darrow need not disclose the affidavit, because he does not plan to use it at trial.
D. Darrow need not disclose the document, but should describe the nature of the affidavit in his disclosure response and object to disclosing it based on work product protection.

ANALYSIS. In this example, the affidavit was prepared by Darrow in anticipation of litigation. This "trial preparation" material is protected from discovery by Rule 26(b)(3). Is it also protected from automatic disclosure?

B is probably wrong, since Quinn's affidavit fits the definition in Rule 26(a)(1)(A)(ii). It is a document in Casteneda's possession that she may use to support her defense that she was not negligent in causing the accident — indeed, she created the document for that purpose. Even though the document was created by counsel, it still seems to fit the Rule 26(a)(1)(A)(ii) definition, since Darrow plans to use it to support Casteneda's defense.

C is also a weak answer. While Darrow does not plan to use the affidavit at trial, she does plan to use it in support of the motion for summary judgment. Rule 26(a)(1)(A)(ii) requires disclosure of documents the party "may use to support its claims or defenses." The Advisory Committee Note confirms that materials that will be used to support a pre-trial motion, as well as those that will be used at trial, must be disclosed. Advisory Committee Note to 2000 Amendment (note on Subdivision (a)(1)).

A states that Darrow must disclose the document. But this document is work product, since it was created by Casteneda's counsel in preparation of her case, which would ordinarily be protected from discovery under Rule 26(b)(3). It seems doubtful that it should enjoy any lesser protection from disclosure at the outset of the case. When Darrow files it in court with a summary judgment motion, the affidavit will lose work product protection, since filing makes the document public. But Casteneda would still prefer not to produce the affidavit at the outset, since she is not sure that she will use it at all.

A careful reading of the Rules suggests that she should reveal the existence of the affidavit, but assert the work product protection to protect it from disclosure. There is no reason why the doctrine should bar production of work product through regular discovery, but not through disclosure. And a careful reading of Rule 26(a)(1)(A)(ii) indicates that Darrow may comply with it by disclosing *a description by category and location* of the affidavit. At the same time, Darrow may object to producing it based on work product protection. Rule 26(b)(5) confirms this. It requires the objecting party

> to describe the nature of the documents, communications, or things *not produced or disclosed* — and do so in a manner that, without revealing information itself privileged or protected, will enable other parties to assess the applicability of the privilege or protection. [emphasis added]

The reference to materials "not produced or disclosed" certainly suggests that a party may resist disclosure as well as discovery based on work product protection.

This reading makes sense and makes **D** the best answer. It provides the opposing party with information about relevant documents in the hands of her adversary, but in a way that preserves the protection of the work product doctrine. Roberge will still learn that Quinn has relevant evidence, because, under Rule 26(a)(1)(A)(i), Darrow will have to disclose that Quinn is a witness she may use to support Casteneda's defense. The identity of a witness, even if discovered through counsel's own efforts, is not protected work product.

B. Supplementation of initial disclosures

As its name suggests, "initial" disclosure under Rule 26(a)(1) takes place shortly after the case is filed. The parties' initial disclosures will be based on "the information then reasonably available" to them. Rule 26(a)(1)(E). That subsection further provides that a party is "not excused from making its disclosures because it has not fully investigated the case. . . ."

Because of their preliminary nature, initial disclosures will frequently be incomplete. Parties are likely to learn of further witnesses and documents relevant to their claims and defenses in the course of subsequent investigation and discovery. So the Rule contemplates further disclosures in certain situations:

Rule 26(e)(1). A party who has made a disclosure under Rule 26(a) . . . must supplement or correct its disclosure. . . .

> (A) in a timely manner if the party learns that in some material respect the disclosure or response is incomplete or incorrect, and if the additional or corrective information has not otherwise been made known to the other parties during the discovery process or in writing. . . .

Rule 37(c)(1) spells out the potential consequences of failure to properly supplement initial disclosures. It allows the court to bar use of the information or witness, unless the failure was "substantially justified or is harmless." Alternatively, the rule provides an array of other possible sanctions the court can impose for the insufficient disclosure.

Consider how you would apply these provisions, if you were the judge, to the following example.

QUESTION 3. The latest news.   Build-Rite Construction Company and Xifares Construction Company engaged in a joint venture for the construction of an apartment building, agreeing to share the profits equally after payment of all expenses. Build-Rite later sues Xifares for an accounting, claiming that Xifares has overstated its expenses on the project and reported smaller profits than it actually realized on the venture.

Three months after initial disclosures were exchanged, counsel for Xifares discovers an itemization of its construction expenses on the apartment building. Xifares's employees had searched for relevant documents but this itemization had been misfiled with forms for another Xifares project, and it was missed. When he discovers the itemization, Xifares's counsel forgets to disclose it to opposing counsel. Six months later, and three months before the date for trial, Xifares's counsel is organizing exhibits and realizes that he has not disclosed it. Xifares's counsel will probably want to use the itemization, which supports its position, at trial.

A. Xifares did not violate Rule 26(a)(1)(A), because its employees made a reasonable search for relevant documents before making initial disclosures.

B. Xifares will be barred from using the itemization at trial, since it should have been in the initial disclosure.

C. The judge must bar Xifares from using the itemization at trial, because it did not supplement its disclosure "in a timely manner" (Rule 26(e)(1)(A)) to include the itemization.

D. Xifares has violated its disclosure obligations, but will not necessarily be barred from using the information at trial.

ANALYSIS. This question considers the consequences of making an incomplete initial disclosure of the evidence described in Rule 26(a)(1). Xifares failed to disclose the expense itemization at the outset of the case because its employees made a reasonable investigation but missed it. Rule 26 contemplates that this may happen, since it requires supplementation where a disclosure is "incomplete or incorrect." Surely, Xifares will not be forever barred from using the evidence based on this good faith mistake. Thus **B** suggests too drastic a penalty for the initial failure to disclose.

However, when Xifares's counsel became aware of the document, Rule 26(e)(1) required him to make a supplemental disclosure, since he has learned that "the information disclosed is incomplete or incorrect." Clearly the drafters intended parties to supplement their disclosures in light of their evolving knowledge of the witnesses and documents in the case. See the Advisory Committee note to the 1993 amendments, which provides that "supplementation need not be made as each new item of information is learned but should be made at appropriate intervals during the discovery period. . . ." Since Xifares's counsel may want to use the itemization to support its claims, it should have sent a supplemental disclosure including the itemization or a description of it. **A**, which suggests that later disclosure is not required, so long as a reasonable search was made initially, is off the mark. That leaves us to choose between **C** and **D**.

C states that Xifares will be barred from using the itemization since it has not been disclosed in a timely manner. Yet it is doubtful that the rule leads inexorably to that conclusion or that a practical judge would so rule. Although Rule 37(c)(1) provides that the party who failed to make disclosure may be barred from using the information, it also provides alternative, lesser sanctions where such a drastic sanction is not warranted. Here, the information won't be barred if the failure to disclose it was harmless (as it would be, for example, if the opposing party already knew of it). If the failure to disclose did affect Build-Rite's trial preparation, some sanction less than a blanket exclusion of the document is likely warranted. The failure to disclose was inadvertent. Discovery is not yet complete in the case, so disclosure at this point should provide Build-Rite an adequate opportunity to develop its case in response to the itemization. Thus, **D** is the best answer; Xifares has likely violated the rule, by failing to disclose the itemization sooner, but it will not necessarily suffer the sanction of having it excluded from evidence.

C.   Interrogatories to parties under Rule 33

While disclosure was added to the discovery rules in 1993, interrogatories, depositions, and requests for production of documents have been available under the Federal Rules since their adoption in 1938.

Interrogatories are simply questions, sent by one party to the case to be answered by another. (They may not be used to obtain information from nonparties.) A major advantage of interrogatories is that they are inexpensive. You just write them and send them, and hopefully get useful information back in the answers. However, the answers are not spontaneous; they are written by the responding party's lawyer, who, as an advocate for the opposing party, tends to construe interrogatories narrowly and respond with as little information as possible. Interrogatories should be precise and specific, in order to get something precise and specific in return. Thus they are best used to obtain objective factual information such as names of witnesses, itemizations of damages, dates of relevant events, and the location of known documents. This type of information can be clearly described in an interrogatory, in a manner that is not subject to a limiting construction by opposing counsel. For more subjective inquiries, interrogatories tend to produce unsatisfying results.

A long-running source of debate has been the extent to which parties may ask interrogatories that call for opinions or contentions. For example, an interrogatory might ask the plaintiff in a contracts case to specify "each act upon which the plaintiff relies in support of her contention that the defendant breached the contract." This is not a purely factual question, like "Please state where the meeting between Smith and Jones took place." Instead, such "contention interrogatories" call for the application of law to fact, for the party to provide factual support for a position taken in the pleadings. Rule 33(a)(2) confirms that such interrogatories are proper, though the court may allow a party to defer answering them until discovery is complete:

> An interrogatory is not objectionable merely because it asks for an opinion or contention that relates to fact or the application of law to fact, but the court may order that the interrogatory need not be answered until designated discovery is complete, or until a pretrial conference or some other time.

Such contention interrogatories provide a means for opponents to gain an understanding of the factual basis for general allegations in the pleadings. Consider the interrogatory in the following example.

QUESTION 4. Just deserts. Arena sues Shukla for negligence, for injuries suffered in an accident. Shukla's eleventh interrogatory to Arena is as follows:

"11. Why do you contend that the defendant is liable for your injury?"

> Arena's lawyer submits the following answer to interrogatory #11:
>
> **"11. Answer:** The defendant is liable for the accident because the defendant was negligent in operating his vehicle, leading to the collision which injured the plaintiff."
>
> Arena's answer is probably
>
> A. a proper response to the interrogatory.
> B. not proper under the rules, because it does not specify the negligent act Shukla committed.
> C. inadequate, because it fails to state the facts on which Arena bases his response.
> D. unnecessary. Arena's lawyer should object to the interrogatory, because it asks Arena to specify the basis for his legal contentions.

ANALYSIS.   Shukla has asked Arena a question, and Arena has answered it. The answer hasn't helped much, but is it sufficient under the Rules?

D is clearly not right. Rule 33(c)(a)(2) allows parties to ask interrogatories that require a party to flesh out their contentions about the case. I think **C** is wrong too. Rule 33 does not require a party responding to an interrogatory to give all factual details, unless asked. Here, Shukla's general "why do you claim I'm liable" question does not ask for supporting factual evidence. And **B** fails as well for the same reason: Arena's question does not clearly call for a specification of the negligent act Arena relies upon. Shukla's answer seems, in a common sense reading of the question, to be a perfectly satisfactory answer. Of course, it probably isn't what Arena wanted by way of an answer, but since it fairly responds to the question, it is probably sufficient under the rules. As one judge opined in a discovery case, "a cryptic question invites an inscrutable answer. It is said colloquially, 'Ask me a foolish question, and I'll give you a foolish answer.'" *Preslye v. Boehlke*, 33 F. R.D. 316, 317 (D.N.C. 1963). If Arena wants hard information about Shukla's case, or about her contentions, he had better ask a more precise, focused question. **A** is the best answer.

The general learning is that interrogatories do not provide much useful information, since they are not answered spontaneously, but labored over by grudging lawyers trying to protect their clients' interests. But in one respect they can be more effective than depositions. An interrogatory to a corporate party requires the party "to furnish such information as is *available to the party*," (emphasis added) not just information that the person answering them personally knows. Fed. R. Civ. P. 33(b)(1)(B). Thus, the party answering the interrogatories must make a reasonable inquiry to obtain the information requested. By contrast, a deponent will generally answer at a deposition based solely on personal knowledge.

If a party believes that the information sought is not within the scope of discovery, or is protected from disclosure, the party should respond by objecting to the interrogatory. For example, if an interrogatory asked for all statements taken from any witness, the responding party could object based on work product protection under Rule 26(b)(3). The responding party signs the interrogatories under oath, but any objections raised are to be signed by the attorney making them. Rule 33(b)(5). This emphasizes that it is the lawyers who interpose legal objections to discovery (and, consequently, may be sanctioned if such objections are not justified).

Which is the proper response to the interrogatory below?

QUESTION 5. Reasonable inquiry.   Melchior brings a products liability action in federal court against Atmosphere Aviation Corporation, a national airline. She seeks damages for personal injuries suffered in the crash of an Atmosphere plane. She also sues General Engines Corporation, which manufactured the engines on the plane. General Engines has offices in five states. Atmosphere Aviation sends interrogatories to General Engines, requesting it to list all reports it has in its possession concerning accidents over the last ten years involving the type of engine involved in the crash, and the names of the persons conducting those investigations.

Branch, the vice president for operations of General Engines, is designated to respond to the interrogatories for the corporation. While Branch oversees all General's operations, she does not have all the information sought by the interrogatory; much of it is located in files in offices at other corporate locations. Branch should

A. conduct an investigation to determine what relevant documents General has, and answer based on that investigation.

B. respond by listing whatever documents she has in her own files about accidents involving the engine.

C. object to the interrogatory, because the information sought is covered by the disclosures required by Rule 26(a)(1)(B).

D. not respond to the interrogatory, since it is not sent by an opposing party.

ANALYSIS.   This interrogatory calls for information located in various offices in five locations. Doubtless, Branch, when she receives the interrogatory, would not be able, of her own knowledge, to specify how many documents fit the description in the interrogatory, or perhaps even which employees have such documents. The only way to find out is to conduct an investigation, which may require considerable effort by numerous General Engines employees.

Let's dispose of **D** first. It states that Branch should not respond, since the interrogatories were sent by a codefendant, not by the plaintiff. This would be bad advice for several reasons. *First,* ignoring interrogatories is not one of the options under the Rule, even if you think they are improper. If the receiving party has objections to the interrogatories, she should respond with those objections, not drop them in the circular file. *Second,* the rule authorizes interrogatories to "any other party" (Fed. R. Civ. P. 33(a)(1)), so the interrogatory is not objectionable on this basis anyway.

The argument for **C** is interesting. The initial disclosure requirements in Rule 26(a)(1) mandate disclosure of documents about the case. Since that rule covers the ground, why should a party be required to answer an interrogatory on the same point?

It's a nice argument, but doesn't fly. Rule 26(a)(1)(A)(ii) requires a party to disclose the documents that it "may use to support its claims and defenses," not all documents it has concerning issues in the case. Indeed, the documents other parties will be most interested in probably won't be disclosed, since they are likely to be adverse to the disclosing party and therefore would not be "used to support [that party's] claims or defenses." Rule 26(b)(1), which authorizes discovery of any information relevant to a claim or defense of any party, clearly permits interrogatories seeking information about such documents, including information adverse to that party. This is true, even though some relevant documents will be disclosed under Rule 26(a)(1). Indeed, parties will almost always send interrogatories or document requests that partially duplicate the disclosure requirements, since they will want *all* the documents, not just those favorable to the other side.

So, it seems that Branch will have to answer the interrogatory. The remaining question is whether she should do so based on the information she personally has (**B**), or must go beyond that to gather information available throughout the company (as **A** suggests). Rule 33(b)(1)(B) provides that a party must respond to interrogatories by providing "the information available to the party." "The party" here is General Engines, not Branch. Thus the Rule requires that Branch determine what documents the company has concerning such accidents, and respond based on that investigation. See generally Wright & Miller §2174. Choose **A**.

You can imagine how enthusiastic Branch will be about conducting that investigation. At the very least, it is a major distraction from her job; at worst, it can be an enormous burden leading to production of lots of damaging evidence. In some cases, interrogatories may be objectionable on the ground that the burden of responding is too great or that they require the responding party to conduct analyses or gather information that the requesting party should obtain itself. But here, the request probably is not unduly burdensome, since the interrogatory describes precisely the documents to be listed, and there are not likely to be huge numbers of such reports.

D. Requests for production of documents under Rule 34

Perhaps the most intrusive of the discovery tools is the request for production of documents. Rule 34 allows parties to request production of documents from other parties that are relevant to claims and defenses in the case. The request must describe the documents sought with "reasonable particularity." Fed. R. Civ. P. 34(b)(1)(A). A request for "all documents relevant to the plaintiff's claims against the defendant" would be too broad, but it is permissible to describe the requested documents by category (Rule 34(b)(1)(A)), such as "all documents relevant to the plaintiff's medical treatment from the date of the accident to the date of this request."

Requests for production require a party to open its files, to provide other parties access to documents that are otherwise confidential and may be damaging to the producing party's case. It is indeed intrusive. It isn't surprising that parties — especially corporations with extensive operations and complex filing and computer systems — frequently view such discovery as unwarranted. It can be extremely burdensome to comply with even a narrowly crafted request for production, and may interfere significantly with corporate operations.

Rule 34 provides one means of limiting this burden. Rule 34(b) authorizes a party to comply with a Rule 34 request by producing the relevant documents as kept in the usual course of business. Thus, a corporation could simply make its files available to the requesting party, and let the requesting party do the work of culling through them for relevant documents. This course has several problems, however. *First*, it provides the other party with wide access to files, both relevant and irrelevant. There is likely to be information in the files that the producing party would prefer to keep confidential, and that would not be within the scope of the Rule 34 request. *Second*, allowing access to the files waives the producing party's objection to production of documents that are protected from discovery. For example, allowing the other side to review files that contain documents that are privileged or enjoy work product protection will waive the privilege or protection.

Nor would opening the files to the other side save the responding party much effort. The responding party will have to review those files anyway, in order to prepare for trial and to determine what documents the other side has found. Consequently, when a request is made, the producing party is likely to take the alternative course available under Rule 34: to cull through its files, extract relevant documents, "organize and label them to correspond to the categories in the request," and produce them for the requesting party. Fed. R. Civ. P. 34(b)(2)(E)(i).

Consider how the producing party should respond to the request for production of documents in the following question.

QUESTION 6. A matter of opinion. Paragon Corporation is involved in litigation with Omniplex Corporation, which alleges that Paragon breached its contract to supply Omniplex with wiring assemblies for its high-speed printing presses. In particular, the parties dispute the meaning of a clause that requires Paragon to "supply Omniplex's needs for wiring assemblies for the period of the contract." Omniplex argues that this requires Paragon to supply as many assemblies as Omniplex requires. Paragon argues that it only requires them to supply the number Omniplex was using yearly when the contract was made. Paragon receives a Request for Production of Documents under Rule 34 seeking "all documents relating to the drafting, negotiation, or execution of the contract in issue in this litigation."

At its counsel's request, Paragon officers order a search of the files for documents responsive to the request. They come up with quite a few. One, however, is particularly troubling. It is a memo written by Paragon's contracts administrator, detailing her discussions with Omniplex negotiators. The memo questions whether Paragon should accept this provision, since "I read this language in the agreement to commit Paragon to supplying *all* of Omniplex's requirements for wiring assemblies for five years, regardless of conditions in the market or alternative opportunities with other customers."

A. Paragon will have to produce the document in response to the request.
B. Paragon should describe the document as required by Rule 26(b)(5), but raise the work product objection to avoid producing it.
C. Paragon should interpret the Rule 34 request narrowly, and not produce the document.
D. Paragon need not produce the document, because it simply states an opinion as to the meaning of the disputed term in the contract.
E. Paragon should not produce the document, since it would be very damaging to its case.

ANALYSIS. Perhaps a few students, imbued with the concept that litigation means a scorched-earth defense of the client's cause at all costs, would choose **E**. This is understandable. Once you represent a client, you naturally identify with that client's interests, and producing this document is clearly going to adversely affect Paragon's defense. But Rule 34 contains no exception for documents likely to hurt the producing party's case. If it did, there'd be little point in using the rule! It requires production of all relevant documents, favorable and unfavorable, unless the producing party has a valid objection.

So ignoring the document — or, worse, destroying it — would be a clear violation of Paragon's obligation under Rule 34, which, if discovered, would subject it to potentially severe sanctions under Rule 37. A lawyer advising such a course would violate both the Rules of Civil Procedure and applicable rules of professional conduct, and possibly even criminal statutes. Nor would Paragon be likely to "get away with it." Paragon employees who received the memo will likely be deposed. Unless they are willing to commit perjury, they are likely to testify to the existence of the memo, making its absence extremely awkward. If they are deposed, the document would likely be subpoenaed in conjunction with the deposition. Unless all these employees are willing to violate their obligations to testify truthfully under oath, the memo is going to surface. Thus, ignoring its existence would be an unwise as well as an unethical course.

D is also wrong. Nothing in the discovery rules suggests that documents stating opinions are exempt from discovery. Perhaps the memo would not be admissible, at least for the truth of the statement about the meaning of the contract provision.[2] But admissibility and *discoverability* are two different concepts. "Relevant information need not be admissible at the trial if the discovery appears reasonably calculated to lead to the discovery of admissible evidence." Fed. R. Civ. P. 26(b)(1). Here, for example, production of this document would likely lead Omniplex to take the contracts administrator's deposition, which clearly could lead to admissible evidence.

Moving on up the line, **C** also fails. It is hard to think of any reasonable interpretation of the document request that does not encompass this document. Although it involves internal debate at Paragon about the contract, it certainly does relate to the negotiation of the contract. And **B** fails as well. This document was not drafted in anticipation of litigation; it was in the normal course of business.

So, **A** is the best answer. Painful as it may be, Paragon will have to produce this document. And your job, as counsel, will be to give them the bad news.

---

2. Very likely it would be admissible to show the state of mind of Paragon officials when they entered into the contract.

Here's another question that considers objections to requests for production.

QUESTION 7. Full disclosure. Rangeley sues Plante Laboratories for injuries allegedly caused by its asthma drug, Pro-Nosatrol. Suit is brought in federal court in Arizona where Plante has its principal place of business. Rangeley's lawyer sends Plante a Rule 34 Request for "all documents, files and other records relating to the pre-market testing of the drug Pro-Nosatrol, whether in hard copy or electronic form, including e-mail and voice mail, deleted files, hard drives, laptops and other electronic devices or storage systems." Most documents concerning the testing are in the possession of Advanced Testing Company, an independent testing laboratory in Florida that contracts with Plante to test its new pharmaceutical products.

Plante's counsel should object to the request because

A. the records at Advanced Testing are in the possession of an independent company, not the defendant.
B. the records at Advanced Testing are not present in Arizona, and therefore are not subject to the jurisdiction of the court.
C. the request is too broad, since it seeks records in electronic form as well as hard copy, which would have to be retrieved by computer professionals.
D. the request does not describe the records sought with reasonable particularity.
E. None of the listed objections is likely to be accepted by the court.

ANALYSIS. **E** is the best answer. None of the arguments in the other choices is likely to carry the day. Although the records are in the hands of Advanced Testing, the court would likely conclude that they are in Plante's "control" (Rule 34(a)(1)), since Advanced did the work for Plante and has an ongoing contractual relationship with Plante that would likely lead them to cooperate in producing documents they created for Plante. So **A** fails. So does **D**, since the records are described reasonably clearly, by the "category" (Rule 34(b)(1)) of documents relating to pre-market testing of the drug. This is a recognizable, reasonably discrete category.

   C has some appeal. Reviewing all the relevant sources, many of them electronic, is going to be a substantial and technically sophisticated undertaking. Plante may object on the ground that it is burdensome, but it will be required to search its computers for relevant information as well. See Fed. R. Civ. P. 34(a)(1)(A) (mandating production of "electronically stored information"). The producing party will even be required to translate electronic records into "a reasonably usable form." Id.[3] Plante may claim it cannot produce deleted files, but it is scary how frequently these can be resurrected by sophisticated techies. It they can, they will likely be required to be produced as well.

B is also a weak objection. While many of the records are not in Arizona, Plante is subject to the jurisdiction of the Arizona court and may be ordered to produce its records, or those within its control, wherever located.

E. Problems posed by electronic discovery

In large scale litigation these days, many problems are posed by the fact that the "documents" parties need are in electronic form. "It is estimated that over 90 percent of all business information is created electronically and never printed out."[4] Computers have facilitated the creation, storage and retrieval of vast amounts of information. When litigation eventuates, opposing lawyers generally want it all. In big cases, this can make discovery hugely expensive and especially contentious.

In 2006, the Federal Rules were amended to assist judges in handling problems posed by electronic discovery. The amendments addressed several problems:

- Rules 33(d) and 34(a)(1)(A) expressly provide that "electronically stored information" is subject to discovery. There wasn't much doubt that such information was discoverable before, but it's clear now that it is.
- Rule 26(b)(2)(B) provides that parties need not provide electronic information that is "not reasonably accessible because of undue burden or cost." The burden falls on the party who objects on this basis to show that the information is not reasonably accessible. If the party carries that burden, the court may still order production, but only for good cause and under appropriate provisions (such as cost sharing). This doesn't really seem to change much either, but it emphasizes that the burden of producing information is an important factor in limiting discovery and calls on the judge to make careful judgments about whether and how much of this information must be produced.

---

3. This can get very costly, especially since most records these days are in electronic form. Usually the expense will fall initially on the producing party, though some of the expense may be shifted to a losing party as court costs after judgment.

4. R. Marcus, M. Redish, and F. Sherman, Civil Procedure: A Modern Approach, Updated Fourth ed. 377 (2008).

- Rule 37(e) was added to deal with the problem of automatic destruction of documents by computer systems. Many large institutions have inaptly named "document retention policies" that call for destruction or overwriting of electronic files after a specified period of time. Rule 37(e) protects parties from being sanctioned due to the loss of such information through "the routine, good-faith operation of an electronic information system." The rule would not protect a party, however, once litigation commences and it is ordered or expected to retain documents relevant to the case.
- Rule 26(b)(5)(B) addresses another problem intensified by electronic discovery. Because parties often produce huge masses of material in electronic discovery exchanges, they will sometimes discover that, without meaning to, they have produced documents that were privileged or subject to work product protection. Rule 26(b)(5)(B) allows a party who has made such an "inadvertent disclosure" to notify the receiving party of the mistake. If so notified, the receiving party

> must promptly return, sequester, or destroy the specified information and any copies it has; must not use or disclose the information until the claim is resolved; must take reasonable steps to retrieve the information if the party disclosed it before being notified; and may promptly present the information to the court under seal for a determination of the claim. The producing party must preserve the information until the claim is resolved.

This provision attempts to freeze the status quo until the producing party's claim of privilege can be resolved. It does not provide that the information is still privileged despite its inadvertent production; rather, it bars any use of it until a court determines whether producing it in discovery has waived the right to keep it confidential. The question below probes the meaning of this quizzical provision.

QUESTION 8. **Gimme, Gimme!** Black Corporation sues White Corporation for patent infringement. The case involves very large numbers of files, some electronic, others in print, that contain technical data about the development of a complex turbine for generating energy from the tides. After Black produces its files in response to White's request for production, it discovers that it has mistakenly produced to White's lawyers a hard copy of a memo written by its chief engineer, Pasco. Pasco wrote the memo, after the suit was filed, offering her assessment to Black's board of directors of the overlap between Black's turbine design and White's, to assist the board in deciding whether to litigate or settle the case. Shortly after producing it, Black's lawyers ask for it back, claiming that it is protected as work product and citing Fed. R. Civ. P. 26(b)(5)(B). That rule

A. requires White's lawyers not to reveal or use the document until the court assesses whether Black has waived the work product protection by producing the document in discovery.
B. requires White's lawyers to return it to Black's lawyers.
C. does not apply, because the report was not an electronic document.
D. does not apply, because the work product privilege does not apply to this document.
E. does not apply to work product material, just to privilege objections.

ANALYSIS. **E** is a clear loser, because Rule 26(b)(5)(B) expressly applies to inadvertent disclosure of "trial preparation material" as well as claims of privilege. **D** also falls short, because the work product privilege would apply to a document produced by an agent of Black Corporation, a party to the case, to assist the party in planning litigation strategy. Although it is written for a party, not the party's lawyer, it falls within the scope of Rule 26(b)(3)(A) ("prepared in anticipation of litigation or for trial by or for another party . . .").

Although inadvertent disclosure tends to occur most frequently in exchange of electronic discovery, Rule 26(b)(5)(B) does not apply solely to electronic documents. It speaks of the production of "information," and Pasco's memo certainly satisfies that standard, even if it's an old fashioned hard copy. So **C** fails as well.

That brings us to the crux of the matter: What exactly does Rule 26(b)(5)(B) require White's lawyers to do when informed of an inadvertent disclosure? **B** is wrong: It does not require them to return the document, although that is one of the options under the rule. Alternatively, it may "sequester" the document, lock it away until a court tells it whether Black has waived work product protection by mistakenly producing it. Some courts hold that inadvertent disclosure waives a privilege or work product protection. If the court hearing Black's case so holds, White's lawyers may unlock the drawer and use the document as they please. Thus, the main purpose of the rule is to put matters on hold until a court rules; the Rule itself does not determine whether the claimed privilege has or has not been waived by inadvertent disclosure. Choose **A**.

F. Depositions

A deposition is the examination of a witness under oath. Depositions are the most effective means of previewing the detailed testimony of witnesses. The party wishing to depose the witness sends a notice of the deposition to the deponent and to all other parties. If the deponent is not a party, a subpoena must also be sent to ensure the witness's attendance. The subpoena is a court order to appear and give testimony. A witness who ignores it may be punished by the court. (Parties do not have to be subpoenaed, because they are already before the court and subject to the rules of discovery and to court orders enforcing them.)

Depositions serve several purposes. They "get the witness on the record." That is, the witness tells her story under oath. If she contradicts that story at trial, she can be impeached with her deposition testimony. Depositions also allow deposing counsel to learn what the witness knows and to ask follow-up questions to get the details of what the witness knows. In addition, taking a witness's deposition gives opposing counsel the opportunity to look the witness in the eye, to form a judgment about her credibility and about how she will likely perform as a witness at trial.

Ordinarily, parties will depose the *other side's* witnesses rather than their own. After all, they can talk to their own witnesses privately, without revealing the witness's testimony or counsel's line of reasoning by the questions they ask. For the same reason, counsel do not usually cross-examine in detail at a deposition, except to clarify points on which the deponent's testimony may create a misimpression. However, in some cases a party may depose a witness in order to obtain the party's testimony for use at trial. If, for example, a witness is moving out of the country, the party who wants to use that witness's testimony at trial may take her deposition as a substitute for her live testimony at the trial. The deposition will be admissible at trial if the witness is not available to testify in person. Fed. R. Civ. P. 32(a)(4). Note that in this scenario, unlike the typical deposition, the party noticing the deposition will be the party who plans to use that witness's testimony, not the opposing party.

Consider what the plaintiff's counsel should do in the following scenario.

QUESTION 9. Your witness.   Czonka is fired from his job at fifty-nine, after twenty-one years with NorthStar Corporation. He sues in federal court under the Federal Age Discrimination in Employment Act (ADEA), claiming that he was fired based on his age. Two months after filing suit, Czonka's counsel learns that Roh, one of his supervisors at NorthStar, has just retired, and is about to move to South Korea. Although discovery has just begun, NorthStar has noticed Roh's deposition.

Czonka's counsel should

A. prepare as fully as possible for the deposition, and cross-examine Roh as if she were doing so at trial.

> **B.** object and move for a protective order under Rule 26(c), on the ground that discovery has just begun, so that she is not yet prepared to cross-examine Roh at the deposition.
> **C.** attend the deposition, but not cross-examine Roh, if Roh is willing to talk privately to her about the case.
> **D.** object on the ground that Roh cannot be deposed, since Roh is not a party to the case.

ANALYSIS. The usual purpose of the deposition is to gather information, or to pin down the opposing party's witnesses on the record. But that isn't the purpose of *this* deposition. Here, NorthStar has noticed the deposition of Roh, a former supervisor who is likely to be "their" witness, in the sense that he is likely to testify favorably to them. (If he were likely to testify unfavorably to NorthStar, they would presumably allow him to disappear undeposed.) Clearly, they have decided to take his deposition because he may not be available for trial. If he is unavailable, they plan to use his deposition testimony at trial instead, as Rule 32(a)(4)(B) allows.

The fact that Roh's deposition is likely to be used at trial changes the equation. At such a "trial deposition," NorthStar will be conducting direct examination of Roh, their own witness, as they would at trial, and Czonka's counsel had better be prepared to cross-examine Roh just as though she were doing so at trial. However, since the deposition is being conducted so early, Czonka's counsel is not fully ready to do so.

Let's dispose quickly of **D.** Rule 30(a)(1) authorizes taking the deposition of "any person, including a party." Roh isn't a party, but he is a person, so he may be deposed.

As the introduction states, the lawyer who did not notice the deposition (said to be "defending the deposition") usually does not cross-examine extensively at a deposition, if she can discuss the case privately with the witness. But **C** is wrong here, because the deposition is being taken to perpetuate the witness's testimony for trial, not to obtain information. If Roh does not appear at trial, cross-examining at the deposition will be the only opportunity Czonka's counsel has to cross-examine Roh under oath. She had better do it as well as she can. On this logic, **A** is the best answer. Czonka's counsel could move for a protective order postponing the deposition till later in discovery, as **B** suggests. But she isn't likely to succeed if Roh is about to leave the country. Once he's gone, he's gone. He no longer works for NorthStar, so it could not make him return for trial. Consequently, the judge is not likely to prevent the taking of his deposition, even though it leaves Czonka at a disadvantage.

G.   The Closer: Instructions not to answer at a deposition

While depositions produce sworn testimony, they are not taken in front of a judge. They are usually taken in the office of the lawyer taking the deposition. A court reporter, hired privately by deposing counsel, swears the witness and records the testimony. The testimony is then transcribed and provided to counsel for each party. Counsel for all parties are entitled to attend the deposition, and usually do. An interesting problem arises if the deponent's lawyer has objections to the deposing counsel's questions. Since there's no judge present to rule on objections, what happens?

Several provisions of Rule 30 address this problem. Rule 30(c)(2) provides:

> An objection at the time of the examination — whether to evidence, to a party's conduct, to the officer's qualifications, to the manner of taking the deposition, or to any other aspect of the deposition — must be noted on the record, but the examination still proceeds; the testimony is taken subject to any objection.

That rule further provides that "A person may instruct a deponent not to answer only when necessary to preserve a privilege, to enforce a limitation ordered by the court, or to present a motion under Rule 30(d)(3)." Rule 30(d)(3)(A) authorizes a party to seek a protective order from the court if the deposition is being conducted "in bad faith or in a manner that unreasonably annoys, embarrasses, or oppresses the deponent or party."

Under these provisions, the deponent's counsel may raise objections to the questions asked, but the deponent must usually answer despite the objection. For example, if the witness is asked a question her counsel considers irrelevant to the issues in the case, her counsel may object, but the witness should still answer the question ("the examination still proceeds; the testimony is taken subject to any objection" — Fed. R. Civ. P. 30(c)(2)). This approach generally makes sense: most objections are meant to protect against the *use of evidence at trial,* not against providing the testimony per se. Since most deposition testimony is never used at trial, most of the objections raised to the testimony will never have to be resolved. If the disputed deposition testimony is offered at trial, the judge can rule on the objections when it is offered in evidence.

So, the questioning at the deposition is fairly unconstrained. How about this case?

QUESTION 10. Gag order.   Unger, a real estate appraiser, sues First American Bank for defamation, alleging that First American's officers had told other bankers not to use Unger for appraisals, because he took bribes to fraudulently inflate his appraisals of residential properties. Unger's counsel takes the deposition of Huffman, First American's vice president. She asks Huffman about an analysis of Unger's appraisals done by Zervos, the bank's mortgage officer. Here's the question:

> *Plaintiff's counsel:* "Did Mr. Zervos ever tell you that, after this action was filed, he did an analysis of appraisals done by Robert Unger on commercial real estate, and found that his appraisals were consistently within proper appraisal guidelines?"

> *Defendant's counsel:* "Objection. The question asks for inadmissible hearsay and for irrelevant information, since it pertains to commercial loans, not residential loans. In addition, the information sought is protected as work product, since it calls for material developed by an agent of the defendant in preparation for the trial of this case. I instruct the witness not to answer the question."

Counsel's instruction to the witness not to answer the question is

A. proper, since the question calls for information that would be inadmissible at trial as hearsay.
B. proper, because the information is irrelevant.
C. proper under Fed. R. Civ. P. 30(d)(2), if the question calls for information protected as work product.
D. not proper. Under Fed. R. Civ. P. 30(c)(2) the Bank's counsel should object, with the testimony being taken subject to the objection.

ANALYSIS. As the introduction indicates, it is not usually appropriate to instruct a witness not to answer deposition questions based on an objection to the evidence. For example, it is improper to instruct a witness not to answer a question on the ground that it is irrelevant, as **B** suggests. If the questioning were abusive ("How many times have you beaten your wife?"), the proper response would be to suspend the deposition to present a motion to the court, under Rule 30(d)(3), on the ground that the deposition is being conducted "in a manner that unreasonably annoys, embarrasses, or oppresses the deponent."

Similarly, it is improper to instruct a witness not to answer on the ground that the evidence the question calls for would be inadmissible at trial. First, evidence is discoverable whether or not admissible at trial. See Fed. R. Civ. P. 26(b)(1): "Relevant information need not be admissible at the trial if the discovery appears reasonably calculated to lead to the discovery of admissible evidence." Second, under Rule 30(c)(2) it is not permissible to instruct the witness not to answer, except for three purposes: to preserve a privilege, to enforce a court-ordered limitation on discovery, or to present a motion for a protective order to the court. So **A** fails as well.

So the proper response must be **C** or **D**. **C** states that counsel could instruct the witness not to answer if the question calls for information that constitutes work product. Rule 30(c)(2) authorizes counsel to instruct a witness not to answer in order to "preserve a privilege." So the question is whether a work product objection is based on a "privilege." Work product is often referred to as a "protection" rather than a privilege. But interpretation of Rule 30(c)(2) here should turn on the policy underlying that subsection, not on the terminology. The rationale for allowing instructions not to answer questions that call for privileged information is that the information should be protected from disclosure *at all*, not just from use at trial. Based on this rational, counsel should be able to instruct a deponent not to answer a question that would reveal work product information as well, because work product is protected from pre-trial disclosure unless a showing of substantial need is made. Here, the question calls not only for the fact of Zervos's investigation, but for the results, which is probably protected work product. Thus, **C** seems like the best answer. If the question calls for information protected by the privilege, it is proper to instruct the deponent not to answer, under Rule 30(c)(2).[5]

 ## Glannon's Picks

1. Missing in action	C
2. Disclosure and protection	D
3. The latest news	D
4. Just deserts	A
5. Reasonable inquiry	A
6. A matter of opinion	A
7. Full disclosure	E
8. Gimme, Gimme!	A
9. Your witness	A
10. Gag order	C

---

5. Note that the question does not call for work product protected by Rule 26(b)(3), since it is not a document or tangible thing; it is testimony about such a document. See the Closer in Chapter 18, p. 375, which discusses this problem.

20

Dispositive Motions: Dismissal for Failure to State a Claim and Summary Judgment

~

Though she filed suit with considerable emotion
Of the law Jill had scarcely a notion.
So her pro se complaint —
Though exceedingly quaint —
Came up short on a 12(b)(6) motion.

~

CHAPTER OVERVIEW

A. The meaning of "failure to state a claim"
B. Hard cases make new law
C. Summary judgment compared: "Piercing the pleadings"
D. Summary judgment, if appropriate
E. Mixed motions: Rule 12(b)(6) and the "speaking motion"
F. Summary judgment for the plaintiff
G. The Closer: Summary judgment, jurisdiction, and the merits
◆ Glannon's Picks

A plaintiff doesn't always get her case to a jury just by filing a lawsuit. Well before trial, the defendant may challenge the legal sufficiency of her claim. If the plaintiff's claim doesn't state a right to relief under applicable law, it will be dismissed without trial. Similarly, the defendant may challenge the plaintiff's factual support for the elements of her claim. If the plaintiff does not have credible proof of each element of her claim, it will also be dismissed without trial.

Challenges to the legal sufficiency of the claim are usually raised by a "motion to dismiss for failure to state a claim upon which relief can be granted." See Fed. R. Civ. P. 12(b)(6), 12(c). A challenge to the plaintiff's ability to prove her case is raised by a motion for summary judgment under Fed. R. Civ. P. 56. This chapter will address each of these motions in turn.

A. The meaning of "failure to state a claim"

It makes sense that a party should not be able to take a case to trial if she seeks relief that a court is not able to grant. Suppose, for example, that Arkwright, owner of a car dealership, sues Miranda for negligence. He claims that Miranda caused an accident on Main Street, that because of the accident traffic was unable to reach his dealership for three hours during his President's Day sale, and as a result he lost profits. Many states limit recovery in negligence cases to direct personal injury or property damage, and would not recognize a right to recover for secondary economic damages like Arkwright's. See generally J. Diamond, L. Levine & S. Madden, *Understanding Torts* 167-169 (4th ed. 2010). In these states, a court looking at Arkwright's complaint could tell that he seeks relief that is not available under the law. Since there is no right to relief, even if Arkwright proves all the facts he has alleged, the court would dismiss the complaint for failure to state a claim upon which relief can be granted.

The purpose of a motion to dismiss for failure to state a claim is to test the legal validity of the plaintiff's allegations, not their factual truth. Consequently, in considering the motion, the court does not ask whether the plaintiff is likely to prove them. The motion does not challenge the plaintiff's ability to prove her case — as a summary judgment motion does — but only the validity of the legal cause of action she asserts. In ruling on the motion, the court must assume that the facts alleged in the complaint are true. The question for the judge is, if they are all true, do they set forth a claim for which the court could grant the plaintiff some kind of remedy.

Here's a question to illustrate the point.

> **QUESTION 1. Law and facts.** Snow sues Petrillo for emotional distress he suffered when he witnessed an accident in which Petrillo's car careened into his parents' car. The action is brought in federal court in the state of Euphoria, which applies the "impact rule" to claims for negligent infliction of emotional distress. Under the impact rule a plaintiff can only recover for emotional distress if she actually suffered a physical impact in the accident caused by the defendant. Mere "bystanders" cannot recover.
>
> Snow was not in his parents' car at the time of the accident. He was waving goodbye to them from the curb, where they had just dropped him off. He claims, however, that Petrillo's car, when it careened into his parents' car, threw water on his leg, and that this satisfies the impact rule. Petrillo denies that his car threw water on Snow. He also denies that water splashing is sufficient to satisfy the impact rule under Euphoria law; the impact, Petrillo argues, must be with the defendant's car itself. He answers the complaint, denying that his car splashed Snow, and then moves to dismiss it for failure to state a claim upon which relief can be granted. The trial judge should
>
> A. refuse to entertain the motion, since it should have been made before answering the complaint.
> B. consider the motion, but deny it if she concludes that water splashing satisfies the impact rule.
> C. deny the motion, because Petrillo has denied that his car splashed Snow, raising a question of fact to be litigated.
> D. grant the motion, because Petrillo has denied that his car splashed Snow, and Snow cannot recover without proving an impact.

ANALYSIS. **D** is wrong, because it confuses pleading with proof. It is true that Snow cannot recover without proving impact. If in fact Petrillo did not splash Snow, Snow cannot recover, even if splashing suffices as an "impact" under Euphoria law. However, the motion to dismiss for failure to state a claim is not meant to test whether the facts are true, only whether, *if they are true,* they state a right to relief. In passing on the motion, the judge will assume that the facts Snow has alleged are true. So, Petrillo cannot obtain dismissal of the claim by denying that he splashed Snow. The issue posed by the motion is, "assuming that Petrillo did splash Snow, is that sufficient to state a legal wrong for which the court could award damages to Snow?" Whether Petrillo did in fact splash Snow is a question of fact to be litigated later . . . but only if the allegations in the complaint state a legally recognized claim to relief.

　　A is also wrong, though you need to think back to Chapter 15 to recall why. The objection that a complaint fails to state a legally sufficient claim may be raised by a "pre-answer" motion. See Fed. R. Civ. P. 12(b)(6). But it also may be made later. The defendant may raise it in the answer, or she may assert it after answering by a motion for "judgment on the pleadings." Fed. R. Civ. P. 12(c). Petrillo did not waive this fundamental objection to the suit by failing to make a pre-answer motion, or by leaving it out of his answer. Fed. R. Civ. P. 12(h)(2).

C is also wrong. It states that the motion should be denied because there is a question of fact as to whether Petrillo splashed Snow. True, the parties dispute whether he did, but this would not prevent dismissal for failure to state a claim if that fact is legally irrelevant. If the court assumes (as it will on the motion) that Petrillo *did* splash Snow, but concludes that he is not liable *even if he did*, then it should dismiss the complaint. Snow must lose even if he was splashed, if splashing doesn't satisfy the impact requirement. Consequently, there's no need to decide whether he was splashed. On the motion, the court takes the facts alleged in the complaint as true and asks whether, assuming they are true, they would establish a right to relief from the court. If we assume that Petrillo splashed Snow, but splashing doesn't satisfy the impact requirement under Euphoria law, Snow doesn't state a claim that would entitle him to relief. Even if the court tried the case, and found that Petrillo did splash him, it could not award any relief to Snow. Consequently, there is no reason to litigate the truth of those allegations.

So **B** is right. If the court concludes that splashing doesn't satisfy the impact rule under Euphoria law, there is no need to prolong the case. The complaint should be dismissed for failure to state a claim upon which relief can be granted. But if the court concludes that water splashing satisfies the impact requirement, the plaintiff will have stated a compensable claim, and the parties will then litigate the contested question of whether the splashing actually occurred.

B.   Hard cases make new law

Why would a plaintiff assert a claim in her complaint that fails to state a compensable claim under applicable law? Well, it may happen for a number of reasons. First, the plaintiff's lawyer may not have done her homework, so she doesn't realize that a particular claim is legally insufficient. In other cases (unfortunately), lawyers may include legally dubious claims for tactical reasons, even if they doubt that they will ultimately support recovery. And, in another set of cases, it simply may not be clear under applicable law whether the complaint states a legally compensable claim or not. There may not be case law from the state appellate courts that clearly delineates the limits of a legal theory. If that is true, the trial judge faces a difficult task when a plaintiff files a claim and the defendant challenges it as legally insufficient to support relief.

Here's a question that illustrates the trial judge's dilemma.

QUESTION 2. Authority on point. Angeles sues Centerville Hospital, a hospital in the state of Euphoria, for medical malpractice by Dr. Kildare, who operated on her at Centerville. Angeles alleges that Dr. Kildare negligently performed the operation, and that Centerville is liable for Kildare's negligence, even if Kildare was an independent contractor rather than an employee of Centerville. Her theory is that, to the patient, the surgeon *appears to be* an employee of the hospital, even though surgeons are often actually independent contractors who merely contract for use of hospital facilities. Euphoria courts have never decided whether a hospital is liable for acts of surgeons who use its facilities, under this "apparent authority" theory. Courts in a few other states have accepted the argument, however.

In her complaint, Angeles alleges that she reasonably believed that Dr. Kildare was an employee of Centerville. She further alleges that Centerville is liable for Kildare's negligence, based on this "apparent authority" theory.

A. The court should dismiss the complaint, because Euphoria has never ruled on the "apparent authority" theory.

B. The court should dismiss the complaint if it concludes that Euphoria does not recognize the "apparent authority" theory, even though Angeles has pleaded that she reasonably believed that Dr. Kildare was an employee of the hospital.

C. The court should not dismiss the complaint, because Angeles's reasonable belief that Dr. Kildare was an employee is a question of fact, and the motion is only meant to determine the legal sufficiency of the complaint.

D. The court should not dismiss the complaint, because it must take the allegations in the complaint as true on a motion to dismiss under Rule 12(b)(6), and Angeles has alleged that Centerville is liable for the acts of Dr. Kildare.

ANALYSIS. In this case, Angeles has asserted a claim that may or may not be legally valid. The Euphoria appellate courts have never ruled on the question, so the trial judge has no authority to guide her in reaching the legal conclusion as to whether the complaint "states a claim upon which relief can be granted." What should she do?

A suggests that the judge should dismiss the complaint, because no Euphoria case has recognized a claim based on the "apparent authority" theory before. This appears to be based on the premise that no new theory is a valid theory, or else that a trial court should always reject novel claims, leaving it to the appellate courts to recognize them. This is too narrow a conception of a trial court's authority. Generally, a trial court must decide whether the claim is valid or not, and it may conclude that it is valid, even if no appellate court has addressed the point. The trial judge might conclude, for example, that appellate cases recognizing the "apparent authority" argument in other contexts indicate that it would be accepted here as well. Or it might rely on the reasoning of courts from other states that have recognized the claim. In the absence of controlling authority from the appellate courts, the question for the trial judge is whether the claim the plaintiff asserts should be recognized, not whether it has been. Trial judges, as well as appellate judges, can pronounce rules of common law, though of course they can also be reversed on appeal if the appellate court disagrees with their holdings.

D is tempting, but wrong. It asserts that the motion should be denied, because the allegations in the complaint must be taken as true in ruling on the motion, and Angeles has alleged that Centerville is liable. Can you see the fallacy in this argument? Surely, the court must take factual allegations in a complaint as true, for purposes of ruling on a motion to dismiss for failure to state a claim, but it need not assume the truth of *legal* allegations. The legal validity of the claim the plaintiff asserts is exactly what the motion is designed to assess. If the court had to accept the plaintiff's allegation that the cause of action she asserts exists, the motion could never be granted! No, the court will assume the truth of Angeles's *factual* allegation that she reasonably believed that Kildare was a Centerville employee, but not her *legal* assertion that Centerville is liable for his acts if she did.

C asserts that the complaint should not be dismissed, because there is a dispute of fact as to whether Angeles reasonably believed that Dr. Kildare worked for the hospital. The court cannot decide facts on the motion to dismiss for failure to state a claim, only the legal sufficiency of the complaint. So doesn't the court have to let the case go forward?

As in the last question, the parties will only need to litigate the factual issues if they are relevant to a valid claim. Here, whether Angeles thought Kildare worked for the hospital is irrelevant, if that belief would not make the hospital liable. Even if Angeles believed that Kildare worked for the hospital, her claim must be dismissed if, under Euphoria law, the patient's belief is not enough to make the hospital vicariously liable for Kildare's negligence. So, if the court holds that apparent authority is insufficient to impose liability on the hospital, it will dismiss Angeles's claim, regardless of whether Angeles reasonably believed that Kildare worked for it.

So **B** is the best answer. If the trial court concludes that Euphoria law doesn't impose liability on a hospital for the acts of an independent contractor/surgeon (even if the patient thought she worked for the hospital), the trial court will dismiss the claim for "failure to state a claim upon which relief can be granted." In so doing, the trial court is "making" Euphoria law. If Angeles thinks the trial judge is wrong in rejecting her claim, she can appeal the dismissal, and get a decision from an appellate court on the apparent authority theory.

C. Summary judgment compared: "Piercing the pleadings"

In most cases, the plaintiff's complaint *does* state a claim for which relief can be granted. It isn't usually that hard to allege a valid cause of action. But it is one thing to *allege* the required elements and quite another to prove that they are true. Frequently, the defendant will doubt that the plaintiff can prove all of the elements of her complaint, and wish to challenge her ability to do so before trial. The motion for summary judgment under Fed. R. Civ. P. 56 provides a mechanism for doing so, and for disposing of cases if that challenge demonstrates that the plaintiff has no proof of a required element.[1]

Suppose, for example, that Fuentes, the beneficiary on Carello's life insurance policy, seeks to recover the proceeds of the policy from Reliable Insurance Company. Reliable refuses to pay, arguing that Carello committed suicide; the insurance company would not be liable on the policy if he did. Fuentes sues, alleging that Carello owned the policy, that she was the beneficiary, that Carello died accidentally, and Reliable has breached the contract by failing to pay the proceeds. These allegations state a good claim for breach of contract. If Fuentes proves them, she would be entitled to recover.

But suppose that Reliable had good reason to refuse to pay. Reliable investigators had interviewed a witness, Herrera, who will testify that Carello, who was seriously ill, had deliberately jumped from a seventh-story window. Convinced that Fuentes cannot prove an essential element of her claim — that Carello died accidentally — it moves for summary judgment, attaching Herrera's affidavit swearing that Carello deliberately jumped.

Reliable's motion, supported by admissible evidence (sworn eyewitness testimony) challenges Fuentes's ability to prove an element of her case. It says to the court, "Fuentes may have alleged accidental death, but she can't prove that allegation. Our evidence shows that Carello did not die accidentally, so Fuentes cannot recover under the policy. Consequently, there is no dispute of fact about how he died, and we are entitled to judgment as a matter of law under Fed. R. Civ. P. 56(a)."

---

1. Plaintiffs as well as defendants may move for summary judgment. For simplicity's sake, the text usually refers to motions made by the defendant.

This sounds pretty convincing, doesn't it? There's no need to convene a jury and try the case if there's nothing to try, and Reliable has argued that there really isn't anything to try, because there is "no genuine dispute" of material fact about how Carello died. If Reliable is right about that, it ought to win, right now, "as a matter of law."

When Reliable makes the motion, challenging Fuentes's ability to prove an element of her case, and supports the motion with admissible evidence, Fuentes must respond by demonstrating that there *is* a "genuine issue of material fact," or the motion will be granted. To defeat the motion, Fuentes must demonstrate that she has admissible evidence—proof that she could put before a jury—to support her allegation that the death was accidental. Fed. R. Civ. P. 56(c)(1), (4). If she has such evidence, the motion will flush it out. If she doesn't, the motion has done its job; it has demonstrated that she cannot prove an essential element of her case, and therefore must lose.

Consider how the judge should rule in the following example.

QUESTION 3. Evidence of allegations. Fuentes, the beneficiary of a life insurance policy owned by Carello, sues Reliable Insurance to collect the proceeds of the policy. In its answer, Reliable claims that Carello committed suicide, and it is therefor not liable on the policy. (As a matter of law, it would not be liable if this is true.) Reliable moves for summary judgment, attaching the affidavit of Herrera, who swears that he saw Carello deliberately jump from the seventh-story window. It also attaches an excerpt from a deposition of Carello's family physician, in which she states that she had told Carello that he was dangerously ill and not likely to live more than a few more months.

Fuentes files an affidavit in opposition to the motion, in which she testifies under oath that "Carello did not commit suicide." The trial judge should

A. grant the motion, since Fuentes's affidavit does not satisfy the requirements of Rule 56 for materials sufficient to defeat the motion.
B. deny the motion because Fuentes has submitted an affidavit contradicting Reliable's materials.
C. deny the motion, because there is a genuine issue of material fact as to whether Carello committed suicide.
D. deny the motion if she believes that Herrera's testimony may be biased.

ANALYSIS. When a party supports a summary judgment motion with admissible evidence, as Reliable has done here, the opposing party must respond with countervailing admissible evidence, to show that there is a real issue to be tried.

Fuentes hasn't done that here. Instead, she has filed an affidavit that simply restates the position in her complaint, that Carello died accidentally.

A motion for summary judgment requires more; it requires the party to go beyond stating a position to produce *proof* of that position. There's a difference between reasserting her opinion that Carello died accidentally, as Fuentes has done here, and supporting it with admissible evidence (Fed. R. Civ. P. 56(c)(1)) that supports her position. Fuentes has not done that here.

A is right. The motion should be granted, because Fuentes's reassertion that Carello did not commit suicide is mere opinion, it does not provide any admissible evidence to support that position. If she has such evidence, the motion requires her to produce it. For example, she might submit an affidavit from D'Urso, another witness to Carrello's fall, who states that she was there and saw Carello accidentally fall out of the window while trying to adjust a shade. That would pose a direct conflict in the testimony for a jury to resolve. Fuentes's burden, when the motion is properly supported, is to show that she has admissible evidence to support "her side of the story." If she has no evidence to support her allegation that Carello died accidentally, she cannot carry her burden of proof at trial, and the judge would grant summary judgment for Reliable.

D is clearly inadequate. In ruling on the motion, the judge does not evaluate the quality of the evidence or the credibility of witnesses. Indeed, she has very little basis to do so based on written affidavits. Her only job is to determine if the evidence is genuinely contradictory, if there is a real dispute on the challenged point. If there is, she denies the motion; if there isn't she may grant it.

C also fails, because Fuentes's affidavit does not establish that there is a genuine dispute *in the evidence* about whether Carello committed suicide. Surely, she and Reliable take different positions on the point, but that isn't enough to keep the case going, without some proof from Fuentes that she can back up her position with evidence. And **B** is wrong, because it isn't enough for Fuentes to contradict Reliable's affidavits at the summary judgment stage. When the motion is made and supported with admissible evidence, she must contradict that evidence with countervailing evidence the jury could use to find for her on the cause-of-death issue. She hasn't done that. Summary judgment should be granted for Reliable.

Here's another example that considers the burden of the party opposing a motion for summary judgment.

QUESTION 4. A matter of life and death. Fuentes, the beneficiary of a life insurance policy owned by Carello, sues Reliable Insurance to collect the proceeds of the policy. In its answer, Reliable claims that Carello committed suicide, and it is therefore not liable on the policy. (As a matter of law, it would not be liable if this is true.) Reliable moves for summary judgment, attaching the affidavit of Herrera, who swears that he saw Carello deliberately jump from the seventh-story window. It also attaches an excerpt from a deposition of Carello's family physician, in which she states that she had told Carello that he was dangerously ill and not likely to live more than a few more months.

Fuentes files an affidavit in opposition to the motion, in which she states that she had had a conversation with Carello a week before he died, in which he expressed disbelief that he was seriously ill, and the hope that he would recover. The trial judge should

A. grant the motion if she concludes that Carello committed suicide.
B. deny the motion because Fuentes has submitted an affidavit opposing the motion.
C. deny the motion if she concludes that Fuentes's affidavit is truthful.
D. deny the motion if she concludes that there is a question of fact as to whether Carello committed suicide.

ANALYSIS.   Reliable's motion has posed an issue of life and death to Fuentes's case. If Fuentes has not raised a triable issue of fact on the cause of Carello's death, her case will meet an untimely demise on summary judgment. She cannot win if Carello committed suicide, and Reliable's evidence suggests that he did. To keep her case alive, she must bring forth opposing evidence that could lead a jury to reject Reliable's evidence and to find that he died accidentally.

A is wrong, because the judge's role in ruling on this summary judgment motion is not to determine whether Carello committed suicide. It is only to decide whether Fuentes has produced credible evidence that he did not. If she has produced such evidence, then there is a "genuine dispute as to any material fact" on the issue, and the jury must resolve it, not the judge.

B is also inaccurate. It isn't enough for Fuentes to submit some opposing materials. She has to submit opposing materials that demonstrate that there is "a genuine dispute" as to the factual issue challenged by Reliable. It isn't at all clear that she has done that here. Even if Carello wasn't sure he was mortally ill a week earlier, it is doubtful that, based on this general evidence of his earlier state of mind, a jury could ignore the testimony of Herrera, who was on the spot and testifies that he jumped. But you don't have to decide that to reject B. It suggests that the motion must be denied as long as Fuentes submitted *something*, and that clearly isn't enough to avoid summary judgment.

C fails as well: First, the judge does not decide the truth of Fuentes's affidavit. How could he? The motion is not a trial, Fuentes is not testifying in person, and the judge does not hear all the evidence. The judge's role on the motion is simply to decide if the affidavit provides admissible evidence that Carello's death was accidental, not whether it is true. Second, the affidavit could be true yet not prevent entry of judgment for Reliable. The judge might conclude that, even if it is true that Carello was hopeful the week before, this is not inconsistent with the uncontradicted evidence that he committed suicide a week later.

So **D** is the best answer. The judge should deny the motion only if she concludes that Fuentes has demonstrated a genuine dispute of fact for the jury to decide as to whether Carello committed suicide. Her affidavit here is probably insufficient to do that. If I were the judge, and a disinterested witness testified that he saw Carello jump out the window, and the only countervailing evidence was testimony that a week earlier he didn't believe he was mortally ill, I would likely grant judgment for the insurer. Testimony that Cavallo had hoped to live and earlier thought that he would does not contradict the testimony that he jumped; it simply provides evidence of his earlier state of mind. It hardly seems sufficient to allow a jury to conclude that he didn't commit suicide, in the face of disinterested testimony that he did.

Under Rule 56(a) summary judgment should be granted only if there is "no genuine dispute as to any material fact" and the moving party is entitled to judgment as a matter of law. This is a somewhat misleading provision, unless you parse it very, very closely. Consider this question.

QUESTION 5. Immaterial materials? Tang sues Crucible Laboratories, Inc., for injuries suffered in an accident with Jericho, who was driving a Crucible van at the time of the accident. His complaint alleges that Jericho's negligence caused the accident, that Jericho was acting in the scope of his employment for Crucible at the time, and that Tang suffered a serious back injury as a result of the accident.

In its answer, Crucible denies that Jericho was negligent, denies that Tang suffered a back injury from the accident, and denies that Jericho was acting in the scope of employment at the time of the accident. (Crucible would only be liable for Jericho's negligence if he had been acting in the scope of employment at the time of the accident.) Crucible subsequently moves for summary judgment, attaching an affidavit of Gomez, a shift supervisor for Crucible. Gomez states that on the day of the accident, Jericho had received a call that his mother had been rushed to the hospital and borrowed the van to drive to the hospital to visit her. Based on this affidavit, it argues that it is entitled to judgment as a matter of law, since the evidence shows that Jericho was not acting in the scope of employment at the time of the accident.

Tang responds with two affidavits. One, from his doctor, explains Tang's serious back symptoms, and expresses the opinion that they were caused by the accident. The other is the affidavit of a witness to the accident, stating that before the accident Jericho had swerved into the opposite lane in front of Tang, causing the accident. Summary judgment for Crucible should

A. be granted.
B. be denied, because Tang has submitted evidentiary materials with his opposition to the motion.
C. be denied, because Tang's supporting evidence shows that there are genuine issues of material fact concerning Jericho's negligence and the cause of Tang's back injury.
D. be denied, because the pleadings show that three issues of fact are in dispute: Jericho's negligence, whether he was in the scope of employment, and the cause of Tang's back injury.

ANALYSIS. In a tort case, the plaintiff can only recover if she establishes each element of her claim. If an employer is sued for the tort of an employee, it is only liable if the employee caused the injury in the scope of employment. Tang alleged in his complaint that Jericho did act in the scope, but Crucible's motion for summary judgment challenges Tang to produce some proof that Jericho did. The Gomez affidavit provides admissible evidence that Jericho acted for his own purposes, not Crucible's, in driving at the time of the accident. If that is true, Tang must lose. To avoid summary judgment, he must produce admissible evidence that Jericho acted in the scope of employment at the time of the accident. He didn't do that. Summary judgment should be granted for Crucible. **A** is right.

D is the weakest answer. It takes the position that, if an issue is contested in the pleadings, summary judgment can't be granted on that issue, because the parties obviously take different positions on it. But summary judgment virtually always is sought on issues contested in the pleadings. The motion says, "all right, Tang, you claim Jericho acted in the scope of employment, but I denied that. And now here's proof that my denial is true. If you have contrary proof, let's see it. I'm challenging you to show that you can not only allege scope of employment, but back it up with admissible evidence." If Tang can't do that, summary judgment may be granted for Crucible, even though Tang alleged that Jericho acted in the scope of employment.

C is the most distracting distractor. What makes it tempting is that puzzling language in Fed. R. Civ. P. 56(a), that summary judgment can only be granted if there is "no genuine dispute as to any material fact. . . ." Tang's affidavits show that he has admissible evidence to show that Jericho was negligent, and that his negligence caused Tang's back injury. If those issues are disputed, how can summary judgment be granted? Well, in the language of Rule 56(a), these facts are not *material* if Jericho did not act in the scope of employment. A chain is only as strong as its weakest link: If Jericho did not act in the scope of employment, Crucible is not liable for his negligence. *Even if* he was negligent in causing the accident, and *even if* the accident did cause Tang's sore back, Tang will not recover without establishing the scope-of-employment allegation. So, if Crucible demonstrates that Tang cannot prove any one element of his claim, Crucible is entitled to summary judgment. The rule is confusing on this, but Crucible certainly can get summary judgment without showing that there is "no genuine dispute of fact" about *every* issue in the case.

B is clearly wrong. It is not sufficient for the party opposing summary judgment to submit something. She must submit evidence that shows a genuine factual dispute about the element challenged by the motion, here scope of employment. Tang's materials show that Tang has admissible evidence about two other issues in the case, but do not present anything to contradict Crucible's evidence that Jericho acted on a personal errand rather than in the scope of employment. Tang needs to produce such counter-vailing evidence to avoid summary judgment.

D. Summary judgment, if appropriate

The purpose of the summary judgment motion is to challenge a party's ability to prove an allegation in the pleadings. The moving party supports her motion by submitting evidence that, if uncontradicted, would establish the claim or defense she asserts. To avoid summary judgment, the opposing party then must come forward with evidence showing that she has con-tradictory evidence. Fed. R. Civ. P. 56(c)(1). But suppose the party opposing the motion doesn't produce such evidence?

Consider how the judge should rule on the summary judgment motion in this case.

QUESTION 6. Inherent contradiction. Fuentes, the beneficiary of a life insurance policy owned by Carello, sues Reliable Insurance to collect the proceeds of the policy. Before answering the complaint, Reliable files a motion for summary judgment. Its ground for the motion is that Carello, who was seriously ill, committed suicide by taking an overdose of sleeping pills, and it is therefor not liable on the policy. (As a matter of law, it would not be liable if this is true.) Reliable attaches the affidavit of Allen to the motion. Allen's affidavit states that on the day before he died,

> Carello told her that he was miserable, that he couldn't get any rest due to pain caused by his illness, and that he was glad he had a full bottle of sleeping pills.
>
> Assume that Fuentes files no affidavit or other admissible evidence in opposition to the motion. The trial judge should
>
> A. grant the motion, because Allen's affidavit supports Reliable's position that Carello committed suicide.
> B. grant the motion, because Fuentes has failed to respond to it with supporting materials, as required by Rule 56(c)(1).
> C. deny the motion, because it is not clear that Reliable is entitled to judgment as a matter of law.
> D. deny the motion, because it may not be filed until Reliable has answered the complaint.

ANALYSIS.   D is belied by the language of Rule 56(b), which allows a defendant to make the motion "at any time until 30 days after the close of discovery." Reliable's motion itself shows that it denies an essential element of Fuentes' case — that Carello died accidentally. If Reliable's materials demonstrate that Fuentes cannot establish that point, the court could dismiss the case without ever requiring an answer.

At first glance, it seems that **B** is right. Rule 56(c)(1) states that when a summary judgment motion is made and supported as required under Rule 56, the opposing party must produce opposing evidence to show that there is a dispute of fact for the jury to consider. Here, Fuentes has not produced any evidence to contradict Allen's affidavit.

However, summary judgment still is not warranted if the moving party's materials — here, Reliable's — do not suffice to establish the issue of fact on which the motion is based. If Reliable's materials do not establish that there is no dispute of fact as to whether Carello committed suicide, summary judgment should be denied, even if Fuentes did not submit materials to contradict Reliable's evidence. So **B** is wrong; Reliable does not win automatically simply on the procedural ground that Fuentes failed to file opposing evidence.

A is also a weak answer. Under Rule 56(a), the judge should grant summary judgment only if the moving party's materials themselves show that there is no genuine dispute of material fact to be determined, and that the moving party is entitled to judgment. Here, Reliable's affidavit doesn't show that there is no genuine issue of fact about how Carello died. The evidence in Allen's affidavit is ambiguous. It would support an inference that Carello intended to commit suicide, but it would also support an inference that he simply intended to use the pills to help him sleep. Consider what would happen if this case went to trial, and Reliable presented Allen's testimony to prove that Carello committed suicide. That testimony might suffice to support a finding that Carello committed suicide, but it certainly does not compel such a finding, even in the absence of countervailing evidence. Thus, Allen's evidence, even if uncontradicted, does not show that there is "no genuine dispute of material fact" as to how Carello died. C is right; it is not appropriate to grant summary judgment where Reliable's own materials do not clearly support a finding that Carello committed suicide. Of course, the safer course would be for Fuentes to produce any evidence she has that Carello did not commit suicide. But she will not automatically lose if she does not.

E.   Mixed motions: Rule 12(b)(6) and the "speaking motion"

In deciding a Rule 12(b)(6) motion for failure to state a claim for which relief can be granted, the court only considers the complaint itself, to determine whether, if the allegations in the complaint are proved, the plaintiff would be entitled to some form of relief.

Clear though that proposition may be, litigants frequently disregard it — sometimes consciously, sometimes mistakenly — in filing Rule 12(b)(6) motions. It is very common for defendants to use the Rule 12(b)(6) motion not to challenge whether the plaintiff has *pleaded* a compensable claim — the intended role of the Rule 12(b)(6) motion — but rather to challenge her ability to *prove* her case. To do that, they frequently submit evidence with a Rule 12(b)(6) motion to show that she can't prove a necessary element of her claim.

For example, suppose that Van Dam, a sailor, sues Jimenez, owner of a ship, under a federal statute authorizing recovery from the owner for injuries at sea. In the complaint, he alleges that his injuries took place at sea. Jimenez, however, has evidence that Van Dam's injury took place on the dock before sailing, which would not be compensable under the statute. So he moves to dismiss under Rule 12(b)(6), claiming that the complaint "fails to state a claim upon which relief can be granted," because the injury took place on land, not at sea. And he attaches to the motion affidavits from witnesses stating that the injury took place before the ship sailed.

Although Jimenez's motion isn't strictly proper — it confuses the role of Rule 12 with that of Rule 56 — motions like it are filed so often that Rule 12 acknowledges the practice and instructs the court how to deal with such "speaking motions" (so called because they go beyond a legal challenge to introduce factual evidence outside of the complaint).

If, on a motion under Rule 12(b)(6) or 12(c), matters outside the pleadings are presented to and not excluded by the court, the motion must be treated as one for summary judgment under Rule 56. All parties must be given a reasonable opportunity to present all the material that is pertinent to the motion.

Fed. R. Civ. P. 12(d).

Under this provision, if the defendant has in effect moved for summary judgment, by submitting *evidence* about the truth of the allegations, rather than challenging their legal sufficiency, the court can convert the motion to a motion for summary judgment and treat it accordingly. The judge will consider the motion not under the Rule 12(b)(6) standard, but the Rule 56 "no-genuine-dispute-of-material-fact" standard in Fed. R. Civ. P. 56(a), and both parties will be given an opportunity to submit admissible evidence relevant to the disputed allegation.

The defendant isn't really getting away with something by this less than rigorous use of the Rule 12(b)(6) motion. Rule 56(b) provides that a defending party can move for summary judgment at any time until after the close of discovery, so the court is just treating the motion as the summary judgment motion the defendant could have filed anyway.

With this background, the example should be pretty straightforward.

QUESTION 7. **Speaking of motions.**   Fenske is injured in an auto accident with Shea, a driver for Consolidated Fabricators, Inc. She sues Consolidated for her injuries, alleging that she was injured due to Shea's negligent driving in the scope of employment. Consolidated answers the complaint, and a week later files a motion to dismiss it for failure to state a claim upon which relief can be granted. It attaches an affidavit of Spenser, Shea's supervisor, to the motion, stating that Shea was not at work that day, and a short brief citing authority for the proposition that it is not liable if he was not acting in the scope of employment at the time of the accident.

The judge should

A. grant the motion, since Consolidated's affidavits establish that Shea was not working at the time of the accident.
B. treat the motion as a motion for summary judgment, and grant it if it is clear that the plaintiff's complaint fails to state a claim upon which relief can be granted.
C. treat the motion as a motion for summary judgment, but deny it, since Fenske's complaint states a valid legal claim. If she proves that Shea acted in the scope of employment she could recover damages from Consolidated.

> **D.** treat the motion as a motion for summary judgment, allow Fenske to file countervailing evidence to oppose it, and then decide if there is a genuine issue of material fact as to whether Shea acted in the scope of employment.

ANALYSIS.   In this case the defendant has filed a "speaking motion" challenging Fenske's case. Although it has styled it as a motion to dismiss for failure to state a claim, it has actually challenged Fenske's ability to prove her case, by submitting an affidavit contradicting her allegation that Shea acted in the scope of employment. The sentence from Rule 12(b) quoted before the question tells the court how to deal with the motion.

C is wrong, because it suggests that the court should treat the motion as one for summary judgment, but then decide it under the Rule 12(b)(6) failure-to-state-a-claim standard. That wouldn't make sense. If the judge is going to consider evidence about the scope-of-employment question, she is making a decision not about legal sufficiency, but the presence or absence of evidentiary support for the allegation, and she should use the Rule 56 standard. She should determine whether there is a genuine dispute of fact about whether Shea acted in the scope of employment. If there is, she should deny the motion. If there isn't she should grant it, since Consolidated would be entitled to judgment as a matter of law if Shea did not act in the scope of employment.

B fares no better. It suggests that the judge should deny the motion if she concludes that the complaint is legally sufficient to state a claim. But again, the "speaking motion" doesn't challenge legal sufficiency; it challenges the plaintiff's ability to prove an allegation in the complaint—here, that Shea acted in the scope of employment. If the judge treats the motion as one for summary judgment, she should decide it under the summary judgment standard.

A suggests that the judge should treat the motion as one for summary judgment, and grant it if Consolidated's affidavits show that Shea wasn't working at the time of the accident. The problem here is that, if the motion is going to challenge Fenske's *proof* that Shea acted in the scope of employment, Fenske ought to have a chance to present proof that Shea *did* act in the scope, before the court grants summary judgment for Consolidated. When a judge converts a purported Rule 12(b)(6) motion to a motion for summary judgment, she must give the opposing party time to respond to the moving party's supporting materials, to produce her own admissible evidence to show that the challenged fact is genuinely contested. See Fed. R. Civ. P. 56(c)(1). In the question, Fenske hasn't had her chance to do that yet.

So **D** is the proper choice. If the judge allows Consolidated to challenge Fenske's ability to prove scope of employment, it should allow Fenske the opportunity to submit her own evidence tending to prove that Shea did act in the scope of employment, and then decide whether there is a dispute of fact on that question. If there is, the case is for the jury, and summary judgment should be denied.

F. Summary judgment for the plaintiff

The discussion so far has focused on motions by the defendant. But the plaintiff may seek summary judgment as well, under the same standard: that there is no genuine issue of material fact and she is entitled to judgment as a matter of law. However, the effect of summary judgment for the plaintiff is often different from the grant of the motion for a defendant.

Here's an example:

QUESTION 8. Insulation from liability. Maxwell sues Chao for breach of a contract to insulate Chao's house. He alleges that they had a contract, and that he did the work, but Chao refused to pay the agreed price for the work. Maxwell seeks recovery in the alternative on a quantum meruit theory.

Chao denies that Maxwell can sue for breach of contract, because the writing Maxwell relies on as the contract—a scribbled note indicating the price for the job—fails to satisfy the requirements for a valid contract under the relevant statute of frauds. Chao also claims that the insulation used was substandard and improperly installed.

Maxwell moves for summary judgment on the question of whether the parties had a contract. In support of his motion, he submits the scribbled note itself, an affidavit attesting that it was signed by Chao in his presence, and a brief arguing that the note is sufficient to constitute a binding contract under the statute of frauds. Chao submits no opposing materials, but submits a brief arguing that the note does not constitute a contract, because the terms are insufficiently described in it.

A. If the judge concludes that the note constitutes a valid contract, Maxwell is "entitled to judgment as a matter of law." She should enter judgment for Maxwell for the damages sought in the complaint.
B. If the judge concludes that the note does not meet the requirements of a valid contract, she should enter a final judgment for Chao, dismissing Maxwell's case.
C. The judge should grant Maxwell's motion, because Chao has not submitted any evidence contradicting Maxwell's supporting materials.

D. If the judge concludes that the note meets the requirements of a valid contract, she should enter partial summary judgment for Maxwell on the issue of the validity of the written contract.

ANALYSIS. In this case, Maxwell uses summary judgment to seek a holding from the court that there is no issue of fact with regard to the validity of the contract and that, as a matter of law, it is enforceable. If the court agrees, and grants his motion, what will happen?

A indicates that, since Maxwell would be "entitled to judgment as a matter of law," the judge should enter judgment for Maxwell for the damages he seeks in the complaint. However, Maxwell would not automatically win the entire case if the contract is valid. He would still have to establish that he had performed under the contract in order to recover the price of the work. The judge could grant *partial* summary judgment, establishing that the contract is valid. See Fed. R. Civ. P. 56(g). However, since the issue of whether Maxwell performed the contract would still be in dispute, she could not enter judgment on the entire case for Maxwell.

B is wrong too. It indicates that, if the judge concludes that the writing does not constitute a valid contract, she should enter judgment for Chao, dismissing the complaint. However, Maxwell has also sought quantum meruit recovery in the other count of his complaint, which he could recover even if the contract is not enforceable. So his case should not be dismissed, even if his count based on the written contract is.

C focuses on Chao's failure to submit opposing evidence. Rule 56 usually requires the party opposing summary judgment to submit supporting evidentiary materials, to convince the judge that there is a factual issue to be tried. Here, however, Chao does not disagree with the facts set forth by Maxwell in support of the motion. He agrees that the note is the only writing evidencing the contract, but takes the position that, as a matter of law, it is insufficient to satisfy the statute of frauds. In effect, he admits that there is "no genuine dispute of material fact" about the writing, but takes the position that Maxwell is *not* entitled to judgment as a matter of law, since the writing he has produced doesn't satisfy the statute of frauds. This is permissible under Rule 56. Indeed, summary judgment provides an excellent vehicle for resolving cases in which the parties' disagreement is not about the facts themselves, but about the legal effect of the facts. Chao might well have made a cross-motion for summary judgment here, arguing that *she* is entitled to judgment as a matter of law, because the note is insufficient to evidence a contract. If the judge agreed, she could grant judgment for Chao on the written-contract claim, since Maxwell could not win on it if the writing is insufficient.

So, **D** takes the prize. If the judge concludes that the note suffices as a writing, she should grant partial summary judgment for Maxwell on the issue of the sufficiency of the note as a contract. But she would not enter judgment for Maxwell on the claim as a whole, because his motion only establishes one element of the claim, existence of the contract. Maxwell still has to establish other elements of the contract claim (such as adequate performance) or the quantum meruit claim, in order to recover from Chao.

G.   The Closer: Summary judgment, jurisdiction, and the merits

Sometimes it can be hard to distinguish challenges to a court's subject matter jurisdiction from challenges to the merits of a claim. Frequently, a court must decide facts in order to determine whether it has subject matter jurisdiction over a case. For example, a court may have to determine a party's domicile, or a corporation's principal place of business, in order to decide whether the court has subject matter jurisdiction based on diversity.

When facts must be found in order to determine jurisdiction, the court is the fact finder on the jurisdictional issues. To determine diversity, it does not ask whether there is a genuine dispute of material fact as to whether the plaintiff is domiciled in Wisconsin; it *decides* whether she is domiciled there. Thus, the court's role in dealing with disputed issues of fact about jurisdiction is fundamentally different from its role in determining whether issues of fact about the merits are disputed. In considering a motion for summary judgment on issues going to the merits, the court only decides whether a genuine issue of fact exists about those issues; it does not decide those issues itself.

Consider what motion the defendant should file in the following case, and whether the court should decide the relevant facts itself or determine, under the summary judgment standard, whether an issue of fact is posed for the jury.

QUESTION 9. Substance and procedure.   Conway Corporation sues FunSoft Corporation in federal court for selling Voop, a card game, in Illinois. Conway claims that FunSoft's sale of Voop in Illinois infringes its trademark on Vooper, its own card game. Conway asserts that the court has subject matter jurisdiction because the claim arises under federal law, specifically, the federal trademark statute.

FunSoft claims that it did not sell Voop in Illinois, so it cannot be liable for trademark infringement for selling there. It has affidavits from three FunSoft employees who testify that FunSoft did not market Voop in Illinois.

FunSoft should

A. move to dismiss the case for lack of subject matter jurisdiction. The trial judge should determine whether FunSoft sold Voop in Illinois, and dismiss the case for lack of subject matter jurisdiction if she finds that it did not.

B. move for summary judgment on the issue of whether the court has subject matter jurisdiction over the case. The court should allow Conway to file countervailing materials under Rule 56, determine whether there is a genuine dispute of fact as to whether FunSoft sold Voop in Illinois, and take jurisdiction if it finds that there is a dispute of fact on the issue.

C. move for summary judgment on the merits of the trademark claim. The court should allow Conway to file countervailing materials under Rule 56, determine as a matter of fact whether FunSoft marketed Voop in Illinois, and dismiss Conway's claim on the merits if she determines that it did not.

D. move for summary judgment on the merits of the trademark claim. The court should allow Conway to file countervailing materials under Rule 56, and determine whether there is a disputed issue of fact as to whether FunSoft marketed Voop in Illinois. If it finds that there is, it should deny summary judgment, and the parties should prepare to try the case.

ANALYSIS. The point here is to figure out whether FunSoft is really challenging the court's power to hear the case, or the plaintiff's ability to prove it. If it is challenging jurisdiction, and the court needs to decide facts to determine its jurisdiction, the court would be the fact finder. If it is challenging Conway's ability to establish an element of its claim on the merits, it should move for summary judgment. The court would then determine whether there is a genuine dispute in the evidence, and deny summary judgment if it finds that there is.

FunSoft is not really challenging the court's subject matter jurisdiction. Under the *Mottley* rule, the federal court has arising-under jurisdiction if Conway has alleged a right to relief arising under federal law. Conway has done so; it alleges that FunSoft sold Voop in Illinois, infringing its trademark. This allegation is sufficient to confer arising-under jurisdiction on the court. Even if it turns out that Conway is wrong, that FunSoft didn't sell Voop in Illinois, it has still filed a claim alleging relief under federal law. Unless it is utterly frivolous, the court has subject matter jurisdiction over the case. FunSoft is really saying, "You can't prove that we violated the trademark statute, because your allegation that we sold in Illinois isn't true." Thus, FunSoft challenges Conway's ability to prove the federal claim it has alleged; it does not claim that Conway hasn't alleged a claim under federal law.

So **A** is wrong. FunSoft should file a motion for summary judgment on the allegation that it sold Voop in Illinois, not a motion to dismiss for lack of subject matter jurisdiction. And the judge should not decide, as a fact, whether FunSoft sold there, but only whether there is a genuine issue of fact as to whether it did. And **B** is wrong, because it suggests that the decision is jurisdictional, and that the court should decide its jurisdiction by applying the summary judgment standard. If the judge needs to decide jurisdictional facts, she will do so by the preponderance of the evidence, because she is the fact finder on such facts. But here, so long as there is a colorable allegation that FunSoft violated the federal trademark laws, the court has jurisdiction. It does not have to decide whether FunSoft actually violated those laws to determine its jurisdiction. To do so would be to turn the ultimate merits issue into a jurisdictional issue.

C is also wrong, because it suggests as well that the judge should decide whether FunSoft sold Voop in Illinois. This is an issue that goes to the merits, not the court's jurisdiction. If FunSoft wishes to challenge Conway's ability to prove that it sold in Illinois, it should move for summary judgment, submitting its evidence to establish that it did not. The court should then decide (after Conway has its opportunity to submit counter-vailing evidence) whether there is a genuine dispute about whether FunSoft sold in Illinois, *not* decide the factual question itself. If it finds a meaningful dispute in the evidence, it would deny summary judgment, since the issue is then for the jury. So, **D** is the right answer.

 Glannon's Picks

1. Law and facts	B
2. Authority on point	B
3. Evidence of allegations	A
4. A matter of life and death	D
5. Immaterial materials?	A
6. Inherent contradiction	C
7. Speaking of motions	D
8. Insulation from liability	D
9. Substance and procedure	D

21

Judgment as a Matter of Law in the Federal Courts

Defendant's counsel let out a guffaw,
When at the close of the trial she saw,
That the plaintiff couldn't win,
No matter how great the spin,
So she sought judgment as a matter of law.
—M.G., Harvard

CHAPTER OVERVIEW

A. The function of the directed verdict motion (judgment as a matter of law before verdict)

B. The meaning of a "legally insufficient evidentiary basis"

C. Reviewing the entry of judgment as a matter of law on appeal

D. Judgment notwithstanding the verdict (judgment as a matter of law after the verdict)

E. Prerequisites for judgment as a matter of law under Rule 50(b)

F. The Closer: "Directing the verdict" in a judge-tried case

✦ Glannon's Picks

Surprisingly, the plaintiff who survives jurisdictional challenges, the travail of discovery, and the likely motion for summary judgment, and gets to trial, may still not have the jury decide her case. Even at trial, the judge has several devices for controlling the jury's consideration of the case, or for withdrawing it entirely from the jury's consideration. This chapter considers two devices — the motions for a directed verdict and for judgment notwithstanding the verdict — that a judge may use to restrict the jury's decision-making in cases that go to trial.

In the federal courts, these motions are both called "motions for judgment as a matter of law." Fed. R. Civ. P. 50(a), (b). However, functionally the motion is the same as the traditional directed verdict motion if it is made before the jury deliberates, and the same as the traditional motion for judgment notwithstanding the verdict, if it is made after the jury returns its verdict.

These motions may be granted for either the plaintiff or the defendant. However, because the plaintiff bears the burden of proof in a civil case, to establish all elements of her claim, these motions are much more frequently made by the defendant, challenging the sufficiency of the plaintiff's proof of one or more elements of her claim. In this chapter I'll talk in terms of the defendant as the party making the motion; just remember that I'm oversimplifying a bit for illustration purposes.

A.   The function of the directed verdict motion (judgment as a matter of law before verdict)

The purpose of the directed verdict motion is to ask the trial judge to take the case away from the jury, on the ground that the evidence is insufficient to support a verdict for the plaintiff. See Fed. R. Civ. P. 50(a) (motion should be granted where there is "no legally sufficient evidentiary basis" for the jury to find for the party opposing the motion). In a case where the plaintiff's proof is patently inadequate to establish her claim, the judge has the authority to bar the jury from deciding the case, by "directing a verdict" against her. This older name, "directed verdict," is suggestive of the motion's purpose: the judge in a sense orders the jury to find a verdict for the defendant, since no other verdict is supportable on the evidence submitted to them.

At one time, judges apparently did literally "direct the verdict," that is, they ordered the jury in such cases to go out and come back with a verdict for the defendant. These days, the judge simply orders a judgment entered for the defendant. The jury has been empaneled and heard the evidence, but doesn't get to deliberate and reach a verdict, because the judge has concluded, as a matter of law, that the evidence is too weak to support a plaintiff's verdict.

How can the judge do this? What about the constitutional right to jury trial? Well, that right is generally interpreted to guarantee a jury decision only where there is a legitimate dispute in the evidence, where a meaningful dispute exists about whether the facts the plaintiff must establish are true. If there is such a conflict in the evidence, so that reasonable jurors could find for either party, the jury should resolve that conflict by "finding the facts." However, if the plaintiff has no evidence, or clearly insufficient evidence, to establish a required element of that claim, courts have held that the jury has no legitimate role to play, because its constitutional role as the finder of facts is not required. See Wright & Miller, Federal Practice and Procedure §2522. If it is clear that the plaintiff cannot establish a required element of her claim, there is no need for the jury to consider the case.

Courts often speak of two burdens the plaintiff must carry in order to obtain a valid verdict in her favor. *First*, she bears the burden to convince *the judge* that her evidence is strong enough on each element of her claim to support a rational verdict in her favor. This is often referred to as the "burden of production." To avoid a directed verdict, the plaintiff must produce enough evidence that a jury, acting rationally upon that evidence, could find that the elements she must prove are met. It is the judge who decides whether the plaintiff has met the burden of production. In making that decision, she does not ask whether she, were she the fact finder, would be convinced of the truth of the disputed element. Instead, she must ask whether a jury, looking at that evidence, could rationally be convinced of it, that is, if the decision is in the debatable range. If she concludes that the plaintiff has met the burden of production on each element of her claim, she denies the motion for judgment as a matter of law and sends the case to the jury.

If the judge concludes that the plaintiff has satisfied the burden to produce credible evidence on each element of her claim, and lets the case go to the jury, it must then decide whether she has met her *second* burden, the burden to prove her case by a preponderance of the evidence. The judge has concluded that a jury rationally *could* find for her on the evidence produced. Now the jury must decide whether it *will* find for her, under a more-probable-than-not standard of proof. The jury's job is to determine whether she has met the "burden of proof" on each element of her claim, while the judge's role is to decide whether she has met the less onerous burden to produce credible evidence of those elements.

Consider the defendant's motion in the following example. It's a negligence case. As you have learned or will learn in Torts, there are four elements to a claim for negligence. To recover for negligence, a plaintiff must establish that the defendant owed her a duty of due care, that the defendant breached that duty, that she suffered damages, and that the defendant's breach of the duty of due care caused her damages.

> **QUESTION 1. Elementary principles.** Powers sues Dr. Vicaro in federal court for negligence in medical treatment. The case goes to trial, and the plaintiff presents all of her evidence. That evidence shows that she went to Vicaro with complaints of pain in her arm, that he treated her with

various drugs, and that the arm has gotten progressively worse, so that now she can barely use it. Her evidence further shows the damages she has suffered due to the loss of use of the arm, including the loss of her job. At the close of the plaintiff's evidence, the defendant moves for judgment as a matter of law under Fed. R. Civ. P. 50(a).

A. The motion should be denied. If the jury believes the plaintiff's evidence, they may conclude that she is disabled and find for her.
B. The motion should be denied because the trial is not yet complete. The defendant hasn't yet put on his case, which might (unintentionally) strengthen the plaintiff's proof.
C. The motion should be granted, since the plaintiff has not established the right to relief for a negligence claim.
D. The motion should be denied, because it can only be made after the jury deliberates, not before.

ANALYSIS.   Let's quickly dispose of the last choice. **D** is wrong because, if a plaintiff's proof is legally insufficient (if she has failed to meet her "burden of production"), the judge has the power to order a judgment as a matter of law for the defendant without letting the jury decide the case. True, she could deny the motion, let the jury deliberate and reach a verdict, and then reconsider whether the evidence is sufficient on a motion for judgment notwithstanding the verdict. See Fed. R. Civ. P. 50(b). But she also has the authority, under Rule 50(a), to withdraw the case from the jury before it deliberates, by granting judgment as a matter of law. If she does, the jury never will deliberate on the case.

   B is also incorrect. It suggests that the defendant must wait until the close of all the evidence to challenge the sufficiency of the plaintiff's case. Under the Federal Rules — and, I'll wager, under those of most states — the defendant may raise that challenge as soon as the plaintiff has had her full chance to present sufficient evidence to get to the jury. When the plaintiff "rests her case," that is, announces that she has put on all her evidence, she has had her full opportunity to establish a credible case on each element of her claim. At that point, she has presumably presented everything she's got to establish breach, causation, and damages,[1] so it's fair to stop the process if, having had that full opportunity, she has failed to produce a submissible case. So the defendant can challenge the sufficiency of the plaintiff's case as soon as the plaintiff has fully presented it. See Fed. R. Civ. P. 50(a) (once "a party has been fully heard on an issue" the court can consider directing a verdict). The defendant need not wait until the close of all the evidence, though the motion may be made then as well, or may be *renewed* then if it was made earlier and denied.

---

1. Duty, the fourth element, is a question of law for the court, not a question of fact for the jury. If the case gets to trial, the court has presumably concluded that the defendant owed the plaintiff a duty of care.

C is the best answer here. Powers has presented credible evidence that Vicaro treated her, and that her arm has gotten worse. But if that were enough to establish a claim, doctors would be liable every time a patient had a bad outcome. Recovery for malpractice requires something more: proof that the doctor was negligent, that her treatment fell below the standard of reasonable care. Nothing in the question suggests that Powers presented any evidence to establish what good medical practice required in treatment of Powers' condition, that Vicaro's treatment failed to live up to that standard, or that any substandard treatment was the cause of Powers' loss of use of the arm. Thus, A fails, because the evidence does not suffice to support recovery without a finding that Vicaro was at fault.

On the evidence presented, Vicaro may have provided excellent treatment, but still been unable to prevent the loss of use of the arm. Many health problems, alas, remain beyond the power of the medical profession to remedy. Powers bears the burden to produce evidence that Vicaro's treatment was substandard, that he "breached the duty of due care," and that the breach caused his damages. Powers can not recover without submitting credible evidence of *all* the elements of her claim, not just some of them, or a majority, but every element of her cause of action. Here, she put on credible evidence that she suffered damages, evidence that could lead a reasonable jury to find that she has become debilitated. That's good! But it's not enough to establish a right to recover, only to prove the damages element of her claim.

If the judge allowed Powers's case to go to the jury on the evidence described, the jury would be licensed to find for her without any proof of a crucial element of her claim. A verdict for her without proof of negligence would be based on legally insufficient evidence. The motion for judgment as a matter of law allows the judge to prevent such legally unsupported verdicts, by refusing to allow the jury to reach them.

The "burden of production/burden of proof" terminology is a little confusing. Basically, the judge is acting as a gatekeeper to ensure that only cases that could reasonably be decided in the plaintiff's favor make it to the jury. If this "burden of production" is met, the jury then decides whether the plaintiff wins. The two "burdens" serve different purposes and are addressed to different participants in the trial. Here's another question that requires you to sort out these burdens.

QUESTION 2. Double trouble. Powers sues Dr. Vicaro for medical malpractice. After both parties have put on their cases Vicaro makes a motion for judgment as a matter of law under Rule 50(a).

A. The judge should grant the motion if she concludes that Powers
   has failed to meet the burden of proof on *any* element of her claim.
B. The judge should grant the motion if she concludes that Powers has
   failed to meet the burden of production on *any* element of her claim.
C. If the judge denies the motion, the jury should determine whether
   Powers has failed to meet the burden of production on *any* element
   of her claim.
D. If the judge denies the motion, the jury should determine whether
   Powers has met the burden of production on each element, *and* the
   burden of proof on each element.

ANALYSIS.   Burdens, burdens, burdens. Which is whose and what do they
require? **A** indicates that the judge should grant the Rule 50(a) motion if she
concludes that Powers has failed to meet the burden of proof on any element
of her claim. This suggests that the judge should decide whether Powers
has proved the elements of her claim, but that's not the judge's job in a case
tried to a jury. The judge's job is to decide whether there's a legitimate
dispute in the evidence on each element of the claim, so that there's a job for
the jury to do.

To decide that, the judge considers whether Powers had produced
enough evidence on each element that a jury, acting rationally on that
evidence, could find for Powers. This is the "burden of production," to
submit adequate evidence on each element to raise a legitimate dispute of
fact about that element. Certainly, the judge could conclude that the result is
debatable (that the burden of production is met) in many cases, even though
she believes the defendant has the better part of the debate (that the plaintiff
has not met the burden of proof). The judge, as gatekeeper, may only
consider whether Powers has met the burden of production. If she has, the
jury decides whether she has carried the burden of proof. **A** confuses the
burdens.

Because the question of meeting the burden of production is a preliminary question for the judge in deciding whether to submit the case to the
jury, **C** and **D** are both also wrong. The jury won't be told anything about the
burden of production, and never considers whether it has been met. Burden
of production is a concept used by the judge in determining whether the case
is "jury-worthy," whether the plaintiff has produced enough evidence to get
into the debatable range. If the case gets to the jury, they will decide whether
the burden of proof has been met, not the burden of production.

That leaves **B**, which correctly distinguishes the burdens. If the judge,
looking at Powers's case, concludes that she has failed to produce adequate
evidence on any element of her claim to support a verdict for her on that
element, she should grant judgment as a matter of law (direct a verdict) for

the defendant. To get to the jury, Powers must submit enough evidence on each element to meet the "burden of production," that is, enough evidence that a rational jury could find the element proved. This does not mean enough that the judge believes it is proved, but enough that she couldn't say a verdict for Powers on the element would be legally insupportable.

B. The meaning of a "legally insufficient evidentiary basis"

So, we've established that one of the judge's roles is to make sure that the plaintiff has presented enough evidence on each element of her claim that a jury could reason to a rational verdict for her on each element. If she has, the jury gets the case; if she hasn't, the judge may order entry of judgment for the defendant. Still, it looks perilously like the judge is finding facts herself, by restraining the jury's ability to do so where the evidence is weak. Isn't the conclusion that the evidence is "too weak to support a verdict" for the plaintiff a subjective judgment by the judge on the facts themselves?

Well, it is somewhat subjective. It's hard to dispute that the judge does, in some degree, pass upon the strength of the plaintiff's case, unless it's a case like that in Question 1, where there was literally *no* evidence on a required element. But the cases at least establish some guidelines to constrain the judge in making the too-weak-for-a-jury determination. *First*, the judge isn't to direct a verdict because she thinks the defendant's proof (on one or more of the elements of the claim) is stronger than the plaintiff's. That would be substituting her judgment about the facts for the jury's. She's not supposed to do that; she's supposed to decide whether a jury could rationally reach a verdict for the plaintiff on the evidence before it.

Second, in deciding whether to direct a verdict, the judge does not decide for herself whether the witnesses are telling the truth. Except where testimony is literally incredible, she must assume that the jury will construe the evidence in favor of the nonmoving party. The standard is "whether the evidence is such that, without weighing the credibility of the witnesses or otherwise considering the weight of the evidence, there can be but one conclusion as to the verdict that reasonable [persons] could have reached." *Simblest v. Maynard*, 427 F.2d 1, 4 (2d Cir. 1970). The judge must assume that the jury will believe the plaintiff's witnesses, even if their testimony is impeached or contradicted by the defendant's. It's up to the jury to decide whom to believe, not the judge, so legitimate conflicts in the testimony about who ran the red light should go to the jury. *Third*, if certain testimony would support two inferences, one that supports recovery and one that doesn't, it is the jury's job to decide which inference to make. The judge, in passing on the motion, must assume that the jury will make the inference that favors the plaintiff. In other words, she is supposed to take the case in the light most favorable to the plaintiff, assume that the jury will resolve conflicts in the testimony in the plaintiff's favor, and ask, *if it does*, would there be adequate evidence to support a plaintiff's verdict.

Here's a question (based on facts shamelessly cribbed from another source)[2] that illustrates the application of these guidelines.

QUESTION 3. Found facts? Pavarotti sues Sills for negligence, after he is hit by a car on Maple Street. The driver did not stop after the accident. At trial, Pavarotti presents the testimony of a bystander that the car was a red Chevrolet, that two of the numbers on the license plate were "3" and "1," and that the driver was a blonde woman. He further presents evidence that Sills, a blonde woman, lives three blocks from the scene of the accident, owns a red Chevrolet with license plate number 74J-311, and often commutes home along Maple Street in the early evening. Sills testifies that she was home cooking dinner at the time of the accident, and her car was in her garage. This is the entire evidence on the issue of whether Sills was the driver of the car that hit Pavarotti. At the close of the evidence, Sills moves for judgment as a matter of law under Rule 50(a), arguing that the evidence is insufficient to establish that it was her car that hit Pavarotti.

A. The judge should grant the motion only if she concludes that Sills is telling the truth.

B. The judge should grant the motion for Sills. She has given direct testimony that it was not her that hit Pavarotti, and Pavarotti's evidence that it was is based on inferences from circumstantial evidence.

C. The judge should grant the motion, since the evidence does not clearly establish that it was Sills who hit Pavarotti.

D. The judge should deny the motion. The evidence is sufficient to support an inference that Sills was the driver, and the judge in passing on the motion would disregard Sills's testimony that she was not.

ANALYSIS. The crux of the matter here is that there's some evidence to support a finding that Sills hit Pavarotti, and some that suggests that she didn't. Should the judge allow the case to go to the jury or not?

The first choice, **A**, is the most clearly deficient. The judge is definitely not there to decide for herself whom she believes, and take the case from the jury if she is convinced that Sills is telling the truth. Whether Sills was the driver is a classic question of fact, for the jury to resolve if there is a genuine

---

2. J. Glannon, *Civil Procedure: Examples & Explanations* 502 (7th ed. 2013).

dispute in the evidence. If there's enough evidence that a jury could, reasoning from that evidence, rationally conclude that Sills was the driver, the jury should make the finding one way or the other, and Sills's motion for judgment as a matter of law should be denied.

C is also a loser. It suggests that the judge should grant the motion for the defendant unless she is convinced that the plaintiff has established each element of her claim. But it isn't the judge who has to be convinced: It's the jury. If the evidence is in the debatable range, where a jury might find one way or the other, it is for the jury to make the decision. The question the judge has to ask is not whether Sills was probably the driver, but whether Pavarotti has satisfied his burden of production, has produced enough evidence that the jury could rationally conclude that she was. If there's a legitimate basis in the evidence for the jury to find that Sills was the driver, the jury should decide that issue, even if the judge believes that the evidence for Sills is stronger.

Now let's consider **B**. Pavarotti's case that Sills was the driver requires an inference from circumstantial evidence. To find for Pavarotti on that issue, the jury would have to look at the evidence — that the driver was a blonde woman, that the car was a red Chevrolet, that the license number had a "3" and "1" in it, that Sills lives nearby and has a red Chevrolet with those numbers, and so on — and make an inference that it was probably her. The evidence is less than overwhelming, but it is probably sufficient to support that inference. A rational jury could conclude that Sills was the driver . . . or, that she wasn't. It's true that Pavarotti's evidence is circumstantial (that is, it requires an inference of one fact from proof of others), while Sills's evidence is direct, through her testimony. But people do lie, and sometimes circumstantial evidence can be very convincing.[3] Thus, **B** is also wrong. Since there is a legitimate conflict in the evidence, it is for the jury to resolve it. The motion for judgment as a matter of law should be denied. **D** is the best choice.

One difficulty in applying the judgment-as-a-matter-of-law standard is deciding how to treat the defendant's evidence.[4] If the plaintiff's evidence contradicts it, as Pavarotti's does in the question above, the judge should assume in passing on the motion that the jury will believe the plaintiff's evidence. But suppose that it doesn't directly contradict the plaintiff's, and is not challenged in any way by the plaintiff. Some courts have said that the judge, in passing on a motion for judgment as a matter of law, should only

---

3. "There are footprints in the mud, and a hundred eyewitnesses testify on oath that they sat there the whole time and no one passed by. Can the jury find that someone did? Would you expect them to?" Schwartz, Kelly & Partlett, *Prosser, Wade & Schwartz's Torts: Cases and Materials* 228 (10th ed. 2000).

4. That is, the evidence of the party making the Rule 50 motion, which usually is the defendant.

look at the evidence that supports the plaintiff's case, and disregard the defendant's evidence entirely. I'll call this the "plaintiff's evidence" standard. But other courts have concluded — and this is the clear majority position — that the judge should consider evidence that supports the defendant's position, if the jury would have no reason to disbelieve it. These courts hold that the judge should consider all the evidence supporting the plaintiff's case, make all inferences that the jury could make in the plaintiff's favor, but also consider the uncontradicted, unimpeached evidence for the defendant. See generally Friedenthal, Kane & Miller, *Civil Procedure* 585-587 (4th ed. 2005).

In the Pavarotti example above, the judge should properly disregard Sills's testimony in deciding whether to grant her motion for judgment as a matter of law. Pavarotti's evidence supports an inference that Sills was the driver, and Sills, who testified to the contrary, has a clear motive to lie, so the jury would have a basis for ignoring her testimony. Assuming that the jury doesn't believe Sills, and makes the supportable inference from the other evidence that she was the one who hit Pavarotti, it could rationally find that she was. So it should be allowed to decide the case.

Now, consider this variant on the Pavarotti case.

QUESTION 4. Singing the blues. Pavarotti sues Sills for negligence, after he is hit by a car on Maple Street in Albany, New York. The driver did not stop after the accident. At trial, Pavarotti presents the testimony of a bystander that the car was a red Chevrolet, that two of the numbers on the license plate were "3" and "1," and that the driver was a blonde woman. He further presents evidence that Sills, a blonde woman, lives three blocks from the scene of the accident, commutes down Maple Street, and owns a red Chevrolet with license plate number 74J-311.

Sills testifies that she was not the driver, and that she was in Miami performing in an opera at the time of the accident. She submits the program from the performance, which shows her billed as the star, and a review from the Miami Herald, dated the day after the accident, lauding her performance the night before. The stage manager from the Miami theater also testifies that Sills performed that day.

At the close of the evidence, Sills moves for a judgment as a matter of law, arguing that the evidence is insufficient to establish that she was the person who hit Pavarotti.

A. Under the "plaintiff's evidence" standard, the judge would deny the motion.

B. Under the standard that considers unimpeached, uncontradicted evidence of the defendant, the judge would deny the motion.

> **C.** Under the standard that considers unimpeached, uncontradicted evidence of the defendant, the judge would grant the motion.
> **D.** Both **A** and **B** are true.
> **E.** Both **A** and **C** are true.

ANALYSIS. In this example, the result may differ depending on which standard the judge uses to assess the evidence. The "plaintiff's evidence" standard requires her to consider only the evidence that supports Pavarotti's case. If she does, the answer should be the same here as it was in the last question: She should deny the motion, because his evidence would support an inference that it was Sills who had hit him, and — under the plaintiff's evidence standard — the rather powerful contradictory evidence would be ignored. So **A** is a correct answer.

That doesn't end the matter, however. We have to consider whether two answers may be correct, given the last two pesky choices. Most multiple-choice questions don't include multiple-right-answer choices. This suggests that, when they are included, they may very well be the right answer. Not always, but you should consider the "**A** and **C** are both right" choice very carefully when it is offered. So we have to decide how the judge would rule if she uses the other, more common standard, under which she is to consider the evidence for the plaintiff, in the light most favorable to the plaintiff, but also any evidence for the defendant that the jury would be required to believe. Would the judge grant the motion (C) or deny it (B)?

Here, the jury certainly could discount Sills's own testimony that it was not her; they could conclude that she is lying to avoid liability. That's certainly been done before. But how could they ignore the other evidence that she was in Miami at the time? If the newspaper article was a fraud, you would think Pavarotti could have exposed it by getting the real Miami Herald for the day. If she was listed in the program, but didn't actually perform that night, plaintiff could have found that out. If the stage manager was lying, or had an incentive to, you would expect that Pavarotti could show through cross-examination what his incentive was. It's hard to see how a jury could ignore such uncontradicted evidence that Sills wasn't the driver.

But doesn't Pavarotti's circumstantial evidence about the driver and the car, and the fact that Sills lives nearby and commutes down Maple Street contradict this defendant's evidence? Not really. Pavarotti's evidence, alone, would support a rational inference that Sills was the driver. But the basis for that inference is eliminated by her evidence that she was in Miami. Unless the jury has some credible reason to disregard Sill's evidence, they could not rationally make the inference that it was Sills that hit Pavarotti. Since the article and the stage manager's testimony are not challenged, it seems very likely that the judge would grant Sills' motion. Thus, **C** is also a correct statement, but **B** is not. So **E** is the best choice.

C.   Reviewing the entry of judgment as a matter of law on appeal

If a party persists all the way to trial, and goes to the trouble and expense to try her case, she probably thinks that her case is credible. And her lawyer, who has taken the case, lived with it for a year or more, and assumed the expense of preparing it and bringing it to trial, probably does too. When you make that kind of financial and psychological investment in a case, you aren't likely to agree that it is so drastically weak that "no reasonable jury" could find it proved.

Consequently, if the judge puts a spike through the heart of the plaintiff's case, by granting a directed verdict without letting the jury decide it, the plaintiff is likely to appeal, to try to get that decision reversed. In theory, the judge's decision is a legal conclusion that, as a matter of law, the evidence is insufficient to support a verdict for the nonmoving party. But the decision certainly involves an assessment of evidence, as the prior questions show, and where human beings make such assessments, other human beings — such as appellate judges — may disagree. So it may be worth an appeal.

This question considers what the appellate court should do if it disagrees with the trial judge's assessment of the strength of the plaintiff's case.

QUESTION 5. Encore, encore.   Assume, on the facts of Question 3, that the trial judge granted judgment as a matter of law for Sills at the close of all the evidence, on the ground that the evidence was too weak to support a finding that she was the driver who hit Pavarotti. Pavarotti appeals. If the appeals court concludes that the evidence was sufficient to support a rational inference that Sills was the driver, it will

A. reverse the entry of judgment for Sills, and order a new trial of the entire case.
B. order the judge to reconvene the jury, have counsel give their closing arguments, instruct the jury, and allow them to deliberate and reach a verdict.
C. grant judgment for Pavarotti, since it has rejected Sills's argument that the case is too weak to support recovery for him.
D. reverse the judgment and order a retrial of the negligence issue only. Since Sills did not claim the evidence was insufficient on the other issues, they will be established in favor of Pavarotti.

ANALYSIS.   The point of this question is to highlight the reason why a judge might allow the case to go to the jury, even if she doubts the sufficiency of the plaintiff's evidence.

If the appellate court concludes that the judge should not have granted the motion for judgment as a matter of law, the case is going to have to go back to the trial court to continue. It may seem that the most sensible next step would be that suggested by **B**, to pick up the case where the judge had erroneously stopped it. That is, the court should reconvene the jury (which had already heard all the evidence when the judge so abruptly interrupted the process), instruct the jury, and allow it to deliberate and reach a verdict, now that the appellate court has pronounced the case jury-worthy. That's essentially what would happen in a judge-tried case, but, alas, it isn't practical in a jury case. An appeal takes time, perhaps a year, perhaps longer. Even apart from the effect of the lapse of time on jurors' memories, the jury that heard Pavarotti's case will long since have been released from service. Some of them may have moved away, or not be available for other reasons. As a practical matter they can't be reunited to deal with Pavarotti's case.

D is tempting. It's true that Sills only moved for a judgment as a matter of law on the issue of whether she was the driver. But that doesn't mean that she concedes that Pavarotti has satisfied the burden of *proof* on the other issues in the case. It only means that she concedes that there is *sufficient evidence on those other issues to go to the jury*—that Pavarotti has met the burden of production on those issues. She would, of course, still hope that the jury would find that Pavarotti had not established negligence or damages by a preponderance of the evidence. At this point, the jury hasn't decided either of these issues, and might well find for Sills on one or both of them. So, if anything is to be retried, *everything* will have to be. So **D** is rather radically off base.

Nor would the court grant judgment for Pavarotti, as **C** suggests. The judge may have wrongly entered judgment as a matter of law for Sills, but that does not mean that Pavarotti will automatically win if the appellate court overturns that decision. It will simply rule that judgment as a matter of law should not have been entered for Sills, that the case should have gone to the jury to decide the facts one way or the other. Since the case is jury-worthy, it will have to go back to the trial court to give a jury the chance to decide it. There's only one way to do that: to remand the case to the trial court for a new trial, from scratch. **A** is the unfortunate winner here.

So, granting the motion can lead to a wasteful sequence of events. The case is tried; the judge grants a directed verdict motion; the plaintiff appeals; the appellate court reverses; the case goes back to the trial court and starts over from the beginning. This is hardly an optimal use of everyone's time.

D.   Judgment notwithstanding the verdict (judgment as a matter of law after the verdict)

The trial judge can avoid the scenario just described by holding her fire, denying the defendant's motion for judgment as a matter of law under Rule 50(a), and letting the jury deliberate, even if she views Pavarotti's case as too weak to support a rational verdict. Usually, things will work out. If the judge thinks that Pavarotti has failed to meet the burden of *production*, that his proof is so desperately weak that she is tempted to direct a verdict, the jury will likely conclude that he has not met his burden of *proof*, the more-probable-than-not standard of proof in a civil case, and return a verdict for Sills anyway. That's a great outcome from the system's point of view. Pavarotti will have had every opportunity to prove his case, and will have no complaint that the judge interfered with his right to a jury. And, the party that the judge and jury think should win did win.

If the jury does return a verdict for Pavarotti, the judge has another remedy: she can grant judgment for Sills "notwithstanding the verdict." That is, she may order a judgment entered for Sills *even though* the jury rendered a verdict for Pavarotti. Essentially, a motion for judgment notwithstanding the verdict (in federal court, judgment as a matter of law under Rule 50(b)) is a delayed motion for a directed verdict. The standard for granting the motion after verdict is the same as the standard used if the motion is made before the case goes to the jury, that the evidence is too weak to support a rational verdict for the plaintiff. The difference is timing, and, of course, the fact that the jury *has* rendered a verdict for the plaintiff, so the judge, by granting the motion for judgment notwithstanding the verdict, is declaring the jury's verdict insupportable. While this is awkward, it has the distinct advantage illustrated below.

> **QUESTION 6. Your verdict or mine?**   Assume, on the facts of Question 3 (the first Sills hypo on p. 432) that the trial judge denied Sills's motion for judgment as a matter of law at the close of all the evidence. The case went to the jury, which returned a verdict for Pavarotti. Sills then moves for judgment notwithstanding the verdict, and the judge grants the motion, on the ground that the evidence was too weak to support a finding that she was the driver who hit Pavarotti. Pavarotti appeals. If the appeals court concludes that the evidence was sufficient to support a rational inference that Sills was the driver, it will
>
> **A.** reverse the entry of judgment for Sills, and order a new trial on the issue of whether Sills was the driver.

> **B.** reverse the entry of judgment for Sills and order entry of a new judgment on the jury's verdict for Pavarotti.
> **C.** reverse the entry of judgment for Sills and order a full new trial.
> **D.** enter an order that Sills was the driver, and remand for retrial of the other issues in the case.

ANALYSIS. Here, the judge allows the case to go to the jury, it finds for the plaintiff, the judge takes the verdict away on the motion for judgment notwithstanding the verdict, and the appellate court reverses, concluding that Pavarotti had satisfied the burden of production after all. What should the appellate court order?

In this scenario, the jury deliberated and reached a verdict for Pavarotti. While the judge took that verdict away, the appellate court concludes that she should not have done so. The remedy is easy: Order judgment entered for Pavarotti on the jury's verdict, assuming there were no other errors in the trial process. **A, C,** and **D** are all wrong; by postponing the decision to order judgment for Sills, and getting the jury's verdict, the trial judge has avoided any need to retry the case. If the appellate court declares that the case was "jury-worthy," the jury's verdict is there to resolve the case. The trial court will be ordered to enter judgment for Pavarotti on that verdict. Choose **B.** None of the issues need be retried, because they all were tried already, and resolved by the jury in Pavarotti's favor.

Given this advantage of waiting, why would a judge ever direct a verdict, instead of using judgment notwithstanding the verdict? Well, consider Question 1, in which Powers produced no evidence that Dr. Vicaro was negligent. Sometimes, the decision on whether the case is fatally weak is clear, because the plaintiff produces literally nothing on an essential element of the claim. Where that is true, the judge will be confident that her decision won't be reversed — or likely even appealed. And there are substantial savings from cutting the trial short. The time spent on closing arguments, formulating and giving the instructions to the jury, and the jury deliberations themselves, will be saved.[5]

E. Prerequisites for judgment as a matter of law under Rule 50(b)

In federal court, the motion for judgment notwithstanding the verdict is governed by Fed. R. Civ. P. 50(b). Rule 50(b) provides that, if a motion for a

---

5. If the motion is granted at the close of the plaintiff's case, the time for presentation of the defendant's evidence will also be saved.

judgment as a matter of law is denied, the motion may be renewed no later than twenty-eight days after entry of judgment. This establishes two prerequisites for the motion. First, it must be made within twenty-eight days after judgment is entered on the jury's verdict for the plaintiff. Second, the party moving for judgment notwithstanding the verdict must have moved for judgment as a matter of law under Rule 50(a) before the case went to the jury.

There is an important practical reason for the requirement that a party who seeks judgment notwithstanding the verdict must have moved for a judgment before the case is submitted to the jury. A party seeking judgment as a matter of law before the case goes to the jury must state the grounds for her position that the plaintiff's case is too weak. In Question 1, for example, Vicaro would state as grounds for the motion the lack of evidence of the relevant standard of medical care, that his treatment fell below that standard of care, or that his treatment caused Powers's condition. Now (while it's unlikely with such a glaring omission), it may be that Powers has this evidence and simply neglected to introduce it. If that is true, Vicaro's motion acts as a wake-up call to Powers's lawyer. When the defendant points out the gap in her evidence, she will ask the judge to allow her to reopen her case to offer the omitted evidence. Since a trial is a quest for truth rather than a game of skill, the judge should allow her to do so, absent unfair surprise to Vicaro. So, by requiring the challenge to the sufficiency of the plaintiff's case at a point where the omission can be remedied, Rule 50(b) facilitates the trial of the case on the merits.

In the federal courts, there is a second reason for the prior-motion requirement in order to move for judgment notwithstanding the verdict. The Supreme Court held, in a dubious decision, that reconsidering the jury's verdict violates the Seventh Amendment right to jury trial, unless the judge reserved the right to do so on a motion made before the case went to the jury. *Baltimore & Carolina Line, Inc. v. Redman*, 295 U.S. 654 (1935).

Consider how the prior-motion rule should apply in the following case.

QUESTION 7. **Second time around.** Uberoth, a venture capitalist, sues Colon, an investment broker, in federal court. He alleges that Colon fraudulently induced Uberoth to invest in an internet start-up company, by knowingly making false statements about its prospects and the backgrounds of its officers. The case goes to trial. At the close of the evidence, Colon moves for a judgment as a matter of law, on the ground that Uberoth has not produced enough evidence to support a verdict that Colon knew, at the time he made the statements, that they were false. The judge denies the motion, and the jury subsequently returns a verdict finding Colon liable for the misrepresentation.

After the jury's verdict, but before a judgment has been entered on the verdict, Colon moves for judgment notwithstanding the verdict. He argues that Uberoth had produced no evidence that he had actually relied on Colon's statements about the company's prospects in making his investment. Reliance on the defendant's misrepresentation is a required element of a claim for negligent misrepresentation. The trial judge should

A. deny Colon's motion, because it was made before the entry of judgment on the jury's verdict.
B. deny Colon's motion, since it was made on a different ground from that raised in Colon's prior motion for judgment as a matter of law.
C. deny the motion, since she already determined, by denying the prior motion, that Uberoth's evidence was sufficient to go to the jury.
D. grant the motion if she concludes that no reasonable jury could conclude that Uberoth relied on Colon's statements in making the investment.

ANALYSIS. Let's start by eliminating C. It suggests that the judge, by denying the earlier motion for judgment as a matter of law, has determined that Uberoth's evidence is sufficient, so this issue is settled. The fact that the judge denies a motion for a directed verdict does not always mean that she has concluded that the plaintiff's case is adequately supported by the evidence. It may simply mean that she is reserving judgment, perhaps hoping that the jury will settle the issue by finding for the defendant. The very point of Rule 50(b) is that the denial of a prior motion under Rule 50(a) does not inevitably mean that the judge considers the evidence sufficient. It may simply reflect her desire to "save the trial" by ruling on the sufficiency of the evidence after the verdict rather than before.

The right answer here flows from the rationale for the Rule 50(b) requirement that the motion for judgment be made before the case goes to the jury, in order to preserve the right to seek judgment notwithstanding the verdict after a verdict. Here, Colon moved for a directed verdict before the case went to the jury, on the ground that the evidence did not show that he knew that the statements he made about the investment were false. This motion put Uberoth on notice of a possible weakness in his proof of this element of his case. If he had further evidence about Colon's knowledge that the statements were false, he could ask the court to allow him to reopen his case, and submit that proof.

But the motion on this ground did *not* put Uberoth on notice that his proof of reliance, a separate element, was inadequate. When Colon moves for judgment notwithstanding the verdict on this ground, the challenge comes out of the blue, at a time when Uberoth can no longer do anything about it. In the language of poker, Colon has "sandbagged" Uberoth by keeping this objection in his back pocket, letting the case go to the jury and raising the reliance issue after the jury's verdict, when it is too late to offer any further evidence of reliance.

Of course, it's true that it's Uberoth's case to prove. He should know the elements of a claim for fraud, and assumes the responsibility of proving them at trial. If he hasn't proven one of them, perhaps he should take the consequences. But the point of Rule 50(b) is to put him on notice of the defect before the case goes to the jury, and Colon didn't put him on notice of the defect in proof of reliance at that point. It is not enough that he moved for judgment as a matter of law on *some* ground to preserve his right to judgment as a matter of law after the verdict. His motion must raise the objection he renews in the motion for judgment notwithstanding the verdict. So **B** is the right answer here; the motion will be denied based on Colon's failure to raise this challenge to Uberoth's proof before the case went to the jury. Although **D** seems like it should be right, Colon will have forfeited his right to judgment on this ground by failing to raise it before the case goes to the jury. This is one more illustration of a basic point: procedure matters.

A is a little tricky. Rule 50(b) provides that the motion may be made "within twenty-eight days of the entry of judgment." But there's no reason it can't be made *before* entry of judgment. As soon as the jury returns a verdict for Uberoth, Colon will be in a position to raise the objection. He could make the motion right then, in open court. The twenty-eight-days-after-judgment rule is an outer limit on when it can be made; it doesn't mean that it couldn't be made sooner. See, e.g., *Boehringer Ingelheim Vetmedica, Inc. v. Schering-Plough Corp.*, 106 F. Supp. 2d 696, 698-699 (D.N.J. 2000).[6]

F.   The Closer: "Directing the verdict" in a judge-tried case

The function of the motion for judgment as a matter of law is to allow the judge to control the jury, in cases where it is not clear that they have a meaningful role to play. But in many cases there is no jury; the judge not only administers the trial, but also hears the evidence and finds the facts. Judges act as the fact finder where neither party requests a jury, and in many cases in which the parties do not have a right to jury trial.

How do motions for judgment as a matter of law work in a judge-tried case, where the judge is finding the facts? How does she apply the concepts covered in this chapter, particularly the burden of production and the burden of proof?

---

6. While it makes sense that the motion could be made before entry of judgment, there's really no reason why a first-year student would know it. And the language of the rule might give rise to an inference that it has to be made after judgment is entered. So, if I hadn't made this point in class, I think it would be a little sneaky to give this choice in the question.

The short answer is that Federal Rules 50(a) and (b) don't apply at all in a judge-tried case. See the heading of the rule, "Judgment as a Matter of Law in a Jury Trial." And there's a good reason for this. These motions exist to prevent the jury from deciding for a party on the basis of insufficient evidence. The judge doesn't have to constrain *herself* from doing that, where she is the fact finder. If the judge thinks the plaintiff's evidence is too weak to support a verdict for her, she can simply rule that the plaintiff hasn't proved her case! And, because she is the fact finder, she is not required to assess the evidence in the light most favorable to the plaintiff, and assume that the jury will believe her witnesses. She does that in a jury case because she has to give the plaintiff the benefit of the doubt, to preserve the jury's role. But there's no jury role to preserve in a judge-tried case. So, the judge can decide what she believes about the facts and rule for the defendant if she concludes that the plaintiff's proof on any required element is inadequate. See Fed. R. Civ. P. 52(c) (once a party has been fully heard on an issue, the judge may enter judgment against the party if the court finds against her on the issue).

Perhaps this question will help you to understand the difference in the judge's role when she is the fact finder.

QUESTION 8. The judge's judgment. Uberoth, a venture capitalist, sues Colon, an investment broker, in federal court. He alleges that Colon fraudulently induced Uberoth to invest in an internet start-up company, by knowingly making false statements about its prospects and the backgrounds of its officers. Because the parties waived their right to jury trial, the case goes to trial before Judge Fortera, without a jury. At the close of the plaintiff's evidence, Colon moves for entry of judgment in his favor, on the ground that Uberoth has not proved by a preponderance of the evidence that Colon knew, at the time he made the statements, that they were false.

A. Colon has invoked the wrong standard, by arguing that Uberoth failed to meet his burden of proof. He should have argued that Uberoth has not met the burden of production, that is, introduced sufficient evidence to support a rational verdict that Cologne knew, at the time he made the statements, that the statements were false. If the judge finds that Uberoth has met the burden of production, she should deny the motion.

B. Colon has invoked the proper standard. If the judge concludes that Uberoth has not established, by a preponderance of the evidence, that Colon knew the statements were false, she should order judgment entered for Colon.

C. Colon has invoked the proper standard. If the judge concludes that Uberoth has not established, by a preponderance of the evidence,

> that Colon knew the statements were false, she should enter a finding that Colon did not make the statements knowing them to be false, and proceed to hear the rest of the case.
> **D.** Colon has invoked the proper standard, but would have to make the motion at the close of all the evidence.

ANALYSIS. In this case, Judge Fortera is deciding the facts. In order to find for Uberoth, she must be satisfied that he has established each element of his claim by a preponderance of the evidence. After Uberoth finishes presenting his case, Colon challenges its sufficiency, arguing that Uberoth's evidence is insufficient to establish a necessary element — that he knew the statements were false when he made them. What standard should Judge Fortera use in evaluating the evidence at this point?

A indicates that Judge Fortera should ask herself whether Uberoth has produced enough evidence to support a rational verdict for him. But why should the judge use that standard? She isn't deciding whether the case is worth of jury consideration. It's a judge trial; she is deciding the facts. She doesn't have to ask whether a jury could be convinced by Uberoth's evidence. She has to ask whether she, as the fact finder, *is* convinced by it.

When Colon moved for judgment in his favor, Uberoth had had his full opportunity to prove that Colon knew his statements were false — to meet his burden of proof on the point. So **A** is wrong. Judge Fortera should not ask whether Uberoth has produced rational evidence on the issue of Colon's knowledge, but whether he has carried his burden of proof on it. Uberoth has had his shot at it, presented what he has. If it doesn't convince Judge Fortera, the fact finder, the case need go no further. She can enter judgment against Uberoth on the issue.

D isn't right either: The judge need not wait until Colon presents his case. There's no need to hear Colon's rebuttal evidence if the plaintiff has had a full shot at proving the knowledge-of-falsity issue, and her own evidence hasn't established it by the preponderance-of-the-evidence standard. **C** also fails. Uberoth must establish that Colon knew the statements were false in order to recover, and hasn't. There's no need to hear more evidence or make any findings about the other elements of the claim; a tort claim is only as strong as its weakest link. If Judge Fortera concludes that knowledge of falsity is unproved, she should enter judgment dismissing Uberoth's case. **B** wins.

 ## Glannon's Picks

1. Elementary principles	C
2. Double trouble	B

3. Found facts?   D
4. Singing the blues   E
5. Encore, encore   A
6. Your verdict or mine?   B
7. Second time around   B
8. The judge's judgment   B

22

Second Time Around: The Grounds and Procedure for Motions for New Trial

[ ]*

CHAPTER OVERVIEW

A. New trial motions based on legal errors at trial

B. New trial motions on the ground that the verdict is against the weight of the evidence

C. New trials based on newly discovered evidence

D. New trials based on excessive or inadequate damages

E. New trials based on improper influence on the jury

F. Appellate review of the grant of a new trial

G. Double Closer: Combined motions for new trial and judgment as a matter of law

◆ Glannon's Picks

The last chapter analyzed judgment as a matter of law (the directed verdict and judgment notwithstanding the verdict), which allows a judge to take a case away from a jury and decide it as a matter of law. This chapter addresses the motion for a new trial, a tool the judge may use,

---

* Send your limerick offerings to j.glannon@suffolk.edu.

not to take the case away from the jury, but to send it to another one. The motion for a new trial asks the court, in a case that has already been tried, to order it tried again.

A.   New trial motions based on legal errors at trial

Assume that a case has been tried, it has gone to the jury, and the jury has returned a verdict. Why would a judge, instead of entering judgment for the verdict winner, grant a new trial? If she does, the first jury's verdict is disregarded. All their work, and that of the court and the parties in trying the case the first time, goes for naught. The trial process starts over, with the selection of a new jury, opening statements, and so forth. This seems like a waste.

There are a number of reasons why a court might choose to nullify the jury's verdict and start over. One common reason is for an error of law in the conduct of the first trial. Suppose, for example, that Brown sues Little for injuries suffered in an accident. At trial, the judge admits important evidence offered by Brown to establish Little's negligence, over Little's objection, and the jury finds for Brown. Little moves for a new trial, arguing that the judge wrongly admitted the evidence. If the judge concludes that the evidence was inadmissible under the rules of evidence, she could, and probably would, grant a new trial. Little has a right to have the case tried properly under the established trial rules. If the judge is convinced that she made a mistake of law in admitting the evidence, Little has not had a trial by the proper rules, so it seems fair to start over and do it by the book.

Consider what will happen in Little's case if the judge *doesn't* grant a new trial. Little will likely appeal, arguing that the trial was unfair due to the admission of the improper evidence. If the appellate court agrees, it will order the case remanded for a new trial, at which the improper evidence will not be admitted. So, if the judge doesn't correct the error herself, by granting a new trial, the parties will likely end up going through the expense and delay of an appeal, probably giving rise to a published opinion reversing Her Honor's decision. No trial judge enjoys being reversed. So, for several reasons, if the judge is convinced that she committed reversible error at the first trial, she would be well advised to order a new one herself.

If the evidence wasn't admissible, why did the judge admit it? Well, things happen fast at trial, and many decisions have to be made on the spot. A decision may seem right at the time but on quieter reflection and further research prove ill-advised. So Little might convince the judge, after the fact, that she made a mistake of law, and that the wisest course would be to try the case again. In the federal courts, Fed. R. Civ. P. 59 authorizes the trial judge to order a new trial for errors of law. State courts have similar new trial rules as well.

Of course, Little should not keep objections like this in her back pocket and spring them on the judge after the jury reaches a verdict. She should object to any ruling that might prejudice her case when the judge makes it. That way the judge, if convinced, can change her mind and prevent reversible error. Consequently, the court will not ordinarily grant a new trial for trial mistakes unless an objection was made at the time the judge made the mistaken ruling.

The trial judge makes many legal rulings at trial that might form the basis for a new trial motion. Another example is improper jury instructions. The judge has to instruct the jury, before they deliberate, on the legal rules that govern the plaintiff's claim — the rules of negligence in a tort case, or the elements of a contract claim in a contract case, and so on. If she gives a mistaken instruction, the jury will apply the wrong legal rules in reaching their verdict. Suppose, for example, that she instructs the jury that "the plaintiff cannot recover if she is more negligent than *any* defendant," and the jury concludes that Brown, the plaintiff, was 20 percent at fault, the first defendant, Little, was 10 percent at fault, and Berle, the other defendant, was 70 percent at fault. Under the judge's instruction, the jury would be bound to return a verdict for the defendants, since Brown was more negligent than one defendant. If the proper instruction should be that "the plaintiff may not recover if she was more negligent than the defendants" (i.e., the defendants as a group), the judge's error has led the jury to return the wrong verdict. If the judge reads the statute and the cases and concludes that her instruction was wrong, she should bite the bullet and start the process over again. And the same is true for other mistakes of law during the trial.

Here's a tricky question to get us started. Reading Rule 59 will be useful in answering it.

> **QUESTION 1. Objection, objection.** Hazak sues Keller in federal court for violation of his federal civil rights, alleging that Keller used excessive force in arresting Hazak, injuring him seriously. At trial, the judge admits evidence of three other assaults by Keller on arrestees. Keller's counsel does not object.
>
> The case goes to the jury, which returns a verdict finding Keller liable. Keller's counsel is surprised; she thought the case had gone well and expected a defendant's verdict. She obtains a transcript of the trial and reviews it, hoping to find grounds for a motion for a new trial. She concludes that the evidence concerning other assaults by Keller should have been excluded and that it may have swayed the jury in reaching a

verdict for Hazak. Four days after the court enters judgment for Hazak, Keller's counsel files a motion for a new trial, on the ground that the evidence of other assaults was improperly admitted.

Assuming that the evidence was improperly admitted, the trial judge should

A. grant a new trial. If she doesn't, Keller will likely appeal, and the appellate court will order a new trial at which the improper evidence is excluded.
B. deny the motion. Although the evidence may have influenced the jury's decision, they might have found for Hazak even without the evidence of the other assaults.
C. deny the motion, since Keller's counsel never objected to the evidence at the time it was admitted.
D. deny the motion, since it was made after judgment was entered on the jury's verdict. The proper motion would be a motion for relief from judgment under Rule 60(b) instead.

ANALYSIS. In this case, the judge made a mistake at trial by allowing the plaintiff to introduce inadmissible evidence. Defendant's counsel didn't do anything about it at the time. In retrospect, she casts around for some ground to undo an unfavorable result. She uncovers the judge's mistake of law in admitting the evidence and moves for a new trial on that ground.

D is refuted by Rule 59 itself, which provides that a motion for a new trial "must be filed no later than 28 days after the entry of judgment." Fed. R. Civ. P. 59(b). Even though judgment has been entered, the rule gives litigants a short window after entry of judgment to seek a new trial. (They may also seek it after the verdict but before judgment is entered on the verdict as well.)

B makes an interesting point. Who is to say that the jury found for Hazak based on this improper evidence? They may have based their verdict on the other, proper evidence instead, so that Hazak would have won whether or not the improper evidence was admitted. If the motion for a new trial is granted, and the case is retried without this evidence, Hazak may well win again.

That's true. We don't know for sure that the improper evidence led to the verdict. But we don't know for sure that it *didn't* either. Where the error may have affected the outcome, the appropriate remedy is generally to grant the motion for a new trial, since the verdict might have been different if the mistake of law had not been made. Only if the judge is convinced that the error was "harmless," that is, that the erroneous admission of evidence of other assaults clearly did not affect the result, should she refuse to grant the motion for a new trial.

But there is another problem here. In this case, Keller's counsel did not object to the improper evidence when it was offered at trial. Had she done so, the court would presumably have recognized the problem and excluded the evidence, avoiding the error and saving the trial. It is counsel's job to assist the court in avoiding error by raising objections when a judge's ruling may prejudice her client's rights. If she doesn't do so, she will usually be precluded from relying on the judge's error as grounds for a new trial or on appeal. Thus, **C** is the best answer.

Consider the possibilities for manipulation if courts allowed counsel to seek new trials based on trial mistakes they had not pointed out during the trial. Counsel might deliberately withhold her objection to one or more of the judge's rulings at trial. Then, if she loses the verdict, she could pull these out and argue for a new trial. This would give counsel an incentive for manipulation that the system ought not to countenance. Hence, the court will not ordinarily grant a new trial on a ground not brought to its attention at the time the error was made. See generally Wright & Miller §2805. (The exception sometimes suggested is that a judge has the power to grant the motion if the error, though not raised by the losing party's counsel, "was so fundamental that gross injustice would result." Id.)

Why is **A** not correct here? If the judge refuses to grant the new trial, won't Keller take an appeal based on the admission of the improper evidence? And won't the appellate court reverse based on the error? Again, not if Keller's counsel failed to object at the time of its admission: The appellate court, like the trial court, usually will not allow Keller to "sandbag" Hazak by appealing on the basis of an error that she did not bring to the judge's attention when it was made. Keller has waived the objection by failing to raise it at the time of the trial judge's ruling.

B. New trial motions based on the ground that the verdict is against the weight of the evidence

It seems fairly obvious that a litigant should get a new trial if the judge made an error of law. You have a right to have the process done right, and if it wasn't, to have it done again.

Granting a new trial where the jury's verdict is against the weight of the evidence is more perplexing. The case is tried; the jury deliberates and reaches a verdict. Now the loser moves for a new trial, arguing not that the judge made a mistake of law at the trial, but that the jury made a mistake in rendering a verdict for the other side. This just seems like sour grapes.

Sour grapes it may be on the losing party's part, but the judge does have the authority, in the federal system and many state systems as well, to order the case retried if she is convinced that the verdict is seriously suspect. The idea is that the judge should have the authority, in egregious cases, to protect against improper jury behavior based on sympathy for a plaintiff or other improper grounds.

Which cases are egregious enough for the judge to invoke this considerable power? Rule 59 doesn't expressly tell us, but a variety of verbal formulas are used in the cases. Some hold that the judge may order a new trial if the jury's verdict is "against the great weight of the evidence,"[1] represents "a miscarriage of justice,"[2] or the jury has reached a result which is "seriously erroneous."[3] And, in making the assessment whether the verdict is "this wrong," the judge may consider the credibility of the evidence. She is not asking — as she does on a directed verdict motion — whether the jury *could* find for the plaintiff if they believe the evidence. Rather, she is asking whether the jury was clearly, seriously wrong in choosing to believe it. Although this standard intrudes more on the jury's role as fact finder, it is usually justified on the ground that granting the motion sends the case to a new jury rather than leading to entry of a judgment for the party who lost before the first one.

Consider, in answering the following question, how this standard relates to the standard for directed verdict or judgment notwithstanding the verdict.

QUESTION 2. Judging the jury.   Angelos sues Faithful Investment Co. for fraudulently misrepresenting the value of an investment that Faithful had solicited from Angelos. He claims that their investment brochure contained deliberate fraudulent statements about the investment. At trial, Angelos's expert testifies that the brochure contained several errors which seriously inflated the value of the investment and understated the risk. Faithful's employees testify that these were simply good faith mistakes, and that they had no intent to defraud Angelos.

The jury returns a special verdict finding that Faithful had not intentionally misled Angelos. Angelos moves for a new trial, on the ground that the jury's verdict is not supported by the evidence.

A. The trial judge must deny the motion unless she concludes that no reasonable jury could have found as the jury did.

---

1. See, e.g., *United States v. Sullivan*, 1 F.3d 1191, 1196 (11th Cir. 1993).

2. See, e.g., *Fleet National Bank v. Anchor Media Television, Inc.*, 831 F. Supp. 16, 32 (D.R.I. 1993).

3. See, e.g., *Datskow v. Teledyne Continental Motors Aircraft Products*, 826 F. Supp. 677, 683 (W.D.N.Y. 1993).

> **B.** The trial judge must deny the motion unless, taking all the evidence and inferences in the light most favorable to Faithful, the verdict is against the great weight of the evidence.
>
> **C.** The trial judge may grant the motion if she is firmly convinced that Faithful's witnesses are not credible, so that a verdict for Faithful is against the clear weight of the evidence.
>
> **D.** The trial judge may grant the motion if she believes that Angelos had established fraud by a preponderance of the evidence.

ANALYSIS.   This question compares the standard for granting a new trial and the standard for directing a verdict. Recall that when the judge directs a verdict, she takes the case away from the jury and decides it herself, because, as a matter of law, the evidence is too weak to support a verdict for the nonmoving party. The standard for doing that should be rigorous, and it is. The judge should not direct a verdict unless the evidence is so one-sided that no reasonable jury could find for the other party. But granting a new trial is less drastic, since it doesn't deprive the parties of a jury decision, but rather submits the case to another jury. So, the standard for doing so is a bit looser as well.

If **D** were true, the standard would be too loose. It asserts that the judge should order a new trial if she believes that the losing party should have prevailed. This would allow the judge to grant new trials whenever she disagreed with the verdict. That standard would give the trial judge too much discretion to disregard the jury's finding, simply on the ground that the judge disagreed with it.

A sets too stringent a standard. It equates the power to grant a new trial based on the weight of the evidence with the standard for directing a verdict. It would only allow the judge to grant a new trial in cases in which no reasonable jury could find for the plaintiff. There would be little point to the separate new trial option if it were only available in those cases.

B is close. It states the great-weight-of-the-evidence standard, which is a commonly stated standard for new trials based on the strength of the evidence. But it suggests that the judge, in applying that standard, must take all inferences in favor of Faithful, the party that won the verdict. That is required when deciding whether to direct a verdict, but not when deciding whether to grant a new trial. In deciding whether to grant a new trial based on the weight of the evidence, the judge may make judgments about whether an inference is appropriate from the evidence, and may discount evidence she finds clearly unworthy of belief. For example, suppose that Angelos had testified at the trial that Faithful's sale rep had provided inaccurate explanations about the meaning of the brochure. And suppose that this testimony, if believed, would support a verdict for Angelos on the fraud claim — but the judge is strongly convinced that Angelos is lying. In passing on the motion for a new trial (unlike a motion for judgment as a matter of law under Rule 50(b)), the judge does not have to assume that Angelos's testimony will be accepted by the jury. If she (the judge) is firmly convinced that it is false, and therefore the jury's verdict is wrong, she can order a new trial. Admittedly, this does indeed substitute her judgment for that of the jury, in a sense, but again, the result is a new jury trial, not a judgment for Faithful. So **C** takes the prize. If the judge is firmly convinced that the witnesses Faithful relies upon are not credible, she may grant a new trial.

C. New trials based on newly discovered evidence

Suppose that Baker and Whitney are involved in an accident, and Baker sues Whitney for his injuries. The parties are the only witnesses at trial, and each testifies that the other ran the red light. The jury finds for Baker, awarding a large verdict. Before the judgment is entered, the award is reported in the paper, and a week later Motz contacts Whitney's lawyer. He tells her that he was looking out the window of a nearby building and saw *Baker* run the light, but had not come down to the scene or notified the police that he had witnessed the collision. Whitney's lawyer moves for a new trial, arguing that she has "newly discovered evidence" that should be considered in determining whether Whitney is liable for the injuries.

There is certainly an argument for allowing a new trial here. The jury's verdict was based on the testimony of the parties, who both have an interest in skewing the facts in their favor. Here's an impartial witness whose testimony might be very persuasive. Shouldn't we give Whitney another chance? How could we *not* do so?

The primary argument for refusing new trials based on the discovery of new evidence is that the system is burdened enough trying to process cases once, without retrying them every time a party comes up with something they didn't present before. In addition, if counsel know that a new trial will probably not be an option, they will have a significant incentive to find all the relevant evidence the first time. Last, if courts routinely granted new trials on this basis, lawyers might be tempted to game the system, by withholding some marginal evidence, and then — if they lose at trial — asserting it as the ground for a motion for a new trial.

So, there are policy considerations on both sides. Typically, the rules and cases take a middle ground. They give the trial judge discretion to grant new trials based on newly discovered evidence, but with limits. *First*, most courts will deny the motion if the evidence should have been discovered earlier if the moving party's counsel had been diligent in preparing for trial. And, *second*, they will scrutinize the new evidence to determine whether it could significantly impact the jury's evaluation of the case. If the new evidence is marginal, or purely cumulative of other evidence the jury heard, the motion is likely to be denied.[4]

In Whitney's case, the motion would likely be granted. Motz's evidence is very significant — the only evidence available from a disinterested witness. And nothing suggests that Whitney's counsel should have found out about Motz before trial.

Consider whether a new trial should be granted in this case, and on what ground.

QUESTION 3. The ungrateful guest.   Knox, a recreational pilot, crashes his plane on takeoff one January morning in Maine. Sardinha, his passenger, sues him for damages in federal court. Sardinha's theory is that the wings of the plane had iced up, causing the flaps to freeze and preventing Knox from controlling the plane. The case is tried to a jury. Six witnesses at the field that morning, including three flight mechanics on duty at the time of the flight, testify about the weather conditions at the field that morning and the condition of the plane. Experts for both parties testify about whether it was negligent to attempt the flight given the weather conditions at the time. The jury returns a verdict finding that Knox, the defendant, was not negligent.

After the verdict, but before judgment is entered upon it, Sardinha moves for a new trial. He supports his motion with an affidavit stating that he has located a Federal Aviation Administration manual setting standards for bad weather flights, which he argues Knox failed to follow. He also states that he has located a witness, Lindbergh, who checked out icing conditions on the field shortly before Knox's takeoff, and decided not to fly himself. Lindbergh had not previously come forward, and no one had identified him as a potential witness before the first trial. The judge will probably

A. deny the motion.
B. grant the motion based on the evidence of the FAA manual.
C. grant the motion based on Lindbergh's testimony.
D. grant the motion only if Sardinha's counsel was unaware of the existence of the FAA manual at the time of trial.

---

4. Such evidence may also come to light after the period for seeking a new trial under Rule 59 has elapsed. The Federal Rules, and many state rules based on them, authorize a motion for "relief from judgment" on the ground of newly discovered evidence, but restrict such motions to one year from the entry of judgment. Fed. R. Civ. P. 60(b).

ANALYSIS.   This question is more a matter of judgment than most. But some professors gravitate to such questions, because they want to evaluate students' ability to exercise judgment in close situations. A trial judge's decision on a new trial motion requires just such an exercise of discretion. (Of course, the judge would have more information on which to base the decision than most multiple-choice questions can provide.)

The problem with granting the motion based on the FAA manual is that Sardinha's counsel almost certainly should have found it in preparing for trial. Surely, his expert would be familiar with relevant FAA materials. They are very likely public documents commonly available, and the witnesses — both Sardinha's and Knox's — would likely be aware that FAA standards exist. It will be extremely hard for Sardinha's counsel to explain why this is new evidence that could not have been discovered with due diligence prior to the first trial. So **B** is not the best answer. Nor is **D**. If Sardinha's counsel was unaware of the existence of the manual, but *should have* known of it, the motion should be denied.

How about Lindbergh's testimony? Does it support grant of a new trial? I wouldn't think so. The question suggests that Sardinha's counsel, in the exercise of due diligence, probably would not have found out about Lindbergh, so that shouldn't prevent the grant of a new trial. However, Lindbergh's evidence seems both marginal and cumulative. Numerous witnesses who were on the spot testified as to the weather conditions at the time of the flight. Lindbergh's testimony doesn't seem likely to add much about the conditions that the jury hasn't already heard. Given the interest in repose, and the waste of resources involved in retrying decided cases, new evidence should be pretty compelling to merit starting over. The best choice is **A**, that the judge should deny the motion.

D. New trials based on excessive or inadequate damages

A judge may also grant a new trial if the damages awarded are grossly excessive or inadequate. If the evidence supports an award of $40,000, and the jury awards $500,000, that verdict is "against the great weight of the evidence" or "a serious miscarriage of justice." Thus, new trials on this basis are simply a specific application of the principle that a judge may order a new trial where the original verdict is seriously erroneous.

However, where a new trial is sought on this ground, it may not be necessary to retry the entire case. The judge might conclude that the jury's finding that the defendant is liable for the claim is proper, but that they awarded too much in damages . . . or too little. In that case, she may order a partial new trial, limited to the proper amount of damages. (New trials may similarly be limited to discrete liability issues, such as an affirmative defense or one element of a claim.)

The judge may also use the device of remittitur if she concludes that liability was properly determined but the damages awarded are so high as to "shock the conscience" of the court. Remittitur offers the plaintiff a kind of settlement. The judge says to the plaintiff, "All right, I'm willing to accept the jury's finding that the defendant is liable to you, but the $800,000 in damages that they awarded is clearly unsupported by the evidence. I could grant a new trial. In fact, I *will* grant a new trial . . . unless you are willing to accept $200,000. If you'll accept that, I'll enter judgment on the jury's verdict for that amount. If you won't, we'll start over and do it again."

The judge's offer of a remittitur (usually prompted by a defendant's motion for it) puts the plaintiff in a tough spot. Two hundred thousand dollars is a lot of money. If the damages are uncertain, as where intangible injuries like pain and suffering and emotional distress are being valued, another jury might give $75,000. It takes steady nerves to "roll the bones" by refusing the remittitur and taking your chances on a new trial.[5] I'll wager that, for this reason, plaintiffs accept remittiturs a good deal more often than they refuse.

If the judge offers a remittitur, and the plaintiff acquiesces, judgment will enter for the plaintiff for the remitted amount. The plaintiff may still be very unhappy, having had $600,000 lopped off of the jury's award. However, in the federal courts, the plaintiff cannot accept the remittitur and then appeal the trial judge's decision to make her choose between taking a remitted award and facing a new trial. The plaintiff is viewed as having made a deal that bars her from appealing the judgment she accepted. *Donovan v. Penn Shipping Co.*, 429 U.S. 648 (1977). If she wants to appeal, she must refuse the remittitur, go through the new trial, and (if she gets a smaller award in the new trial, or loses entirely), *then* appeal the judge's decision to grant the new trial after the first jury's verdict. This is an unenviable position for the plaintiff, to say the least. Very probably, she has waited long enough to get to trial the first time and needs funds to deal with the consequences of her injury, rather than to go back into the queue for another trial.

Suppose the jury finds for the plaintiff, but awards a damage amount that the judge finds unconscionably low? In some states, the judge may grant an "additur," that is, offer the *defendant* the choice between facing a new trial and agreeing to an increased award. Why would the defendant agree to pay *more* than the jury awarded? Presumably, the incentive is to avoid the

---

5. It would be a particularly difficult decision if the trial judge threatened to order a *complete* new trial, rather than a new trial on the issue of damages only.

expense of a new trial and the risk of an even larger award from a second jury. However, federal courts cannot use the additur device. In a dubious decision, *Dimick v. Schiedt*, 293 U.S. 474 (1935), the Supreme Court concluded that it would be unconstitutional for a federal court to give an additur, since it would grant the plaintiff damages that the jury had not awarded.

This question explores the judge's options where the jury renders an arguably improper damage verdict.

> **QUESTION 4. A jury of your miserly peers.**   Dimick sues Schiedt in federal court, for personal injuries suffered in a construction accident.
>
> The jury returns a verdict finding Schiedt liable, and assessing the damages at $5,000. The judge concludes that the jury's finding that Schiedt's negligence caused the accident is supported by the evidence, but that the amount awarded is unconscionably low, since the uncontested testimony shows that Dimick suffered substantial pain and suffering and a partial disability, as well as $3,000 in medical bills. The judge should
>
> A. order the case retried.
> B. order the issue of damages retried.
> C. order the case retried unless Schiedt agrees to pay an increased award.
> D. enter judgment on the jury's verdict, since additur is not permissible in the federal courts.

ANALYSIS.   This question simply requires an understanding of the judge's options where the jury's liability finding is supported by the evidence, but the damages are well below the reasonable range.

We know that one option the judge does *not* have is to offer an additur, since additurs have been ruled unconstitutional in the federal courts. So **C** is wrong; the judge can't "make a deal" with the defendant to pay a higher award and avoid a new trial. But that doesn't mean that the judge is powerless to avoid what she considers an insupportable result.

Although the judge can't use additur, she doesn't have to enter judgment on the verdict if it would be a miscarriage of justice to do so. **D** isn't right, because we know that the judge still has the authority to order a new trial where the jury has reached a seriously erroneous result, whether the error is in the amount of damages or in finding liability at all. *Dimick* did not bar new trials based on improper damage awards, only additurs based on them. So the judge has the option to order a retrial if she is convinced that the size of the jury's verdict is outside the range of permissible results.

The only question, then, is whether she should order a full retrial, or a partial retrial of damages only. Since the question indicates that the judge considers the liability verdict sound, there is no reason to retry the liability issues. The judge should order a retrial of damages only. **B** is the best answer.

E. New trials based on improper influence on the jury

Another ground for granting a new trial is that the jury, or some of them, were subject to some improper influence that may have affected their deliberations. This could happen in a number of ways. A juror might talk to counsel for one of the parties, or to a party, or to a witness, either in the courthouse or on the street. A trial is a ritualized process, tightly protected from outside influences. The court and counsel orchestrate the production of the evidence the jury is to consider, and test that evidence through presentation and cross-examination. If a juror gets additional evidence from some other source, this untested information may affect the jury, without being subject to scrutiny through the rules of evidence or cross-examination.

In re Beverley Hills Supper Club Litigation, 695 F.2d 207 (6th Cir. 1982), provides a dramatic example. In the *Beverly Hills Supper Club* case, a fire in a night club caused many deaths. A major issue was whether aluminum wiring in the walls had started the fire. The plaintiffs argued that such wiring overheats at the connection to receptacles, creating a risk of fire. After a twenty-two day trial, the jury returned a verdict for the defendant, rejecting this theory. Later a juror wrote to a local newspaper, explaining that the fire couldn't have happened that way: He had that wiring in his house, and had gone home, taken the plates off the outlets, and found none of the conditions that the plaintiffs argued had caused the fire. Based on this juror experiment, the court ordered a new trial, since the juror had not only conducted the experiment, but had communicated his findings to other jurors.

While this seems counterintuitive, barring real world information from the jury, it makes good sense. This evidence may have been very persuasive to the jury, yet improperly so. Who is to say that the juror's receptacles were the same as those in the night club, or that they were installed in the same way, under the same conditions or using the same wire? Had this evidence been introduced at trial, the plaintiffs' counsel could have challenged it on such grounds, but if it goes directly to the jury instead, it is not subject to correction or explanation.

If a judge finds that extraneous information has found its way into the jury room, she will not automatically grant a new trial motion. Very likely, she will hold a hearing to ascertain how the jury considered the information, whether the evidence was too peripheral to affect the outcome, was simply repetitive of information already before them from the trial, or did not prejudice the party who lost the verdict (where, for example, the extraneous information actually supports the losing party's case). Only if she is convinced that there is a significant possibility that the improper evidence has affected the jury's decision will she bite the bullet and order a new trial.

Of course, jurors bring a great deal of knowledge and experience with them into the jury room. Jurors do rely on their experience, and this is one of the strengths of the jury system. But there is a distinction — sometimes a fine one — between testing the evidence against one's general experience, and introducing evidence into the jury's deliberations that was not placed before the jury by the parties. Here's a question that explores that distinction.

QUESTION 5. **The voice of experience.** Ewald sues Stein for injuries suffered when Stein's sixteen-foot truck rolled down a hill into his car. Ewald alleges, and submits evidence at trial to show that Stein was negligent, because he left the truck parked on a hill, with the emergency brake on, but did not turn the wheels toward the curb. His theory is that the brake was insufficient to hold the truck, so that Stein should have pointed the wheels toward the curb, to prevent it from rolling down the hill into his car. Stein argues that he acted reasonably in relying on the emergency brake.

After the parties have presented their proof, the jury is instructed on the basic standard of negligence, and proceeds to its deliberations. During the deliberations, Stepner, one of the jurors, states that he had rented trucks about the size of Stein's a number of times, and that he always had trouble with the emergency brake on those trucks because the size of the truck requires a very strong brake to hold it. In fact, one time he had a brake let go, causing the truck to roll.

The jury renders a verdict for Ewald. A week later, before judgment has entered, Stein's lawyer runs into one of the other jurors on the street, and the juror mentions Stepner's comments. Stein's lawyer files a motion for a new trial, based on the jury's consideration of extraneous information. The judge should

A. grant the motion for a new trial.
B. conduct a hearing to determine whether the jury's decision was influenced by Stepner's information.
C. grant a new trial if she believes the information may have influenced the other jurors in reaching a verdict.
D. deny the new trial motion.

ANALYSIS. If Stepner's comments were an improper extraneous influence on the jury, **B** would be the appropriate answer. But it seems doubtful that they were improper. Surely, jurors can contribute information about a case from their general experience. If they couldn't, how could they decide? They are meant to bring their understanding of the world to bear on the issues they are deciding. If a driver is alleged to be negligent for driving at the speed limit on a rainy day, the jurors have to consider, based on their life experience, whether that was a reasonable thing to do. This is not to say that they should ignore the evidence, but that they are there to *evaluate* the evidence, and they use their judgment and experience to do so.

Isn't that what Stepner has done here? He's used his own experience with similar vehicles in similar circumstances to evaluate the reasonableness of Stein's conduct. If this were considered to "infect" the jury's deliberations with outside information, a jury's verdict would seldom be safe from impeachment. **D** is the best answer. Stepner's consideration of his own experience, and sharing that experience with the other jurors, is a permissible part of the jury's deliberations, and would not support the grant of a new trial. **C** is wrong, because Stepner's comments were permissible, and therefore would not taint the verdict even if they did influence the jury. **A** is also wrong, because there was no inappropriate outside influence that has tainted the verdict, only appropriate consideration of the evidence in light of experience.

It would be different if Stepner went out and rented a similar truck and conducted experiments parking it on various hills. That would surely be an improper experiment that would lead to a new trial. But using his general knowledge of trucks to help form a judgment about the reasonableness of Stein's conduct is Stepner's job as a juror, not his fault.

F.   Appellate review of the grant of a new trial

If the judge grants a new trial, for any of the reasons reviewed above, what happens next? In the federal courts, the new trial happens next. Since the judge has ruled that the first trial was improper, and ordered another, the case is not over. It will go back into the queue for a new trial. Imagine how frustrating this is for the verdict winner, who got a verdict, believes it a fair one, and has the verdict snatched away on a motion for a new trial. She must go through the new trial and, if she loses the second time (or wins a substantially smaller verdict), then appeal the trial judge's decision to grant the new trial.[6]

Consider how this scenario plays out on appeal.

---

6. State practice differs on this, however. Evidently it is possible to obtain interlocutory review — that is, immediate review, without going through the new trial first — in some state court systems. See, e.g., *Wolfe v. Welton*, 558 S.E.2d 363, 374 (W. Va. 2001). However, apparently most state systems do not allow interlocutory review.

QUESTION 6. Justice delayed. Vivens sues Parker in federal court for fraud in a real estate transaction. After trial, the jury returns a verdict for Vivens. Three days after judgment enters, the judge grants a new trial under Fed. R. Civ. P. 59, on the ground that certain evidence Parker had offered concerning the transaction was improperly excluded. Parker had not moved for a new trial on that ground.

The case is now retried. At this trial the disputed evidence is admitted, and a new jury considers the case. It returns a verdict for Parker. The judge enters a final judgment for Parker. Vivens now appeals.

A. If the appellate court concludes that the evidence was inadmissible, it will order a third trial.

B. If the appellate court concludes that the evidence was inadmissible, it will order judgment entered on the original verdict for Vivens.

C. The appellate court will reverse, since Parker never moved for a new trial on the ground of the exclusion of the evidence.

D. The appellate court will affirm, since Vivens has waived his objection to the admission of the evidence by failing to appeal after the first trial.

ANALYSIS. This question explores the procedural implications of the grant of a new trial. Here, the case was tried. The plaintiff won. The judge snatched the verdict away by granting a new trial. At the second trial, the defendant won. Now the plaintiff is unhappy and wants to appeal on the ground that the judge erred in granting the new trial. Can she do that? And what will happen if the appellate court agrees that the new trial should not have been granted?

C argues that the judge should not have granted the new trial on this ground, since Parker never asked for it. But the rule itself refutes the argument. Rule 59(d), captioned "New Trial on the Court's Initiative . . . ," authorizes the trial judge to grant a new trial even if not asked to do so (or if asked to on other grounds) within twenty-eight days of the entry of judgment.

D also misses the boat. As the discussion indicates, in federal court the party who loses the verdict because the judge grants a new trial cannot appeal at that point. The decision is "interlocutory"; it does not result in the entry of a final judgment, but rather in the order for a retrial. Thus, the frustrated Vivens must wait until there is a final judgment, after the second trial, before he can appeal the grant of that trial. Doubtless, Vivens would prefer to take an immediate appeal, but that isn't an option in federal court.

So what should the appellate court do if it concludes that the evidence was inadmissible, so that the first trial was actually without error? If that is true, the new trial should not have been granted. Consequently, there's no need to do it a *third* time, as **A** suggests. (Thank goodness!) Vivens should have the benefit of his verdict at the *first* trial. The court should order entry of judgment on the jury's verdict for Vivens at the first trial. **B** rules again.

G.   Double Closer: Combined motions for new trial and judgment as a matter of law

Suppose that the losing party at trial believes that she has grounds both to seek a new trial and to seek judgment as a matter of law? (Remember, under Federal Rule 50(b), a motion for judgment as a matter of law after the verdict is the equivalent of the common law motion for "judgment notwithstanding the verdict.") Suppose, for example, in the plane crash case in Question 3, that Knox loses at trial and believes that Sardinha's evidence of negligence was so weak that the jury's verdict is irrational. In federal court, she would presumably move for judgment as a matter of law under Rule 50(b) on that ground. And, if she views the evidence as that weak, she must also view the jury's verdict as "against the great weight of the evidence," a ground for a new trial. And, just to make things more interesting, assume as well that she believes the judge's instruction on causation was wrong. What should Knox do?

Well, what would *you* do? You would make both motions, of course. Naturally, you would prefer that the judge granted your motion for judgment as a matter of law under Rule 50(b), because then you would win outright. But if she won't do that, you'd certainly like to live to fight another day, by getting a new trial.

Federal Rule 50(c) deals with such combined motions. It requires the judge to rule on both motions. If she is inclined to grant the motion for judgment as a matter of law, she should do so, but, under Rule 50(c), she should *also* rule "conditionally" on the motion for a new trial as well. For example, she might rule as follows:

> The defendant's motion for judgment as a matter of law is granted, since the jury's finding that the accident resulted from the negligence of Knox is not supported by sufficient evidence to support a rational verdict. However, in the alternative, I find that the jury's verdict is also against the great weight of the evidence, and I therefore conditionally grant the defendant's motion for a new trial. However, I deny the motion for a new trial based on the causation instruction, since the instruction given accurately reflects the law in this jurisdiction.

The trial judge, by ruling on all the motions, facilitates full appellate review of the case. If there is an appeal, the appellate court can review all of the trial judge's rulings in a single, consolidated appeal.

So, if the judge does rule on both motions, what happens next, and how do the parties obtain appellate review of the judge's rulings on these motions? Here's a question that illustrates how these decisions will be reviewed on appeal. (Reading Rule 50(c) will help with it.)

QUESTION 7. Interim finality. Parkins sues Orwell Corporation in federal court under the Federal Age Discrimination in Employment Act. At trial, Orwell moves for judgment as a matter of law under Rule 50(a) before the case goes to the jury. The motion is denied. The jury finds for Parkins. Orwell then moves for judgment as a matter of law under Rule 50(b) and in the alternative for a new trial on the ground that the jury's verdict was against the great weight of the evidence. The judge grants Orwell's motion for judgment as a matter of law, and conditionally grants the motion for a new trial as well, on the ground that the verdict is against the great weight of the evidence.

A. Parkins may appeal both orders, since a final judgment will enter for Orwell.
B. Parkins may appeal, but only the grant of the motion for judgment as a matter of law, because the grant of the new trial was conditional.
C. Parkins may not appeal now, because the grant of the new trial prevents the judgment from being final. The case will be scheduled for a second trial.
D. Parkins may appeal the grant of judgment as a matter of law, but not the decision to grant the new trial, since the new trial has not yet taken place.

ANALYSIS. The crux of the matter here is that the judge has granted the defendant's motion for judgment as a matter of law. She has concluded that the evidence is too weak to support a verdict for Parkins. Consequently, Orwell is the winner. Judgment should enter for him.

But Rule 50(c)(1) tells the trial judge not to leave it at that, to rule "conditionally" on the motion for a new trial too. When the judge does that, she is saying, "I've taken the verdict away from Parkins and ordered judgment entered for Orwell, because the evidence is too weak to support a rational verdict for Parkins. So I'm granting judgment as a matter of law under Rule 50(b) for Orwell. Rule 50(c)(1) tells me I have to rule on the new trial motion too, so I'm stating that, if the appellate court reverses my Rule 50(b) ruling, I would grant a new trial in this case, because the verdict is against the great weight of the evidence."

Fine, but where does the case go from there? **C** is wrong, because Rule 50(c)(2) provides that a conditional grant of a new trial "does not affect the judgment's finality." The judge has ordered final judgment entered for the defendant, and that will happen. The case is over in the trial court. If no appeal is taken, the judgment for Orwell will stand as the final adjudication of the case. True, the judge has said that, if her order is overturned, there should be a new trial, but only if the order is overturned on appeal.

So there is a final judgment, and the case is therefore appealable. But which order is appealable, the order for judgment as a matter of law, or the new trial order, or both? **D** is wrong, because both orders are appealable. That's the reason for having the trial judge make both rulings, so that the appellate court can review both and properly dispose of the case. Even though the ruling on the new trial is "conditional," that is, it will only take effect if the grant of judgment as a matter of law is reversed, that ruling is still reviewable. If the appellate court reverses the entry of judgment for Orwell under Rule 50(b), it can then decide whether the motion for new trial was appropriately granted. Thus, **B** fails as well. Both orders are appealable. If the appellate court concludes (after reversing the judgment for Orwell) that the new trial was properly granted, it will remand for the new trial. If the court concludes that this motion also should not have been granted, it will reverse the new trial order too, and order entry of judgment for Parkins on the jury's verdict. **A** takes the cake.

Just to nail this complex concept down, here's another Closer. This one also considers what the appellate court should do if it disagrees with the trial judge's rulings, or some of them.

QUESTION 8. Reversal of fortune. Sardinha sues Knox in federal court for injuries in the crash of a single-engine plane. The case is tried to a jury, which returns a verdict for Sardinha. Knox moves for judgment as a matter of law under Rule 50(b) and for a new trial on the ground that the verdict is against the great weight of the evidence. He also seeks a new trial on the ground that the judge had given the jury the wrong instruction on causation.

The judge rules as follows on Knox's motions.

> The defendant's motion for judgment notwithstanding the verdict is granted, since the evidence that the accident resulted from the negligence of Knox is not sufficient to support a rational verdict. However, in the alternative, I find that the jury's verdict is against the great weight of the evidence, and conditionally grant the defendant's motion for a new trial. I deny the motion for a new trial based on the causation instruction, since the instruction given accurately reflects the law in this jurisdiction.

Sardinha appeals. The appellate court views Sardinha's evidence as considerably stronger than the trial judge did. Consequently, it concludes that judgment notwithstanding the verdict should not have been entered, and that the verdict was not against the great weight of the evidence.

However, Knox argues on appeal, and the appellate court finds, that a new trial should have been granted because the judge gave the jury the wrong instruction on causation.

A. The court should remand the case for entry of a judgment for Sardinha.
B. The court should remand the case for entry of a judgment for Knox.
C. The court should remand the case for a new trial.
D. The court should remand the case for the judge to rule again on the motion for a new trial based on the causation instruction.

ANALYSIS.   This one should not have given trouble. Here, the appellate court has concluded that the evidence was strong enough to support a verdict for Sardinha, so that entry of judgment for Knox as a matter of law was wrong. And, it has concluded that the evidence was not against the great weight of the evidence, so that the trial judge should not have "conditionally" granted the motion for a new trial on that ground. If those were the only rulings before the appellate court, it would have remanded the case for entry of a judgment for Sardinha, since it has concluded that the verdict for him was supported by the evidence.

However, Knox also sought a new trial on the ground that the judge's instruction on causation was wrong. He now argues that, if the entry of judgment as a matter of law for him is overturned, he should get a new trial. The trial judge denied that motion, but the appellate court agrees with Knox on this point, though not on the judgment notwithstanding the verdict. So, what happens next?

Surely, there is no reason for the trial judge to pass on the causation issue again, as **D** suggests. The appellate court is the last word on the proper legal rules to tell the jury. If it says the right instruction is "X," then the trial judge must give the "X" jury instruction. Nor is there any ground to enter judgment for Sardinha, as **A** suggests. Since the jury was wrongly instructed on causation, affirming its verdict for Sardinha would be unfair to Knox. Judgment should not enter for Knox either, as **B** suggests. After all, Sardinha won at the trial, though it was not a proper trial leading to a valid verdict. The proper ruling is to remand the case to the trial court for a new trial with the proper causation instruction. Choose **C**.

These two questions illustrate, I hope, the way in which the trial judge's conditional ruling on the new trial motion allows the appellate court to review all the alleged problems with the trial in one appeal, rather than *seriatim* in several. In the last example, if the trial judge had not ruled on the new trial motions, the appellate court would have had to remand for her to do so. After she did, those rulings would still be open to review on a second appeal. By requiring conditional rulings that may be appealed, Rule 50(c) provides a more efficient process for reviewing these various rulings.

 ## Glannon's Picks

1. Objection, objection	C
2. Judging the jury	C
3. The ungrateful guest	A
4. A jury of your miserly peers	B
5. The voice of experience	D
6. Justice delayed	B
7. Interim finality	A
8. Reversal of fortune	C

23

The Quest for Finality: Claim Preclusion Under the Second Restatement of Judgments

There once was a backbencher named Motta
Who had been grilled in Civ Pro quite a lotta,
The prof's question was hard,
So she pled it was barred . . .
By the doctrine of res judicata!

CHAPTER OVERVIEW

A. The importance of joinder to claim preclusion analysis
B. The scope of the "claim" that is precluded
C. The type of judgment that triggers claim preclusion
D. The "same parties" requirement for claim preclusion
E. Closer plus: A taste of intersystem claim preclusion
◈ Glannon's Picks

Once a claim has been litigated and resolved by a judgment in favor of one of the parties, the usual rule is that there can be no further litigation on that claim. If the plaintiff wins, and gets a judgment for damages, she may enforce that judgment, but she can't relitigate the underlying claim. If the defendant wins, the judgment in her favor bars any further litigation on the claim. This chapter addresses the requirements of this mystic doctrine of "claim preclusion" or "res judicata."[1]

Traditionally, res judicata only applies if four prerequisites are met: (1) the claim in the second action must be the same as that litigated in the first; (2) the parties must be the same; (3) the judgment rendered in the first action must be final; and (4) the judgment must have been rendered on the merits of the case. The questions will explore each of these requirements.

A. The importance of joinder to claim preclusion analysis

The premise underlying claim preclusion is that, once a party has litigated a claim, she should be barred from doing so a second time. Respect for the first court's authority, the parties' reliance on settled rights, and the need to conserve judicial resources all support a refusal of the second court — either the same court that originally decided the case or another court — to relitigate it.

However, fairness suggests that a party should only be precluded from litigating a claim in a second action if she litigated it in the first action, or was *entitled* to litigate it there. Claim preclusion would deprive a party of due process of law if it barred a court from considering a claim in a second action that the party could not have presented in the first. Thus, in determining what claims are barred by claim preclusion in a second action, it is important to know what claims could have been — or could not have been — asserted in the first.

Today, most procedural systems allow much broader joinder of claims than courts did a hundred years ago. In the federal courts, and in many state court systems as well, a plaintiff may join any claims she has against a defendant, even if they are based on different theories or seek different types of relief. Under earlier procedural rules, plaintiffs were much more constricted in joining claims. They might, for example, under the common law "forms of action," have been barred from joining claims based on different types of legal theories, such as tort and contract. They might also have had to seek different types of relief, such as money damages or equitable relief (an injunction, rescission of a contract, or an accounting, for example) from different courts.

---

1. "Claim preclusion" is the more modern term for barring relitigation of a claim that has already been litigated. The more traditional term is "res judicata." However, res judicata is sometimes used more broadly, to include all forms of preclusion, including issue preclusion (collateral estoppel).

Here's a simple example to illustrate the relationship between the scope of joinder under civil procedure rules and the operation of claim preclusion.

QUESTION 1. Ruin and res judicata. Mulligan hires DeLay to restore his 1933 Rolls Royce, but claims that DeLay ruined it rather than restored it. He sues DeLay in the state courts of Emporia. The State of Emporia does not jump at fancy new concepts, like the unified civil action recognized in Rule 2 of the Federal Rules of Civil Procedure. It remains content with the old common law forms of action. Under Emporia procedure, a plaintiff who brings suit under a writ of assumpsit may assert any contract claims she has against the defendant, even for breach of two unrelated contracts. However, she could not assert claims based on a tort theory under a writ of assumpsit, even if the tort claim arose out of the same underlying facts as the contract claim.

Mulligan brings an action in assumpsit against DeLay, seeking damages for breach of contract for the work on the Rolls. Mulligan's action is dismissed on a motion for summary judgment, on the ground that his contract is unenforceable under the Emporia statute of frauds. A final judgment enters for DeLay. Shortly thereafter, Mulligan brings a new action against DeLay, based on the writ of trespass on the case, alleging that his negligent work on the Rolls rendered it worthless. Under Emporia procedure, an action on the case allows assertion of claims based on negligence. Mulligan's second action will probably

A. not be barred, because he never asserted it in the first action.
B. not be barred, because he could not have asserted it in the first action.
C. be barred, because it is based on the same transaction as the first.
D. be barred, because he should have joined it in his first action.

ANALYSIS. The fundamental point here is that Mulligan was unable to assert his negligence claim in his initial action based on the writ of assumpsit. The joinder rules of Emporia, which limit claims under a writ of assumpsit to contract claims, simply didn't allow it. So the question is, having sued on the assumpsit claim and lost, can he now bring a second action on the negligence claim?

It would certainly be tough on a litigant in Mulligan's position if he could not. He would have to choose between his two possible theories of relief, bring one or the other, and lose the one he did not pursue in the first action. I suppose one could make a rational argument for such a system of claim preclusion, but it would certainly force plaintiffs to make some tough tactical decisions.

No system your author knows of operates that way. Instead, claim preclusion rules generally bar a party from bringing claims that he either did join in the first action or *could have* joined in that action. Once a judgment is rendered on a claim, it is final "not only as to every matter which was offered and received to sustain or defeat the claim or demand, but as to any other admissible matter which might have been offered for that purpose." *Cromwell v. County of Sac,* 94 U.S. 351, 352-353 (1876). However, if the first court was unable to entertain a claim, for lack of jurisdiction or lack of authority under the joinder rules, a second action on the omitted claim will not be barred.

Here, **D** is wrong because Mulligan could not join his negligence claim in the first action. Under Emporia procedure, the writ of assumpsit limited him to asserting contract-based claims. And **C** is wrong because, as just stated, where a claim could not have been joined in the first action, a second action on that claim will generally not be barred, even if it arose (as this one did) from the same transaction as that asserted in the first action. **A** is not quite wrong, but it isn't the best answer. It implies that a claim is not barred, as long as it was not asserted in a prior action. But frequently, claims will be barred that were not asserted in the first suit. The key question is not whether the claim was asserted, but rather whether it *could have been* asserted in the prior suit. If it could have been joined, but was left out, it usually will be barred.

But here the claim could not have been asserted in the first suit, because of the very limited Emporia joinder rules. So **B** is right. Where a party leaves out a claim because it could not be included, claim preclusion will not bar a second action on that claim.

Under modern procedure, this will rarely happen. Most American procedural systems allow very broad joinder of claims arising from a single dispute. Since the right to join such claims is broad, the bar on later actions based on that dispute is equally broad.

B.   The scope of the "claim" that is precluded

So, claims that could not have been joined will almost certainly not be barred by res judicata. But how about the converse situation, where a plaintiff could have joined a claim, but doesn't? Will all such omitted claims be barred from assertion in a later action, or, if not, which will and which will not?

Today, the federal courts, and many state courts, apply the "transactional" approach to claim preclusion set forth in the Second Restatement of Judgments. Under the Second Restatement approach, parties who have litigated a transaction are barred from litigating any further claims that arise from the same set of underlying facts. For example, if they had an accident, and litigated whether the defendant was liable for it, the judgment in that action would bar any further lawsuit between them arising out of that accident. Or if they entered into a contract for repair of the plaintiff's computer system and, after the work was done, litigated the adequacy of the defendant's performance of the contract, the judgment in that action would bar any further action seeking relief arising out of that transaction.

The premise of this approach is that, if the parties are going to litigate a set of historical facts — the accident, the repair transaction, whatever — they should resolve all their disputes arising from that set of events together in the first action, rather than nickel-and-diming each other (and the courts) by successive law suits involving the same dispute. This "transactional" approach is permissible today because most courts apply broad rules of joinder that authorize a plaintiff to assert all claims she has arising out of the same underlying facts in a single suit. Because the joinder rules authorize the plaintiff to seek all the relief she may be entitled to in the first action, the doctrine of claim preclusion or res judicata may fairly force her to do so. Thus, under the Second Restatement, a party is held to waive any claims she leaves out of the first action, if they arise from the transaction that was litigated in that action.

The language used in claim preclusion analysis can be confusing. Most courts hold that a plaintiff who has previously sued the defendant will be barred from suing her again on the "same claim." But this does not mean that, if Mulligan sues DeLay on a contract claim arising from his work on the Rolls, he can sue DeLay again on a tort "claim" arising from that work. The term "claim" in this context means the underlying transaction or set of facts that gave rise to the dispute, not a particular legal theory.

> The present trend is to see claim in factual terms and to make it coterminous with the transaction regardless of the number of substantive theories, or variant forms of relief flowing from those theories, that may be available to the plaintiff; regardless of the number of primary rights that may have been invaded; and regardless of the variations in the evidence needed to support the theories or rights. The transaction is the basis of the litigative unit or entity which may not be split.

Restatement (Second) of Judgments §24, cmt. a. Under Second Restatement analysis, if Mulligan sued DeLay for the Rolls job on a contract theory, he would be barred from suing him a second time for that work on a tort theory. Both suits would be for the same "claim," because both would seek relief based on the same underlying set of facts. Thus, while Mulligan might have tort and contract "claims" (in the sense of legal theories for relief) arising from DeLay's restoration work, he only has one "claim" arising out of it for purposes of claim preclusion analysis.

This chapter focuses on the Second Restatement approach, which continues to gain adherents. But there are other approaches to claim preclusion. These approaches tend to cling to older conceptions that prevailed when the forms of action and law/equity distinctions loomed larger than they do today.

For example, some courts hold that a plaintiff who has sued the defendant may assert a new claim based on a different "primary right" arising out of the underlying events. This approach focuses on the legal theory of recovery in the two actions, allowing a second action on a different theory or for invasion of a distinct interest. For example, under this approach, some courts have allowed a plaintiff who sued a defendant for property damage arising out of a motor vehicle accident to bring a second action for personal injuries arising from the accident, on the ground that the two claims involve invasion of different rights. See, e.g., *Carter v. Hinkle*, 52 S.E.2d 135 (Va. 1949). This would clearly be impermissible under the Second Restatement approach, since both claims arise out of the same "transaction," the accident.

Here's a straightforward question for a warm-up.

QUESTION 2. **Reconstruction.**   Aronson sues Miller in a court in the State of Arcadia, which applies the "transactional" approach of the Second Restatement to claim preclusion, and allows broad joinder of claims. He seeks damages for breach of a contract to build an addition on his house. He claims that Miller breached the contract by using substandard construction materials. The jury renders a verdict for Miller, and judgment is entered on the verdict.

Subsequently, Aronson sues Miller again, in Arcadia, this time for negligence. He claims that Miller's employees were negligent in interpreting the contract specifications, and consequently built the addition one hundred square feet smaller than the plans required.

A. Aronson's second suit will be barred, because the first action determined that the house was built correctly.
B. Aronson's second suit will not be barred, because Miller never raised or litigated a claim that the addition was too small in the first action.
C. Aronson's second suit will be barred, because it is the "same claim" that was litigated in the first action.
D. Aronson's second suit will not be barred. It is not the "same claim" as that litigated in the first action, because it is based on negligence, not breach of contract.

ANALYSIS.   A is a bit muddled. It suggests that the first action resolved the issue Aronson seeks to litigate here, the size of the house, so that collateral estoppel will bar relitigation of that issue. But the size issue was never litigated in the first action, only the quality of the materials.

B is also a loser, since it suggests that Aronson's too-small argument will only be barred if it was litigated in the first action. Under the Second Restatement's transactional approach, claims that arise from a single transaction are barred if they were raised or *could have been* raised. This one clearly could have been asserted in the first action, since Arcadia (like federal courts under the Federal Rules of Civil Procedure) allows broad joinder of claims. Under the Second Restatement approach, Aronson will be barred from suing on this theory in a second action. Because his second claim arises out of the same transaction that was litigated in the first action — the construction of the addition — Aronson had to assert it in Suit One, or lose it. **C** is the right answer.

D proceeds on the premise that a party may "split" her claims if they are based on different legal theories. Again, some older approaches to preclusion, such as the "primary right" approach, would allow this, but under the "transactional" approach of the Second Restatement of Judgments, all claims, regardless of the legal theory they assert, must be brought in the first action if they arise from the same underlying facts.

Here's another question to help distinguish a plaintiff's claims in an action from her "claim" under res judicata principles.

QUESTION 3. Roadblock. The Town of Jasper, in the State of Arcadia, hires Montrose Paving Company to pave the roadway and parking areas at its transfer station. The Town claims that Montrose did a shoddy job, forcing it to hire another contractor to redo the job. Assume that the joinder rules of Arcadia would allow broad joinder of any claims the Town had against Montrose. It sues Montrose for breach of contract, and recovers $30,000.

Subsequently, the Town brings a new action against Montrose. In its second action, the Town asserts a negligence claim against Montrose for destruction of trees and shrubs caused when Montrose brought in its large paving machine to do the transfer station paving job. It also sought a refund of advance payments made to Montrose on a contract to pave the school parking lot, which Montrose had contracted to complete before the transfer station job, but had never performed. Assuming that Arcadia applies the Second Restatement's transactional approach to the "same claim" requirement,

A. neither of the town's claims in the second action will be barred.
B. the town's contract claim will be barred, but its negligence claim will not.
C. the town's negligence claim will be barred, but its contract claim will not.
D. both of the town's claims in the second action will be barred.

ANALYSIS. If you keep the basic Second Restatement test in mind, this example shouldn't be heavy lifting. The crucial point is that, under the

Second Restatement, a plaintiff who brings a claim against a defendant for a particular set of events must assert all claims she has against the defendant that arise from that set of events. Any such claims that could have been brought, but were not, will be barred by claim preclusion.

Here, the Town sued Montrose for the transfer station paving job. Arcadia's broad joinder rules would have allowed it to join any other claims it had arising from that job. The claim for damage to the shrubbery *does* arise from the same events as the Town's first action, the paving work at the transfer station. Consequently, under the "same claim" approach of the Second Restatement, it will be barred from asserting that claim in a second action. The basic idea is simple: If you are going to sue Montrose for the paving job, you must seek all the relief you might be entitled to arising from that job in the first action. If you don't, res judicata will bar you from seeking it in a second. While the shrubbery claim is based on a different theory, and involves collateral damage from the paving, it does arise from the transfer station paving work, so it had to be asserted in the first suit. Since it was not, it is barred by res judicata. Thus, **A** is wrong.

However, the school paving job is a different transaction from the transfer station job. Consequently, **D** is wrong. The Town was not required to assert its claim for the school job when it sued Montrose for the transfer station job. Although the school-paving claim had already accrued, and under Arcadia procedural rules it *could have been* asserted in the first action, the claim preclusion principles of the Second Restatement do not force the plaintiff to join all claims she has against a defendant in her first suit. It only provides that any further claims that arise from the transaction that was the basis of the first action are barred. Since the school paving claim arises from a different set of events, the Town did not have to assert it in the first action, and is not barred from suing on it separately.

B implies that the Town's contract claim based on the school paving job would be barred. This appears to be based on the logic that the Town sued before on a contract theory, so it should have joined all contract claims it had against Montrose in the first action. But this isn't right. Since the second contract claim arises from a different transaction from the first, the Town was not required to join it and will not be barred from suing on it separately. The key to preclusion is not that the second action is based on the same *legal theory*; it's that it arises from the same *underlying facts* that were litigated in the first.

Thus, the right answer is **C**. The negligence claim will be barred, since it arises from the same transaction as the first suit. But the claim based on the school paving contract is not barred, since it arises from a different transaction that the town did not litigate in the first action.

Since the scope of a "claim" under the Second Restatement is the most basic claim preclusion issue — and the most tested — let's try another example. This one has a twist or two. Consider what the answer *should* be, in light of the policies that underlie claim preclusion.

QUESTION 4. Pipe dreams. Carzis Company, an Arcadia construction contractor, orders two thousand feet of PVC pipe it plans to use in a sewer construction project from Hassan Supply. Hassan fails to deliver the pipe on time, so Carzis buys the pipe from another supplier, and finishes the job, though with a serious delay. A year later, Carzis sues Hassan in the courts of Arcadia to recover a $7,000 deposit it had paid Hassan toward the cost of the pipe, and recovers a judgment for that amount.

At the time of Carzis' action, consequential damages (that is, secondary damages such as the delay Carzis suffered here) for breach of contract were not available under Arcadia contract law. However, a year later the Arcadia Supreme Court held that, where the seller is specifically notified of the intended use and that time is of the essence, consequential damages may be recovered. After the Arcadia Supreme Court's decision, Carzis sues Hassan again, in the Arcadia court. It claims consequential damages for the delay it suffered in completing the sewer project.

Carzis also asserts a claim in the second action under the Arcadia Consumer Protection Act, which authorizes treble damages for deceptive acts in a trade or business, claiming that Hassan's salesperson had misrepresented its ability to deliver the pipe in a timely manner. Last, relying on the same statements by Hassan's salesperson, he includes a claim under the Federal Interstate Deliveries Act (FIDA), which authorizes damages for fraudulent misrepresentation in interstate sales. Assume that claims under the FIDA may be filed in state court. Assume also that the joinder rules of Arcadia would allow broad joinder of any claims Carzis had against Hassan in the first action.

A. None of the claims in the second action are barred.
B. All of the claims in the second action are barred except the federal claim.
C. All of the claims in the second action are barred except the claim for consequential damages.
D. All of the claims in the second action are barred.

ANALYSIS. A can't be right. Certainly the state Consumer Protection Act claim should be barred. It arises out of the same transaction — the agreement to supply pipe to Carzis for the sewer construction project — as the initial action. No reason appears why it could not have been asserted in the first suit. Thus, it should have been. Remember, the key to preclusion under the Second Restatement approach is whether the claim arises out of the transaction that was litigated in the first action, *not* whether the particular theory was asserted or litigated in that action. While Carzis never asserted a claim under the Consumer Protection Act, it could have, and since this claim arose from the same pipe supply contract as the initial suit for a refund, it should have been joined. The penalty for failing to do so is that it is barred by res judicata.

The same is true for the claim arising under federal law. This claim also arises out of the negotiations for the pipe contract for the project. Thus, under the Second Restatement's transactional test, it is part of the same claim that was litigated in the first action. The fact that the claim arises under federal law rather than state law does not change this result. The question indicates that FIDA claims (like most claims that arise under federal law) may be asserted in state court. Since the federal claim arose from the same events as the refund claim, and could have been brought in the first action, Carzis is barred from suing on it later.

That knocks out **B**. The tough issue here is posed by **C**, and admittedly, I didn't lay out the governing black letter rule before the question. But the principle of repose that underlies res judicata should suggest the result. Here, Carzis sued on his contract claim, and obtained a judgment. Case closed. Normally, res judicata would attach to that final judgment, and bar Carzis from seeking any further relief based on the pipe transaction. But here Carzis will argue, "when I sued the first time, the law did not allow consequential damages. Now that the Arcadia Supreme Court has changed the law to allow such damages, I want 'em! Since the claim could not have been asserted in the original action, I should be allowed to assert it now."

It isn't hard to see that Carzis's argument would unsettle many settled cases. If parties could bring a new action whenever the law changed, cases would be only provisionally over; they might still be resurrected if the legal rules changed. In most situations, Carzis's argument will be rejected. Parties have the right to one decision on their cases, under the law as it exists at the time of decision, not to multiple decisions under the law of 1999, the law of 2009, and again under the law of 2013!

In addition, note that Carzis *could* have asserted his claim for consequential damages in his original action. He would have lost on it in the trial court, of course, since at the time Arcadia appellate case law did not recognize a right to consequential damages. The trial judge in Carzis's case would have been bound by those decisions. But Carzis could have taken an appeal, and the Arcadia Supreme Court, which changed the rule a year later, might well have changed it in his case instead. Better to leave Carzis to this remedy, than to revisit old judgments every time the legal rules change in the future.

So, the best answer is **D**. All of Carzis's claims in his second action arise out of the same sale that he sued upon before, and are barred by claim judicata and res preclusion, or whatever you call it.

C.   The type of judgment that triggers claim preclusion

It is commonly said that res judicata only applies if the judgment in the prior action was rendered on the merits of the case. This requirement is deceiving, however, since a party is frequently precluded from relitigating even though she never litigated anything "on the merits" in the prior action.

The point of the "on the merits" requirement is to prevent courts from giving claim preclusive effect to certain procedural dismissals of the first action. For example, if Reynoso sues in federal court, and her case is dismissed for lack of subject matter jurisdiction, no court would bar her from suing on the same claim in state court. She never had a full opportunity to have her case heard in the first action. Indeed, the court's reason for dismissal was that it could not hear the claim. As we saw at the outset of the chapter, where a legal theory can't be asserted in the first action, a second action on that theory will not be barred. So dismissals for lack of subject matter jurisdiction, and similarly, for lack of personal jurisdiction or improper venue, are not viewed as "on the merits," and do not preclude a second action in another court competent to entertain the claim.

In other situations, however, dismissals that clearly do not involve litigation of the claim itself do bar a second action, even though we would not think of them as decisions "on the merits." (For this reason, the Second Restatement shies away from the phrase entirely.) If a defendant fails to respond to the suit, for example, and judgment is entered by default for the plaintiff, there has clearly been no litigation on the merits. Yet most courts give res judicata effect to a default judgment. That is, they would not allow the defendant, having abandoned his opportunity to defend in Suit One, to try to relitigate the transaction later. The rationale is that the defendant had the *opportunity* to litigate in Suit One, and is not entitled to ignore the pending action in favor of another action later at a time and place of his own choosing. On the same rationale, a plaintiff who files an action and does not pursue it, leading to a "dismissal for failure to prosecute," will be barred from bringing a second action. If litigation was commenced, and there was no procedural impediment to prevent the court from hearing it, the parties have had their opportunity to litigate and should either grasp it or recognize that they have waived it.

In some cases, the parties may reach the merits but not go to trial. For example, a claim may be resolved on summary judgment, when the court finds that there is no dispute of material fact and one of the parties is entitled to judgment as a matter of law. Or, a case may be dismissed at the outset for "failure to state a claim upon which relief can be granted." In both of these situations, the court has concluded that the plaintiff cannot recover, though neither involves a trial. Virtually all courts would give claim preclusive effect to a summary judgment, and a good many treat the dismissal of a case under Fed. R. Civ. P. 12(b)(6) (or similar state court rules) for failure to state a claim as a bar to a new action. When a complaint is dismissed for failure to state a claim, the plaintiff will be given the opportunity to replead, to try to state a compensable claim for relief. She may also seek to dismiss the action "without prejudice," that is, with express recognition by the court that the dismissal of the first action will not bar another suit on the same claim. If the plaintiff takes neither of these avenues to avoid the demise of her claim, it is probably because she cannot state one.

Consider whether the second claim would be barred in the following example.

QUESTION 5. Procedure and substance. Akbar sues Rajiv Motors in an Emporia court for injuries suffered while driving a used snowmobile that Rajiv had sold to him. His suit is based on breach of warranty (a contract theory) and strict products liability, a tort theory. Rajiv moves to dismiss the contracts claim, on the ground that the Emporia long-arm statute does not authorize jurisdiction over it. The judge concludes that the long-arm statute allows suit against Rajiv for tort claims, but not contract claims, and dismisses the breach of warranty claim. The case goes to trial on the strict liability claim. After Akbar presents his evidence, the trial judge grants a directed verdict for Rajiv, on the ground that Akbar has not presented sufficient evidence that the snowmobile was defective. Judgment is entered for Rajiv.

Later, Akbar sues Rajiv again, for the same injuries, again in the Emporia courts. He bases his claim in this action on a negligence theory. Assuming that the principles of the Second Restatement of Judgments apply, Akbar's second action

A. will be barred, because the negligence claim could have been brought in the first action but was omitted.
B. will not be barred, because the contract claim was dismissed for lack of jurisdiction, so there has been no final decision "on the merits."
C. will not be barred, because the grant of the directed verdict motion did not decide the case on the merits in the first action.
D. will not be barred, since his claim in the second action is not the same claim as his claim in the first.

ANALYSIS. This case is something of a hybrid, since part of it was dismissed for lack of personal jurisdiction, while the rest of it was litigated to a final judgment in favor of the defendant. But basic principles should point you to the answer.

If Akbar had brought a second action (perhaps in another court) on the contract claim, it would not have been barred, since the first court determined that it lacked personal jurisdiction to entertain that claim. As we said at the outset, a party is almost never precluded from bringing a claim that it *could not* have litigated in an earlier action.

But here Akbar did not sue a second time on the claim that was dismissed for procedural reasons. He brought a new claim on a new tort theory. **D** is wrong here, because the negligence claim is "the same claim" as the strict products liability claim: They both arise out of the same accident. And, since the court in the prior action concluded that it had jurisdiction to hear tort claims arising from that accident under the long-arm statute, it presumably had jurisdiction to hear the negligence claim as well as the strict liability claim. Thus, the negligence claim was based on the "same claim" as Akbar's first suit, could have been heard in the first case, and was left out. Under Second Restatement claim preclusion principles, it will be barred . . . if the first case was decided on the merits.

It was decided on the merits. **C** is wrong, because the parties here went to trial on the strict liability claim. Akbar had his full opportunity to present his evidence, and the judge determined that it was insufficient to support a reasonable verdict in his favor. Like the grant of a motion for summary judgment, the grant of a directed verdict motion resolves the case on substantive grounds: The judge has determined that the plaintiff's proof is not strong enough to prevail, and orders a judgment for the defendant. Thus, claim preclusion will apply to bar the negligence claim here. **A** is right.

D. The "same parties" requirement for claim preclusion

Although a judgment in a suit against a defendant bars the plaintiff from asserting any further claims against that defendant arising from the same events, it does not bar claims against other actors the plaintiff *might have* sued for the same injuries. "The basic premise of preclusion is that parties to a prior action are bound and nonparties are not bound." Wright & Miller §4449. Thus, in the common terminology of claim preclusion, preclusion requires that the parties to the second action be the "same parties" as the parties to the first.

The simplest example of this involves a plaintiff who sues one defendant for injuries arising from an accident, loses, and then sues another. Generally, this is permissible. Jones, by suing Smith, does not lose the right to sue Doe at another time in another court . . . or at the same time in another court, for that matter. His claims against different defendants are viewed, for claim preclusion purposes, as distinct, so that the assertion of his "claim" against

Smith does not affect his right to assert his separate "claim" against Doe in another action. Similarly, if Jones and Gomez, two passengers in Smith's car, are injured due to his negligence, each has a separate claim against Smith. If Jones sues for her injuries, and the case goes to judgment, it will not affect Gomez's right to sue separately for his.

The litigation world would be a lot more complicated if res judicata theory did not include this "same parties" limitation on the effect of a judgment. If suing one defendant gave rise to a res judicata bar on Jones's claims against all possible defendants, he would be forced to sue them together in a single action, or lose his claims against the omitted defendants. Jones may not wish to do that, or even be able to do that, due to limits on joinder, personal jurisdiction, or subject matter jurisdiction in the court he prefers. Thus, the "same parties" limit appropriately reconciles res judicata theory with the rules on joinder and jurisdiction.

Even if a person was a party to a prior action, preclusion may not apply if she was not a direct adversary of another party in the case. Suppose, for example, that Puckett sues Caribe and Ostend, two defendants, in an action arising out of a business deal. He claims that Caribe breached her contract to deliver 50,000 widgets he needed for his business, and that Ostend, the agent who arranged the transaction, misrepresented Caribe's ability to deliver. Although Caribe and Ostend are codefendants, they are not adversaries. Neither has asserted a claim for relief against the other, and, in fact, they may both be raising the same defenses to Puckett's claim. Suppose that Puckett loses, because the jury concludes that Caribe had complied with her obligations under the contract. If Ostend had a claim against Caribe for his commission, he would be free to sue Caribe for it in a separate action. Even though he and Caribe were both parties to the prior action, they were not adversaries. Ostend could have asserted a cross-claim for his commission (at least, under Federal Rules practice—see Rule 13(g))—but chose not to. Because his "claim" for the commission is not the same as Puckett's claim against him and Caribe, he could still bring a separate action for his commission against Caribe.

There are a few situations in which a nonparty will be bound by a judgment. These usually arise where one of the litigants in the prior action expressly represented the interests of the nonparty. Suppose, for example, that the trustee of a trust sues a bank, claiming that the bank mismanaged the assets of the trust, leading to a loss of value. If the trustee lost, a beneficiary of the trust could not then sue on the same theory. The trustee was empowered to represent the interests of the beneficiaries, and sued on their behalf. Because he litigated on behalf of the beneficiaries, they would be bound. Similarly, legatees of a will would be bound by litigation on their behalf by an executor. On a similar rationale, a buyer of property would be bound by a judgment against the seller. Suppose, for example, that Estrada sued to keep a neighbor from walking across her property to the beach, and the court determined that the neighbor had an easement to do so. A purchaser from Estrada would be bound by that determination of Estrada's interest in the property, on the theory that Estrada could only convey the interest she actually held. In cases like these, it is held that the represented party is "in privity" with the party who sued and therefore bound by the result in the prior litigation. But such situations are rare. In most contexts, one party is not bound by the results in another party's suit, even if she has a similar interest in establishing liability of a defendant.

With this warm-up, have a try at the following question.

QUESTION 6. Through the roof. Granite State Crane Company was working on a job installing air conditioning equipment on the roof of a warehouse owned by Regal Property Management. Its crane operator landed a large mechanical ventilator on the roof a bit too hard, causing cracks in the seams of the roof. Three rainy days later, water leaks through the cracks, ruining electronic products stored in the warehouse by Conductrol Products, Inc.

Regal sues Granite State in federal court for the cost of repair to its roof, and recovers. Although it could have joined as a coplaintiff (see Fed. R. Civ. P. 20(a)), Conductrol did not. Subsequently, Conductrol sues Granite State, again in federal court, for damages to its products stored in the warehouse. Conductrol's action will be

A. barred, because Conductrol shared the same interest as Regal in proving negligence of Granite State.

B. barred, because Conductrol, the lessee, was in privity with Regal, the lessor of the warehouse space.

C. barred, because Conductrol could have joined as a coplaintiff in Owner's action.

D. not barred, because Conductrol's claim is different from Regal's for res judicata purposes.

ANALYSIS. In this example, the defendant's negligence causes an invasion of the interests of both the owner and a lessee who stored goods in the warehouse. One sues and recovers for his damages. What effect does that have on the other's right to sue?

The general rule is that each party has her own claim, and may choose, within the limits of the joinder rules and principles of jurisdiction, to sue when and where she wants. In a few narrow circumstances, however, where one party's interests are clearly asserted by another, the represented party may be barred from relitigation.

A suggests that Conductrol will be barred from bringing its own action, because it has the same interest in proving Granite State's negligence that

Regal does. It does share an interest in establishing Granite State's negligence, but that isn't enough to make Regal its representative and bar Conductrol from suing separately. Imagine that it were, and Regal sued first and lost. That would bar actions by anyone who had goods stored in the warehouse, just because the owner had sued and failed to recover. Unlike the situation of a trustee or executor, no one has expressly designated Regal to represent Conductrol's interests, nor could it sue for Conductrol's losses. It can only sue for its own. True, when it sues for its own damages, Regal will try to establish Granite State's negligence, just as Conductrol will when it sues for its losses. But there's a world of difference between having a mutual interest in establishing a defendant's negligence and one party representing another's interests in a way that will bar the other from bringing its own claim. **A** is wrong; although Regal and Conductrol both have an incentive to establish Granite State's liability, Regal did not represent Conductrol's interests or sue for its losses. Conductrol may bring its own action to collect those losses.

B is wrong for the same reason; Conductrol is not "in privity" with Regal just because it rents space from Regal. By renting space from Regal, Conductrol does not delegate authority to Regal to represent its interests in a suit against third parties. Indeed, their interests may be adverse to Regal's in some respects: Conductrol might want to sue Regal on the theory that it caused the damage due to negligent maintenance or should have discovered the leak and limited the damage. Thus, there is hardly the unity of interest between the two that makes it fair to conclude that Regal represented Conductrol's interests in the first action.

C also fails. It suggests that, if a party could join in another's action against the defendant, she must do so or lose her claim. Under the basic elements of claim preclusion, that isn't so. Each party has her own "claim," and is entitled to sue on it separately. Had Conductrol joined in Regal's action, it would be barred from suing again. But, having decided not to, it is free to sue separately. This is consistent with the Federal Rules's approach to party joinder, which allows, but does not require parties with claims arising out of the same transaction to sue together. See Fed. R. Civ. P. 20(a)(1) (parties "may" join as plaintiffs if they seek relief arising out of the same transaction or occurrence).

So **D** takes the prize. Conductrol is not barred from bringing its own action for its damages, since it is not the same party as Regal for claim preclusion purposes.

In some cases, a lessee might be bound by litigation by the lessor. Suppose that the owner of property sued to prevent trespass by a neighbor, and it was held that the neighbor had an easement to cross the property. If the owner then leased the property to Jones, Jones would be bound by that prior litigation. The owner can only convey to Jones the interest he holds in the property. If it has been determined that his interest is subject to the easement, Jones takes the owner's interest subject to that limitation.

See generally Restatement (Second) of Judgments §43 and accompanying commentary. But the situation here is clearly different.

E.   Closer plus: A taste of intersystem claim preclusion

A frequent claim preclusion scenario involves a plaintiff who sues in federal court on federal claims, and then brings a later action in state court on related state law claims. This scenario is different from the previous examples, because it involves a court in one system determining what res judicata effect to give to the decision of a court in a different system. These "intersystem preclusion" issues can be complex. But a fair working rule is that a court in one system will give the same res judicata effect to a judgment that it would be given *in the court that rendered it*. See Friedenthal, Kane & Miller, *Civil Procedure* 730-733 (4th ed. 2005).

Thus, a state court, confronted with a decision of a federal court, will ask, "could the plaintiff have gone back and tried again in federal court?" If she could not have tried again in the rendering court, she will almost always be barred from trying again in another court, in either the state or federal system. Similarly, a federal court, confronted with a second action after a previous action in state court, will apply the claim preclusion rules of the state court that rendered the previous decision.

On that premise, consider the following two examples. Keep in mind that the federal courts follow the Second Restatement approach to claim preclusion problems.

> **QUESTION 7. Round One.** Pelham sues Correro, a police officer who arrested him. He brings suit in federal court under 42 U.S.C. §1983, a federal statute that authorizes suits against persons acting on behalf of the state for violation of federal civil rights. Pelham alleges that Correro's conduct in using excessive force in making the arrest violated his Fourth and Fourteenth Amendment rights. He loses, because the federal court determines that Correro is entitled to qualified immunity from liability on the federal civil rights claim.
>
> Subsequently, Pelham sues Correro in state court for assault and battery, based on the same conduct that gave rise to his federal civil rights action. Assume that the state court uses a narrower, "primary rights" approach to claim preclusion, that the assault and battery claims, under that approach, would be viewed as based on different primary rights from the federal civil rights claim and could be brought in a separate action. Pelham's second action

A. will not be barred, because he did not assert his state law claims in the initial suit.
B. will not be barred, because he could not have asserted his state law claims in the initial suit.
C. will be barred, because he could have joined the state law claims in the initial action and they are part of the "same claim" under the Second Restatement approach to claim preclusion.
D. will not be barred, because the state court will view his assault and battery claims as based on different primary rights from the claims asserted in his first action.

ANALYSIS. This example should not give trouble, if you keep our basic working rule in mind. The court in which the second action is filed will apply the preclusion law of the court that decided the first. That is, it will bar relitigation if the rendering court (here, the federal court) would bar a second action in its own courts.

In his original action, Pelham sued in federal court, and left out the state law claims for assault and battery. When he sues again in Emporia state court, that court must determine whether Pelham could have brought a second action on those claims in *federal* court, the court that rendered the judgment. Here, he could not have brought a second federal court action. The federal courts follow the Second Restatement's transactional approach to preclusion. Under that approach, the assault and battery claims will be barred if they arise from the same events as the federal civil rights claim and could have been brought in the first suit. **B** suggests that a second action should be allowed because these state law claims could not have been asserted in the federal suit. However, they could have been asserted there: His assault and battery claims would have been proper supplemental claims under 28 U.S.C. §1367(a), since they arise from the same events as his federal civil rights claim. Thus, **B** fails.

Since the two state law claims could have been asserted in the first action, they would be barred under the Second Restatement approach to claim preclusion. **A** is wrong too, because preclusion under the transactional approach does not turn on whether the omitted claim was joined, but on whether it *could have been* joined.

D also fails, because the Emporia court will not ask whether Emporia's res judicata principles would bar a second action, but rather whether federal res judicata principles would. Once again, the second court, even in a different state or a different court system, will usually look to the preclusion principles of the rendering court, not its own.

Since Pelham could not have brought a second action in federal court, under our "working rule" that the second court looks to the preclusion law of the first, he cannot bring it in state court either. **C** is the best answer: Pelham will be barred, under federal preclusion law, because the assault and battery claims arise from the same arrest as the civil rights claim. Because he could have joined those supplemental claims in the first action and didn't, he is barred from raising them in a second suit.

Of course, a federal court has discretion under the supplemental jurisdiction statute to entertain or dismiss supplemental claims. Isn't it possible that, if Pelham had asserted these claims in federal court, the court would have declined the invitation to hear them? Yes, that is possible, but by failing to present the claims in Suit One, Pelham has denied the court the opportunity to litigate the entire controversy in one action. Res judicata will apply.

Had Pelham asserted his assault and battery claims in the first suit, and the federal court decided, in its discretion, to dismiss them, Pelham would have been allowed to bring a second action in state court on those claims. At that point, the principle we started with, that a party is not precluded from later asserting a claim that could not be heard in the first action, would apply.

Let's try another example, keeping in mind our same basic intersystem preclusion premise.

QUESTION 8. Round Two.   Pelham sues Correro, a police officer who arrested him. He brings suit against Correro in an Emporia state court for assault and battery. He recovers damages.

Subsequently, Pelham sues Correro in federal court under 42 U.S.C. §1983, for violation of his federal civil rights, based on the same conduct that gave rise to his prior action. Assume that Emporia applies narrow claim preclusion rules, under which a second action on the federal civil rights claim would not be barred in the Emporia courts, because it asserts a right to relief based on a different "primary right." Federal courts, however, apply the Second Restatement's claim preclusion approach. Assume also that the Emporia state court would have had subject matter jurisdiction to hear Pelham's §1983 claim. Pelham's federal court action

A. will be barred, because the federal courts apply the transactional claim preclusion rules of the Second Restatement of Judgments.
B. will be barred, because federal civil rights claims may be brought in state court.
C. will not be barred, because, if it were, the federal court would be barred from hearing a claim arising under federal law.
D. will not be barred, because a second suit on the federal claim could have been brought in the Emporia courts.

ANALYSIS.   Round Two illustrates the converse situation from Round One. In the first action in state court, Pelham left out the federal civil rights claim, though it could have been joined. Now he sues on it in federal court. Under our "working rule" for intersystem preclusion problems, we ask whether Pelham could have brought this second action in an Emporia court. If he could have, the federal court will allow a second action, even though, if it applied its own preclusion rules, it would not.

Here, Pelham could have brought a second action in Emporia, since the Emporia courts view the civil rights action as based on a different "primary right" that would not be barred by the previous action. **A** is wrong in Round Two, because the question for the federal court is not whether the second action would be barred under federal preclusion rules, but whether it would be barred under *Emporia* preclusion rules. And **B** is wrong because, while the federal claim could have been brought in Pelham's first action, Emporia's preclusion rules provide that it is not barred, even though it could have been but was not included in that action.

C is wrong too. It implies that a state court action could not bar a later suit on a federal claim in federal court. That isn't true, under our "working rule." Suppose that Pelham had brought his first action in Massachusetts, a state that (like the federal courts) applies the transactional approach to res judicata. Suppose again that the federal claim was left out. In that case, a federal suit on the federal claim would be barred. The federal court would ask whether a second suit on the federal civil rights claim could have been brought in the Massachusetts courts. Under Massachusetts's transactional approach to res judicata it could not, since it arose from the same events as the first claim, and could have been asserted in the first action but was left out. In this scenario, the prior state court action would prevent the federal court from hearing the §1983 claim, even though it arises under federal law. However, because Emporia allows second suits to enforce different "primary rights," and the federal court will look to the preclusion rules of the first forum, the second suit based on the §1983 claim is not barred here. **D** is the right answer.

✵ Glannon's Picks

1. Ruin and res judicata	B	
2. Reconstruction	C	
3. Roadblock	C	
4. Pipe dreams	D	
5. Procedure and substance	A	
6. Through the roof	D	
7. Round One	C	
8. Round Two	D	

24

Collateral Estoppel, Issue Preclusion, Whatever

~

Perkins sued Jones who sued Koppel
Who sued Sax who sued Chan who sued Popple;
They all thought they'd prevail
With little travail
By invoking non-mutual estoppel!

~

CHAPTER OVERVIEW
A. Fundamentals: The "same issue" requirement
B. Psychoanalyzing old lawsuits: The "actually decided" requirement
C. Collateral estoppel where multiple defenses are raised
D. Two early Closers: The "necessary to the judgment" requirement
E. A taste of "non-mutual" collateral estoppel
✦ Glannon's Picks

All courts recognize the principle that, once parties have litigated an issue and decided it, there is no point in litigating that issue again. *First*, it isn't fair to the party who litigated and won on the issue to make her relitigate it just because it comes up again in a later action. *Second*, the courts have better things to do than revisiting issues that they have settled before. So the doctrine — called collateral estoppel by some courts, issue preclusion by others — is universally recognized and frequently applied. This chapter will address the basic requirements for estoppel, and briefly introduce, at the end, the concept of "non-mutual" estoppel.

Like many common law doctrines, collateral estoppel varies somewhat from court to court. But increasingly, the requirements set forth in Section 27 of the Restatement (Second) of Judgments are accepted as the elements of the doctrine:

> When an issue of fact or law is actually litigated and determined by a valid and final judgment, and the determination is essential to the judgment, the determination is conclusive in a subsequent action between the parties, whether on the same or a different claim.

This formulation specifies four requirements for estoppel to apply to an issue: (1) the issue to be precluded in the second action must be the same as that litigated in the first; (2) it must have been actually litigated in the first action; (3) it must have been actually decided in the first action by the court or jury; and (4) the decision of the issue in the first action must have been necessary to reach the judgment rendered in the first action.

Note that the "elements" or requirements for estoppel differ from those for res judicata. For example, res judicata will preclude claims that never were litigated; collateral estoppel only applies to issues actually litigated and decided. In addition, collateral estoppel does not require a judgment "on the merits." For example, a court's finding that it lacks personal jurisdiction over a defendant for a particular claim would estop relitigation of that issue, even though the case was dismissed for lack of jurisdiction, not on the merits.

A.   Fundamentals: The "same issue" requirement

If an issue was litigated between the parties in an action, and comes up again in a later suit, there's little point in litigating it again. But, obviously, estoppel should only apply if the issue in the second action *really is the same* as the one resolved in the prior action. The court can hardly take an issue as decided if it wasn't.

Suppose that Higgins agrees to buy a small business from DeVito. After the sale contract is signed, but before closing the deal, he sues to rescind the transaction, claiming that DeVito had misrepresented the annual income of the business. The court finds that DeVito had not misrepresented the income, and refuses to order rescission. After the sale, when Higgins fails to make an installment payment due on the sale, DeVito sues to collect. Higgins now defends again on the ground that the sale is void, because DeVito misrepresented the income of the business.

In this example, there is no reason to relitigate the misrepresentation issue. It is the same issue the parties litigated before. The judge heard the evidence and decided the issue in the prior suit. And that decision was necessary to reach the judgment in the prior suit: The reason the judge denied rescission was that she concluded that there had been no misrepresentation, so that the transaction was valid. It would be unfair to DeVito to make him muster the evidence on the point again, and take the risk of losing before a new finder of fact. And it would be a waste of the court's time to retry the misrepresentation issue in the second action. So, assuming that DeVito raises collateral estoppel as a defense, the court in the second action will estop Higgins from asserting misrepresentation as a defense to the second action.

Always begin the analysis of a collateral estoppel problem by asking, "What issue was decided in the earlier lawsuit?" and "Is the issue in the second action the same as the one decided in the first?" Consider how this "same-issue" requirement applies in the following question.

QUESTION 1. The long arm of collateral estoppel. Collins, from Virginia, sues Mora, from Pennsylvania, in Virginia. He claims that Mora had agreed to provide software consulting services for Collins in Virginia and then refused to do so. Mora moved to dismiss, arguing that the Virginia long-arm statute did not authorize jurisdiction over her. Assume that the Virginia long-arm statute authorizes jurisdiction for claims that arise out of "contracting to supply goods or services in the state" and for claims that arise out of "transacting business" in the state. The judge takes evidence regarding the parties' negotiations, and concludes that Mora had never accepted the contract, so that the "contracting to supply" provision does not apply. She further concludes that, since none of the negotiations took place in Virginia, the claim did not arise out of the transaction of business by Mora in Virginia. She dismisses the case for lack of personal jurisdiction.

Collins now sues Mora in Maryland, where her office is, to recover for the same transaction. Assume that Maryland's long-arm statute has the same two provisions, and Collins argues that both apply. Mora moves to dismiss, claiming that collateral estoppel bars Collins from claiming that the Maryland long-arm statute applies. Collins will probably

A. be estopped from arguing that either provision of the Maryland long-arm statute applies.
B. not be estopped from arguing that either provision of the Maryland long-arm statute applies.
C. be estopped from arguing that the "contracting to supply" provision applies, but not the "transacting business" provision.
D. not be estopped, because the first case was dismissed for lack of jurisdiction.

ANALYSIS.   As indicated above, the analysis of a collateral estoppel question should start by asking what issues were decided in the first case, and whether those issues are the same issues being litigated in the second. If the issues in the second action aren't the same as those litigated in the first, estoppel doesn't apply, even if the issues were "actually litigated," "actually decided," and "necessary to the judgment" in Suit One.

Here, the Virginia judge decided several issues. She decided that Mora never accepted the contract. Consequently, she rejected jurisdiction under the "contracting to supply" provision of the Virginia long-arm statute. She also decided that Mora had not transacted business in Virginia, so she rejected jurisdiction under the "transacting business" section as well.

In Suit Two, Collins claims that Mora "contracted to supply services" in Maryland, and "transacted business" there. Assuming that the Maryland "contracting-to-supply" provision would not apply if the parties didn't have a contract at all, estoppel should apply to the question of whether the parties had a contract. The Virginia court held that they did not, so Mora may invoke collateral estoppel to prevent Collins from establishing that they did. They already litigated that issue in the Virginia action, it was decided against Collins, and the issue of whether the parties had a contract is the same in Suit Two.[1] Collins will likely be barred from relitigating the contract issue.

The Virginia court also decided that Mora had not "transacted business" in Virginia, because none of the negotiations concerning the software services took place there. But the issue of whether Mora transacted business in Maryland is different from the issue of whether he did so in Virginia. The Virginia court never decided whether Mora transacted business in Maryland, since that issue was irrelevant to jurisdiction under Virginia's long-arm statute. Maybe the negotiations *did* take place in Maryland, and would support jurisdiction under its "transacting business" long-arm provision. Collins is not estopped on that question, since it is a different issue from the one he litigated and lost on in the Virginia action. So, estoppel will bar Collins from relying on the contracting prong of the Maryland statute, but not the transacting prong. **C** is right. **A** is wrong, because Collins clearly will not be estopped from arguing that Mora transacted business in Maryland. **B** is also wrong, because he *will* be estopped on the contracting provision, since the Virginia court concluded that no contract was formed.

But how about **D**? Isn't it true that this case was never decided on the merits, since it was dismissed for lack of personal jurisdiction? That is true, but the issue of whether the parties had a contract was still litigated, decided, and necessary to the judgment dismissing the Virginia action. There is no point in allowing relitigation of that issue, even though the ultimate

---

1. Let's leave aside the remote possibility that the Maryland court would apply a different state's contract law to the issue, and that a contract was formed under that law but not under the law applied by the Virginia court.

disposition of the case was a judgment of dismissal for lack of jurisdiction. A decision "on the merits" is a requirement for res judicata, but not for collateral estoppel. A factual finding that leads to a jurisdictional dismissal may be the basis for estoppel on that factual issue in a later action.

This same-issue requirement is fundamental. Let's try another example.

QUESTION 2. Food for thought. O'Hara sues Area Harvesting Company for breach of a written contract under which Area allegedly agreed to harvest the wheat on O'Hara's farm for a five-year period. Area defends on the ground that Cameco, the Area employee who had negotiated the contract, had no authority to bind the company, and that Area had notified O'Hara that it would not honor the agreement.

The judge grants summary judgment for O'Hara, finding that Cameco, as a sales agent for Area, had implied authority to enter into the contract. She orders specific performance of the contract.

In the third year of the contract, Area again refuses to perform. This time it seeks to avoid the contract by arguing that there was a mutual mistake as to the acreage covered by the contract, because Cameco had not understood that it was to include acreage rented by O'Hara to other farmers. (Assume for purposes of the question that res judicata (claim preclusion) does not bar the second action.)

A. Area will not be estopped from raising this defense, since it was not litigated and decided in the first action.
B. Area will not be estopped from raising this defense, since the first case was decided on summary judgment in the prior action, not after trial on the merits.
C. Area will be estopped from raising this defense, because it could have been raised in the first action.
D. Area will be estopped from raising this defense, since the prior judgment determined that the contract was valid.

ANALYSIS. In the previous chapter, we saw that res judicata bars relitigation even of claims that were not raised in the prior action, if they could have been raised. But that isn't true of collateral estoppel; it only bars an issue if it was litigated and decided in the prior action. Here, the issue of Cameco's authority to enter into the contract was litigated and decided, but the mutual mistake issue was not. It could have been raised there, but it wasn't. **C** is wrong, because collateral estoppel will only bar litigation in a second action of issues that were actually litigated and decided in the first.

B suggests that the first action can't have collateral estoppel effect because it was resolved on summary judgment, not after trial. Not so; issues decided by judges have the same collateral estoppel effect as issues decided by juries. (In the first question, the issues were decided by the judge, too.) When a judge enters summary judgment on an issue, she decides that one party is entitled to win on it, because there is no dispute of fact and its position is established as a matter of law. For example, the judge's conclusion that Cameco had implied authority to enter into a contract with O'Hara disposes of that issue, and could bar relitigation of the point in a later action.

D is probably wrong too, though there's an intelligent argument for it. The argument runs like this: "The parties litigated the validity of the contract in Suit One. It was held valid. So Area can't relitigate that issue." But this states the issue litigated in Suit One at too high a level of generality. The issue actually litigated in the first action was whether the contract was invalid because Cameco lacked authority to enter into it. If we precluded Area from arguing mutual mistake in Suit Two because it argued lack of authority in Suit One, Area would have to raise all possible defenses to the contract in Suit One, or lose them all in Suit Two. This might actually lead to an *increase* in litigation, since parties would have to assert *every* possible defense in the first case or lose the omitted defenses in later actions. Instead, courts focus on the specific issue — here, Cameco's implied authority — that the parties did raise and litigate in the prior action, and bar relitigation of that defense, but not other defenses to the contract that Area might have raised but did not.

So **A** is the best answer. Since Area did not litigate the mutual mistake issue before, it will not be estopped from raising it now.

How about another same-issue problem, with an interesting twist.

> **QUESTION 3. Issues and arguments.**   Renfrow sues Gillespie for negligence. He claims that Gillespie was negligent because he ran the red light just before their cars collided. The case is tried, and the jury finds for Gillespie. Renfrow loses.
>
> Now, Gillespie sues Renfrow for *his* injuries in the accident. (Assume that the jurisdiction does not have a compulsory counterclaim rule, so Gillespie can do this.) Renfrow raises the defense that Gillespie was negligent in running the red light and also because he swerved into Renfrow's car rather than swerving to avoid it.
>
> Gillespie moves to strike these defenses, on the ground that Renfrow is estopped from raising them, since he litigated and lost on the issue of

Gillespie's negligence in the prior action. Renfrow argues that he now has an additional witness on the question of whether Gillespie ran the red light. He also argues that he should be allowed to litigate whether Gillespie swerved into him, because he did not litigate that issue in the prior action.

A. Renfrow will be barred from asserting either of these arguments to establish the defense that Gillespie was negligent.

B. Renfrow will be barred from asserting the red light argument, but not the negligent swerving argument.

C. Renfrow will not be barred from asserting either of these arguments, since they were not fully litigated in the first action.

D. Renfrow will not be barred from raising either argument, because this action is a new suit in which Renfrow asserts Gillespie's negligence as a defense, not to establish liability.

ANALYSIS. **D** is a dog. The whole point of collateral estoppel is to preclude relitigation of issues when they arise in other actions and different contexts. As long as the issue of Gillespie's negligence was litigated and decided in the prior action, it is fair to preclude Renfrow from litigating it again, even if he is raising the issue to defeat Gillespie's claim rather than to establish his own. There is no requirement that the plaintiff be the same in both actions, or that the estopped party litigate the issue to establish liability (as opposed to a defense) in both actions.

The crux of the matter is, again, "what issue was litigated and decided in Suit One?" How we define the original issue will determine the scope of preclusion. If we define the issue as, "Did Renfrow prove that Gillespie was negligent with the evidence he submitted in Suit One?" then the issue isn't the same in the second suit, since Renfrow now offers different evidence to establish that Gillespie ran the light. But a little thought suggests that defining the issue in Suit One that narrowly would pretty much eviscerate collateral estoppel. A party who lost on an issue before would simply offer slightly different evidence to prove the point, and argue that he can't be estopped. This is not going to fly. If the issue is the same one that was litigated before, the loser will be precluded on it, even though she argues that she could do a better job of proving it the second time. No court will allow Renfrow to relitigate whether Gillespie ran the light, just because he claims he'll offer more evidence the second time.[2] Indeed, the specter of collateral

---

2. If Renfrow really has new evidence, he should move for relief from judgment in the first action. Fed. R. Civ. P. 60(b)(2) allows the judge to reopen the original case based on newly discovered evidence within one year of the entry of judgment. (The question here does not say that the evidence is newly discovered; if it was available at the time of the prior trial relief from judgment would be denied.)

estoppel (and res judicata) is what gives parties the incentive to do it right the *first* time.

So, **C** is also wrong, since estoppel will apply to the jury's finding that Gillespie didn't run the light. But how about his other argument, that Gillespie was negligent in swerving into his car, instead of turning the other way? Is this a new issue, or is it simply another argument in support of his prior claim that Gillespie's negligence contributed to the accident?

Very likely, a court would hold that the issue litigated in the prior action was "whether negligence of Gillespie was a cause of the accident," rather than "whether negligence of Gillespie in running the red light was a cause of the accident." Presumably, Renfrow would have pleaded the defense at this level of generality, and would be expected to produce all the evidence he had of negligent acts by Gillespie. See generally Restatement (Second) of Judgments §27, Ill. 4. If the court accepted the more specific ran-the-light formulation of the issue, it would allow Renfrow to relitigate the cause of the accident time and again by coming up with other negligent acts Gillespie may have committed. Since any negligence by Gillespie would bar his recovery, Renfrow should raise all his arguments for negligence in the first action, or be estopped from switching to new arguments in support of this issue in a later one. While we have to limit estoppel to the issues actually litigated, we don't have to break an issue like "Gillespie's negligence" down into atomic particles and limit estoppel to individual bits of evidence about it.

Thus, **A** is the best answer. The parties litigated the issue of Gillespie's negligence in Suit One. Renfrow lost on that issue, and will be estopped from relitigating it in Suit Two.

Admittedly, there is a subtle line between a new issue, illustrated in Question 2, and a new argument in support of the same issue, illustrated here. Law, a discipline that deals with human experience, is full of such close distinctions. It can't be helped.

B.   Psychoanalyzing old lawsuits: The "actually decided" requirement

The assumption underlying collateral estoppel is that, where the fact finder (either judge or jury) heard the evidence on an issue, and resolved it in one party's favor, there is no point in doing so a second time. However, if the fact finder heard the evidence on an issue, but *did not* decide it one way or the other, collateral estoppel cannot apply. How can the court apply estoppel if it doesn't know which party to estop? This is the logic of the "actually decided" element of collateral estoppel. Collateral estoppel will not apply every time the parties litigated an issue, or the judge or jury heard evidence on it at a trial. Estoppel can only apply if the issue was decided by the fact finder in the first case. So again, we have to look back to Suit One and figure out what issues were decided there.

The classic example used to illustrate this point is the negligence/contributory negligence example. Here it is in multiple-choice format.

QUESTION 4. Verdicts and decisions.   Watkins and Pasquale are in an accident. Watkins sues Pasquale for his injuries. Pasquale answers, denying negligence and pleading that Watkins was negligent in causing the accident. Under applicable negligence law, contributory negligence of the plaintiff would be a complete defense. That is, if the plaintiff was negligent at all in causing the accident, she would lose, even if the defendant was negligent too.

The action is tried to a jury, and both parties present evidence in support of their negligence allegations. The jury renders a general verdict finding that Pasquale is not liable to Watkins. That is, they return a verdict that Watkins take nothing, without recording their specific findings of fact on the two negligence issues.

Later, Pasquale sues Watkins for her injuries in the accident. In the second action

A. Pasquale can invoke collateral estoppel to establish that Watkins was negligent.
B. Pasquale can invoke collateral estoppel to establish that he was not negligent.
C. Pasquale can invoke collateral estoppel on both negligence issues.
D. Pasquale cannot invoke collateral estoppel on either party's negligence.

ANALYSIS.   This scenario could not happen under the Federal Rules of Civil Procedure. Pasquale's negligence claim would be a compulsory counterclaim in the first action, and he would waive the right to sue on it if he failed to assert it as a counterclaim in Watkins's suit. But not all states make counterclaims compulsory, so this scenario could happen in a number of courts, and used to arise in many.

The key to estoppel questions is to look back at Suit One, to determine what issues were litigated and decided in that suit. Here, the question indicates that the parties litigated the negligence of Watkins and of Pasquale. Both issues were raised in the pleadings, and evidence about both parties' negligence was submitted to the finder of fact. But that isn't enough to support estoppel. We also have to figure out *what the jury decided* about those issues. Did they find Watkins negligent (which would preclude him from recovery)? Did they find that Pasquale was not negligent (which also would have led to a verdict for Pasquale)? Or both? Only if we can re-construct the jury's reasoning, and determine that a particular issue was decided, can we estop relitigation of that issue in the second suit.

Here, we can't tell which conclusion led them to render their verdict. There are two trains of thought that would have led to the bottom line — a verdict for Pasquale. The jurors may have found that Watkins was negligent, so that he could not recover under the doctrine of contributory negligence. Or, they may have found that Pasquale was not negligent, so that he is not liable under basic negligence law. The jury must have reached one of these conclusions (or both), but we don't know which one. So estoppel can't be used, because we don't know what issue was decided in Suit One. **A, B,** and **C** are all wrong, because without knowing what was decided in Suit One, the court cannot apply estoppel in Suit Two. Too bad, but the parties will have to relitigate both issues. Choose **D** for five points.

The result might be different if the judge had asked the jury to render a special verdict in Suit One, specifying their factual findings about the negligence of each party. If they had rendered a special verdict, for example, finding that Watkins was negligent and Pasquale was not, we would know exactly what they had decided. If those issues arose again in Pasquale's suit, the court could estop Watkins from relitigating at least one of them.

Now, consider this variation on the Watkins case. Again, remember that the question to ask is what we can tell from the jury's verdict in Suit One about what issues were decided in that case.

QUESTION 5. Reprise. Watkins and Pasquale are in an accident. Watkins sues Pasquale for his injuries. Pasquale answers, denying negligence and pleading that Watkins was negligent in causing the accident. Under applicable negligence law, contributory negligence of the plaintiff would be a complete defense. That is, if the plaintiff was negligent at all in causing the accident, she loses, even if the defendant was negligent too.

The action is tried to a jury, and both parties present evidence in support of their negligence allegations. The jury renders a general verdict finding Pasquale liable to Watkins. Later, Pasquale sues Watkins for her injuries in the accident. In the second action

A. Watkins can invoke collateral estoppel to establish that Pasquale was negligent, but will have to relitigate his own negligence.
B. Watkins can invoke collateral estoppel to establish that he was not negligent, but will have to relitigate Pasquale's negligence.
C. Watkins can invoke collateral estoppel on both negligence issues.
D. Watkins cannot invoke collateral estoppel on either party's negligence.

ANALYSIS.   When Watkins *wins* the first action, it is possible to sort out how the jury decided the issues of his negligence and Pasquale's. Watkins couldn't have won the first action, under applicable negligence principles, unless he proved that Pasquale was negligent *and* that he, Watkins, was not. Thus, his recovery in the first action necessarily decided both of those issues. He couldn't have recovered if the jury found that he was negligent, because contributory negligence would bar recovery under applicable law. He couldn't have recovered, even if he was *not* negligent, unless Pasquale was, because a defendant is only liable if he caused the accident through negligent conduct. So here we can reconstruct the jury's reasoning process, and confidently conclude that they found that Pasquale was negligent and Watkins was not. That's the only train of thought that could have led to the verdict the jury rendered. Consequently, **C** is the right answer. Watkins can estop Pasquale on both issues, since both were litigated and decided in the first action, and both led to the judgment for Watkins.

C.   Collateral estoppel where multiple defenses are raised

A similar estoppel problem arises where a plaintiff brings suit, and the defendant asserts multiple defenses to the claim. Here again, we can only apply estoppel in a later action if we can figure out, from the pleadings, the trial and the verdict in the first action, what was decided in that action. Consider this case.

QUESTION 6. **Patent medicine.**   Amalgamated Manufacturing Company sues Sempco Products Company for patent infringement, claiming that Sempco has been using a switch component in its electrical transformers that is identical to one covered by Amalgamated's patent. Sempco defends on two grounds. First, it alleges that Amalgamated's patent is invalid. Second, it alleges that Amalgamated agreed to let Sempco use the switch in their transformers if Sempco would not challenge the validity of Amalgamated's patent on the switch.

Sempco moves for summary judgment on the invalidity of Amalgamated's patent. The court denies the motion. The case is then tried to a jury, which returns a general verdict finding Sempco not liable to Amalgamated. Two years later, Amalgamated sues Sempco again, this time alleging that it is using the same switch in making circuit boards for lighting systems. Sempco raises the defense that Amalgamated's patent on the

> switch is invalid, and argues that Amalgamated is estopped from proving that the patent is valid, since it lost the prior action involving the same issue.
>
> A. Amalgamated will be estopped from proving that its patent on the switch is valid, since this issue was litigated and decided in the prior suit.
> B. Amalgamated will not be estopped from proving that its patent on the switch is valid, since this issue was not decided in the prior suit.
> C. Amalgamated will estop Sempco from proving that the patent on the switch is invalid. The denial of summary judgment for Sempco in the prior action established the validity of Amalgamated's patent.
> D. Amalgamated will not be estopped from proving that its patent on the switch is valid, since it is not clear whether that issue was decided in the prior action.

ANALYSIS. Note that **C** requires you to apply summary judgment doctrine as well as collateral estoppel. In this book, I've generally confined the choices in each question to the topic of the chapter, but many multiple-choice questions, in Civil Procedure and other courses, will require you to draw on your knowledge of more than one topic in the course. Fair enough; legal analysis often requires consideration of multiple issues and rules. But such choices do make the questions more challenging. The last chapter in this book, "Closing Closers," offers a smorgasbord of such multi-topic morsels.

Here, anyway, it should be clear that **C** doesn't cut the mustard. *Denial* of summary judgment does not decide any factual issue. In denying Sempco's motion, the court did not decide that the patent was valid, or that it wasn't. It simply decided that there was sufficient evidence on both sides of the patent-validity issue to leave that question to the jury.

Turning to the other choices, the key again is to ask what the jury decided in Suit One. We know the parties litigated two issues at trial: validity of the patent and whether Amalgamated had agreed to let them use the switches. Which of these issues did the jury decide, and what did they decide about them?

Unfortunately, we don't know. The jury rendered a general verdict for Sempco. It won; it wasn't found liable. But, *why* did it win? We can't tell for sure. The jury may have found that Amalgamated's patent was invalid, or they may have found that it was valid, but Amalgamated allowed them to use the switches anyway. **A** is wrong, because estoppel cannot apply unless the court in the second action can tell that the issue was decided in the first. **B** is wrong too: The jury may have decided the case on the patent issue, or they may not. Amalgamated cannot be estopped on the validity of its patent, because we simply don't know whether it was held invalid in the prior action. Choose **D** for another five points.

Compare the following question, which also involves the situation in which two defenses are raised and litigated in Suit One.

QUESTION 7. Switching switches. Amalgamated Manufacturing Company sues Sempco Products Company for patent infringement, claiming that it has been using a switch component in its electrical transformers that is identical to one on which Amalgamated holds a patent. Sempco defends on two grounds. First, Sempco alleges that Amalgamated's patent is invalid. Second, it alleges that Amalgamated agreed to allow Sempco to use the switch in their transformers if Sempco would not challenge the validity of Amalgamated's patent on it. The case is tried to a jury, which renders a general verdict for Amalgamated and awards damages to it.

Two years later, Amalgamated sues Sempco again, this time alleging that it is using the same switch in making circuit boards for lighting systems. Sempco raises the defense that Amalgamated's patent on the switch is invalid. Amalgamated argues that Sempco is estopped from proving that the patent is invalid, since Sempco lost the prior action involving the same issue.

A. Sempco will be estopped from proving that Amalgamated's patent is invalid, since this issue was litigated and decided in the prior suit.

B. Sempco will not be estopped from proving that Amalgamated's patent is invalid, since this issue was not decided in the prior suit.

C. Sempco will not be estopped from proving that Amalgamated's patent is invalid, since it is not clear whether that issue was decided in the prior action.

ANALYSIS. Once again, we know that the parties litigated both the validity issue and the permission issue in the first case. We need to look back to the verdict and reconstruct the jury's train of thought in order to figure out, if we can, what issues they decided in reaching their verdict.

In the last example, we couldn't reconstruct their reasoning. There were two possibilities, but it was impossible to know which finding led to their no-liability verdict. So estoppel didn't apply. But here, we can do better. The plaintiff sued for infringement, and the defendant raised two defenses. The plaintiff won. It could only have won if the jury rejected both defenses. They must have rejected the defense that Sempco had permission to use the switch design. Otherwise, they would not have awarded damages for its use. And, they must have rejected the argument that the patent was invalid. Even if Sempco didn't have permission to use the switch, it would not be liable for patent infringement if Amalgamated did not have a valid patent on the switch. Since Amalgamated sued for patent infringement, and Sempco argued that the patent was invalid, the jury's award of damages for infringement tells us that they must have concluded that the patent was valid.

So **B** is wrong; from a careful analysis of the prior action it is apparent that the patent issue was decided in Suit One. And **C** is wrong, since we *can tell* that the issue was decided. **A** is the winner.

D. Two early Closers: The "necessary to the judgment" requirement

Necessary-to-the-judgment hypos make natural closers, because they are so difficult for students to grasp. This requirement seems arbitrary and technical, even silly. But let's try to understand why courts have consistently included this mysterious limitation on collateral estoppel.

Cambria v. Jeffrey, 307 Mass. 49 (1940), provides a classic example of the problem. In slightly simplified form, the facts were as follows: Cambria had an accident with Jeffrey and sued Jeffrey for negligence in causing his injuries. Jeffrey pleaded contributory negligence. At the time of this crusty case, contributory negligence of a plaintiff barred recovery entirely, even if the defendant was negligent too. The case was tried before a judge, not a jury. The judge found that Cambria was negligent, and that Jeffrey was negligent as well.

Question: What judgment should the judge enter based on these factual findings?

He should dismiss Cambria's suit. Under the contributory negligence doctrine, a plaintiff who was partially at fault in causing the accident could not recover. The plaintiff had to be blameless to recover, and Cambria was negligent, so he lost.

But that wasn't the end of it. After the judge dismissed Cambria's suit, Jeffrey sued Cambria for *his* injuries. (At the time Massachusetts had no compulsory counterclaim rule, so Jeffrey had not waived his claim by failing to assert it in the first action.) Predictably, Cambria pleaded that Jeffrey was contributorily negligent, and asserted that Jeffrey was estopped from denying his negligence, since the judge in the first suit had found that he was. This isn't a bad argument; the parties litigated Jeffrey's negligence in Suit One, and the judge decided that he was negligent, so why should Jeffrey be allowed to litigate it again?

Despite this logic, the court in *Cambria v. Jeffrey* held that Jeffrey *could* litigate it again, because the judge's finding in the first suit that Jeffrey was negligent was not "necessary to the judgment."

Question: What finding *was* necessary to the judgment in Suit One? Why did Cambria lose?

If you think about it, it's clear that Cambria did not lose because Jeffrey was negligent . . . that finding would tend to support liability! No, he lost because *he* (Cambria) was negligent. At the time, a contributorily negligent plaintiff could not win, *whether the defendant was negligent or not*. Thus, Cambria's negligence led to the judgment, but the finding that Jeffrey was negligent was irrelevant to the outcome in the first action.

Because the judge in the first action never had to decide whether Jeffrey was negligent, that finding was a form of dicta. The finding didn't affect the outcome, so the judge may not have given it the same serious consideration he would have if it would affect the result. Thus, we can't have quite the level of confidence in this irrelevant conclusion that we have in a finding that *leads to* the judgment in the case.

There's another problem with findings that don't lead to the judgment. They are, usually, unreviewable:

Question: Put yourself in Jeffrey's shoes. The judge has found him negligent. He contemplates a suit against Cambria for his own injuries in the accident. What would he want to do if he feared that he would be estopped from relitigating his negligence in the second action?

> Naturally, if Jeffrey fears being stuck with the finding that he was negligent, he would want to appeal it and get it reversed, so it would not come back to haunt him in his later suit for his own injuries.

Question: If Jeffrey appealed the judge's finding in the first action that he was negligent, what would the appellate court do?

> Very likely, the appellate court would say, "What are you doing here, Jeffrey? You won below. Why should we review the finding that you were negligent? The issue is moot. Even if we agreed with you, it wouldn't change the outcome, so why should we waste our time reviewing an irrelevant conclusion?" And how could they meaningfully review it? If Jeffrey appealed, why would Cambria spend the money to oppose the appeal? He lost anyway, he isn't likely to litigate an appeal about Jeffrey's negligence out of pure curiosity.

So, Jeffrey would probably not be able to obtain appellate review of the trial judge's finding that he was negligent. Since the finding did not affect the outcome, and can't be corrected on appeal, most courts would not give collateral estoppel effect to it.

The trick, of course, is to distinguish such miscellaneous findings from those that *do* affect the outcome, that are "necessary to the judgment." Consider this case.

QUESTION 8. **Here we go again.** Arrowmark Products Company sues Sentry Manufacturing Company for trademark infringement. Arrowmark claims that Sentry is liable for trademark infringement, because it used a logo for its products that is the same as one on which Arrowmark holds a trademark, and sold the products in Arrowmark's market area. Sentry admits using the logo, but argues that Arrowmark's trademark is invalid and that it did not sell its products in Arrowmark's market area, so it did not infringe the trademark anyway.

The case is tried to a jury, which returns a special verdict specifying its findings on the issues. It finds that Arrowmark's trademark is valid. It also finds that Sentry did not sell in Arrowmark's market area. Consequently, the judge enters judgment for Sentry.

Later, Sentry begins selling products with the same logo again, in another state. Arrowmark sues Sentry again for infringement of its trademark. Sentry defends on the ground that Arrowmark's trademark is invalid.

A. Arrowmark can invoke collateral estoppel to preclude Sentry from relitigating the validity of Arrowmark's trademark, because the issue was litigated, decided, and necessary to the judgment in the prior action.
B. Arrowmark can invoke collateral estoppel to preclude Sentry from relitigating the validity of Arrowmark's trademark, because that issue was clearly decided by the jury's special verdict in the prior action.
C. Arrowmark cannot invoke collateral estoppel to preclude Sentry from relitigating the validity of Arrowmark's trademark, because that issue was not necessary to the judgment in the prior action.
D. Arrowmark cannot invoke collateral estoppel to preclude Sentry from litigating the validity of Arrowmark's trademark, because it is not the same issue that was litigated in the first action.

ANALYSIS. D as in Dog once more. Sentry's defense in the second case challenges the same trademark that was challenged in the first case. The question is whether that trademark is valid, just as it was in the first suit.

It is true, as **B** states, that the trademark issue was decided in the first suit, but that is not sufficient to allow estoppel. The finding must also, as *Cambria v. Jeffrey* illustrates, be necessary to the judgment in the earlier case. And the decision here that Arrowmark's trademark is valid was not necessary to the judgment in its first suit against Sentry. Arrowmark did not win because the jury found its trademark valid. It did not win *at all*. The judgment in the suit was for Sentry, on the ground that it did not infringe the trademark because it did not sell in Arrowmark's market area. So the finding that the trademark was valid did not lead to the judgment that ended the case; indeed, it would tend to support a different judgment. Thus, while that issue was litigated and decided in Suit One, Sentry will be able to relitigate the issue in the later action. Both **A** and **B** are wrong; **C** is the best answer.

This doesn't seem to make sense. At trial, the parties don't know whether the jury will find that Sentry sold in Arrowmark's market area, so they have every incentive to litigate the other issue — validity — aggressively. The jury's decision on the validity issue could well lead to the judgment — for either party. And the jury, who may not understand much about how their factual findings will be used to fashion a final judgment, probably gave the validity issue as serious consideration as the infringement issue. Why relitigate it later?

The jury may have considered the validity issue seriously. But they may have concluded first that there was no infringement, so given validity less thought. Even if they did conscientiously decide the issue, Sentry can't appeal it, since it won the case. So, while there's an argument for giving estoppel effect to findings like this, it has not generally been accepted by the courts.

Let's try one more on the necessary-to-the judgment problem. Again, ask what findings by the jury necessarily led to the judgment in the first action.

QUESTION 9. Triple play. Perez sues the City of Atlantis, alleging that the mayor violated his First Amendment rights by demoting him from his city job to a lower-paying one because he had supported Appolonia, the losing candidate for mayor in the 2002 election. The City raises three defenses. It denies that Perez was demoted, arguing that he was transferred to an equivalent position. Second, it claims that the mayor never believed that Perez supported Appolonia, so could not have discriminated against him on that basis. Last, it claims that Perez had waived any claim for demotion when he agreed to accept his new position.

The case went to trial on all three issues. The jury rendered a general verdict, finding the City liable to Perez for violating his First Amendment rights.

A year later, Perez is fired. He sues again, claiming that he was fired in violation of his First Amendment rights, because the mayor believed he had supported Appolonia in the 2002 election.

A. Perez may not estop the City on the issue of whether the mayor believed Perez had supported Appolonia. Since the City raised three defenses, we cannot tell what issues were decided in the first case.

B. Perez may estop the City on the issue of whether the mayor believed that Perez had supported Appolonia. The jury's verdict indicates that they found that he had believed it, and that finding was necessary to the judgment in the first case.

C. Perez may not estop the City from relitigating whether the mayor believed that Perez had supported Appolonia. Since the City raised three defenses, we cannot tell which findings were necessary to the judgment in the first case.

ANALYSIS. Not to belabor the point, but again the analysis has to start by looking back to the first case, to determine what issues the jury decided in that case.

The suggestion in **A**, that we can't tell what was decided in the first case, fails. The City raised three defenses. Any one of these defenses, if accepted, would lead to a defendant's verdict. Since Perez won, the jury must have rejected all three defenses. They must have found that the mayor believed that Perez had supported Appolonia, that he was demoted for it, and that he had not waived his claim to damages. So we know what they decided on each of these issues.

Which of these findings was necessary to the judgment? They all were. The jury had to reject all three defenses in order to render a verdict for Perez. They couldn't find for Perez *without* rejecting all three defenses. If, for example, they had found that the mayor had not believed that Perez had supported Appolonia, they would not have awarded damages for violation of his First Amendment rights in demoting him for it. Consequently, their finding on this issue was necessary to the outcome in the first suit. And the same is true of the other two defenses. Thus, **C** is wrong, because, if the jury had reached a different result on any one of these three defenses, the City would have won. But it didn't, so the jury must have rejected them all, and rejecting all three *led to* the verdict they returned. Here, it's **B** as in "Best."

E.   A taste of "non-mutual" collateral estoppel

The cases we've analyzed so far have involved situations in which one of the parties to Suit One invokes collateral estoppel in a later action between the same parties. Suppose, for example, that Smith sues Doe, and loses on Issue A. The same issue then arises again in a later suit between Smith and Doe, and Doe invokes collateral estoppel to bar Smith from relitigating it. This is a case of "mutual collateral estoppel," because Doe, the party invoking estoppel in the second action was a party to the first, litigated it against Smith in that action, and prevailed on the issue in Suit One.

However, an issue previously litigated and decided may arise in later litigation involving a new party as well. Suppose, for example, that Forrestal Corporation sues Quantum Software for infringing its patent, and loses because the jury finds that the patent is invalid. Subsequently, Forrestal sues Apex Corporation for infringing on the patent. Apex would like to invoke collateral estoppel, arguing that Forrestal litigated and lost on the patent issue in Suit One and should not be able to relitigate the issue.

Under traditional principles of collateral estoppel, Apex could not invoke estoppel, because it was not a party to the first suit. Under the "mutuality" doctrine, which still reigns in some jurisdictions, only the parties to the first action could invoke estoppel based on findings in that action. Apex, a stranger to Suit One, could not step in and use the finding from that suit to bar Forrestal from relitigating the validity issue.

Other courts have moved away from mutuality, recognizing that, under some conditions, allowing a new party to invoke estoppel is fair. The key case on the point is *Parklane Hosiery Co. v. Shore*, 439 U.S. 322 (1979), in which the Supreme Court cautiously authorized federal trial judges to apply non-mutual estoppel in circumstances that ensure that the issue was fairly decided in the first action. However, while the federal courts and a good many state courts now allow non-mutual estoppel, *all courts* adhere to a fundamental requirement: that the party who is being estopped must have litigated and lost on the issue in the prior suit. The party invoking estoppel may be new, but the party who is barred from relitigating must have had its fair bite at the apple in the first suit. Otherwise, it wouldn't be fair to invoke estoppel to bar her from litigating the issue.

In analyzing a non-mutual preclusion problem, start by asking who litigated the issues in the prior action. In a mutuality jurisdiction, only those parties may use estoppel in a later action. In a non-mutuality jurisdiction, estoppel can be used *against* a party who litigated and lost on an issue in the first suit. Here's a case that makes the point.

QUESTION 10. First Principles. Gotchall invested one million dollars with Faithful Investments Inc., on the basis of a brochure describing its mutual fund. Later, he sued Faithful in federal court. He claimed that Faithful's brochure promised a return of at least 15 percent. Faithful denied this, arguing that the materials were ambiguous about the likely return. After a trial without a jury, the judge found that the brochure did not guarantee any particular rate of return. She therefore entered judgment dismissing Gotschall's claim for damages.

Later, Carmichael, who had also invested in the fund, sued Faithful for damages, basing his claim on the same argument as Gotschall's, that Faithful's brochure promised a return of at least 15 percent. Faithful moves for summary judgment, arguing that Carmichael is estopped from proving that the brochure misrepresented the likely return, since the judge had found for Faithful on the issue in the first suit. The court should hold that

A. Carmichael's claim is barred, because he should have joined as a coplaintiff with Gotschall in the prior action.

B. Carmichael's claim is barred, because the issue was litigated in the prior action, decided in favor of Faithful, and the issue was necessary to the judgment in the prior action.

C. the claim is not barred, because the finding that the brochure did not promise a particular rate of return was not necessary to the judgment in the prior action.

D. the action is not barred. Carmichael was not a party to the prior action and therefor cannot be estopped on the issue.

ANALYSIS. Scratch **C** from the beginning. The finding that the brochure did not promise a particular rate of return *was* necessary to the judgment. Gotschall based his claim on the fact that the brochure promised a 15 percent return, and he lost his case *because* the judge found that the brochure did not promise a specific rate of return, so that finding of fact did lead to the judgment. It was not dicta; it was the very basis for the decision that Gotschall could not recover.

A suggests that Carmichael is barred because he should have joined as a coplaintiff with Gotschall. However, while Rule 20(a) would allow him to join in that suit, it does not require him to do so; Rule 20(a) is permissive. (In fact there might be various reasons why Carmichael could not have joined, such as diversity problems.) More practically, who says he even knew about Gotschall's action? It would be a tough rule that forced him to join even though he never learned of the other action!

B argues that he is barred because the requirements for collateral estoppel are met — the issue is the same, it was actually litigated in suit one and decided by the court. All that is true . . . but it was not litigated *by Carmichael*. Due process of law requires that he have his bite at the apple before he is estopped on the issue, and he hasn't had it. This is indeed a "first principle": No party will be estopped (absent some form of privity) until she has had her day in court. My students frequently lose sight of this fundamental, ineluctable requirement for applying issue preclusion. Always ask whether the party who is being barred from litigating the issue litigated it before. If not, no estoppel! Estoppel — in a mutuality jurisdiction or in a non-mutuality jurisdiction — only bars a party from *relitigating* an issue, not from litigating it the first time. **D** is right.

OK. With that basic point resolved, let's try another version of Faithful's litigation saga.

> **QUESTION 11. Investment in litigation.** Gotschall invested one million dollars with Faithful Investments Inc. on the basis of a brochure describing its mutual fund. Later, he sued Faithful in federal court. He claimed that the brochure fraudulently promised a 15 percent rate of return on his investment. He also alleged that his contract with Faithful agreed to return his money after one year if the fund had not made a profit during the year, which Faithful had subsequently refused to do. Faithful denied both claims.
>
> After a trial without a jury, the judge found that the contract did not guarantee any particular rate of return. However, she also found that the contract did provide for a refund at the close of the first year if there had not been a profit. The court entered judgment awarding no damages to Gotschall for misrepresentation, but ordering return of his original investment.
>
> Later, Carmichael, who had also invested in the fund, learned of the action and sued Faithful for breach of contract and fraud, raising the same two claims that Gotschall had asserted in his suit. Faithful raised the same defenses. Under federal collateral estoppel principles, the court would probably
>
> A. bar Carmichael from relitigating either issue, based on issue preclusion, since the same issues were already litigated and decided in Gotschall's action.
> B. allow Carmichael to relitigate whether the brochure guaranteed a 15 percent rate of return, since Carmichael has not litigated that issue.
> C. allow Faithful to relitigate whether the contract provided for a refund after one year, because they have not litigated that issue against Carmichael.
> D. require Carmichael to relitigate whether the brochure guaranteed a 15 percent rate of return, because the finding in Faithful's favor on that issue was not necessary to the judgment in the prior action.

ANALYSIS. D is wrong. Gotschall sued for the 15 percent profit he claimed he was entitled to. But he didn't get it, because the court held he wasn't entitled to it. He lost on this claim *because of* the court's ruling against him on his misrepresentation claim. Thus, that finding was necessary to the judgment denying him those damages. He got his original investment back but did not collect the alleged profits.

C is close. Faithful litigated and lost on the issue of the right to return of the principal in Gotschall's suit. So the first requirement for estoppel is met — the party to be estopped litigated and lost on the issue in the prior action. But we know from *Parklane* that the court does not automatically estop a party just because they litigated and lost on the issue in the prior action. The trial court will consider whether estopping Faithful is fair under the circumstances. Here it probably is. Both actions are in federal court, so Faithful is not likely to have a better procedural opportunity to prevail on the return-of-principal issue in the second action. There are no inconsistent judgments. And Carmichael did not hang back to see whether Gotschall would win on the issue — the question indicates that he only learned of Gotschall's suit after it was over. So the federal court probably would allow Carmichael to estop Faithful on the issue. So **C** is probably not right.

B takes the prize. Carmichael, as a new party, has not litigated whether the brochure promised a 15 percent return, so he will get his chance to do that, even though Gotschall failed to prove it in his action.

 ## Glannon's Picks

1. The long arm of collateral estoppel	C
2. Food for thought	A
3. Issues and arguments	A
4. Verdicts and decisions	D
5. Reprise	C
6. Patent medicine	D
7. Switching switches	A
8. Here we go again	C
9. Triple play	B
10. First principles	D
11. Investment in litigation	B

25

Closing Closers: Some Practice Questions that Cross Jurisdictional Lines

Despite all the questions and gimmicks,
I hope that you've mastered the right Picks;
The book wouldn't be bad
But the author went mad
And threw in those terrible limericks!

Tis chapter is different from the others. It includes fifteen questions without introductory discussion of the black letter law. The questions are intended to serve two purposes. First, they provide a chance to practice on questions without introductory text. And second, unlike most of the questions in the earlier chapters, these questions require consideration of multiple issues in the course. Many professors will give questions like this on exams, so these provide both a review and an opportunity to test your understanding of how different procedure concepts relate to one another.

I have included short analyses of the questions at the end of the chapter. But to get full value out of this chapter, analyze these questions fully before looking at my analysis. And again, if any of my questions, in this chapter or the others, seem wrong or confusing, send me an e-mail and I'll try to fix my mistakes.

So, here goes.

QUESTION 1. Inflated expectations.   Apex Tire Company manufactures bicycle tires in Florida and sells them to Vanguard Bicycle Corporation in Alabama, which installs them on its bicycles. Vanguard sells large numbers of its bicycles in Illinois, where it maintains a network of dealerships and sales agents to assist its customers. Argenti buys a Vanguard bike from a dealership in Illinois and is injured when the tire explodes, in Illinois. She sues Vanguard and Apex in Illinois.

A. The Illinois court will have personal jurisdiction over Apex, because Vanguard maintained a network of dealerships and agents to serve and provide advice to customers in Illinois.

B. The Illinois court will have personal jurisdiction over Apex, because Illinois' long-arm statute (as interpreted in *Gray v. American Radiator*) authorizes jurisdiction over nonresidents who "commit a tortious act" in Illinois, and the bicycle tire exploded there.

C. The Illinois court will probably not have personal jurisdiction over Apex, even if the Illinois long-arm statute applies, if the court follows the plurality opinions in *Asahi Metal Industry Co. v. Superior Court* and *J. McIntyre Machinery, Ltd. v. Nicastro*.

D. The Illinois court will not have personal jurisdiction over Apex, because it did not commit a tortious act in Illinois within the meaning of the Illinois long-arm statute.

QUESTION 2. The inconvenient forum.   Jackson, a New Yorker, sues Ace Corporation, incorporated in Delaware with its principal place of business in Massachusetts, for injuries suffered in an accident with Wong, an employee of Ace. The accident took place in Richmond, Virginia. Jackson brings suit in state court in Worcester County, Massachusetts, where Ace has a major factory. He believes that Worcester jurors will be unfavorably disposed toward Ace, which has laid off 1500 workers in Worcester over the past year. Ace prefers to avoid litigating in the Massachusetts state court. Ace's best chance for getting the case out of the Massachusetts state court would be to

A. remove the case to federal court in Virginia.

B. remove the case to federal court in Massachusetts.

C. move to transfer the case, under 28 U.S.C. §1404(a), to the state court in Virginia.

D. move to transfer the case under 28 U.S.C. §1404(a), to the federal court in Virginia which embraces the place where the accident happened.

E. move to dismiss for forum non conveniens.

QUESTION 3. **A drug on the market.**   Cortez sued General Chemical Corporation in a Texas federal court for injuries suffered when he took a medication manufactured by General in Delaware. Although Cortez took the medication in Texas, General Chemical moved to dismiss under Fed. R. Civ. P. 12(b)(2). The Texas court dismissed the case on the ground that the medication had been sold into Texas by a pharmaceutical distributor, not by General, so that the claim did not arise out of the "transaction of business" by General in Texas, within the meaning of the Texas long-arm statute.

After the Texas action was dismissed, Cortez sued General in Delaware for his injuries. His second action will

A. not be barred, since the first claim was not dismissed on the merits.
B. be barred by res judicata, since he already sued on this claim in another court.
C. be barred by collateral estoppel if the Delaware long-arm statute has the same "transaction of business" provision as Texas has.
D. not be barred, because General has already made a Rule 12(b)(2) motion and cannot make another pre-answer motion on this ground.

QUESTION 4. **Charges and discharges.**   In which of the following cases will the court *lack* jurisdiction over the last-mentioned claim?

A. Summers, from Illinois, was discharged from her job by Cruz, president of High-Tech Corporation. She sues High-Tech (incorporated in Delaware with its principal place of business in Ohio) for violation of the Federal Age Discrimination in Employment Act, seeking $100,000 in damages. She also adds a claim against Michaels, her immediate supervisor (an Illinois citizen), for breach of contract arising from the same events.
B. Summers, from Illinois, was discharged from her job with High-Tech. She sues High-Tech for violation of the Federal Age Discrimination in Employment Act, seeking $100,000 in damages. High-Tech impleads

Michaels, from Illinois, seeking $50,000 in contribution if it is held liable to Summers.

C. Summers, from Illinois, was discharged from her job with High-Tech. She sues High-Tech for violation of the Federal Age Discrimination in Employment Act, seeking $100,000 in damages. High-Tech impleads Michaels, from Illinois, seeking $50,000 in contribution if it is held liable to Summers. Summers then asserts a claim directly against Michaels for breach of contract.

D. The court has jurisdiction over all the claims asserted in choices A, B, and C.

QUESTION 5. Crossfire. Able, Baker, and Correro, all from different states, were involved in a three-car collision in Arcadia. All suffered serious injuries that would support six-figure recoveries. Able sued Baker for his injuries in federal court. Baker answered, denying negligence, and asserting contributory negligence of Able, which would be a full defense under Arcadia law. Baker also filed a third-party complaint against Correro under Fed. R. Civ. P. 14(a)(1), claiming contribution on the ground that her negligence was also a cause of the accident.

The case was tried to a jury, which found that Able was negligent, and that Baker was too. (It made no finding on Correro's negligence, since it was not necessary to do so to reach its verdict.) Judgment is entered dismissing the claim against Baker and Baker's third-party claim against Correro. Correro now brings an action against Able for her own injuries. She sues in federal court, seeking $150,000 in damages. Correro's claim

A. is not barred, because it could not have been asserted in the first action.

B. is barred by res judicata, since she was a party to the prior action.

C. is not barred by res judicata, but Correro will not be able to invoke collateral estoppel against Able, since she did not assert a claim against Able in the first action.

D. is not barred by res judicata, and Correro may be able to assert offensive non-mutual estoppel to establish Able's negligence.

QUESTION 6. Lost chance?   Hlavety brings a negligence action against Simons, owner of a car, for injuries in an accident. At the time of the accident, the car was driven by Cohen; Hlavety bases his claim against Simons on a statute making an owner liable for injuries negligently caused by a driver while driving the owner's car with permission. Simons defends on the ground that Cohen was not using the car with his permission at the time of the accident. Hlavety recovers damages from Simons.

Simons now sues Cohen, to recover indemnification for the damages he had to pay because of Cohen's negligence. In Simons' action against Cohen,

A. neither res judicata nor collateral estoppel will bar Simons from pursuing his indemnification claim against Cohen.

B. the court will not dismiss, but will bar Cohen from relitigating the issue of his negligence, since Hlavety could not have prevailed against Simons without establishing Cohen's negligence.

C. the court will dismiss the claim, since Simons had the opportunity to litigate this claim against Cohen in the first action by impleading him under Rule 14.

D. the court will dismiss on res judicata grounds, since Simons already litigated this transaction or occurrence against Hlavety.

Sometimes it seems as though there aren't enough choices in life. So try this question, with nine.

QUESTION 7. Take your pick.   Harkness, from Illinois, sues Steinberg Electronics, a Colorado corporation with its principal place of business in Colorado, seeking recovery based on strict liability for an injury suffered using a Steinberg pacemaker. His damages are $125,000. He also sues Dr. Armand, the doctor who implanted the pacemaker, for failing to recognize the problems it was causing and removing it sooner. He seeks $23,000 from Armand, an Indiana citizen. The suit is brought in state court in Illinois and removed by Steinberg to federal court.

Steinberg had manufactured the pacemaker in Oklahoma and sold it to Quality Medical Supply Company in Texas, from which it was ordered by the Illinois hospital where Dr. Armand implanted it. Quality, under its agreement with Steinberg, is required to (and does) advertise in Illinois and visit doctors there to market Steinberg's products. Illinois has a long-arm statute authorizing the assertion of jurisdiction over a defendant who "commits a tortious act in Illinois." The Illinois courts interpret the statute to apply if the injury to the plaintiff takes place in Illinois. *Gray v. American Radiator & Standard Sanitary Corp.*, 176 N.E.2d 761 (Ill. 1961). Which of the following is true?

A. Venue is improper, since Steinberg does not "reside" in Illinois.
B. The court lacks power to exercise personal jurisdiction over Steinberg, even though, under Illinois's interpretation of its long-arm statute, it "committed a tortious act in Illinois" under *Gray.*
C. Removal is proper.
D. Removal is improper, because Harkness is from Illinois.
E. The federal court lacks original subject matter jurisdiction over the case.
F. Under stream-of-commerce analysis, the court lacks personal jurisdiction over Steinberg.
G. Venue is improper under 28 U.S.C. §1391(b), because the pacemaker was manufactured in Colorado.
H. Joinder of the two defendants is improper, since Harkness seeks different damages from them.
I. Venue is proper under 28 U.S.C. §1391(b)(3).

QUESTION 8. **Wrong target?**   Wise, from Idaho, sues Spinelli, from Louisiana, for damages arising out of the cancellation of a computer programming contract he had signed with Spinelli, a customer for his programing services. The action is filed in federal court, and seeks damages of $125,000. Spinelli counterclaims, seeking $60,000 from Wise for failure to deliver the program on time. He adds Pope, from Ohio, as an additional party on the counterclaim, demanding $25,000 from Pope for poor programing he did, which increased the delay.

A. The court has jurisdiction over the entire action.
B. The court lacks supplemental jurisdiction over the claim against Pope.
C. The court has jurisdiction over the claim against Pope, but joinder is improper, since Spinelli does not claim that Pope is liable for "all or part of the" plaintiff's claim against him (i.e., Spinelli).
D. The court has original jurisdiction over the claim against Pope, because the total damages sought on the counterclaims is $85,000.

QUESTION 9. Mismatch?   Charlie, from Maine, sues Mary, from Ohio, in federal court, for injuries in a motor vehicle accident. He also joins Specific Motors, which sold Mary the car she was driving, as a second defendant. Specific is incorporated in Ohio with its principal place of business in Ohio. Mary's counsel believes that she may have a $40,000 claim against Specific for contribution for Charlie's damages, since it sold her the car with bad brakes, and also a $10,000 claim for misrepresentation in the sale, based on statements Specific had made to her about the mileage of the car when it sold it to her. Which of the following is most likely true.

A. Mary could assert the contribution claim against Specific, but not the misrepresentation claim, under the joinder rules.
B. Mary could assert both claims against Specific under the joinder rules, but the court would not have jurisdiction over the misrepresentation claim.
C. Mary could assert both claims against Specific under the joinder rules, and the court would have jurisdiction over both claims.
D. Mary could assert both claims against Specific under the joinder rules, but the court will not have jurisdiction over either claim, because Mary and Specific are both from Ohio.

QUESTION 10. Going through the motions.   Delirio sues Parquette Packaging Company, his employer, for injuries in an accident he was in riding in a truck driven by another Parquette employee in the course of their employment. He sues Parquette in state court. Parquette files a special appearance to contest the court's jurisdiction (the proper procedure for challenging personal jurisdiction in the state where suit was filed).

A week after filing its special appearance, Parquette removes the action to federal court. Three days after that, it files a motion to dismiss under Rule 12(b)(6) for failure to state a claim upon which relief can be granted. It argues that Delirio is limited to recovery under the workers compensation statute, and cannot bring a tort action for damages for an accident in the scope of employment.

A. Parquette's Rule 12(b)(6) motion is improper, because it already made a pre-answer motion.

B. Parquette's Rule 12(b)(6) motion is proper, but it will waive Parquette's objection to personal jurisdiction, since it raises an additional defense besides lack of jurisdiction.

C. Parquette's Rule 12(b)(6) motion is improper, because it was not asserted in the state court before removal.

D. Parquette's Rule 12(b)(6) motion is proper, but Parquette has waived its objection to personal jurisdiction by removing to federal court.

E. None of the above is true.

QUESTION 11. Going through more motions.   Publice sues Dr. Stowalski in federal court for negligence, claiming that she suffered injuries from a diet medication Stowalski prescribed for her. At trial, the evidence is hotly contested as to whether the drug caused Publice's injuries and whether Dr. Stowalski was negligent to prescribe the drug for her.

At the close of the plaintiff's case, Dr. Stowalski moves for judgment as a matter of law on both grounds, lack of negligence and lack of causation. The motion is denied. At the close of all the evidence Dr. Stowalski renews the motion for judgment as a matter of law, stating as the ground lack of sufficient evidence of causation. The case goes to the jury, which finds for Publice. Dr. Stowalski then moves for judgment as a matter of law under Rule 50(b), arguing that Publice has failed to introduce sufficient proof of negligence and of causation. She also seeks a new trial on both grounds. Under Rules 50 and 59, the judge would have the authority to

A. grant judgment as a matter of law on either ground, but could not grant a new trial, since it was not sought before the jury's deliberations.

B. grant judgment as a matter of law on causation only. She could grant a new trial on either ground.

C. grant judgment as a matter of law or new trial on causation only.

D. grant judgment as a matter of law on either ground and a new trial on either ground.

QUESTION 12. Here and there. Luis, a New York citizen, sues Orion Corporation, incorporated in Delaware with its principal place of business in the Eastern District of Virginia. Orion has a large factory in the Northern District of California, but no other activities in California. Luis's claim arises out of a motor vehicle accident caused by one of Orion's drivers in the Northern District of California. Luis sues in the federal district court for the District of Delaware (Delaware has only one federal district).

A. The action should be dismissed, because the Delaware federal court is not a proper forum.

B. If Orion seeks to dismiss for forum non conveniens, the judge would likely grant the motion.

C. If Orion moves for transfer under 28 U.S.C. §1404(a) to the Central District of California, the judge would have the authority to grant the motion, and probably would.

D. If Orion moves to transfer under 28 U.S.C. §1404(a) to the Eastern District of Virginia, the judge would have the authority to grant the motion, but probably would not.

QUESTION 13. Hopping to conclusions. Merton, from California, sues Colonial Reprints Inc., a publisher incorporated in California with its principal place of business in New York. Colonial had published the first edition of Merton's book, *Grasshoppers of the Azores.* Merton sues Colonial for violation of the federal Copyright Act, by publishing a second edition of the book without his permission. Suit is brought in California, and in federal court (as it must be, since federal courts have exclusive jurisdiction over claims arising under the federal copyright laws. 28 U.S.C. §1338(a)).

Colonial asserts a counterclaim against Merton for breach of contract, claiming Merton's refusal to allow a second edition violates a clause in the publication contract authorizing Colonial to publish later editions as well. In adjudicating the counterclaim, the federal court must

A. apply federal law to determine the contract claim, since the federal court has exclusive jurisdiction over the copyright claim.

B. apply the contract law of California, because the suit is brought in California.

C. apply whatever contract law the California courts would apply to the claim.

D. dismiss the claim because, while it is permitted under the joinder rules, it is not based on federal law.

QUESTION 14. Additions and objections.   In July 2006, a week before the three-year statute of limitations passes, Carson sues Herrera in federal court for breach of a contract to design a computer system for his store in Calpurnia, Illinois. In July 2007, he moves to amend his complaint to add a claim for violation of the state Consumer Protection Act, based on the same dispute. The Consumer Protection Act has a two-year statute of limitations.

A. The second claim would not be barred by the limitations period, as long as the judge grants the motion to amend.

B. The second claim would "relate back" to the date of the original filing of the case, and therefore would not be barred by the statute of limitations.

C. The second claim will be barred by the limitations period, because it will not "relate back" to the original filing under Rule 15.

D. The amendment will be barred, even if it relates back to the filing of the original complaint.

QUESTION 15. Grounds for objection.   Rogers sues Foremost Motor Company for injuries suffered in an accident involving his Foremost station wagon. He also sues Schlempel, the driver of another car involved in the accident. Foremost includes in its answer an allegation that Rogers was negligent because he had been drinking before the accident. Schlempel defends on the ground that she was not negligent; she does not raise Rogers's negligence as an affirmative defense. Schlempel sends an interrogatory to Rogers asking if he had been drinking before the accident and if so how many drinks he had had.

A. Rogers may object on the ground that the information is beyond the scope of discovery, because Schlempel has not pleaded negligence of Rogers.

> **B.** Rogers may object on the basis of the attorney/client privilege if he had revealed to counsel in confidence that he had been drinking before the accident.
>
> **C.** Rogers's counsel could object on the basis of the work product doctrine, if Rogers had given his counsel a statement admitting that he had been drinking before the accident.
>
> **D.** Schlempel's interrogatory is proper and Rogers must answer it.

 Glannon's Picks

1. **Inflated expectations. C** is the best answer. Apex made a component, bicycle tires, and sold them to a final manufacturer in another state, which then distributed them to other states. Justice O'Connor's plurality opinion in *Asahi* would very likely conclude that more was needed to establish that Apex had "purposely availed itself" of the opportunity to conduct activities in Illinois. Similarly, Justice Kennedy in *J. McIntyre* would probably reject jurisdiction in this stream of commerce case:

   > The defendant's transmission of goods permits the exercise of jurisdiction only where the defendant can be said to have targeted the forum; as a general rule, it is not enough that the defendant might have predicted that its goods will reach the forum State.

   131 S. Ct. at 2788.[1]

2. **The inconvenient forum.** Choose **E.** Removal may only be to a court in the state in which the case is brought. But this diversity case can't be removed, since there is an in-state defendant. And it can't be transferred to any court, state or federal, under §1404(a), which only authorizes a *federal* court to transfer a case to another federal court. Ace's best argument is that the case should be heard in Virginia, so the Massachusetts court should dismiss it, under the common law forum non conveniens doctrine, leaving Jackson to refile in the more sensible forum, Virginia.

3. **A drug on the market. A** is right. Cortez's first suit was dismissed for lack of personal jurisdiction. Res judicata will not bar bringing an action in another court that has jurisdiction, because the first case was not resolved on the merits. Even if the Delaware long-arm has the same language as the

---

1. As an aside, however, it is not clear to me that the other six *J. McIntyre* justices would refuse jurisdiction on these facts. Clearly the three dissenters would find jurisdiction proper, and Justice Breyer's concurrence suggests that he is open to jurisdiction in stream-of-commerce cases if there is a regular flow of the defendant's goods into the forum state. 131 S. Ct. at 2792.

Texas statute, the issue of whether Cortez's claim arises out of General's "transaction of business" in Texas is different from the issue of whether it arises from its "transaction of business" in Delaware, so collateral estoppel would not bar him from suing under the Delaware statute. And, the second motion under Rule 12(b) is fine, because it is in a different law suit from the first one.

4. **Charges and discharges. D** is right. Each of these cases is properly brought in federal court based on arising-under jurisdiction. In each, the added claim arises out of the same events, so it meets the §1367(a) standard for supplemental jurisdiction. And, the last sentence of §1367(a) allows supplemental jurisdiction over added parties. Since the main claim in each case is based on arising-under jurisdiction, not diversity, the exceptions in §1367(b) are irrelevant.

5. **Crossfire. D** is the best answer. Correro is not barred from asserting the claim in a new action. A claim by a third-party defendant against a plaintiff is permissive under Rule 14(a); Correro could have asserted it, but was not required to. Correro chose to hold her fire, which she may do, and sue separately. Under *Parklane Hosiery Co. v. Shore*, 439 U.S. 322 (1979), she may be able to use offensive non-mutual estoppel to establish that Able was negligent. Able litigated and lost on the issue of his negligence in Suit One, so he could be estopped on that issue in Suit Two. Note that the jury also found in Suit One that Baker was negligent. But clearly, it was the finding on Able's negligence that was "necessary to the judgment." Able lost because he was negligent, not because Baker was.

Although estoppel may be available under *Parklane*, a court might hold that Correro's failure to assert her claim in the prior action reflected a "wait and see" attitude and refuse to allow her to invoke estoppel.

6. **Lost chance?** Choose **A**. Simons is not barred by res judicata, since he has not litigated this set of facts against Cohen. He was under no obligation to join him in the prior action. Collateral estoppel won't bar Cohen on any issue, since he was not a party to the prior action.

An argument might be fielded that Cohen and Simons were "in privity." But the argument is weak. Surely, they do not represent the same interest, nor does Simons represent Cohen's position in the litigation or act on Cohen's behalf: He simply tries to fend off liability by asserting a separate defense (not using with permission) that does not protect Cohen from liability.

7. **Take your pick.** I won't go through all the wrong choices. **E** takes the prize. The court lacks subject matter jurisdiction over the claim against Dr. Armand, because it doesn't meet the amount-in-controversy requirement. When a plaintiff sues multiple defendants in a diversity case,

the traditional aggregation rules require that she meet the amount-in-controversy requirement independently against each. The Supreme Court held in *Exxon Mobil Corp. v. Allapattah Services*, 545 U.S. 546 (2005), that 28 U.S.C. §1367(b) allows plaintiffs who do not meet the amount requirement to "tag along," as long as one plaintiff sues in a diversity case for more than $75,000. However, *Allapatah* does not affect the traditional rule with regard to claims by a plaintiff against multiple defendants. Section 1367(b) bars claims "by plaintiffs against persons made parties under Rule . . . 20 [the joinder-of-plaintiffs-and-defendants rule]" that would not meet the jurisdictional requirements of §1332. So there is no jurisdiction over Harkness's claim against Armand.

8. **Wrong target? A** is right. The claim against Pope is properly added under Rule 13(h). The claim need not be for indemnification or contribution, which is the standard for impleader of third parties under Rule 14. Instead, Pope may be added if Spinelli's claim against him arises from the same transaction or occurrence as his claim against Wise, and there will be a question of law or fact common to the two claims. Rule 13(h). The court has supplemental jurisdiction over it because it arises from the same events as the main claim. And §1367(b) does not except the claim from the broad reach of supplemental jurisdiction, since it is not a claim brought by a plaintiff or intervenor, etc.

9. **Mismatch? B** is the best answer. Once Mary asserts a proper cross-claim for contribution against Specific under Rule 13(g), she may add on her misrepresentation claim under Rule 18(a). However, because it arises out of different events — the sale rather than the accident with Charlie — the court will lack supplemental jurisdiction over it. There is a shaky argument that this is a series of transactions, but it seems doubtful. One is a commercial claim for the sale, which arose independently of the accident; the other is a claim based on a defect that caused the accident.

10. **Going through the motions. E** is the best answer. Parquette properly raised its objection to personal jurisdiction in the state court by making a special appearance before removing. Removal to federal court did not waive that objection; it just means that the objection will be ruled on by a federal judge rather than a state judge. Nor did Parquette waive its right to move to dismiss under Rule 12(b)(6) by failing to assert it in the state court. Parquette couldn't do that; if it had asserted the failure-to-state-a-claim objection when it appeared in state court, it would have waived the objection to personal jurisdiction under the state's special appearance rule. However, once the case is removed, Parquette may assert other pre-answer objections along with the objection to personal jurisdiction, without waiving it. See Fed. R. Civ. P. 12(b), last sentence, which provides that a party does not waive any defense by asserting it along with others in a pre-answer motion or a responsive pleading.

But what about Fed. R. Civ. P. 12(b), which bars a party from making a later pre-answer motion in some circumstances? That rule bars a second pre-answer motion to raise an objection "that was available to the party but omitted from its earlier motion." Here, the earlier motion was the special appearance in state court, and the Rule 12 (b)(6) objection could not have been asserted with that. Since it was not "available" at the time Parquette made its first motion, it may raise it in a second.

11. **Going through more motions.** The question tests two points. First, to preserve the right to seek judgment as a matter of law under Rule 50(b), the defendant must seek judgment as a matter of law under Rule 50(a) after the plaintiff has presented her evidence on the issue. Here, Stowalski moved for judgment as a matter of law on both issues at the close of the plaintiff's case, but only renewed her motion based on the causation issue. However, she did make a Rule 50(a) motion on this ground after plaintiff had been "fully heard on [the] issue" Rule 50(a)(1)), so I think she has preserved her right to seek judgment as a matter of law on the issue after verdict as well. See Rule 50(b) ("if the court does not grant a motion for judgment as a matter of law made under Rule 50(a)" it may be renewed after verdict). I suppose Publice might argue that Stowalski waived the motion based on lack of evidence of negligence, by renewing the one motion but not the other. But I think the rule suggests that Stowalski did not waive the argument, since she made that motion after the plaintiff had put in her full case, at a time when she could have presented more evidence if she had something to cure the problem.

The other problem posed by the question is whether the judge can grant a new trial on either ground, where Stowalski never moved for a new trial on either ground before the case went to the jury. Rule 59(d) authorizes the trial judge to grant a new trial "on the court's initiative," that is, even if no party has moved for it. Thus, the fact that Stowalski did not seek a new trial before the case went to the jury would not prevent the judge from granting a new trial on either ground. So **D** is the best answer; the judge could grant either motion on either ground.

12. **Here and there.** The federal court in Delaware is a proper forum. It's a proper diversity case, and Delaware would have general in personam jurisdiction over Orion, based on its incorporation in Delaware. Venue would also be proper in the District of Delaware under 28 U.S.C. §1391(b)(1) and (c)(2), since all defendants (Orion only) reside there. Section 1391(c)(2) tells us that Orion "resides" in Delaware for venue purposes because it is subject to general in personam jurisdiction there based on its incorporation in Delaware.

B fails, because forum non conveniens does not apply if the appropriate forum would be in another federal district. Since the more appropriate district would be the Northern District of California, the proper motion would be a motion to transfer under 28 U.S.C. §1404(a), not a motion to dismiss for forum non conveniens. But the motion to transfer to the Central District of California would not be granted. Under §1404(a), the action can only be transferred to a district "where it might have been brought." This case could not have been brought in the Central District of California, since venue would not be proper there: No events giving rise to the claim took place there, and Orion does not "reside" there under the §1391(c)(2) test.

So **D** is the best answer. The federal court would have authority to transfer to the Eastern District of Virginia, because Orion "resides" there under §1391(b)(1) and (d), based on having its principal place of business there, and would be subject to personal jurisdiction there. But that district would not be any more convenient or appropriate for the case than the District of Delaware. The Northern District of California would be the proper district to transfer to, but that's not one of the choices.

13. **Hopping to conclusions.** Colonial's counterclaim is a state law claim. Even though the main claim is based on federal law, not on diversity, it is axiomatic, under *Erie*, that the federal court will have to apply state law to Colonial's state law counterclaim: The federal court can't "make up" the law on supplemental claims any more than it can on diversity claims.

So, the only question is, which state's law? *Klaxon Co. v. Stentor Manufacturing Co.* held that the federal court, when it hears a state law claim, must apply the choice-of-law rules that would be applied by the state courts of the state in which the federal court sits. Thus, the federal court in California should apply whatever state's law the California courts would apply, under California choice-of-law rules. **C** is the proper answer.

14. **Additions and objections.** The twist here is that the statute of limitations had passed on the added claim *before the original claim was filed*. Thus, even though the amended claim (if the amendment were allowed) would relate back to July 2007, when the original claim was filed, that would not make the claim timely. It was already barred by the limitations period on that date, so "relating back" to that date does not help Carson. If Carson had filed a suit on that date, alleging violation of the Consumer Protection Act, the limitations period would have barred it. **D** is the right answer; the claim is barred.

This one flummoxed lots of students.

15. **Grounds for objection.** Schlempel has sought discovery concerning a defense asserted by Foremost, not by her. However, **A** is wrong, because Rule 26(b)(1) allows a party to seek discovery as to "the claim or defense of any party," not just her own claims and defenses. **B** is also wrong, since

Rogers must answer factual questions whether he has discussed the issue with his counsel or not. And **C** is wrong, because the work product doctrine does not bar discovery of facts, only of documents and other work product created in the process of defending the action. **D** is the best answer.

———————————

So, there you are. I hope this guide through the expanses of civil procedure has been helpful, perhaps even enjoyable. I really enjoyed writing it.

26

Closing Openers:
Some Looney Limericks

There once was a prof named Glannon
His books were a great companion.
When we read it we feel fine,
Before that, Procedure blew our mind.
And now law school we don't have to abandon!

—M.D., Loyola/Chicago

In the earlier editions of this book, I solicited limericks for chapters that didn't have one. I've gotten some doozies. Here, without editorial comment, are some of the offerings of your fellow law students. I'll let you decide which shall become immortal.

Diversity

While the married Mases were sleeping
Their landlord he was a-peeping
He defended his perversity,
By claiming no diversity
But the court said this case we're a keeping!

—*T.D., John Marshall*

Removal

It seems everyone wanted to write about removal . . .

> Texas Jo in Maine state court sued Wayne,
> For a million for suffering and pain.
> When Wayne tries to remove it
> District Court won't approve it
> So poor Wayne must in state court remain.
>
> — *C.S., New York Law School*

> The laws to removal aren't great,
> But since learning is to be your fate,
> Just know you'll be fine.
> And make sure you're on time,
> Can't be more than 30 days late!
>
> — *C.F. [???]*

> She chose the best court for approval
> Did all to defeat the removal
> She alleged facts misleading
> Tried to hide artful pleading,
> But the feds kept the case, with reproval.
>
> — *L.A., Loyola of L.A.*

> The state court granted approval
> Its long arm was most unusual,
> But arising under the averment
> John's lawyer came fervent
> Bearing a notice of removal.
>
> — *M.G., Suffolk*

The defendant's not happy in court
In a biased setting for tort.
To avoid being outdone,
He'll use fourteen forty-one
And might just hit a home run.

     —M. O'C. [???]

Plaintiff brought the case in state.
Defendant became quite irate
Federal courts had approval
Defendant moved for removal,
They'll grant if he doesn't file late.

     —T.H. & J.B., Suffolk

There once was a man who sued in state court,
from a claim arising from a negligent tort.
The defendant tried for removal,
but got no federal approval,
because the law wasn't of the right sort.

     —M.H., Harvard

There once was a plaintiff who decided to sue
and thought that a state court would nicely do.
The defendant thought federal was better,
but the judge wouldn't let her
remove so she's feeling quite blue.

     —M.H., Harvard

There once was a Congress who declared concurrence,
But along came a Senator who asked for, "Deterrence!"
So what once got removal
Now gets exclusive approval
And the Feds complain of over-recurrence.

     —E.L., O.S.U.

Joe was a very old lawyer
(He even once met Pennoyer)
And, from law, a bit removed
He made a fool of himself
By not knowing 1441(f)
And so missed a chance to remove.

—*P.G., U. Texas*

Plaintiff files a state court suit
Defendant wants to give state court the boot
He files for removal
Gets federal approval
to the state court he says, "NaNa, you're moot."

—*D. M-C., Boston College*

"If party wishes the case be gone,
And state-judge offers but a yawn,
He or she has one more thing to prove,
Look to the feds and so remove."

—*M.D., University of Connecticut*

Service

Mullane says, if you know where defendants are
You better serve them near and far.
Due process does require
A real effort to transpire.
Otherwise, your service won't reach the bar.

—*C.P., University of Southern California*

Erie

Federal Common Law had made them all weary,
So the Court did answer a query:
"When it comes to the test,
State law is best;
It's not that it's scary, it's Erie."

—*S.B., St. John's*

Pleading

Mick and Keith brought an action
but were shocked by the Judge's reaction
She said: "Your pleadings are lacking . . .
I'm sending you packing—
The law will give no satisfaction!"

—*A.S., University of Miami*

Failure to state a claim

I did not state a claim,
for which I did not think I was to blame,
Obviously I did not have a clue
Because now I cannot sue.

—*A.M., Emory*

Ed thought the suit against him was for kicks
No cause of action found in the mix
He looked for a federal rule
Found himself quite a jewel
And dismissed under Rule 12(b)(6).

—*A.C., Suffolk*

Discovery

> Well Jack got his shot at discovery
> And has proven his grounds for recovery
> He used the basic tools
> Lined out in the Rules
> That can be used by a party seeking victory.
>
> — *D.D., University of Arkansas*

> She thought she could hide under cover
> Her facts and proof all aflutter
> But letters were sent
> By lawyers hell bent
> Demanding the right to discover.
>
> — *M.G., Suffolk*

Tools of Discovery

> An attorney asks Fortenbaugh what he knows
> But Fortenbaugh does not want to disclose
> The work was done in anticipation
> Of substantial litigation
> So the attorney had to find some witnesses to depose.
>
> — *A.C., Suffolk*

> The courts have given devices
> to help lawyers discover surprises;
> you must follow the rules
> and make use of the tools
> as 26(a)(1) advises.
>
> — *B.M., University of Iowa*

Summary judgment

Jill came to class with a motion she'd been lent;
Her professor asked her what the motion meant
As Jill cracked smile
She said, "no need for a trial"
The case ended in summary judgment.

—*J.S., Loyola*

She thought she could score with the court
By showing an outrageous tort
But lo and behold
Her theory had holes
And no jury would hear her retort.

—*M.G., Suffolk*

Judgment as a matter of law

The plaintiff thought that his case had no flaw
Getting ready to recover he stuck out his paw
he'd survived summary judgement and a 12(b)(6)
He thought the defendant had to be out of tricks
But then Defendant moved for judgment as a matter of law.

—*A.R., Barry University*

The defendant didn't like what he saw
No scintilla of evidence from which to draw
So he caused a commotion
And filed a motion
For judgment as a matter of law.

—*A.C., Suffolk*

Jack prevailed through it all
through daunting motions and discovery
this gave him lots of hope, while his opponent began to pout
but just then, the Judge told Jack, "Sorry, but the jury is still out."

— *B.C., George Washington*

Res judicata

I went sailing, it was regatta
I got injured, it hurt a whole lotta,
I filed a claim
I lost — so lame,
I could not refile due to res judicata.

— *M.C., DePaul*

And, in closing, an encomium from a convert.

There once was a teacher named Glannon,
Whose civpro hornbooks are practically canon;
I'll admit at the start of the year
I looked at Glannonites with a sneer,
But now I'm ready to join his fandom.

— *R.B., University of California, Irvine*

Naturally, Dear Reader, I am always open to improvements. If you can write a better limerick, on any of the chapter topics, send it to *jglannon@suffolk. edu.*

INDEX